SYNTHESIS: LEGAL READING, REASONING, AND WRITING

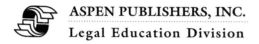

SYNTHESIS

Legal Reading, Reasoning, and Writing

Deborah A. Schmedemann
Professor of Law

Christina L. Kunz
Professor of Law

both of William Mitchell College of Law

ASPEN LAW & BUSINESS
A Division of Aspen Publishers, Inc.
Gaithersburg   New York

Permissions
Aspen Law & Business
1185 Avenue of the Americas
New York, NY 10036

Printed in the United States of America

1 2 3 4 5 6 7 8 9 0

Library of Congress Cataloging-in-Publication Data

Schmedemann, Deborah A., 1956–
    Synthesis : legal reading, reasoning, and writing / Deborah A.
Schmedemann, Christina L. Kunz.
      p. cm.
    Includes index.
    ISBN 0-7355-0312-5
    1. Legal composition.   2. Law—United States—Interpretation and
construction.   3. Forensic oratory.   I. Kunz, Christina L.
II. Title.
KF250.S36   1999
808′.06634—dc21   98-54842
                                                CIP

ABOUT ASPEN LAW & BUSINESS, LEGAL EDUCATION DIVISION

In 1996, Aspen Law & Business welcomed the Legal Education Division of Little, Brown and Company into its growing business—already established as a leading provider of practical information to legal practitioners.

Acquiring much more than a prestigious collection of educational publications by the country's foremost authors, Aspen Law & Business inherited the long-standing Little, Brown tradition of excellence—born over 150 years ago. As one of America's oldest and most venerable publishing houses, Little, Brown and Company commenced in a world of change and challenge, innovation and growth. Sharing that same spirit, Aspen Law & Business has dedicated itself to continuing and strengthening the integrity begun so many years ago.

ASPEN LAW & BUSINESS
A Division of Aspen Publishers, Inc.
A Wolters Kluwer Company

DEDICATION

We dedicate this book to Professor Ken Kirwin, our fellow Legal Writing co-coordinator, and to the terrific attorneys who take time from the practice of law to devote their talents and creativity to teaching Legal Writing at the College.

On a personal note, we dedicate this book to Craig, Mary, Karen, Keith, Anna Mary, Barb and Joan; and to Rachel, Barbara, Carol, Suzy, Ruth, and Hal.

SUMMARY OF CONTENTS

CONTENTS

CHAPTER 1

INTRODUCTION: THE LAWYER'S ROLES AND THE LEGAL SYSTEM

CHAPTER 2

THE STRUCTURE OF LEGAL RULES

CHAPTER 3

CHAPTER 4

CHAPTER 5

CHAPTER 6

INTERPRETING STATUTES   65

CHAPTER 7

READING COMMENTARY   77

CHAPTER 8

APPLYING A RULE TO FACTS: DEDUCTIVE REASONING   81

CHAPTER 12

THE OFFICE MEMO: ISSUES, SHORT ANSWERS, AND CONCLUSION 131

CHAPTER 13

THE OFFICE MEMO: THE FACTS 139

CHAPTER 17

ADVOCACY WRITING IN THE APPELLATE SETTING: THE FUNCTION AND FORMAT OF THE APPELLATE BRIEF

CHAPTER 18

THE ART AND PHILOSOPHY OF ADVOCACY

APPENDIX B

APPENDIX C

LIST OF EXHIBITS

PREFACE

If you are reading this book, you probably have heard the phrase, "thinking like a lawyer." This book is about thinking like a lawyer—thinking that is both structured and open-ended, expansive and precise, rigorous and creative; thinking that is grounded in careful reading of legal texts and insightful understanding of the situations of real people; thinking that is both intellectually rewarding in its own right and critically important to the lives of people involved in the case at hand.

We worked on this book for six years before we came up with the first word in its title: synthesis. We chose "synthesis" as the flagship concept for this book for several reasons. According to the tenth edition of Merriam Webster's Collegiate Dictionary, "synthesis" means "the composition or combination of parts or elements so as to form a whole." Each phase of legal analysis discussed in this book—reading the law, reasoning about a client's situation, writing about it—entails combining parts or elements to form a whole. More specifically, the two chief forms of law, cases and codes, both consist of parts that form the whole. Reasoning consists of deductive reasoning, reasoning by example, and policy analysis. Every legal document you will write has standard components that work together to form the whole. Furthermore, the overall process of legal analysis combines reading, reasoning, and writing to form a whole.

"Synthesis" also means "the dialectic combination of thesis and antithesis into a higher stage of truth." In turn, "dialectic" means "any systematic reasoning . . . that juxtaposes opposed or contradictory ideas and usually seeks to resolve their conflict." Much of the time, law is about disputes between people, conflicting interests, opposed or contradictory ideas. To resolve conflict in a fair and just way is the purpose of the legal system and the highest calling of a lawyer.

This book is itself a synthesis of elements that, we believe, make for effective learning of the skills discussed here. As you will see, this book:

■ describes each skill in general terms, setting out steps to follow, identifying factors to consider, detailing criteria for your work, and exploring pertinent ethical principles;

- presents many processes and products of legal analysis in traditional textual form and in drawings or diagrams;
- draws analogies between the skills discussed here and other fields of endeavor, such as architecture;
- demonstrates the skills through the HomeElderCare case file, a lawyer's case file that documents a case from initial client interview to appellate argument; and
- provides an opportunity for practice in the exercises, which explore an evolving area of tort law.

During each of the six years we have worked on this book, close to 300 students have used these materials in the first-year Legal Research and Writing course at William Mitchell College of Law. Each year, twenty-five practicing lawyers, teaching the course as adjunct professors, have taught from these materials. We have learned much from these "co-authors" and are pleased to pass their insights along to you in the following pages.

We hope you are stimulated by the process of learning to think like a lawyer. And we hope you use what you learn from this book to think like a highly competent, creative, and caring lawyer.

Deborah A. Schmedemann
Christina L. Kunz
St. Paul, Minnesota
April, 1999

ACKNOWLEDGMENTS

We had the good fortune to be able to write and revise this book during six years of classroom use. We were able to revise each chapter many times and to incorporate the valuable suggestions of our students and our Legal Writing faculty. Also important was the wholehearted and long-term support of this project by former Dean James Hogg and current Dean Harry Haynsworth.

We also had the good fortune of working with talented research assistants, many of whom worked on bits and pieces of the book in the course of their other duties. We note here those who made major contributions: Anthony Massaros and Katie Crosby Lehmann wrote the initial drafts of the HomeElderCare office memos, motion practice memoranda, and appellate briefs; they also delivered the appellate oral argument that appears in transcript form in the HomeElderCare case file. Tony also developed the library for the torts exercises. Lynn Bebeau Psihos, Kerry Cork, Renee Michalow, and Jodi Sharrow worked closely with us to produce this multi-faceted book. We thank them for their excellent work.

Our colleagues generously contributed their insights and feedback on a wide variety of topics: Professor Kenneth Kirwin as a fellow co-coordinator of the Legal Writing course, Professor Daniel Kleinberger on rule structure and on levels of organization, Professor Russell Pannier on logic, Professors Eric Janus and Robert Oliphant on civil procedure, Professor Phebe Haugen on living wills, and Professor Curtis Stine on legal issues affecting the elderly. Professor Kirwin, Professor Stine, and Professor Denise Roy were the judges for the appellate oral argument that appears in the transcript in the Home-ElderCare case file.

An evolving manuscript of this size and complexity depends on high-quality production work, as each year's manuscript is made ready for the incoming students. Cal Bonde contributed superb word processing skills and overall document management for our countless revisions. During the last stretch, she was assisted by Linda Thorstad. Dawn Ives and, this past year, Tom Donnellan copied and bound each year's manuscript for our students. Judy Holmes, the administrator of the Legal Writing course, coordinated this production work for five years, until she handed the reins over to Darlene Finch last summer. We are grateful to each one of them for every way in which they helped us bring this project to fruition.

The original encouragement for this project came from some of our favorite people at what was then the law division of Little, Brown and Company. Rick Heuser, Carol McGeehan, and Nick Niemeyer each played an important role in moving this book forward. Carol McGeehan has our special gratitude for bridging the contract transition from Little, Brown to Aspen Law and Business. Elizabeth Kenny, Ellen Greenblatt, and Melody Davies on the editorial end of the process, and Karen Quigley and Kathy Porzio in design and production matters, have skillfully brought this book to press for Aspen Law and Business.

This textbook owes much of its richness to the ideas of colleagues in the field of legal reading, reasoning, and writing across the country. Their presentations, publications, and personal observations over the years have made legal writing a rigorous and vibrant discipline. We deeply appreciate being part of a national community of legal writing teachers with a strong ethic of teaching each other.

Six years is a very long time for friends, family, and colleagues to bear with the long hours and intense concentration that a book project demands. From the bottom of our hearts, we thank our families and friends for the many ways in which they supported us and worked around us, while we worked on this book.

We also would like to acknowledge those publishers who permitted us to reprint copyrighted material in this book.

Illustration 11.6: Lynn B. Squires et al., *Legal Writing in a Nutshell* 95-98 (2d ed. 1996). Reprinted with permission of the West Group.

Robert Frost, "The Road Not Taken," in *The Complete Poems of Robert Frost,* ed. Edward Connery Lathem, page 124 (1949). Reprinted with permission of the Estate of Robert Frost and the publisher, Jonathan Cape, Ltd., as to English-language rights in the British Commonwealth. Other English-language rights are in the public domain.

HomeElderCare case file:

> *Dick Weatherston's Assoc'd Mech'l Servs. v. Minnesota Mut. Life Ins. Co.,* 100 N.W.2d 819 (Minn. 1960): Reprinted with permission of the West Group.
>
> *Buckley v. Humason,* 52 N.W. 385 (Minn. 1892): Reprinted with permission of the West Group.
>
> Minn. Stat. § 481.02 (1992): Reprinted with permission of the Revisor of Statutes, State of Minnesota.
>
> Minn. Stat. §§ 145B.01.-.06 (1992): Reprinted with permission of the Revisor of Statues, State of Minnesota.
>
> *Peterson v. Hovland (In re Peterson's Estate),* 42 N.W.2d 59 (Minn. 1950): Reprinted with permission of the West Group.

Gardner v. Conway, 48 N.W.2d 788 (Minn. 1951): Reprinted with permission of the West Group.

Annotation, *Activities of Law Clerks as Illegal Practice of Law,* 13 A.L.R.3d 1137 (1967): Reprinted with permission of the West Group.

8 Dunnell's Minn. Digest *Contracts* § 3.20, at 163-64 (4th ed. 1990): Copyright 1990. Reprinted with permission from *Dunnell's Minn. Digest Contracts* (4th ed. 1990) by Lexis Law Publishing, Charlottesville, Va., (800) 446-3410. All Rights Reserved.

Howard Orenstein et al., *Minnesota's Living Will . . . ,* Bench & B. Minn., Aug. 1989, at 21: Reprinted with permission of Howard Orenstein, David Bishop, and Leigh D. Mathison.

Restatement (Second) of Contracts § 181 (1979) (with comments and illustrations): © 1981 by The American Law Institute. Reprinted with permission.

E. Allan Farnsworth, *Contracts* § 5.6, at 377-79 (2d ed. 1990): Reprinted with permission of Aspen Law & Business.

Exercises:

Moore v. Bunk, 228 A.2d 510 (Conn. 1967): Reprinted with permission of the West Group.

4 Fowler V. Harper, *The Law of Torts* § 20.5 (2d ed. 1986 & Supp. 1999): Reprinted with permission of Aspen Law & Business.

SYNTHESIS: LEGAL READING, REASONING, AND WRITING

INTRODUCTION:

THE LAWYER'S ROLES

AND THE LEGAL SYSTEM

A. Introduction
B. The Lawyer's Roles
C. The Legal System
D. About This Book
E. The HomeElderCare Situation
F. Conclusion

> Every calling is great when greatly pursued.
> —Oliver Wendell Holmes
> "The Law," *Speeches* (1913)

A. INTRODUCTION

"A lawyer is a representative of clients, an officer of the legal system and a public citizen having special responsibility for the quality of justice," according to the Preamble to the Model Rules of Professional Conduct for lawyers, drafted by the American Bar Association. To write well in the law, you must understand these roles and the legal system. This chapter introduces these topics and describes the organization of this book.

B. THE LAWYER'S ROLES

1. Problem-Solver for Clients

Whether law practice is a calling, an art, a science, or a business, practicing law entails solving problems. Lawyers help clients solve their problems by operating as advisor or advocate.

As an advisor, a lawyer acts prospectively, counseling the client about the law that governs actions the client may take. The lawyer identifies options, assesses their legal implications, and often executes the option selected by the client. Lawyers act as advisors when they draft wills, write employee handbooks, prepare stock prospectuses, and review license applications.

As an advocate, a lawyer acts retrospectively, pleading the client's case before a decision-making body so as to obtain a fair and favorable resolution of an existing dispute between the client and the opponent. The lawyer constructs legal arguments based on the facts and the law, then presents them, sometimes orally, sometimes in writing, sometimes both. Lawyers act as advocates when they prosecute or defend an individual charged with a crime, represent an employer in labor arbitration, present a landowner's argument before a zoning commission, or argue before an appeals court on behalf of a patent-holder. In a broader sense, lawyers act as advocates when they lobby the legislature or administrative agencies for laws benefiting client interests.

In all of these instances, the lawyer's fundamental contribution is to provide a legal analysis of the client's situation. The lawyer develops a legal meaning for the client's situation by placing the facts of the client's experience within certain legal rules and assigning to the experience the legal significance suggested by the rules. "[I]n the law: we convert immediate experience into the subject of thought of a particular kind, which has at its center the question of meaning: what this event means, and should mean, in the language of the law; and what that language itself means, as a way in which we articulate our deepest values and attain collective being." James Boyd White, *Meaning in the Life of the Lawyer*, 26 Cumb. L. Rev. 763, 770 (1996). This assignment of legal meaning occurs through several steps, as depicted in Exhibit 1.1. Although the exhibit shows the usual order of steps, legal analysis is not entirely linear, as signified by the arrows looping back to earlier steps. Ethical considerations enter in at every step.

Of course, the client ultimately controls the solution to the problem on which the lawyer works. The client may rely not only on the lawyer's expertise, but also on the counsel of other professionals as well as the client's own values. There is no such thing as a purely "legal problem."

Nor is legal analysis radically different from the types of analysis performed by other professionals. Rather, sound legal analysis resembles other forms of rigorous problem-solving. It requires the engineer's precision, the literary critic's close attention to text, the physician's openness to alternatives, and the minister's concern for social good and individual well-being. Thus, no matter what background you bring to the law, your skills will be useful in the study and practice of law.

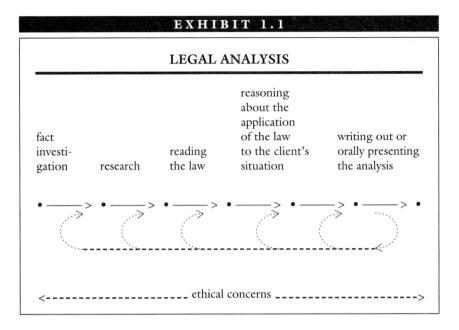

EXHIBIT 1.1

LEGAL ANALYSIS

| fact investigation | research | reading the law | reasoning about the application of the law to the client's situation | writing out or orally presenting the analysis |

ethical concerns

2. Servant of the Public

As lawyers help clients solve problems, they also serve the public. Lawyers act as officers of the legal system and public citizens in several ways.

First, a lawyer acting as an advisor aids in the implementation of the law. The lawyer advises the client on how to conform its conduct to the law and implements a legally permitted solution. The public benefits from the client's law-abiding conduct.

Second, a lawyer acting as an advocate assures that legal disputes are resolved properly. As a gatekeeper limiting access to the courts and other legal processes, the lawyer screens out frivolous claims. The lawyer guides the dispute into civil litigation or into less formal and less costly forms of dispute resolution. Furthermore, the lawyer presents the client's case so as to assure a fair depiction of the facts and statement of the governing law. The lawyer thus serves the public interest in fair and efficient resolution of disputes.

Third, also while acting as an advocate, a lawyer helps to make new law. Law is a reiterative system of client problems and legal rules. Lawmakers create legal rules in response to conflicts brought to their attention—typically by the disputants' lawyers. The new rule then applies to other persons involved in similar situations. When the application of the rule proves troublesome, a new conflict arises, and lawmakers may revise the rule—again with the guidance of the disputants' lawyers. Thus, when a lawyer pleads a client's case, the lawyer also influences the direction of the law for the future.

Acting both as a client representative and as an officer of the legal system often entails difficult judgment calls. For example, the lawyer must decide how to protect client confidences, how to present testimony in court, and whether to facilitate transactions that push the boundaries of the law. In making these decisions, a lawyer is guided by his or her own personal values, as well as codes of professional ethics, which operate as the policies of the profession and the standards by which lawyers are judged.

3. Some Examples

To provide a glimpse into law practice, we asked practicing attorneys from a range of settings to describe their day-to-day activities. Here are several responses from litigators (advocates) in private law firms:

> I am on the phone five hours a day talking to clients and other lawyers. I listen sympathetically to everything they say, guide them, and lay the foundation for future calls when bad news may come. Talking to plaintiffs is a matter of providing reassurance, much like in the ministry, but you need to be efficient. I also go to hearings, write briefs, take clients to lunch.

> I write—research and write. I'm usually part of a team. We spend lots of time developing a strategy, constructing arguments, figuring out what will happen down the road. I spend some time in client contact, advising them. Sometimes I go to court (motion practice and appellate work). I take depositions and spend a lot of time working with documents. [Note: A deposition is a pre-trial interview of a witness or a party.]

> Currently I am setting up mediation for a large piece of litigation. [Note: Mediation is a negotiation process aided by a third-party neutral.] So I talk on the phone with ten other attorneys. I keep in mind what the client wants, what the issues are, what procedures to follow. At the same time, I'm preparing for trial, in case mediation doesn't work: preparing a chronology of the facts, deciding which witnesses to call, analyzing evidentiary issues. I do all of this because the client has been sued: try mediation to avoid the time and expenses of trial for everyone, prepare for trial so I know the case well and can anticipate what the other side will do.

Here are two responses from transactional lawyers (advisors) in private firms.

> I talk on the phone a lot of the day. I attend periodic day-long board meetings of my clients. The week before, I prepare opinions on new issues and status reports on pending matters. During the meetings, I advise on matters that were referred earlier, answer questions that come up. When I leave the meeting, I have a list of things to do for the next meeting. I consult with the client's in-house staff often, indeed on a daily basis.

> My work is like *Bonfire of the Vanities*. I work for government entities or private individuals that want to build and need funding. I write documents that run over 100 pages to accomplish the deal and draft opinions about the deal. These must be written by an attorney in the "red book," a guild-like system.

Other lawyers work within their clients, such as corporations or the government. Here is an excerpt from an in-house corporate lawyer and one from a state assistant attorney general:

We handle every day-to-day problem that comes in the door. For example, how do we fire an employee, accept service of process on an employee who is hiding from it, draft articles of incorporation, manage litigation, pay off a mortgage, arrange executive compensation, modify an employee handbook? I do whatever I can to comply with the law and get the project off my desk: research, draft a letter or call someone, talk to the other side, talk to the client (the corporation's officers) or employees. I try to see what the problem is and what I can do to fix it, by contract, or phone call, or letter, or getting people to work together to work it out, or by paying a little money.

I do a lot of litigation—courtroom work—and heavy-duty brief writing. I research the applicable law, both sides of it; synthesize the cases; write the brief in support of the client's position. I write it to win, by making all arguments within the bounds of ethical conduct. Then I review it, file it, prepare for oral argument.

I also advise the department I work for, when the department wants to do something new. So I research, brainstorm, think about it, give the best opinion as to whether the new action will withstand legal action. When there is a pervasive problem, I advise on initiating legislative action and consider: What is the evil to remedy? What is the solution? How can we write up the solution so it will be understandable to many people?

The following two excerpts are from lawyers on either side of the criminal justice system, a county attorney (prosecutor) and a public defender:

I review police reports and decide what offense to charge. I advise police officers in ongoing investigations by answering the question on the other end of a ringing phone. I try cases: plan out the presentation of the evidence, meet with witnesses, prepare exhibits. I negotiate out most cases, since ninety-eight percent settle, which entails offering a plea to the defense attorney and agreeing to the sentence. I also research, write, and argue cases on appeal.

My time is spent in client interviews, brief writing, oral arguments, as well as some trial court hearings. Because our clients have an absolute right to an appeal, we are not bound by professional responsibility rules on frivolous appeals, but we do retain the right to choose issues. It takes creativity to find colorable issues sometimes, although some cases do have real appealable issues.

As these excerpts demonstrate, the day-to-day activities of law practice vary, depending on the lawyer's setting. Yet all lawyers aim to solve problems for their clients by assigning them a legal meaning, that is, by use of the mechanisms afforded by the legal system and by reference to the rules afforded by the law.

C. THE LEGAL SYSTEM

The American legal system is rather complex, reflecting the intricate structure of American government. Exhibit 1.2 presents the institutions of our government and the forms of law each creates.

The three *levels* of government are federal, state, and local. The federal government generally occupies the highest position in a hierarchy, with state government in the middle and local government at the lowest position. In some areas of law, the federal government is the primary lawmaker, with state and local governments thereby either supplementing the federal law or being precluded from lawmaking. In other fields, state or local law is the traditional and predominant source of law.

Under our tripartite system of government, the three *branches* of government are the legislature, the judiciary, and the executive. Each has its essential function in the legal system: the legislature making the law, the judiciary interpreting and applying the law to resolve specific disputes, and

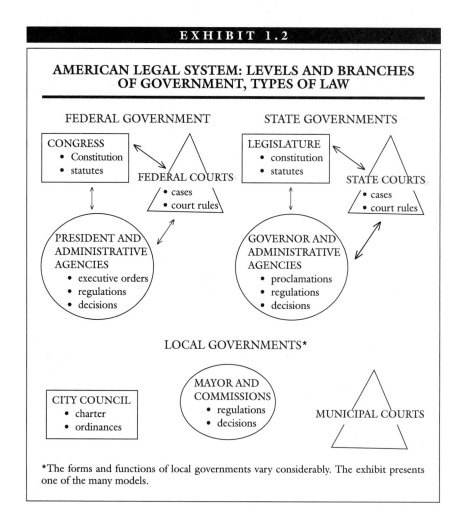

EXHIBIT 1.2

AMERICAN LEGAL SYSTEM: LEVELS AND BRANCHES OF GOVERNMENT, TYPES OF LAW

FEDERAL GOVERNMENT   STATE GOVERNMENTS

CONGRESS
• Constitution
• statutes
FEDERAL COURTS
• cases
• court rules

LEGISLATURE
• constitution
• statutes
STATE COURTS
• cases
• court rules

PRESIDENT AND ADMINISTRATIVE AGENCIES
• executive orders
• regulations
• decisions

GOVERNOR AND ADMINISTRATIVE AGENCIES
• proclamations
• regulations
• decisions

LOCAL GOVERNMENTS*

CITY COUNCIL
• charter
• ordinances

MAYOR AND COMMISSIONS
• regulations
• decisions

MUNICIPAL COURTS

*The forms and functions of local governments vary considerably. The exhibit presents one of the many models.

the executive implementing the law. There is, however, considerable overlap. For example, the judiciary makes law via the common law and court rules, and the executive branch also may do so via executive order. Administrative agencies in the executive branch resolve specific disputes much as courts do, although within limited spheres. The genius of the tripartite system lies not only in the allocation of functions to each branch, but also in the checks and balances among the branches. For example, the judiciary may overturn legislation or agency actions that exceed the legislature's or agency's power. The legislature may overturn decisions of the courts deemed contrary to the public's will.

The three branches and three levels of government engage in a continual process of lawmaking that can yield complex results. Thus, it is not surprising that a substantial body of legal scholarship explains the law and proposes reforms. Legal scholarship, also called "commentary" or "secondary authority" because it is not the law itself, is written by lawyers, law professors, law students, and occasionally lawmakers. Although commentary is not law, it can be a helpful aid to legal analysis.

D. ABOUT THIS BOOK

This book covers three linked processes: reading the law, reasoning about the application of the rules of law to your client's situation, and writing (or otherwise communicating) your legal analysis. As noted above, the processes are closely related; nonetheless, they are distinct enough to be presented sequentially. Throughout, the book emphasizes four criteria by which to judge all of your work: completeness, correctness, coherence, and comprehensibility. In addition, advocacy work is judged by how well it convinces the reader and advisory work by its creativity.

This book has three major units: The first unit (Chapters 2 through 7) explores how to read the law. Chapter 2 develops the concept of rules of law. Chapters 3 and 4 explain how to read a single case, one of the two dominant forms in which the law appears, and how to fuse multiple cases. Chapters 5 and 6 explain how to read codes, the second dominant form in which the law appears, and then how to integrate codes and cases. The first unit closes with Chapter 7, which covers how to read legal commentary.

The second unit (Chapters 8 and 9) explores how to reason about a client's situation in light of a given rule of law. Chapter 8 discusses the framework of legal reasoning: deductive reasoning, or reasoning from general to specific. Chapter 9 discusses reasoning by example and the use of public policy.

The third unit (Chapters 10 through 19) explores how to write or speak about the analysis of a client's situation. Chapters 10 through 13 cover the classic document in which most legal analysis is first presented: the office memo. Chapter 14 covers the advice letter, the key document by which the lawyer communicates the analysis to the client. The remaining chapters cover the standard tools by which advocates communicate with courts: the motion practice memorandum (Chapters 15 and 16), the appellate brief (Chapters 17 and 18), and oral argument (Chapter 19).

Three appendices to this text cover facets of writing that are critical to any document you may write as a lawyer: sentence structure and word usage (Appendix A), editing (Appendix B), and citation (Appendix C). We encourage you to consult them from time to time as you refine your written work.

This book offers two presentations of each topic. Each skill is first described in general terms. Then, each skill is demonstrated in the context of a representative (although fictional) client problem: the HomeElderCare case. The preliminary HomeElderCare situation appears at the end of this chapter. The HomeElderCare case file at the end of the book contains some of the legal authorities consulted, notes taken along the way, final written documents, and an oral argument transcript. Please note that the cases, statutes, and other authorities presented in the HomeElderCare example are for example only. They were current as of the early 1990s, when the HomeElderCare case file was developed; they are cited accordingly. The facts unfold as the file progresses, as indeed a client's situation unfolds during the course of representation.

This book aims to meet the needs of various readers. Some readers are abstract thinkers, while others are concrete thinkers. Some prefer traditional text, while others prefer diagrams, analogies, or examples. Some modes of presentation may prove more effective for you than others. We encourage you to concentrate on the modes of presentation that work well for you and to consider the rest for how they may enhance your abilities to analyze legal problems and to communicate with people whose thought processes differ from yours.

E. THE HOMEELDERCARE SITUATION

Client representation typically begins with a conversation between lawyer and client. Notes from that conversation in the HomeElderCare case appear on page 9.

F. CONCLUSION

There are many ways to "think like a lawyer," that is, to read, reason, and write in the law. This book presents some of the common methods used by lawyers, and we hope that you find these methods useful.

Meeting with Mary Mahoney, Executive Director
of HomeElderCare, Sept. 9, 1992

HomeElderCare (HEC)
    NFP corp.
    clients = elderly
    250 clients
    staff = 10 social workers, variable # of volunteers
    social worker duties:
        initial interview to find needs (finances, family concerns, home
            cleaning, etc.)
        set up schedule
        monthly ck-in
        liaison to atty or physician is possible
    fee per service, differs for each client
problem area
    some clients want living wills & help with health care decisions
    has form living will that looks straightforward (gave me copy)
        is it?
        does an atty need to do it?
        if not done by atty, will it be valid?
        will HEC's fees be collectible?
    social workers' role (not volunteers)
        need training
        would ask Qs on form and fill in client's answers
        would help get form notarized
        would charge fee for those services
    clients would save $ by not hiring an atty
    social workers' background/training
        minimum = bachelor's degree in social work, licensed (5 staff)
        some have master's degree + second-level licensing (5 staff)
        4 possible levels of licensing
        some master's degree classes focus on care of elderly
        do they need additional 1-2 seminars?
I'll send her opinion letter soon, before her trip, then call re addi-
    tional Qs

THE STRUCTURE

OF LEGAL RULES

> Logical consequences are the scarecrows of fools and the
> beacons of wise men.
> —Thomas H. Huxley
> *Animal Automatism* (1884)

A. INTRODUCTION

The law is formed of rules. A rule of law is "an abstract or general statement of what the law permits or requires of classes of persons in classes of circumstances."[1] Rules of law appear in many legal authorities, such as cases, statutes, regulations, and court rules. Regardless of form, all rules have the same function: to identify the legal consequences that flow from specified factual conditions.

Rules of law benefit society. They specify predictable legal consequences of particular actions; this predictability allows people and other legal entities (such as corporations and public agencies) to plan and order their affairs in reliance on the law. Rules of law also give guidance to disputants and judges as to how to resolve disputes, so that similarly situated disputants obtain similar outcomes.

---

1. Steven J. Burton, *An Introduction to Law and Legal Reasoning* 13 (1985).

This chapter introduces you to the structure of rules of law. It first demonstrates how to state rules in an if/then form and how to deconstruct the rule into its elements and consequences, then analyzes the different relationships that can exist among the elements of a rule, discusses the types of legal consequences a rule may involve, and concludes with suggestions for depicting a rule.

B. STATING RULES IN IF/THEN FORM

Even though legal rules may come in many forms, they all can be rephrased in an if/then statement as follows:

IF   the required *factual conditions* exist,

THEN   the specified *legal consequences* follow.

The if-clause contains words or phrases describing a class of situations lawmakers wished to address. Typically the if-clause refers to one or more actors (whether individuals or legal entities such as corporations), one or more actions, and circumstances under which the actions occur.

The then-clause identifies the legal consequence that follows when the factual conditions are met. The consequence may be a benefit to or burden on a specified party, and it may be multi-faceted. Often a benefit flows to one party, and a burden is imposed on another, as when one is ordered to pay monetary damages to the other.

The analytical task of the lawyer is first to discern the if/then statement from the legal authorities on the topic, and then to determine how the client's facts fit the factual conditions set out in the if-clause. Because lawmakers do not always phrase the law according to this pattern, often you will need to distill your own if/then statement. This part describes several steps in that process.

1. Separating Factual Conditions from Legal Consequences

Stating a rule of law in if- and then-clauses is an important step in legal analysis. If you do not know what factual conditions are required, you might apply an inapplicable rule to your facts. Or you might misperceive the legal consequences of a client's situation.

Sometimes the rule as originally stated consists of two clauses. If so, evaluate whether the factual conditions and legal consequences are in separate clauses; the words "where" and "when" often mean "if." If the rule is not so constructed, you will need to identify each concept as a factual condition (actors, actions, and circumstances) or legal consequence, and group them accordingly.

For example, consider the following rule, which could apply to the HomeElderCare case:

If a person not admitted or licensed to practice law in this state renders legal advice or counsel to another, the unlicensed practitioner generally shall be guilty of a misdemeanor, upon the charging of a fee, and punished therefor.

This rule has two clauses, suggesting an if/then structure.

IF   a person not admitted or licensed to practice law in this state renders legal advice or counsel to another,

THEN   the unlicensed practitioner generally shall be guilty of a misdemeanor, upon the charging of a fee, and punished therefor.

But the then-clause contains a factual condition (charging of a fee), which needs to be moved to the if-clause. The result is as follows:

IF   a person not admitted or licensed to practice law in this state renders legal advice or counsel to another and charges a fee,

THEN   the unlicensed practitioner generally shall be guilty of a misdemeanor and punished therefor.

Some legal rules are stated in complex and wordy sentences. Thus, the next step may be to carefully paraphrase the rule, making sure that you do not remove meaning from the rule, in an effort to make it easier to work with.[2] A legal dictionary can help you to determine which words carry legal meaning, what that meaning is, and which synonyms you can safely use in your paraphrasing. Where the if-clause is long and cumbersome, you may find the sentence easier to read if you place the then-clause before the if-clause. This rewording may clarify the rule for you.

In the example, you could delete "admitted" or "licensed"; you also could delete "advice" or "counsel." The then-clause refers to both guilt and punishment; it also uses a legalistic term ("therefor"). One simpler phrasing reads as follows:

IF   a person not licensed to practice law in this state renders legal advice to another and charges a fee,

THEN   the unlicensed practitioner generally commits a misdemeanor.

2. Dealing with Rules with Exceptions

Some rules state not only factual conditions necessary for the legal consequence to follow, but also factual conditions that stave off the legal consequence. These rules take the following form:

IF   some factual conditions exist,

THEN   the specified legal consequences follow,

---

2. *See generally* Richard Wydick, *Plain English for Lawyers* (4th ed. 1998).

UNLESS   other factual conditions exist.

The unless-clause contains exceptions to the if-clause. Fortunately, a rule in if/then/unless form can be stated in a simpler if/then form in the following way:

IF   some factual conditions do exist
      and other factual conditions do *not* exist,
THEN   the specified legal consequences follow.

For example, consider the following sample rule and elaboration:

If a person not admitted or licensed to practice law in this state renders legal advice or counsel to another, the unlicensed practitioner generally shall be guilty of a misdemeanor, upon the charging of a fee, and punished therefor. However, where the legal advice is incidental to another legitimate professional service and addresses only settled legal points, the unlicensed practitioner shall not be guilty of a misdemeanor.

The second sentence introduces an exception, an idea that could be expressed in an unless-clause. Note that the exception clarifies why the first sentence includes the word "generally." Here is a simplified restatement of the more complete rule, using an extensive if-clause, rather than a second sentence or an unless-clause:

IF   a person not licensed to practice law in this state renders legal advice to another and charges a fee, and the advice is not incidental to another legitimate service and confined to settled points,

THEN   the unlicensed practitioner commits a misdemeanor.

C. DERIVING INDIVIDUAL ELEMENTS AND CONSEQUENCES

Some factual conditions in if-clauses are complex, giving rise to more than one element. An element is a factual condition that can be analyzed as a unit. Most elements can be stated in a simple clause, and some have subelements. Thus, once you have developed your if/then statement, your next goal is to restate the if-clause so that each element (with or without subelements) is stated separately.

For example, the if-clause of the rule developed above can be dissected into the following elements and subelements:

IF   (1) a person is not licensed to practice law in this state, and
      (2) that person renders legal advice to another, and
      (3) that person charges a fee, and

  (4) the advice is not
       (a) incident to another legitimate service and
       (b) confined to settled points,

THEN   that person commits a misdemeanor.

   Then-clauses also can be broken into parts if the rule contains more than
one legal consequence. For instance, if the rule developed above also indicated that an injunction could be brought against the unlicensed practice,
the resulting then-clause would look like this:

THEN   (1) that person commits a misdemeanor, and
        (2) the unlicensed practice may be enjoined.

D. ANALYZING THE RULE'S ELEMENTS

The elements in a rule must be connected to each other in some discernible
way. Virtually every rule follows one of four patterns—conjunctive, disjunctive, aggregate, balancing—or is a mixture of these. Exhibit 2.1 summarizes
the four patterns.

EXHIBIT 2.1

RULE STRUCTURES

Rule Structure	Linguistic Concept	Applicability of Rule	Characteristics
Conjunctive	and	must satisfy all elements	predictable; easy to apply relative lack of discretion in application
Disjunctive	or	need satisfy only one of multiple elements	predictable; easy to apply relative lack of discretion in application
Aggregate	some but not all of the listed elements:	depends on weight accorded to various factors	vests considerable discretion in judge potentially inconsistent application; unpredictable; difficult to apply
Balancing	If [x] outweighs [y], then. . . . Balance [x] against [y] to determine whether. . . .	depends on weight accorded to each side	vests considerable discretion in judge potentially inconsistent application; unpredictable; difficult to apply

Some rules have multiple elements connected by the word "and." The "and" connector tells you that all of the elements of the if-clause must exist in order for the legal consequences of the then-clause to apply. This kind of rule is a *conjunctive rule* ("conjunctive" meaning joining or coming together). Conjunctive rules are fairly simple in structure and relatively predictable in application because courts have relatively little discretion in applying them. The major rule discussed in this lesson is a conjunctive rule. Note that the consequence occurs only when all of the following elements are met:

IF   (1) person is not licensed to practice law, *and*
        (2) person renders legal advice, *and*
        (3) person charges a fee, *and*
        (4) advice is not
              (a) incidental to another legitimate service and
              (b) confined to settled points

THEN   that person commits a misdemeanor.

A second type of rule contains multiple elements connected by the word "or." The "or" connector tells you that only one of the alternative elements of the if-clause must exist in order for the legal consequences of the then-clause to apply. This kind of rule is a *disjunctive rule* ("disjunctive" meaning separating or presenting alternatives). For example, consider the following rule:

IF   the parties form a contract
        (1) involving fraud in the inducement, *or*
        (2) involving mutual mistake, *or*
        (3) contravening public policy,

THEN   that contract is unenforceable against the disadvantaged party.

Note that the consequences of unenforceability can occur when only one of the disjunctive elements is met.

Few rules are completely disjunctive, but many are conjunctive as to the major elements and disjunctive as to one or more subelements. For example, consider the following rule:

IF   (1) a person is not licensed to practice law in this state *and*
        (2) that person
              (a) renders legal advice, *or*
              (b) prepares legal documents, *or*
              (c) appears in court for another, *and*
        (3) that person charges a fee,

THEN   that person commits a misdemeanor.

The second element has disjunctive subelements, and the three elements are conjunctive. For there to be a misdemeanor, (1) and (3) must occur along with 2(a) or (2)(b) or (2)(c).

The third and fourth types of rules are similar in that they state factors for the court to consider; no specific factor is necessarily critical by itself. An *aggregate rule* requires a determination whether enough of the suggested factors have been met to justify applying the legal consequences. A *balancing rule* requires you to balance factors favoring either outcome in order to determine whether the legal consequences will apply. A rule may be purely aggregate or balancing, or it may be a mix, for example, aggregate and conjunctive. Aggregate and balancing rules are difficult to apply. Courts may come to varying holdings on similar facts, so that parties seeking to order their behavior in reliance on these rules may have a difficult time trying to predict the rule's impact on their conduct. The advantage of these rules is that the courts have discretion to come to results called for by particular circumstances.

For example, consider the following rule, which covers the same topic as the other samples presented in this chapter:

IF   (1) a person is not licensed to practice law in this state and
     (2) that person engages in significant legal advising, *as determined by:*
          (a) the difficulty of the legal issue,
          (b) the impact of the advice on the client,
          (c) the duration of the relationship, and
          (d) the charging of a fee,

THEN   that person commits a misdemeanor.

This rule is aggregate as to element (2). That is, factors (2)(a), (b), (c), and (d) are all to be considered together; the absence or presence of any one is not dispositive. (The rule's overall structure is conjunctive.)

As an example of a balancing rule, consider the following sample:

IF   (1) a person is not licensed to practice law in this state, and
     (2) that person renders legal advice to another, and
     (3) (a) *the harm* caused by that advice—measured by any cost to the client, other loss suffered by the client, loss suffered by third parties, and fraud perpetrated on the client or others—
          (b) *outweighs the benefits* of the advice—measured by any advantage received by the client and the person's interest in practicing a related profession—

THEN   that person commits a misdemeanor.

This rule is balancing as to element (3). That is, the factors in (3)(a) are to be weighed against those in (3)(b) to determine whether element (3) is met. (This rule's overall structure is conjunctive).

E. ANALYZING THE LEGAL CONSEQUENCES

Just as if-clauses merit careful analysis, so too should you analyze the then-clause carefully to discern the number and nature of the legal consequence(s).

Many legal rules state a clear legal consequence, and some provide for more than one consequence. In the latter situation, you must discern the relationship between those consequences. Some rules provide for *plural* consequences; they have conjunctive then-clauses. For example, a rule may provide for fines *and* imprisonment.

IF   a person engages in unauthorized practice of law

THEN   that person pays a fine *and*
          that person may be imprisoned.

Other rules provide for *alternative* consequences; they have disjunctive then-clauses. For example, a rule may provide for a fine *or* imprisonment.

IF   a person engages in unauthorized practice of law

THEN   that person pays a fine *or*
          that person may be imprisoned.

Some legal rules identify the *ultimate practical* consequence of conduct fitting within the if-clause; that is, they directly state the impact on the people involved. An example of this sort of rule is a rule providing for a fine or stating that damages may be recovered.

IF   unauthorized practice of law

THEN   fine [ultimate practical consequence]

Other rules identify an *intermediate legal* consequence of conduct fitting within the if-clause; that is, they affix a legal label to the conduct, which then must be linked to an additional rule which in turn determines the ultimate practical consequence. For example, the rule featured in this section has as its consequence that the unlicensed practitioner is guilty of a misdemeanor; you would need to consult another rule on misdemeanors to discern what practical consequence (such as a fine) flows from that label.

IF   unauthorized practice of law

THEN   misdemeanor [intermediate legal consequence]

IF   misdemeanor

THEN   fine [ultimate practical consequence]

Careful attention to these dimensions of the then-clause will permit you to identify properly the significance of a legal rule for your client's case.

F. DEPICTING A RULE IN VARIOUS WAYS

Rules of law can be depicted in a variety of ways. Your choice should be based on the nature of the rule and your needs in working with the rule. If the rule has a simple structure, it may be best understood in sentence or paragraph form. As shown throughout this chapter, tabulation and enumeration can aid you in displaying structure for more complex rules. Another way to depict complex rules is a flowchart. See Exhibit 2.2, below. Generally the elements precede the consequences. Disjunctive elements are depicted across horizontal lines, while conjunctive elements are depicted along vertical lines. A double arrow can show the transition from the factual conditions to the legal consequences.

G. REVIEW OF CHAPTER 2

This chapter has covered the following analytical steps in stating rules of law as if/then statements with clearly identified elements and consequences:

(1) Segregate the factual conditions and the legal consequences into if- and then-clauses. As needed, carefully paraphrase the rule for ease of use.
(2) Reword factual conditions framed as exceptions to read as negative conditions in the if-clause.
(3) Separate the if-clause into individual elements and list distinct consequences separately.

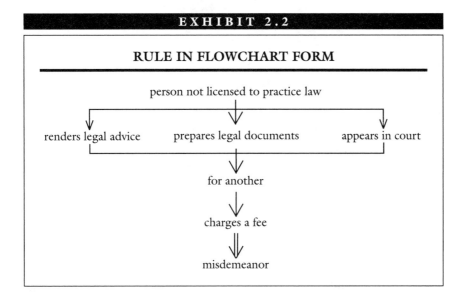

EXHIBIT 2.2

RULE IN FLOWCHART FORM

person not licensed to practice law

renders legal advice   prepares legal documents   appears in court

for another

charges a fee

misdemeanor

(4) Determine whether the rule's elements are conjunctive, disjunctive, aggregate, balancing, or some combination.
(5) Discern the number and nature of the legal consequences.
(6) Depict the rule in an appropriate way.

As you will see in the next few chapters, you will derive rules to work with in this way from various types of legal authority.

READING CASES

A. Introduction
B. Court Structure
C. Stare Decisis and Precedent
D. Reading a Case
E. Briefing a Case
F. Federalism
G. Review of Chapter 3

> The prophecies of what the courts will do in fact, and nothing
> more pretentious, are what I mean by the law.
> —Oliver Wendell Holmes
> *The Path of the Law,* 10 Harv. L. Rev. 457, 461 (1897)

A. INTRODUCTION

This chapter introduces case law, that is, the law that emanates from decisions of various tribunals in specific disputes. In law, the word "case" has several related meanings. Many lawyers use "case" to refer to a client's situation or problem. Once a dispute enters litigation, it becomes a "case" in a more formal sense; it is referred to by the names of the litigants. When a tribunal renders a written decision, that decision also is referred to as a "case." This book uses the word "case" in all of these ways.

This chapter focuses on decisions of courts because they are present in virtually every area of law and constitute the final and weightiest decisions. Nonetheless, it is important to remember that other tribunals decide cases. For example, federal administrative agencies render decisions on such topics as labor, immigration, and Social Security benefits. State and local commissions render decisions on such diverse topics as discrimination and zoning. In more and more areas of law, such as commercial and securities arbitration, the parties may choose a private decisionmaker as the primary tribunal, subject to limited review by the courts.

This chapter covers court systems and "stare decisis," the foundation of case law; a process for reading cases and writing a "case brief," a set of notes on a case; and the relationship between the federal and state lawmaking functions. Much of this chapter pertains not only to decisions of the courts, but also to decisions of other tribunals.

Along the way, this chapter refers to a specific case, *Dick Weatherston's Associated Mechanical Services v. Minnesota Mutual Life Insurance Co.* This case is a leading authority that a lawyer would use in analyzing the Home-ElderCare case, because it addresses a contract for professional services by an unlicensed professional. *Weatherston's* appears in the HomeElderCare case file at page 247, and you may wish to scan it before reading this chapter.

B. COURT STRUCTURE

1. Levels of Courts

The judiciary is one of the three branches of government. Hence, most areas of law involve lawmaking by either the federal or state courts, or both. Exhibit 3.1 illustrates the federal courts and representative state court structures. Although each court system has unique features, all court systems share certain fundamental features and procedures.

Every court system has trial courts, sometimes called "district courts." Cases enter the legal system at this level, and most conclude there. Many cases settle through negotiations conducted by the parties' lawyers. Some court systems require or encourage litigants to pursue informal means of resolving their disputes, such as mediation (negotiations aided by a neutral) or arbitration (an informal trial leading to a decision by an expert neutral).

If these efforts do not succeed, the case is decided formally through the court. The function of the trial court is to resolve disputes about the facts, to apply the law to the facts, and to determine an outcome. A jury may decide the case after a trial, by a jury verdict. At trial, witnesses testify, and the decisionmaker closely views objects and documents. Alternatively a case may be resolved by the judge, either after a bench trial (a trial without a jury) or through motions. A motion is a request by one party that the judge take a specified action, which may entail deciding the case without trial. An example is summary judgment, in which the judge decides the case based on written materials developed during discovery, which is the pre-trial process by which lawyers gather factual information about the case.

Every court system also has one or more appellate courts. The appellate courts exist for two essential purposes. First, an appellate court reviews the trial court's work to determine whether the trial court made errors that are significant enough to have produced an improper result. These errors may include misunderstanding of the law, failure to conduct the trial according to rules of evidence, failure to handle motions according to the rules of civil or criminal procedure, and coming to judgment contrary to the facts. Second,

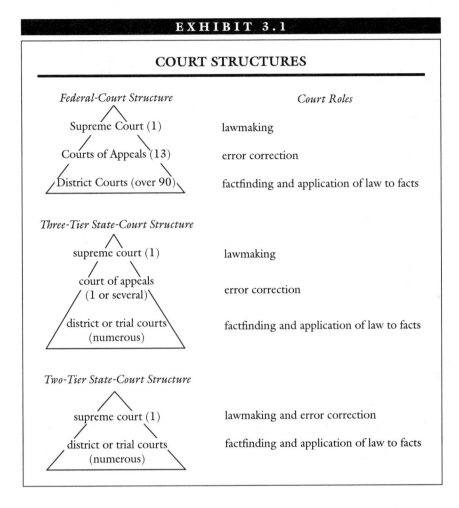

EXHIBIT 3.1

COURT STRUCTURES

Federal-Court Structure   *Court Roles*

Supreme Court (1)   lawmaking

Courts of Appeals (13)   error correction

District Courts (over 90)   factfinding and application of law to facts

Three-Tier State-Court Structure

supreme court (1)   lawmaking

court of appeals
(1 or several)   error correction

district or trial courts
(numerous)   factfinding and application of law to facts

Two-Tier State-Court Structure

supreme court (1)   lawmaking and error correction

district or trial courts   factfinding and application of law to facts
(numerous)

an appellate court uses the case to make law, as described further in Part C below.

Because the appellate court's function is to review the trial court's work, not re-do it, the appellate court does not conduct trials. Rather, the appellate court reviews the written record created at the trial court and the written and oral arguments of the parties' attorneys.

A two-tier court system has a single appellate court. That court handles all cases coming out of the trial courts, and that court both corrects error and makes law.

A three-tier court system has two tiers of appellate courts, in addition to the trial court. In these systems, the intermediate court, typically called the "court of appeals," handles virtually all cases coming out of the trial courts and focuses on correction of error. Some systems have multiple intermediate courts, each handling cases coming out of the trial courts in its region of the state. Other systems have a single intermediate court; all cases from around the state are heard by a panel of several judges or the entire court. The highest court in a three-tier appellate court system, typically called the "supreme court," handles a fairly small percentage of the cases coming out of the intermediate court(s). To assure that the supreme court's resources are concentrated on significant cases, the supreme court has the power to select most of its cases through grant of certiorari or grant of petition for review. The court selects cases with new or especially difficult legal questions or broad impact, because the supreme court's task is not so much to correct error as to make law. Some supreme courts also are required to handle certain limited categories of cases.

As noted in Exhibit 3.1, the federal court system includes the United States Supreme Court; thirteen intermediate appellate courts, called the courts of appeals, for eleven numbered circuits as well as the Federal and the District of Columbia Circuits; and more than ninety federal district trial courts for the fifty states, the District of Columbia, and American territories. Each federal district (trial) court covers either an entire state or a portion of a large state.

The Minnesota state court system, which created the law applicable to the HomeElderCare situation, has resembled both the three-tier and two-tier state-court structures in Exhibit 3.1. The Minnesota state court system currently includes the Minnesota Supreme Court; the Minnesota Court of Appeals (a single court with multiple panels); and ten trial courts, called district courts. Before the court of appeals was created in 1983, Minnesota had a simpler court structure, with the Minnesota Supreme Court the only appellate court.[1]

The sample case for this lesson, *Weatherston's*, proceeded through the Minnesota state courts. Dick Weatherston, an air-conditioning contractor not licensed as an engineer, sought to contract with Minnesota Mutual Life Insurance Company (MMLIC) for work on MMLIC's building. The negotiations failed, and a dispute arose. Mr. Weatherston's business brought suit against MMLIC in Minnesota state district court. The case was tried to a jury, which returned a verdict in favor of Weatherston's business for $5,691. MMLIC moved to set aside the verdict, and the trial judge denied the motion.

MMLIC appealed to the only appellate court at that time, the Minnesota Supreme Court, arguing that (1) it never really entered into a binding contract with Weatherston's business, (2) any such contract would be illegal because Mr. Weatherston would be performing engineering services without a license, and (3) the figure of $5,691 was too large. Had the appeal arisen in 1983 or thereafter, the Minnesota Court of Appeals would have decided the initial appeal. MMLIC's first and third arguments pertain to errors in factfinding. Had those been MMLIC's only arguments, the Minnesota Supreme Court probably would not have chosen to review the case. By contrast, the supreme court probably would have chosen to address the second argument, because it was an issue the supreme court had not addressed recently or extensively.

Note that the dealings between Mr. Weatherston and MMLIC occurred in 1956 and 1957. The Minnesota Supreme Court ruled on the case in 1960. Litigation takes time.

---

1. Table T.1 of *The Bluebook* provides basic information about the courts in each state.

2. Jurisdiction

All courts have the power to decide only certain classes of cases.[2] A court has jurisdiction over a case when the court is empowered to decide the case and enforce its decision. There are two types of jurisdiction, both necessary for a court to handle a case. First, a court has *personal* jurisdiction over a *party* based on the party's contact with the state, based on such factors as the location of the events and the party's citizenship. Second, a court has *subject matter* jurisdiction over a *dispute* when the subject matter of the litigation is within a category the court has the power to decide. The term "jurisdiction" also is used to describe the geographic range of a particular court.

In terms of subject matter jurisdiction, most court systems have courts of general jurisdiction and courts of limited jurisdiction. Courts of general jurisdiction handle a wide range of cases not assigned to courts of limited jurisdiction. The latter have very specialized roles. For example, at the federal level, specialized courts handle military matters, bankruptcies, and patent cases. Some state courts use relatively informal procedures to handle relatively small cases, such as landlord-tenant disputes.

Weatherston's, the sample case, came within the jurisdiction of the Minnesota state courts. They had *personal* jurisdiction because MMLIC had numerous contacts with Minnesota (it was a Minnesota company) and the litigation involved a contract to provide services on MMLIC's office building in St. Paul, Minnesota. Weatherston's claim that MMLIC breached the contract arises under the law of contracts, a *subject* governed by state law and commonly handled by state courts of general jurisdiction.

C. STARE DECISIS AND PRECEDENT

1. Stare Decisis

Judges write opinions explaining their decisions for various reasons. In difficult cases, the process of explaining the decision no doubt helps the judge actually come to the decision. In addition, the opinion justifies the result so that the parties (and in some cases the public) will accept it as just. Finally, in the American common law system, which emanates from the English common law, the opinion operates as law under the doctrine of stare decisis.

"Stare decisis et non quieta movere" means "to stand by precedents and not disturb settled points." The term "precedent" refers to decisions in past cases. Stare decisis is a doctrine based on consistency with the past; it compels a court to decide a present case in accord with decisions rendered in similar cases in the past.[3]

Stare decisis has several advantages. Litigants perceive that they are treated fairly, because similarly situated persons receive the same results. The

---

2. Jurisdiction is a complex topic. For a more complete explanation, see Charles Alan Wright, Arthur R. Miller et al., *Federal Practice and Procedure* (various editions and publication dates).
3. For a more extended discussion, see Oliver Wendell Holmes, *The Common Law* (1881); Edward Levi, *An Introduction to Legal Reasoning* (1949).

doctrine promotes predictability; a lawyer can predict the legal outcome of a present or future situation by examining the outcome in a similar situation that has been adjudicated. Stare decisis preserves scarce judicial resources, by eliminating the need to reinvent solutions where one already has been developed.

If stare decisis operated inflexibly, however, it would be counterproductive. As circumstances, information, and societal values change, so too should the law. In addition, as the membership of a court changes, pressure to change some areas of the law can arise. Fortunately, the doctrine of stare decisis permits change. Where the needed change is not dramatic, the courts modify the existing rule, typically by adding a new element or reframing an element of the existing rule. Where the needed change is dramatic, the courts overrule the precedent and create a new rule in the new case.

2. Mandatory and Persuasive Precedent

Stare decisis operates within a court system, according to its internal hierarchy. Courts are bound by decisions of courts higher in the same court structure and are expected to decide cases consistently with their own prior decisions. Decisions that a court must follow are called "mandatory precedent" or "binding precedent."

By way of illustration, the Minnesota state district courts are bound by the decisions of the Minnesota Court of Appeals and the Minnesota Supreme Court. The single court of appeals is bound by the decisions of the supreme court and is expected to decide cases consistently with its own decisions. And the supreme court is expected to decide cases consistently with its own prior decisions or explain why it has chosen to chart a new course. As a second illustration, in the federal system, a federal district court is bound by the decisions of its circuit court of appeals and the United States Supreme Court. Each circuit court of appeals is bound by the decisions of the Supreme Court and is expected to decide cases consistently with its own decisions, but need not align with the other circuits; the Supreme Court is expected to decide cases consistently with its prior decisions or explain why it has chosen to chart a new course.

In some situations, a court may choose to follow a decision from a court it is not bound to follow, such as a decision from the highest court in a neighboring state. That decision thereby functions as a persuasive precedent. Courts typically rely on persuasive precedent when there is as yet no binding precedent, or when the law is undergoing change in the direction set forth in the persuasive precedent.

Especially when a court is considering persuasive precedent, but also when a court is considering only binding precedent, there may be several applicable precedents from which to choose. Several factors determine the weightiness of various cases. Obviously, a binding precedent carries more weight than a persuasive precedent. Furthermore, a precedent from the highest court within a system carries more weight than a precedent from a lower court. As a general principle, the newer the precedent, the weightier it is, although longstanding precedent followed in recent decisions also carries significant weight. Unanimous decisions are weightier than split decisions.

The more thorough and cogent the court's reasoning is, the weightier the case. The greater the factual and legal similarity between the precedent and the client's case, the more useful the precedent. Furthermore, some courts command more respect than others, because the general quality of their research and reasoning is high or because their decisions frequently are the leading edge in an area of law. Finally, many courts make a practice of turning to certain courts within the same broad region of the country or with similar orientations toward broad issues of policy.

Some courts designate some of their decisions for publication and designate other decisions as unpublished decisions. Through various tools of legal research, you will be able to locate unpublished decisions. However, you should be alert to the reduced precedential weight of an unpublished decision. Typically the court views an unpublished decision as not adding to the common law, but rather as presenting the application of settled law to unremarkable facts in a routine way. Indeed, an unpublished decision may not be precedential.

For example, in reasoning through the *Weatherston's* case, the Minnesota Supreme Court referred to previous decisions of the Minnesota Supreme Court in somewhat similar cases. See, for example, footnote 7 at page 824, where the opinion refers to *Peterson, Minter,* and *Brimhall.* In turn, *Weatherston's* is itself a significant precedent. As a Minnesota Supreme Court decision from 1960 with a significant discussion of an aspect of contract law, it is binding precedent for later cases arising in the Minnesota state courts with similar contract claims.

3. Retroactive Effect of Cases

As a general rule, judicial decisions are retroactive in that they apply to a set of facts that arose in the past.[4] The court applies the rules of law set out in the case to yield an outcome to the present dispute. Furthermore, the case governs the resolution of similar disputes currently in litigation.

The retroactivity of case law can be troublesome where the decision creates a shift in the law, most clearly where the court overrules an existing precedent. The difficulty arises because the parties may well have relied on previous law. Courts sometimes apply the new precedent retroactively, despite this reliance. At other times, courts overrule their precedents prospectively, by declaring a new rule of law effective as of the date of decision, not applying the new rule to the case currently before the court, and not applying the new rule to other cases now in litigation based on disputes that occurred before the new rule was recognized. In making this judgment, courts consider how the law has developed and the equities of the situation.

As for *Weatherston's,* the rule there, which permits enforcement of some contracts for unlicensed professional services where public policy is not violated, does not diverge sharply from pre-existing law. It was used to resolve the case in favor of Mr. Weatherston and his business.

---

4. For more detail, see Edgar Bodenheimer et al., *An Introduction to the Anglo-American Legal System* (2d ed. 1988).

D. READING A CASE

1. Two Narratives

To use a case as a precedent, you must know how to read a case. A case contains two narratives, as shown in Exhibit 3.2. The first narrative consists of the occurrences prompting the litigation—what lawyers call the "real-world facts." The second narrative consists of the response within the legal system. As to both narratives, it is helpful to ask the six standard questions journalists are trained to ask: Who? What? When? Where? Why? How?

More particularly, as you read the real-world facts, ask yourself: Who is litigating against whom, and are there other important people? What happened between the parties? When did that happen? Where did that happen? Why did that happen? How have the events between the parties become the basis of litigation?

Similarly, ask comparable questions about the legal system's response, the second narrative. Note that there may be more than one response by the legal system if the case you are reading is not a trial-court opinion but an appellate opinion. Because few trial-court decisions are published, most cases you will read will be appellate opinions. Hence, the preliminary set of questions to ask is: Who—which courts—have considered this case before the court whose opinion I am reading, and what did that court or those courts decide? Then ask: Who wrote the opinion I am reading now? When did this court rule? Where does this opinion appear? What has this court decided—who wins, who loses, or is it unsettled? Why did this court rule this way? How did this court respond to the rulings below?

2. An Analogy: Cases as Fables

Cases are like fables. Fables consist of two components: the story and its moral, which suggests an outcome for similar stories occurring in the future. Cases, too, contain a story and a moral, or prediction. The story is the real-world narrative. The moral or prediction derives from the second narrative,

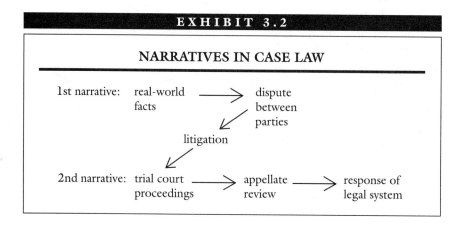

EXHIBIT 3.2

NARRATIVES IN CASE LAW

1st narrative: real-world ——→ dispute
                  facts   between
                                     parties
                          litigation

2nd narrative: trial court ——→ appellate ——→ response of
                  proceedings   review   legal system

the court's response, in which the court assigns a legal meaning to the real-world facts, thereby setting a precedent for the resolution of future similar disputes.

Both the real-world story and the legal-system story are important to your understanding of the case. It is difficult to appreciate the moral without the story, and vice versa.

3. Organization of a Case Report

Most published cases follow a standard organization, which includes the components described in this part. The *Weatherston's* case at page 247 has these components labeled.

Citation information: Located at the top of the first or second page, this information identifies where the case is published. Lawyers must provide citations to cases so that readers may locate them.

Case name: This critical information identifies the parties, which helps you understand both the real-world facts and the legal-system response to the case. The most common party designations are as follows:

Plaintiff: the party that brought the lawsuit
Defendant: the party sued by the plaintiff
Appellant or petitioner: the party that brought the appeal (and hence lost in lower court)
Appellee or respondent: the party opposing the appeal

The plaintiff generally is listed first, but some courts list the defendant first if it is the appellant. Some party designations are complicated; examples include cross-appeals, in which both sides won and lost below and both seek reversal of their losses, and litigation with more than two parties.

Court, date, and docket number: This information tells you which court decided the case, when it did so, and what docket number was assigned to the case by the clerk of the court. The latter can be useful in the rare situation when you wish to contact the court for more information than the published decision provides.

Publisher's editorial matter: The publisher's staff may insert a synopsis of the case and short paragraphs summarizing various points made in the opinion. (In the case of opinions published by West Publishing Company, the short paragraphs are called "headnotes.") This editorial matter plays an important role in researching cases. However, this editorial matter is not written by the court, has not been written with any particular client's situation in mind, and thus cannot substitute for your own careful reading of the case.

Court's editorial matter: Some courts provide their own synopses of their opinions. These synopses may be written by the court's staff or designee, not by the judges themselves. Hence they also should not be relied on in lieu of the opinion itself.

Attorneys: If you have questions not answered by the case itself or you are looking for an expert in the precise type of case you are reading, you may wish to note who represented the parties.

Authoring judge: Immediately before the opinion itself is the name of the author of the opinion. In appellate cases, which involve three or more judges, if the court was not unanimous, you also will learn which other judges agreed with the lead opinion. Some brief opinions on which the judges were generally in agreement are not signed, but are labeled "per curiam." As a general rule, the judges on the highest court of a jurisdiction are referred to as "justices," while others are referred to as "judges."

Opinion(s): The lengthiest portion of a case report—and obviously the most important—is the opinion itself. Each judge has his or her own way of organizing the material in the opinion. Generally one or more of the following appears at the beginning to orient the reader: the procedure in any lower court(s) before the case reached this court, the issue(s) raised by the case, and the outcome(s). Typically the next segment is a recitation of the real-world facts. The bulk of the opinion is devoted to a discussion of the legal issues raised by the parties and a statement of the court's resolution of those issues. The concluding paragraph indicates the court's ultimate decision: to affirm, modify, or reverse the decision of the lower court, and to remand the case. When a court remands a case, it sends the case back to the trial court with instructions as to how to proceed.

A case decided by an appellate court may yield more than one opinion. The opinion receiving over half the votes is called a "majority opinion." A judge concurs when he or she agrees with the result but wishes to state reasoning different than the majority's. A judge dissents when he or she disagrees with the majority result. On occasion, a court splits so significantly that there is no majority opinion; the opinion drawing the largest number of votes, although less than half, is called the "plurality opinion" and generally is viewed as the most influential of the opinions.

4. Reading Stages

You most likely will find that you must read a case several times before you understand it fully. It is generally wise to scan the case first, without marking it or taking notes, to obtain an overview and general sense of the case. Then read it more carefully, highlighting important points and making marginal notes, such as key phrases or the components of the case brief (illustrated in Exhibit 3.3 and covered in the next part). Be sure to look up terms you do not know in a legal dictionary. Then ponder the case for a few moments, asking yourself the who, what, when, where, why, and how questions suggested above. Once you believe that you have good answers to all of them, you are ready to brief the case.

E. BRIEFING A CASE

A case brief is a structured set of notes on a case. Writing a case brief affords an excellent means of testing, as well as recording, your understanding of a case. There is no standard case brief format; you may well develop your own

---

EXHIBIT 3.3

SAMPLE CASE BRIEF

Dick Weatherston's Associated Mechanical Services v. Minnesota Mutual Life Insurance Co., 100 N.W.2d 819 (Minn. 1960).

FACTS: P is contractor in air conditioning in MN. Although P's assignor Dick Weatherston (DW) had B.S. in mechanical engineering, he was not registered as engr in MN. D needed air conditioning for new building & asked P to submit design plans & pricing. DW told D he wasn't licensed & raised concern about conflict w/Ellerbe, D's architects & engrs. Ellerbe agreed to act as consultant. P submitted plans; they were modified after review by Ellerbe & approved. No charge for design or plan was included. P was told to start, but 2 weeks later, P was informed that D had given project to different contractor (also not reg'd engr).

PROCEDURE: P sued D for damages for breach of K. Jury found offer & acceptance & awarded damages. D moved for new trial or JNOV; denied. D appealed.

*ISSUE: Is K illegal, or can unregistered engr recover damages for breach of K, where statute requires regn as engr to practice engrg, work covered by K includes professional engr services, engr has training as engr, services are subject to approval of architect/engr retained by D, & D knows engr isn't regd?

HOLDING: Affirmed & remanded to trial ct w/directions re damages. Unregistered engr can recover damages for breach of K including engr services where engr has training, D's engr approves plans, & engr tells D of non-regn.

REASONING: General rule: Ks made in violation of licensing statutes typically are illegal & void. But statute must be viewed as whole to avoid arbitrary result & to determine whether legislature intended K to be illegal.
   Minn. Stat. § 326.02 requires that person who practices as profl engr be registered in MN. Statutory purpose is to protect public against fraud & incompetence & to promote public health & welfare.
   Here K should be enforced: K was incidental to & part of entire job. DW had training. Work was approved by registered engrs. D sought out P, & DW told D of unregd status. Case does not raise concerns about incompetence, harm to public welfare, fraud.
   Policy: Assure that parties who K for engr services are not harmed by fraud or work done by incompetent persons. Safeguard public welfare through properly engrd buildings (presumably).
   Nor does P's claim for "designing & preparing drawings" establish P's work was illegal engrg practice.

*Challenge to jury verdict & damages award are not covered.

EXHIBIT 3.4

QUESTIONS TO ASK
AND CASE BRIEF COMPONENTS

Six Questions	Case Brief Components
First narrative: real-world facts	
■ Who are the parties and other important people?	heading; facts
■ What happened between the parties?	facts
■ When did that happen?	facts
■ Where did that happen?	facts
■ Why did that happen?	facts
■ How have these events become the basis of litigation?	procedure
Second narrative: response of legal system Lower court(s)	
■ Which courts considered this case prior to the current court, and what did they decide?	procedure
Appellate court opinion	
■ Who wrote this opinion?	heading
■ When did this court rule?	heading
■ Where does this opinion appear?	heading
■ What has this court decided: who wins, and who loses?	issue, holding (also rule of law)
■ How did this court respond to the lower court's outcome?	holding
■ Why did this court rule this way?	reasoning (also rule of law)

---

or use different formats for different cases. This part discusses the classic components found in many case briefs. As illustrated in Exhibit 3.4 above, these components encompass the answers to the six questions about the two narratives described previously. At this point, you may wish to read the sample *Weatherston's* brief in Exhibit 3.3.

1. Opening Components

The opening components set the context for the core components discussed in Section 2.

Heading: The heading typically includes the case name, court, date, and citation of the case.

Facts: This component contains the real-world facts. Be sure to answer the journalist's questions set forth in Part D.

You should present material that is critical to the court's decision and its reasoning; omit extraneous material. To sift the facts effectively, first ask yourself which facts you must know to understand the court's thinking on the case; these relevant facts belong in the case brief. Then ask yourself which other facts provide important context for the relevant facts; these background facts also belong in the case brief. Facts failing these two tests should not be included.

Take care to state the facts in a useful way. Some writers prefer to use P and D for plaintiff and defendant, while others prefer proper names or functional labels, such as attorney and client. Present the facts in a logical order, which generally is chronological. Indeed where timing is critical and intricate, you may wish to draw a timeline. Condense what can be stated briefly. Avoid excessive detail. Use abbreviations for a more compact presentation.

In the *Weatherston's* example, the major issue was whether the contract between Weatherston's and MMLIC was illegal because Mr. Weatherston was doing engineering work without a license. Hence it is relevant that Mr. Weatherston did not have a current license to perform engineering work. The fact that MMLIC contracted with Weatherston to work on an air-conditioning project in its office building provides useful context. The fact that MMLIC was having difficulty providing ventilation in a particular area for computing equipment need not be included.

Procedure: This component chronicles events within the legal system that predate the opinion being briefed. First state who sued whom, on what type of claim, and what remedy was sought. Then, as applicable, state who won in the trial court and how (by motion, judge trial, or jury verdict); then the outcome in the intermediate appellate court; and finally who has brought the current appeal.

2. Core Components

The remaining components of the case brief address the most important dimensions of the legal system's response, that is, what the current court decided, as well as how and why the court so decided the case. The answers to these questions constitute the precedent established by the case.

Issue(s): The issue is the question the court had to answer in order to decide the case. Because the court resolves specific situations involving real people and real events, and because the court applies the law to these events, the issue combines a reference to a rule of law and real-world facts. In other words, *issue = (law + facts) in question form.*

Issues vary on several dimensions. First, some issues are primarily questions about what the law is or should be, with the real-world facts in a clearly secondary role. Other issues involve the application of settled law to facts, so that the law is in the secondary role and the facts are in the primary role. Others involve evenly balanced interactions between law and facts. Most of the time, the issue should be neither a question solely about what happened in the real world nor an abstract question about what the law is or should be.

Second, some issues involve primarily substantive legal rules, while others involve primarily procedural legal rules, and others are mixtures of the two. Substantive legal rules govern the conduct of people in the real world, while procedural rules govern the conduct of litigation, that is, events in the legal system.

Third, some issues are quite simple, dealing with a single legal concept. Others are more complex, involving several legal concepts that are so closely related that they raise subissues of the main issue.

A case may well involve several distinct issues. For example, the plaintiff may have brought several claims against the defendant, or the defendant may have asserted several defenses. Either may challenge the conduct of a trial on several grounds or be concerned with both the validity of the claim and the remedy. You generally will not be concerned with all of the issues in a multi-issue case, but instead will want to focus on issues parallel to the legal questions raised by your client's case. Even so, you should read through the entire opinion at least once to be sure that seemingly extraneous discussion really does not pertain to your client's case.

You can deduce the issue(s) in a case in several ways: First, the court may state the issue (although not necessarily artfully or completely). Second, the court may summarize the arguments of the parties; often you can convert a party's argument into an issue. Third, put yourself in the position of the court, and ask yourself what questions you would have to address to decide the case. Finally, you may wish to read the court's syllabus and the publisher's editorial matter to confirm your understanding.

If you were to brief *Weatherston's* for purposes of advising HomeElderCare, you would focus on MMLIC's argument that Mr. Weatherston contracted illegally when he agreed to perform engineering services without an engineer's license. The sample brief focuses on that issue. Note that the issue in the brief combines legal concepts (recover damages for breach of contract) and real-world facts (unregistered engineer, work includes professional engineering services, etc.). The issue involves discerning what the law should be and how that law should be applied to the facts—an evenly balanced issue. It is a substantive (not procedural) issue, because it addresses whether the parties contracted legally. The issue in the brief draws from the court's issue statement at page 821.

The issues of whether there was a contract based on the parties' discussions and how to calculate the damages are far less important to HomeElderCare. These issues are both primarily fact issues.

Holding(s): The holding is the court's answer to the issue. Mirroring the issue, it connects the law to the facts of the case to reveal the legal significance of those facts. In other words, *holding = (law + facts) in statement form.* Generally, the holding is neither an abstract statement of legal concepts nor a mere statement of what occurred in the real world. As with issues, some holdings are more legal than factual, or vice versa; some are substantive, while others are procedural; some are simple, while others are complex. Note that the court will make multiple holdings if it decides multiple issues.

The holding not only is the answer to the issue; it also constitutes precedent. Under stare decisis, the court should come to a similar holding on similar facts in the future.

One way of discerning a holding is to determine who won the case. You may find it easiest to ascertain the procedural outcome. For example, if the lower court's ruling is affirmed, the appellant has lost, and the court has resolved the issue against the appellant. Indeed, it often is useful to note this procedural outcome at the beginning of the holding. On the other hand, you may wish to focus on the court's discussion of the real-world facts and how the parties' dispute concludes. Of course, if the court states a holding in so many words ("We therefore hold . . ."), this statement merits close attention.

Holdings can be phrased narrowly, broadly, or in-between. A narrow phrasing refers specifically to the facts before the court and thus suggests that the case's impact does not extend much beyond the specific facts addressed by the court. A broad phrasing states the facts in more abstract terms, suggesting that the case's reach is expansive. The court may signal the breadth of its holding, and this statement commands respect. More often, a holding can be legitimately stated in varying degrees of generality.

In practice, your choice among these approaches will be driven by your client's situation. If your client's case is very similar to the facts of the case, a narrowly phrased holding is appropriate. If your client's case is similar only in a broad sense to the facts of the case, you may need to use a broadly phrased holding to draw out the case's significance for your client's case. You may be tempted to state a case with an unfavorable outcome narrowly or state a case with a favorable outcome broadly. However, you must be faithful to the decided case and mindful of your client's situation. In an advisory context, a neutral or cautious approach is preferable, to provide your client a margin of safety as your client contemplates various possible options. When you are advocating for a client who has already taken action, it is more appropriate to read an unfavorable precedent narrowly and a favorable precedent broadly; then your task is to persuade the tribunal to decide the case favorably to the client.

For example, the *Weatherston's* holding could be framed in terms of Mr. Weatherston himself, engineers who lack licenses, or unlicensed professionals generally. The sample case brief takes the middle ground, which most closely reflects the court's approach. As so stated, the case's significance for the HomeElderCare case is not obvious. A lawyer representing HomeElderCare probably would read the case somewhat broadly, as covering unlicensed professionals who nonetheless are trained, supervised, and honest about their status. This reading would be especially likely if the lawyer were advocating for HomeElderCare in a suit to enforce the living will contracts, because *Weatherston's* is a favorable precedent.

Rule(s) of law: In reasoning to its holding, a court employs one or more rules of law. A rule of law states the legal consequences that flow from certain broadly stated factual conditions. The court's task is to determine how the facts of the case compare to the factual conditions of the rule and deduce thereby what legal outcome to order. The rule of law is similar to the holding in that the case stands for the rules of law stated within it. Indeed, a broadly stated holding closely resembles a rule of law.

As you draft your case brief, you should look for a statement of legal consequences paired with a set of factual conditions. The legal consequences may be implied, rather than stated explicitly. The factual conditions will be described in fairly general terms, so as to cover not only the circumstances of the particular case but also other similar cases. The rule of law may be derived by the court from existing authority; in such a case, there ordinarily will be a citation to legal authority, such as a binding precedent, following the rule of law. Or the court may create a rule of law in the case you are reading, if the court has not addressed the area before or is turning in a new direction. In these situations, the court may well use a signal such as "we thus rule . . . ."

You may wish to state the rules in a separate component of your case brief. Or you may wish to state the rules—clearly labeled as such—within the reasoning component, discussed next. Either way, you should be sure you have presented the rules carefully. You may wish to follow the court's formulation or, as needed, re-work the court's statement into an if/then statement, as discussed in Chapter 2.

For example, the sample *Weatherston's* brief refers to a general rule at the opening of the reasoning component. That rule is a consolidation of sentences at pages 823 and 824. Those sentences are supported by footnotes containing references to commentary and Minnesota case law. Note that the rule is phrased more broadly (by reference to licensing statutes) than the holding (by reference to engineers).

Reasoning: As just noted, the reasoning component may cover the rules of law stated in the case. It also should synopsize the court's explanation of its holding. The court's reasoning is important because it provides guidance on how narrowly or broadly to read a case and insight into how the court will analyze future cases.

The court typically does not simply identify a rule of law and then pronounce a holding. Rather, the court shows how the rule applies to the specific facts of the case before it. In many cases, the court also identifies the competing arguments of the parties (as to what rule of law is applicable or should be created or how the facts should be analyzed), evaluates those arguments, and then accepts or rejects them. The court sometimes describes the public policy or broad social goals it seeks to serve. Finally, the court usually cites the major authorities it relied upon in reasoning to its conclusion.

For example, the *Weatherston's* court was especially concerned about fraud, incompetence, and the public welfare in that case; these concerns are certainly pertinent to HomeElderCare's case as well. Therefore the sample case brief emphasizes these points. So, too, the brief emphasizes the court's statements of public policy. The sample brief provides fairly little reference to authorities the court relied upon because the court itself did not emphasize them much; you too are unlikely to provide citations in a case brief, except where an authority is pivotal.

3. Optional, Concluding Components

Some components do not occur in every case brief, but only where needed.

Dictum: On occasion, the court remarks upon matters not essential to the holding(s). When the court does so, no matter how clear and unequivocal the remarks seem to be, the remarks are considered dicta. The plural term "dicta," or the singular "dictum," derives from "obiter dictum," which means "a remark by the way." Dicta are not considered precedent by which the court is bound. The court is bound only by statements that were fully considered because they were critical to the outcome of the case.

Dicta typically arise in two situations. First, the court may rule on one of several issues in a case in such a way as to make it unnecessary to address the remaining issues, yet the court may provide a discussion of the remaining issues. Second, to clarify its reasoning, the court may hypothesize about how it would handle a slightly or even radically different case.

You should note pertinent dicta in your case brief because the statements do emanate from the court. In the future, the dictum may become law, or the court may repudiate the dictum. In the meantime, the dictum does provide some insight into the court's current thinking.

For example, had the *Weatherston's* court concluded that the contacts between Weatherston and MMLIC did not in fact form a contract, any comments on the legality of such a contract would have been a dicta. As another example, had the court noted that it would consider cases involving attorneys or other professionals similarly to the *Weatherston's* case, this statement would have been dictum. The *Weatherston's* case does not contain dicta, so there is no dictum component in the sample brief.

Concurring and dissenting opinions: If the court has split, you should note briefly who voted differently than the majority and how they would have decided the case. Dissents are not precedent. Concurrences only rarely are, in situations where the concurrence adds to a plurality to form a majority. Nonetheless, some of these opinions eventually do inspire the court to change the law in a future case, and all of them show the thinking of the members of the particular court.

In the example, the court ruled unanimously for Weatherston's. A dissenting justice might have written, for example, that there was no evidence of a contract or that the contract was illegal because Mr. Weatherston was practicing engineering without a license. A concurring justice might have written that none of Mr. Weatherston's work would have constituted engineering practices.

Questions: Here you may note any questions the court explicitly reserved for a future case—or questions you had as you read the case.

4. Some Drafting Suggestions

Because you are the primary reader of your case brief, it must be useful to you. It also is important to produce case briefs efficiently (as indeed all lawyering tasks must be performed efficiently). Your goal is to provide the information you need to understand the case, but no more.

As you practice reading the law, you will build efficiency fairly naturally. In the meantime, you can conserve your time and energy by use of such timesavers as a standard set of abbreviations for various common terms and a form tailored to your own preferences.

You may find it easier to draft your briefs if you begin with the part of the case you generally understand the most readily. Your starting point may stay constant from case to case, or you may find that it shifts from case to case.

Be sure to review the draft of your case brief carefully. At least where the case is complicated or central to your analysis of the client's situation, consider skimming the case again after writing the brief, to check the brief against the case. Check the brief against itself, to be sure, for example, that the facts alluded to in the reasoning section are covered in the facts component. As you evaluate your own case briefs, consider the following four criteria of sound legal writing:

- *Completeness:* Is everything present that is needed for a sound understanding?
- *Correctness:* Are all points stated accurately?
- *Coherence:* Do all parts of the brief fit together?
- *Comprehensibility:* Can you understand the document readily?

F. FEDERALISM

Thus far, this chapter has presented a fairly uncomplicated image of the court system and precedent by focusing on a purely state case, that is, a case handled by a state court, discussing several related issues of state law. Many cases are more complex because they span the federal and state systems or involve the law of more than one state. This section briefly discusses several of the more common complexities (which are covered more fully in procedure courses).[5]

In two fairly common situations, the federal courts handle issues of state law. First, where citizens of two different states have a case with an amount in controversy of more than $75,000, the plaintiff may opt to sue in federal court rather than state court, even though all claims raised are state law claims. This situation is called "diversity jurisdiction." Second, where the case involves related federal and state claims and is brought in federal court, the federal court will consider the state claims, along with the federal claims, under its supplemental jurisdiction.

In both of these situations, as to issues of state law, the federal court is bound by the precedent of the highest state court, which is the ultimate authority on issues of state law. The federal court most likely will also follow decisions of higher federal courts ruling on the same issue under the same state law, but the decisions of the federal courts in these types of cases are really only persuasive precedents.

For example, if *Weatherston's* had arisen in federal court because Mr. Weatherston's business and MMLIC were citizens of different states and the amount in controversy was large enough, the federal court would have tried to decide the case as the Minnesota Supreme Court would have. It probably would have relied on much the same sources as the supreme court actually

---

5. *See* Wright et al., *supra* note 1.

did. It would not have been likely to develop a new rule unless it was fairly certain that the Minnesota Supreme Court would so rule.

Similarly, state courts on occasion address issues of federal law. This situation occurs when the federal Congress has chosen not to deny jurisdiction to the state courts on a claim arising out of federal law. In these concurrent jurisdiction cases, the state courts must follow United States Supreme Court case law and are equal to the lower federal courts.

Finally, from time to time state courts handle issues that are governed by the law of sister states. For example, if a contract involving events taking place in more than one state indicates that the law of one of those states shall govern the contract, that law usually would govern a dispute under the contract, even if the litigation occurred in a different state. In other situations, when it is not readily apparent whose law should govern, the court will have to resolve the choice-of-law question.

G. REVIEW OF CHAPTER 3

Because courts follow precedent created in earlier cases in the particular court system, legal cases have tremendous authority. Decided cases are like fables, with real-world facts constituting the story and the holding constituting the moral. This chapter has set out the following steps for reading and understanding cases:

(1) Read the case several times, and look up unfamiliar terms.
(2) Annotate the case, perhaps by labeling the paragraphs according to the components of the case brief.
(3) Ponder the two narratives in the case: Who did what, when, where, why, and how in the real world? Who did what, when, where, why, and how in the legal system?
(4) Write a case brief with the following components:
    opening: heading, facts, procedure
    core: issue, holding, rule of law, reasoning
    optional: dictum, dissent, concurrence, questions
(5) Review your brief against the case and itself. Verify that it is complete, correct, coherent, and comprehensible.

Following these steps should yield sound case briefs, permitting you to move on to fusing multiple cases—the topic of Chapter 4.

FUSING CASES

> [Common law] stands as a monument slowly raised, like a coral reef, from the minute accretions of past individuals, of whom each built upon the relics which his predecessors left, and in his turn left a foundation upon which his successors might work.
>   —Learned Hand
>   Book Review, 35 Harv. L. Rev. 479, 479 (1922) (reviewing Benjamin N. Cardozo's *The Nature of the Judicial Process*).

A. INTRODUCTION

You no doubt have synthesized material in order to discern an overall governing rule or pattern. Perhaps you have followed an employer's responses to various co-workers' performances so that you could deduce how to perform your job, or tracked customers' responses to new products so that you could make appropriate marketing decisions, or gathered the results of medical tests to make a diagnosis.

So too do lawyers synthesize information. Rarely is any single case so similar to the client's situation that the lawyer can ignore other cases on the same topic. Rather, the lawyer needs to take account of multiple close cases, "fusing" them into a single rule or pattern on that topic that then can be applied to the client's facts.

This chapter first discusses the context in which case fusion occurs and why it is necessary. It then demonstrates five fusion tools: timeline array, hierarchical array, textual fusion, rule flowchart, and features chart.

The examples in this chapter refer to *Weatherston's* and two additional cases: *Buckley v. Humason* and *Solomon v. Dreschler.* The new cases deal with an issue similar to the illegal contract issue in *Weatherston's.* You should look over those cases and briefs at pages 256 through 264 before you read further.

B. UNDERSTANDING FUSION IN THE LEGAL CONTEXT

Generally, when you fuse cases, you derive a rule of law. Sometimes, you develop a pattern of outcomes based on factual features. Other times, you also discover a policy driving the courts' decisions.

If you did not fuse your cases, you would have to apply each case separately to your client's facts, reach a conclusion as to each case, then try to merge those conclusions, some of which might differ from each other. This analysis would be time-consuming, cumbersome, and sometimes unproductive. Thus, fusing the cases before you apply them promotes efficiency.

Furthermore, the whole is greater than the sum of the parts. That is, a fusion of cases is a stronger basis for further legal analysis than a series of case briefs. The fusion permits you to explore the big picture and to avoid focusing too much on distracting details of specific cases.

Ordinarily, you can fuse cases on the same topic from the same jurisdiction, because they should be consistent with each other or they should explain why they seem inconsistent. Sometimes cases seem inconsistent because they address different classes of facts or because a later case overrules the earlier cases.

Cases from different jurisdictions may or may not be consistent with each other, because those courts are not bound by each other's precedents. Thus, inconsistent cases from other jurisdictions need not be fused with cases from your jurisdiction.

C. ARRAYING AND FUSING CASES

Occasionally the fusion process is easy, because you can use a statement in a secondary source or a recent case that surveys the case law to date. When you cannot find such a statement or when you doubt its merits, you must fuse the cases yourself.

The first step is to array the cases hierarchically (if they are from different courts) and chronologically (if they are from different years). This step is essential to understanding the relationship among the cases. The second step is to fuse the cases, by use of the textual fusion, rule flowchart, or features chart. As you do so, you should note not only the elements the court has evolved, but also elaborations on and examples of the elements. Finally, you should check the validity of the result.

1. Arraying Cases Hierarchically and Chronologically

Of course a necessary starting point is to read and brief the cases carefully. Separate the binding cases from the persuasive cases. You may wish to read from oldest to newest (or vice versa) or from the highest to the lowest court. Focus on the relationship of each case to the cases that preceded it.

To focus your attention on the relative precedential values of the cases, array them hierarchically, using the triangular court diagram of Exhibit 3.1. If there is more than one case from a particular court, list those cases from top to bottom in reverse chronological order. This hierarchical array is especially useful when you have cases from multiple levels of the same court system or sets of cases from different jurisdictions.

Exhibit 4.1 is a hierarchical array of the three HomeElderCare cases, all decided by the high court of the binding jurisdiction.

EXHIBIT 4.1

HIERARCHICAL AND CHRONOLOGICAL ARRAYS OF CASES

S.Ct.:

Weatherston's (1960)
Buckley (1892)
Solomon (1860)

Ct. App. (after 1983):

trial cts.:

Minnesota
(binding)

Solomon (Minn. 1860): unlicensed liquor dealer's K invalid, bcz stat. policy to protect public v. evils of unrestrained liquor sales

Buckley (Minn. 1892): unlicensed realty broker's comm'n K invalid, no discussion of stat. policy

Weatherston's (Minn. 1960): unlicensed eng'r's K valid, bcz incidental part of larger K., public protected agst fraud & incompetence by P's training & D's supervision; public health & safety protect'd

Then array your cases on a timeline from oldest to most recent, placing cases with one result above the line and cases with the other result below the line. For each case, sketch out the key facts and reasoning. You can begin to discern a pattern by looking for what is true of all cases above the line *and* not true of cases below the line.

From the chronological array of HomeElderCare cases in Exhibit 4.1, you can see that two of the three cases, the older ones, came out the same way: the contract was not enforced. But the most recent case came out differently (the contract was enforced), perhaps because the court's approach has shifted after seventy years, or because the facts were more favorable for the unlicensed practitioner, or both.

2. Fusing the Cases

There are various ways to fuse cases. If the cases all have fully articulated (albeit somewhat different) rules, you can choose between textual fusion and the rule flowchart. On the other hand, if the rule is not well articulated, you may want to use the features chart to unearth patterns in the facts or policies of the cases. For the strongest fusion, you would combine methods.

a. Focusing on Rules

You may wonder why the statement of a rule is not the same in every case. As the opening quote to this chapter notes, the common law is built by "minute accretions of past" cases, as each case builds upon past cases and adds to the foundation for future cases. Because a court can decide only the controversy presented to it, the court's opinion in each case should discuss only so much of a rule as it needed for that case. Other cases on the same general topic may entail other aspects of the rule. Or the court may adjust the elements stated in previous cases without overturning the previously stated rule, to keep the rule current. Or the court may alter the phrasing of a rule, while not intending to change the meaning.

i. Textual Fusion
Textual fusion involves a word-by-word analysis of the similarities and differences between or among two or more rules drawn from the cases to be fused. First, compare each word and phrase of the rules to be fused. Separate the language into four categories: material that is *identical* in all rules, material that is *similar* in all rules, material that *appears in only some* rules, or material that *differs* from rule to rule.

Begin to assemble the fused rule with the material that is *identical* in all rules. If *similar* material can be rephrased into a single broader term that still adequately describes the original material, use that new term in the fused rule. If it cannot, use one or more of the similar phrasings for this material.

Then turn to the material *appearing in only some* cases. Add this material to the fused rule, one item at a time. Test each new item by asking whether its addition would change the results of cases in which that item does not appear. If the addition would not change any of the cases, add the new item to the fused rule. If the addition would change any of the cases, try to adjust the new item by rewording it to eliminate the change in the case result or by presenting the item as a disjunctive element (alternatives connected by "or"). Often the new item appears in a newer case and reflects a factor the court simply did not consider or articulate earlier. As for material that is *different* in the various rules, refer to Part D of this chapter.

As you work through these steps, ask yourself whether your fused formulation accurately states the law. More precisely, consider whether the fused rule would change the result in any of the cases.

Exhibit 4.2 presents a textual fusion of the primary rule of law from *Weatherston's* and the rule from *Buckley*. Many of the words in those rules are identical and therefore are not italicized or in boldface; these identical items appear in the fused rule. Four boldface concepts are phrased in similar but

---

EXHIBIT 4.2

TEXTUAL FUSION OF RULES

italics = appears only in one case
boldface = similar terms

Weatherston's	*Buckley*
IF (1) stat. req's person practic'g particular **profess'n** to obtain **license or certificate,** &	IF (1) *valid* stat. req's **license** for particular **business,** &
(2) person in that **profess'n** enters into **agr'mt** of **profess'l** character w/o license or certificate, &	(2) person in that **business** enters into **contract** for the **bus.** w/o license,
(3) *circumstances surround'g agr'mt violate any reason for licens'g stat's existence,*	
THEN that agr'mt is **illegal** & void.	THEN contract is void & **unenforceable.**

Fused Rule

IF (1) a statute requires a person practicing a particular profession or engaging in a particular business to obtain a license or certificate, and
(2) a person in that profession or business enters into a business or professional contract without a license or certificate, and
(3) the circumstances surrounding the contract violate any reason for the statute's existence,

THEN   that contract is void and unenforceable.

not identical terms. The fused rule uses both terms as to some concepts (business and profession), only one term as to others (contract, not agreement). One underlined term is unique to *Buckley,* and one is unique to *Weatherston's.* The word "valid" from *Buckley* can safely be eliminated, because an invalid statute no longer has the force and effect of a statute. The second unique item, element 3 in *Weatherston's,* is a pivotal portion of that rule. It is difficult to test its consistency with *Buckley* because the *Buckley* facts are so sparely stated. Because *Weatherston's* was decided much later than *Buckley,* the additional element in *Weatherston's* signals the rule's evolution. Thus, you should include element 3 in the fused rule. There are no different items in this example.

ii. Rule Flowchart

A rule flowchart also focuses closely on the language of the rule. A rule flowchart presents the elements and legal consequences, showing how time affected each aspect of the rule. Note the names and dates of the cases beside the wording each contributes.

EXHIBIT 4.3

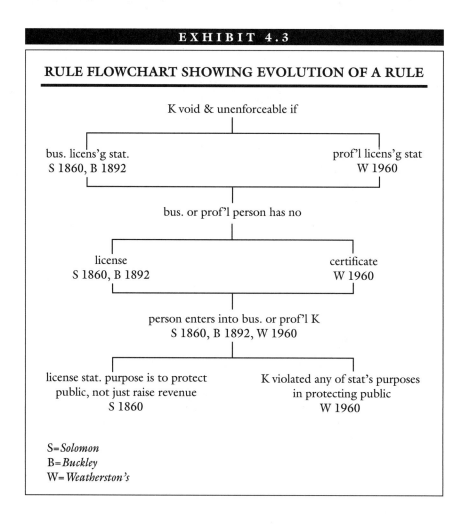

RULE FLOWCHART SHOWING EVOLUTION OF A RULE

K void & unenforceable if

bus. licens'g stat.
S 1860, B 1892

prof'l licens'g stat
W 1960

bus. or prof'l person has no

license
S 1860, B 1892

certificate
W 1960

person enters into bus. or prof'l K
S 1860, B 1892, W 1960

license stat. purpose is to protect
public, not just raise revenue
S 1860

K violated any of stat's purposes
in protecting public
W 1960

S=*Solomon*
B=*Buckley*
W=*Weatherston's*

For instance, in Exhibit 4.3, opposite, the rule flowchart starts with the legal consequence (contract void and unenforceable) and then sets out the if-clause. The horizontal branches show the disjunctive subelements, while the vertical arrows show the conjunctive relationships among the elements. Exhibit 4.3 shows that the court gradually added words and phrases. At the bottom, the flowchart shows that *Weatherston's* revised an element alluded to in *Solomon*, but omitted in *Buckley*.

iii. Presentation of Rule-Based Fusion

Whichever method of rule-based fusion you use, you would depict the resulting rule using one of the methods from Chapter 2. Exhibit 4.2 shows a textual depiction, while Exhibit 4.3 presents a flowchart depiction.

As you work with cases, you no doubt will notice how the rule applied to the various facts of the cases. Furthermore, in most cases, the court will discuss what one or more elements mean. This information, which exemplifies and elaborates upon the rule, can be helpful to you as you seek to apply the rule to your client's situation, so you may wish to incorporate it into your statement of the rule.

For example, the three HomeElderCare cases provide three examples of the concept of licensed profession: liquor dealer, realty broker, and engineer. As another example, the *Weatherston's* court elaborated on how a contract may or may not violate the purpose of a licensing statute; the court focused on the incidental nature of the engineering services, fraud, incompetence, and risks to public safety. Exhibit 4.4, a textual depiction of the rule distilled by fusing the three cases, incorporates these points.

EXHIBIT 4.4

IF/THEN PRESENTATION OF FUSED RULE

IF   (1) statute requires licensure or certificate of person practicing
            profession/business, and
                  exs: liquor dealer, realty broker, engineer
       (2) person in that profession/business enters into contract with-
            out license/certificate, and
       (3) circumstances violate reason for statute
                  such as fraud, incompetence, danger to public safety &
                  health [not so where engr is an incidental part of larger
                  contract, professional told client of unlicensed status, unli-
                  censed professional is licensed in another state and super-
                  vised by licensed professional],
THEN   contract is void and unenforceable.

b. Focusing on Facts or Policies: Features Chart

Another approach is to look for patterns in the cases' facts, results, and reasonings, including policies. This approach is especially effective where the court has not articulated the rule fully or clearly. Hidden rules generally occur where the law is unsettled, because a rule is new or changing. The fusion method best suited to this approach is the features chart.

This chart is a matrix of potentially significant features of the cases. In addition to the case name, court, and year, possible features include the real-world roles of the parties, the claim (also known as "cause of action"), the relief sought (also known as "remedy"), the salient facts, policies stated by the court, and the holding(s) of each case on the issue(s) being examined. If the court stresses a feature, it should appear in your features chart. Be sure to list the cases in a logical order, such as oldest to most recent.

The next step is to look for patterns that explain the holdings: Does a particular holding always follow from a particular fact or combination of facts? Does a particular policy consideration result in one holding or the other? Does one result occur until a certain date, and then another result appear? These patterns may be cause/effect relationships, or they may be coincidences. A close reading of the cases should tell you which is true.

Your work with a features chart is not complete until you can discern the pattern from the columns in the matrix. If you cannot find a pattern that explains the holdings, reread the cases to find additional facts that may not have seemed significant on first reading. Be sure to look for the possibility that two or more columns, acting together, provide the pattern. If the cases truly conflict, concentrate on the later cases and the cases from the highest binding court.

Finally, align the findings from your features chart with whatever rule material the court has presented. The aspects you have identified as important should be consistent with the concepts identified by the court.

Exhibit 4.5 is a features chart comparing *Solomon*, *Buckley*, and *Weatherston's*. The columns to the right of center suggest that the key aspect is violation of the statute's policy. Note, however, that this is not a certain pattern because this aspect was not analyzed in *Buckley*.

3. Checking Your Work

However you perform your case fusion, be sure to check it for compliance with the four criteria of sound legal writing:

- *Completeness:* Are all cases, elements, and consequences included?
- *Correctness:* Have you accurately reflected the cases? Have you attended closely to the court's language? Have you accurately represented the holdings?
- *Coherence:* Does the fusion make sense? Are the elements consistent with each other?
- *Comprehensibility:* Can you understand the fusion?

If you have prepared both a rule-based fusion and a features chart, check the results of each against the other.

EXHIBIT 4.5

FEATURES CHART

Case	Court/ Year	Parties	Claim	Additional Facts	Purpose of License Statute	Purpose Violated Here?	Contract Valid?
Solomon	Minn. 1860	Unlicensed liquor dealer and buyer	Recover price of liquor delivered	NA	Protect public from evils of unrestrained liquor sales	Yes	No
Buckley	Minn. 1892	Unlicensed realty broker and client	Recover broker's commission	NA	None stated	NA	No
Weatherston's	Minn. 1960	Unlicensed engineer and client	Recover damages for breach of contract	Engineer was competent; no fraud; services were incidental to permitted transaction	Protect public from fraud and incompetence; protect public health and safety	No	Yes

D. RECOGNIZING THE LIMITS OF FUSION

On occasion, you may find yourself trying to fuse material that cannot be fused. For instance, your work with the rules might yield an element as to which the cases differ dramatically, in a way that cannot be accommodated by a disjunctive element or a wording change. In other situations, your features chart may not yield a pattern that explains all of the cases' holdings. Material cannot be fused in three situations.

First, the court may not merely modify a rule over time, but instead impliedly overrule previous case law, without saying so. It is not possible or desirable to fuse cases that are meant to conflict.

Second, the cases may concern topics that are related but not the same. For example, different rules may develop for different actors in a class of situations, based on differences in their roles toward the harmed party. Or different rules may develop for various legal consequences; the elements of a rule imposing criminal penalties may differ from the elements of the rule imposing civil liability. Fusing these rules will produce a murky and complex rule not useful for analyzing a client's situation. The solution is to develop two or more rules.

Third, you may have an anomalous case (or two) in an otherwise fusible set of cases. While anomalous cases frustrate lawyers seeking to understand an area of case law, they do not surprise most experienced lawyers. Recall that courts do not only make precedent; they also resolve real-world disputes. Some litigants have facts sympathetic enough to persuade a court—despite the legal weaknesses of their cases. If you have discovered a truly anomalous case, consider omitting it from your fusion. This omission is especially justifiable if later cases discount the anomalous case or do not take note of it.

For example, if the following cases existed, you would not have included them in the sample fusion: an 1850s case indicating that contracts for unlicensed professional services are valid and enforceable, on the theory that the penalty for unlicensed practice should be criminal, not civil, liability (not included because *Solomon* and *Buckley* subsequently overruled it); a case denying enforcement of a contract because it was procured by fraud (not included because it deals with a different legal problem); a case finding for an unwitting unlicensed professional and against a sophisticated client (not included because of its unusual, sympathetic facts).

E. REVIEW OF CHAPTER 4

The goal of the fusion process is to generate a rule or pattern that encompasses the content of many cases. The steps of fusion are as follows:

(1)   Prepare hierarchical and chronological arrays, to help you to understand the precedential relationships among cases.

(2)(a) Where possible, fuse the rules stated in the cases by use of textual fusion or a rule flowchart, and note examples and elaborations.

(b) Where appropriate and useful, seek a pattern or policy in the cases by constructing a features chart.

(3)   Check your fusion for completeness, correctness, coherence, and comprehensibility.

Fusing cases before you apply them to your client's case will strengthen your understanding of the law and your analysis of your client's legal position.

5

READING STATUTES

> The law is a living growth, not a changeless code.
> —Inscription carved over the entrance to the Yale Law
> School, 1929–1931

A. INTRODUCTION

This chapter introduces codified law—law in the form of a code, that is, a set of rules of general applicability. The discussion will focus on statutes, the codes enacted by legislatures. Statutes are both an increasingly prevalent and a highly authoritative form of law. Nonetheless, it is important to remember that there are other types of codified law. Legislatures (and voters) create constitutions. Administrative agencies create rules and regulations. Courts create rules governing the procedures to be followed in various types of litigation. These forms of law stand in a hierarchical relationship: constitutions at the top, statutes and court rules in the middle, administrative regulations at the bottom. Thus, for example, statutes must accord with constitutional requirements, and regulations must accord with statutes.

This chapter first provides a brief overview of the legislative process and discusses the importance of legislative intent, then presents a process for reading and briefing statutes, and closes with a discussion of federalism.

Much of this chapter, especially the material on reading and briefing statutes, pertains not only to statutes, but also to other forms of codified law.

Along the way, this chapter discusses two specific statutes. Section 481.02 of the Minnesota Statutes, which governs the unauthorized practice of law, is the major statute governing the HomeElderCare situation. Minn. Stat. § 481.02 (1992). Minnesota's living will statute, Minn. Stat. §§ 145B.01-.17 (1992), is also relevant.[1] Relevant portions of both appear at pages 265-74, and you may find it helpful to read them now.

B. LEGISLATIVE PROCESS AND LEGISLATIVE INTENT

1. Legislative Process

The legislative process[2] is a highly collaborative and loosely structured process, in which legislators, the executive, and interested members of the public participate. See Exhibit 5.1. Proposals for new legislation or amendments to existing statutes come from many sources: legislators, the executive branch, individual citizens, organizations such as industry associations and public-interest groups, and law-reform commissions. Ultimately, for a proposal to receive the legislature's official attention, it must become a bill and be introduced by legislators.

In the United States, most legislatures, including the federal Congress, are bicameral, consisting of both a house of representatives and a senate. For a bill to become law, it must be passed in identical form by both chambers. Sometimes a bill begins in and is passed by one chamber, then proceeds to the second. Other times, companion bills are considered simultaneously by both chambers. Both chambers typically consider bills in several stages; at each successive stage, legislators' participation broadens, and the public's involvement decreases.

In the first stage (1), a subcommittee specializing in the general area of the bill's topic considers the bill. The subcommittee may hold a public hearing and receive testimony from interested individuals and groups, then report to the full committee.

In the second stage (2), the committee deliberates on the bill, discussing its strengths and weaknesses and honing its language. The committee either reports the bill favorably to the full chamber or tables it, the latter precluding further action on the bill. Although the public's role at this stage is not as formal as at the subcommittee stage, lobbyists may be in contact with committee members. When a committee reports a bill favorably, it usually generates a report summarizing the bill and explaining the need for it.

---

1. Because the HomeElderCare case file was developed in the early 1990s, the citations are current to that time.
2. For further detail, see Jack Davies, *Legislative Law and Process in a Nutshell* (2d ed. 1986).

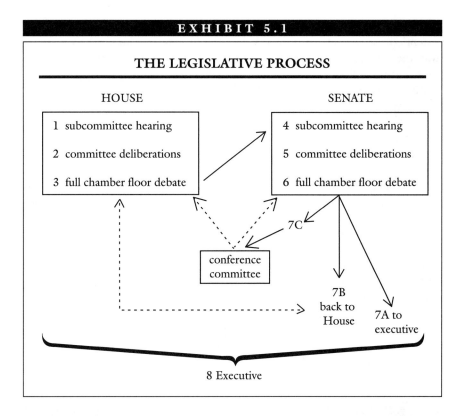

EXHIBIT 5.1

THE LEGISLATIVE PROCESS

HOUSE   SENATE

1 subcommittee hearing   4 subcommittee hearing

2 committee deliberations   5 committee deliberations

3 full chamber floor debate   6 full chamber floor debate

7C

conference
committee

7B
back to
House

7A to
executive

8 Executive

The third stage (3) is debate by the full chamber. When the bill is controversial, the debate may actually be a true airing of competing views involving most members of the chamber. In other situations, the so-called debate entails a series of speeches by the bill's supporters that go unheard by most other legislators. Ultimately, the legislators vote on the bill. At this stage, the public does not have a formal role, but lobbyists may be active behind the scenes.

After the same process, or an abbreviated process, occurs in the other chamber (stages 4–6), the bill may clear the legislature, or it may be the subject of further consideration. If both chambers have passed identical bills (7A), that bill clears the legislature and goes to the executive (president or governor). If the two chambers considered non-identical bills and the differences are minor, one chamber may accede to the other's changes; then the bill clears the legislature (7B). If the differences are major, a conference committee (7C), with members from both chambers, resolves the differences and reports a consensus bill back to the two chambers, which may then pass the consensus bill. Again, lobbyists may be involved.

Once both chambers pass the same bill, it proceeds to the executive for signature (8). The executive may disagree with the bill and veto it, subject to override by the legislature. On the other hand, if the executive signs it, or, in some systems, permits it to become law without his or her signature, the bill becomes law and is labeled a "statute."

The legislature may amend the statute at a later time. Statutes are amended for several reasons. The legislature may not be satisfied with the way the statute has worked out and may modify troublesome language to more closely reflect what the legislature intended. Or the legislature may become aware of facts it did not initially have and revise the statute to reflect that new knowledge. Or the legislature may change its collective mind about what the law should be and alter the statute accordingly.

In some respects, the legislative process is similar to the judicial process. For example, both are lawmaking processes, both involve participation by those governed, and both have mechanisms for adjusting the law.

However, the two processes also differ in important ways, as shown in Exhibit 5.2. The courts are reactive, considering only cases brought to their attention by the parties; the legislature acts both reactively and proactively, taking on problems brought forth by the public and also those discerned by the legislators themselves. The courts take the issues as framed by the parties' dispute; the legislature defines its own issues, broadening, narrowing, or shifting its focus as it wishes. A small segment of the public participates in judicial lawmaking through litigation, which is a very formal process defined by rules of procedure; a wider segment participates in legislative lawmaking through lobbying, a quite informal and ill defined process. The judicial process is intended to be non-political; the legislative process is intended to be highly political.

EXHIBIT 5.2

COMPARISON OF CASES AND STATUTES

	Cases	Statutes
Lawmaking process	■ reactive ■ parties frame issues ■ litigation ■ non-political	■ reactive and proactive ■ legislature frames issues ■ lobbying ■ political
Focus	■ facts of current litigation ■ case before the court	■ future situations ■ broad class of situations
Effect	■ generally retroactive	■ generally prospective
Form	■ primarily narratives with embedded rule ■ narrative in parties' case ■ fable with story and moral	■ primarily rule with implied narrative ■ narrative in paradigm case ■ rules of game

As an example, consider the Minnesota statute on living wills, chapter 145B, which has an interesting legislative history. For five years, two sides with strongly held views battled: on one side, Minnesota Citizens Concerned for Life (MCCL); on the other, a coalition of senior citizen groups, the state bar association, and medical provider associations. Eventually, the chair of the House committee sought to mediate the conflict, and in 1987 and 1988, the House committee held thirty-five hours of hearings around the state. Various events occurred, easing the stalemate. The chief voice for the MCCL in the House lost his seat, and the coalition in favor of the bill enlisted a new chief author in the Senate (who was a prominent lawyer). Ten more hours of hearings were held. Several changes were made in committee and on the floor, and the bill passed as the Adult Health Care Decisions Act, ch. 3, 1989 Minn. Laws 8. *See* Howard Orenstein, et al., *Minnesota's Living Will . . . ,* Bench & B. Minn., Aug. 1989, at 21. Incidentally, the statute has been amended since 1989, including a new title, the Minnesota Living Will Act. *See* Act of May 20, 1991, ch. 148, 1991 Minn. Laws 308.

2. Legislative Intent and Word Choice

The ultimate product of the legislative process is a statute: a collection of words chosen to express the will of the legislature. The premise of a statute is that it expresses legislative intent. To a certain extent, "legislative intent" is a legal fiction. In any statutory provision, some legislators probably intended to state one idea, others intended another, and yet others did not think seriously enough about it to have a clear intent. Although there may be individual legislators' intentions, rarely is there a single legislative intent. Furthermore, a particular factual situation may pose a question that the legislature never even contemplated. Nonetheless, the premise of legislative intent is powerful. For whatever reasons, the legislature has enacted the precise language in the statute—each word, each phrase, each punctuation mark— and this language commands respect.

Statutes thus differ from case law. Again, see Exhibit 5.2. Judges write most directly to the parties to the case, explaining the outcome of the litigation for them. However, certain portions of an opinion, chiefly the rules of law and the holding, are written with an eye toward unknown participants in future disputes, and these portions are quite carefully worded. In comparison, the legislature writes entirely to unknown persons whose future activities fall within the statute's scope. Thus, every word in a statute carries the potential impact of the rule of law and the holding from a case.

3. Prospective Effect of Statutes

Unlike case law, which typically is retroactive, statutes typically have prospective effect. A statute covers conduct occurring on or after the statute's effective date. Some statutes take effect on the date of enactment, which generally is the date of signature by the executive. Others do not take effect until a date specified in the statute, which is usually some months after the date of enactment. Others take effect on the default effective date for statutes with no effective date.

There are some limited exceptions to this general rule of prospectivity. The legislature may provide that the statute is to be applied retroactively. A statute addressing procedures or remedies for a wronged party may be retroactive in the sense that a party whose loss occurred before the statute's enactment would proceed under the new statute if the litigation occurs after the effective date.

Thus it is critical to discern which language was effective at the time of the events you are analyzing, especially if a statute has been amended. That version (not necessarily the current version) of the statute governs the law for your situation.

C. READING A STATUTE

1. An Analogy: Rules of a Game

Statutes resemble the rules of a game. Both are written in fairly abstract terms. Some statutes govern discrete, uncomplicated situations, and the rules are quite simple. Others govern a wider range of complicated situations, and the rules are quite elaborate. In either event, you may find it helpful to imagine that you are seeking certain information about how to play the game: What is the name of the game? What is its purpose? Who can play? What kind of conduct is generally encouraged or prohibited? Are there any exceptions to these general rules? What are the consequences of playing or not playing the game as described?

2. Organization of a Statute

A statute reads like an expansive rule of law. It thus differs from a case, because only a small portion of a case is framed as a rule of law. At first reading, a statute may seem to lack a narrative of specific real-world events, as there always is in a judicial opinion. However, if you think carefully about the statute, you will be able to envision a specific situation that would clearly bring the statute into play. This situation may be understood as a paradigm case and is discussed further in Chapter 6.

Although each statute is unique, statutes have some standard components. The following material outlines the components you are likely to find in longer statutes, such as the living will statute, although the components seldom will be set out with these labels. Shorter statutes, such as the unauthorized practice statute, do not contain all of these components or do not have them separately labeled. The copies of the two statutes in the Home-ElderCare case file at pages 265-74 are labeled according to these components.

Title: Legislatures occasionally name major statutes, and some statutes come to be called by their names, rather than their section numbers. The living will statute's name is the Minnesota Living Will Act, according to Minn. Stat. § 145B.01.

Preamble, purpose statement: On occasion, the legislature includes a statement of its purpose in enacting the statute: the problems the legislature sought to address, the interests the legislature sought to serve, or the results the legislature desired. Although this language does not itself constitute any portion of the statute's rule, it can provide helpful insight into the legislature's intent. Neither sample statute contains a purpose statement.

Definitions: Many statutes employ particular meanings for terms used in the statute. These statutory terms of art generally are set out in a definition section, or they may appear in the scope section (see below) or elsewhere. Regardless of location, these definitions are critical, because they help to define the factual conditions leading to the statute's legal consequences. Absent a clear contrary indication, every time a defined term appears in the statute, it carries this definition. For example, the living will statute provides a very narrow meaning of "health care" in section 145B.02 subdivision 3.

Scope: Some statutes contain scope provisions, generally found near the beginning of the statute, which state the situations to which the statute does apply and thereby imply which situations are not within the statute's reach. A statute's scope typically has three dimensions: the actors (whether natural persons or entities) covered by the statute, their actions, and the circumstances in which they act. If there is no separate scope provision, you must infer the statute's scope from the definitions and other components. For example, section 145B.03 subdivision 1 of the living will statute indicates that the statute governs living wills regarding health care, entered into by competent adults.

The following three components constitute the operative provisions of the statute. All statutes contain general rules; most also contain exceptions; nearly all contain consequences/enforcement provisions, although some require reference to other statutes or case law for this information.

General rule: The core of the statute describes the conduct the legislature has chosen to encourage or prohibit. Many statutes contain multiple general rules, because the legislature has chosen to govern several forms of related conduct in one statute. Section 481.02 subdivision 1 of the unauthorized practice statute is a general rule prohibiting unauthorized practice of law.

Exceptions: Frequently, the legislature grapples with competing policies in enacting a statute. The legislature may favor one policy in the general rule, but seek to accommodate a competing policy by carving out an exception. For example, section 481.02 subdivision 3 of the unauthorized practice statute delineates numerous situations that would have fallen within the general rule prohibiting unauthorized law practice, except that the legislature chose to exempt them.

Consequences and enforcement: The purpose of the general rule is to link the identified conduct to a specific legal consequence. If the conduct is encouraged, the consequence is a legal benefit, such as recognition of a transaction as legally enforceable or exemption from a fee. If the conduct is prohibited, the consequence is a legal penalty, such as a criminal sanction, a civil fine, nonenforcement of the transaction, or payment of damages to a harmed party. These consequences may be stated in the same section as the general rule, or they may be stated in a separate section. The statement of the consequences may refer explicitly to an enforcement mechanism, or the enforcement mechanism may be implied. For example, if a statute indicated that a party is liable for damages, one could infer that the harmed party would bring a lawsuit to obtain damages. In the unauthorized practice statute, section 481.02 subdivision 8 identifies both the consequences of engaging in the unauthorized practice of law and the means by which the statute is enforced.

Severability or saving clause: Some statutes include a provision indicating that, should any specific provisions be deemed unconstitutional, the rest of the statute is intended by the legislature to stand. Neither sample statute includes a severability provision.

Effective date: As noted above, the legislature may specify an effective date. Neither sample statute has a stated effective date.

3. Reading Stages

You should read a statute several times. The first time through, read the entire statute to discern its overall design and scope. Second, identify which provisions are pertinent to your client's case and which (if any) are not; err on the side of including information that may or may not be pertinent. Third, identify which material fits into each of the components set forth above.

For example, the copy of section 481.02 at pages 265–268 shows that a lawyer would disregard much of that section in an analysis of the HomeElderCare situation. The insignificance of many provisions is quite obvious; others require careful consideration before they can be eliminated. For example, subdivision 2 applies only to corporations "operated for pecuniary profit"; HomeElderCare is a corporation, but it is not organized for pecuniary profit. The provisions on drafting of testamentary wills might be retained for further consideration, although they probably apply only to wills disposing of property upon death.

D. BRIEFING A STATUTE

Statutory briefing is a means of analyzing and taking notes on a statute. You can organize your brief by statutory components or, ideally, by the if/then rule structure introduced in Chapter 2. And you can use various means of depicting the statutory rule.

1. Brief Based on Statutory Components

A brief based on statutory components parallels the case brief (discussed in Chapter 3) in that it presents the material under component headings. Although you can simply copy the statutory language under each heading, the

---

EXHIBIT 5.3

COMPONENTS-BASED STATUTORY BRIEF

TITLE: Unauthorized practice of law.

DEFINITIONS: None expressly stated, tho atty is member of MN bar admitted & licensed. Subd. 1.

SCOPE: None expressly stated; governs actions of non-attys as stated below. Subd. 1.

GENERAL RULES: Subd. 1 states: Unlawful for non-attys to:

- give legal advice or counsel
  perform for or furnish legal services
  to another
  for fee or considn
  OR
- prepare directly or thru another
  for another person, firm, corp
  will, testamentary disp'n, instrument of trust serving purposes
  similar to will
  for or w/o fee or considn
  OR
- prepare for another person, firm, corp
  any other legal document
  for fee or considn.

EXCEPTIONS: Permissible for:

- person to draw will for another
  in emergency if imminence of death leaves insuff. time for atty
  superv'n—Subd. 3(2).
- person to confer or cooperate with atty of another
  in preparing any legal document
  if atty is not empd by non-atty or by person, firm, corp.
  repd by non-atty—Subd. 3(6).
- corp. to furnish
  to person lawfully engaged in practice of law
  information or clerical service that is lawful
  provided that atty maintains responsibility to clients for
  information & services—Subd. 7.

CONSEQUENCES/ENFORCEMENT: (1) Misdemeanor. County attys prosecute; jurisdiction in dist. ct. (2) Injunction against illegal actions, brought by county atty or atty general. Subd. 8.

brief will be more useful if you condense the key ideas and use enumeration or spacing so that the language most pertinent to your client's situation is highlighted. You may find it helpful to note the sections or subsections where the information appears.

Exhibit 5.3 is an example of such a brief for section 481.02. Note how the key material in a lengthy statute has been extracted and is presented in a more accessible form.

2. Briefs Based on If/Then Format

Because a statute is an expansive rule statement, it makes sense to brief a statute by creating one or more if/then rule statements. You can derive an if/then brief from the brief based on statutory components, according to the following formula:

IF   the client situation (actor/action/circumstances)
           meets the *definitions,* and
           falls within the *scope,* and
           falls within the *general rule,* and
           does not qualify for any of the *exceptions,*

THEN   the *consequences* follow,
           through the *enforcemen*t mechanism.

.   This if/then brief is more useful than the components-based brief. Although the components-based brief conveys the statute's design well, the if/then brief synthesizes functionally related information that may appear in various provisions of the statute. All information related to the factual conditions appears in one location, the if-clause, although this information may be scattered throughout the statute in definition, scope, general rule, and exception provisions. Similarly, all information related to the legal consequences appears in the then-clause, even though this information may be scattered in the statute among the general rule, consequences, and enforcement provisions.

This if/then statement of a statute can be presented in various ways. Options include a traditional paragraph, a quasi-outline using tabulation or enumeration, and flowchart.

Exhibits 5.4 and 5.5 (see pages 61 and 62) are examples of if/then briefs for section 481.02, in quasi-outline and flowchart form. Note that both present the same material as the components-based brief, but the elements and consequences are easier to discern.

3. Drafting Carefully and Checking Your Work

As you create either of the briefs described above, you will reconfigure the statute's own structure and language slightly. Make sure that the brief accurately reflects the overall design of the statute. For example, the statute may address several forms of related conduct or several actors, and the brief should reflect these distinct items.

EXHIBIT 5.4

IF/THEN STATUTORY BRIEF

IF   any person/assn except members of MN bar admitted & licensed
to practice

A. does 1 OR 2 OR 3 (all in Subd. 1)
1. gives legal advice or counsel
performs for or furnishes legal services
to another
for fee or considn
2. prepares directly or thru another
for another person/firm/corp.
any will or testamentary disp'n or instrument of trust serving purposes similar to will
(for or w/o fee or considn)
3. prepares for another person/firm/corp.
any other legal document
for fee or considn

B. AND NOT person drafting will
for another
in emergency leaving insuff. time for atty supervn
Subd. 3(2)

C. AND NOT person conferring or cooperating
with licensed atty of another
in preparing any legal document
if atty is not empd by that person or by person/firm/corp.
repd by that person
Subd. 3(6)

D. AND NOT corp. furnishing
lawful info or clerical services
to atty
who maintains responsibility to clients
for info & services
Subd. 7

THEN   misdemeanor prosecuted by county atty in dist. ct; injunction
brought by county atty or atty genl—Subd. 8

Guard against a very understandable temptation to paraphrase the
statute into language that is easier to work with or more desirable from the
client's perspective but does not capture the statute's meaning. Take care not
to lose relevant content in the statute when you paraphrase or condense lan-

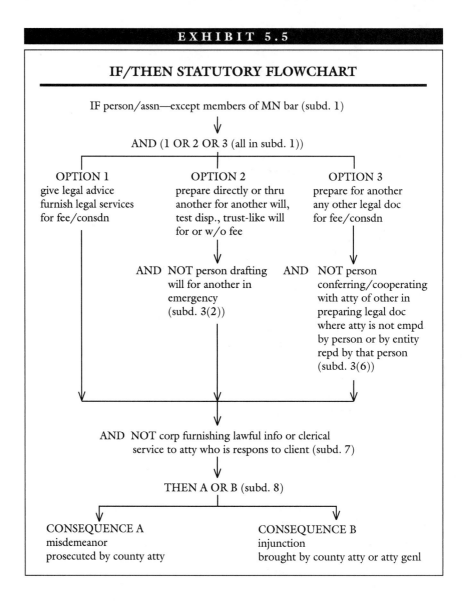

EXHIBIT 5.5

IF/THEN STATUTORY FLOWCHART

IF person/assn—except members of MN bar (subd. 1)

AND (1 OR 2 OR 3 (all in subd. 1))

OPTION 1	OPTION 2	OPTION 3
give legal advice furnish legal services for fee/consdn	prepare directly or thru another for another will, test disp., trust-like will for or w/o fee	prepare for another any other legal doc for fee/consdn

AND NOT person drafting will for another in emergency (subd. 3(2))

AND NOT person conferring/cooperating with atty of other in preparing legal doc where atty is not empd by person or by entity repd by that person (subd. 3(6))

AND NOT corp furnishing lawful info or clerical service to atty who is respons to client (subd. 7)

THEN A OR B (subd. 8)

CONSEQUENCE A
misdemeanor
prosecuted by county atty

CONSEQUENCE B
injunction
brought by county atty or atty genl

guage. More specifically, pay special attention to the grammatical units in the statute's provisions. These units typically are nouns, verbs or verb phrases, and modifiers. Attend closely to details. For example, there is a major difference between "and" and "or" in a statute. Be sure you know what a modifying phrase modifies. Statutory terms of art should be employed as defined throughout the statute, even though a statutorily defined term might have a different meaning in everyday speech.

Finally, insert section and subdivision references, to allow you easily to locate the statutory provisions you have briefed.

Following these suggestions should enable you to satisfy the four criteria:

- *Completeness:* Are all pertinent provisions included?
- *Correctness:* Have you accurately captured the concepts the legislature meant to convey in the specific words it chose?
- *Coherence:* Do the parts of the brief fit together well? Does the overall point (that the specified legal consequence will follow the specified factual conditions) make sense?
- *Comprehensibility:* Can you understand the brief?

By way of illustration, section 481.02 subdivision 1 prohibits five separate activities (three pertinent to HomeElderCare's situation), all in one massive paragraph. It is easier to understand this lengthy subdivision when the verb phrases ("to appear," "to hold out," etc.) are separated from each other (as revealed by the numbers in circles on the copy at page 265). These five major activities are stated in the disjunctive. Note how important it is to link the modifying phrases "for or without a fee or any consideration" and "for a fee or any consideration" in the last six lines to the appropriate activities. Although the statute has no definition provision, it implies a definition of "attorney" (someone admitted and licensed to practice in Minnesota) which should be carried throughout the statute. The sample briefs in Exhibits 5.4 and 5.5 reflect these intricacies and include subdivision citations for future reference.

E. FEDERALISM

Statutes exist at multiple levels of government. Some areas, such as the HomeElderCare situation, are governed by state statutes; other areas are governed by federal statute or local ordinance; others are governed by a combination of these.

Federal statutes govern matters Congress has perceived to be of national interest. Examples include air and water pollution, the operation of the securities market, and union-management relations. The Constitution has reserved to the states matters deemed to be primarily of local interest. For example, most statutes relating to property, contract, and tort issues are state statutes.

Where both federal and state statutes exist, you must discern the relationship between the two. The federal statute typically identifies the permissible role of state law. In some areas, Congress has sought to cover a field with federal law, so state statutes cannot also exist. In other areas, Congress has sought to assure minimum standards to a class of persons protected by the statute while permitting the states to enact supplemental legislation to provide similar or additional protections. In yet other areas, Congress has created a federal model that the states may opt in or out of; states opting out may be required to enact comparable state statutes.

F. REVIEW OF CHAPTER 5

Statutes and other forms of codified law resemble the rules of a game. They state rules of law in broad terms applicable to classes of situations occurring in the future. Your chief focus in reading statutes is on the words chosen by the legislature to express its intended meaning. This chapter has set out the following steps for reading and understanding statutes:

(1) Read the entire statute to discern its overall design and coverage.
(2) Identify the statutory provisions that are pertinent to your client situation.
(3) Label the pertinent provisions according to the standard statutory components.
(4) Create a brief based on the statutory components. Create a brief based on the if/then rule stated in the statute—with due care taken to respect the words chosen by the legislature.
(5) Review your brief against the statute to verify that it is complete, correct, coherent, and comprehensible.

Following these steps should provide you with an accurate understanding of the statute and prepare you to explore aids to interpretation of the statute, described in Chapter 6.

INTERPRETING

STATUTES

> Law is merely the expression of the will of the strongest for the time being, and therefore laws have no fixity, but shift from generation to generation.
> —Brooks Adams (American historian)
> *The Law of Civilization and Decay* (1896)

A. INTRODUCTION

Statutes do not exist in isolation, and you need not confine your analysis to the statute itself as you interpret its language.[1] This chapter discusses ambiguity in statutory language, which makes statutory interpretation necessary, and then compares and reconciles two competing principles of statutory interpretation: the plain meaning rule and the purpose approach. This chapter then describes various sources used to resolve ambiguity: case law; indications of the legislature's intent; "canons of construction," or maxims for

---

1. *See generally* Norman J. Singer, *Statutes and Statutory Construction* (5th ed. 1992).

reading the words chosen by the legislature; and the use of similar statutes and persuasive precedent.

Most examples in this chapter are drawn from the unauthorized practice of law statute, while a few are drawn from the living will statute. The statutes appear at pages 265 and 270. This chapter introduces a new case, *Peterson v. Hovland;* you may wish to read it and its brief at pages 275-83.

B. AMBIGUITY IN STATUTORY LANGUAGE

1. Why and How Ambiguity Arises

As a rule of law, a statute provides for certain legal consequences to follow certain actions, undertaken by certain actors, in certain circumstances. When the statute is applied to a specific client's facts, there are boundaries to be drawn as to all of these matters: Which actors fall within the statute, and which do not? Which actions fall within the statute, and which do not? Which circumstances matter, and which do not? Which consequences follow, and which do not?

Ambiguity in statutory language makes answers to these questions uncertain. Statutory language is ambiguous when more than one meaning is possible. Some statutes are ambiguous because the language is vague or puzzling; others are ambiguous because a point logically related to the statute's topic is omitted.

Statutory ambiguity has several causes. The legislature may have intentionally chosen ambiguous language because legislators were unable to agree on clearer language and were willing to defer the issue to the courts or a later session of the legislature. Or the legislators may have tried but been unable to write less ambiguous language. Or the legislature may not have perceived an ambiguity in its choice of words; one can think of only so much when writing any document. Or new situations may have arisen since the statute's enactment, turning language that once was clear into ambiguous language.

For example, two clauses in section 481.02 subdivision 1 prohibit the drafting of "any will or testamentary disposition or instrument of trust serving purposes similar to those of a will" and the drafting of "any other legal document." Minn. Stat. § 481.02 (1992). Does a living will come within either of these clauses? This ambiguity stems from the use of a puzzling word, "will," and the use of a vague, undefined term, the phrase "any other legal document." Most likely, the legislature did not think about living wills in drafting this language since living wills postdate its enactment.

As a second example, section 481.02 subdivision 8 specifies that someone who violates the statute is subject to prosecution for a misdemeanor or an injunction. But is the transaction thereby void? This latter consequence is simply not addressed in the statute. Perhaps the legislature did not think of this question; perhaps it chose to leave the question for the courts to resolve.

2. An Analogy: Rules of a Game

As noted in Chapter 5, statutes are like the rules of a game. When the rules of a game are unclear, there are several possible means of clarification. You can puzzle through the language. You can seek an authoritative interpretation. You can try to discern the point of the game and interpret the unclear rule accordingly. You can draw on your knowledge of the rules of other similar games.

These options have parallels in statutory interpretation, which is sketched in Exhibit 6.1. Keep in mind that the legislature's words must be respected at all times. These tools help you interpret the statute; they do not supplant it.

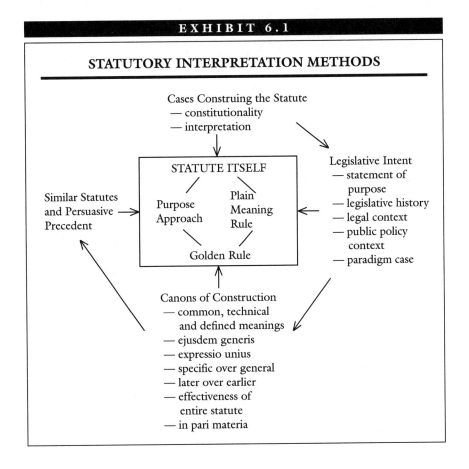

EXHIBIT 6.1

STATUTORY INTERPRETATION METHODS

Cases Construing the Statute
— constitutionality
— interpretation

STATUTE ITSELF

Purpose Approach

Plain Meaning Rule

Golden Rule

Legislative Intent
— statement of purpose
— legislative history
— legal context
— public policy context
— paradigm case

Similar Statutes and Persuasive Precedent

Canons of Construction
— common, technical and defined meanings
— ejusdem generis
— expressio unius
— specific over general
— later over earlier
— effectiveness of entire statute
— in pari materia

C. EMPLOYING THE PLAIN MEANING RULE, PURPOSE APPROACH, AND GOLDEN RULE

Statutory interpretation can be approached in various ways. One is the plain meaning rule. According to this rule, the lawyer's task is to follow the letter of the law, that is, the words chosen by the legislature. When the statute's meaning is plain, one need not use the methods of interpretation discussed in this chapter.

A second is the purpose approach. According to the purpose approach, the lawyer's task is to ascertain and then give meaning to the legislature's purpose in enacting the statute, that is, to respect legislative intent.

In many situations, these two approaches converge because the legislature's purpose is well articulated in the statute's language. But the two approaches diverge when the statutory language leads to a result probably unintended by the legislature. The bridge between the plain meaning rule and the purpose approach is the golden rule. The golden rule instructs lawyers not to honor the wording of a statute when it produces an absurd or unreasonable result, calls for an impossible outcome, or yields an unconstitutional result. The meshing of the purpose approach and plain meaning rule is thus left to the sound discretion of the lawyer interpreting the statute.

For example, imagine that the legislature prohibited the drafting of "any document" by a nonlawyer. According to the plain meaning rule, the statute could prohibit government employees from completing birth certificates and coroners from completing death certificates. By contrast, according to the purpose approach, the statute would not be construed to prohibit these actions because these results would not serve the statute's purpose of precluding nonlawyers from engaging in work requiring legal expertise. The golden rule suggests that the latter interpretation is the better one.

D. RELYING ON CASES INTERPRETING STATUTES

In many situations, the lawyer's choice among various statutory meanings is firmly guided by the decisions of the courts. When a dispute is governed by a statute and the parties are unable to settle the dispute themselves, they bring the dispute to the courts (not the legislature) for resolution. In addition to resolving the dispute for the parties, the court undertakes two very important tasks in relation to the statute.

First, the courts assess whether the legislature acted within constitutional bounds when it enacted the statute. The court will attempt to read the statute to render it constitutional, if possible. If not, the statute is declared unconstitutional in whole or in part, and the unconstitutional portion has no further legal effect.

Second, courts provide authoritative interpretation of a statute and thereby reduce the ambiguity in the legislature's language. The statute provides the rule of law by which the case is decided. The court may elaborate on this rule, give definition to unclear language, or fill gaps left in the statute. It then links the abstract language of the statute to the facts of a specific dispute. The rule of law, holding, and reasoning have precedential effect.

The lawmaking process can also work in the opposite direction. When the court deems a statute unconstitutional, the legislature may enact a revised statute. When the court interprets a statute, the legislature generally accepts the interpretation by not amending the statute. On occasion, however, the legislature registers its objection to the court's interpretation by amending the statute. Where the law consists of an original statute with amendments as well as case law, you may well wish to make a timeline of the various statutory enactments and cases pertinent to your problem. You must fully understand the dialogue between the legislature and courts.

In the HomeElderCare situation, neither the living will statute nor the unauthorized practice statute has been declared unconstitutional. The living will statute does touch upon a patient's constitutional right of privacy to refuse invasive medical treatment, under the Minnesota Constitution, *see Jarvis v. Levine*, 418 N.W.2d 139 (Minn. 1988). Had the statute impaired, rather than facilitated, the exercise of this right, it may well have been unconstitutional.

An important case interpreting section 481.02 is *Peterson v. Hovland* (*In re Peterson's Estate*), 42 N.W.2d 59 (Minn. 1950), involving a challenge to a will on the grounds it had been drawn by a bank cashier several weeks prior to the testator's death. The court resolved the issue created by the legislature's failure to address the effectiveness of a document tainted by unauthorized practice of law. The court reasoned that the statute was intended to forestall the drafting of wills by incompetent nonlawyers and that the statute focuses on penalizing the incompetent drafter. The statute was intended to protect the testator, who should not be deemed a wrongdoer or suffer adverse consequences because of the drafter's violation of the statute. The legislature chose to enact penalties only against the drafter and opted against imposing other consequences. Therefore, the will was not void by virtue of the unauthorized practice by the drafter. *Id.* at 61-66.

Peterson thus adds the following elaboration to the consequences portion of the if/then statutory brief for section 481.02 developed in Chapter 5: the statutory consequences do not include voiding of an illegally drafted document. Exhibit 6.2 is an expanded version of that brief with the bulleted items showing the points from this chapter that elaborate on the statute's elements.

E.   INCORPORATING LEGISLATIVE INTENT

The touchstone of statutory interpretation is to effectuate legislative intent. Although the most straightforward indication of legislative intent is a statement of purpose in the statute itself, few statutes contain this statement. Generally, you must rely on a statute's legislative history, legal and public policy context, and paradigm case.

EXHIBIT 6.2

EXPANDED IF/THEN STATUTORY BRIEF

IF   any person/assn except members of MN bar admitted & licensed
      to practice

    A. does 1 OR 2 OR 3 (all in Subd. 1)
        1. gives legal advice or counsel
            or performs for or furnishes legal services
            to another
            for fee or considn
        2. prepares directly or thru another
            for another person/firm/corp.
            any will or testamentary disposition or instrument of trust
                serving purposes similar to will
            (for or w/o fee or considn)
        3. prepares for another person/firm/corp.
            any other legal document
            for fee or considn

              ■ common meaning of "legal" "document": official paper
                 relied on as basis or proof, established by law or con-
                 forming to law
              ■ in pari materia: § 145B.04 equates living will with "legal
                 document"

    B. AND NOT person drafting will
        for another
        in emergency leaving insuff. time for atty supervn
        Subd. 3(2)

    C. AND NOT person conferring or cooperating
        with licensed atty of another
        in preparing any legal document
        where atty is not empd by that person or by
            person/firm/corp. repd by that person
        Subd. 3(6)

    D. AND NOT corp. furnishing
        lawful info or clerical services
        to atty
        who maintains responsibility to clients
        for info & services
        Subd. 7

THEN   misdemeanor prosecuted by county atty in dist. ct OR
           injunction brought by county atty or atty genl—Subd. 8.

              ■ *Peterson:* illegally drafted doc. is *not* voided
                 —policy of statute is to penalize drafter, not testator
                 —expressio unius

1. Legislative History

First you might turn to the record developed during the legislature's consideration of the bill and enactment of the statute, known as "legislative history." Some legislative history materials are more authoritative than others. For example, the committee report is very authoritative, because it is a formal document prepared by the legislators most involved in the statute's enactment. The comments of legislators during the debates vary in significance, with the sponsor's comments generally viewed as the most authoritative.

In most situations, there are two practical obstacles to using legislative history. First, legislative history is difficult to research. It may not have been preserved in any form; if it was preserved, it may be fairly inaccessible; often, it is bulky and poorly indexed. Second, there may be nothing pertinent on any particular point or conflicting statements by different legislators.

In the HomeElderCare example, you could trace the key language in the unauthorized practice statute back to 1931. *See* Act of April 4, 1931, ch. 114, 1931 Minn. Laws 119. The legislative history of this language would be difficult to research, if indeed it was recorded.

2. Legal Context

Fairly few statutes represent the first law on a topic; most join an existing body of law, of which the legislature presumably is aware. A statute's common law, statutory, and constitutional context can provide helpful background information about the legislature's intent.

Statutes relate to the common law in several ways. In some areas, the legislature acts to codify or clarify the common law. In other areas, the legislature acts to overturn or substantially modify the common law. In yet other areas, the common law and statutory law operate in tandem, each addressing an aspect of the behavior they regulate.

A new statute may affect existing statutory law in several ways. The new statute may cover a topic not yet addressed by existing statutes, or it may revisit a topic that already has been addressed. Amendments clarify or add to existing statutes, while repealers delete existing statutes and thus signify a dramatic change in the law. When the legislature has revisited an area, it may be possible to make inferences about the legislative intent behind a particular version of the statute by examining its previous and subsequent forms.

Finally, one can presume that the legislature acted with knowledge of and in accordance with constitutional provisions. Statutes are interpreted so as to avoid unconstitutional applications.

As an example, the unauthorized practice statute operates in the context of a common law rule: that transactions in violation of licensing statutes typically are void. The unauthorized practice statute also has a rich statutory context, because the legislature has added exceptions to the unauthorized practice statute a number of times since its original enactment in the late 1800s.

As another example, the living will statute provides that it is not intended to impair the existing rights of any patient to control his or her health care. Minn. Stat. § 145B.17 (1992). Those rights include the right to refuse invasive medical procedures, based in the state constitution and case law, as described above in Part D.

3. Public Policy Context

In some situations, there are no clear indications of legislative intent in a purpose statement, legislative history, or legal context. Nonetheless, you may be able to deduce the legislature's intent from the public policy issues at the time of enactment. Sometimes the statutory language itself suggests what these issues were. In other situations, you may be able to find extrinsic evidence of them.

For example, the *Peterson* court engaged in this type of analysis regarding the unauthorized practice statute. The court observed that the legislature must have been concerned with how testators and survivors were affected by the bungled drafting of wills by nonlawyers. Bungled drafting could cause estates to be overtaxed, bequests to fail, and wills to be held invalid. This analysis prompted the court to view the testator as a person protected by the statute and to decline to void the will drafted by the bank cashier. *Peterson*, 42 N.W.2d at 63-64.

As a different example, some of the legislators involved in the passage of the living will statute wrote an article on the statute, which describes their concern that medical care will be given to persons who have not requested and do not want such care, yet at the time are not able to speak for themselves. *See* Howard Orenstein et al., *Minnesota's Living Will . . .*, Bench & B. Minn., Aug. 1989, at 21. This information provides insight into that statute's public policy context.

4. The Paradigm Case

Although a statute does not state a specific story as a case does, it may imply one or more paradigm cases. A paradigm case is a situation that clearly would bring the statute into play. It entails actors, actions, and circumstances that fall squarely within the statute. You can discern a paradigm case by reading the statute carefully and then asking what situation (or situations) clearly falls within this language. (Indeed, legislators often act on specific stories heard from constituents or the media.)

The value of a paradigm case is that it permits inferences about legislative intent. If you can assume that the legislature was concerned with your paradigm case, then you can ask what broader concerns underlie that paradigm case.

For example, a paradigm case implied by the unauthorized practice statute is the drafting by a nonlawyer of a document that is significant primarily in a legal sense and requires a lawyer's expertise to draft correctly, such as divorce settlements or articles of incorporation for a new company. The document would be drafted by someone without legal training or other basis for competent performance; the interests of the client would be imperiled. And the drafter would charge a fee, thus gaining financially from his or her dubious endeavor. This paradigm case reveals the legislature's concern with incompetence, harm to the client and the public from botched transactions, and financial gain by the unauthorized practitioner.

F.   APPLYING CANONS OF CONSTRUCTION

Canons of construction are maxims for reading—and writing—statutes. Each is based on a psychological principle of language use. Because some have Latin names, they appear more mystical than they really are. Seven of the more commonly used canons are:

Defined, common, and technical meanings: Some terms are defined in the statute itself. Otherwise, according to this canon, which reflects the importance of context in word choice, terms should be understood in their everyday sense or, where the context suggests it, in a technical sense.

This canon provides one basis for interpreting the term "legal document" in section 481.02. According to the dictionary, "legal" means "established by law; statutory; conforming to or permitted by law or established rules." *Webster's New Collegiate Dictionary* 651 (1981). "Document" means "an original or official paper relied on as the basis, proof, or support of something." *Id.* at 333.

Ejusdem generis: The phrase means "of the same class," and the canon applies where the legislature has created a list and included a general term as a catch-all. The catch-all term then refers to items of the same class as the specific items in the list, as one would expect from standard list-making practice.

By way of example, assume that the list "will or testamentary disposition or instrument of trust" was followed by "or other legal document." According to this canon, the phrase "other legal document" would be construed to refer to documents similar to those listed, namely will-like documents.

Expressio unius: The full phrase, "expressio unius est exclusio alterius," means "expression of one excludes others." According to this canon, where the legislature created a list with specific items, but did not mention others or include a catch-all term, unmentioned items are not included, again, as one would expect.

It was this canon that the *Peterson* court used. The legislature's choice of misdemeanor penalties and injunctions precluded voiding Mr. Peterson's will as an additional consequence for the unlicensed practice of law. *Peterson,* 42 N.W.2d at 64.

Specific prevails over general: Where there is a conflict between two provisions, the more specific provision should take precedence over the more general provision, since specific information is more salient than general. In essence, all exceptions to general rules rest on this principle.

For example, even if there were no statement in the unauthorized practiced statute making the general rule of subdivision 1 subject to the exceptions of subdivision 3, one would give effect to the exception of will drafting in an emergency over the general prohibition against will drafting.

Later prevails over earlier: Later enacted provisions prevail over earlier provisions, when there is a conflict, since recent information is more reliable than older information.

If, for example, the legislature had written two exceptions relating to drafting of a will by a nonlawyer—one permitting it only in emergencies, the other allowing it only by a licensed legal assistant without any limitation as to circumstance—a conflict could arise. The more recent of the two provisions would govern.

Effectiveness of entire statute: This canon assumes that all statutory language is meant to communicate some meaning. Hence, language that could be construed to add nothing should, if possible, be construed to add meaning.

For example, consider the effect of adding the following statement to the existing penalty provisions of the unauthorized practice statute: "The courts shall consider any action in violation of this statute illegal." Because the existing language already provides for misdemeanor penalties and injunctions, perhaps one should infer an additional consequence from this language, such as voiding the transaction.

In pari materia: This phrase means "of the same matter," and the canon comes into play when two or more statutes relate to the same topic. The statutes must be considered together; consistency is assumed. One application of this canon is that a word should carry over its meaning from one statute to a related statute.

For example, the unauthorized practice statute prohibits drafting of "legal documents." The living will statute contains a form will, which states: "This is an important legal document." Minn. Stat. § 145B.04. This equation of a living will with the category of legal document should carry over to the unauthorized practice statute.

Other canons: Finally, some canons pertain to particular types of statutes. For example, penal (criminal) statutes are to be construed narrowly to avoid criminal sanctions where conduct was not clearly forbidden.

You may well find that different canons of construction point in different directions. If so, consider the application of these canons in the context of the other methods described in this chapter.

G. LOOKING TO SIMILAR STATUTES AND PERSUASIVE PRECEDENT

In interpreting a statute, a court may choose to rely on the interpretation that a sister court has given a similar or identical statute in the sister jurisdiction, even though that case is not binding precedent.

In selecting a precedent to follow, the court will be guided by the factors set forth in Chapter 3 along with an additional set of factors. The court will look for an opinion interpreting a similar, if not identical, statute. The court also will examine the opinion to determine whether the two statutes rest on the same policy.

Reliance on persuasive precedent for statutory interpretation occurs most regularly in two situations. First, some state statutes are based on a model law promulgated by a law reform organization. Use of persuasive precedent to interpret these statutes is common because the language is (nearly) identical from state to state and the origins of the statutes are the same. Second, some state statutes are based on federal statutes on the same topic. The state court may wish to provide for uniformity in state and federal law through use of federal persuasive precedent.

In the HomeElderCare situation, the courts have not been particularly prone to using persuasive precedent in interpreting unauthorized practice statutes, as they differ from state to state. It is more likely that the courts will use persuasive precedent to interpret the living will statute, because Minnesota was the fortieth state to pass such legislation in a fairly short period of time; presumably there are only a few models for such legislation.

H. REVIEW OF CHAPTER 6

You can use various methods to reduce ambiguity in statutory language, all aimed at deducing the legislature's intent and giving meaning to the words the legislators chose. This chapter has set out the following methods:

(1) Seek an authoritative interpretation in a case construing the statute.
(2) Seek information about the legislature's intent in the statute's purpose statement, its legislative history, the legal context of the statute, its public policy context, or its paradigm case.
(3) Apply canons of construction to the statute's language.
(4) Seek guidance in cases from other jurisdictions that interpret highly similar statutes.

All of these methods require you to exercise judgment to reach an appropriate result. Proper use of these options reduces statutory ambiguity and prepares you for the next stage of analysis.

READING COMMENTARY

> Delusive exactness is a source of fallacy throughout the law.
> —Oliver Wendell Holmes
> *Truax v. Corrigan*, 257 U.S. 312, 342 (1921)

A. INTRODUCTION

In many areas, the law is complex, or controversial, or both; furthermore, the law changes over time. It is not always easy to understand fully how the law has evolved, what the law is, or what the law should be. Legal scholarship, or commentary, addresses these matters. Commentary is written by persons without lawmaking authority (professors, students, attorneys) or persons with lawmaking authority (judges, legislators, agency heads) acting in other than a lawmaking capacity. Commentary, also called "secondary authority," cannot substitute for the law itself (i.e., "primary authority") in your analysis, but it can further your analysis in several ways.

This brief chapter first describes various forms of legal commentary and then explains the best uses of commentary in your legal analysis. It refers to several examples pertinent to the HomeElderCare problem; they appear at pages 297 to 313. You should scan them before reading further.

B. TYPES OF COMMENTARY

In most situations, you are likely to find commentary that falls into one of these five categories: annotations, encyclopedias, periodicals (law reviews), Restatements, and treatises. Exhibit 7.1 provides brief information about the purpose, authoritativeness, format, and coverage of each.

EXHIBIT 7.1

TYPES OF COMMENTARY

Type	Purpose	Authoritative-ness	Authors	Format	Coverage/ Updating
American Law Reports annotations	summarize case law, especially splits among jurisdictions	minimal, except to document jurisdictional splits	attorneys and editors	overview; then series of case descriptions, grouped by holdings	selected topics discussed in considerable depth; updated
Encyclopedias	summarize statutory and case law	depends on credibility of particular encyclopedia	attorneys and editors	overview of legal rules supported by footnotes	very wide range of topics described in general terms; updated
Periodical articles	describe and explain the law; advocate for change	varies, depending on author; highly authoritative if well regarded judge or professor; less so if student	attorneys, judges, legislators, professors, students	essay with extensive supporting footnotes	selected narrow topics discussed in great detail; not updated
Restatements	"restate" the law, although some state what the law should be in the view of the drafters	generally highly authoritative, with some sections adopted by courts	American Law Institute (attorneys, professors)	rule statement followed by explanations (comments) and examples (illustrations)	broad statement of selected general areas of law; some statements are infrequently updated; recent cases are listed
Treatises	primarily describe and explain the law; may also advocate for change	varies according to author's prestige	professors, attorneys	textual discussion supplemented with fairly extensive footnotes	each covers discrete broad or narrow topic in fair depth; may or may not be updated

C. USING COMMENTARY TO ADVANCE YOUR LEGAL ANALYSIS

As you research the law applicable to a client's case, commentary can assist you in locating the law. In the analysis stage, although commentary cannot substitute for the law, it does have several important roles.

First, and most commonly, you may use commentary to solidify your understanding of the law. Commentary may provide clarification where the law is murky, complex, or fragmented. Most commentary distills out details and presents general principles on a legal topic; this broad perspective often is helpful when you have been, by necessity, focusing on fine points of each case or statute. However, keep in mind that the author did not have your client's situation in mind and thus may not have discussed a pertinent nuance. In addition, authors of legal commentary can err. So you may use commentary to solidify, but not supplant, your own understanding of the law.

Second, commentary may provide background information not stated in the cases, statutes, and other legal authorities. The most common type of insight afforded by commentary is historical; commentary may provide information about the background of a case or line of cases, the history of a statute, or the purpose of a court rule. Or commentary may document a trend in the law, so that you can better predict upcoming changes. Again, this information generally is helpful, but it does not, of course, replace the rule as it now stands.

Third, commentary presents perspectives on the law. These perspectives may derive from such diverse intellectual schools as feminist jurisprudence and law and economics. You are most likely to look to the discussion of public policy in commentary in several situations: when you must make a close call in advising a client, when you need additional support for the argument you are making on a client's behalf in an advocacy setting, or when you are seeking change in the law.

Although you have little discretion in selecting which cases, statutes, and other primary authorities to analyze (at least within the realm of binding authority), you do have considerable discretion in choosing commentary. Obviously, the more pertinent the commentary the better. Additional factors weighing in favor of a particular source are its credibility (in turn, a function of the author), currency, comprehensiveness, and quality of analysis.

The materials in the HomeElderCare case file are all commentary you might consult in analyzing that case. The first sample, an *American Law Reports* annotation, is on the general topic of unauthorized practice of law, but the fact settings are rather different from the HomeElderCare situation; hence it does not merit much attention. The second sample, an encyclopedia excerpt, provides a summary of the law and thus could serve to confirm your own reading of the cases. Because it is devoted to Minnesota law, it is tightly focused on your binding precedent. The third sample, a periodical article, provides insight into the legislative purpose of the living will statute; that information could be useful in clarifying the statute's ambiguous provisions. The fourth sample, a Restatement section, comes from a very credible source and underscores the common law rule. The fifth sample, an excerpt from a highly influential contracts treatise, provides a potentially useful statement of general legal principles on the enforcement of contracts for unlicensed work as well as a statement of the modern trend.

D. REVIEW OF CHAPTER 7

Although much of the commentary you read will seem more familiar in form than the law, it is not the law. It should be used not to supplant, but only to supplement your analysis of the law itself by solidifying your understanding, providing background information, and providing additional perspectives. Look for material that is pertinent to your situation, comes from a credible source, is current, and presents a comprehensive and cogent discussion.

APPLYING A RULE

TO FACTS:

DEDUCTIVE REASONING

A. Introduction
B. What is Deductive Reasoning?
C. Linking Elements and Client Facts
D. Alternative Depictions of Deductive Reasoning
E. Cautions about the Negative of the Rule
F. Review of Chapter 8

> Reasoning is an ancient subject but an everyday practice.
> —David A. Conway and Ronald Munson,
> *The Elements of Reasoning* (1990)

A. INTRODUCTION

So far, this text has discussed how to read the law and legal commentary. Lawyers read these materials for a specific purpose: so they can bring legal meaning to the facts of the client's experience. This chapter and the next focus on three reasoning processes that enable you to connect the law you have read to the facts of a client's case, to yield a prediction about the legal outcome of the case.

The first process is *deductive reasoning*. In deductive reasoning, you apply elements of a rule from case law, codified law, or both to the facts of a client's situation, in order to reach a preliminary conclusion. Deductive reasoning is a necessary phase of all legal analysis. This chapter focuses on deductive reasoning, beginning with a discussion of what deductive reasoning is and then showing several methods for performing this process.

The second reasoning process is analogical reasoning, or *reasoning by example*. In reasoning by example, you compare the facts from a client's case, which has no known legal result, to the facts of a decided case, which has a known legal result. Chapter 9 discusses this kind of reasoning. Reasoning by example is a helpful, but not necessary, phase of legal reasoning.

Chapter 9 also covers the third type of reasoning: *analysis of policy considerations* to predict the outcome of the client's case. Like reasoning by example, policy analysis is very helpful, but not necessary.

Both chapters draw on the rules, cases, and statutes referred to in the previous chapters. In addition, this chapter draws on a new case, *Gardner v. Conway,* beginning on page 284 and briefed at page 295. You should review that brief and the HomeElderCare facts at page 9 before reading on.

B. WHAT IS DEDUCTIVE REASONING?

Deductive reasoning is common in many fields. It involves using known general principles to solve a specific unknown situation. For instance, a mathematician uses theorems and corollaries to solve a geometric proof. A physician uses diagnostic principles to diagnose a patient's disease. A parent uses family rules to decide how to discipline a misbehaving child.

Deductive reasoning in a legal setting is the process of using rules from legal authorities to draw a prediction about the outcome of a client's case. The rule you apply, whether it be from case law or codified law or both, should be stated in if/then form and separated into elements and legal consequences. Then you assess whether the elements required by the rule are present in the facts of the client's case. The structure of the rule dictates what is required—that is, all elements of a conjunctive rule, only one of several disjunctive subelements, or some critical mass of the factors in aggregate and balancing rules. If the elements are met, then the legal consequences in the rule will follow.

If the rule cannot be applied with certainty, you may need to supplement your deductive reasoning with reasoning by example and policy analysis. Even so, deductive reasoning remains the core of legal analysis; everything else is supplementary.

C. LINKING ELEMENTS AND CLIENT FACTS

Deductive reasoning is a structured, but not a mechanical, process. Typically, the most difficult aspect of deductive reasoning is drawing out the relevant facts from the client's situation to align with each element of the rule.

Each element of the rule directs your attention to some aspect of the client's situation; relevant facts pertain to that aspect. Most elements of a rule focus your attention on one or perhaps two of the six classic questions journalists ask: who, what, when, where, why, and how. An element describing an actor focuses on the "who" aspect of the situation. An element focusing on the action taken is a "what" element. An element focusing on the circumstances may be a "when," "where," "why," or "how" element. Once you know which question the element addresses, you generally will be able to identify the relevant client facts.

Sometimes this linkage process is not straightforward. If you are unsure of the factual focus of a case law element, reread the case, and study the facts that the court saw as relevant to that element. Similarly, if you are unsure of the focus of a statutory element, examine a case interpreting the statute, or consider a statutory paradigm case. Finally, you may find commentary helpful in identifying the focus of murky elements.

Sometimes, even once you understand an element well, discerning the relevant facts in your client's situation can be difficult. The facts may be complex; if so, consider separating them according to the six classic journalist's questions. Or the difficulty may arise because you are missing key facts. In your analysis, you will need to note the omission and the uncertainty it creates; make one or more sensible assumptions, given the facts you do know; and proceed on your assumption(s). If there is more than one sensible assumption, you may need to pursue more than one analysis of the case. The difficulty may arise because you have conflicting information, because different individuals perceived an event differently. These conflicts require much the same handling as omissions.

As a simple example, consider the statutory prohibition on unauthorized practice of law, which applies to any person except members of the Minnesota bar admitted and licensed to practice. This element is a "who" element with a narrow focus. In analyzing the HomeElderCare facts, you would link this element with the social workers and their lack of licensure as attorneys in Minnesota. You would conclude that this element is met.

For a more difficult example, consider the case law requirement that the circumstances surrounding the contract violate the reason for the licensing statute. This element is a "how" element with a very broad sweep. To find an example, you would review *Weatherston's,* noting the court's consideration of the client's awareness of the nonlicensure and the supervision of the unlicensed work by a licensed professional, among other facts. You then would look for HomeElderCare facts relating to the clients' knowledge of the social workers' status, the supervision of the social workers, or other facts bearing on their competence. You can assume that the HomeElderCare clients will be informed that the social workers are not attorneys. Yet it is difficult to assess how much competence the social workers can gain from a brief training session. Because two alternative assumptions are sensible, you would pursue two analyses of the case.

D. ALTERNATIVE DEPICTIONS OF DEDUCTIVE REASONING

You can depict deductive reasoning various ways. Two quite different options are presented here. Any depiction must use a rule of law as its point of departure and reflect the structure of the if-clause of the rule: conjunctive, disjunctive, aggregate, or balancing.

EXHIBIT 8.1

COLUMN CHARTS

Conjunctive Rule

	Elements	Client Facts	Element Met / Not Met
IF	1 and	xxxxxxxxx	✓
	2 and	xxxxxxxxx	✓
	3	xxxxxxxxx	✓
	Consequences	Effect on Client Facts	
THEN	x and	x results	
	y	y results	

Mixed Conjunctive and Disjunctive Rule

	Elements	Client Facts	Element Met / Not Met
IF	1 and	xxxxxxxxx	✓
	2 and	xxxxxxxxx	✓
	(3 or	xxxxxxxxx	✓
	3')	xxxxxxxxx	✓
	Consequences	Effect on Client Facts	
THEN	x and	None—consequence does	
	y	not result under this rule	

Aggregate Rule

	Factors	Client Facts	Factor Present / Absent
IF	some but not necessarily all of the following are present:		
	a	xxxxxxxxx	++
	b	xxxxxxxxx	+
	c	xxxxxxxxx	–
	d	xxxxxxxxx	+++
	e	xxxxxxxxx	–
	Consequences	Effect on Client Facts	
THEN	x	x results	

Note: + signifies that the factor is present, in some degree.
– signifies that the factor is lacking, in some degree.

Balancing Rule

	Factors	Client Facts	Factor Present / Absent
IF	a	xxxxxxxxx	++
	outweighs		
	b	xxxxxxxxx	+
	Consequences	Effect on Client Facts	
THEN	x	x results	

Note: + signifies that the factor is present, in some degree.
– signifies that the factor is lacking, in some degree.

1. Column Chart

The first depiction is the column chart. In this chart, elements of the rule line up with relevant facts of your client's case. If the required elements are met by the client's facts, then the legal consequences follow.

Exhibit 8.1 above shows four formats that you might wish to use for the four different forms of legal rules. With conjunctive and disjunctive elements, you can use a check mark to signify that an element is met. With aggregate and balancing rules, you can use plus and minus marks to represent the extent of the presence or absence of the factors.

Exhibit 8.2, on pages 86-87, is a sample HomeElderCare column chart addressing the issue of whether the living will services would constitute unauthorized practice of law under section 481.02 and two cases, *Gardner* and *Peterson*. According to the analysis presented in Exhibit 8.2, it is likely that some aspect of the living will service would constitute unauthorized practice and no exception applies. The possible legal consequences of meeting the elements of the unauthorized practice statute are misdemeanor penalties or an injunction. Exhibit 8.2 also notes the *Peterson* case holding that the document resulting from unauthorized practice is not invalid for that reason.

2. Syllogism

An alternative to the column chart is the syllogism with major and minor premises. The major premise is the rule of law; the minor premise is the specific set of facts presented by the client. Deductive reasoning is the process of matching the minor premise to the major premise to generate a conclusion about the outcome of the client's case.[1] In other words:

Major Premise:	[rule of law]
Minor Premise:	[relevant client facts]
Conclusion:	Therefore [probable legal consequence]

As an example, in Exhibit 8.3, the major premise is the *Weatherston's* rule on enforcement of contracts for unlicensed professional services. Assume at this point that you had determined that the living will services would indeed amount to law practice. This conclusion and the other relevant facts from the HomeElderCare case appear in the minor premise. Because the fourth element is not met, the prediction is that the contracts would not be void under this rule.

---

1. In the study of logic, this syllogism, known as modus ponens, can be expressed as "if P, then Q. P is true. Therefore Q is true."

EXHIBIT 8.2

HomeElderCare COLUMN CHART

Elements	Client Facts	Element Met / Not Met
IF any person/assn except members of MN bar admitted & licensed to practice	social workers not members of MN bar	✓
A. does 1 OR 2 OR 3 (all in subd. 1)		
1. gives legal advice or counsel or performs for or furnishes legal services to other for fee or considn	not clear if HEC is giving legal advice/ counsel or performing/furnishing legal services; HEC will charge fee	?
■ *Gardner:* acts must be more than incidental, or if acts are incidental, they must involve difficult/ doubtful legal issues	act will be incidental, but it's not clear what "difficult or doubtful legal issues" are	
2. prepares directly or thru another for another person/firm/corp. any will or testamentary dis- position or instrument of trust serving purposes similar to will for or w/o fee or considn	probably living will is not will (testamentary disposition . . .)	✓
3. prepares for another person/ firm/corp. any other legal document for fee or considn	living will is legal doc, and HEC is preparing it for a fee	✓
■ common meaning of "legal" "document": official paper relied on as basis or proof, established by law or conforming to law		
■ in pari materia: § 145B.04 equates living will with "legal document"		
B. AND NOT person drafting will for another in emergency leaving insuff. time for atty supervn (Subd. 3(2))	living wills not drawn in emergency	✓
C. AND NOT person conferring or cooperating with licensed atty of another in preparing any legal document where atty is not empd by that person or person/firm/corp. repd by that person (Subd. 3(6))	social workers—not licensed attor- neys—are doing work	✓

EXHIBIT 8.2 (continued)		

HOMEELDERCARE COLUMN CHART

Elements	Client Facts	Element Met / Not Met
D. AND NOT corp. furnishing lawful info or clerical services to atty who maintains responsibility to clients for info & services (Subd. 7)	no atty involved in this transaction	✓

Consequences	Effect on Client Facts
THEN X or Y Subd. 8. X. misdemeanor prosecuted by county atty in dist. ct. Y. injunction brought by county atty or atty genl ■ *Peterson:* illegally drafted doc. is *not* voided —policy of statute is to penalize drafter, not testator —expressio unius	HEC would be guilty of misdmnr or subject to injcn.; living wills would still be valid

E. CAUTIONS ABOUT THE NEGATIVE OF THE RULE

When at least one element of a rule is not met, you might be tempted to re-cast the rule in a negative form, so that you can figure out the legal consequence of that element not being met. To do so, carefully follow the steps described below.

First, recast the if-clause in a negative form. In recasting the elements of a conjunctive rule, "and" becomes "or,"[2] as shown below:

IF	1 and	becomes	IF	not 1 or
	2 and			not 2 or
	3			not 3

---

2. In logic, the change in connectors is based on De Morgan's Rules, which can be restated as follows:

"Not (P and Q)" is equivalent to "not P or not Q."
"Not (P or Q)" is equivalent to "not P and not Q."

EXHIBIT 8.3

SYLLOGISM

Major Premise: [rule of law]	IF (1) a statute requires a person practicing a particular profession or engaging in a particular business to obtain a license or certificate, and (2) a person in that profession or business lacks license or certificate, and (3) that person enters into a business or professional contract, and (4) the circumstances surrounding the contract violate any reason for the statute's existence, THEN that contract is void and unenforceable.
Minor Premise: [relevant client facts]	(1) A statute requires persons practicing law to obtain a license, and (2) the HEC social workers lack that license, and (3) they probably will be practicing law or entering into contracts to practice law in drafting living wills, and (4) these contracts nonetheless would *not* violate any policy underlying the licensing statute, given the social workers' training and knowledge of their status by HEC clients.
Conclusion: [legal consequence]	Therefore, the consequence does not result, so the contracts would *not* be void and unenforceable under this rule.

This change in connectors makes sense because a conjunctive rule can be defeated by *just one* element not being met. The opposite change in connectors occurs when you recast the elements of a disjunctive rule into a negative form, as follows:

IF	1 or	becomes	IF not 1 and
	2 or		not 2 and
	3		not 3

This change in connectors makes sense because a disjunctive rule can be defeated only by *all* of the elements not being met. Sometimes, negating an element that already contains a negative concept results in a pair of negatives, which—true to common sense—cancel each other out. For example, in Exhibit 8.3, the second element becomes "a person in that profession or business *does not lack* a license or certificate," which is equivalent to "a person . . . *has* a license or certificate."

Because of the flexible nature of aggregate and balancing rules, you are less likely to recast them in negative form. If you were to do so, the elements would be expressed as follows:

IF enough of factors a, b, c,	becomes	IF not enough of factors a b, c
IF factors a, b, c outweigh d, e, f	becomes	IF factors a, b, c do not outweigh d, e, f

After negating the if-clause, the second step is to apply the newly negated if-clause to the client's facts. See Exhibits 8.2 and 8.3 for examples of how to apply an if-clause to the client's facts. If the client's facts meet the required elements of the negated if-clause, then move on to the next step.

The third step is to recast the then-clause in a negative form. If the then-clause contains more than one consequence (plural or alternative), negate each consequence and change the connector(s): "and" becomes "or"; "or" becomes "and." For example, in Exhibit 8.2, "then misdemeanor or injunction" becomes "then *not* misdemeanor *and not* injunction."

The fourth step is to evaluate the overall meaning of negating the then-clause. In most rules, the most you can conclude is that the consequence does not result under this rule, but it might result under some other rule. For example, in Exhibit 8.3, the client's facts do not meet the fourth of the conjunctive elements, so the consequence of the rule does not result under that rule. However, you would need to perform additional research to determine whether another rule voids the contract.

Occasionally, though, a rule will be the only rule with that particular legal consequence. In that situation, you can safely negate the conclusion without any caveats. You might think of these kinds of rules as exclusive rules.[3] For example, the following exclusive rule appears in section 145B.05 of Minnesota's living will act:

IF   a living will is delivered to the declarant's physician or other health care provider,

THEN   the living will becomes operative upon delivery.

The negative of that rule would be the following:

IF   a living will is *not* delivered to the declarant's physician or other health care provider,

THEN   the living will does *not* become operative.

---

3. Students of logic may recognize the exclusive rule as an "if and only if" rule. A non-exclusive rule can be rephrased as "if P, then Q," or "P is sufficient for Q." An exclusive rule can be rephrased as "if and only if P, then Q," or "P is sufficient and necessary for Q."

Nonexclusive rules are not conclusive when restated in the negative. Accordingly, a non-exclusive rule represented by "if P, then Q" cannot be restated in the negative as "if not P, then not Q." To do so is the classic fallacy of denying the antecedent.

On the other hand, exclusive rules are conclusive when restated in the negative, as in "if not P, then not Q."

In other words, no other rule makes the living will operative if it is not delivered, so the negative of the consequence is true without any caveats. You will need to evaluate each rule that you negate to determine how exclusive that rule really is and how many other rules might alter your negative conclusion.

F. REVIEW OF CHAPTER 8

Deductive reasoning—applying a rule to the facts of the client's situation in order to predict the legal consequence for the client—is the fundamental form of legal reasoning. Based on a careful reading of the law, deductive reasoning involves the following steps:

(1) Analyze each element in an if/then rule statement; focus on who, what, when, where, why, or how.
(2) Identify the facts in the client's situation that are relevant to each element.
(3) Analyze whether each element is met by the facts of the client's situation.
(4) If the necessary elements are not met, then the legal consequence does not result under this rule. If they are, then the legal consequences of the rule will result.

The process of deductive reasoning can be shown various ways, including a column chart and a syllogism.

The deductive reasoning process sometimes leaves unanswered questions. You may be able to answer those questions with the tools covered in Chapter 9: reasoning by example and policy analysis.

APPLYING A RULE
TO FACTS: REASONING
BY EXAMPLE AND
POLICY ANALYSIS

A. Introduction
B. Reasoning by Example
C. Policy Analysis
D. Meshing Deductive Reasoning, Reasoning by Example, and Policy Analysis
E. Review of Chapter 9

> We are all able to reason. Someone totally unable to assess claims and arrive at conclusions would believe anything and act in wild and arbitrary ways. That we do not generally behave in this fashion shows how we rely on reasoning to guide our actions and ground our beliefs.
> —David A. Conway and Ronald Munson,
> *The Elements of Reasoning* (1990)

A. INTRODUCTION

Often some uncertainty remains at the end of the deductive reasoning process. This chapter introduces two tools for resolving this uncertainty: reasoning by example and policy analysis. This chapter first explores what reasoning by example is, how it works in a legal setting, and how to do it. The second half of the chapter examines the role of policy in the law, its derivation, and its uses. The chapter concludes with a discussion of how to mesh the three forms of legal reasoning: deductive reasoning, reasoning by example, and policy analysis. As always, this chapter draws examples from the HomeElderCare case file.

B. REASONING BY EXAMPLE

1. What Is Reasoning by Example?

Law relies not only on deductive reasoning, but also on analogical reasoning, or reasoning by example. Reasoning by example involves using the known outcome(s) of one or more resolved situations to draw a conclusion about a current situation with an unknown outcome. It is based on a formal principle of justice: that similar facts should be treated similarly.[1] Reasoning by example is common outside the law. For instance, a student who turns in a paper late expects that he or she will be treated similarly to other students who have turned in late papers previously. An employee who performs an employment obligation poorly or well expects to be treated like other similarly performing employees. In law, reasoning by example is called analogizing and distinguishing, or the drawing of analogies and distinctions.

Reasoning by example may involve drawing sufficient parallels between the client's situation and a decided case so that you can conclude that the client's situation should be handled in the same manner as was the decided case. This kind of reasoning is called "drawing an analogy." The verb "should" is used because there always is some uncertainty in reasoning by example. Inexactitude is inherent in the process of judging how much and what kind of similarity is needed for an analogy.

You may, of course, conclude that an analogy is not appropriate because the resemblance between the decided case and the client's case is not close enough; hence the outcome in the decided case would not be the result in the client's case. This kind of reasoning is called "distinguishing a case." Again, there may be uncertainty as to how much and what kind of dissimilarity is needed to justify the distinction.

Distinguishing a particular case does not allow you to conclude that a result opposite to that of the distinguished case should occur. For example, if the closest tort liability case to your client's case is distinguishable, your client may not be required to pay tort damages, but still may have to pay contract damages. However, if the distinction is strong and buttresses other reasoning that points in the same direction, then the distinction may suggest the outcome opposite to that in the decided case.

---

1. David A. Conway & Ronald Munson, *The Elements of Reasoning* 123–24 (1990).

2. Judging Similarity and Difference

a. With a Single Case

To reason by example, you first decide which case to work with, then evaluate its similarities to and differences from your case, and then determine whether that case and your client's case are analogous or distinguishable. All three steps require you to exercise considerable judgment.

As for the first step, a decided case is a possible candidate for reasoning by example if it meets two criteria: First, it must address the same or very nearly the same legal rule or element that you are analyzing in your client's case. Second, the facts pertaining to that rule or element should be similar to your client's case, although they almost certainly will not be identical or even nearly so. You should focus on the client's facts that are relevant to the rule or element and select a decided case with facts similar to those client facts.

The second step is to compare and contrast the decided case and your client's case in detail, focusing on the facts relevant to the rule or element under consideration. There inevitably will be both similarities and differences, and you should begin by listing both. Determine the relative importance of each fact to the court's reasoning and holding in the decided case. In some situations, a single striking difference or similarity drives the analysis. In others, you will rely on a collection of less obvious similarities or differences.

Comparisons and contrasts can be drawn broadly or narrowly. If your focus is too narrow, the client's case will appear utterly different. If your focus is broad, every decided case will begin to look similar to your client's case. You must judge how much "elasticity" is justifiable, based primarily on language in the decided case. If the decided case discusses the law or the facts in broad terms, then a broadly drawn comparison is justifiable; a narrowly drawn comparison is appropriate when the decided case is narrowly worded as to its law or its facts. Other authorities discussing the decided case may also help you decide how elastic it is. You may be tempted to stretch or constrict a comparison to bring your client's case within a favorable decided case or to save your client from the impact of an unfavorable decided case. However, you should make the intellectually better judgment, especially in an advisory setting where caution can forestall future legal problems.

The final step is to conclude whether the case is (overall) analogous or distinguishable.

For an illustration of reasoning by example, consider the *Gardner* case, briefed at page 295, and the HomeElderCare situation. Both involve unauthorized practice of law; both raise the question of whether the practitioner addressed "difficult or doubtful legal questions." *See Gardner v. Conway,* 48 N.W.2d 788, 794, 796 (Minn. 1951). Although it would be more helpful to have a case involving living wills and social workers, that case does not exist. The *Gardner* case, which involves tax preparation and a tax preparer, is fairly close.

The relevant facts under the "difficult or doubtful legal question" element are the activities of the nonlawyer and the extent to which those activities are legal in nature. In a broad sense, the *Gardner* and HomeElderCare activities are the same, because both involve advice on matters with legal implications and the eventual filling out of forms. Yet in a narrow sense, the two activities are not the same, as one involves taxes and the other involves medical determinations. The analysis should focus on whether the legal dimensions of the two activities are comparably complicated and would take into account, for example, the complexity of the two statutes. The tax code is a lengthy and complex statute, more so than the living will statute; yet the living will statute has an intricate legal background and no case law to resolve its ambiguities. Because valid arguments can be made on both sides, *Gardner* is neither clearly analogous nor clearly distinguishable.

b. With Multiple Cases

You may be uncertain at various points in reasoning by example. One way to resolve the uncertainty is to use more than one case for comparison. You could engage in reasoning by example more than once, with more than one decided case. Or, better yet, you can fuse several decided cases into a pattern and reason from that pattern to the client's case. This process is known as "inductive generalization"—reasoning from specific (the decided cases) to a generalization (their pattern) to specific (the client's case). Inductive generalization relates closely to the fusion process described in Chapter 4.

As an example, assume that the court decided in three cases that an unlicensed liquor seller could enforce his contract, while an unlicensed real-estate broker and an unlicensed engineer could not. You could infer that if licensure is a means of assuring technical competence, the unlicensed professional cannot enforce the contract; but if licensure is a means of generating revenue for the state, the unlicensed person can enforce the contract. The HomeElderCare social workers would have difficulty enforcing their contracts because licensure as an attorney assures technical competence.

EXHIBIT 9.1

VENN DIAGRAM

Gardner	filling out form	HomeElderCare
accounting	filling out form	social work
business/tax decisions	form has important legal consequences	medical decisions
long and complicated statute with lots of case law and regulations	form could be done by client alone	new, short statute with little case law
	separate field with training and standards	

3. Depicting Reasoning by Example

Just as with deductive reasoning, you can depict reasoning by example in various ways. In addition to textual forms, such as an expansion of the syllogism in Chapter 8, you may want to consider visual forms.

Exhibit 9.1 is a Venn diagram. The purpose of a Venn diagram is to illustrate the areas of similarity and difference between two sets—in this instance, two sets of facts. The areas of similarity appear in the center, the areas of difference at the sides. Exhibit 9.1 captures aspects of the *Gardner* analogy discussed above.

Exhibit 9.2 is a checkerboard chart that lines up the holding and facts from the decided case with the issue and facts of the client's case; it also sketches out a conclusion. Exhibit 9.2 illustrates the analogy to *Gardner* on the unauthorized practice issue of a difficult or doubtful legal question. Both *Gardner* and the client's case deal with the same rule and element, as shown in the issue boxes. Relevant facts appear in the two facts boxes. The implications of the comparison appear in the final row.

EXHIBIT 9.2

CHECKERBOARD CHART

Client's Case		Decided Case—*Gardner*
Issue(s)		Issue(s)
Will these laypersons be engaged in unauth'd practice of law? Will they be answering difficult or doubtful legal questions?	same? $\longrightarrow$	same as client's issues
Facts		Facts
Social workers will fill out form and answer questions about living wills, e.g., guardian selection, choice of medical treatment; form contains instructions.	similar $\longrightarrow$ enough?	Tax preparer provided client with advice on partnership, tax exemption, filing status, and deductions; form has some instructions.
Predicted result		Holding
HEC social workers will be practicing law if they answer client Qs on difficult or doubtful legal questions; living will issues may well be difficult or doubtful, given newness of statute and related regulations.	analogy or distinction justified? $\longleftarrow$	Advice on four legal topics was unauthorized law practice because these were difficult or doubtful legal questions that require a legally trained mind.

4. Using Reasoning by Example

Reasoning by example cannot stand alone. Rather, reasoning by example supplements deductive reasoning. The rule, in interaction with a concrete example, becomes less abstract and more specific, and your reasoning becomes more certain. Not insignificantly, the use of the decided case as an example adds a human side to the law and demonstrates how the rule has affected the lives of others.

In many situations, the conclusion begins to emerge in the deductive reasoning stage and is reinforced during reasoning by example. In other situations, the conclusion suggested by deductive reasoning is uncertain, and it is sharpened and directed by way of reasoning by example. In yet others, the deductive reasoning conclusion is at odds with the reasoning by example conclusion, necessitating further analysis.

C. POLICY ANALYSIS

1. What is Policy Analysis?

Sometimes, your deductive reasoning and reasoning by example may not prove conclusive. The rule may employ vague terms. There may be no decided cases to use, or your conclusion as to analogy or distinction may be tentative. The third phase of legal reasoning, policy analysis, is useful in these situations.

You no doubt use policy analysis in nonlegal contexts. Whenever you make a decision based on the ultimate goal inherent in a situation, you are engaging in policy analysis. For example, your spending decisions may be based in part on a budget or rules that you have developed for yourself, and in part on examples of how friends and relatives have made similar decisions. Most likely, you also consider your personal and financial goals, which might include furthering your education, providing for your family, or traveling.

In the context of legal reasoning, policy is the broad societal goal to be achieved by application of the legal rule to various situations. A policy is a general principle or goal, more abstractly expressed than a rule of law. Policy considerations drive the creation of legal rules. Judges, especially in the highest court, derive rules and select outcomes in particular cases based in part on their judgment of how to further society's interests. Legislators enact statutes based on their conceptions of the social good.

In many areas of law, society has more than one competing interest. In some situations, lawmakers select one interest to serve, and the resulting law arises from a fairly unitary and perhaps one-sided policy. In other situations, lawmakers seek to serve more than one interest, and the resulting law rests on two or more policies. The single-policy law typically is simpler in form and content than the law resting on multiple policies.

Competition among policies also causes jurisdictions to diverge in their choice of rules on the same subject, favoring different sides of the same policy struggle. These jurisdictional splits can occur in the judicial or legislative branches.

   Legal policy sometimes is supplemented by other disciplines such as philosophy and economics that also address how to achieve the public good.
Legal rules about who should bear the risk of loss in accidents, for example,
are informed by our philosophical conceptions of fault and responsibility. As
another example, economic principles about efficient markets underlie many
rules of contract law.

2. Deriving Policy

To apply policy to a client's situation, you first must discern the policy underlying the law. In some situations, the court or legislature states its policy
in so many words, in the reasoning portion of a judicial opinion or in the
purpose section of a statute. When there is no such statement, you may be
able to find it in commentary on your rule of law, because commentary writers often discuss the underlying policy of a rule in the process of describing
and critiquing it.

   In addition, you may find stakeholder analysis to be useful in deriving
underlying policies. Stakeholder analysis is a method of discerning the ethical
implications of a situation. It entails thinking broadly about the stakeholders
in a situation, their respective interests, and possible resolutions. You probably will find it helpful to focus on a specific application of the legal rule, such
as a major decided case or the statute's paradigm case. First, identify the immediate participants in the situation (the parties) as well as persons who are
less immediately involved but nonetheless affected by the case's resolution.
Second, identify the stakes, or interests, of each stakeholder. Third, identify
the legal consequences that follow from application of the rule, such as payment or receipt of damages, and the impact of the rule's application on the
various stakeholders' interests, such as economic security. The final step is to
identify the winners and losers in the case. The winner's interest, stated in
broad terms, constitutes the major policy behind the legal rule.

   Consider, as an example, the *Buckley* case at page 256. The two major
stakeholders were the parties: the real estate agent, who sought his contract
fee as well as the freedom to pursue his occupation unfettered by licensure
requirements, and the client, who sought to avoid paying the agent's fee and
to be protected against possibly incompetent work. Less immediately involved were the buyer of the property, any company for which the agent
worked, and other buyers and sellers in the real estate market who could have
been adversely affected by botched transactions. The client's interests won
out, along with those of the real-estate market; the court probably saw them
as more compelling than the fairly narrow and self-serving interests of the
agent and his employer. Accordingly, the client won the case.

   There are various ways to depict stakeholder analysis. Exhibit 9.3, on page
98, uses a spider-web diagram to depict the analysis of the interests in *Buckley*.

3. Employing Policy Analysis

Once you have discerned the policy underlying a legal rule, you can incorporate this information into your reasoning about the client's case. To apply
policy, you evaluate potential outcomes—and ways of reasoning that arrive at

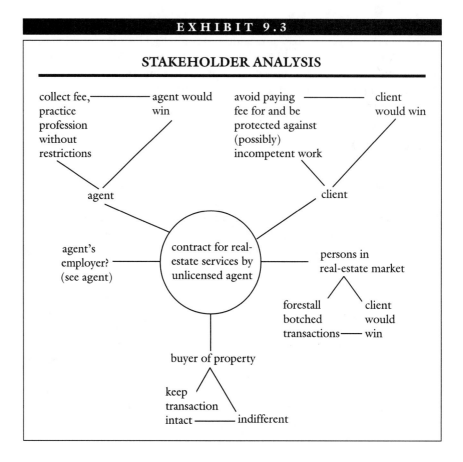

EXHIBIT 9.3

STAKEHOLDER ANALYSIS

those outcomes—by asking how well each outcome would serve the identified policy.

Policy can be incorporated in various ways. Assume that you are not certain of the elements in a rule, even after carefully reading the law. You can examine the possible interpretations of the rule in light of what you know about the rule's policy, then select the interpretation that best serves the policy. Assume that you have identified an element of the rule, matched it to your client's facts, and concluded that it probably does meet the requirement of the rule. This conclusion will be more certain if you also can reason that the policy is well served by the conclusion. Assume that you are uncertain whether your client's case is analogous to or distinguishable from a decided case. Policy permits you to resolve the tie, by focusing on the factual comparisons relevant to the law's policy.

You may find that more than one policy is inherent in a complex rule. The two chief questions to ask yourself are: First, is either policy preferred over the other by lawmakers? For example, has the court cited or relied on one policy more than the other recently? Second, which policy is more clearly served by the possible outcomes in the client's case? If one outcome would clearly serve one policy while the other outcome would only somewhat serve the competing policy, the former outcome might be favored by the courts.

By way of example, whether the activities of the HomeElderCare social worker would constitute the unauthorized practice of law raises major policy concerns. Legislators sponsoring the living will statute sought to safeguard a terminally ill patient's right to autonomy in medical care decisions and to avoid allocation of scarce medical resources to a person who does not want medical care. Howard Orenstein, et al., *Minnesota's Living Will . . .*, Bench & B. Minn., Aug. 1989, at 21. These policies favor HomeElderCare because, presumably, the clients will be a little more likely to draft living wills if they can be assisted by a social worker, not just by a lawyer. This policy analysis is buttressed by the *Gardner* principle that the rule on the unauthorized practice of law should not be applied to produce "impractical and technical restrictions." *Gardner*, 48 N.W.2d at 797. On the other hand, the policy favoring living wills is served even if HomeElderCare's service would be deemed unauthorized law practice, because the wills would nonetheless be valid under *Peterson*.

Yet the policy of the rule on unauthorized practice of law also is important: "to protect the public from the intolerable evils which are brought upon people by those who assume to practice law without having the proper qualifications." *Gardner*, 48 N.W.2d at 794. If questions addressed in a living will are primarily legal, permitting the social workers to draft the living wills raises the potential of incompetent legal work. On the other hand, the potential for incompetent work is not large if the living will addresses primarily medical questions and the social workers receive training. This analysis points out how close a call this issue is and how clearly HomeElderCare needs to be informed of the risks of its plan.

As always, there are various ways to depict your analysis. Exhibit 9.4 on page 100 presents a simple flowchart depicting the HomeElderCare policy analysis.

D. MESHING DEDUCTIVE REASONING, REASONING BY EXAMPLE, AND POLICY ANALYSIS

The reasoning stages described here can help you structure your analysis, but they cannot make difficult calls easy. You will need to exercise your judgment in the end. As your experience increases, your judgment will improve. You will learn how to inform a client of the uncertainty in your analysis and how to develop options or arguments to minimize the risks and maximize the strengths of the client's position.

If you have proceeded through a fairly complex reasoning process, you may wish to mesh major points in your analysis. The depictions of deductive reasoning presented in Chapter 8 can be expanded to incorporate the key points of reasoning by example and policy analysis, as shown in Exhibits 9.5 and 9.6, on pages 101 and 102 respectively.

Be sure to review your meshed analysis for compliance with the four criteria of sound legal writing:

- *Completeness:* Have you included all pertinent rules (their elements and factors) and all relevant facts?

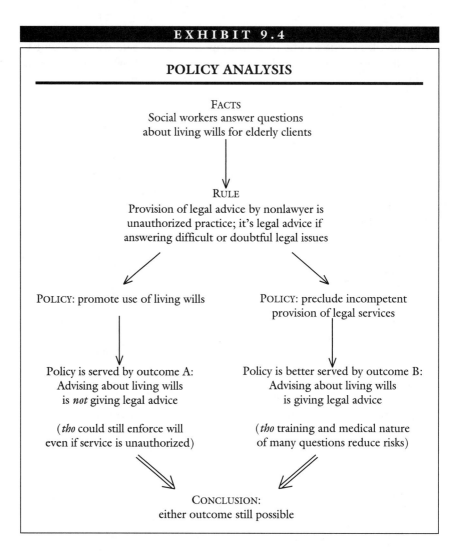

EXHIBIT 9.4

POLICY ANALYSIS

FACTS
Social workers answer questions
about living wills for elderly clients

RULE
Provision of legal advice by nonlawyer is
unauthorized practice; it's legal advice if
answering difficult or doubtful legal issues

POLICY: promote use of living wills

POLICY: preclude incompetent
provision of legal services

Policy is served by outcome A:
Advising about living wills
is *not* giving legal advice

(*tho* could still enforce will
even if service is unauthorized)

Policy is better served by outcome B:
Advising about living wills
is giving legal advice

(*tho* training and medical nature
of many questions reduce risks)

CONCLUSION:
either outcome still possible

- *Correctness:* Have you expressed the legal rules accurately? Have you depicted the facts accurately?
- *Coherence:* Does the analysis hold together? Do the facts match the elements? Is the probable outcome a sensible resolution of the case?
- *Comprehensibility:* Can you understand fully all steps of the analysis?

E. REVIEW OF CHAPTER 9

Both reasoning by example and policy analysis can supplement deductive reasoning, to reduce uncertainty in the rule or its application to the client's case. The process of reasoning by example, from specific to specific, involves the following steps:

(1) Select a decided case involving the same legal rule and element that you are analyzing in your client's situation.

EXHIBIT 9.5

COLUMN CHART SHOWING DEDUCTIVE REASONING, REASONING BY EXAMPLE, AND POLICY ANALYSIS

	Elements	Client Facts	Case Comparison	Policy Analysis	Element Met / Not Met
IF	any person/assn	HEC social workers	tax preparer		✓
	except members of MN bar admitted & licensed to practice	not licensed	not licensed		✓
	AND				
	gives legal advice or counsel, that is,	talk to elderly clients about issues re living will as part of social work	answered questions about how certain transactions are handled by law, e.g., marital status, business expenses; analogous in overall complexity and uncertainty of legal topics	1. avoid incompetence in legal services—contra HEC	✓ (probably)
	acts are more than incidental to other calling				
	OR			2. promote living wills—favors HEC	
	acts are incidental and involve difficult/ doubtful legal issues				
	Consequences	Effect on Client Situation			
THEN	prohibited as unauthorized practice of law (misdemeanor or injunction)	legal consequences probably result			

(2) Evaluate the similarities and differences between the relevant facts in the client's case and those of the decided case.
(3) Determine whether the client's case and the decided case are analogous or distinguishable.

Uncertainty in reasoning by example can be reduced by inductive generalization.

While reasoning by example is based on specifics, policy analysis entails application of broad principles to your client's case. The broad principle is the purpose of your legal rule—the goal sought by lawmakers. Policy analysis entails the following steps:

(1) Discern the policies from a statement in the law itself or from commentary on the law.
(2) If there is no satisfactory statement of policy, conduct a stakeholder analysis to draw out the policies; identify the stakeholders, their interests and preferred outcomes, and the interests favored by the law.

EXHIBIT 9.6

LEGAL SYLLOGISM SHOWING DEDUCTIVE REASONING, REASONING BY EXAMPLE, AND POLICY ANALYSIS

Major Premise:	IF any person/assn except members of MN bar admitted & licensed to practice gives legal advice, that is, ■ acts are more than incidental to other calling *or* ■ acts are incidental and involve difficult/doubtful legal issues THEN conduct is prohibited as unauthorized practice of law (misdemeanor, injunction).
Comparison Case:	Tax preparer not licensed in MN answered questions about tax treatment of transactions, e.g., marital status, business expenses; he was addressing difficult or doubtful legal issues; this conduct was unauthorized practice of law.
Policies:	1. to preclude provision of legal services by incompetent persons 2. to promote living wills
Minor Premise and Reasons:	HEC social workers are not licensed, and they will be giving advice on living wills incidental to their social work, and the issues probably involve doubtful or difficult legal questions because: Case analogy: Parallel between tax issues (complex statute) and living will issues (simpler statute, but complex and uncertain area of law). Policy analysis: Forestall drafting by incompetent laypersons; living wills may be harder to draft if lawyers are required, but improperly drafted wills may still be valid.
Conclusion:	HEC's conduct *probably* is prohibited as unauthorized practice of law.

(3) Apply the policies by testing your tentative outcome against them.

Once you have read the law and commentary carefully and reasoned carefully through your client's case, you are ready to communicate your analysis. The next several chapters describe the office memo, the standard form in which legal analysis is first communicated.

ADVISORY WRITING:

THE FUNCTION

AND FORMAT

OF THE OFFICE MEMO

> You may write for the joy of it, but the act of writing is not complete in itself. It has its end in its audience.
> —Flannery O'Connor, in *The Habit of Being* (Sally Fitzgerald, ed., 1979)

A. INTRODUCTION

To this point, this book has focused on the processes of reading the law and legal reasoning. The writings discussed thus far, such as the case fusion and statutory brief, are tools to further your reading and reasoning; they are not tools for communication to someone else.

This and the remaining chapters discuss ways in which lawyers communicate legal analysis to other people. The basic written form in which a legal analysis is presented is the office memo. Other written forms include the client letter, motion practice memorandum, and appellate brief. Of course, lawyers communicate orally as well, in such varied settings as client conferences, legislative hearings, and judicial proceedings.

Although the following chapters depict communication as a distinct stage, the reading, reasoning, and writing processes are not truly separable. You may write a rough outline of a memo midway through the reasoning process, to record your thoughts or test your analysis. You may return to a key case or statute, to re-read it, as you write about it. As you write, you not only memorialize your analysis, but also clarify and often modify it.

This chapter discusses several topics: reader-centered prose, the importance of audience and purpose, and the framework of the office memo. The next three chapters look more closely at the main components of the office memo: the discussion in Chapter 11; the issues, short answers, and conclusion in Chapter 12; and the facts in Chapter 13.

You will find two sample office memos on the HomeElderCare case at pages 312 and 319. Please read them before reading the rest of this chapter. You will see that they come to different conclusions. This is not surprising; legal analysis rarely is a mechanical process leading to certain outcomes. Note that there are similarities as well as differences in the two memos; some aspects of the HomeElderCare case are fairly straightforward. The first sample memo is annotated and analyzed in the coming chapters; the second is left for your analysis.

B. Reader-Centered Writing (and the Writer's Voice)

1. Reader-Centered Writing

The aim of legal writing is to communicate the writer's legal analysis of a situation to the reader. The writer aims to present the results of his or her research, reading of the law, and reasoning about the client's case. If the writer does so successfully, the reader will fully understand the writer's analysis, without having to retrace all of the writer's steps. The reader will be ready to adopt the legal meaning the writer has ascribed to the case and act accordingly.

Legal writers (indeed, all writers who wish to be understood) should keep in mind basic principles of communication. Communication is a form of social interaction, which succeeds when the writer honors these principles:

(1) Take the reader's characteristics into account.
(2) Convey the truth as you see it.
(3) Try to be understood; write coherently and comprehensibly.
(4) Give neither too much nor too little information.
(5) Keep to relevant points.
(6) Produce a writing that is appropriate to the context and circumstances.
(7) Produce a message that is appropriate to your purpose.[1]

---

1. *See generally* C. Douglas McCann & E. Tory Higgins, Personal and Contextual Factors in Communication: A Review of the *"Communication Game,"* in *Language, Interaction and Social Cognition* 144 (Gun R. Semin & Klaus Fiedler, eds., 1992).

Some of these principles restate the four hallmarks of sound legal writing: completeness (items 4 and 5), correctness (item 2), and coherence and comprehensibility (item 3). Others highlight the importance of the reader's characteristics (item 1) and the paper's context, circumstances, and purpose (items 6 and 7). In other words, you must attend to the paper's audience and purpose—its function.

If you do so, you will structure the paper with the reader in mind. From the overall format of the paper to the sequence of points in individual paragraphs to the design of each sentence, you should consider how the reader will peruse and use your paper. What will the reader already know? What does the reader still need to know? What should come first? Next? At the end? How much detail is needed? How can the information be presented so as to maximize understanding? How will the reader best grasp the big picture and still see the nuances?

To a significant extent, the answers to these questions are provided by the conventions of legal writing. Every discipline has its own writing conventions; law is no exception. Following these conventions is advantageous for several reasons. First, legal writing conventions closely reflect the ways lawyers approach and solve problems. Second, because your readers are familiar with the conventions, they process legal writing that follows the conventions more efficiently than they process writing that does not. Third, your writing will seem more credible when it follows the profession's conventions. Fourth, the better you address the needs and expectations of your audience, the better you serve your client.

2. The Writer's Voice

It may seem that focusing on the reader means that your voice, as a writer, is muffled. Admittedly, your aim in legal writing is not primarily self-expression, as it would be in some other forms of writing, such as poetry or journals. And your personal preferences may differ from the language and conventions of the legal community. Nonetheless, it is your analysis—your research, your reading of the law, and your reasoning about your client's case—that is presented within the conventional form. Your analysis inevitably will reflect your values, your creative ways of thinking about problems, and your choice of words. No two lawyers, writing about the same client's case, will generate the same paper.

Many lawyers have been trained never to use the first person ("I think . . .") in legal writing. A typical explanation is that the reader does not care what you think, but is concerned only with what the law is. A better explanation is that the reader does in fact care what you think, but the reader also realizes full well, without a reminder, that your paper reflects your thinking. Moreover, if you forgo the use of the first person, your analysis will seem more objective and, hence, more credible. Whether you refer to yourself expressly or not, your paper will bear your stamp. It also will bear your name, because most formats include the writer's name in a prominent location.

C. THE FUNCTION AND FORMAT OF THE OFFICE MEMO

1. The Function of the Office Memo: Audience and Purpose

The office memo (also known as a file memo, intraoffice memo, or internal memo) is standard in most settings where more than one lawyer practices, whether in a law firm, corporate counsel office, or legal department of a government agency or other organization. Office memos are written for various purposes. Some simply record conversations with the client or opposing counsel, information recently obtained from other sources, or ideas generated in discussions among lawyers working on the case. Other office memos are more elaborate and substantial, presenting the lawyer's analysis of the client's case at a particular time.

The analytical office memo records the facts as currently known; documents the research conducted on the file, along with citations to the sources; presents the lawyer's reading of the pertinent legal authorities; and sets out the lawyer's reasoning about the case. The memo culminates in predictions about how a court would handle the client's case, should this come to pass, and recommendations for appropriate action. The memo states the best judgment of the writer and permits informed judgment by other lawyers working on the file. The memo also forms the basis of advice to the client, which in turn leads to steps taken on the client's behalf, such as the structuring of a transaction, arguments made to courts or other tribunals, or discussions to settle the dispute.

The most obvious audience for the analytical office memo is the named recipient, typically the senior lawyer who has requested the memo from a junior lawyer. Other lawyers working on the same case also may read it. The office memo may be read again if a similar case involving a different client arises within the office. The writer also is a member of the audience, because he or she is likely to return to the memo as the client's case progresses. The client also may read the memo, although the lawyer typically sends the client a letter based on the memo, rather than the memo itself.

In writing the office memo, the lawyer, even though acting on behalf of the client, must act objectively. The lawyer's role as an officer of the legal system compels this perspective. The requirement of objectivity also stems from considerations of practicality and trust. The lawyer assesses both the strengths and weaknesses of the client's legal position. The lawyer best serves a client contemplating a legally risky transaction by telling the client the risks and how to avoid them, rather than permitting the transaction to go forward and hoping that liability will not follow. For a client in a difficult position in litigation, the lawyer's most valuable service is to alert the client to the difficulties and to help the client obtain a realistic outcome, rather than to pursue a losing position until the case is lost at great expense. The lawyer's job is to tell the client "yes" only if "yes" is warranted, and to say "no" or present options if "yes" is not warranted.

2. The Format of the Office Memo

There is no single office memo format on which lawyers everywhere agree. On the other hand, several components are common to almost every format. This section discusses those components from the perspective of the reader; Chapters 11 through 13 describe how to write them.

Caption: The caption identifies the memo. It typically consists of the recipient's name, the writer's name, the date, and the subject. The date is important because every office memo is time-bound, reflecting only what the writer knew and thought about the client's facts and the law as of the date the memo was written. The subject of the memo usually consists of the client's name and file number, along with a brief description of the topic of the memo. The topic description facilitates access in future similar situations not involving the same client.

Issue(s): The issues orient the reader to the legal questions arising in the client's case and to the organization of the memo. Legal analysis involves asking and answering one or more questions about the legal implications of the client's facts. The issues link rules of law to the relevant facts of the client's case. They appear in the same order as the main topics appear in the discussion.

Short answer(s): The short answers further orient the reader and provide the reader with the writer's position on the issues, permitting the reader to read the rest of the memo in light of the writer's position. The short answers present bottom-line answers, an indication of the degree of certainty the lawyer can provide, and a word or two of explanation. They do not fully explain the answers or give legal support for them. They parallel the issues in number and sequence.

Facts: The fact statement tells the reader the client's story. If the lawyer has talked only to the client, the story is told through the client's eyes. If the lawyer has investigated the facts, the facts include information obtained from other sources. If the entire story has not yet unfolded, because the client has sought advice before taking action, the facts not only recount past events but also refer to future possibilities.

Discussion: The bulk of the office memo is the discussion, in which the writer systematically analyzes each issue and justifies each short answer for the reader. The discussion of most issues involves an introduction, a presentation of the rule of law (including alternative legal rules if they exist), application of the rules to the facts (again, including alternative approaches if they exist), and the lawyer's conclusion. Transitions clarify the links among the issues, and headings signal the major and minor topics.

Conclusion (and Recommendations): The conclusion both summarizes the preceding material for the reader and recommends actions to be taken for or by the client. The recommendations should flow from the legal analysis in the discussion and may also be based on nonlegal factors, which should be stated.

Some office memos also contain appendices. Some lawyers attach copies of key authorities, such as a key statute or new case, especially if the authority is not well known to the recipient of the memo. Where the facts involve a

EXHIBIT 10.1

PARALLELS BETWEEN JUDICIAL OPINIONS AND OFFICE MEMOS

Judicial Opinion	Office Memo
Case name, court, date, docket number	Caption (client's name, writer's name, date, file number, etc.)
Issues	Issues
Holdings	Short answers
Fact statement	Facts
Reasoning	Discussion
Concluding paragraph with procedural outcome	Conclusion with recommendations

contract, map, or other document, it often is more efficient to attach the document than to describe it in full detail in the facts. If there are many specific events and their timing is crucial, a timeline can be a helpful appendix.

In some ways, office memos parallel judicial opinions. See Exhibit 10.1. The lawyer writing an office memo is, in essence, seeking to anticipate what a court would do when faced with the client's case. Indeed, one way to maintain objectivity is to imagine that you are a judge deciding the client's case.

3. An Analogy: The Architecture of a House

The upcoming chapters develop a nonlegal analogy: An office memo resembles a building, specifically, a house. The issues and short answers together constitute the facade, the facts the foundation, the discussion the interior, the conclusion the roof. Just as one must attend to function and structure in building a house, so one must attend to function and structure in constructing an office memo.

D. WRITING THE OFFICE MEMO COMPONENTS

The next three chapters discuss the writing of office memo components in the following order: discussion; issues, short answers, and conclusions; facts. You may well write these components in this order, because the discussion flows most directly from your reasoning; the issues, short answers, and conclusion derive from the discussion; and the facts must support the rest of the memo. However, if you are a big-picture thinker, you might begin with the issues and short answers. If you are more fact-oriented, you may write the facts first, to set the foundation for the legal analysis.

No matter what order you choose for your writing, you should assemble the memo components in the order set out in this chapter. Then, check each component for consistency with the other components. The key to a successful memo is that the components work together well and meet the criteria discussed in the next three chapters.

E.   REVIEW OF CHAPTER 10

As the basic form of legal writing, the office memo communicates the writer's legal analysis of a client's case to the reader. The audience consists of lawyers working on the client file (yourself included), and the purpose is to present an objective analysis that will support sound advice for the client. You will meet your audience's need and serve your purpose well if you structure the memo according to the following conventional format: caption, issues, short answers, facts, discussion, and conclusion.

THE OFFICE MEMO:

THE DISCUSSION

> Never be afraid to sit awhile and think.
> —Lorraine Hansberry,
> *A Raisin in the Sun* (1958)

A. INTRODUCTION

The core, as well as the bulk, of the office memo is the discussion component. There, the writer systematically analyzes each issue and justifies each short answer for the reader. This chapter describes how to convert your ideas from reading the law and reasoning about your client's case into a discussion that communicates effectively to your reader. They key to an effective discussion is its structure, or organization. And the driving force behind the organization of a discussion is the rule of law, or rules of law, pertinent to the client's case. Hence analysis and organization are intertwined.

This chapter discusses how to gather and group your thoughts to produce a preliminary organization; how to organize material at three levels—large, middle, and small scale; how to deal with branchpoints at which the analysis could proceed in two (or more) directions; how to use transitions and headings; and additional considerations in writing the discussion.

To write an effective discussion, you will need to attend to all of these matters. You might proceed according to the sequence suggested here: first determining the large-scale design, next working on the middle-scale and then small-scale designs, and finally developing the transitions. Alternatively, you might write small, discrete passages of the discussion and then assemble the small passages into large stretches of material. Yet another possibility is to write your headings and transitions at the outset and then fill in the development of your points.

As an illustration, this chapter refers to the discussion from the first sample HomeElderCare office memo, found at page 314. You should re-read that memo now.

B. GATHERING AND GROUPING THOUGHTS

Your first task is to gather your thoughts. If you have proceeded carefully through the steps suggested in Chapters 2 through 9, you will have thought through the case thoroughly. And your thoughts will be organized by legal rules when you turn to writing your memo.

At the same time, some thoughts may occur to you when you are not deliberately working on the analysis. Further, you may wish to spend some time brainstorming about the analysis, without focusing on the rules of law applicable to the case; creative ideas often arise when you let yourself think freely. Be sure to jot down these random thoughts.

However you generate your thoughts, be sure to develop them fully. To do so, ask yourself two questions: Does this thought presuppose any other thought? What is the implication of this thought?

The next major step is to group your thoughts, to sort them into literal or metaphorical piles of closely related thoughts. Presumably the major piles or topics will derive from the rules of law. For example, you may have piles for each of the following: the procedural rule, the claims, the defenses, and the remedies. You may want to sketch out what you think your major topics will be and then see whether your thoughts fit within the topics. Or you may want to shuffle and sift the thoughts you have generated until you develop piles of logically connected thoughts, each pile representing a major topic. Some thoughts may not fit into any pile particularly well, and some thoughts may seem to span piles; put those thoughts in every potential pile. If you have quite a few stray thoughts or thoughts that span piles, you may discover a topic that eluded you earlier on, or you may discover a new way to group your thoughts.

C. AN ANALOGY: THE INTERIOR OF A HOUSE

In the analogy between office memos and houses, the discussion constitutes the interior. Just as the interior of a house is organized at several levels, so is an office memo. See Exhibit 11.1.

At the large-scale level, ordering legal rules parallels arranging the stories of a house. Each story in a house should have its own function or set of related functions, and the stories should be stacked in a sensible order. So, too, each part of the discussion should have its own legal rule (or set of related rules), and the parts should be presented in a logical order. Just as there is more than one way to arrange the stories of a house, there often is more than one way to order the parts of a discussion, some being more conventional than others.

At the middle-scale level, ordering the elements of a rule in subparts of the discussion parallels configuring the various rooms in a story of a house. The rooms should be arranged well, so that the occupant need not backtrack or pass through unnecessary rooms when undertaking a particular activity. So too, the subparts of a memo should be arranged so the reader can proceed straight through the subparts about a particular rule, becoming well informed at each point, not needing to backtrack. As with configuring the rooms in a house, there may be more than one logical way to order the subparts of a discussion.

At the small-scale level, ordering the points about a particular element parallels designing a room in a house. Rooms have standard features, such as doors and windows, that relate to each other in ways that make sense, given the use of the particular room. So too, the discussion of an element has a standard sequence that makes sense to lawyers, yet the sequence varies somewhat from one element to another.

Finally, as with a house's interior, a well structured discussion has transitional elements. Paralleling the stairs and hallways of a house are transitional passages, phrases, and words, as well as graphics.

EXHIBIT 11.1

LEVELS OF ORGANIZATION
OF OFFICE MEMO DISCUSSION

Level of Organization	Task Involved	Organizational Unit	House Analogy
Large-scale organization	how to order rules	parts of discussion	arranging the stories in a house
Middle-scale organization	how to order elements of a rule	subparts	configuring rooms in a story
Small-scale organization	how to discuss an element	paragraphs or paragraph blocks	designing rooms

D. LARGE-SCALE ORGANIZATION: HOW RULES RELATE TO PARTS

Many office memos have a wide scope, covering more than one legal rule. Each rule and the application of that rule to your client's case is a distinct topic, to be discussed in its separate part of the discussion. These office memos present large-scale organizational challenges: Which legal rule, or topic, should you discuss first? Which comes second? And so on.

You should order the parts of the discussion according to either the logic of the law or the factual logic of the client's case. It is more common to follow the logic of the law, whereas factual logic may be used if there is no clear legal logic to follow. Sometimes you can discern the legal logic for a discussion by examining models you discovered through your legal research, for example, in a commentary source or leading case on your topic. Of course, you should be sure that the borrowed organization is logical and fits your client's case. You also may find some standard legal conventions helpful in creating a logical organization for your discussion:

Intermediate to ultimate consequences: As discussed in Chapter 2, some rules identify an intermediate legal consequence; others identify ultimate practical consequences. An intermediate-consequence rule must be linked to an ultimate-consequence rule. You should discuss the intermediate-consequence rule first, because the discussion of the ultimate-consequence rule presupposes the intermediate consequence.

Threshold rules first: A threshold rule nearly always appears first because its application dictates whether analysis of the other rules is necessary. For example, if the court clearly lacks jurisdiction or the statute of limitations certainly has run, issues of liability and remedies are beside the point. However, unless a threshold rule unequivocally forecloses further analysis, you should discuss the remaining issues. The rationale of this convention is efficiency.

Claim/defense/remedy: It is typical to start with the rules applicable to the plaintiff's claim, proceed to the rules governing the defendant's defense, and then discuss any rules pertaining to remedies. The rationale is that the plaintiff must present its case before the defendant must produce a defense or before the plaintiff is entitled to a remedy.

General to specific: Generally, discussion of a broad rule precedes discussion of a narrower rule. This convention parallels the way most people process information, by making broad conclusions and then more particular conclusions.

More to less important alternatives: In some situations, certain conduct may be covered by more than one rule, as in the cases of overlapping common law and statutory rules, or two widely recognized common law rules, neither of which has yet been selected in your jurisdiction. The discussion should begin with the rule that is the more probable or better established in your situation. This convention presents the more important information first.

Procedural/substantive or substantive/procedural: Procedural rules often appear together, and substantive rules often appear together. Which set comes first depends on the logic of the law as applied to the client's case. For example, a procedural rule may be a threshold rule, or a substantive rule may be pivotal.

Chronology: In some areas, rules of law arise chronologically. For instance, nearly any area of law related to contract law is constructed chronologically in the order that the transaction unfolds (formation, terms, performance, breach, and remedies).

Actors: Discussion focuses first on all rules pertaining to a particular actor, then proceeds to the rules pertaining to another actor, and so on. This convention is most useful when you are analyzing a transaction involving multiple actors or a single complicated event.

Even in a simple memo, you may employ two or more of these conventions. For instance, you may proceed through procedural rules chronologically, then move to substantive rules by claim/defense/remedy. However, be wary of combining so many conventions that the reader will find it difficult to follow the logic of the organization.

Sometimes a rule may be moved to the beginning of a discussion rather than appear in its most logical place. If a rule is easily applied and can be gotten out of the way early in the discussion to make way for the tougher analysis, then that easily applied rule sometimes can be moved up, if that presentation would not confuse the reader. Similarly, if a rule is clearly met and thereby eliminates the need to consider one or more other rules (or at least makes their consideration less important), then that rule sometimes can be moved up, if that presentation would not confuse the reader.

Some complex discussions entail overlap between legal rules. For example, the same rule may apply to two different sets of parties involved in closely related transactions. One option is to discuss all claims involving one set of parties, then all claims involving the other set:

Parties	*Claim 1*	*Claim 2*
A and B	first	second
A and C	third	fourth

Another option is to discuss all instances of one claim, then all instances of the other claim:

Parties	*Claim 1*	*Claim 2*
A and B	first	third
A and C	second	fourth

A third option is a hybrid, e.g., to discuss the topics on which there is no difference across the parties, then discuss the topics that are unique to each party. All options involve some repetition, but that is inherent in the situation. You should select a clear and logical large-scale organization and use shortened discussions and cross-references in the later portions of the discussion to reduce repetitiousness.

These large-scale organizational principles are followed in the discussion in the first HomeElderCare sample memo, sketched in Exhibit 11.2, in which the main topics are numbered with roman numerals. The memo addresses three topics, each with its own rule, in this order: (1) whether the drafting of the wills would be an unauthorized practice of law, (2) whether

EXHIBIT 11.2

CLASSIC OUTLINE OF DISCUSSION

    I. Unauthorized practice of law
       A. Statutory quote with overall rule re non-attorney;
          application—non-attorney
       B. Drafting legal documents (all one paragraph)
          1. Introduction: conclusion
          2. Rule: construing UPL and LW statutes together;
             dictionary definitions
          3. Application: living will as legal document, fee
          4. Conclusion: there is UPL
       C. Giving legal advice or counsel (eight paragraphs)
          1. Introduction: transition
          2. Rule: statute, *Gardner* rule and example
          3. Application in several stages
            ■ Review of activities and LW statute
            ■ Comparison to *Gardner*
            ■ Policy argument: protect public
            ■ Other side: inconvenience, impracticality
            ■ Refutation
            ■ Charging fee
          4. Conclusion: there likely is UPL; consequences
       D. Link between UPL and two remaining questions
   II. Contract enforceability (seven paragraphs)
       [No A, B level because simpler rule]
          1. Introduction: topic
          2. Rule: *Buckley* and *Weatherston's*
            ■ Including summary of latter
          3. Application in several stages
            ■ Practice probably contrary to statute
            ■ Purpose of UPL statute
            ■ Protections against incompetence
            ■ No fraud or misrepresentation
            ■ Incidental to other service
            ■ Supporting public policy
          4. Conclusion: enforceable contract
  III. Validity of living will (four paragraphs)
       [Again, no A, B]
          1. Introduction: conclusion
          2. Rule: UPL statute and *Peterson*
          3. Application in two stages
            ■ Comparison to *Peterson*
            ■ Policy analysis based on LW statute
          4. Conclusion: valid living wills

the contracts between HomeElderCare and the clients would be enforceable, and (3) whether the wills would be valid. This organization reflects the convention regarding intermediate- and ultimate-consequences rules. Because the validity of the contract and living will could hinge on whether there is unauthorized practice, the unauthorized practice rule is addressed first. Either of the remaining rules could be addressed next because they do not hinge on each other. The discussion's organization also is based on actors and chronology. The rule pertaining primarily to HomeElderCare comes first, and the rule pertaining solely to the clients comes last, with their issue of mutual concern in the middle. Viewed another way: chronologically, the first event would be the drafting of the living wills, which raises the possibility of unauthorized practice; then conflicts might arise over the enforceability of the contract or the validity of the wills.

E. MIDDLE-SCALE ORGANIZATION: HOW ELEMENTS RELATE TO SUBPARTS

Once you have decided how to order the rules in the discussion on a large-scale level, you next must decide on your middle-scale organization, that is, how to order the elements within each multi-element rule. The middle-scale organizational challenge is: Which element of the rule should be addressed in the first subpart? Which comes second? And so on. (For simple rules with only one element, you can skip this step and move directly to small-scale organization.)

Sometimes the elements of a rule have their own logical order, as shown in the sources setting out the rule using that order. Other times, if you have synthesized all or part of the rule, you will need to order the elements of that rule yourself. In doing so, keep in mind the rule's structure. For example, you will want to cover the two (or more) options in a disjunctive rule together and the factors in an aggregate or balancing rule together.

In addition, some of the large-scale organizing conventions discussed in Part D, with some variations, are also helpful at the middle-scale level. For example, ordinarily you would discuss threshold elements first, proceed from general to specific, or work through a chronology, as appropriate.

In many situations, the application of one or more elements will be straightforward, requiring very little discussion, while the application of others will require extended discussion. You may wish to combine the straightforward elements into a subpart to present first, then work through the more difficult elements, each with its own subpart.

Once you have finished discussing the elements of a rule, you should state the consequences of the rule. If there is more than one consequence, first discuss the consequence that is more probable or more effective in your case.

In the HomeElderCare situation, the rule on the unauthorized practice of law is a multi-element rule. As shown in Exhibit 11.3, in which the middle-scale organization is depicted in boldface uncapped type, the discussion of unauthorized practice has three subparts as suggested by the statute.

EXHIBIT 11.3

TYPEFACE OUTLINE OF DISCUSSION

UNAUTHORIZED PRACTICE OF LAW (first rule)
Statutory quote with overall rule re non-attorney (first element)
—Application: non-attorney
Drafting legal documents (second element)
—Introduction by way of conclusion
—Rule: construe UPL and LW statutes together, dictionary definitions
—Application: living will as legal document, charging fee
= Conclusion: there is UPL
Giving legal advice or counsel (third element)
—Introduction by way of transition
—Rule: statute, *Gardner* rule and example
—Application: review of activities and LW statute
            comparison to *Gardner*
            policy argument: protect public
            other side: inconvenience, impracticality
            refutation
            charging fee
= Conclusion: there likely is UPL; consequences
Link between UPL and two remaining questions (transition)
CONTRACT ENFORCEABILITY (second rule)
—Introduction by way of topic
—Rule: *Buckley* and *Weatherston's,* including summary of latter
—Application: practice probably contrary to statute
            purpose of UPL statute
            protections against incompetence
            no fraud or misrepresentation
            incidental to other service
            supporting public policy
= Conclusion: enforceable contract
VALIDITY OF LIVING WILL (third rule)
—Introduction by way of conclusion
—Rule: UPL statute and *Peterson*
—Application: comparison to *Peterson*
            policy analysis based on LW statute
= Conclusion: valid living wills

The first subpart, whether the social workers are attorneys, is a threshold element. Drafting and advising are disjunctive elements; the simpler discussion precedes the more elaborate.

F. SMALL-SCALE ORGANIZATION: HOW ANALYSIS IS DEVELOPED IN PARAGRAPH BLOCKS

1. IRAC

Once you have set the order in which you will discuss the pertinent rules and elements within multi-element rules, you are ready for small-scale organization. Small-scale organization pertains to the discussion of either a single element of a multi-element rule or an entire single-element rule. The small-scale organizational challenge is: In what order should the discussion present the law, its application to the client's case, any pertinent case comparisons, policy analysis, and the conclusion?

For this task, many lawyers use a standard sequence known by the mnemonic IRAC (easily the most popular mnemonic in legal education):

Introduction	(Topic)
Rule	(Elaboration)
Application	(Elaboration)
Conclusion	(Conclusion)

(For some, "I" stands for issue. We have chosen a broader term, introduction, for reasons stated below.)

The rationale of IRAC is quite simple: introduce the reader to the point under discussion, provide the legal rule (because the legal analysis is driven by the rule), show how the law applies to the client's facts, and then draw a conclusion. As shown in the right-hand column above, IRAC is a legal version of the classic paragraph template, TEC.

Although IRAC is not the only way to organize the discussion of an element, IRAC has two significant advantages. First, it mirrors the order in which lawyers think about problems. Second, IRAC is very flexible, as the discussion below shows. As a result, IRAC is widely followed. Thus, although you will learn about alternatives in later chapters involving advocacy, you first should master IRAC.

Within each of the four IRAC components, you can choose among several options. Your choice should reflect the material you are discussing.

Introduction: The introduction orients the reader to the precise point you are about to discuss and is typically one sentence long. You may state any of the following:

■ the topic—that is, a reference to the subject of the upcoming paragraph block;

- the issue you are about to address—that is, a question linking law to facts (as in a case brief);
- the conclusion you have come to—again, linking law to facts, but in statement form; and
- a transition—that is, a sentence linking the previous topic to the up-coming topic.

The topic option is shorter than the others. The issue and conclusion options tend to be longer than the others and thus work best at the start of a lengthy part. The transition is a good choice if consecutive topics have important links that the reader may miss unless they are pointed out. Consider using the same option consistently within the discussion of a particular rule, for stylistic coherence.

Rule: The rule component informs the reader of the law pertinent to the client's situation. It may be an entire rule or an element of a multi-element rule. Lawyers must cite the legal authorities they use in analyzing a client's case. (Appendix C covers citation.)

The derivation of the legal rule determines how you should present the rule. If your rule is derived from a single case, you will present the court's statement of the rule from the case, along with a summary of the facts and holding if the facts are quite similar to your client's case. If your rule is derived from a set of cases, you will state the fused rule and refer to the set of cases. You also might summarize the case that most resembles your client's case, or you might briefly present two cases with different facts and outcomes. If your rule is derived solely from a statute, you will quote the pertinent statutory language. If your rule is derived from a statute supplemented by case law or other materials, you will first quote the statute and then present the supplementary material.

Whether your rule is from a statute or case law, if the reader would benefit from knowledge of the rule's underlying policy at this point, you could state that policy immediately following the statement of the rule.

Application: The application component presents your reasoning about the client's facts in light of the law. Your goal is not simply to restate the facts, but rather to show whether they meet the factual conditions in the element or rule under discussion.

Sometimes the reasoning process involves only deductive reasoning. If the conclusion from deductive reasoning needs support or clarification, then reasoning by example or policy analysis or both can be used. Deductive reasoning usually comes first, followed by reasoning by example or policy analysis; if all three are presented, policy analysis frequently is placed last. On occasion, reasoning by example or policy analysis may be used as a lead-in to deductive reasoning. Although the application relies in large part on the development of the law in the rule component, the application may refer to and cite legal authorities to expand upon the rule or to present policy.

Throughout your application, you should draw clear links between the law and your facts. As you deal with the language of a statute, set out the relevant facts of your client's case and tell the reader whether the element is met or not. As you deal with a decided case, identify the similarity or difference between the facts of that case and the client's case, then tell the reader the significance of the comparison. As you deal with policy, spell out for the reader how the various possible outcomes would or would not serve the policy you have identified. To test whether your analysis is explicit enough, ask yourself "why?" after each sentence, and keep explaining your thinking until nothing remains to be stated.

In many situations, there are good arguments on both sides of the question. To fully inform your reader, you must present both sides. Thus, you would present parallel discussions, with differing implications. The more conventional approach is to lead with the better argument (whether it favors the client or not), follow it with the weaker one, and then explain why you have chosen the first. Often, policy forms the basis for the choice among competing applications and thus is discussed near the end.

Conclusion: The IRAC discussion closes with a statement of your conclusion, that is, whether the requirements of the element of a complex rule or the entire simple rule are met or not. If the element under discussion is the last one for the rule, or the IRAC sequence covers an entire legal rule, the conclusion also should refer to the legal consequences flowing from that rule.

2. Paragraphs and Paragraph Blocks

The length of an IRAC discussion varies, depending on the complexity of the analysis. IRAC can be rather brief if the law applies to the client's situation in a quite obvious way, and IRAC can be completed within a single paragraph. For instance, a single sentence could introduce the topic and present the rule, and a second sentence could apply the rule and state the conclusion. As another example, a single sentence could present the rule and its application.

On the other hand, IRAC likely will run a page or more where both statutory and case law is involved, if there are good arguments on both sides, or where an extended comparison to a decided case or policy analysis would be instructive. Then, IRAC requires a sequence of paragraphs, that is, a paragraph block. A common break in a two-paragraph block is:

Para. 1: Introduction (topic) and **R**ule
Para. 2: **A**pplication of rule and **C**onclusion

A more complex and lengthy paragraph block might be divided as follows:

Para. 1: Introduction (issue) and statutory **R**ule
Para. 2: **R**ule/major case interpreting statute
Para. 3: **A**pplication/parallel between case and client situation
Para. 4: **A**pplication/contrast between case and client situation
Para. 5: **A**pplication/policy analysis
Para. 6: **C**onclusion as to this element and consequences

The key to using IRAC effectively is to follow the IRAC sequence and to break for a new paragraph when your discussion moves to a new stage.

The sample HomeElderCare discussion includes many examples of IRAC, as sketched in Exhibit 11.4. Drafting legal documents is discussed in

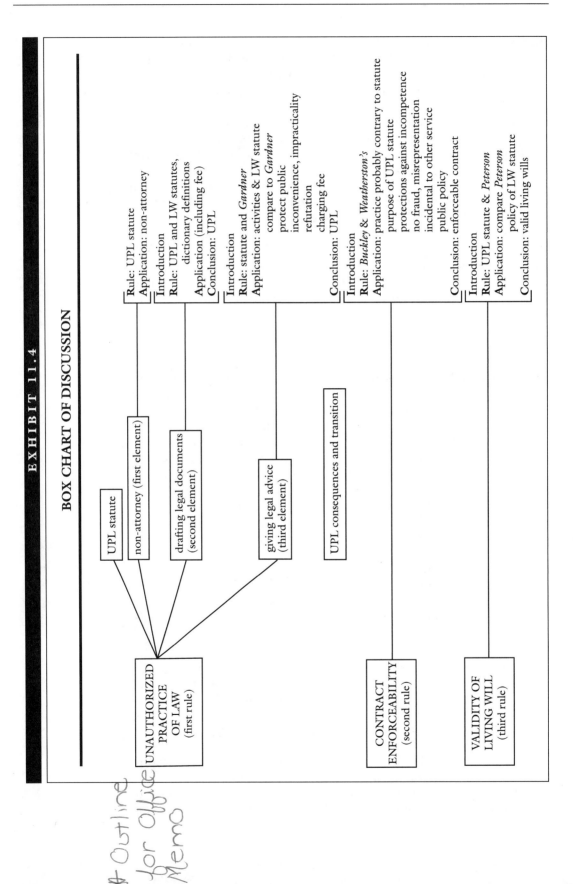

EXHIBIT 11.4

BOX CHART OF DISCUSSION

a single IRAC paragraph near the beginning of the discussion. By contrast, the discussion of the contract's enforceability under the *Weatherston's* case is more complex and runs several paragraphs. The first paragraph contains the introduction (the topic) as well as the overarching rule, the second paragraph summarizes *Weatherston's,* the following five paragraphs present the comparison of *Weatherston's* to the HomeElderCare facts and include policy analysis, and the final paragraph presents the conclusion.

3. IRAC Packages

Sometimes one IRAC sequence will cover an entire single-element rule. More often, though, as discussed above with regard to middle-scale organization, it will take several IRACs to cover a rule. You need to package these IRACs together, so the reader properly sees them as connected to the same rule. The mechanisms for doing so are bookend paragraphs or sentences: a roadmap at the beginning and an overall conclusion at the end. In other words:

Roadmap
IRAC for element #1
IRAC for element #2
IRAC for element #3
Overall conclusion

The overall conclusion, which follows the intermediate conclusion as to the last element, should state what the legal consequences are; it may begin with a brief summary of all intermediate conclusions.

The same package can also be looked at as one big IRAC. The initial introduction and rule are followed by the IRAC sequences for each element of the rule. The package finishes with an overall conclusion. In other words:

Introduction
Rule
IRAC for element 1
IRAC for element 2
IRAC for element 3
Conclusion

In a sense, the element's IRACs are the A for the overall IRAC.

The first sample HomeElderCare memo presents such a package on the unauthorized practice of law issue. See Exhibit 11.4. The statutory quotation serves as the roadmap. Three IRACs of various sizes follow. The package concludes with an overall conclusion that states the legal consequences, along with a branchpoint transition paragraph.

G. BRANCHPOINTS

The discussion thus far has skirted a major organizational challenge present in some analyses: branchpoints. Branchpoints occur when an analysis can proceed down one of two "roads," each with its own analysis and implications. Unlike the narrator in the Robert Frost poem about two roads diverging in a yellow wood,[1] a legal writer should proceed down the first road and loop back to proceed down the second. Otherwise, the analysis will not be complete.

Branchpoints commonly occur in the following situations: an ambiguous rule, so that you have to apply two or more possible versions of the law; an unknown rule, so that you have to consider two or more rules from persuasive authority; unknown or disputed facts, or facts that have yet to occur because the client has sought advice before acting, so that you have to apply the law to two or more alternative versions of the facts; facts that are known but fit awkwardly within the rule, so that your reasoning could lead to two or more results; and interlocking rules, such that the debatable outcome of the analysis of the pivotal rule dictates the analysis of the other rule(s). Exhibit 11.5 presents these situations in flowchart form.

Branchpoints are particularly likely to occur in transactional settings, when the events have not yet occurred. The client may seek advice about more than one option, or you may generate options as you analyze the client's situation. Sometimes, the different options will be governed by different rules; each option will appear in its own part of the discussion. Other times the different options will lead to different results under the same rule; there will be a branchpoint at the application point.

The organizational challenge is to make the branchpoint design clear to the reader. Generally the most straightforward approach is to provide an initial roadmap, complete one path of the analysis, indicate that the discussion is about to loop back to an earlier point where the analyses diverge, pursue the second path, and conclude with a summary. Carefully crafted roadmaps and transitions are very important.

For example, in the first HomeElderCare sample memo, at the end of the first part of the discussion, a branchpoint arises. If HomeElderCare is not engaging in unauthorized practice of law, it need not be concerned about the enforceability of the contract or the validity of the living wills based on the drafting activities of the social workers. If, however, HomeElderCare is en-

---

1. "Two roads diverged in a yellow wood,
   And sorry I could not travel both
   And be one traveler, long I stood
   And looked down one as far as I could
   To where it bent in the undergrowth
   Then took the other, just as fair, . . .
   Oh, I kept the first for another day!
   Yet knowing how way leads on to way,
   I doubted if I should ever come back."
   —Robert Frost, "The Road Not Taken,"
   in *The Complete Poems of Robert Frost* (1949).

EXHIBIT 11.5

TYPES OF BRANCHPOINTS

Issue → first interpretation of rule → application, conclusion #1
Issue → second interpretation of rule → application, conclusion #2

Issue → potential rule #1 → application, conclusion #1
Issue → potential rule #2 → application, conclusion #2

Issue → rule → fact A → application, conclusion A
Issue → rule → fact B → application, conclusion B

Issue → rule → application → conclusion A
Issue → rule → application → conclusion B

unauthorized practice of law → no → no need to assess validity of contract or will based on drafting process

unauthorized practice of law → yes → *Weatherston's* rule on contract enforceability + *Peterson* rule on will validity

gaging in unauthorized practice, the analysis should proceed to the next steps. The first sample memo begins the discussion with unauthorized practice, ends the unauthorized practice part with a paragraph describing the branchpoint, and makes a transition to the next two parts.

H. SKETCHING AND CHECKING YOUR ORGANIZATION

Once you have tentatively committed yourself to an organizational scheme, you should sketch it somehow, at some point well before you write the bulk of your paper. The classic means is an outline; the parts that form your large-scale structure would appear as Roman numeral items, the subparts as capital letters, and so on. See Exhibit 11.2. An alternative is to use a typeface outline, typing or writing the rules in boldface and all capitals, the elements in boldface but not capitalized, and so on. See Exhibit 11.3. A third alternative is a box chart in which the rules occupy large boxes, the elements middle-sized boxes, and so on. See Exhibit 11.4. All three of these depictions are somewhat linear, because the discussion component is inherently linear.

As you review your draft, ask yourself whether you can follow your organization without difficulty. Is anything omitted? Does any material appear more than once, without a compelling reason? Do you need to know about a later point to understand an earlier point? Have you adhered to your organizational scheme? Indeed, you may wish to sketch out the organization of your actual draft discussion and check it against your pre-writing sketch.

Furthermore, review how you have allocated your space to various topics. Your sketch should demonstrate how complex each rule and element is as applied to your facts, and your draft should allocate space so that the complex topics receive more space than the straightforward ones. Avoid overly long discussions of straightforward material and overly compact discussions of complex material. For your memo to be effective, it must be efficient, each sentence conveying its fair share of the information to be communicated.

I. OVERVIEWS AND TRANSITIONS

No matter how simple or complex your analysis, you should alert your reader to the discussion's structure. There are two devices for this purpose: overviews and transitions.

An overview briefly states the points in the order they appear in the text. It usually does not contain any citations or reasoning. It can occur at the large-, middle-, or small-scale level. You can provide an overview of the parts of the discussion, or of the subparts (that is, elements) within a part of the discussion, or indeed of the points made within a lengthy IRAC paragraph block. There are two types of overview: a roadmap, which appears at the outset of material it previews, and a summary, which reviews the material just presented.

A transition builds links between segments of the analysis, alerting the reader that one segment has finished and the next is starting. Some transitions link phrases or sentences; examples include "as well as," "because," "but," "furthermore," "thus." Other transitions link larger units of material; examples include "Under the second element . . . ," "If the court has jurisdiction, the rule applicable to the claim is . . . ." A transition can be a mere word, a phrase, a sentence, or even a paragraph, depending on the complexity of the material and the size of the units being linked. If you have laid out a clear roadmap, your reader may not need substantial transitions. In all events, take care to use words that truly convey the nexus between the units you are linking. Exhibit 11.6 lists transitional words and phrases, grouped by meaning.

EXHIBIT 11.6

LIST OF TRANSITIONS*

Introducing
first
initially
to begin, to begin with
the first reason
primarily
in general

Sequencing
first, second, third
finally
initially
next
then
last
before

Restating
that is
in other words
more simply
in brief
as noted

Exemplifying
for example
for instance
to illustrate
in particular
namely

Emphasizing
indeed
certainly
above all
especially
not only . . . but also

Contrasting
however
but
on the other hand
yet
unlike *x*
in contrast
nevertheless
nonetheless
rather
although
despite

Adding or Amplifying
again
furthermore
moreover
additionally
similarly
also
alternatively
a further reason

Connecting Logically
thereby
therefore
thus
as a result
hence
accordingly
consequently
since
because

Concluding
to conclude
in summary
to review
finally
as a result
as we have seen

*Adapted from Lynn B. Squires et al., *Legal Writing in a Nutshell* 95-98 (2d ed. 1996).

Graphics also serve as signals for the reader. For example, the indentation at the beginning of a paragraph tells the reader that a new idea is coming. Office memos also typically use headings, surrounded by white space, to demarcate portions of the memo. The most prominent headings announce the components of the office memo. Within the discussion, less prominent headings announce the major and minor topics. Topic headings typically are words or phrases, not full sentences. Generally, textual transitions can be brief or even nonexistent where a topic heading is present.

The sample HomeElderCare memo uses overviews, such as the introduction paragraph (roadmap) and the penultimate paragraph of the unauthorized practice discussion. The sample memo also uses transitions, including phrases ("first," "second," "on the other hand," "in conclusion"), sentences ("The remaining questions are the enforceability of the contract and the validity of the living will."), and headings.

J. ADDITIONAL CONSIDERATIONS

As you write your discussion, keep in mind the principles of communication presented in Chapter 10, part B, as well as the four criteria for sound legal writing:

- *Completeness:* Have you covered the material completely?
- *Correctness:* Have you stated both the law and the facts accurately?
- *Coherence:* Does each part connect clearly to the others? Does each conclusion on each topic fit with the others?
- *Comprehensibility:* Will your reader be able to understand your discussion in one careful reading?

Furthermore, think carefully about issues of breadth, depth, and slant. You should present the information the reader needs in order to understand and evaluate your analysis of the client's case. On the other hand, you should not write the legal equivalent of an encyclopedia, providing more background on the law than a reader really needs. Nor should you write an epitaph, a cursory statement of your bottom line without an explanation. Nor should you write an editorial, with the primary aim of persuading the reader of the wisdom of your personal point of view. Rather, you should write a balanced, analytical paper—an essay.

For example, the reader of the HomeElderCare memo would not need a statement of the law of contract formation in the HomeElderCare analysis. The reader would look for an assessment of why there is no concern about fraud, not simply a statement that there is none. Because the unauthorized practice issue in the HomeElderCare situation is a close call, the reader will want to know about both perspectives.

K. REVIEW OF CHAPTER 11

The success of the discussion of an office memo depends on a sound structure. The first step is to gather and group your thoughts. Then, as you develop your discussion, attend to the following structural concerns:

(1) large-scale organization, so that the rules you discuss appear in a logical order;
(2) middle-scale organization, so that the elements of each rule appear in a logical order;

    (3) small-scale organization, so that the discussion of each element or
         simple rule follows IRAC in some way;
    (4) clear presentation of branchpoints; and
    (5) use of overviews, transitions, and graphics to signal the organiza-
         tion to the reader.

Once the discussion is drafted, you are ready to capture its key points by
writing the opening and closing sections of the memo—the issues, short answers, and conclusion. Chapter 12 covers these three components.

THE OFFICE MEMO:
ISSUES,
SHORT ANSWERS,
AND CONCLUSION

> What is the answer?[no response] Then, what is the question?
> —Gertrude Stein's last words, quoted in
> Elizabeth Sprigge, *Gertrude Stein* (1957)

A. INTRODUCTION

Although the discussion constitutes the core of the office memo, it neither opens nor closes the memo. Rather, the memo opens with two closely linked sections—the issues and short answers—and it closes with the conclusion. This chapter discusses the roles and drafting of these three components.

This chapter uses as examples the issues, short answers, and conclusion of the first sample office memo on the HomeElderCare case at page 314. You may want to re-read those segments before continuing.

131

B. An Analogy: Parts of a House

In the analogy between a house and an office memo, the exterior walls of the house parallel the issues and short answers. The issues and short answers link the main legal and factual concepts covered in each part of the discussion. They let you see the memo at a glance, just as the exterior walls allow you to deduce the basics of a house's design.

Similarly, the conclusion is like the roof. The roof rests on the rest of the house and can be constructed only after the house is framed. So, too, the conclusion rests on the rest of the memo and can be written only after the rest of the memo is drafted. Just as a roof protects the house's occupants and contents, so too should the recommendations in the conclusion protect the client's interests.

C. Issues

1. The Function of the Issues

In most memo formats, the caption is followed immediately by the issues. Some formats call this component the "questions presented." Whichever label you prefer, its purpose is threefold. First, the issues orient the reader to the scope of the memo. Second, questions attract and focus the reader's attention. The issues in an office memo thus focus the reader's attention on the key legal topics and facts addressed in the discussion. Third, the issues show the reader how the memo is organized. Well written issues alert the reader to the number and order of major topics and to the relationships among them.

2. Drafting Issues

The basic formula for an issue is *law + facts in question form*. In most situations, the issue links a major legal concept to the most important relevant fact(s) of the client's case. To maximize your reader's understanding, you generally should present the legal concept at one end of the issue and the factual material at the other, rather than interweaving the two. You can lead with the law and proceed to the facts, or vice versa: *Is [law] when [facts]? Do [facts] result in [law]?*

On occasion, your issue will be almost purely legal or factual. For example, when the rules of law are very unsettled and your primary task is to determine what the rule is, with the application to your client's case following as a matter of course, your issue will read as a primarily legal issue. On the other hand, when your task is to develop and assess the facts under a straightforward rule, the issue will read as primarily factual.

Whichever situation applies, your goal is to state the topic(s) of the discussion clearly and in a question that is informative and fully readable the first time through. Chart a middle course between generality and specificity.

Present only the most important legal concepts and facts, not every detail. Refer to the concepts in a pertinent rule, rather than using general terms like "liability" or "illegality" or presenting citations to specific authorities. Refer to actors by using labels that identify their roles under the rule, rather than using general references to "person" or using proper names (except perhaps for the client, whose identity is known).

Furthermore, because the office memo should be objective, the issue should be phrased objectively. Avoid slanted language, which plays on the reader's emotions; rather, use language that a neutral observer, such as a court, would use. Present the most important facts and legal concepts, whether they are favorable or unfavorable to your client.

Many memos cover more than one rule, so the discussion consists of multiple parts. Generally, you should write an issue for each rule you cover in the discussion. The issues should signal the relationships among the rules through transitional phrases or cross-references; for example, where one rule follows from another, the next issue could begin with "if so" or "as a result."

In some situations, you may wish to write your issues so as to reflect subparts of your discussion as well. The classic approach is to present an introductory segment or question referring to the main topic, followed by specific questions referring to the subparts.

Most lawyers start a new, numbered paragraph with each new issue and use a lettered, tabbed, or bulleted list for subissues. Finally, although some writers introduce an issue with "whether," this construction is undesirable because the result is a sentence fragment, which is sometimes difficult for the reader to understand.

The first sample HomeElderCare memo contains three issues, because three rules are discussed in the memo. The issues are numbered and appear in the order in which the rules appear in the discussion. The first issue begins with the legal concept (practicing law illegally) and closes with the key facts (elderly clients, living will, set fee). It is phrased objectively and uses labels rather than proper names. Because the first issue provides the key facts, the second and third issues refer back to the first—"such a service"—and are quite concise as a result.

D. SHORT ANSWERS

1. The Function of the Short Answers

In most memo formats, the issues are followed by short answers, also labeled "brief answers" in some formats. They answer the questions posed in the issues, and they have three purposes. First, the short answers orient the reader to the scope of the memo. Second, they tell the reader the legal meaning you would ascribe to the client's case. Knowing the answers at the outset permits the reader to examine along the way how well the analysis supports the answers. Third, the short answers show the reader how the memo is organized.

2. Drafting Short Answers

The basic formula for a short answer is *law + facts + a reason in statement form*.

Many of the principles of issue-writing apply as well to the writing of short answers. There should be an answer for every issue. The short answer ordinarily should combine facts and law, read well the first time through, be neither too abstract nor too detailed, and be phrased objectively. You should use transitional phrases, cross-references, and formatting to convey the relationships among the answers. The answers should be numbered, lettered, bulleted, or tabbed.

Short answers are more extensive than issues because they include brief statements of your reasoning. Take care not to synopsize all steps of your reasoning, or the answer will no longer be short. Ordinarily, you will not include citations in your short answers. Rather, you should state, in simple and concise terms, the main reason for each answer.

A challenge in writing short answers is how to convey the (un)certainty inherent in your answer. In some situations, you will be certain how the law applies to your client's situation; in other situations, you will be quite unsure. In both situations, you should clearly state your best prediction about how the court would handle your client's situation, should litigation actually arise. At the same time, you may phrase your short answer to reflect any uncertainty you have about the conclusion, possibly by using a hedging phrase, such as "probably" or "most likely," or by noting that the situation presents a close call. Some lawyers include probabilities in their predictions; for example, in stating that "there is a seventy-five percent chance" that the court will rule a particular way, a lawyer is opining that three out of four courts faced with the case would rule a particular way, while the fourth would rule differently. (Your instincts for predicting legal outcomes will develop as you develop expertise in a particular area of law.)

The first sample HomeElderCare memo contains three short answers, paralleling the three issues and the order the issues are covered in the discussion. All three short answers provide clear responses to the issues. Each short answer includes a brief explanation: the first refers to legal documents and difficult or doubtful legal questions, and the second and third refer to statutory policy. The short answers are linked in subtle ways; "such a service" and "nonetheless" in the second answer refer back to the first. Each short answer reflects the writer's relative uncertainty or certainty ("most likely," "probably," "would").

E. CONCLUSION

1. The Function of the Conclusion

At the end of the memo comes the conclusion. In some formats, this component is labeled "summary" or "recommendations." The conclusion has two purposes. First, the conclusion provides closure and should prompt the reader to make a final judgment about whether he or she accepts the answers arrived at by the writer. Second, the conclusion presents the writer's recommendations as to how the case should be handled. Here the memo shifts from predicting how the legal system will respond to the client's case to recommending actions that will lead to the best possible legal results for the client.

2. Giving Legal Advice

As you turn to the conclusion, keep in mind the following statement about legal advice, from the Model Rules of Professional Conduct:

> In representing a client, a lawyer shall exercise independent professional judgment and render candid advice. In rendering advice, a lawyer may refer not only to law but to other considerations as well, such as moral, economic, social and political factors, that may be relevant to the client's situation.
>
> Model Rules of Professional Conduct Rule 2.1 (1983).

Legal advice is to be "candid" and based on "independent professional judgment." The lawyer's job is to inform the client about how the law governs the client's case, not only when the law favors the client's plans, but especially when the law constrains the client. Lawyers must know how to say "no" effectively. Of course, the lawyer should also provide the client with alternatives that avoid or minimize the legal problems.

Although legal advice is grounded in the law, it also may incorporate nonlegal factors. Many cases call for consideration of other disciplines, such as economics, management, or psychology. It often is both practical and valuable for a lawyer to give advice mixing law and nonlegal factors, especially when the lawyer has training in another relevant discipline and when the client has come to value the lawyer's counsel over time. The comments to the Model Rule also state that a lawyer should recommend that a client consult a professional in a different discipline if the case calls for that expertise.

Good legal advice typically entails creative and expansive thinking similar to that used in other forms of problem-solving. Although you should start with the client's plan, you should then generate alternatives that have the potential of serving the client's interests. Once you have generated a list of possibilities, you should assess each and select those that best serve the interests of the client and conform to the law.

A useful way of sketching the options available to a client is a decision tree. A decision tree charts the client's options, linking each to the most likely legal outcome and nonlegal outcomes. The decision tree in Exhibit 12.1 depicts the reasoning behind the conclusion in the first HomeElderCare sample memo.

3. Drafting the Conclusion

Unlike the issues and short answers, the conclusion is written in conventional paragraph form. The conclusion should begin with a restatement of the answers to the issues, although in briefer form than in the short answers. Unless

EXHIBIT 12.1

DECISION TREE

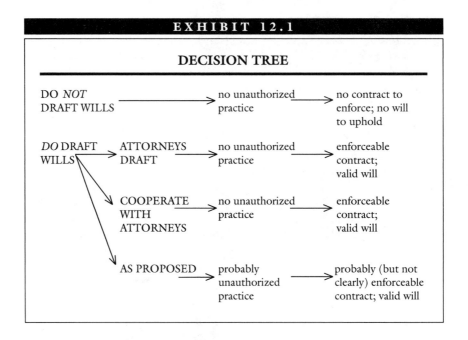

the memo is quite long, you need not restate the reasoning, and it is rare to refer to legal authorities.

The bulk of the conclusion should be devoted to a discussion of the client's options including the plan(s) identified by the client itself. If the case involves litigation, the advice will be framed as litigation strategy and may cover such options as settling, employing alternative forms of dispute resolution (such as mediation or arbitration), bringing a pre-trial motion, going to trial, or appealing. If the situation involves a pending transaction, the advice will address whether to go forward at all and, if so, how to structure the transaction. In both the litigation and transaction contexts, the probable legal outcome of each option should be noted. As noted in Chapter 11, when more than one option is under serious consideration, these options may be analyzed in the discussion component.

In the conclusion in the first HomeElderCare sample memo, the first sentence states answers to all three legal issues, and the next sentence presents the writer's assessment of whether the client should proceed as planned. The following two paragraphs present other options, along with their practical and legal implications.

F. OVERARCHING CONSIDERATIONS

You should, of course, review all three components discussed in this chapter to verify that they fit the four criteria:

- *Completeness:* Does your work incorporate the important main legal and factual concepts? Are the main topics in the discussion alluded to?
- *Correctness:* Have you referred to both facts and law accurately?
- *Coherence:* Do the components track each other, so that the same topics appear in all three? Do the short answers and the issues align with each other, and do the recommendations flow from the answers?
- *Comprehensibility:* Will your reader be able to follow your prose in one careful reading?

Finally, in assessing your advice to your client, consider whether you have approached your client's situation with creativity.

G. REVIEW OF CHAPTER 12

The issues, short answers, and conclusion share important attributes: All three orient the reader, by focusing his or her attention and by paralleling the organization of the discussion. All three advance the reader's understanding—the issue by posing a question, the short answer by answering the question, and the conclusion by tracing out the implications of that answer. More specifically:

The issues should

- combine law and facts in question form,
- be neither too abstract nor too detailed,
- be phrased objectively, and
- reflect the organization of the discussion.

The short answers should

- combine law, facts, and a brief reason in statement form;
- be neither too abstract nor too detailed;
- be phrased objectively;
- reflect the organization of the discussion; and
- convey your degree of (un)certainty about the answer.

The conclusion should

- briefly restate your answers to the issues,
- provide candid and creative advice,

- incorporate nonlegal principles as needed, and
- present and assess your client's options.

Issues, short answers, and a conclusion fulfilling these criteria will serve the needs of your reader well.

THE OFFICE MEMO:

THE FACTS

> Fact and fancy look alike across the years that link the past with
> the present.
> —Helen Keller
> *The Story of My Life* (1903)

A. INTRODUCTION

Between the short answers and discussion in the office memo comes the fact statement. The fact statement is precisely what the name suggests: a recounting of the important facts of the client's case. This chapter first discusses the functions of this component and then presents strategies for assembling and presenting the facts. The fact statement from the first sample memo on the HomeElderCare case at page 314 serves as an example.

B. FUNCTIONS OF THE FACT STATEMENT

The fact statement tells the client's story to the reader. If the reader is unfamiliar with the client's situation, the reader learns of it through the facts. If the reader is familiar with the client's situation, but has learned it in bits and pieces through interviews and review of documents and items, the facts help the reader to see the important facts, assembled and presented in a coherent narrative. The fact statement does not simply duplicate the coverage of the facts in the discussion, where facts are interspersed among legal rules and elements. To serve a client with understanding, a lawyer must see the client's situation as a cohesive story, not merely as bits of factual material tied to legal rules.

For the writer of the memo, writing the fact statement presents an opportunity to revisit the facts and think through them carefully. It is easy to lose track of the facts as you research the law, read it, and reason about the client's case. Committing the facts to paper in a carefully organized narrative forces you to concentrate on them. Indeed, you may grasp the import of a particular fact for the first time when you write out the fact statement.

In addition, the fact statement serves as a useful record of the facts as of the date the memo is written. In many situations, you will learn facts gradually, over days, weeks, months, or even years. You must take stock periodically to determine which facts are fully known, which facts are not known, and which are disputed; this information can be noted in the fact statement. The legal analysis in the memo is then tied to this specific set of facts. When new facts come to light, you will see whether you need to revise portions of the analysis.

C. AN ANALOGY: FOUNDATION OF A HOUSE

In the analogy of an office memo to a house, the facts form the foundation on which the office memo is built. Just as a house's foundation sets the shape for the house, so the facts set the topics for the office memo. If the factual foundation is weak, the analysis in the discussion also will be weak.

D. ASSEMBLING THE FACTS

Assembling the facts from the bits of factual information you have gathered entails two steps: weaving together information from various sources and then sorting out the facts to be included.

1. Weaving Facts Together

Facts rarely come in a single tidy statement. Rather, you gather facts by talking to your client and other participants, reading documents, visiting the location of the events, handling the items, and so on. Then you must weave together these bits of information.

EXHIBIT 13.1

FACTUAL MATRIX

	PARTICIPANT X	PARTICIPANT Y	DOCUMENT A	VISIT TO SITE
description of location				
background of X-Y relationship				
1st event				
2nd event				
etc.				

Of course, the first step is to read (or otherwise process) each source carefully, so that you have a very good idea of the information it provides. As you work through the sources one by one, you should start a list of topics and, as needed, subtopics. These topics may be events, relationships, locations, options, or other matters. Then you can array these topics along the left side of a matrix, as in Exhibit 13.1 above, and array the sources you have along the top. Next, fill in the boxes by extracting and synopsizing pertinent information from each source. A slightly different technique is to write all of the information about each topic on its own page, along with shorthand references to the sources of the information.

Another classic way to organize factual information is the timeline, as shown in Exhibit 13.2 below. The line itself contains relevant dates. The material above and below the line consists of date-specific information. You can use the timeline as a dividing line, by writing information from one source above the line and information from another below the line, or by writing information about one of two simultaneous events above the line and information about the other below the line.

EXHIBIT 13.2

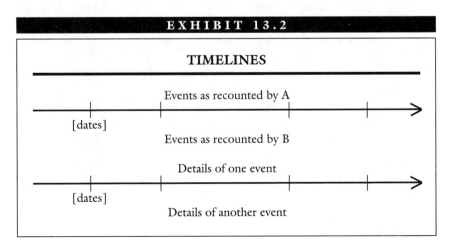

TIMELINES

Events as recounted by A

[dates]

Events as recounted by B

Details of one event

[dates]

Details of another event

You may well discover some discrepancies, as well as considerable overlap, in the information from various sources. Experienced lawyers expect this discrepancy. Participants or observers of an event often differ in their recollections of what they have experienced or perceived. The differing recollections are due to varying abilities to perceive, understand, and recall situations, as well as varying perspectives and interests.

Your task is to reconcile these discrepancies. If the discrepancy is minor, you may be able to cover both versions with a somewhat broadly phrased fact, such as a numerical range rather than a precise number. Another approach is to discern any core area of agreement and leave the details in dispute, as long as the details are not critical. If one source has greater credibility, a clearer perspective, or less self-interest than the other, you could choose the version provided by that source and state the reason for your selection. If these methods fail, you may need to state both versions and their sources—in which case the discussion may diverge into a branchpoint and proceed along two paths.

2. Sorting Facts

Once you have synthesized the information from your various sources, you need to choose which facts to include in the fact statement. Facts fall into three categories: legally relevant facts, background facts, and residual facts. You should include the first and second, but not the third.

Legally relevant facts pertain directly to the elements in the legal rules; they are used in your deductive reasoning, reasoning by example, or policy analysis. As a court or legislature makes law, it sets the factual focus of the rule of law. The rule may not focus on every fact you would deem important, but you are bound by the court's or legislature's selection of which facts to focus on (although you may argue for a new or revised legal rule in a compelling case). To identify legally relevant facts, read your discussion. All facts appearing in your discussion should appear in the fact statement.

Background facts are facts that the reader needs to know to make sense of the client's situation, even though they do not pertain directly to the elements of the rule. To identify the background facts, ask yourself: What does the reader need to know to link the relevant facts in a coherent narrative? Focus on what the reader needs to know, not on what might be interesting to know.

Residual facts are neither legally relevant nor background. Some residual facts are emotionally charged, causing one to feel sympathy or distaste for your client or another participant. You should exclude these facts, because they clutter the narrative and distract the reader's attention. In particular, you should not include emotionally charged residual facts, which may cloud the reader's ability to assess the client's situation objectively.

Of course, you will be quite aware that some facts are favorable to your client and others are unfavorable. This distinction is not an appropriate basis on which to include or exclude facts. Both favorable and unfavorable facts belong in the fact statement, just as they do in the discussion, if they are legally relevant or needed for background.

As an example, the fact statement in the first sample memo covers the current business of HomeElderCare and what it has done so far on the living will project, as well as the process the social workers would follow. Most of the facts are legally relevant, prime examples of which are the proposed activities set out in the final paragraph. There are some background facts, such as the elderly client's requests for the service. No residual facts are stated. Both favorable and unfavorable facts are stated.

3. Timing

You probably will find that you must work with your facts several times. In particular, you may weave your facts together early on, before you write your analysis or conduct your research. You may even write an outline or tentative statement at that early stage, if you need to orient yourself. However, you should not sort your facts until you have analyzed the case in light of the law, because only at that point will you appreciate the legal significance of the various facts.

E. PRESENTING THE FACTS

1. Format

The relevant and background facts should appear in your fact statement in a sequence that makes for a coherent story. The classic organization entails an introductory paragraph, several paragraphs or pages of development, and a wrap-up or transition paragraph as needed.

The introductory paragraph (or paragraph block) sets the stage and orients the reader. It should identify the client and other important people or organizations, describe the client's goals or the basic nature of the dispute, and give the location and time of the events.

The body of the fact statement should present the events that constitute the client's situation. The most common organizational scheme is chronological. A fact statement organized by chronology begins with the first important event and moves forward in time to the most recent. Chronology typically works best where a dispute has already occurred. The next most common is topical organization, in which each paragraph or paragraph block covers a facet of the situation, such as relationships among people or features of transactions. Topical organization typically works well when you are advising a client about its future plans. Least common is perceptual organization, in which the events are presented first from one person's perspective, then from another's. It is used when key people, due to their different vantage points, know different parts of the story. On occasion, a mixed organization may work well; for example, several topical paragraphs may be used to set the scene for a series of chronologically organized paragraphs.

The last paragraph typically draws a link between the facts and the upcoming discussion of their legal implications. If there is an existing dispute, the last paragraph may summarize the current procedural posture of the litigation. If the client has sought advice about a transaction, the last paragraph may note the client's legal and nonlegal concerns. This wrap-up paragraph may not be necessary if the fact statement is brief.

In the first HomeElderCare sample memo, the first paragraph introduces the facts by identifying the client and its situation. The overall organization is topical: HomeElderCare's business, living wills, staff competence and training, and the proposal. The paragraph detailing the proposal follows a chronological organization. A statement of the client's legal concerns concludes the fact statement.

2. Perspective and Flow

Your fact statement is unlikely to have the flair or drama of a prizewinning short story. A short story writer can use tools that are inappropriate to memo writing, such as first-person point of view, shifts in time, symbolism, and ambiguity.

Nonetheless, your fact statement need not be clinical or wooden. Keep in mind that you are telling a story. As the "narrator," you have the advantage of an omniscient third-person point of view; you know whatever there is to be known for purposes of writing the memo and can recount the story fully. To help your reader fully understand the situation, show how one event led to another, why a participant selected the course of conduct he or she engaged in, and how an event affected a participant. In other words, link the events to each other and the participants to each other.

In the sample HomeElderCare memo, the writer has drawn these links. For example, the statement indicates why the clients are interested in living wills (third paragraph), how that interest has prompted HomeElderCare to seek to respond (fourth paragraph), what HomeElderCare believes about the benefits of the service (also fourth paragraph), and why HomeElderCare's executive director nonetheless is concerned (final paragraph).

3. Wording

An important dimension of your facts is verb tense. In many situations, you will advise a client about how to resolve an existing dispute. The facts will have occurred by the time you write the memo, so the fact statement will be written mostly in past tenses. In other situations, you will advise a client about a course of future behavior. You will know few facts in the traditional sense of the term, but you will know what the client plans to do, if permitted by law. Furthermore, there may be several scenarios to describe, if the client has requested consideration of several options. This type of fact statement is a contingent account of future events, written in subjunctive mood ("client would . . .") or future tenses ("client will . . .").

Throughout the fact statement, you should follow several principles developed in the preceding chapters on office memos. First and most obviously, you must recount your facts accurately. Furthermore, you must state the facts objectively. For example, use quantitative measures, rather than adjectives such as "large" and "small." Use nouns and verbs with straightforward meanings. Minimize the use of adjectives and adverbs. Refer to people respectfully; use neutral labels or proper names. Do not use words that imply legal conclusions, such as "negligently."

Second, provide an indication of where you derived your facts. Although you need not provide formal citations, your phrasing should inform the reader whose statement or which document yielded your information, for instance, "according to Ms. Smith," or "as indicated in the contract."

Third, the facts should be readable. Strike a balance between detail and abstraction. Decide how much detail the reader needs on each topic, and condense the facts to provide only needed detail. Consider attaching material that would otherwise require a lengthy explanation, such as a contract or map.

Finally, check your work against the four criteria for effective legal writing:

- *Completeness:* Have you included the favorable and unfavorable relevant and background facts your reader needs?
- *Correctness:* Are the facts stated true, according to your sources?
- *Coherence:* Does your narrative present a story that could occur as you have stated it? Are the events, people, places, and times properly aligned?
- *Comprehensibility:* Will your reader follow the story in one careful reading?

In the first HomeElderCare sample memo, the present tense is used to describe HomeElderCare's present operations, and the subjunctive mood is used to describe its proposal. The facts are stated objectively, with neutral labels ("clients," "social workers") and few adjectives and adverbs. The reader can tell where the facts came from (the document, the social work director). The statement is readable. The writer might have attached the form, if the reader would be unfamiliar with it.

F. REVIEW OF CHAPTER 13

The fact statement informs the reader of the client's story and stands as a record, for the reader and writer, of the facts known at the time the memo was written. To assure that you fully understand the facts, you must first weave the information from various sources together, reconciling any discrepancies, and then sort out the relevant and background facts from residual facts. A well presented fact statement

- includes relevant and background facts, whether favorable or unfavorable to the client;
- begins with an introductory paragraph or paragraph block;

- follows a chronological, topical, or perceptual organization (or combination);
- closes with a wrap-up paragraph, as needed; and
- states the facts accurately, objectively, with attribution, and at an appropriate level of detail.

This chapter is the last of four chapters on the office memo, the basic form of advisory writing. You may want to review the appendices on sentence structure and word usage, editing, and citation, because all three skills are critical to writing a polished office memo.

14

ADVISORY WRITING: THE FUNCTION AND FORMAT OF THE ADVICE LETTER

> Letters are expectation packed in an envelope.
> — Shana Alexander
> "The Surprises of the Mail," *Life* (1967)

A. INTRODUCTION

As important as the office memo is, it rarely serves as the final expression of the lawyer's analysis. The lawyer still must take the next critical step: sharing the lawyer's analysis and conclusions with the client. This step almost always involves a conversation and generally also involves a written document — the advice letter. It is through the advice letter that the client is informed of the legal meaning of the situation.

The advice letter is only one of many types of letters lawyers write. They write other letters to clients to ask for information, inform the client of new developments, enclose documents related to the case, seek payment, and so forth. Lawyers also write letters on behalf of clients to other people, demanding payment or other relief from opposing parties, seeking records or information from third parties, making arrangements with opposing counsel, enclosing briefs sent to courts, and similar matters. Some lawyers specialize in writing formal "opinion letters." An opinion letter discusses the client's compliance with a particular rule and is used to induce others to transact business with the client.

This chapter focuses on advice letters because of their importance. Moreover, the formal opinion letter aside, the advice letter is the most challenging type of letter to write. If you can master the advice letter, other types of client letters should come relatively easily.

This chapter first presents ethics rules on advisory work, then discusses considerations of audience and purpose, suggests a conventional set of components, and explores such considerations as tone and caveats. A sample letter to HomeElderCare, drawing on the analysis in the first sample office memo, appears at page 327. You should read it before proceeding.

B. THE ADVISOR'S ETHICS

Model Rule of Professional Conduct 1.2 states: "A lawyer shall abide by a client's decisions concerning the objectives of representation [subject to certain limitations] and shall consult with the client as to the means by which they are to be pursued." The client's case is just that—the *client's* dispute or transaction. So, the client sets the objectives of the representation, subject to legal constraints and the lawyer's professional obligations. As to the means for obtaining the client's objectives, the lawyer is responsible for "technical and legal tactical issues" while the client controls such matters as "the expense to be incurred and concern for third persons who might be adversely affected," according to the comment to Rule 1.2. In practice, the lawyer and the client jointly delineate their respective roles, reflecting the client's desire for control or involvement, the degree of trust between client and lawyer, the lawyer's experience with the type of situation at hand, and similar factors.

Rule 2.1 makes two important points. First, "[i]n representing a client, a lawyer shall exercise independent professional judgment and render candid advice." The lawyer serves the client not by telling the client what the client wants to hear, but by telling the client what the law permits or prohibits. The lawyer thereby serves the legal system and the client's interest in conforming its conduct to the law. Second, "[i]n rendering advice, a lawyer may refer not only to law but to other considerations such as moral, economic, social and political factors, that may be relevant to the client's situation." Situations raising legal issues typically have moral, economic, social, or political dimensions as well. Although these dimensions may be primarily within the client's realm, the lawyer's objective observations may help the client assess these factors.

Compare these rules to the standard conception of the lawyer as "hired gun"—an agent who acts at the client's direction, without regard to the impact the client's actions may have on others. The hired-gun conception places high value on the autonomy of the client. Other conceptions of the lawyer-client relationship also exist. Thomas Shaffer and Robert Cochran posit three alternative images:[1] The "godfather" lawyer, focusing on client victory, makes choices, with fairly little client involvement, so as to produce victory for the client. The "guru" lawyer, focusing on client rectitude, makes choices, with fairly little client involvement, so as to prompt the client to do what the lawyer sees as the right thing. The "friend" lawyer, focusing on client goodness, engages the client in a discussion of what is good for the client and others affected by the case. In reality, lawyers often use a blend of these conceptions, switching back and forth, depending on the client and the situation. As you learn more about lawyering, you may want to consider which models are true to practice and professional principles.

Finally, Model Rule 1.4 reads:

> (a) A lawyer shall keep a client reasonably informed about the status of a matter and promptly comply with reasonable requests for information.
> (b) A lawyer shall explain a matter to the extent reasonably necessary to permit the client to make informed decisions regarding the representation.

This rule not only requires the lawyer to respond to the client's request for information, but also to initiate communication when needed to keep the client fully informed. In addition, the rule sets a standard for the content of that communication: what is "reasonably necessary to permit the client to make informed decisions."

C. THE FUNCTION OF THE ADVICE LETTER: AUDIENCE AND PURPOSE

If the client is an individual, the primary reader of the advice letter is, of course, the client. If the client is a legal entity, such as a corporation or government agency, the primary reader is the person empowered to act for the client in the case.

Every reader has his or her own preferences, which the lawyer must take into account. Some readers prefer considerable detail about legal authorities; for others, summary information suffices. Some readers prefer extensive discussion of the nonlegal dimensions of the case; others view such analysis as overstepping by the lawyer. Some readers prefer a no-nonsense approach; others prefer a more empathetic style. And so on. These preferences reflect the reader's personal attributes and the client's situation. For example, a reader with legal training may prefer a detailed legal analysis. A reader who has suffered personal injury or lost a loved one typically looks for empathy as well as legal analysis.

---

1. Thomas L. Shaffer & Robert F. Cochran, Jr., *Lawyer, Clients, and Moral Responsibilities* (1994).

Thus, an important first step in writing an advice letter is analyzing the situation and thinking about the client. Take care not to act on stereotypes. For instance, the elderly widow with little formal education and no paid work experience may be a savvy reader due to her volunteer work or civic activities. Learn what you can about your reader's preferences by getting to know the reader before writing the letter.

Some advice letters will be read by more than one reader. For example, a letter advising a corporation may be read by its president, in-house counsel, board members, and key managers. Sometimes it is possible for a single letter to address both primary and secondary readers. In other instances, you may need to write to the primary reader and cover the different needs of the secondary reader another way, for example, by providing a more detailed memo for a more sophisticated secondary reader.

Regardless of the reader or readers, the advice letter has two main purposes: (1) to inform the reader of the lawyer's legal analysis of the client's case, that is, to convey to the reader the legal meaning of the client's situation, and (2) to persuade the client to take action that has sound legal support, whether relating to an existing dispute or an upcoming transaction. Subsidiary purposes include establishing rapport with the client, verifying the facts and tasks the client has presented to the lawyer, and obtaining direction from the client. From time to time, these purposes may conflict. For example, it may be difficult to establish rapport with a client who strongly desires to engage in behavior that is illegal or legally risky. When a conflict among purposes arises, be sure to serve the main purposes of informing the client and persuading the client to take legally sound actions.

D. THE FORMAT OF THE ADVICE LETTER

The format of the advice letter is similar in several ways to that of the office memo. First, its format is governed not by rule, but by convention. Second, it differs from law office to law office and across client situations. Third, as Exhibit 14.1 shows, the conventional components parallel those of the office memo. In a long or formal letter, headings may be used to set off some of these components; in short or less formal letters, transitional phrases or sentences are used instead.

Heading: As with any business letter, the heading includes the sender's letterhead; the date of the letter; the name, position, and address of the reader (or readers); and the salutation. The heading also may include a one-line reference to the topic of the letter; this feature makes the letter more formal and is most common when the letter is sent to an organization or individual that has frequent contact with lawyers.

Introduction: One purpose of the introduction is to provide an overview of the main points made in the letter. The introduction has an additional purpose: to establish rapport with the reader.

The first sentence or two typically refers to the previous contact between the lawyer and the client and to the occasion for the request for legal advice.

EXHIBIT 14.1

COMPARISON OF ADVICE LETTER
AND OFFICE MEMO

Advice Letter	Office Memo
heading ■ letterhead ■ date ■ addressee ■ topic reference ■ salutation	caption ■ to _____ ■ from _____ ■ date ■ topic
introduction	issues short answers
summary of facts	facts
explanation	discussion
advice and closing	conclusion

You should personalize this opening; do not use a canned sentence such as "This letter is in response to yours of October 14th."

The next part of the introduction is the overview of the legal points covered in the letter. Often, the reader will have asked an open-ended bottom-line question; the overview helps the reader to see how the law frames the client's concern. You can state the conclusions you have come to, the issues you have addressed, or both. In part, your choice should reflect how formal you want the letter to be; the options are listed from least to most formal. In part, your choice should reflect how ready the reader will be for your conclusions at the outset of the letter. Generally, stating your conclusions at the outset will benefit the reader; however, if the conclusions are complex or significantly adverse, you may wish to present an overview of the issues instead.

The overview is not stated as completely or technically as the issues or short answers in an office memo. See Exhibit 14.2. Nonetheless, be sure to state the overview with great care. It should be precise enough that the scope of the advice is apparent to the reader. In addition, any conclusions you state in the overview should convey how certain you are.

Some lawyers include a third part in the introduction: a brief paragraph about ground rules of a legal advice letter. Many lawyers alert the client to the need to keep the letter confidential. You may want to note that the letter states the facts of the client's case, identify the source of the facts, and ask the client to verify those facts. You also might note that the conclusions are based on the facts currently known or assumed as well as on current law, and that the conclusions could change with changes in the facts or law. If you have any reason for concern that you have not addressed all of your client's issues, you could urge the client to contact you if there seem to be omissions. Alternatively, you could state these points in the summary of the facts or in the ex-

EXHIBIT 14.2

SHORT ANSWERS VERSUS INTRODUCTION

Short Answers

1. Social workers most likely practice law illegally when they pre-pare living wills and advise clients about them, because they thereby draft legal documents and answer difficult or doubtful legal questions.

2. A contract to provide such a service for a fee probably would be enforceable nonetheless, for public policy reasons.

3. The living will would be valid, based on the intent of the legis-lature in enacting the Minnesota Living Will Act and the unauthorized practice of law statute.

Introduction

. . . as this letter explains, there could be some legal risks. One concern is avoiding the illegal practice of law, which could lead to prosecution for a misdemeanor or a court order prohibiting the ser-vice. On the other hand, HEC probably would be able to enforce the contracts with its clients. Furthermore, the living wills would be valid.

planation, or you could omit these points if it is likely the reader is well aware of them.

The introduction in the sample advice letter takes this tripartite ap-proach. The first paragraph seeks to establish rapport with Ms. Mahoney, the second provides an overview of the three topics, and the third alerts Ms. Ma-honey to the limitations of the letter. Because theirs is not a longstanding re-lationship, the writer chose to state the ground rules of an advice letter.

Summary of facts: As with the fact statement in the office memo, the summary of facts tells the reader the facts of the client's case. You may wonder why this is necessary, if the reader is the client or represents the client. The summary of facts serves five critical purposes: to show the reader you have heard the story; to permit the reader to verify your account; to help the reader see the facts from an objective point of view; to identify for the reader which facts are important from the law's perspective; and, where ap-plicable, to show the reader how information from various sources comes to-gether.

You should include facts that are legally relevant facts or important back-ground facts, whether favorable or unfavorable to the client's case. You also may wish to include other residual facts that are very significant to the client; do so sparingly, so as not to blur your focus on what is legally relevant. The source(s) of the facts should be noted informally; proper citation is not nec-essary. The organization should be clear and logical; chronological and topi-cal approaches typically work well. On the rare occasion when you know the differing perspectives of two or more people regarding the situation, you may employ perceptual organization.

Some lawyers also include caveats about the facts. In addition to the points mentioned above under "introduction," you may wish to note that you have not yourself investigated the facts, especially if you have doubts about them or believe your client may assume that you have investigated them yourself.

In the sample HomeElderCare summary of facts, virtually all facts are either legally relevant facts or important background facts. The only arguable exception is that HomeElderCare is responding to requests from its clients; this fact merits inclusion because the executive director probably considers it significant. The summary notes that the source of the facts is the conversation with the client. The overall organization is topical, with a chronological scheme in the fifth paragraph.

Explanation: The explanation presents your objective legal analysis of the client's situation. It should proceed in a logical way through the issues, presenting the legal rules and linking them to the relevant facts. It should explore both sides of issues as to which there is a reasonable debate. The organization should be made clear through transitions, especially if there are branchpoints in the analysis.

The explanation differs from the discussion in an office memo primarily in how it presents the law. See Exhibit 14.3, which shows portions of each. The explanation focuses not on the origins of the law, but on its concepts. Those concepts typically are stated in concrete terms paralleling the client's

---

EXHIBIT 14.3

DISCUSSION VERSUS EXPLANATION

Discussion

First, HEC social workers would prepare "legal documents" for a fee by preparing living wills for their clients. Although the unauthorized practice of law statute does not define "legal document," the Minnesota Living Will Act provides a suggested form for living wills that plainly states that the form is a legal document. Minn. Stat. § 145B.04 (1992). This interpretation accords with the dictionary definitions of "legal" and "document": "an original or official paper relied on as the basis, proof, or support" of matters that are "established by law; statutory; conforming to or permitted by law or established rules." *Webster's New Collegiate Dictionary* 333, 651 (1981). HEC would draft these legal documents for clients and charge a fee for this service, thereby violating the statute.

Explanation

The first ground is that preparing legal documents for someone else for a fee constitutes practicing law. The official form itself indicates that the living will is a "legal document."

case. Indeed, where the legal concept is fairly straightforward and its link to the facts is obvious, you may merge the law and pertinent facts into a single statement. On the other hand, if similar situations may arise in the future for the same client or if the law is complex, it may make sense to state the law in abstract terms before linking it to the facts. Unless the reader is a lawyer or otherwise sophisticated in the law, the explanation does not include citations.

The explanation in the sample HomeElderCare letter proceeds logically through the three issues. It raises the unauthorized practice issue first, because it plays a part in the analysis of the other two issues and has the most serious consequences for HomeElderCare. The law is stated precisely, yet simply and concisely, without citations (although with an occasional reference to the courts or the statute). The legal rules on unauthorized practice are stated in abstract terms ("Minnesota law prohibits persons who are not licensed lawyers from practicing law."). This client should know the rules outside the living will context. The remaining rules are stated in the context of this particular situation ("The risk of incompetent service would be fairly minor . . ."). The uncertainty in the unauthorized practice analysis is revealed in a paragraph of counterarguments, while the analysis of the validity of the living wills is presented as much more certain. Because the analysis is fairly involved, the letter features various transitional devices.

Advice: The purpose of the advice component is to link the legal analysis presented in the letter to concrete actions to be taken by or on behalf of the client. The advice component typically has two, sometimes intertwined, parts: a summary of the legal analysis and a discussion of the client's options.

The summary helps the reader recall the conclusions you have drawn. It may not be necessary to include one if the explanation is fairly brief and you have stated your conclusions clearly in the explanation. Another approach is to reiterate your conclusions as they arise in your discussion of the client's options. In either event, your statement of your conclusions in the summary should parallel the order of topics in the introduction and in the explanation, and you should convey whatever uncertainty you may have.

Most clients have more than one option. The client may have suggested one or more options; you may have thought of others. You should present the relative legal advantages and disadvantages of each option, noting how certain each assessment is. As suggested above, if you know the client has nonlegal concerns, you may bring these into the discussion as well.

Whether to advance a particular option as the best option is a matter of considerable judgment. In part, the law may decide for you—that is, there may be only one good option from a legal perspective. Where various options are legally sound, in deciding whether to indicate your preference, you should think about your relationship with the client: For instance, do you know all of the facts regarding the client's financial situation? Do you know for sure how the client weighs various nonlegal factors? Do you have an established relationship of trust with the client? If you do indicate your preference, you should take care to convey that the choice is ultimately the client's.

The advice conveyed in the HomeElderCare sample letter has two prongs. First, the letter clearly, but gracefully, tells the client not to pursue the proposal it brought to the lawyer. Second, the letter suggests several options with fewer legal risks. Because the lawyer does not know the client well and has not discussed these options with the client, the letter leaves the non-legal issues as well as the ultimate choice to the client.

Closing: The closing is not simply the end of the letter, but rather the basis for the continuation of the representation. It has three parts: an indication of what you plan to do next, instructions as to what the client should do next, and the signature block. Your next step should be to follow up with some communication so you are sure that the client fully understands the letter. After that, the client may contact you to implement the client's choice of action, such as sending a demand letter to the opponent in a dispute, proceeding with a transaction, or doing nothing further.

The closing in the sample HomeElderCare letter simply refers to a follow-up phone conversation, initiated by the lawyer or the client.

E. ADDITIONAL CONSIDERATIONS

The artistry of an advice letter comes in its tone. Its tone conveys much about the lawyer as a person and directly influences the relationship between the lawyer and the client. The letter should convey that the lawyer is professional, focused, thorough, analytical, objective, careful, involved, creative, cooperative, and reasonable. Other impressions may be more or less appropriate in particular settings: assertive and efficient, for example, or sympathetic and supportive, as another example.

These impressions are created through subtle stylistic variations. Consider, for example, how to use personal pronouns. A certain intimacy results when the letter uses the first person ("I recommend . . ."), perhaps even drawing the client into the first person plural ("We could contact their lawyer . . ."). Distance results when an organizational client is referred to by name ("HomeElderCare could take the following actions . . ."), rather than second person pronoun ("You could take the following actions . . .").

As a second example, consider the use of active versus passive voice. The active voice has a harder edge to it than the passive voice, especially when used to refer to the actions of the client. Active voice may be appropriate if the lawyer wishes to appear emphatic or businesslike, whereas passive voice may be appropriate if the lawyer wishes to appear compassionate and empathetic.

As always, be sure that the letter fulfills the following four criteria:

- *Completeness:* Does the letter address all topics brought to you by the client? Have you covered the pertinent legal rules and relevant facts?
- *Correctness:* Have you stated the client's facts with scrupulous accuracy? Do your statements of the law fairly reflect the concepts pertinent to the client's case?
- *Coherence:* Do the various components mesh well? Do the conclusions make sense in light of the rules and facts? Do they fit with each other?

■ *Comprehensibility:* Will your reader probably be able to understand the letter in one careful reading? Is the letter written to fit the reader's attributes and situation?

F. REVIEW OF CHAPTER 14

The advice letter is a critical document because it communicates your legal advice to your client and forms a basis for the client's future actions. To write it successfully, you should follow these steps:

(1) Respect the relative roles of yourself and your client.
(2) Carefully consider how best to communicate with the probable reader(s) of the letter.
(3) Present the information in the following components: heading, introduction, summary of facts, explanation, advice, and closing.
(4) Bring creativity to your advice; develop various options for the client and assess their wisdom in light of current legal and nonlegal factors.
(5) Meet the criteria of completeness, correctness, coherence, comprehensibility, and creativity.

Following these steps should enable you to meet your professional obligation to communicate with your client so that the client can make well informed decisions about its case.

15

ADVOCACY WRITING IN THE PRE-TRIAL AND TRIAL SETTING: THE FUNCTION AND FORMAT OF THE MOTION PRACTICE MEMORANDUM

> Of every hundred cases, ninety win themselves, three are won by advocacy, and seven are lost by advocacy.
> —A. Fountain
> *Wit of Wig*, 1980

A. INTRODUCTION

Legal advocacy, the topic of Chapters 15 through 19, occurs in three major settings.

First, lawyers help clients to resolve specific, concrete disputes over past events, in a wide variety of legal settings: civil or criminal litigation in the courts; administrative agency proceedings; and alternative means of dispute resolution, such as arbitration and mediation. These are not entirely distinct processes. For example, a case that is in litigation in the courts may be resolved through arbitration. Of course, the parties may resolve the case themselves at virtually any time. Indeed, the vast majority of American lawsuits settle, fortunately for both the legal system (which could not handle more trials without additional resources) and the parties (for whom litigation is generally very stressful and expensive).

Second, lawyers advocate for client interests by engaging in lawmaking activities. Lawyers lobby legislatures to promote client interests in upcoming legislation. Lawyers present client positions on pending agency regulations as well. Of course, litigation also may yield a significant rule of law if a case proceeds to an appeals court.

Third, lawyers advocate for clients in negotiating contracts and other facets of transactions with other parties. This kind of law practice, commonly called "transactional practice," involves advocacy because the attorney seeks to convince the other party that his or her client's terms should be included and that unfavorable terms should be changed.

The remaining chapters in this book focus on advocacy in the litigation setting. We have chosen this setting for several reasons. Most areas of law involve civil litigation. In addition, many principles of advocacy have developed and are applied in the litigation setting. Finally, litigation has more technical procedures and standards than other settings. As you learn about other forms of advocacy, you may want to consider how the general principles taught in the following chapters transfer to those settings.

More specifically, Chapters 15 through 19 look closely at two stages of civil litigation: pre-trial and trial practice, and appellate practice. Chapter 15 explores pre-trial and trial practice and the motion practice memorandum, a common written form of advocacy in that setting. Chapter 16 covers fundamentals of advocacy—which we call the "science" of advocacy—applicable to all settings of legal advocacy. Chapter 17 explores appellate practice and the appellate brief, which is more complex than the motion practice memorandum. Chapter 18 covers advanced advocacy, which we call the "art and philosophy" of advocacy. Chapter 19 discusses oral argument, which commonly accompanies the written argument.

This chapter discusses ethical rules governing advocacy, provides background on civil litigation and pre-trial and trial—or "motion"—practice, and then covers the function and format of the motion practice memorandum. Two sample memoranda based on the HomeElderCare case appear at 333 and 343, along with several other documents used in motion practice; you should read through these materials before reading further.

B. THE ADVOCATE'S ETHICS

The lawyer who serves as a client's zealous advocate simultaneously takes on another role: "an officer of the legal system and a public citizen having special responsibility for the quality of justice." Preamble to Model Rules of Professional Conduct (1983). At times, you may perceive conflict, or at least tension, between these roles. But they are intended to be complementary; clients should be interested in a fair process and just outcome, as well as a favorable result.

A lawyer, as an officer of the legal system, may pursue only nonfrivolous claims and defenses. Model Rule of Professional Conduct 3.1 states: "A lawyer shall not bring or defend a proceeding, or assert or controvert an issue therein, unless there is a basis for doing so that is not frivolous, which includes a good faith argument for an extension, modification or reversal of existing law." A lawyer who violates this rule faces professional sanctions such as reprimand and disbarment. Similarly, Federal Rule of Civil Procedure 11 provides for sanctions when a lawyer signs a document that is not, according to the lawyer's informed belief, "warranted by existing law or by a nonfrivolous argument" for a change in the law. Many states have similar rules.

A lawyer must be candid with the court. It is a violation of professional ethics to knowingly make a false statement of material fact, offer evidence the lawyer knows to be false, or fail to disclose a material fact if nondisclosure would deceive the court. Model Rules of Professional Conduct 3.3 (1983). Similarly, it is a violation to knowingly fail to disclose known, adverse, binding precedent not disclosed by opposing counsel. *Id.*

Finally, a lawyer must expedite litigation and refrain from engaging in unfair, harassing, or delaying tactics. Examples of the latter include obstructing access to potentially relevant material and resisting proper requests for information from opposing counsel. *See id.* Rule 3.4; Fed. R. Civ. P. 11.

For many lawyers, these rules serve as minimum standards. Their own personal values prompt them to act according to even more stringent standards of respect for the law, candor, and fairness.

C. CIVIL LITIGATION AND MOTION PRACTICE

These ethical rules govern a lawyer's conduct in a range of settings, including the complex task of litigating a case on behalf of a client. The central purpose of litigation is to resolve disputes through the application of legal rules to proven facts by decisionmakers empowered by the government. The following discussion presents a generic model of civil litigation; the details of each jurisdiction's procedures vary.

In general terms, as illustrated in Exhibit 15.1, civil litigation entails framing the case, ascertaining the facts through discovery, and obtaining a decision. At various points in the litigation, one side or the other may bring a motion requesting the court to grant the relief desired by the moving party,

EXHIBIT 15.1

OUTLINE OF CIVIL LITIGATION

Phases of Litigation	Illustrative Motions
Framing the Case	
■ complaint ■ answer ■ joinder of parties ■ counterclaims ■ class certification	■ dismissal for lack of jurisdiction ■ dismissal for failure to state a claim ■ class certification ■ temporary injunction
Ascertaining Facts **Through Discovery**	
■ depositions ■ production of documents ■ interrogatories ■ admissions	■ compel discovery
Obtaining a Decision	
summary judgment (pre-trial)	■ summary judgment
trial ■ selection of jury ■ opening statements ■ presentation of evidence ■ closing arguments ■ instruction of jury ■ deliberations by jury ■ entry of judgment	■ in limine ■ judgment as matter of law ■ new trial
Appeal (see Exhibit 17.2)	

or movant, against the opposing party. Exhibit 15.1 lists common motions. The movant may seek to move the litigation along (a nondispositive motion), or the movant may seek a resolution of the case in its favor (a dispositive motion). Courts either grant or deny motions.

1. Phases of Civil Litigation and Accompanying Motions

In the first phase of litigation, the parties frame the case through the plaintiff's complaint and the defendant's answer. The two sides name the persons or entities involved, assert various facts to be true or deny the opponent's assertions, identify legal claims or defenses arising out of those facts, and state their desired outcomes. In complicated cases, there may be three or more parties, or the defendant may sue the plaintiff as well as be sued, or a group of similarly situated individuals may sue as a class.

Motions are quite common at this initial stage of litigation. For example, the defendant may seek to dismiss the case on various grounds, such as the court's lack of jurisdiction (power to decide the case), the plaintiff's excessive delay in bringing the lawsuit, or inadequate legal support for the plaintiff's claim. The plaintiff may seek certification of a class. Or the plaintiff may seek a temporary injunction to preserve the status quo pending litigation.

In discovery, the second phase of litigation (which may overlap some-what with the first), the parties exchange information about the relevant facts through several methods: depositions (interviews) of parties and witnesses, production of documents or other items, answers to interrogatories (written questions), and admissions (statements of agreement as to certain facts).

Motions arise during discovery if the parties are unable to manage the process themselves. A party may resist discovery if it believes the opposing party is seeking irrelevant or protected information or is asking for discovery that is exceedingly burdensome. Then the party seeking discovery brings a motion to compel discovery.

Discovery concludes as the case nears the trial date. The parties may avoid trial in various ways. They may settle the case based on what they have learned through discovery, or they may resolve it with the assistance of a third-party neutral. If one party believes the key facts to be undisputed and its position to be supported by the law, it may move for summary judgment. Summary judgment is a decision by the court based on the pleadings, factual documents supporting the motion (such as a portion of a deposition or an affidavit), and arguments of counsel. Summary judgment may cover all claims or defenses in the case or only some portions of the case. A grant of summary judgment obviates the need for trial on that portion of the case.

If the case has not been resolved during the pre-trial phases, it will pro-ceed to trial. The trial process consists of selection of the jury; opening state-ments by the lawyers; each side's presentation of evidence through witnesses, documents, and items; closing arguments; the judge's instruction of the jury on the law; jury deliberations; and the verdict. The judge then reviews the jury's work and decides whether to enter judgment on the verdict. Some cases are tried to a judge without a jury (a bench trial), in which case the judge determines what the facts are and applies the law to the facts.

Motions are common at various phases of trial. For example, one party may bring a motion in limine, to obtain a ruling on the admissibility of cer-tain evidence. The defendant may bring a motion for judgment as a matter of law at the end of the plaintiff's case, seeking a ruling that the plaintiff failed to carry its burden of proof and that the defendant therefore wins. Or either party may move for judgment as a matter of law before the case goes to the jury. The party that lost before the jury may seek a new trial based on erro-neous rulings by the judge on such matters as admissibility of evidence.

If a party that loses at the trial court level is sufficiently disturbed by the loss and wishes to pursue the case further, it may appeal. The appeals process is described in Chapter 17.

The sample memoranda at the end of this lesson are based on a fictional lawsuit brought by the county attorney of LaSalle County, Minnesota, on behalf of the State of Minnesota. Assume that the Complaint (not included) asserted that HomeElderCare was engaging in certain acts amounting to unauthorized practice of law and that this conduct should be enjoined pursuant to the unauthorized practice statute. Assume further that HomeElderCare's Answer admitted some of the county's factual assertions, denied others, presented facts HomeElderCare deemed important, and asserted that HomeElderCare was not violating the statute. The likely types of discovery in such a case would be depositions of the social workers and some clients, production of living will forms and actual living wills, interrogatories, and admissions on uncontroverted topics. Assume that the county attorney moved for a temporary injunction, that is, an order by the court restraining HomeElderCare from continuing to draft living wills pending the resolution of the litigation.

2. Motion Practice

a. Procedures

Motion practice can be oral, written, or both. Some motions are made and argued orally, frequently on the spot. For example, an evidentiary motion generally is made and argued orally while the trial is in progress. The judge can ask for a written motion and written memoranda to support the oral motion.

More typically, the movant brings a motion by filing a notice of motion and motion. (See the sample at 331.) The notice alerts the opponent to the motion and provides information about the time and location of the hearing. The motion itself constitutes the request to the court to take the action desired by the movant. Generally the movant also provides a proposed order for the court's consideration, should the court grant the motion. (See the sample at 332.)

The movant and opponent may write memoranda of law for and against the motion. The movant writes first, filing the memorandum in support of the motion with the court and serving it on opposing counsel. The party opposing the motion writes its memorandum in opposition to the motion, in response to the movant's memorandum, and then serves and files it. The movant then may prepare, serve, and file a reply memorandum if the memorandum in opposition raises matters unaddressed by the movant's initial memorandum.

These memoranda set out and analyze the law governing the case and apply that law to the facts of the case. These memoranda cite to the law and to the documentation compiled thus far as needed to support statements about the facts of the case. For example, a defendant writing in support of a motion to dismiss a case for failure to state a legal claim would refer to the complaint. A party seeking summary judgment would refer to the affidavits, depositions, interrogatories, admissions, and documents generated during discovery.

In addition to submitting written materials, the lawyers usually argue orally before the judge. Motion practice arguments may be very formal (in the courtroom with each lawyer standing in turn at a lectern) or quite informal (with the lawyers seated around the judge's desk in chambers). Formal oral arguments typically follow the same sequence as the memoranda: movant, opponent, movant. Informal oral argument resembles a discussion. Oral arguments are based on the material in the memoranda and include questions by the judge.

Judges are assigned to hear motions under one of several systems. In a block system, each case is assigned to a judge to handle from the very earliest stages through trial; that judge hears motions in the case. In a calendar system, cases are not assigned to judges early on; rather, each judge rotates through a schedule in which he or she hears all motions scheduled for a specific day. Furthermore, in federal court, judges typically hear and decide dispositive motions while magistrates (assistant judges) typically hear and decide nondispositive motions.

b. Court Rules

Federal and state rules of procedure define the types of motions that commonly are made and state the standards for granting them. In addition, local rules (or court rules), which supplement the rules of procedure and are drafted by a single court or by a set of trial courts, cover matters of detail.

Court rules may impose page limits. To provide a specific example, in the state courts in Minnesota, in which the hypothetical HomeElderCare case has been brought, memoranda can be no longer than thirty-five pages, exclusive of facts. In the case of the movant, the page limit covers the sum of the initial and reply memoranda. Minn. Gen. R. Prac. Dist. Ct. 115.05.

Another important detail is timing. For example, Minnesota state courts require the parties to file their memoranda at fixed intervals before the date of the hearing. One rule governs dispositive motions, i.e., motions that could resolve the case; the other governs less significant motions.

	Dispositive Motions	Nondispositive Motions
movant's initial memorandum	28 days	14 days
opponent's memorandum	9 days	7 days
movant's reply memorandum	3 days	3 days

Minn. Gen. R. Prac. Dist. Cts. 115.03, 115.04. If these dates are not met, the hearing may be cancelled (if the movant is in violation), or the motion may be granted as unopposed (if the non-movant is in violation). Either party may lose the opportunity to argue orally, and attorney fees may be imposed. Minn. Gen. R. 115.06.

The message should be clear: Know and comply with the rules of procedure and the local rules in your jurisdiction.

c. Strategy

Bringing a motion should reflect a well considered choice. The most obvious reason for bringing a motion is to obtain the relief sought, whether it be dismissal of the case, a temporary injunction, or a discovery order. In addition, if the case has been assigned to a specific judge, motions provide an opportunity to educate the judge about the case and, in turn, to see how the judge assesses the case. Furthermore, because the opponent typically defends against the motion, motions provide an opportunity to learn about the opponent's strategy.

Nonetheless, there are distinct disadvantages to motions, especially ill-considered ones. Making a motion can be costly in time, energy, and therefore money. A motion that is premature or only weakly supported will present a poor impression of the case (and the lawyer) to the judge, and the opponent's position will seem strong by comparison. Finally, excessive use of motions can undermine the relationships among the lawyers and between them and the judge, who must work together throughout the litigation.

The party opposing the motion typically chooses to defend against the motion. Alternatively, the opponent may offer to negotiate about the matter in dispute. For example, a party facing a motion to compel discovery may seek to work out a revised date for submitting its response, or a party facing a summary judgment motion may offer to settle the case.

In the hypothetical HomeElderCare case, the county attorney moved for a temporary injunction for several reasons: to obtain the injunction so as to preclude further unauthorized practice of law during the litigation, to begin to sway the court in the State's favor, to ascertain the court's first reaction to the case, and to learn of HomeElderCare's approach to the case. HomeElderCare probably would not settle but rather would defend against the motion, which goes to the heart of the dispute—HomeElderCare's ability to provide its living will service.

D. THE FUNCTION OF THE MOTION PRACTICE MEMORANDUM: AUDIENCE AND PURPOSE

As you prepare your motion practice memorandum, keep in mind who will be reading it and why you are writing it. The immediate audience is the judge, as well as his or her law clerk. Law clerks typically are recent law school graduates who assist judges by researching cases and writing memos analyzing the cases. Other important readers are opposing counsel and your client.

Judges, of course, are familiar with the law in general and the legal system. Every judge has a few areas of expertise and some areas that he or she has not studied since law school (if then). Most law clerks also have only general knowledge of issues that are presented to the court. With this background, the task of the judge and clerk is to render a correct decision by assigning the proper legal meaning to the case. To do so, they need to know the facts of the dispute, the applicable substantive law, the procedural law on the motion at hand, and the application of the law to the facts of the case. They need to know the complete picture, not just the material favoring your position. To find in your favor, they need to believe your position; they need to find you and your client credible. Additionally, the judge and law clerk need to understand the case with a minimum of time and effort on their part. Most judges are very pressed for time, because of heavy caseloads.

As for opposing counsel, your primary purpose is to convince him or her of the merits of your position. If your opponent becomes at least somewhat convinced of your position, settlement in your client's favor becomes more likely. Even if the case does not settle, your opponent may contest fewer points at trial or in pre-trial motions. Your secondary purpose regarding opposing counsel is to develop a good working relationship; modern litigation requires considerable cooperation between the attorneys, even as they pursue their clients' divergent interests.

As for your client, your purpose is to earn the client's confidence by presenting the client's position in the best light possible, consistent with the law and the facts. Your client should see his or her story told in an effective way, and your client should understand the main legal arguments, if not the intricacies of the law. Your client should see that you believe in his or her position and want the court to do so as well.

E. THE FORMAT OF THE MOTION PRACTICE MEMORANDUM

As diverse as these readers' perspectives are, you can serve all of your audiences and purposes well by writing your memorandum to meet the criteria developed earlier in this book, as well as one new criterion. Legal advocacy should be complete, correct, coherent, comprehensible — and convincing.

1. Format Choices

No single format for the motion practice memorandum is used in courts across the country. Many courts do not dictate a format; nonetheless, you should check for any applicable local court rules. You also should consult other attorneys about any informal local practices. Consider as well the following suggestions based on common practices (which probably align fairly closely with any court rules you may come across).

The movant's initial memorandum follows this sequence: caption, opening components, argument, conclusion with signature. The variation comes in the opening components. Virtually all formats include a fact statement. Optional opening components are issues, introduction or summary, and procedure. The order in which these opening components appear can vary. See Exhibit 15.2 for several classic sequences.

The formats for the opponent's memorandum are similar. The opponent need not, of course, follow the format selected by the movant. The opponent generally does not include a procedure statement. Also, the opponent occasionally elects not to include a fact statement if the movant's statement is acceptable, as occurs when the parties are not disputing the facts and may even have an agreed-upon (stipulated) fact statement. More often, the opposing party tells its own story in a fact statement. Again, see Exhibit 15.2.

EXHIBIT 15.2

FORMAT CHOICES FOR MOTION PRACTICE MEMORANDA

Initial Memorandum (Movant and Opponent)			Reply Memorandum (Movant)	
Caption	Caption	Caption	Caption	Caption
Introduction or Summary	Procedure**		Introduction or Summary	Introduction or Summary
Facts*	Facts*	Facts*		Facts
	Issues	Issues		
Argument	Argument	Argument	Argument	Argument
Conclusion with signature	Conclusion with signature	Conclusion with signature	Conclusion with signature	Conclusion with signature

*On occasion, the party opposing the motion may omit the fact statement.

**The party opposing the motion generally omits the procedure statement.

The movant's reply memorandum is the most flexibly structured. Its purpose is to respond to points raised by the opponent and not addressed in the initial movant's memorandum. The reply memorandum may address factual matters in a short fact statement, legal matters in a short argument, or both. It is fairly common to include an introduction and fairly uncommon to include a statement of the issues. The reply memorandum always includes a conclusion and a signature. See Exhibit 15.2.

As for the sample memoranda, Plaintiff's memorandum uses the first format listed in Exhibit 15.2; this format allows Plaintiff to begin with the big picture of the case, followed by the fact statement. On the other hand, Defendant's memorandum uses the third format listed in Exhibit 15.2; this format introduces the court to the facts before raising the legal issues arising out of the facts. There is no reply memorandum.

2. Seven Components

The following discusses the seven components in the order the reader generally encounters them. You need not write the motion practice memorandum in this order. For example, you may decide to write the argument before the facts, or you may decide to write the introduction last.

Caption: The chief purpose of the caption is to permit easy recognition and accurate processing of the document. The caption lists the parties, the court in which the case is venued, the docket number for the case, and the title of the document. Court rules may require additional information, such as the type of case and the judge's name. The layout of the caption should follow the layout of other documents filed with that court.

Note that the captions of the two HomeElderCare sample memoranda are nearly identical. They both present the information just listed. The only difference is in the titles: "Plaintiff's Memorandum in Support of Plaintiff's Motion for Temporary Injunction" versus "Defendant's Memorandum in Opposition to Plaintiff's Motion for Temporary Injunction."

Introduction or Summary: When done well, the introduction serves two very important purposes: It orients the reader to the motion, and it begins to persuade the reader to adopt the client's position.

The introduction should briefly identify the parties, the nature of their dispute, and the relief sought by the movant or the result sought by the opponent. It also should present a key point or two in favor of the client, whether a key fact or point of legal reasoning. If you also present an overview of the legal arguments in the memorandum, "summary" is the preferred title.

The sample State's memorandum includes a summary. The first paragraph acquaints the reader with the factual dispute, the second paragraph identifies the legal dispute, and the third paragraph provides an overview of the argument.

Procedure: This component sets out the history of the litigation, up to the current motion. It identifies the main events, typically in chronological order, and provides citations to pertinent documents, such as the complaint or request for admissions.

This component is most commonly used for cases with complex procedural histories or for motions that are predominantly procedural, rather than substantive, in nature. An example of the former is a motion in a discovery dispute; an example of the latter is a motion to dismiss for failure to state a claim.

Neither sample memorandum in the HomeElderCare case file has a procedure component.

Facts: The fact statement informs the reader of the events in the real world that have given rise to the litigation. Equally important, the fact statement prompts the reader to see the situation from the client's point of view, empathize with the client, and perhaps begin to lean toward the client's legal position.

One key to a successful fact statement is the careful selection of facts. As Chapter 13 explains, a fact can be legally relevant (related to the elements of the rules of law); background (necessary for the reader to make sense of the story); or residual (neither relevant nor background). The fact statement should, of course, include the first two types of facts. Residual facts with no persuasive content should be excluded, but favorable residual facts may be included as long as the memorandum does not become an appeal to emotion rather than a recounting of the important events. Your goal is to prompt the reader to understand the client's situation so that the client's actions and reactions appear reasonable and responsible.

Additionally, rules of legal ethics require that the fact statement present material facts even if they are unfavorable. Without the unfavorable facts, the story is not fully told, and the reader would be misled. Furthermore, it is wise to present unfavorable facts in their most favorable light.

As the case proceeds through the court system, the pleadings, transcripts of oral proceedings, and other material filed with the court become the record of the case. In the fact statement, you must cite to the pertinent portion of the record of the case. (See Rule P.7 of *The Bluebook*.) You need not quote the record verbatim, although you may wish to quote some material directly if the precise wording is important or persuasive. In all events, your presentation must be faithful to the record. For example, inferences drawn from the facts should be clearly identified as inferences, lest they be taken to be stated facts.

The fact statement should have a clear beginning, body, and end. Lengthy fact statements may have subject headings. The opening paragraph should identify the important participants in the situation and establish the labels used for them in the memorandum. If there is no introduction or summary, the opening paragraph also should present a very brief synopsis of the parties' dispute.

The body of the fact statement chronicles what happened between or among these participants. The common modes of organization are chronological, topical, and perceptual. The first two approaches are more strictly objective, while the third introduces an element of subjectivity. In a chronological presentation, events are told in the order they occurred. A topical presentation proceeds from one aspect of the facts, such as location or relationships, to another. In the perceptual mode, the events are presented as a key participant experienced or learned of them; then a competing perspective may be presented if needed. The perceptual organization should be used when the participants' perspectives are critical and differ fundamentally. You should choose the organization that best permits you to tell your client's story, from your client's perspective. Readers are more convinced by a legal argument when the facts are presented in a coherent and interesting narrative.

The end of the fact statement generally states the pertinent procedural history of the litigation up to the point at which the motion was made. There need not be much detail about unimportant procedural matters. However, if the memorandum includes a procedure component, the procedural history appears there instead.

The two sample fact statements contain very much the same facts. Nearly all are legally relevant or background facts, although some details, such as Mr. Nelson's condition, are residual and stated primarily for persuasive effect. Both writers have presented their clients' favorable and unfavorable facts. Both memoranda use a primarily topical organization, with some chronological passages interspersed (in the State's telling of Mr. Nelson's story and in HomeElderCare's account of its experience with living wills). Both fact statements contain cites to the record.

Issues: One purpose of the issue statement is to begin to persuade the reader. In addition, because the issues reveal the scope and sequence of the points covered in the memorandum, the issue statement provides a roadmap.

In most situations, the issues link the law to key facts. Many issues refer both to the law of the motion under consideration (procedural law) and to the law governing the parties' claims or defenses (substantive law). Some issues involve only procedural law, as in a discovery motion, or a pure legal issue, as in an argument that a jurisdiction does not recognize a cause of action. In these situations, the issue's content will be limited accordingly.

The issues as a set should reflect the large- and middle-scale organization of the argument. There generally should be an issue for each major point in the argument, and you may want to flag minor points in the argument with subissues. Use outlining levels (I, II, A, B, C) and transitional words to convey the relationships among the issues and subissues.

The issues should reflect the facts and law accurately, but they need not necessarily be objective in tone. Rather, each issue should be subtly phrased so as to suggest the answer desired by the client. Furthermore, the issues should be relatively concise, so the reader's attention does not flag.

As Exhibit 15.2 suggests, most memoranda have either an introduction or summary or a statement of the issues. Either can serve to frame the central point of the motion and orient the reader. Only in a long and complex memorandum would both components appear.

The sample memorandum for HomeElderCare has a statement of issues. This statement signals the scope and sequence of the upcoming argument: an initial threshold requirement (I) and then a series of three factors (II A, B, and C). The issues incorporate procedural law, substantive law, and facts. They subtly suggest the answer desired by HomeElderCare by focusing on the service of preparing living wills for clients.

Argument—in general: As the longest component of most memoranda, the argument's purpose is to prove to the reader that the client's position is the better one on the facts and the law. The argument states a legal meaning for the client's situation and provides the judge with the legal reasoning needed to adopt that legal meaning. Indeed, the judge may use portions of the successful argument in writing his or her opinion.

To prove its points, the argument first must state the law accurately. Ethics rules require counsel to cover and cite the legal authorities, favorable and unfavorable, that the court will deem important in deciding the motion. The argument must present mandatory authority where it exists, of course; it also may present persuasive precedent and commentary that may be useful to the court and will be favorable to the client. If no mandatory authority exists, the argument should demonstrate how to use persuasive authority and commentary to decide the case and how to handle unfavorable persuasive precedent. The argument should present all analytical steps necessary to develop the applicable rule of law. As appropriate, it should show how to fuse several cases or interpret an ambiguous statute.

The argument should show how the substantive law and the procedural law interact. Some procedural rules operate relatively independently of the substantive law governing the case; an example is a motion to compel discovery where the issue is burdensomeness. Other procedural rules are nearly entirely dependent on the substantive law; an example is a motion to dismiss for failure to state a claim. Still other procedural rules include both elements that rely heavily on substantive law, while others operate relatively independently of substantive law; an example is a motion for temporary injunction, which involves consideration of the likelihood of success on the merits (fixed by substantive law) as well as the burden of harms to the parties from various results (not so fixed). A well written argument clearly demonstrates how to view the facts in light of the substantive law (as needed) and the procedural law.

In all of these situations, you need to do more than present a statement of the law; the argument must connect the law and the facts. The argument should discuss the relevant facts—both favorable and unfavorable—in depth and demonstrate why the court should draw the desired conclusion. In all situations, this task requires clear deductive reasoning; in many cases, it also requires reasoning by example and policy analysis.

On debatable issues, your argument also should address the opposing argument. This discussion commonly arises in one of two postures. If the conflict relates to which rule should apply, you would state the favorable rule and address the unfavorable rule. If the conflict relates to how the rule should be applied, you would state the favorable application and address the unfavorable application. Your discussion of the opposing argument may be woven into your main argument, or it may follow your main argument.

An argument cannot be persuasive if it cannot be followed. To guide your reader through what can be a complex analysis use the following cues within the argument: roadmaps, topic sentences, appropriate transitions, and point headings. The first type of cue, the roadmap, may appear in various places, such as between the argument heading and point heading I, or between point heading I and subpoint heading A. Topic sentences and transition sentences function as they do in office memos. The fourth cue, the point heading, is unique to advocacy writing and is discussed below.

Of course, you must fully and properly cite the law in your argument. In general, the citations to the record in the fact statement support references to the facts within the argument. However, you should provide record citations in the argument when you use a direct quote from the record or want the court to look at a key page.

In the sample memoranda, both arguments present the procedural law (each using six or seven mandatory precedents) and the substantive legal topics (both relying on the two main statutes, the two leading cases, and commentary; the state relying as well on additional cases and a related statute). Both arguments develop the rules of law through references to or quotations from the two statutes, rules drawn from and summaries of the leading precedents, and tools of statutory interpretation. Both use the elements of the procedural rule (the elements of an injunction) as the procedural framework, with the substantive law presented in the context of the procedural framework and the facts in the context of the law, although the schematics differ. See Exhibit 15.3. Both arguments link the rules and the facts through deductive reasoning, reasoning by example, and policy arguments. Both also subtly refute the other's arguments; see, for example, the State's discussion of the policy against technical restrictions and HomeElder-Care's handling of the fee and "legal document" points. Both arguments begin with introductory material to signal the organization of the argument, and they use point headings and transitional phrases to further signal the progression of the argument.

Argument—point headings: Point headings both flag an upcoming topic and make a full-sentence assertion about the topic. Taken together, the point headings state the handful of assertions the court must accept (in total or in part) to rule in the client's favor.

EXHIBIT 15.3

SCHEMATIC OF ARGUMENTS

STATE'S (PLAINTIFF'S) MEMORANDUM
Temporary injunction is warranted because

State likely will succeed on merits, and public policy in statutes favors injunction	Absent an injunction, clients will suffer irreparable harm outweighing harm to HEC from injunction	Injunction will be straightforward to enforce

State likely will succeed on merits, and public policy in statutes favors injunction

↓

Unauthorized practice statute prohibits non-lawyers
■ social workers
from drafting legal documents
■ living wills
or providing legal advice on difficult and doubtful questions
■ advice re physician duties, proxies, etc.
for a fee
■ HEC charges fee

Injunction will promote purposes of unauthorized practice statute
■ prohibit incompetent practice by non-lawyers
and living will statute
■ promote accurate expression of declarant wishes

Absent an injunction, clients will suffer irreparable harm outweighing harm to HEC from injunction

↓

■ improper receipt or denial of medical treatment
vs.
■ impairment of only one of HEC's many services

Injunction will be straightforward to enforce

↓

Unauthorized practice statute calls for injunction
■ short term of statutory remedy
■ notice to employees
■ review of HEC bills

HOMEELDERCARE'S (DEFENDANT'S) MEMORANDUM
Temporary injunction is improper because

State has not proved threshold requirement of great and irreparable injury
↓
laudable service
one allegedly erroneous will is not significant
clients seek assistance

State has not met its burden as to mix of factors:

■ balance of harms   ↓
     clients want and need service
     HEC will suffer business disruption
■ unlikelihood of State succeeding on merits
     because law prohibits legal advice only as to
     difficult and doubtful legal questions
          HEC fills in form; does not deviate from
          form; refers to attorneys
■ law prohibits drafting legal documents
     no drafting here—only filling in form
■ public interest will not be served by injunction
     elderly will not obtain living wills even though
     are favored by law

In most situations, each major point heading ties together the substantive and procedural law and the facts relevant to that topic. For complicated or lengthy topics, minor point headings state the subsidiary assertions, which may combine law and facts, or refer only to the law, or refer only to the facts. If an argument is primarily legal or procedural, the point headings will be too. Unlike the phrases that serve as topic headings in office memos, point headings make a point, and that point need not be restated in the next line of text.

Each point heading should be a single sentence and persuasively worded. The sentence can be compound but should not be so complex that its readability suffers. Multiple headings and subheadings should be numbered and lettered in outline form. Point headings should stand out from the text; major point headings should be more prominent than minor headings. You can use white space (open lines) above and below the heading; you also can use underlining, italics, boldface, initial capital letters, or a different font (if not too flamboyant). All capital letters is also an option, but studies have shown that readers have to work harder and retain less information when reading sentences in all capital letters.

The structures of the two sample arguments are apparent from their point headings, reprinted as Exhibit 15.4. Each major heading makes a main assertion, and most combine law and facts. The minor headings elaborate on the points in the major headings.

Conclusion and signature: The purpose of the conclusion is to remind the reader of the outcome desired by the client. It typically follows a simple formula, in which the writer respectfully requests that the court act in the client's favor. Some writers also synopsize the argument. The closing is usually "Respectfully submitted, . . . ," followed by the attorney's signature, as an endorsement of the preceding material. The signature block also includes the attorney's name, firm affiliation, client representation, address, phone number, attorney registration number, and the date.

Both sample memoranda contain conclusions. The State's conclusion is a short statement of its main points and the relief desired, and HomeElderCare's conclusion includes a slightly longer review of its three main points.

3. Comparison to the Office Memo

There is considerable similarity between the components of the office memo and those of the motion practice memorandum. See Exhibit 15.5 on page 174. However, they also differ in several respects. As you shift from advice to advocacy, the issues should be subtly slanted in the client's favor, persuasive residual facts may appear in the fact statement, the headings in the argument should not simply flag a topic but make a point, and the paper should advance a position rather than objectively assess the case. More broadly, you will want to employ the methods of legal advocacy covered in Chapters 16 and 18.

E X H I B I T   1 5 . 4

POINT HEADINGS

PLAINTIFF'S MEMORANDUM

I. The State likely will succeed in demonstrating that **Defendant's preparation of and counseling about living wills for its elderly clients** *constitutes the illegal practice of law* and affronts the public policies stated in the statutes on *living wills and unauthorized practice of law.*

    A. Defendant's living will service *constitutes the unauthorized practice of law, for a fee,* **by social workers.**

    B. Defendant's living will service affronts the public policies stated in the *unauthorized practice and living will statutes.*

II. **If Defendant incompetently prepares living wills that inaccurately reflect its elderly clients' choices concerning medical treatment or death, its clients** will suffer irreparable harm, with no adequate remedy at law, and this harm will outweigh **Defendant's loss of income** if the injunction is granted.

III. The temporary injunction **sought by the State** will be straightforward to enforce.

DEFENDANT'S MEMORANDUM

I. The State has failed to prove that it will suffer great and irreparable injury if **HomeElderCare continues to offer living will assistance to its clients.**

II. The State has not met its burden as to the factors needed for a temporary injunction to issue.

    A. The State's alleged harm in the absence of a temporary injunction does not outweigh the harm **to HomeElderCare's elderly clients and to the business relationships between HomeElderCare and its clients** if an injunction is granted.

    B. The State is not likely to succeed in convincing the Court that **HomeElderCare's provision of living will services to its clients** *constitutes the unauthorized practice of law.*

    C. The public interest will not be served by **prohibiting HomeElderCare's living will services** during the pendency of the case.

Key: procedural rule
    substantive law
    facts

F. REVIEW OF CHAPTER 15

Lawyers advocate for clients in a range of settings, all governed by the ethical principles of respect for the law, candor, and fairness. These principles reflect the lawyer's dual roles as advocate and public servant. In the setting of civil

EXHIBIT 15.5

COMPARISON OF OFFICE MEMO AND MOTION PRACTICE MEMORANDUM

Office Memo   *Motion Practice Memorandum*

caption ———————————————— caption

issues   introduction or summary

                                                 procedure

short answers   facts

facts   issues

discussion ——————————————— argument

conclusion and recommendations ———— conclusion with signature

litigation, motion practice memoranda serve multiple audiences by persuading the judge, opposing counsel, and indeed the client that the client's position is the better one. The function and format of the motion practice memorandum are as follows:

(1) The caption provides identifying information.

(2) The introduction or summary orients the reader by providing basic information about the case and begins to persuade the reader by featuring a key point or two.

(3) The procedure component recounts the important events in the litigation to date.

(4) The fact statement tells the client's story, thereby evoking understanding.

(5) The issues frame the legal/factual questions to be decided, signal the organization of the argument, and subtly suggest the desired answer.

(6) The argument proves that the client's position is the better one on the facts and the law (both substantive and procedural) and employs point headings as succinct statements of the major propositions.

(7) The conclusion states the relief desired by the client and carries the attorney's signature and the date.

The resulting memorandum should be complete, correct, coherent, comprehensible, and convincing. Chapter 16 develops several foundational principles of legal advocacy to help you accomplish these goals.

THE SCIENCE

OF ADVOCACY

> Among attorneys in Tennessee the saying is: When you have facts on your side, argue the facts. When you have the law on your side, argue the law. When you have neither, holler.
> —Albert Gore, Jr.
> *Washington Post* (July 23, 1982)

A. INTRODUCTION

In all settings, successful legal advocacy involves careful selection and development of points to be made on the client's behalf and then artful presentation of those points. This chapter focuses on the former. More specifically, this chapter first explains what makes a legal argument convincing. It then discusses the following steps for developing your argument: interpreting the facts, selecting legal topics to cover and points to make, arguing in the alternative, accounting for your opponent's arguments, assessing the strengths and weaknesses of your case, developing a theory of the case, stressing your strengths, and working around your weaknesses.

The examples in this chapter are from the sample motion practice memoranda at pages 333 and 343, which you should read before continuing. The topics discussed in this chapter are applicable to all advocacy settings, including appellate arguments.

B.   The Bases of Persuasive Legal Argument

According to principles of Aristotelian rhetoric, persuasion is a function of three elements: logos, pathos, and ethos. In simple translation, these three elements are an appeal to logic or proof, an appeal to emotion, and reliance on the writer's good character. An argument must be logically sound, it must appeal to the reader's sense of what is right on the facts, and the advocate must appear credible and trustworthy.

Similarly, Karl Llewellyn, a prominent legal scholar in the first half of the twentieth century, said that a successful lawyer must "bring in a technically perfect case on the law" and "make the facts talk" to be persuasive. K. N. Llewellyn, *The Modern Approach to Counseling and Advocacy,* 46 Colum. L. Rev. 167, 182-83 (1946). In both of these tasks, the lawyer must fulfill the ethical obligation of candor toward the court, discussed in Chapter 15. If the court is to adopt an advocate's view of the legal meaning to be assigned to the case, the advocate must present the facts and the law in a compelling and credible combination.

C.   An Analogy: Photography

Photographers and lawyers share this task: to present what exists or has happened in a way that informs the observer about the subject and generates a particular response. For the photographer, the subject is the scene, and the goal is to produce the desired response in the viewer. For the lawyer, the subject is the case, and the goal is to convince the reader to assign to the case the legal meaning the client desires.

Both the photographer and the lawyer must accept their subjects as they are. For both, the subject has features that will incline the observer toward the desired response and features that may produce the opposite response. Both the photographer and the lawyer have the opportunity to set boundaries, to decide what is included in the photograph or memorandum and what is not. And both can choose what aspects of the subject to bring into focus and what to leave in the background.

D. INTERPRETING THE FACTS

Rarely are the facts of a case fixed. Rather, most records consist of bits of information that suggest a set of relationships and series of events. The information requires interpretation. Judges expect you to help them understand the facts from your client's perspective.

You must, of course, fully and fairly inform the court. The court needs to be apprised of all relevant facts and necessary background facts. You may include persuasive residual facts, as long as you do so judiciously. Keep in mind that ethical obligations require you to present unfavorable as well as favorable facts.

One situation compelling interpretation is inconsistency, which may arise between the statements of two observers, between the early and later statements of the same observer, or between a document and a witness, among other possibilities. Some inconsistencies are not significant, because, for example, the fact is not relevant or the inconsistency relates to a detail while the general fact is all that matters. Other inconsistencies are significant and can be handled in various ways. You may be able to show that the two sources are only apparently, not truly, in conflict, or you may be able to show that one source is the more credible, based on capacity to perceive the events or lack of bias. In other situations, you may have to discuss both ways of seeing the fact in your analysis. In yet other situations, a legal rule may dictate how you handle an inconsistency. For example, the court must take the plaintiff's view of the facts on a motion to dismiss the complaint for failure to state a claim. As another example, many substantive rules focus on what a reasonable person would perceive in a situation (so that the actual perspectives of various participants are not dispositive).

Often, seemingly fixed facts can give rise to various inferences, depending on whose perspective is taken, and the inferences may be as important as the known fact itself. In such situations, you must take care to delineate what the record itself says. You may go on to present the inference favored by your client if it is an obviously reasonable one or you can explain it well. You should incorporate opposing reasonable inferences into your analysis, as you would incorporate reasonable opposing legal arguments into your analysis.

Finally, it may be significant that evidence of a specific fact does not appear in the record. If it is to your advantage, you may wish to note its absence and who could have testified to it, were that fact true. Of course, absent "facts" are not as weighty as facts that are stated in the record.

In the two sample memoranda, the facts presented in the fact statements and analyzed in the arguments are nearly identical. The only fact requiring interpretation is the cause of the error in Mr. Nelson's living will. Home-ElderCare's fact statement (at 344) states what is known and delicately but fairly intimates that he may have erred ("Perhaps he did not understand . . ."). The State's fact statement (at 334) identifies the error, notes that a lawyer corrected it, and observes that the original erroneous will was drafted by a nonlawyer.

E. SELECTING LEGAL TOPICS AND ARGUMENTS

As you research and reason through your client's case, you are apt to develop a long list of legal topics that could be discussed and points that could be made. It may be tempting to include all items on your list, lest you omit the winning argument. However, succumbing to this temptation is dangerous. If you try to develop too many points, you are unlikely to develop any fully, and you may seem to be relying on quantity, rather than quality, of argument. As judges know, one convincing argument suffices; no number of unconvincing arguments can suffice.

To identify the topics you need to address, consider the structure of the various rules involved in your case, for they impose requirements and offer options to you. For example, if the rule governing the plaintiff's claim is conjunctive, as plaintiff's counsel, you must present an argument for each element; as defendant's counsel, you need only prevail on one element and could omit discussion of one or possibly more elements. As another example, if the situation is governed by an aggregate or balancing rule, both plaintiff and defendant may select the factors to be discussed.

Generally, the court must explore the substantive law in combination with a procedural rule. Thus, in determining the topics you must or may discuss, you should consider the requirements and options of the procedural law. For example, the party opposing a motion for a temporary injunction need not necessarily demonstrate that the movant will lose on the merits; the party opposing the motion may be able to deflect the injunction by demonstrating that the balance of harms favors denial of the injunction.

Once you have selected the topics to cover, you should consider the various assertions to make on each topic. If you have more than one argument to make on a topic, think first about the relative power of each. A legal argument derives its power from the law, the facts, and the strength of the link between them. Ask yourself: Does the law unambiguously say what I am asserting, or is some interpretation necessary? Are my important facts uncontroverted and sympathetic? Is the link between the law and the facts obvious, or is there some murkiness? Would I be convinced if I were the judge or opposing counsel?

Consider as well each potential argument's utility as a response to the arguments likely to be made by your opponent. Legal advocacy entails rebutting your opponent's arguments as well as successfully stating your own. (This topic is discussed below in Part G.)

As you prepare your motion practice memorandum, as at other times in the case, you should consult with your client about the arguments to be made. While the client may not fully grasp the fine points of an argument, the client should be aware of and endorse the gist of the argument. The client may feel strongly about making some arguments or forgoing others, based on important nonlegal considerations.

In the sample memoranda, both parties discussed the same procedural rule. Both parties opted not to cover one factor from the aggregate injunction rule—the parties' previous relationship—on the grounds it is not apt and would only clutter already intricate arguments. The State addressed one factor—ease in enforcing the injunction—that HomeElderCare chose to skim by in one line. That factor favors the State; HomeElderCare can downplay it to focus on other stronger factors. Both parties focused on the obviously central concerns: harms to the parties, likelihood of success on the merits, and statutory expressions of public policy.

F.   ARGUING IN THE ALTERNATIVE

Ideally your best assertions will form a coherent whole argument. Each legal and factual assertion will flow smoothly from the previous assertion and lead naturally into the upcoming assertion.

Not infrequently, however, your best assertions will not be consistent with each other. There may be a break, but not a conflict, between two assertions; that is: "X is true. Whether X is true or not, Y is true." Or there may be a conflict between two assertions; that is: "X is true. Even if X is false, Y is true."

Although it may seem intellectually dishonest to make such arguments, lawyers commonly argue in the alternative. Arguing in the alternative is common in the law because both facts and law are malleable enough that more than one legal meaning may reasonably be ascribed to a situation. One of two rules may apply to a situation. For example, a statute may be amenable to two interpretations, both of which call for analysis; or a situation may fit into one of two closely related common law claims or defenses. Another possibility is that a rule may apply in more than one way; for example, a fact may be unknown or ambiguous, and both possibilities merit exploration. As these examples suggest, arguments in the alternative can occur at the topic level or within a topic. Judges are accustomed to arguments in the alternative; indeed, they use reasoning in the alternative to justify some of their own decisions.

Arguing in the alternative does have its drawbacks. It entails complexity and risks confusing the reader. The initial assertion or argument may seem weakened by the presence of the alternative, which suggests that the initial assertion or argument is not strong enough to stand on its own. In general, alternative arguments involving breaks are more convincing than alternative arguments involving conflicts.

The key to a successful argument in the alternative is clarity of presentation. You should begin with a clear roadmap, and you should introduce each assertion or argument with a signpost calling attention to the alternative relationship, such as, "Even if the Plaintiff's conduct were covered by the statute, it nonetheless would be permissible because. . . ."

Neither sample memorandum presents any arguments in the alternative. However, HomeElderCare's arguments on page 346 could have been phrased in the alternative, as follows: "Mr. Nelson failed to follow through on the social worker's advice to consult an attorney. But even if he did not, one inaccurate living will out of forty does not amount to great harm."

G. ACCOUNTING FOR YOUR OPPONENT'S ARGUMENTS

Legal advocacy has both offensive and defensive aspects. Not only must you convince the court of the merits of your argument; you also must deflect your opposition's arguments. Thus, an important step in developing your argument is to take stock of your opponent's argument.

Often this entails anticipating your opponent's argument, for instance, when your memorandum is the first to be written. Ask yourself: What would I argue if I were counsel for my client's opponent? If I were the judge analyzing this case, what are the assertions that I would discuss that would lead to the outcome favored by my client's opponent?

Next, compare your opponent's probable or actual arguments to your own. You very probably will discern both points of concurrence and points of clash. Points of concurrence are propositions on which you and your opponent do not differ; points of clash are propositions on which you and your opponent disagree. Both may involve various matters: You may agree or disagree as to what the governing legal rule is on a topic, how (or whether) to fuse a given set of cases, how to interpret a statute. You may agree or disagree about what the relevant facts are. You may agree or disagree about how the rule applies to the facts, how policy analysis plays out, whether a leading case is analogous or distinguishable.

A useful tool for depicting this analysis is the T-chart, in which you state the main arguments and significant assertions of the two sides in juxtaposition. See Exhibit 16.1. You can use symbols, such as X for points of clash.

You should take care to discern the points of concurrence and clash with precision because your memorandum should be focused accordingly. Your memorandum should focus on the points of clash, providing the court with compelling reasons to resolve them in your client's favor. Although your memorandum should cover the points of concurrence enough to provide context for your discussion of the points of clash, you should not tax the court by overdeveloping them.

In Exhibit 16.1, a T-chart of the HomeElderCare case, note that the parties concur on what the governing legal authorities are, what the rules and elements are, and how some of them apply to the facts. The parties clash as to the application of key elements to their facts and the role of public policy.

H. ASSESSING THE STRENGTHS AND WEAKNESSES OF YOUR CASE

Once you have sorted through the assertions, both legal and factual, that you wish to make, you should assess the overall strengths and weaknesses of your case. Every case in litigation has its strengths and weaknesses; truly one-sided cases generally are resolved before litigation by the parties or their attorneys. Of course, one side's strength is usually the other side's weakness.

EXHIBIT 16.1

T-CHART OF ASSERTIONS

State's Assertions	*HomeElderCare's Assertions*
various factors re injunction	various factors re injunction
■ death etc. is irreparable	✗ ■ no irreparable harm
■ bungled living wills outweigh impairment of HomeElderCare business	✗ ■ improper halting of useful service outweighs single incident
■ no administrative burden	■ no administrative burden
■ no prior relationship	■ no prior relationship
■ will succeed on merits	✗ ■ will not succeed on merits
unauthorized practice prohibitions bind non-lawyers	unauthorized practice prohibitions bind non-lawyers
social workers are not lawyers	social workers are not lawyers
social workers draft documents	✗ social workers fill in form
living will is legal document	✗ living will is not legal document
■ 145B says so	✗ ■ two statutes are separate
■ will has legal effect	✗ ■ issues are medical and moral
social workers give legal advice	✗ social workers avoid giving legal advice
■ service is incidental to nonlegal matters	■ service is incidental to nonlegal matters
■ test is whether Q is difficult & doubtful	■ test is whether Q is difficult & doubtful
■ legal issues abound	✗ ■ social workers avoid law
■ *Gardner* is analogous	✗ ■ *Gardner* is distinguishable
protect elderly from incompetent provision of legal service	✗ assist elderly with living wills
ensure accurate living wills	✗ encourage living wills

Some cases are said to be "strong on the law," while others are "strong on the facts" or "strong on policy." A case is strong on the law when the rule is well established, clearly addresses the client's situation, and calls for the client's desired outcome. A case is strong on the facts, or equities, when the client's situation draws understanding on the part of a reasonable observer and the client's desired outcome seems sensible and fair. A case is strong on policy when the client's goals reflect an important societal interest.

Determining the overall strength of your case may not be a simple matter. If the case raises multiple issues, the strengths and weaknesses may vary across issues. For example, the plaintiff may have the stronger legal position as to one claim, while the defendant has the stronger position as to another. Or the plaintiff's case may be strong on facts as to liability but weak on facts as to damages. Moreover, one party may have the advantage on the substantive law, while the other may have the advantage on the procedural law. Even if this analysis does not yield a unitary impression of your case, it is an important step in your analysis.

In the sample case, the two sides have interesting mixes of strengths and weaknesses. Generally the rule on temporary injunctions favors the opponent, although the State can counter with the statutory authorization of injunctions in the unauthorized practice statute. As for the substantive law, the State has a strong "legal document" argument, while HomeElderCare has a strong "difficult and doubtful question" argument. Mr. Nelson's situation presents a strong basis for argument on the facts for the State, especially since it illustrates the public policy behind the unauthorized practice statute. However, HomeElderCare has a strong record of client service (apart from Mr. Nelson) in an area of articulated client need and legislative concern (living wills).

I.   DEVELOPING A THEORY OF YOUR CASE

Once you have assessed the strengths and weaknesses of your case, you should have in mind some key ideas about the case. The next step is to distill these ideas into your "theory of the case." The theory of the case is what the case is about, in simple (but not simplistic) terms. If you were to write a newspaper article about your case, the headline or first paragraph would state the theory of the case.

Because a case meshes facts, substantive law, procedural law, and policy, the ideal theory of the case partakes of all of these. One or the other may dominate, however. For example, your central concept may be a key factual detail or a phrase representing the pertinent legal rule. Less commonly, a public policy may be your central concept. Whatever your central concept, the court's appreciation of your theory should lead inescapably to the outcome desired by your client and away from the outcome desired by your opponent.

The significance of a theory of the case is that it provides a theme for your argument, indeed for your entire memorandum. A theme is important for you as a writer and for your readers. For you, the theory of the case suggests language to use throughout the memorandum, provides a basis for ultimately deciding which assertions to make or emphasize and which to exclude or downplay, and constitutes a way of unifying what might otherwise seem to be disparate assertions. For the reader, who is unlikely to be able to truly absorb and recall all the distinct assertions of the memorandum, a well communicated theory of the case provides an idea about the case that can be easily grasped and adopted.

One way to depict a theory of the case is a pie chart, divided into thirds, with key phrases allocated to segments labeled "facts," "policy," and "law." See Exhibit 16.2. As you assign each phrase to its appropriate sector, you should see concepts that parallel each other fall into alignment around the circle.

In the sample HomeElderCare case, the strengths detailed above merged into the following theories of the case (sketched in Exhibit 16.2): For the State, "Defendant has illegally drafted legal documents and provided

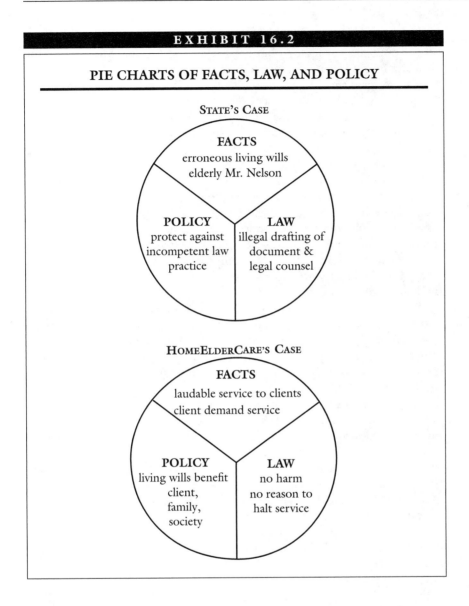

EXHIBIT 16.2

PIE CHARTS OF FACTS, LAW, AND POLICY

STATE'S CASE

FACTS
erroneous living wills
elderly Mr. Nelson

POLICY
protect against
incompetent law
practice

LAW
illegal drafting of
document &
legal counsel

HOMEELDERCARE'S CASE

FACTS
laudable service to clients
client demand service

POLICY
living wills benefit
client,
family,
society

LAW
no harm
no reason to
halt service

legal counsel for a fee to elderly citizens—and erroneously so in at least Mr. Nelson's case." See page 339. For HomeElderCare, "In fact, a laudable service has been done—for the client, for his or her family, and for society. Yet, the State wants to put a halt to this service. . . ." See page 346.

J. STRESSING YOUR STRENGTHS

As you draft your argument, you should hone in on your theory of the case and stress its strengths. The tools for doing so depend on the nature of your strong-suit material.

If your case is strong on the law, overall or in part, emphasize the legal rule. Present the strongest authority possible, and develop it fully. If the rule emanates from a statute, quote and paraphrase the statute, discuss its underlying policy, and provide an illustrative case. If the rule emanates from case law, present the rule itself, and also describe one or two cases in some depth. You could cite an early case to underscore the rule's long standing, and you could cite a recent case to underscore its continued authority. If your case law is largely or entirely persuasive precedent, present the best reasoned cases available, and, where possible, select cases from jurisdictions with economic or social similarities to your jurisdiction.

If your case is strong on the facts, overall or in part, emphasize the facts. Quote from the record. Stack evidence on the key fact by showing that it appears in multiple sources. Note not only what the evidence shows, but also what it does not show. If possible, develop an extended comparison to a decided case, or present several case comparisons, but not so many that the reader loses sight of your client's case. (Remember that a case comparison can be an analogy or a distinction.)

If your case is strong on policy, overall or in part, quote from cases, a statutory purpose section, or commentary that states the policy clearly. Show how the policy plays out in the facts of your case. Refute any opposing policy statements by your opponent by citing authority that downplays that policy, showing its inconsistency with your policy, or demonstrating its irrelevance to the case.

These methods may be used in various parts of your memorandum. You likely will seek to emphasize favorable law or policy in the introduction or summary, issues, and argument. In all these areas, and also in the fact statement, you will seek to emphasize favorable facts.

In the sample HomeElderCare case, you will note an essential contrast between the two memoranda in the State's reliance on the law versus HomeElderCare's emphasis on the facts and equities. This contrast is apparent in the number of authorities cited by the State (three statutes, eight cases, and two articles) and HomeElderCare (two statutes, two cases, one article) as to the substantive law. This contrast also is apparent in the varying emphases on the balance of equities element of the injunction rule, HomeElderCare's argument leading with two versions of the harm factor (at 348), the State's argument presenting a short discussion of this factor (at 341). (As you will see in Chapter 18, space allocation and sequence are two ways to emphasize or de-emphasize material.)

K.   WORKING AROUND YOUR WEAKNESSES

You cannot simply wish that your case's weaknesses will go away and ignore them; they certainly will appear in your opponent's memorandum. On the other hand, you should not dwell on the weaknesses, lest the court also do so. Rather, dispel the weaknesses, even as you make the points you want to make. How to do so depends on the nature of the weakness.

Some weaknesses may be matters of law. If the authority is not mandatory, you should downplay it as merely persuasive and nonbinding; you also should criticize any weaknesses in its reasoning or policy.

If the authority is mandatory case law, you have a range of options: Distinguish the case by showing that the facts or issues differ from your case. Narrow the scope of the case by confining its holding to facts not present in your case. Show that the adverse statement is dictum, not a holding. Demonstrate that the case is inconsistent with other binding precedent and should be discounted. If needed, argue that the case should be overruled because it relies on weak reasoning, the trend of the law is against it, or the case is otherwise outdated.

If the adverse mandatory authority is a statute or procedural rule or regulation, you have several options. Argue that your case falls outside its scope, based on definitions or other scope sections. Demonstrate that the law is ambiguous given the facts of your case; then provide a favorable interpretation based on legislative history or intent, canons of construction, or policy. The most difficult option is to establish that the law is unconstitutional or outside the power of the lawmaking body; a less radical form of this option is to argue for a limiting interpretation that would avoid unconstitutionality and favor the client.

Some weaknesses may be matters of fact. If there is conflicting evidence on the fact, emphasize the helpful evidence. Where possible, discuss other facts that put the unfavorable fact into context, without altering the unfavorable fact. For example, if the client acted unwisely, show why the client did so. Alternatively, you may show that the record does not present an even worse scenario.

Some weaknesses may be matters of policy. Again, you have several options. Show that your case does not truly implicate the policy. Show that the policy is outdated or needs re-evaluation. Shift the focus to a competing policy that is well served by the outcome your client seeks. If the law is clear and favors your client, point out that the law must be followed even if the court would favor a different policy.

These methods for handling weaknesses may be used as follows: the law and policy methods in the introduction or summary, issues, and argument; the fact methods in all those components of the memorandum and additionally in the fact statement.

Of the two sample memoranda, HomeElderCare's memorandum better illustrates how to deal with adverse law. The memorandum downplays the unauthorized practice statute by focusing on case law and pointing out ambiguities in its connection to the living will statute (at 349). The same memorandum distinguishes *Gardner*, the leading case, which has a favorable rule but adverse outcome (at 348). HomeElderCare's memorandum deals with the adverse facts regarding Mr. Nelson's situation by subtly suggesting he may have been at fault and pointing out that no real harm occurred (at 344). The State's memorandum deals with the adverse policy of encouraging living wills by showing how this policy is undercut by incompetent assistance by social workers (at 340), in effect rendering the living will policy subject to the constraints of the unauthorized practice statute.

L. REVIEW OF CHAPTER 16

To write a convincing legal argument, a lawyer must both argue the facts and present the law in a credible manner. To assure that your memorandum reflects these principles and is therefore convincing, you should:

(1) interpret the facts fairly yet persuasively;

(2) select legal topics that you need to cover and assertions that are well grounded in the law and facts;

(3) present arguments that form a coherent whole or are clearly understandable alternatives to each other;

(4) take into account the points of concurrence and points of clash;

(5) assess the strengths and weaknesses of your case;

(6) develop a theory of the case based on those strengths and weaknesses;

(7) as you draft your memorandum, stress your strengths; and

(8) work around your weaknesses.

By following these steps, you will carefully select and develop the arguments to be made on your client's behalf. Chapter 18 covers techniques for artful presentation of the points you have thus developed.

ADVOCACY WRITING IN THE APPELLATE SETTING: THE FUNCTION AND FORMAT OF THE APPELLATE BRIEF

A. Introduction
B. The Appellate Setting
C. The Function of the Appellate Brief: Audience and Purpose
D. The Format of the Appellate Brief
E. Review of Chapter 17

> Be brief, be pointed, let your matter stand
> Lucid in order, solid and at hand;
> Spend not your words on trifles but condense;
> Strike with the mass of thought, not drops of sense;
> Press to the close with vigor, once begun,
> And leave—how hard the task!—leave off when done.
> —Joseph Story
> *Advice to a Young Lawyer*

A. INTRODUCTION

This is the third of five chapters on advocacy, and the first focusing on the appellate setting. Chapter 18 discusses advanced persuasive writing techniques that build on the basic advocacy techniques presented in Chapter 16.

Arguments at the appellate level are delivered both in writing and orally; Chapter 19 discusses oral argument.

This chapter begins with a discussion of why appeals exist, how the appellate process differs from trial court procedures, and how these features are reflected in standards of appellate review. This chapter then discusses the audience, purpose, and format of appellate briefs. For examples, this chapter draws on two opposing briefs in the fictional case of *Nelson v. HomeElderCare,* a lawsuit over the enforceability of a contract for drafting living wills between HomeElderCare and a disgruntled client. The briefs appear at 352 and 364. You should read them in conjunction with this chapter.

B. THE APPELLATE SETTING

1. The Purpose of Appeals in the Legal System

Appeals provide a check on the trial courts. The trial judge is engaged in a venture with some potential for error, which may be due to inadvertence, mistakes in judgment, or, less commonly, bias. Hence, the case may receive a second analysis from a somewhat removed observer, the appellate court.

Appeals also benefit the legal system by providing a mechanism for making and standardizing the law. Appellate courts are collegial bodies of experienced and respected judges who have gained broad perspective on legal issues from seeing a range of lower court results, and so appellate courts have the authority to make precedent. The appellate court seeks to promote uniformity and predictability in the law so that the law in each new case accords with the law in similar or related decided cases.

Yet the appellate system has several disadvantages. Appeals add delay to judicial resolution of disputes and prolong the strain of litigation. They impose costs on the parties and society: salaries for the judges and court personnel, building and equipment costs, and additional attorney and filing fees for the parties.

2. Differences between Appeals and Trials

All courts seek to assure that the process is fair, the parties receive a just result, and the law is well served. As shown in Exhibit 17.1, the various types of courts have different roles to play. Facts are more important to the trial court, law to the intermediate appellate court, and policies to the high court.

A trial court is the court of first impression. Trial judges see the case unfold in person before them, as the parties, experts, other witnesses, documents, and other exhibits come before them. Trial courts focus primarily on ascertaining the facts of the case and applying the law to facts; they focus only secondarily on making law.

Appellate courts determine whether the trial court drew supportable factual findings and focus on whether the trial court properly applied the substantive and procedural law. Cases arrive at the appellate court in file folders and boxes containing the transcript of the trial and hearings, the pleadings

EXHIBIT 17.1

COMPARISON OF TRIALS AND APPEALS

	Trial Court	Appeals Courts	
		Intermediate	High
Primary Role of Court	Initial determination	Review of trial court	Lawmaking
Decisionmakers	Trial judge; sometimes jury	Usually panel of judges	Usually entire court
Parties	Plaintiff Defendant	Appellant (Petitioner) Respondent (Appellee)	
How Court Learns About Case	Pleadings, motions, memoranda, witnesses, exhibits, oral arguments	Transcript of trial, pleadings, motions, memoranda, exhibits; oral argument; briefs; lower court opinion(s)	
Possible Outcomes	Dismissal Judgment for plaintiff Judgment for defendant	Affirm Reverse Modify Remand to trial court	

and other discovery, and the briefs of the parties. The only in-person contact is the oral argument and perhaps a pre-argument conference between the attorneys and a judge.

Most jurisdictions have two levels of appellate courts. While the high court supervises the lower and intermediate courts, it focuses on the task of making the law and its underlying policies. (For brevity's sake, this chapter generally uses "judges" to include both judges of the intermediate court and justices of the supreme court.)

Party titles and case outcomes differ between trials and appeals. At the trial court, the parties are known as the plaintiff and defendant, based on who sued whom. Possible outcomes include dismissal with or without prejudice, judgment for plaintiff or defendant, or a mixed outcome on various counts. At the appellate level, the parties are known as appellant (or petitioner) and respondent (or appellee). The appellant is the party bringing the appeal against the respondent, regardless of who the plaintiff and defendant were in the lower court. Appellate courts differ as to whether they order the parties' names in the case title according to trial court or appellate status. The appellate court may affirm, reverse, or modify the trial court judgment or may remand the case back to the trial court with instructions.

In the fictional HomeElderCare case, Roger Nelson is the Plaintiff and Respondent, while HomeElderCare is the Defendant and Appellant. The trial court entered a declaratory judgment in favor of Mr. Nelson, stating that his contract with HomeElderCare was invalid because the living will service constituted the unauthorized practice of law. HomeElderCare has appealed that ruling, seeking to have the declaratory judgment reversed.

3. Rules Governing the Scope of Appellate Review

Rules on the scope of appellate review define which trial court rulings, facts, and issues are properly before the appellate court. These rules preserve the proper roles of the trial and appellate courts and reduce the likelihood of appeals.

a. The Final Judgment Rule

Most appeals are taken from a "final judgment," which means that the trial court judgment was final as to the entire case (or perhaps as to a claim or party). A final judgment may be, for example, a grant of a motion to dismiss the whole case or a jury verdict followed by a judgment. Decisions that are not final include such actions as denial of a motion to dismiss and rulings on evidence to be admitted at trial. The final judgment rule gives the trial court an opportunity to conclude the case (or a significant portion of it).

Occasionally, a party will wish to appeal a non-final ruling of the trial court; this type of appeal is called an "interlocutory appeal." The appellate court usually has discretion whether to hear an interlocutory appeal. Some interlocutory appeals are routinely granted, such as an appeal from an order granting, denying, or dissolving an injunction. Generally, however, appellate rules discourage interlocutory appeals because the would-be appellant could nonetheless go on to win the case, obviating the need for the appeal, and because a more completely adjudicated case will have a stronger factual record for appeal.

A trial court can obviate the need for an appeal by asking an appellate court to answer an unsettled question of law during the trial court process. This process, variously called "certifying" or "reserving" a question, can occur within the federal court system, within the state court system, or from a federal district court to the high court of the state whose law governs the question. Court rules vary as to when certified questions are allowed.

In the sample case, HomeElderCare appealed a grant of summary judgment. A trial judge grants summary judgment based on the record developed during discovery and other written materials, if the important facts are virtually uncontroverted and the law can be applied without trial. The judge issued a declaratory judgment that disposed of the entire case. Thus, the appeal is from a final judgment.

b. No New Facts on Appeal

An appeal is not a second trial. The appeals court does not receive new evidence. Rather, facts are determined by the factfinder at trial, and the appellate court reviews only whether the evidence supports the factfinder's determination. If the evidence does not support the trial court findings, the appellate court may reverse the trial court judgment or remand the case to the trial court for redetermination. This policy ensures that the appellate court remains in a reviewing capacity, rather than making the first ruling on the matter.

In the HomeElderCare case, the parties did not raise new facts on appeal. Indeed, they submitted the case to the trial court and then the appellate court on stipulated (agreed-to) facts.

c. No New Issues or Theories on Appeal

The appellate court generally does not hear legal issues or theories that the trial court did not have a chance to address. The trial court need not have been apprised of every case, argument, and alternative line of reasoning appearing in the appellate briefs, but the trial court must have had a chance to address the basic issues presented to the appellate court. This rule gives parties the incentive to present the case fully to the trial court. It thereby maximizes the likelihood of a correct ruling in the first instance and ensures that the appellate court functions as a reviewing court.

For any issue one may want to raise on appeal, there is a means of preserving the issue for appeal during the trial court proceedings. These means include motions, such as a motion for a new trial, and objections to evidence during trial.

In the sample HomeElderCare appellant's brief, as the statement of the case indicates, the issues and legal theories presented on appeal are very similar to the issues presented to the trial court.

d. The Reversible Error Rule

The appellate court is interested only in errors that are substantial enough to justify reversal (in whole or in part) of the trial court ruling. An error meeting this test is called "reversible error," "prejudicial error," or "material error." An error not meeting this test is known as "harmless error," "non-prejudicial error," or "immaterial error." An error is not a reversible error if the trial court reached the right result, albeit based on incorrect reasoning. This rule focuses the appellate court on matters of real consequence and forestalls unnecessary remands.

In the sample case, HomeElderCare argued that the trial court misapplied both the law defining the unauthorized practice of law and the law governing the validity of contracts for services not authorized by statute. These errors, if established, would be substantial enough to lead to reversal of the trial court judgment, and therefore each would be reversible.

4. The Range of an Appeal

Usually the appeal is brought by the party that lost at the trial court level. The appellant may appeal all adverse rulings of the trial court. However, sometimes the appellant appeals only a portion of the final judgment, reasoning that there is no reversible error in the unappealed portions of the case, or that a successful appeal as to certain matters would not have enough impact to be worth the cost, or that a portion of the case is better left as is (because, for example, the factual record is weak).

If both parties are unhappy with the trial court ruling, both parties may appeal. In a cross-appeal, both parties are simultaneously appellants and respondents.

In the sample case, only HomeElderCare, the defendant in the trial court, appealed. It appealed the trial court's adverse ruling that the contract was unenforceable on the grounds of unauthorized practice.

5. Standards of Appellate Review

The appellate court has varying amounts of discretion in reviewing the trial court ruling. The applicable standards of appellate review must appear in every appellate brief.

The appellant may challenge various decisions by the trial court judge. A judge's rulings on questions of law can be overturned if the lower court ruled incorrectly on the law and the error was material. Findings of fact by a trial judge can be overturned if they are clearly erroneous or contrary to the manifest weight of evidence. Rulings within the discretion of the trial court, such as whether to allow the plaintiff to amend the complaint a second time, can be overturned only if the ruling was an abuse of discretion—that is, arbitrary, capricious, based on the wrong law, or based on a clearly erroneous factual determination. Thus appellate courts generally defer to varying degrees to the decision of the trial court judge; appellate courts engage in de novo review, looking at the case afresh, as to questions of law.

A civil jury verdict is reviewed through the mechanism of a trial court ruling, such as a motion for judgment notwithstanding the verdict (commonly abbreviated "j.n.o.v.") or a motion for a new trial. In ruling on these motions, the trial court applies various standards, such as whether reasonable minds would differ in finding that the evidence does not support the verdict; whether the jury instructions contained reversible error; or whether the jury disregarded those instructions, resulting in reversible error.

In the HomeElderCare case, the alleged errors were either questions of law or mixed questions of law and fact. Note that, because of the stipulated facts, Appellant did not allege any errors in factfinding. Thus, the standard of review is whether the trial court correctly applied the law to the facts when it ruled that the defendant is entitled to summary judgment as a matter of law.

6. Mandatory versus Discretionary Review

Some appeals arise as a matter of right. In almost every jurisdiction, the intermediate appellate court must take nearly every appeal because a constitution or statute guarantees the right to one appeal. In many jurisdictions, some very serious cases, such as capital punishment or life imprisonment cases, are granted appeal to the high court as a matter of right.

Other appeals depend on the appellate court's decision to grant discretionary review. In a two-tier appellate system, as to most cases, the high court exercises its discretion as to which appeals to hear. In some jurisdictions, the would-be appellant petitions to the high court for a writ of certiorari compelling a lower court to transfer the record to the high court for review of alleged errors. An appeal granted is called a "grant of writ of certiorari," and an appeal denied is "cert. denied," for short. In other jurisdictions, the process involves "grant of review" or "denial of review." In discretionary review cases, the members of the court vote on which cases to hear; for example, four or more of the nine members of the United States Supreme Court must vote in favor of review in order for the petitioner to obtain a writ of certiorari.

A variety of factors influence a high court's decision to grant discretionary review. The high court may grant review because rulings among the intermediate courts of appeals conflict, undermining the predictability of the law. Other factors favoring a grant of review are important or pressing questions, a lower court ruling on the constitutionality of a statute, a departure by the lower courts from an established line of precedent or practice, or the need to harmonize policies or rules across a line of related cases. The factors prompting discretionary review may be published in the court rules, provided for by a statute on the court's jurisdiction, developed on a case-by-case basis, or presented in articles written by the justices. Because the decision to deny review is not a decision on the merits of the case, there is no precedential value to the denial of review.

For reasons of federalism, federal courts sometimes decline, or abstain from, deciding cases in a range of situations, thereby deferring to state courts. For example, the United States Supreme Court generally will not review a state supreme court decision that a government action violates both the state and federal constitutions, since the violation of the state constitution as interpreted by the highest court of that state is sufficient to uphold the judgment.

The appeal in the HomeElderCare sample briefs is an appeal as of right. It is an appeal to the intermediate appellate court, the Minnesota Court of Appeals. In Minnesota, the state constitution guarantees the right to one appeal, generally to that court.

7. Appellate Procedure

As you prepare an appeal, you should research the appellate rules of your jurisdiction. For instance, your failure to file a brief within the prescribed briefing period may deprive your client of the right to oral argument. Although the details of appellate procedure differ among jurisdictions, the major steps do not. See Exhibit 17.2 on page 194.

The initial preparation for an appeal actually occurs during the trial court stage. An appeal is grounded in the pleadings, discovery, motions, and trial, where the important facts and legal theories are first brought to the attention of the court and any errors are preserved for the appeal. The trial attorney should visualize how the case will look in the written trial court record, since that record will provide the appellate court's view of the case.

Within a certain time after the trial court has ruled (ninety days after judgment or thirty days after an order, in the Minnesota state courts), the party wishing to appeal must file a notice of appeal with the appellate court

EXHIBIT 17.2

OUTLINE OF CIVIL APPELLATE LITIGATION*

Preparing for Appeal

- drafting and amending pleadings with care
- making all appropriate motions
- getting all needed facts into evidence
- making needed objections and motions to preserve issues for appeal
- briefing all issues thoroughly with needed theories and authorities

Framing the Appeal

- appellant files and serves notice of appeal
- appellant requests trial court to prepare record and forward it to appellate court
- respondent may cross-appeal
- respondent may add to record
- appellate court judge may hold a pre-hearing conferencee

Presenting the Argument

- appellant files its brief
- respondent files its brief
- appellant may file its reply brief, if any
- amici may file briefs, if allowed by the court
- counsel present oral arguments

*This chart is a continuation of Exhibit 15.1.

and serve it on the opponent, as well as notify the trial court administrator. Soon after (within fifteen days in Minnesota), if the respondent also wants to appeal some issues, it can initiate a cross-appeal.

Meanwhile (in Minnesota, within ten days of filing the notice of appeal), the appellant must request that the trial court reporter prepare and deliver copies of the needed portions of the trial transcript to the trial court administrator and to both attorneys. The typical record of a fully litigated case contains pleadings, motions, orders of the court, exhibits, a transcript of the trial proceedings, the charge to the jury, the verdict, the judgment, and the notice of appeal. The respondent may identify additional portions to be included in the transcript. The trial court administrator then forwards the record, including the transcript, to the appellate court (within ten days after the due date for appellant's brief).

Also during this time, the appellate court may require a prehearing conference between one of the appellate judges or the court's designee and the parties' counsel, to focus or narrow the issues and to discuss what material the court would like covered. During this period, as well as later, settlement talks may occur between counsel.

On a specified date (within thirty days after the delivery of the transcript, in Minnesota state court) the appellant must file and serve its brief. The brief asks the court to reverse or modify the judgment of the trial court and sets out the legal bases for the request.

The respondent's brief (filed and served within thirty days after the appellant's brief is served) responds to appellant's arguments. It also sets forth affirmative arguments as to why the trial court ruled correctly in respondent's favor. Many respondents' attorneys write a rough draft of the respondent's brief during the appellant's briefing period and then add arguments on any unexpected topics after appellant's brief has arrived. This practice prompts respondent's counsel to argue the case affirmatively, rather than reacting only defensively.

The appellant may elect to file a reply brief (in Minnesota, within ten days of service of respondent's brief). The reply brief addresses any unexpected points in the respondent's brief that merit rebuttal.

Some appeals involve a brief by an amicus curiae—"friend of the court." An amicus brief is written by a nonparty with a strong stake in the outcome of the case. The appellate court decides whether to let amici participate in the case, based on whether they will contribute a viewpoint or arguments that the parties are not likely to contribute.

Following the exchange of briefs, the parties may engage in oral arguments before the court. Oral arguments are mandatory before some courts, rare before others; the practice of most courts falls somewhere in between. The oral argument is counsels' last chance to convince the court, but it certainly does not take the place of well written briefs.

The parties then await the court's ruling, which the losing party may decide to appeal further, if an additional appeal is possible.

8. Appellate Strategy and Ethics

When a case moves to the appellate stage, you need to look at the case objectively, to assess the areas of continuing controversy. The task of selecting grounds for the appeal falls primarily on the appellant, although, as already noted, the respondent may cross-appeal. The process of choosing grounds for an appeal entails several steps.

First, you must review the record to ascertain what did in fact occur in the trial court, compared to what you generally recall or impressions based on information from the client or other participants (if a different lawyer handled the case in the lower court). You should verify that witnesses stated what you think they did, that you (or the lawyer at trial) made the necessary motions, and so on.

Second, you must apply the substantive and procedural law to the court's rulings to discern whether any errors occurred and then evaluate whether any errors are within the appellate court's scope of review. As detailed above, the following usually do not receive appellate review: errors that did not culminate in a final judgment by the trial court; errors based on facts not presented to the trial court; errors based on issues or theories not raised at the trial level; and errors which, if corrected by the appellate court, would not result in at least a partial reversal, remand, or modification.

Next, you must evaluate each error according to the applicable standard of appellate review. Some rulings are extremely unlikely candidates for reversal, because the applicable standard of review gives considerable deference to the trial court ruling. In light of the standard of review, you should evaluate the quality of the law, policy, and facts on both sides: Do both sides have plausible arguments? Are your client's arguments supported by statute? mandatory precedent? persuasive precedent? commentary? Which side does public policy favor? How strong are the facts? You should set aside errors that could not overcome the applicable standard of review or could not do so without a stretch that the court is unlikely to make.

Once you have thus discerned the potential bases for appeal, you should explore the scope of the appeal with your client, of course. Your client may not want to pursue one or more points, or your client may have a strong desire to pursue a particular point.

Finally, you should consider the number of points to be raised. Few briefs contain more than three or four major arguments, because including more reduces the space for, and dilutes the effectiveness of, the stronger arguments. On occasion, you may make a larger number of smaller arguments, in hopes of casting doubt on the overall fairness of the trial court proceedings; this tactic is common in the appellant's brief for a losing criminal defendant.

Much of the respondent's task is to respond to the issues or grounds for appeal selected by the appellant. If the appellant does not raise an anticipated issue, the respondent's brief need not address it. (However, if the court might be assisted in its decisionmaking by knowing what respondent's argument would have been, respondent can include a brief comment, perhaps in a footnote or a parenthetical.) If, as respondent's counsel, you are considering raising your own grounds for cross-appeal, you would follow the process just described.

In selecting points to cover and in crafting the brief, both appellant's and respondent's counsel must comply with the ethical principles regarding legal advocacy. The rules (detailed in Chapter 15) preclude pursuing frivolous claims or defenses; knowingly presenting false statements of fact; and knowingly failing to disclose known, adverse, binding precedent not disclosed by opposing counsel. Model Rules of Professional Conduct Rules 3.1, 3.3, 3.4 (1983). These rules are specific expressions of the lawyer's duty to the legal system and justice, as well as to the client, to act with candor and with respect for the law.

The HomeElderCare appeal, framed by the Appellant, raises one major ground for appeal: the invalidity of the living will contract due to any unauthorized practice of law. As already noted, the issue is within the scope of appellate review, and the standard of review is fairly favorable. Although there are weaknesses in HomeElderCare's case, it benefits from favorable mandatory precedent, helpful public policies, and certain favorable facts. Of course, HomeElderCare cares about this issue, especially since its resolution affects more than just Mr. Nelson's contract. And a single ground for appeal makes for a well focused brief.

C. The Function of the Appellate Brief: Audience and Purpose

Your primary audience is the court: the judges and their clerks. At the intermediate appellate court, cases typically are heard by a panel of judges; three is the most common number. Intermediate courts hear only important cases en banc, i.e., as a full court; sometimes after a panel hears a case initially, a full court may rehear the case if the losing party convinces the full court of its significance. Interlocutory appeals may be decided by a single judge or a panel. As a general rule, the highest court hears all cases en banc, which typically involves seven or nine justices. Whatever the number of judges hearing your case, they are likely to have a range of backgrounds, areas of expertise, world views, and preliminary leanings on cases like yours.

The primary purpose of the appellate brief is, of course, to persuade the court to rule in your client's favor and to do so based on sound legal and factual bases. To persuade the court, you must educate those who know little about the area of law involved, inform all of the judges about your client's particular case, and demonstrate the justness of your client's position to those who are skeptical.

Your brief also will be read by opposing counsel and your client. The brief should convince opposing counsel of the strengths of your case, thereby enhancing the chances of settlement, if that possibility exists at such a late stage. For your client, your brief should demonstrate your continuing commitment to the case and provide insight into its legal strengths and weaknesses.

D. The Format of the Appellate Brief

Every court has its own rules as to appellate brief format, so you always should read and follow the applicable rules. The format featured in this part is based on Minnesota's appellate rules, because the sample HomeElderCare case is on appeal to the Minnesota Court of Appeals. Other courts may require different components or sequences of components. Regardless of the required format, you should aim for a brief that is complete, correct, coherent, comprehensible, and convincing.

1. Classic Components of the Main Brief

The following text discusses the components in the appellate brief as they appear to the reader. Of course, you need not write them in this order; indeed, you should save the table of contents and table of authorities until last. As you read this text, you should refer to one or both of the sample briefs at 352 and 364.

Title Page: The title page contains the docket number of the case; the name of the appeals court; the case name; the title of the document, such as

"Appellant's Brief"; and the names, addresses, phone numbers, and attorney registration numbers of the attorneys. The plaintiff typically is listed first and is identified both as plaintiff and by its role in the appeal. The defendant is listed next, identified by its trial and appellate titles. The terms used to identify the parties should be consistent throughout the brief and may be governed by convention or court rule. The title page is color-coded to the identity of the party.

Tables: The table of contents lists page references for the brief components, including all of the point headings within the argument (described below). The table of contents may be the first page the reader consults, so if the point headings are written with care, the reader will have a clear, concise, and logically ordered overview of the argument.

The table of authorities lists cases, statutes, rules, and secondary or other authorities cited in the brief. The table also lists the pages on which each source is cited; "passim" follows an initial page number noted for a very frequently cited source. Generally, authorities are grouped by type and presented alphabetically or numerically within groups. As the rules permit, you may be able to order or group authorities so as to emphasize certain types of authorities over others, thereby driving home a particular view of the case. For example, you may choose not to break out mandatory and persuasive precedent if you are seeking a change in the law and thus are relying heavily on persuasive precedent.

For example, note that HomeElderCare's brief lists cases first, then statutes, reflecting HomeElderCare's emphasis on the common law test of unauthorized practice. See page 354. Mr. Nelson's brief uses the reverse order, reflecting its emphasis on the statutes on unauthorized practice and guardianship. See page 366. His brief also separates Minnesota cases from persuasive precedent, to emphasize that his position is the law elsewhere.

Some jurisdictions merge the information in the tables of contents and authorities into a single table, the table of points and authorities. This table lists the major components of the brief as well as the point headings from the argument, and each point heading is followed by a list of several or all of the authorities cited. The corresponding page numbers appear in the right margin.

Statement of Issues: This component poses the questions the appeals court must answer to resolve the case. Most issues combine law and facts; the law may be either substantive or procedural or both. The trial court's answer is stated after each issue.

Some courts, Minnesota included, require that the issues be phrased neutrally; you can slant the issues only as far as the court would if it were writing an opinion in your favor. The issues usually should be a full question (not a phrase introduced by "whether") and as concise as possible given the ideas to be conveyed. They should be answerable with "yes" or "no." Where there is more than one issue, the set of issues will have more impact if the desired answers are all "yes" or all "no."

The issues are closely related to the point headings in the argument (discussed below). Both reflect the large-scale organization of the argument, and the major point headings usually answer the issues. Some briefs include subissues, which mirror the minor point headings.

The issues from the two HomeElderCare sample briefs are reprinted in Exhibit 17.3, along with the point headings from the two briefs. Note that both sets of issues are neutral enough to be stated by a court, yet both clearly suggest what the favored answer is. The Appellant's fact-centered issue focuses on how HomeElderCare serves its clients and promotes their self-determination. The Respondent's law-centered issues focus on the illegality stemming from the nonlicensure of the social workers, the defectiveness of

---

EXHIBIT 17.3

APPELLATE ISSUES AND POINT HEADINGS

Appellant's Brief

Issues	Point Headings
Is a service contract between Appellant, a private geriatric services agency, and Respondent, an elderly client, invalid on the grounds that the agency practiced law when its trained social worker assisted the elderly client to fill in the blanks on a living will form?	This Court should reverse the summary declaratory judgment in favor of Respondent and should instead grant Appellant's cross-motion for summary judgment, thereby upholding the contract under which a trained social worker for a private geriatric services agency assisted an elderly client to fill in the blanks on a living will form.

      A. The agency did not practice law when its trained social worker assisted the client in filling in the blanks on a living will form.

      B. Even if the social worker practiced law, the contract is valid because the social worker provided the living will services without fraud or incompetence and incidentally to nonlegal counseling.

      C. Public policy favors living wills and therefore also favors a service provider who assists a client in filling in the blanks on the statutory living will form.

Respondent's Brief

Issues	Point Headings
I. Did a social worker—who is not licensed to practice law—engage in unauthorized practice of law when she prepared a defective living will for an elderly client for a fee?	I. The trial court properly ruled that HomeElderCare's social worker engaged in the unauthorized practice of law when she prepared Mr. Nelson's living will for a fee.
II. If there was unauthorized practice of law, is the contract between the social work agency and the client unenforceable, so as to excuse the client from paying for the defective document?	II. Because of this unauthorized practice of law, the contract between HomeElderCare and Mr. Nelson for preparation of the living will is unenforceable, as the trial court properly held.

the living will, and the fee. The issues strongly parallel the major point headings.

In other jurisdictions, the statement of issues may be called "Questions Presented." The trial court's position may not be required. Instead, or in addition, you may be required to list two or three main authorities under each issue.

Statement of the Case: This component contains two portions: (1) the procedural history of the case and (2) the real-world facts of the case. Under the Minnesota rules, this component begins with one or two paragraphs specifying the nature of the case, the court and judge at the trial level, and the procedural history of the case. The procedural history should reflect the direct line of procedural events that led from the outset of the case to the appeal. Appellant may want to show that he or she preserved the right to appeal the pertinent issues, by making the required motions or objections, for instance. Respondent may well emphasize the favorable ruling and reasoning of the trial court, Respondent's hidden ally.

The next portion, a statement of the real-world facts, can be one of the most persuasive parts of the brief. Facts must be stated fully and fairly. Relevant and background facts must be presented; you may include persuasive residual facts, as long as you do so judiciously. Ethical and tactical considerations clearly dictate that unfavorable facts be presented; favorable "facts" may not be created to suit an advocate's purpose. The fact statement should contain all facts discussed in the argument, at least in general terms; in complicated cases, factual details may be reserved for the pertinent portions of the argument. Argumentative statements and legal conclusions should be avoided in the statement of the case. For instance, it would be out of line to characterize an act as "negligent." You are, of course, on firmest ground when stating facts that are plainly and indisputably stated in the record. Nonetheless you may note evidence the other side did not produce, but presumably would have if it had been available (omissions) and what seems to have been true based on what is known (inferences).

Your presentation of the facts should help the court see the events from your client's perspective. For example, although the classic organizational theme for facts is chronology, you may decide to open with a paragraph that highlights the critical event from your client's perspective, even if it did not occur first. Alternatively, you may develop a topical organization that emphasizes the important features from your client's position. You may use perceptual organization to tell the story the way your client experienced it and then present the perspectives of others.

The statement of the case must contain citations to the record to support each fact mentioned. In the appellate setting, you may support a fact in several ways. You must refer the court to the evidence on a fact: for example, a witness' testimony at trial or deposition, or a document admitted at trial. You also may refer to the judge's fact findings or the jury's verdict. Indeed, if the case is on its second round of appeal, you also can refer to the intermediate appellate court's statement of the facts.

In both HomeElderCare sample briefs, the statement of the case begins with the case's procedural history. Both sample briefs convey essentially the same information, yet they convey different subtexts. The HomeElderCare statement (at page 356) underscores the effect of the declaratory judgment in shutting down its living will service for all clients, while Mr. Nelson's state-ment (at page 368) focuses on the favorable trial court ruling.

Both presentations of the real-world facts convey the necessary informa-tion from the stipulated record, including unfavorable facts. Both present the facts persuasively but without relying on argumentative language. Through seemingly minor differences, they create contrasting impressions. For exam-ple, HomeElderCare's brief suggests that Mr. Nelson was responsible for the error (at page 357), while Mr. Nelson's brief intimates the opposite (at page 369); neither asserts that the record clearly answers this question. The HomeElderCare fact statement proceeds topically, while Mr. Nelson's pro-ceeds in a loosely chronological organization. HomeElderCare's statement begins (at page 356) with a description of the valuable services HomeElder-Care provides for its clients, while Mr. Nelson's statement begins (at page 368) with Mr. Nelson's ill health and misdrafted living will.

In other jurisdictions, the two portions of the statement of case may be separately labeled components. Another variation is to present the proce-dural facts at the conclusion of the real-world facts.

Summary of Argument: More than any other component of the brief, the summary of the argument is written to capture the attention of the reader. One to three paragraphs long, it signals what is really at stake and provides an overview of the argument to come, which should appear sensible and straightforward. The tone of the summary should be affirmative; it should not be framed as a rebuttal.

The two sample briefs each contain a summary of the argument, Home-ElderCare's as a separate component (at page 358) and Mr. Nelson's as the first portion of the argument (at page 370). They share these features: me-thodical overview of the main points to come, affirmative language, and a clear statement of the client's position.

Jurisdictions differ on whether a summary is required. Even if it is not required, you often will want to include this material, whether in a separate component so labeled or at the outset of the argument.

Argument—generally: This component presents rules of law, policies, and facts in a demonstration of why the court should find for your client. The appellant concentrates on undermining the trial court's reasoning and rulings, while the respondent uses the trial court as its ally on appeal. That is, the appellant's brief tries to demonstrate reversible error, while the respon-dent's brief tries to maintain the status quo.

Appellate advocacy is four-dimensional involving the facts, substantive law, policy, and procedural law. See Exhibit 17.4 on page 202. Legal advo-cacy entails convincing the court to apply (1) substantive legal rules to (2) the facts of the case so as to favor your client. To do this, you must cite to and explain pertinent mandatory authority; you may cite helpful persuasive authority and may discuss unfavorable persuasive authority. You must reason deductively from the law to the facts, and you should bolster your deductive reasoning with reasoning by example where appropriate. You should directly or indirectly refute the competing authorities and assertions of your oppo-nent, whether they pertain to how to construe the law or how to apply the law to the facts. In most cases, the argument also develops (3) public policy, especially when the case is in the jurisdiction's highest court and challenges the current state of the law. Even in the usual case briefed for an intermedi-

EXHIBIT 17.4

LAW/POLICY/FACT DIAGRAM FOR APPELLATE BRIEF

declaratory judgment ➔ granted on summary judgment by trial court; so, standard of review =
- any genuine issues of material facts? see stipluation
- did trial court err in applying law?

contract valid or invalid?

- lack of licensure? ──────────────⟶ | social workers |

- unauthorized practice—here, law practice?

  - draft legal documents? ──────⟶ | living will |

  - give legal advice or counsel? ──────⟶ | proxy/guardian; medical treatment |

  - answering difficult or doubtful questions
    incidentally to nonlegal services?

- is policy of statute undermined?

  - fraud? ──────────────⟶ | none here |

  - incompetence? ──────────⟶ | 45-minute training |

  - incidental to nonlegal services? ────⟶ | mixture of medical, moral, legal issues |

- -

policy considerations

- avoid incompetence—unauthorized practice statute versus

- promote living wills—living will statute

ate appeals court, policy can be important; appeals courts sometimes create precedent and seek to do so based on solid policy grounds.

In addition, at the appellate level the interaction between (4) procedural law and substantive law is complex. The standard of appellate review envelopes trial-level procedural law, which in turn envelopes the substantive law, which in turn is applied to the facts.

The standard of review can present an organizational challenge. If the same standard of review governs all of the issues, it can be stated at the outset of the argument. If different standards govern different issues, then the discussion of each topic should begin with a paragraph or so on the applicable standard of review. If both sides agree on the applicable standard of review and it is a common one, the statement of the standard of review can be very brief.

Of course, legal propositions must be fully and accurately cited. Generally, you need not provide citations to the record as you refer to facts within the argument, because the citations in the fact statement suffice. However, you should provide appropriate citations to the record if you quote from the record, provide more detail than in the fact statement, or want to highlight a particular passage.

To further promote the flow of your argument, you should be especially careful to use transitional words or phrases, overviews, and summaries to signal the relationships among the parts of the argument.

Footnotes may be used occasionally in appellate briefs. Footnotes should contain only material that is tangential to the main text. That is, the reader should not lose any essential meaning by not reading a footnote. Footnotes are most commonly used to convey information that is needed to make the brief more complete, yet would interrupt the argument's flow.

The arguments in the two HomeElderCare sample briefs both address the package of procedural and substantive law, policy, and facts depicted in Exhibit 17.4. (Exhibit 17.4 is phrased neutrally; the same diagram can be used to sketch arguments to be made for one party or the other.) The two unauthorized-practice arguments demonstrate the types of analysis presented in appellate briefs. Both briefs grapple with statutory language, rely on state case law, and reason by example from the leading case to the facts of this case—arriving at different conclusions, of course. Both briefs use policy arguments (at pages 362, 371, 373); although the court is not the highest court, policy is especially important where the issue is new and the rule of law itself calls for policy analysis. Given the nearly de novo standard of review (which appears near the opening in both briefs), neither brief emphasizes the trial court's opinion; nonetheless, the Respondent's brief refers to the trial court's ruling more often than does the Appellant's brief.

Argument—point headings: Point headings in appellate briefs present the main assertions the court must accept to rule in that party's favor. Point headings can be partisan in their message, but not so much as to lose credibility with the reader. Read together, a set of point headings should provide a clear and logical outline of the brief, showing the order of and relationships among the arguments.

Each point heading should be a single sentence. It should be forcefully phrased: concise, to the point, affirmative in tone. Generally, a major heading should combine legal rules and facts to form a distinct conclusion that the court should reach to rule for the client. Most major headings reflect procedural as well as substantive law, because cases arise in particular procedural postures. Minor point headings provide steps of the analysis, policy, or reasons. They need not always be complete *fact* + *law* combinations.

You should strive to make your point headings informative. Very general point headings are of little help to the court, because they do not focus on a specific legal problem and do not arise from the facts of the case. At the same time, avoid burdensome point headings. Too many facts or legal principles make for point headings that are unduly lengthy, clumsy, and hard to grasp. If the reader must read the heading more than once to understand it, its meaning probably will be lost because the reader may well not read it a second time. A burdensome point heading should be rephrased as multiple major point headings or a major heading with minor headings, or it should state the main point and leave the subordinate points to the text of the argument.

Point headings are organized in outline form, preceded by Roman numerals (I, II), capital letters (A, B), or Arabic numbers (1, 2). Take care not to use headings more detailed than these three levels, or you may lose your reader. As in outlining, if there is no "B," you should not use an "A."

To set point headings apart from the text and show their hierarchical relationships, use whatever format is required by your court. Most commonly, courts do not require a particular format; in that case, use any of the following or a combination: open lines above and below the heading, indentation, underlining, boldface, italics, initial caps, and all capital letters. Use the latter two sparingly, if at all, because they reduce readability.

The point headings from the two HomeElderCare sample briefs, which appear in Exhibit 17.3, share several features. They are assertive, but not overwrought. Taken together, they link facts, law (both procedural and substantive), and policy. Within each set, the relationships among the headings are clear: by the overall issue and A, B, and C in HomeElderCare's brief; by a transitional phrase (as well as I, II) in Mr. Nelson's brief. The point headings convey the key dimensions of the case (the parties, living will drafting, fee, contract validity, unauthorized practice of law) without taxing the reader with excessive detail.

The point headings differ, as they should. Only Mr. Nelson's point headings refer to the proper rulings of the trial court. HomeElderCare's point headings posit the case as a contract case which includes a subtopic of unauthorized practice of law, while Mr. Nelson's headings posit the case as involving primarily the unauthorized practice of law and only secondarily the issue of contract invalidity.

Conclusion and Signature: The conclusion is a concise statement of the relief requested. It need not, but may, restate the argument or cite authority. Keep it short. A signature block follows the conclusion. The closing typically reads "Respectfully submitted, . . . ," followed by the attorney's signature and information (name, client representation, firm affiliation, address, phone number, and attorney registration number).

The conclusions of the two sample briefs contain straightforward statements of the respective clients' desired outcomes. Mr. Nelson's conclusion briefly restates his two main arguments, framed as favorable trial court rulings.

Other components: One or more of the following also may be required in your jurisdiction:

- a request for (or waiver of) oral argument, if oral arguments are not automatically granted;
- a statement of the appellate court's jurisdiction;
- a statement certifying that the brief has been served;

- a citation for any published opinions of lower courts;
- a preliminary statement, which typically covers the identities of the parties, the nature of the case, and its disposition below; and
- citations to or quotations from statutes or constitutional provisions.

Nearly every jurisdiction requires an appendix at the end of appellant's brief that contains pertinent parts of the record. Respondent's brief may include additional appendix material if the needed parts of the record are not in appellant's appendix. In some jurisdictions, the appendix includes constitutional or statutory provisions. Be sure to read the appellate rules on brief format for details of these components.

2. Respondent's Brief and the Reply Brief

As intimated above, in general, the respondent's brief follows the same form as the appellant's brief. The statement of the issues, real-world facts, and procedural posture may be optional, but a savvy advocate usually does not let opposing counsel have the only say on these matters.

The reply brief has no particular format, but its purpose is to respond to points in respondent's brief not covered in appellant's main brief. The most common format includes a summary, argument, and conclusion. It is less common to include a fact or issue statement.

3. Comparison of Appellate Brief to Other Documents

While the appellate brief is the most formal and elaborate of the various documents used to present legal analysis, it has strong parallels to the office memo and the motion practice memorandum, as shown in Exhibit 17.5.

E. REVIEW OF CHAPTER 17

Appeals provide an important safeguard against trial court error. The following rules preserve the proper roles of the trial and appellate courts: the final judgment rule, the prohibition against new facts and theories on appeal, the reversible error rule, standards of review, and mandatory and discretionary review.

An important step in the appellate process is the preparation of the appellate brief, written to convince the court (as well as opposing counsel and the client) of the justness of the client's position. A typical appellate brief format includes the following components:

(1) The title page identifies the case, the court, the lawyers, and the document.
(2) The tables orient the reader to the points made and legal authorities relied on in the brief.

EXHIBIT 17.5

COMPARISON OF OFFICE MEMO, MOTION PRACTICE MEMORANDUM, AND APPELLATE BRIEF

Office Memo	*Motion Practice Memorandum*	*Appellate Brief*

caption ———————————————— caption ———————————————— title page

table of contents
table of authorities

issues   introduction or summary   statement of issues

procedure

short answers   facts   statement of the case
                                                             (covering facts and
                                                             procedure)

facts   issues   summary of argument

discussion ———————————————— argument ———————————————— argument

conclusion ———————————————— conclusion with signature ——— conclusion with signature

(3) The statement of issues frames the questions to be decided by the appellate court.

(4) The statement of the case informs the court of the real-world and procedural facts of the case.

(5) The summary of argument presents a brief distillation of the legal arguments.

(6) The argument component states the client's argument and draws together substantive and procedural law, policy, and facts, with point headings flagging the main assertions.

(7) The conclusion states the relief desired by the client and includes the attorney's signature.

The resulting brief should be complete, correct, cohesive, comprehensible, and convincing. Further strategies for achieving these criteria appear in Chapter 16 (basic advocacy) and Chapter 18 (advanced advocacy).

THE ART AND PHILOSOPHY OF ADVOCACY

> Tell all the Truth but tell it slant—
> Success in Circuit lies—
> —Emily Dickinson

A. INTRODUCTION

Truly successful legal advocacy entails not only careful selection and development of points to be made on the client's behalf, but also artful presentation of those points. Chapter 16 discusses the former; this chapter focuses on the latter. More specifically, this chapter explores ways to "slant" your prose to promote the points you want to make and downplay points that are less important or unfavorable, set the proper tone and pitch, handle concessions and rebuttals with finesse, and accomplish the most challenging task facing the advocate—conceptualizing a change in the law.

For examples, this chapter draws on the sample briefs in the fictional HomeElderCare appeal at pages 352 and 364. The topics discussed in this chapter generally are applicable to other advocacy settings as well.

B. AN ANALOGY: PHOTOGRAPHY

Photographers and lawyers share the same opportunity: to use the tools of their trade to present what exists or has happened in the best light possible. They both seek to make a point about their subjects and do so in part through the tone of the work. Of course, the tools of the two trades are rather different. Photographers use lighting, lenses, film, and development processes in various ways. Lawyers use only words, but words are remarkably powerful and flexible tools.

Ultimately photographers and lawyers can alter how the observer sees a subject. In a compelling photograph, a photographer can alter the viewer's understanding of and future response to the scene. In a compelling argument, the lawyer can alter the court's understanding of the law and, indeed, bring about justice and perhaps also a change in the law.

C. "SLANTING" YOUR PROSE

The way something is said often determines its impact. This part discusses five aspects of writing style that you can use to maximize the persuasive impact of your prose: space allocation, sequence of material, syntax, semantics, and special sentences.

1. Space Allocation

The more we read about a topic, the more we attend to it, the more we recall about it, and the greater the importance we attach to it. Hence you should allocate more space to the material you want the reader to remember and less space to the material you need to include yet want to de-emphasize.

This strategy applies to various components of the brief. For example, in the statement of case or facts, you could write several paragraphs on your client's circumstances and motivations, while covering the adverse effect of the client's actions on the opponent in only a few lines. The summary of argument should be devoted almost entirely to the strong points of the argument, and only a phrase or two to the weak points, if even that. In the argument, you could present several paragraphs on a favorable element of the rule and only one paragraph on a more troublesome element. You could state a favorable rule in some detail, quoting and paraphrasing and illustrating it (without undue repetition), while providing a terser statement of an adverse rule. If you must state your opponent's argument for candor or rebuttal purposes, do so very briefly.

One way to implement this strategy is to allocate percentages to various topics before you write and then monitor how well your draft complies with your allocation. Or, after you have completed a draft, draw brackets around your major topics, label those brackets, and compare the sizes of the brackets.

The sample briefs reveal contrasting space allocations. HomeElderCare's statement of the case allocates only 2 lines to the trial court ruling, while Mr.

EXHIBIT 18.1

SEQUENCE AND SPACE ALLOCATION
IN CASE ARGUMENTS

# lines	Appellant HomeElderCare	# lines	Respondent Nelson
7	Standards of review	6	Standard of review
75	No unauthorized practice	124	Unauthorized practice
46	* ■ no legal advice; not difficult or doubtful	11	* ■ public policy to protect public
10	■ not "legal document"	3	* ■ social worker not attorney
12	* ■ not will	14	* ■ "legal document"
29	Contract is valid	68	■ gave legal advice; difficult and doubtful
4	* ■ no fraud		
8	■ no incompetence	4	* ■ charging fee
3	* ■ incidental professional services	12	* ■ persuasive precedent
		48	Contract unenforceable
34	Public policy	6	* ■ general rule invalidating
10	* ■ right to privacy and control body	11	■ exception based on legislative intent
15	■ role and setting of living wills	14	■ incompetence
7	■ HEC's role in completing living will forms	9	* ■ public policy of unauthorized practice statute
		8	* ■ recovery of fee
	*strong topics		

Nelson's brief explains that ruling in 7 lines. As shown in Exhibit 18.1, Mr. Nelson's discussion of unauthorized practice runs 124 lines; HomeElderCare's, 75 lines. Mr. Nelson's argument includes 12 lines on persuasive precedent; HomeElderCare's brief has none.

2. Sequence of Points

According to the primacy effect, we process most thoroughly and remember best the information that appears at the start of a text. According to the recency effect, we process and remember nearly as well the information that appears last. Information in the middle of a text recedes in memory.

As you organize your brief, you must, of course, follow format requirements, and you must present the material within each component in a logical order. For instance, chronological, topical, or perceptual sequences generally work best for fact statements. In devising your sequence of legal topics, threshold issues generally precede other issues, claims precede defenses, etc.

If several sequences could be proper and logical, you should take advantage of the primacy and recency effects. You may choose to follow one of these sequences:

- ■ The sandwich sequence: Present your strongest material first, "sandwich" your weakest material in the middle, and finish with your second strongest material.

- The running-start sequence: Present your strongest material first, so that it makes a strong impression and dispels most of the doubts the reader might have. Then present your next strongest material, so as to dispel most remaining doubts. And so on, until the last doubt is dispelled.
- The momentum sequence: Start with weaker material and finish with the strongest, thereby starting slowly but finishing with your strongest material.

These sequences can be used in various components. You can use them as you decide which facts should open and close the statement of the case. You can use these sequences in ordering the issues and hence the main legal topics (or rules) within the argument; you also can use these sequences to order the subtopics (or elements) within your argument on a legal rule.

The sample briefs in the HomeElderCare case demonstrate these strategies. Mr. Nelson's statement of the case's facts begins with his situation, while HomeElderCare's begins with the services HomeElderCare provides; both authors led with the client's strong facts, as per the primacy effect. As synopsized in Exhibit 18.1, HomeElderCare's argument on the unauthorized practice of law sandwiches the most difficult topic (legal document) between favorable topics (legal advice and testamentary wills). Mr. Nelson's argument on contract invalidity displays the momentum sequence; after a few lines of general principles, it confronts the leading adverse precedent, then moves on to a discussion of policy and to the clearly favorable argument about HomeElderCare's charging of fees.

At the small-scale level, although you usually will follow the introduction-rule-application-conclusion (IRAC) sequence, you may deviate from this pattern for persuasive purposes. For example, you may lead with a fact discussion or policy if these are your client's strengths.

For example, in footnote 2 of the HomeElderCare brief (see 359), the facts on charging a fee precede the statement of the rule because the facts are far more favorable than the rule. Mr. Nelson's argument on unauthorized practice (at 371) begins with a discussion of the policy underlying that rule; the rule and its application follow.

3. Syntax

Readers respond more to ideas presented in a strongly framed sentence than to ideas couched in an obscure manner. Careful use of syntax allows you to highlight material you wish the reader to remember and downplay material you wish to de-emphasize. For instance, you may wish to de-emphasize concessions and your opponent's arguments that need to be stated for rebuttal purposes. Here are some specific methods:

- State favorable material in short, simple sentences, and state unfavorable material in long, complex (but still understandable) sentences. Readers retain information that is stated simply better than they retain information that is stated in complex sentences that draw attention away from the sentence's content.

- Place unfavorable material in dependent clauses and favorable material in main clauses. Main clauses demand more attention than dependent clauses.
- Use the active voice for verbs relating favorable material, and use the passive voice for verbs relating unfavorable material. Active voice demands more attention than passive voice. Also, with passive voice, you can obscure the actor; this strategy is appropriate where the actor is unknown or unimportant or where you do not want to highlight who the actor is.
- Similarly, use nominalization, instead of a simple verb, for unfavorable information. Nominalization and passive voice have similar purposes and effect.

Exhibit 18.2 shows how these strategies are used for persuasive effect in the HomeElderCare sample briefs' fact statements.

4. Semantics

Readers respond more to concepts stated in vivid terms than to concepts stated in bland terms. Use vivid words for material you want your reader to notice and recall, and use nondescript language for material you wish your reader to notice less.

EXHIBIT 18.2

SYNTAX

Sentence length

- These social workers are not attorneys. (Nelson brief)
- When he was hospitalized, his son realized that the living will made Roger Nelson's proxy for medical decisions also his guardian for financial decisions, although Roger Nelson now desires otherwise. (HomeElderCare brief)

Dependent/main clauses

- While neither Ms. Hall nor Mr. Nelson can remember the details of their interaction leading up to the defective document [dependent clause], HomeElderCare social workers, including Ms. Hall, have followed certain procedures [main clause]. (Nelson brief)

Active/passive voice

- The social workers do not deviate from the form, ... [active] (HomeElderCare brief)
- In this living will, Mr. Nelson's minister was designed as the proxy authorized to make medical decisions . . . . [passive] (Nelson's brief)

Nominalization

- Ms. Hall usually provides a standard explanation of the roles of proxies, guardians, and conservators . . . . (HomeElderCare brief)

Perhaps the most important semantic choice to be made is how to label the parties, where court rules do not mandate or forbid certain labels. One option is procedural labels, such as Plaintiff and Defendant or Appellant and Respondent. A middle ground is labels reflecting the parties' roles in the dispute, such as buyer and seller, landlord and tenant. A final option is their proper names. Generally the first option is the most abstract, and the reader may feel rather distanced from the situation or even confused about who plays which roles in the litigation. In most situations, the second option comes closest to the way the court needs to think about the parties. The third personalizes the parties the most, especially if they are individuals.

If you are writing about individuals and using their names, you have several further options. Some legal writers prefer to use merely last names, which sounds matter-of-fact, while others prefer Mr. Nelson or Dr. Richards, for example, which sounds more respectful. You should use first names only if the individual is a child or if two or more individuals of the same sex have the same last name.

Less obvious but equally important are the labels you use for the key legal concepts in the case. Most legal concepts can be referred to by more than one name, and some labels carry more serious connotations than others. Generally you will want to use the serious label for a cause of action if your client is the wronged party and the milder label if your client is defending.

Finally, pay close attention to the verbs you use to describe the actions of various parties. Some verbs are more vivid than others. Adding an adverb to a dull verb to make it stronger is less effective than using a more vivid verb.

In the sample HomeElderCare briefs, both authors chose to employ proper names for the parties. They chose different phrases for various other concepts, as shown in Exhibit 18.3.

5. Special Sentences

Some statements are more memorable than others, because of the way they present their messages. Within limits, it is appropriate to use rhetorical flourish in legal advocacy. Be sure to use it to make your most important assertions; do not draw undue attention to a minor assertion in this way. Indeed,

---

EXHIBIT 18.3

SEMANTIC CHOICES

HomeElderCare's phrasing	*Mr. Nelson's phrasing*
filling in the blanks on the living will form	prepared Mr. Nelson's living will
medical and ethical issues	legal obligation of doctors issues of client autonomy
patient	declarant
valid contract	enforcement of contract

you may wish to express your theory of the case early on by use of one of the following seven devices, and you would then return to that phrasing in key spots throughout the brief.

First, *juxtaposition* involves a sharp contrast between two ideas presented one after another. The second idea is somewhat startling, given the first.

Second, *allusion* involves an implied or indirect reference to a commonly known situation, typically drawn from history or literature. The allusion prompts the reader to draw the lesson from that situation into the case.

Third, an *aphorism* is a terse statement of a point, designed to draw the reader's attention and linger in the reader's mind. A maxim is an aphorism conveying an important truth or precept.

Fourth, *anaphora* involves the repeated use of a phrase in several consecutive sentences, so as to underscore that phrase and strengthen the connection among the ideas.

Fifth, *alliteration* involves repeated use of a starting letter, typically a consonant, in neighboring words to make a phrase stand out.

Sixth, a *rhetorical question* involves asking a question without answering it. The reader notices the question because we generally attend more closely to questions than to statements and because most of your text is in the form of statements. The question may imply an answer, or it may have no good answer. Either way, the reader ponders the answer or lack thereof. Rhetorical questions are not, of course, used for the issues in the case; your text must provide convincing and clear answers to your issues. Rather, rhetorical questions should be used for smaller points. Some lawyers avoid rhetorical questions on the ground that they are too showy, so you should use this technique sparingly.

Seventh and lastly, consider selective use of *quotes*. To some extent, you must quote the law, especially as to statutory material and key phrases from the common law. You also may quote portions of the record and nonessential passages from legal authorities, such as key portions of the reasoning in a case or helpful commentary. If you quote too much, the reader will not take special note of any of your quotes, and your brief will not flow well. If you quote sparingly, the quotes will stand out.

The brief of Mr. Nelson in the HomeElderCare case has several examples of rhetorical flourish, albeit fairly restrained. These appear in Exhibit 18.4.

EXHIBIT 18.4

SPECIAL SENTENCES

As a consequence of the actions of Ms. Hall, Mr. Nelson designated his minister as both his proxy and guardian—even though this arrangement was not what he desired. (juxtaposition)

A social worker should not be paid for defective legal work. (aphorism)

These social workers are not attorneys. These social workers do not have law degrees. These social workers have not been admitted to practice law in Minnesota or anywhere else. (anaphora)

Note that both briefs quote the statutory language at issue in the case as well as the common law rule, of course. Both quote the court's reasoning in the leading unauthorized practice case—but different language for different purposes. See pages 360 and 372. HomeElderCare's brief also quotes material about the right to privacy, and Mr. Nelson's brief quotes a case law passage about the dangers of unauthorized practice, both important points for their respective clients.

D. SETTING THE PROPER TONE AND PITCH

Words make or break legal cases by setting proper or improper tones. Within a range of reason, you may choose the tone for your brief. Tone is in part a matter of your personal style or voice as a writer and in part a reflection of the needs of the specific case. Some writers routinely choose a measured tone, others a more impassioned tone. Some cases call for a matter-of-fact tone, others for more emotion.

One tone is unacceptable, however: sarcasm. You may be tempted to use sarcasm toward the opposing party or opposing counsel (especially if the case has been in acrimonious litigation for some time). Or you may be tempted to use sarcasm toward the lower court that ruled against your client. You should not succumb to these temptations. Sarcasm would deflect the court from its task, which is to decide between conflicting arguments, not to decide who is the better person. Furthermore, the court may wonder whether you are resorting to sarcasm because your arguments are not strong enough to stand on their own merit. Finally, it is unprofessional to treat the court, your opponent, or others in the case with disrespect.

To avoid sarcasm, focus your brief on the law and facts of the case. Do not write about opposing counsel. Read your brief with this question in mind: If I were opposing counsel, would I find the tone of this brief to be appropriate?

Related to tone is the issue of pitch. Generally, by the time you write a brief, you are well immersed in the facts and law of the case. Two of your audiences, your opposing counsel and your client, will be similarly immersed, but the case will be unknown to your primary reader, the court. If you were to write the entire brief at your level of understanding, you would risk losing the court. Rather, you should see yourself as writing for an intelligent but uninformed reader. A useful strategy is to ask yourself: What did I need to know about the facts and law when I first took on this case? And what has been difficult for me to sort out as I have worked on this case? Your brief should include the former, in compact form, at the outset of a topic, then proceed to focus on the latter.

Both HomeElderCare sample briefs employ a moderate tone. Mr. Nelson's is slightly more impassioned than HomeElderCare's, reflecting Mr. Nelson's frustration at the situation he experienced. HomeElderCare's maintains an even-handed tone, to avoid the impression that HomeElderCare is attacking Mr. Nelson, its own client. Neither attacks the other lawyer or the trial court.

The brief written for HomeElderCare maintains a consistent pitch throughout, the author having judged the topics to be fairly accessible. The brief written for Mr. Nelson reflects a rising pitch in both main arguments, the first starting with the basic concept applied to the facts before proceeding to application of the statute, the second presenting hornbook material before exploring the jurisdiction's cases.

E. FRAMING YOUR ARGUMENTS WITH FINESSE

Many legal arguments entail two potential troublespots: concessions and rebuttals of the opponent's argument. While both enable the court to fully understand the case, they also distract from the argument you want to make on the client's behalf. Hence, both should be presented carefully and with finesse.

1. Concessions

The need to present a concession arises when the two sides concur on a point and that point favors your client's opponent. Concessions may be handled several ways. First, you may implicitly concede the point, neither stating the point nor presenting an argument to the contrary. For example, you could note that the issue concerns a statute and begin your argument with a discussion of the exceptions, implicitly conceding that your client's case falls within the scope and general rule of the statute.

Other techniques for handling concessions involve explicit statements of the conceded point. In the technique known as "confession and avoidance," you state the conceded point but move on to an argument that nullifies the harmful impact of the concession. For example, you could state that the client falls within a statutory definition, yet argue that the client's conduct is permitted by a statutory exception.

In a third technique known as "assuming arguendo," you state the conceded point for purposes of the present argument only, and you emphasize that the point is not conceded beyond the present argument. For example, you would argue first that your client is outside the scope of the statute, then assume arguendo that the client falls within the scope in order to show how its conduct is governed by a statutory exception.

The implicit concession and confession-and-avoidance are true concessions, while assuming-arguendo is a limited-purpose concession. Whenever you are stating a concession, you would use the methods described in this chapter to deflect the reader's attention from the concession. For example, you could allocate little space to the concession, place it in a dependent clause, or state it in passive voice or nominalization. Indeed, if you deem the concession unnecessary to the logical flow of your argument, you could place it in a footnote. Meanwhile, you would allocate more space to your argument responding to the concession, place it in the main clause, or use active voice to express it.

In the sample briefs in the HomeElderCare case, several concessions appear. HomeElderCare implicitly conceded that its social workers are not licensed as lawyers; its argument proceeds directly from a quotation of the unauthorized practice statute to the prohibition against giving legal advice. Exhibit 18.5 presents two explicit concessions; note how affirmative arguments tightly frame both concessions.

2. Rebuttals

Most of your argument should address points of clash in the case, the topics on which the two sides disagree. As to many points of clash, you will find that stating your affirmative argument suffices to rebut your opponent's argument, that the relationship between the two arguments will be apparent to

---

EXHIBIT 18.5

CONCESSIONS AND REBUTTALS

Confession and Avoidance (in Mr. Nelson's brief)

> The *Gardner* rule must be applied in "a common sense way which will protect the public and not hamper or burden that public interest with impractical and technical restrictions which have no reasonable justification." [citation omitted] The restriction on social workers preparing living wills may burden the social worker who wishes to practice law. [confession] But the restriction is not impractical or merely technical; it is more than reasonably justified when viewed from the proper perspective—the client's. [avoidance]
> (*Note:* six sentences developing the client's perspective follow.)

Assuming arguendo (in HomeElderCare brief)

> . . . To avoid the rendering of legal advice, HomeElderCare practice calls for the social worker to suggest that the client consult an attorney if the client wishes to deviate from the form or has legal questions. Thus, the social worker did not provide legal advice. [affirmative argument]
> However, even if the social worker touched on legal matters, [concession for purposes of proceeding], the service would not constitute unauthorized practice of law under Minnesota case law. [next affirmative argument]

Rebuttal (in HomeElderCare brief)

> As it does for all its services, HomeElderCare charged a fee for its living will services. [factual introduction] The charging of a fee should not render this service the practice of law [Mr. Nelson's argument], any more than the charging of a fee for home maintenance services would render that service the practice of law. *Cf. Cardinal v. Merrill Lynch Realty/Burnet, Inc.* . . . [rebuttal]

any reader of the brief, and that little if anything needs to be said in so many words about the opponent's argument.

In other situations, you will determine that your brief should refer to, or perhaps even state, your opponent's argument because the relationship between the two arguments is subtle and will not otherwise be clear to the reader. Or your rebuttal to your opponent's argument may be understandable only as a negation of the opponent's argument, rather than an affirmative assertion.

When you determine that your brief should indeed state or refer to your opponent's argument, do so with care. You will accentuate your opponent's argument if you state it in a position of primacy, at length, in vivid language, or with noteworthy quotes. You should instead minimize the opponent's argument by, for example, referring to it rather than fully stating it, placing the reference in a dependent clause, or sandwiching the reference in the middle of the passage on the topic. Another option is to rebut your opponent's argument in a footnote. Even if you think the opponent's argument is very weak, take care to criticize it in a professional tone, taking aim at the ideas rather than the author.

For example, Exhibit 18.5 presents HomeElderCare's rebuttal of Mr. Nelson's well taken argument that charging a fee suggests unauthorized practice. The brief downplays this topic; it appears in a footnote. Mr. Nelson's legal assertion is stated briefly, sandwiched between two sensible factual assertions.

F.   CONCEPTUALIZING A CHANGE IN THE LAW

Some disputes become litigation because of the parties' inclinations to carry on the dispute. However, most lengthy litigation occurs because the parties (and their lawyers) assign different legal meanings to their dispute. That is, the parties (and their lawyers) disagree about what happened, how the law applies to what happened, what the law is, or what it should be. In the latter two situations, when the law is uncertain, the lawyers have the privilege and responsibility of contributing to the development of the law by proposing a rule of law. The lawyers' task entails not only arguing the client's case, but also conceptualizing the law.

This part first describes some concrete steps lawyers take in such situations. As you seek to conceptualize the law, you may find it useful to step outside the law; this part shows how to use thinking from other disciplines to enrich your conceptualization of the law.

1. Traditional Steps in Advocating for a Rule of Law

Because courts adhere to stare decisis, and because courts are bound to follow statutory language in most situations, it is preferable to argue a case by showing how it fits within established law. You should engage in a discussion of what the rule should be only when your case does not fit an established rule or when an alternative to the established rule would provide a strong basis for your desired outcome.

In general, the less radical your position, the more likely it is to be adopted by the court. Hence an important step is to identify how your rule connects to existing law. For example, show how your rule simply adds an element or defense to an existing common law claim, or show how your rule adapts a common law claim from one setting to your client's setting. Alternatively, you might show how your interpretation of a statute is necessitated by, intimated in, or resolves ambiguity in an existing interpretation of the statute, or show that your approach has been taken by the court in interpreting other statutes.

Another option is to rely on persuasive precedent and legal commentary. This route may be your only option, or you may use these materials to bolster your argument based on binding authority. Select the strongest persuasive material you can, based on its source, reasoning, factual parallels to your case, and currency. If there is an opposing strand of persuasive authority, you should acknowledge it, to fulfill your obligation of candor toward the court, and then show its weaknesses, to bolster your argument.

If the court properly perceives that your request is to make new law, it is likely to be concerned about the wisdom of doing so in your particular case. You therefore must show how the proposed rule would apply to your case, yielding a clearly equitable result. You should dispel the court's concern over ambushing the opposing party with an unforeseen rule, by showing that the opposing party should have foreseen the change you are proposing, by showing that the existing rule improperly favors your client's opponent, or by showing that the opponent does not deserve sympathy, given its actions.

The court also is likely to be concerned about the rule's impact beyond your case. The court may worry that the rule will be taken too far and will be thought to cover related yet different situations (the proverbial "slippery slope"). You must show, as best you can, where the limits of your rule are, so the court will be able to provide guidance for future situations and need not fear a rash of cases exploring the new rule. You should show how the proposed rule yields sound results in the situations it would govern. You also must show why the rule accords with public policy, by identifying those policies and using your case as an illustration of them.

While the fictional HomeElderCare case involves a new application of existing law, it does not involve making new law. The *Weatherston's* case cited by both parties did entail the making of new law. The lawyer for Weatherston's needed to convince the court that it should uphold a contract in violation of a statute that regulates a profession to safeguard the public, although the court's previous case law suggested otherwise. Weatherston's lawyer might have cited the current rule, noted its essential purpose as protecting clients, posited that there could be a case involving a technical statutory violation but no harm to or misleading of the client, highlighted the interests of the unlicensed professional in such a situation and the windfall to the client if the contract is not upheld, and then crafted a rule to reflect the new approach and applied it to the *Weatherston's* facts. If persuasive precedent in favor of the new rule were available, it would be presented for the court's consideration.

2. Stepping Outside the Law

Disciplines other than law also consider issues of justice and fairness. Two important law-related disciplines are economics and psychology.

a. Economics

Economic analysis is premised on the assumption that people usually make rational choices in allocating and using their resources to achieve the best possible result for themselves, whether in terms of wealth as it is traditionally defined, or in terms of utility—that is, intangible benefits such as satisfaction or security. Society benefits as individual members engage in transactions, each maximizing their utilities. Transactions are desirable if both parties gain ground, or one gains and the other does not lose ground, or one gains more ground than the other loses. Accordingly, legal rules that disturb the rational and voluntary distribution of resources are inefficient and therefore undesirable. Legal rules should constrain behavior only when defects in the relationship between the parties impair their ability to make rational and voluntary choices.

If this perspective were brought to bear on the *Weatherston's* case, it would provide a strong rationale for the outcome sought by Weatherston's. Presumably the contract between Weatherston's and Minnesota Mutual was formed because both parties found it beneficial. The evidence did not show that defects in their relationship impaired their contract formation; indeed, Minnesota Mutual was fully informed at the time of formation of the facts it later cited in refusing to perform the contract. If Minnesota Mutual could shirk its responsibilities without more grounds than it actually had, the efficacy of contracts would be undercut.

b. Psychology

An important branch of psychology is the study of moral reasoning. According to one school of thought, often associated with Carol Gilligan, difficult issues are not easily decided by yes/no answers based on ranking of interests according to abstract principles. Rather, moral reasoning involves consideration of a wide range of concerns held by various participants in the situation and then seeking a solution that accommodates as many of these interests as possible.

This approach has strong parallels to the stakeholder analysis discussed in Chapter 9's discussion of policy analysis. In *Weatherston's*, this approach would call for consideration of the interests of at least Weatherston's, Minnesota Mutual, the individuals who would work in or visit the building, and the general public. A ranking of the respective interests of Weatherston's and Minnesota Mutual might suggest that Weatherston's should be paid and Minnesota Mutual should pay according to the contract. But this result does not take into account the safety or welfare of people occupying the building or the public need for effective enforcement of the engineering licensure statute. A solution that would accommodate these less visible interests would be to pay Weatherston's a figure representing the value of the materials provided, for example, but not recovery of his anticipated profit. This outcome would deter unlicensed professionals from crossing the line to the detriment of the public.

G. REVIEW OF CHAPTER 18

This chapter has emphasized the artistry of legal advocacy, showing how you can use the tools of the lawyer's trade—words—to convey the client's case in a convincing way. The methods available to the legal advocate include space allocation, sequence of points, syntax, semantics, and special sentences (such as aphorisms and juxtaposition). Your wording choices fix the tone of your brief to reflect your personal voice, the nature of the case, and your respect for all participants in the litigation; your arguments determine its pitch, which should reflect the needs of your primary reader, the court. The methods discussed in this chapter can be used to present concessions and rebuttals persuasively. In addition, this chapter has explored the steps of legal analysis and the use of other disciplines involved in executing one of the special responsibilities of the lawyer: bringing about change in the law.

ORAL ADVOCACY

> Proceed. You have my biased attention.
> —Learned Hand, speaking to a counsel who sought to re-argue a motion, quoted in M. Frances McNamara, *2000 Famous Legal Quotations*

A. INTRODUCTION

After the memoranda or briefs have been filed and served, the advocates may have a chance to present oral arguments to the court. Oral arguments occur in both trial courts and appellate courts.

This chapter first discusses the role of oral advocacy (as distinct from written advocacy) and typical procedures in trial and appellate courts. It then covers preparation for and delivery of the oral argument, with a focus on the critical task of answering the court's questions. The techniques suggested in this chapter will aid you in presenting an argument that is complete, correct, comprehensible, cohesive, and convincing.

The examples in the text of this chapter are drawn from a sample oral argument on appeal in the fictional case of *Nelson v. HomeElderCare*. You should read the transcript, at page 377, before reading further in this chapter.

B. THE FUNCTION OF ORAL ARGUMENT: AUDIENCE AND PURPOSE

1. A Conversation with the Court

An oral argument is a conversation with the court, not a speech to the court. You should welcome it as a chance to talk with the judge or judges about the arguments in your brief or memorandum, to find out the court's concerns and misgivings, and to dispel them. Rather than give a "book report" on your brief, you should take advantage of the dialogue, truly answering the judges' questions and focusing on the interests of the court.

Your attitude should be one of "respectful intellectual equality" toward the court.[1] Try to think of the court not as an adversary, but rather as individuals who remain to be convinced of the correctness of your arguments. Your goal is to convince them to adopt your reasoning as their own.

Similarly, you have an ethical duty to show respect for opposing counsel. Opposing counsel has a duty to raise arguments that conflict with yours. Your dialogue will be with the court, not opposing counsel, and should focus on the events and the law of the case, not on opposing counsel.

2. The Value of Oral Argument

Oral arguments help judges to clarify the facts, law, and policies, especially in close cases. In two studies, oral arguments were helpful to the judges in eighty to eighty-two percent of argued cases. Moreover, oral arguments influenced the judges' eventual outcomes in twenty-two to thirty-one percent of the cases heard.[2]

United States Supreme Court justices have found oral arguments to be most effective when characterized by clarity, adaptability, and strategy. The first factor, clarity, derives from effective organization, language usage, and delivery. The second factor, adaptability, is counsel's ability to respond to points raised in questions by the court. The third factor, strategy, is how well the argument can withstand tough questioning from the court and attacks by opposing counsel.[3]

3. Oral versus Written Advocacy

The potential scope of an oral argument is the material covered in the parties' briefs. Either party can raise any point or authority covered in any of the briefs, but no new material can be added in oral argument. Courts strongly discourage "surprises" in oral argument. (Newly discovered material may be presented in a supplementary brief, if the court allows it.)

---

1. Fredrick Wiener, *Briefing and Arguing Federal Appeals* § 101 (1967).
2. Myron H. Bright & Richard S. Arnold, *Oral Argument? It May Be Crucial!*, A.B.A. J. Sept. 1984, at 68, 70.
3. Nicholas M. Cripe, *Fundamentals of Persuasive Oral Argument*, 20 Forum 342 (1985).

Rarely will you present the full content of a brief in oral argument. Instead, the oral argument usually focuses on the highly contested issues. Chief Justice Rehnquist has commented that

> [m]any litigators . . . mistakenly approach the two instruments of appellate advocacy, the brief and the oral argument, "as the functional equivalent of one another." Many counsel, the justice contends, view an oral argument as no more than a "brief with gestures." . . . Rather, like the preview of a movie that consists of "dramatic or interesting scenes that are apt to catch the interest of the viewer and make him want to see that entire movie," oral argument should have "flesh and blood . . . insert[ed] into it."[1]

In addition, oral argument gives you a chance to bring the case to life for the court, to humanize the case by using the spoken medium to impart your personality and credibility. The court naturally assesses the lawyer's commitment to the arguments being raised. Furthermore, you can use voice inflection, gestures, body stance, and other means to impart meaning that the written word cannot convey.

At the same time, the spoken medium carries with it some challenges, because it occurs in the moment. Thus, the listener must learn the structure of the presentation from oral roadmaps and signposts, changes in inflection, gestures, and pauses. And the ideas must be presented in terms that the listener can process as quickly as the oral advocate presents them.

Another challenge of an oral argument is that the oral advocate does not control the argument—in sharp contrast to the complete control of the writer over the written brief. The court can, with its questions, dictate almost the entire direction and coverage of the oral argument.

C. ORAL ARGUMENT PROCEDURES

1. The Context of Oral Argument

In the trial court, an oral argument is presented to a single judge. It may occur any time a motion is pending or the judge is about to make a ruling (for instance, on an evidentiary matter or a point of procedure). It may be part of a trial, or it may come up on the motion calendar along with other pending motions. In many jurisdictions, dispositive pre-trial motions, such as summary judgment or dismissal, are argued both in writing and orally, while less critical motions are submitted in writing. In other settings, the trial judge has the discretion whether to ask for briefs and whether to hear oral arguments. In yet others, the practice is to permit oral arguments on all motions. The amount of time allowed for an oral argument on a motion can vary considerably, from a few moments to an hour. Some oral arguments occur in the

---

1. *Justice Rehnquist Emphasizes Importance of Oral Argument,* The Third Branch, Dec. 1983, at 1, 2, 4 (quoting excerpts from two speeches by now-Chief Justice Rehnquist in October 1983).

courtroom; others occur in the less formal setting of the trial judge's chambers, with counsel seated before the judge's desk.

In some appellate courts, all cases are granted oral argument. However, because of increasing caseloads, the trend is toward restricting oral arguments. In some appellate courts, counsel must request and justify oral argument, and the court has full discretion to grant or deny that request. Appellate oral arguments take place in an appellate courtroom; a bench with seats for all of the judges faces a lectern for counsel. The argument may be heard by the full court or a smaller panel, typically three judges. The proceeding generally is amplified and audiotaped. Most appellate courts set a fixed time limit for all but the most unusual cases; these limits usually range from fifteen to thirty-five minutes per side. The time limit may or may not include questions by the court and counsel's answers.

The preparation level of the judge(s) hearing an oral argument can vary considerably. At the trial level, the oral argument may be heard by the motion calendar judge, who may not be familiar with the case, or it may be heard by a judge who has worked on the case for some time. In some appellate courts, before the oral argument, the chief or presiding judge tentatively assigns a judge to write the opinion; other courts do not make that assignment until afterward. Under the former practice, one judge may be extremely well prepared, while others may have done very little preparation. Under the latter practice, all, none, or some of the judges may be well prepared. Lawyers describe these situations as "hot bench" and "cold bench."[1]

The sample HomeElderCare oral argument took place at the appellate level and was heard by three judges. Appellant's counsel was limited to fifteen minutes, and respondent's counsel was limited to twelve minutes. (The actual time permitted before the Minnesota Court of Appeals is fifteen minutes for appellant, fifteen minutes for respondent, and five minutes for appellant's rebuttal. Spec. R. Minn. Ct. App. 2.) It is difficult to gauge the judges' preparation levels from their questions, but the judges all appear fairly familiar with the case and so may be termed a "warm bench."

2. The Format of Oral Argument

You always should study the rules on oral argument before the court hearing your case. You also may want to consult the clerk of the court and local attorneys to learn of any unwritten traditions.

In formal oral arguments at the trial level, the movant speaks first, followed by the non-movant; sometimes the movant is allowed a rebuttal argument as well. The format of these oral arguments is highly variable, although tradition and logic dictate that the issues and the relevant facts be stated near the beginning of the oral argument. Less formal arguments at the trial level resemble a discussion, with the judge asking questions and the lawyers responding to those questions and to each other.

At the appellate level, as appellant's counsel, you would open with an introduction. You may begin with the formal opening, "May it please the

---

1. Myron H. Bright, *How to Win on Appeal: The New Ten Commandments of Oral Argument,* Trial, July 1996, at 68, 69.

court," or you may bypass the formal phrase and directly introduce yourself and your client. You should state right away how much time you wish to reserve for rebuttal and then provide a roadmap of which issues or arguments will be covered and in what order.

It is customary for the appellant to state the facts and procedural posture. This statement should be whittled down to minimal length and stress facts pertinent to the issues being addressed in the oral argument. A longer fact statement is appropriate when the case pivots on a factual dispute or the client's case is strong on the facts and weak on the law. The statement should be fairly balanced, for both ethical and strategic reasons.

Most of your time will be spent discussing the legal arguments, discussed in detail below. The conclusion should be very brief, with any recapping limited to only a few sentences, if that. You should conclude with the disposition you wish the court to grant (reversal, remand, affirmance, modification).

As respondent's counsel, you usually will use this same format. You can choose whether to give your view of the facts and the case; most oral advocates do state additional or reframed facts near the beginning of the argument. Otherwise, you will open with a roadmap of the issues or arguments and then proceed directly to the body of the argument.

With rebuttal, appellant is allowed to end the oral argument. Rebuttal is appellant's chance at the end of the oral argument to refute respondent's arguments and to present the final conclusion. You should not raise new arguments in a rebuttal. You need not answer all of the respondent's points and, indeed, should not address more than two or three topics; you would do well to point out the respondent's omissions or select one or two major topics on which appellant has strong counterarguments. You should conclude by reiterating the relief your client seeks from the court.

The time devoted to rebuttal should be proportional to the length of the argument. Two or three minutes is the norm, but five minutes is appropriate if the argument is long and contains many issues. If appellant's counsel fails to reserve rebuttal time, some courts treat rebuttal as waived.

Exhibits 19.1 and 19.2 present comparisons of oral argument components to the components of motion practice memoranda and appellate briefs.

In the sample HomeElderCare oral argument, both counsel followed the format suggested here. Both counsel used the formal opening, "May it please the court," before introducing themselves and their clients. Appellant's counsel then reserved three minutes for rebuttal and gave a quick roadmap of the two main issues. See page 377. Her fact statement focused on the crucial points and reflected a balanced view of the facts. See page 377. She then recounted the procedural events that led to this appeal and stated the standard of review. See page 378. Respondent's counsel began by introducing the theme of his argument. See page 381. After clarifying the facts in three sentences, he gave a roadmap of his two main arguments. See page 381. The main portions of their arguments are discussed below. Both counsel concluded their arguments by summarizing their points and requesting the appropriate relief from the court. See pages 380 and 385.

Appellant's counsel began her rebuttal by summarizing her main argument and then responding to respondent's assertions as to the two main issues. She concluded her argument by emphasizing the public policy in her client's favor. See pages 384–385.

EXHIBIT 19.1

COMPARISON OF MOTION PRACTICE MEMORANDUM AND ORAL ARGUMENT

Motion Practice Memorandum	Oral Argument
Caption	Introduction (who I am & whom I represent)
Introduction or Summary (optional)	Introduction or Summary (optional)
Procedure (optional)	Issues (optional)
Facts	Facts (with or without procedure)
Argument	Argument (more selective)
Conclusion	Conclusion

EXHIBIT 19.2

COMPARISON OF APPELLATE BRIEF AND ORAL ARGUMENT

Appellate Brief	Oral Argument
Cover page	Introduction (who I am & whom I represent)
Table of contents	Roadmap of issues or arguments
Table of authorities	
Statement of issues	Statement of facts and procedure (albeit briefer)
Statement of case and facts	Argument (more selective)
Summary of argument	Conclusion
Argument	
Conclusion	
Appendix	

D. PREPARING THE ORAL ARGUMENT

Although oral argument is a conversation and not a speech, you nonetheless should prepare carefully for it. You should have a plan for what you wish to accomplish, even though you will not be able to control the course of the argument and must defer to the court's direction.

1. Selecting Arguments to Present

Experts suggest presenting one or two, not more than three, major arguments. The court does not expect the oral argument to cover all topics covered in the briefs.

In choosing arguments for oral presentation, you should consider various factors. First, try to present a coherent picture of your client's case; your arguments should draw in the key facts and outline your theory of the case. Second, choose your strongest arguments; if you cannot win on the strongest argument, you are not likely to win on the weakest. Third, consider which arguments are better suited for oral presentation—generally policy, factual, or equitable arguments, not technical or complex legal questions. A then-Minnesota Supreme Court justice suggested, "Look for a theme [or] . . . trend in the law[,] . . . reasons behind the rules[, and] . . . conflicting interests to be balanced."[1] Fourth, focus on points of clash, the issues on which the parties' positions conflict and which pose the greatest challenge to the court. You will greatly assist the court, and thereby enhance your credibility, by dealing with adverse precedent and troublesome arguments raised by opposing counsel. Fifth, some of the arguments in your brief may affirmatively advance your client's case, while others merely refute opposing arguments. Make sure that the affirmative arguments outweigh the refutations. Sixth, if you still need to pare down your list of arguments, carefully examine arguments in the alternative to see whether you can omit one or more of the alternatives.

In the sample oral argument, as shown in Exhibit 19.3, both counsel selected the same two major issues—unauthorized practice and contract validity—because the scope of the appeal dictated those two issues and because these issues constituted the points of clash. Both addressed these issues in that order because logic compels it. However, their arguments differed quite a bit. The arguments made by each counsel flowed together into a coherent theory of the case for each side.

2. Setting the "Pitch" of the Argument

You generally will not know how prepared your judges will be. Thus you should frame your arguments so that you can reliably educate the trial judge or a majority (at least) of the appellate court. Consider covering the basics initially, then elevating the level of discussion as soon as you are reasonably certain that the judges will be able to follow the more complicated aspects of the case. You may even decide to cover an easier topic at the outset of the argument, so that you can defer the tougher arguments to later in the presentation.

In the appellate setting, resist the temptation to pitch the entire argument to the least prepared judge. You may thereby limit the depth of your argument and its effectiveness for the more informed judges. On the other hand, you do not want to converse exclusively with the judge who seems

---

1. John Simonett, *Oral Argument*, Hennepin Law., Nov.-Dec. 1985, at 10, 11.

EXHIBIT 19.3

SYNOPSIS OF APPELLATE ORAL ARGUMENTS

Appellant's Main Argument	*Respondent's Argument*	*Appellant's Rebuttal*
unauthorized practice of law	unauthorized practice of law	no unauthorized practice of law
statute's content	two violations	because no answers to difficult
difficult and doubtful legal	preparing legal documents for	and doubtful legal questions
question test	a fee	no deviations or alterations in
three examples that were not	providing legal advice and	form
four examples that were	counsel	social workers answer medical
analogizing and distinguishing	meaning of "legal document"	and ethical questions
HEC	reconciling policies of two	clients need this service
HEC guidelines to social workers	statutes	
filling in form, not altering it	policy of protecting the public	
referring client to attorney for	difficult and doubtful legal ques-	
legal advice	tions answered here	
charging a fee not dispositive	purpose of statute	
meaning of "legal document"	lots of other people can assist	
purpose of statute	with form	
contract validity	contract validity	contract is valid
no fraud or incompetent service	evidence of incompetence here	because no incompetence
no evidence of HEC's fault	real estate agents distinguished	HEC guidelines and training
harm to clients if service dis-		
continued		

to understand the case best. This tactic may result in only a muddled understanding among the members of the court who did not follow your argument and, perhaps, a spirited dissent from the judge with whom you conversed.

In the sample oral argument, appellant's counsel started with the basics and then steadily elevated the level of discussion through the progression of arguments stated above. Respondent's counsel did not need to vary the pitch of his arguments because he could build on the material already presented by appellant's counsel.

3. Allocating Time

Just as you should analyze your briefs and memoranda for allocation of space to various components and topics, so too should you plan how to allocate your oral argument time to particular components and topics.

In preparing for your argument, time the fact statement you plan to deliver. In a five-minute motion argument at the trial level, the fact statement may need to be less than a minute long. In a fifteen-minute appellate oral argument, fact statements rarely run longer than three minutes. In a thirty-minute argument, the facts ordinarily would not exceed five minutes. Condense facts that do not need to be presented in detail, and omit facts that pertain to topics you do not intend to argue orally. Another strategy is to present general facts in your fact statement and save the more detailed facts for the body of the argument, when they will mean more to the listener and make the legal argument more understandable. Similarly, limit the procedural history to the rulings that are relevant to the legal issues covered in your oral argument.

In planning the body of your argument, reserve approximately a third of your time for responses to the court's questions, or allocate that time to a less important argument that can be omitted if need be. Of the remaining time, determine how much time to devote to each argument, based on its relative importance and controversy. Furthermore, you may be able to cover some arguments in one or two sentences; other arguments may require factual analogies, extensive development of public policies, or fusion of related cases. For each argument, you must judge how much time you need to make the argument clearly and persuasively, so you can decide whether to attempt the argument if time is running out.

In the sample oral argument, appellant's counsel spent less than three of her fifteen minutes on her introduction and fact statement. Respondent's counsel spent less than a minute on his introduction and facts. Both counsel focused on the essential facts and omitted the unneeded ones. Appellant's counsel saved some of the specific facts for the body of her argument. Both oral advocates spent most of their time on the issue of the unauthorized practice of law, the crucial issue in this lawsuit. Both were able to present far more than the bare minimum on this topic, while they reduced their coverage of the contract validity issue to the bare minimum.

4. Planning for Flexibility

Of course, you never should count on being able to proceed through your argument without adapting it to respond to the judges' questions and concerns. Furthermore, you will want to account for the arguments made by your opponent. You may need to switch the order of topics, drastically expand or condense the coverage of a particular topic, or even change which briefed topics you cover.

In planning for adaptability, you first should determine what material to present if you receive no questions. Then you should decide which arguments you want to make, at a bare minimum, if you receive many questions. In addition, as to each argument, you should figure out how much you would cover if you had no questions, versus the bare minimum you would hope to cover in the face of heavy questioning. You also should plan how to make transitions between arguments if you are forced to cover the arguments in less-than-optimal order.

Adaptability also entails responsiveness to the arguments of your opponent. You should be prepared to answer questions on topics raised by opposing counsel; you must master the authorities and arguments in his or her brief. In the course of your argument, you may want to address some of the questions asked of opposing counsel in the preceding argument. Respondent's counsel responds in his or her argument, while appellant's counsel responds during rebuttal.

In the sample oral argument, the court's questions indicated that the court was interested in two topics: the actions of HomeElderCare's social workers in filling out the living wills, and legislative intent. Both counsel tailored their arguments accordingly.

5. Preparing Written Materials

You should not deliver your argument from a written script, because your presentation will be stilted, and you may fail to respond well to questions. Nor are note cards advisable, because you will find it difficult to adjust your organization or see the entire argument at a glance, and because you may distract the court if you nervously shuffle your cards.

Rather, you should write out a bare-bones outline of the major issues and arguments, as well as abstracts of the leading cases or statutes, quotations from the important legal rules, and notes of the key facts or policies. There are at least three methods for arraying this information.

In the first method, write the outline on one side of an open manila file folder. On the other side, tape a flip-card index of key authorities, favorable and adverse. Each card has the citation on the bottom of the card and the important facts, quotations, and reasoning on the rest. Tape the cards onto the left side of the open folder in layers with the bottom line of each card showing. See Exhibit 19.4. When the court asks a question involving information you have not memorized, you can locate it in your card index.

In the second method, write the introduction to your argument at the top of the left side of an open manila file folder, and write the conclusion at

---

EXHIBIT 19.4

FLIP-CARD AND OUTLINE

Sources

"~~~~~~~~~~~~~~~~~~~~."
~~
treatise
1. rev.
treatise
Rule 12
Rule 56
§ 333
§ 222
§ 111
K v. L
I v. J
G v. H
E v. F
C v. D
A v. B

May it please the court. My name is ~~~~~~~~~; I represent ~~~~~~~~~ ~~~~~~~~~~~~~~. My argument will cover ~~~~~~~~~~~~~~~~~~~~~~~~~ ~~~~~~~~~~~~~~~~~~~~~~~~~~~~.
The facts are uncontested:

- ~~~~~~~~~~~~~~~~~~~~
- ~~~~~~~~~~~~~~~~~~~~
- ~~~~~~~~~~~~~~~~~~~~
- ~~~~~~~~~~~~~~~~~~~~
- ~~~~~~~~~~~~~~~~~~~~

I. ~~~~~~~~~~~~~~~~~~~~~
  A. ~~~~~~~~~~~~~~~~~~
  B. ~~~~~~~~~~~~~~~~~~
II. ~~~~~~~~~~~~~~~~~~~
  A. ~~~~~~~~~~~~~~~~~~
    1. ~~~~~~~~~~~~~~~~
    2. ~~~~~~~~~~~~~~~~
  B. ~~~~~~~~~~~~~~~~~~
In conclusion, ~~~~~~~~~~~~~~~
~~~~~~~~~~~~~~~~~~~~~~~.

the bottom of the right side of the open folder. Then draw a vertical line down the center of the remaining space on either side. Write an outline of the body of the argument in the center column, and jot notes about important authority in the left and right columns. See Exhibit 19.5.

In the third method, assemble a notebook containing an outline of the argument, followed by tabbed sections containing the record and important authority. This technique should be used only for exceedingly complex cases, because the turning of pages can be distracting.

Regardless of which method you use, you should bring the record or a detailed summary of the record with you, in case the court asks you a question about a particular page in the record.

6. Practicing

Write out, memorize, and practice your introduction and your conclusion, so that you can open and close the argument cleanly and with confidence. A sample appellant's introduction might read as follows: "May it please the court. My name is _____, and I represent the appellant, _____. I wish to reserve ____ minutes for rebuttal. I will be addressing the following issues in my argument: . . . ." A sample respondent's conclusion might read as follows: "In conclusion, both of appellant's arguments are unsupported by law. I urge the court to affirm the trial court holding and rule in favor of my client." You also may want to memorize the opening segment of the fact statement, if it is short.

EXHIBIT 19.5

OUTLINE WITH SIDE COLUMNS

May it please the court. My name is ~~~~~; I represent~~~~~~~~~~~~~~~. This argument focuses on ~~~~~~~~ ~~~~~~~~~~~~~~~~~~~~~~~.

Facts: ~~~~~~~~~~~~~~~
~~~~~~~~~~~~~~~~~~~~~
~~~~~~~~~~~~~~~~~~~~~
~~~~~~~~~~~~~~~~~~~~~

§ 111 ~~~~~~~
~~~~~~~~~~~~

I. ~~~~~~~~~~
~~~~~~~~~~~

A v. B ~~~~~~~~~
C v. D ~~~~~~~~~~

§ 222 ~~~~~~
~~~~~~~~~~~~
~~~~~~~~~~~~
~~~~~~~~~~~~
~~~~~~~~~~~~
~~~~~~~~~~~~

A. ~~~~~~~~
~~~~~~~~~

B. ~~~~~~~~
~~~~~~~~~

C. ~~~~~~~~
~~~~~~~~~

~~~~~~~~~~
~~~~~~~~~~

E v. F ~~~~~~~~~
G v. H ~~~~~~~~~~
I v. J ~~~~~~~~~
treatise ~~~~~~~~~

§ 333 ~~~~~~
~~~~~~~~~~
~~~~~~~~~~

II. ~~~~~~~~~~
~~~~~~~~~~~
~~~~~~~~~~~

1. rev. ~~~~~~~~~
~~~~~~~~~~
~~~~~~~~~~

In conclusion, ~~~~~~~~~~~~
~~~~~~~~~~~~~~~~~~~~~~
~~~~~~~~~~~~~~~~~~~~~~

Then practice talking about the case. First, present your entire oral argument without interruptions, perhaps tape-recording it once or twice. Practice presenting your arguments in differing orders. You also should rehearse for the possibility that the court will ask you to skip the facts and proceed to the body of the argument. (This practice is especially common in arguments delivered in law school.) Time your fact statement and each argument, and examine those times for conformance to your desired time allocations, as discussed above. Try to discern how easy or difficult it is to follow your presentation.

Next, find someone to quiz you on the case. Ask your colleagues to ask tough questions and help you figure out how best to handle the tougher questions. Work on connecting your answers to the related arguments you want to make.

Consider presenting in front of a video recorder; then review your performance from the perspective of the listening judges. Watch for distracting nervous mannerisms, like jingling coins in your pocket. Also evaluate your posture, general demeanor, and other aspects of body language. Do you appear confident in your client's case at all times, even when the judges' questions become difficult? Is your posture open to the court, indicating a forthcoming and forthright manner?

E. DELIVERING THE ARGUMENT

1. Making Spoken Communication Clear

A judge listening to an oral argument cannot re-listen to a portion of argument made some minutes ago or stop the argument to consider a statement just made. To help the judges assimilate what is being said, speak at a medium tempo with occasional pauses. These pauses provide you and the judges with time to think; pauses also serve as aural cues equivalent to punctuation and paragraph breaks in written communication. You should pause briefly between sentences, rather than running the sentences into each other, and a longer time between paragraphs. In addition to tempo and pauses, use roadmaps and signposts to assist the listener. These semantic roadmaps and signposts can be emphasized by inflections, pauses, and gestures.

In the sample HomeElderCare oral argument, counsel gave the following roadmaps:

> There are two issues that we will discuss today. The first deals with whether . . . The second issue is whether . . . .

> Respondent must prove two issues to establish the invalidity of the contract. First, . . . Even if . . . .

> [T]he . . . statute was violated . . . in two ways. First, . . . Second, ...

They used the following signposts to mark the beginning of a new topic or subtopic:

The facts have been stipulated . . . .

While opposing counsel has generally stated the facts accurately, I would like to make a few clarifications. . . . .

The main point that I would like you to remember is . . .

The first issue addresses . . . .

The second issue deals with . . . .

They also used the following signposts to mark the end of a topic:

Therefore, ...

So . . . .

In short, ...

In conclusion, ...

Sometimes visual aids, such as a timeline, map, or diagram, may be helpful to the court. You should ask the clerk whether the court receives visual aids, and if so, in what form. You may choose to present the material in a handout, in an appendix to the brief, or on an easel. Of course, the information must have appeared in the briefs in some form and must be within the scope of the court's review.

If possible, you should visit the courtroom in which you will be presenting. Evaluate the distance between yourself and the judges, the adequacy of the lighting, the sightlines of each of the judges, and whether the microphone, if there is one, will amplify your voice if you move from the lectern.

2. Presenting Quotations

Quotations generally are difficult for a listener to process. You are unlikely to read a quote as naturally as you speak in your own words, and the listener must adjust to the style of the quotation and then back to your speaking style. If the quotation was meant to be read, not heard, it may be complex in syntax or semantics.

Yet some material may be so important that it merits a direct quotation: for example, the key phrase of a statute in a statutory interpretation case, or the telling statement of a critical witness. If, on the other hand, the point you wish to make can be made equally well by paraphrasing, do so.

If you do decide to use a quotation, above all else, be sure you state it accurately. Formally introduce the quotation by indicating its source, and be sure to close the quote.

In the sample HomeElderCare argument, both counsel used brief and accurate quotations, which they marked by a pause, a change in inflection, and the use of "quote" and "un-quote."

3. Answering Questions

In most oral arguments, the court will ask you questions. In no circumstance should you treat the court's questions as interruptions. Rather, as a famous appellate advocate exhorted, "Rejoice when the court asks questions."[1] Questions can be of great assistance to a well prepared advocate; like weather vanes, they tell you which way the wind is blowing. Without questions from the court, you are left delivering a speech that may not address the court's real concerns.

Court etiquette dictates that you stop your presentation whenever a member of the court begins a question, even if you are in mid-sentence. Do not interrupt the judge; listen to the entire question; give yourself time to think. Then answer the question, even if the topic is out of the order in which you planned to present your arguments. It is not acceptable to delay the answer to a question, unless the judge asking the question signals that you may do so.

Some questions require only a few words by way of response. Others call for a potentially lengthy response. Once you have answered, you should not wait for the court for a sign of permission to proceed. Rather, you should maintain eye contact with the court so that you can gauge the reaction of the judges to your answer. If the judges seem to have followed your initial response, you should conclude the answer and move on. However, if much of the bench looks puzzled by your answer, you might want to elaborate on it. If the reaction is one of skepticism, you might decide that discretion is the better part of valor and move to an alternative argument or even another topic that the court may view more favorably. If the reaction is mixed, you might quickly count heads and decide whether a majority of the court is with you. When you move back to your prepared comments, try to link your answer to the argument you are about to make.

Above all, do not take tough questioning personally. A seemingly hostile judge may in fact favor your client and may take a devil's advocate stance. At worst, tough questioning represents criticism of your legal arguments, not you personally. The members of the court are usually trying out the reasoning you propose to see whether they are comfortable enough with it to adopt it for the holding.

As the court asks questions, try to discern which of the following types of questions the court is asking and respond accordingly:

Questions about the facts: Judges ask questions about the facts primarily to lock in their understanding of the dispute they are asked to resolve. The judge may not remember a key fact and may seek a reminder from you. Or the judge may ask you to clarify or synthesize evidence that is muddled or conflicting; your answer must be supported by the record and should be as favorable to your client as it can be. Or the judge may ask you about facts that are not in the record; you must respond that the fact is not in the record, and you may draw an inference if the inference is a strong one based on facts in the record. As much as possible, follow up your answer with a comment about the significance of the fact to the legal analysis or equities of the case.

---

1. John Davis, *The Argument of an Appeal*, 26 A.B.A. J. 895, 897 (1940).

In the sample oral argument, for example, the judges asked appellant's counsel the following purely factual question:

Judge 1: Well, don't the facts of this case indicate that the friends and relatives or other people that you mentioned are apparently not filling this need because HomeElderCare apparently did do some forty wills and charged, at least in this case, $80 and that shows there is a need for this service, doesn't it?

Respondent's Counsel: It shows that they did that. I don't know that it shows that that is the only alternative that was available. They do provide other services that require legal expertise in those areas—for example, testamentary wills, with real estate transactions. There they have also provided service to the HomeElderCare clients, and there they have acted primarily as a liaison with attorneys, recognizing that they really don't have the skill and ability to engage in this sort of activity.

Questions about the law: Judges ask questions about the law as they seek to resolve an ambiguity about the legal rule or its application to the facts of the case. In response, you first should state what the law says, as viewed from your client's perspective and within the confines of ethical principles regarding candor with the court. You may need to disagree respectfully with a judge who does not see the law your way; if so, provide a clear rationale for your viewpoint, whether a succinct quotation or policy argument or later legal development. Next, be sure to draw a connection between the law as you have stated it and the facts of your case. In many instances, the law is not clear in the abstract, but becomes so when applied to a specific situation.

In the sample oral argument, the following exchange typifies this kind of question and response:

Judge 2: Counsel, don't you also have to show fraud or incompetence in order to prevail on the contract claim?

Respondent's Counsel: That is true, Your Honor, and we believe that we have clear evidence of incompetence here. The proof of this is that the living will had to be redone; it had to be revised so that the interests of Mr. Nelson were met, so that his desires were satisfied. So we believe that indeed we do have evidence of incompetence in this case.

Questions about public policy: Especially at the highest court, judges ask questions about the societal implications of possible rulings. Your response should show how a ruling in your favor will lead to positive outcomes for similar disputes, by showing why the ruling would promote justice in your client's case. Your response also should show that any concerns about adverse by-products are founded on speculation or that any adverse by-products are outweighed by the positive outcomes. For example, if a new cause of action provides recovery for a class of injured individuals, would-be defendants can avoid liability by reforming their harmful practices, and the courts can avoid excessive litigation by crafting the rule carefully.

In the sample oral argument, the following discussion of public policy occurred:

Judge 3: Counsel, my understanding is that the legislature enacting the living will statute intended for the document to be very easily executed. It did adopt two different ways to execute the document. Wouldn't it be appropriate for this court to authorize persons other than lawyers, such as social workers, to help with the execution of these documents? The legislature has indicated that it is the policy of the state to encourage this document for persons.

Respondent's Counsel: It is true that the legislature has made clear that it believes it is good public policy to encourage the use of living wills. We don't see that there is really any conflict between that policy and the policy underlying the unauthorized practice of law statute. We think the two can coexist very comfortably. What we have here, though, is a situation where the policies that guide the unauthorized practice of law statute—namely, to protect the public from the very serious harm that can result from activities or actions by individuals who are not lawyers—that should be given the primary consideration.

Questions about hypothetical situations: Under stare decisis, judges must write decisions that will work well in the future, lead to just and predictable outcomes, and avoid undue administrative burdens. Thus judges are concerned with, and ask about, hypothetical future situations. Answers to hypotheticals help the judges to foresee the future operation of the rule.

Hypothetical questions are challenging because they often involve facts, law, and policy in a situation the attorneys may not have fully contemplated while preparing oral arguments. The key to a good answer is to take time to think, so that you can provide not only a conclusion, but also an analysis of why the hypothetical would and should be resolved a particular way, in light of the elements of the rule and its policy. If you deem the hypothetical a close call, you should phrase your answer tentatively or provide more than one response and rationale.

If the court asks multiple hypotheticals or engages you in an extended discussion of a single hypothetical, you may feel that your case has become lost in the fray and that you are on unsure ground. If so, you may wish to observe that your client's case does not raise the problem in the hypothetical and then show how the court could rule so as to avoid the problem in the hypothetical.

In the sample oral argument, a judge and respondent's counsel had the following exchange on a hypothetical situation:

Judge 3: Counsel, I'm a bit concerned as to where you would have us draw the line. Are you saying that if a person were brought to a hospital losing consciousness—about to lose the capacity to execute a document of this sort—that the people at the medical facility could not assist in the execution of the document? We'd have to wait until an attorney was called to come?

Respondent's Counsel: No, I don't think that we would say that that was the case. I think if a person in that situation—a hospital worker, for example—just wrote down exactly what the patient wanted, there was no discussion of what the terms mean but basically did it in a sort of clerical way, I don't think that we would have the unauthorized practice of law in such a situation.

Judge 3: But isn't that what happened here?

Respondent's Counsel: Well, we don't believe that it is. In fact, we have the record which indicates that they explain the document to the doctors, they explain it to the proxies, they explain it to the witnesses, and they actually oversee the execution of the document. So we have something very much more involved here than simply completing a form.

Questions seeking concessions: A judge may signal that one of your assertions or arguments is not credible and thereby exert pressure on you to concede that point. Your response to a question seeking a concession can take various forms. Least common is outright retreat, when you say, "That's correct, your honor. We no longer are basing our case on that argument." This response may improve your credibility with the court and thereby strengthen the court's support for your other arguments. For instance, as a plaintiff, you may be able to concede one cause of action, so long as another cause of action secures the recovery sought by your client. As a defendant, you may be able to concede that the plaintiff has a good case on one element of a conjunctive rule, so long as you maintain that another element can be defeated. Of course, to the extent possible, you should know your client's views as to these matters before you enter the courtroom.

More often, oral advocates seek to minimize the impact of any concessions they make by pairing the concession or apparent concession with a strong assertion. You engage in confession and avoidance by saying, "That may be true, your honor, but it doesn't matter because this other [fact or argument] is controlling, rather than the one you raise." You assume arguendo by saying, "Let's assume, for the sake of argument, that these [facts were true, or elements were met]. Even if they were, my client would still prevail because . . . ." Thus, as a general rule, in oral argument you should seek to avoid outright retreat.

In the sample oral argument, the following examples are of the confession-and-avoidance form:

Judge 3: So that any deviation from the form would constitute the practice of law, you think?

Appellant's Counsel: It could be. It's reaching that fuzzy line of what may be the difficult and doubtful question, but it's really not an issue here because our social workers do not deviate from the form whatsoever.

Judge 3: But don't the issues that arise under the content of the living will—they are medical issues, are they not, not legal issues—decisions as to what kind of medical care someone might take? Isn't it true that geriatric social workers might indeed have more knowledge of medical issues than would a lawyer?

Respondent's Counsel: It is true that there are certainly a lot of medical issues involved in the living will form, but there are also a good number of legal issues as well that we believe require expertise in order to provide a proper service to these clients. We see a social worker discussing the role of proxies, guardians, and conservators; explaining the legal obligations of doctors; explaining the document to the client's witness and proxy.

In every case, there are points you cannot concede without sacrificing your client's claim or defense. If the court presses you to concede such a point, you should gracefully convey that you must disagree with the court and perhaps state (or restate) your most persuasive reasons.

In the sample oral argument, respondent's counsel followed this course:

Judge 1: Are those really such difficult and doubtful issues? Isn't it fairly simple to explain in everyday language what a proxy or a conservator is?

Respondent's Counsel: Well, we think that it is difficult and doubtful, and we think the proof of that is actually the fact of this case. And we had a situation here where the person that Mr. Nelson wanted to be his guardian was in fact not made his guardian as a result of the actions of HomeElderCare. So we believe that indeed there are difficult and doubtful legal questions being addressed here, and therefore, the actions of the HomeElderCare social workers did indeed constitute the unauthorized practice of law.

Questions about your opponent's argument: Judges naturally ask counsel to respond to the opponent's argument. Your three basic options are to present your client's approach to the topic, to show the fallacies or weaknesses in the opposing argument, or, less commonly, to make a concession. In any case, you must convey respect for opposing counsel and his or her client, even as you convey disagreement with their assertion, by framing your response in terms of the assertion, not the people involved.

In the sample oral argument, the following exchange occurred:

Judge 1: Well, opposing counsel indicates that the record is unclear as to whether it was maybe Mr. Nelson's own misunderstanding that caused this. We don't really have it clear on the record that it was the HomeElderCare worker's incompetence that produced this. Isn't that true?

Respondent's Counsel: I think that we can make the assumption that indeed it was the incompetence of the HomeElderCare social worker. I think that this further demonstrates why you need somebody with a trained legal background to make these kinds of decisions so that these kinds of questions are not at issue after we have the living will being formed.

Nudging questions: Sometimes a question amounts to a direction to move on. Often these questions are "soft pitches"—that is, a question in which the judge makes a point favorable to your client and thereby encourages you to discuss that point. Resist the cynic's temptation to look for a trap in the question. Rather, to continue the baseball analogy, you should hit the ball out of the ballpark by first concurring with the judge and then developing the point further, by citing authority, or referring to relevant facts, or both.

In the sample oral argument, for instance, the following question, if asked, would have given either counsel the chance to move to the second topic:

Counsel, even if there were unauthorized practice of law, wouldn't there also have to be some incompetence or fraud shown for this contract to be invalid?

Unclear, irrelevant, or unanswerable questions: If the court asks an unclear question, politely tell the court that you are not sure which point the court means to raise and that you need a clarification. For instance, "Your Honor, could you rephrase that question? I'm not sure that I understand it."

If the court asks an irrelevant question, consider asking the judge to repeat the question so you can be sure you have not misunderstood it. Then answer briefly or tactfully explain what the more relevant question is, pose that question, and answer it.

If the court asks a question you cannot answer, say so candidly and offer to submit a supplemental brief on the point. For instance, "I'm sorry, Your Honor; I'm not familiar with that statute. I would be glad to research it and submit a supplemental brief on it, if that would be helpful." Of course, this approach is appropriate only if you are completely unprepared to answer the question. This response likely will decrease your credibility with the court, but it is better to candidly admit lack of knowledge than to risk an erroneous or ill-considered response.

4. Being Your Best Self

Courtroom demeanor varies considerably. Some oral advocates are fairly passionate and demonstrative. Others are more reserved and moderate. To a great extent, your courtroom demeanor will be a matter of your personal style. You also may consider matching your demeanor to the situation, as determined by the nature of the case, the type of argument you are making (equitable arguments calling for more passion than technical legal arguments), and the temperament of the court.

In all cases, of course, you must convey respect for the court, opposing counsel, and the law. Address judges with deference, never familiarity. You may disagree with the merits of opposing counsel's arguments, but you should never convey personal disdain for opposing counsel. Furthermore, oral argument is not an occasion for emotional appeals, pejoratives, abstract speeches about justice, or irrelevant humor. Nor is it an occasion for stating your personal views of the client's case or the state of the law. Indeed, most experts caution against personal references ("I believe . . ."). Rather, your argument should be grounded in the facts as found in the record, the law as it exists or should be, and well founded public policy.

Finally, in all cases, you should convey both credibility and a commitment to the client's cause. Ideally, you actually will believe your client's arguments, and this belief will come through naturally. To maximize the appearance of credibility and commitment during the argument, take care in framing your points so you neither overreach nor understate matters. As much as possible, focus on the material you personally find most compelling. Answer questions honestly; do not try to bluster through awkward situations. Rather than acting according to your image of a lawyer, be yourself.

F. THE DAY OF THE ARGUMENT

1. Before the Argument

You should dress neatly and appropriately, so that your appearance does not distract from your argument. Consult with an attorney who argues often before that court as to local dress conventions.

Bring to the courtroom the transcript, record, all briefs, note materials, and any other materials to which you may need to refer. You need not bring all of these materials to the lectern, but should have them on the counsel's table, where you can retrieve them if you need them.

Arrive early to scout out the courtroom, if it is unfamiliar to you. You will want to note the acoustics, the height of the lectern, and the timing system. Check with the bailiff or clerk for hints as to the procedures of that particular court and the preferences of the judge(s).

The timing system in an appellate courtroom may consist of lights—green for go, yellow for x number of minutes remaining, and red for stop. Or the bailiff or clerk may hold up cards showing the number of minutes left. Or you and the court may keep track of the time yourselves. You always should bring an easy-to-read watch and place it on the lectern.

2. During the Argument

Rise when the court enters and leaves, as well as when you address the court. Wait for the presiding judge to give you permission to begin your argument. Refer to the judge as "Your Honor," "Judge _____," or "Justice _____" (if you are before the high court of the jurisdiction).

To achieve your goal of a conversation, maintain eye contact as much as possible. Give the name of the case or the section number of the statute only if needed to avoid confusion. Do not read citations unless asked for them. Avoid distracting conduct, like jingling coins in your pocket, covering your mouth, or flipping pages over the front edge of the lectern.

According to the recency principle, the last words said carry particular weight, so it is important to conclude well. You need not use all of the allotted time. Courts really do appreciate brevity and may be impressed with the simplicity of a short argument. If you finish early, ask the court if it has any more questions, and, if not, conclude and sit down. If you represent the appellant, you may be able to add your leftover time to your reserved rebuttal time. On the other hand, if you run out of time, you should conclude the sentence or the answer in very brief form, then ask the court if you may have an additional thirty to sixty seconds in which to deliver a very brief conclusion. If the court grants the extension, take care not to exceed the time given. If the court refuses the request, thank the court for its attention, and sit down.

G. Review of Chapter 19

Oral argument is not a speech or book report, but rather a conversation with the court in which your primary goal is to address the court's concerns. Oral argument procedures vary considerably from trial to appellate courts, and you should research the rules and practices of a court before arguing before it.

The movant or appellant argues first. Although oral argument is less fixed than written advocacy, most arguments follow a sequence that bears a loose resemblance to memoranda or briefs: introductory material, including facts and procedure; development of the legal argument; and conclusion. Counsel for the party opposing the motion or appeal speaks next, responding to the points made by opposing counsel and stating his or her own view of the case. The movant or appellant may conclude the argument with a brief rebuttal.

To prepare for an oral presentation, you must select the arguments you wish to present, typically your strongest arguments, the areas of sharpest conflict between the parties, and arguments that can be stated easily in oral form. In addition, you should think through the pitch of your argument, allocation of time among your various topics, and ways to maintain flexibility during the argument. For significant arguments, it is important to prepare written materials to have at the lectern and then to practice.

As you deliver your presentation, speak clearly, use inflection, and employ verbal signals so that your listeners can easily understand your arguments and follow your organization. Analyze the questions you receive by type, for example, as hypotheticals or policy questions, and respond accordingly and fully, moving back into your argument as smoothly as possible. Finally, be sure to follow court etiquette and procedures during the argument so that the court focuses not on your personal mannerisms but rather on the content of your argument.

Your resulting argument will be complete if it addresses what the court wants to know. It will be comprehensible if the court can follow your fact statement, issues, and argument. It will be correct and cohesive if the facts, law, and policy are accurately stated and mesh together into a coherent whole. Lastly, your argument will be convincing if you advocate your client's position with confidence and sincerity, making skillful use of language and speech.

HomeElderCare Case File
TABLE OF CONTENTS

PREFACE TO

HomeElderCare

CASE FILE

This case file contains materials pertinent to a fictional case, the HomeElder-Care case. It includes some of the cases, statutes, and commentary sources on the issues raised by various aspects of that case. Also included are the attorney's interview notes, as well as case and statute briefs. The latter part of the file contains two office memoranda, a letter to the client, two opposing motion practice memoranda, two opposing appellate briefs, and the appellate oral argument transcript.

The initial client interview, office memos, and letter to HomeElderCare preceded HomeElderCare's decision to offer a new service—preparing living wills for its clients. That service gave rise to facts that triggered two concurrent pieces of litigation. One piece of litigation was brought by the State against HomeElderCare. It led to the State's motion for a temporary injunction to shut down HomeElderCare's service during the trial; that motion is the subject of the motion practice memoranda. The other piece of litigation was brought against HomeElderCare by a disgruntled client who sought to invalidate his contract with HomeElderCare because the living will service constituted the unauthorized practice of law and was incompetent. The trial court ruled in favor of the client, and HomeElderCare appealed. This case file contains only the appellate briefs and the appellate oral argument transcript from this latter piece of litigation.

This case file is incomplete in other respects as well. It contains only some of the sources that pertain to the case and only one piece of correspondence. It does not contain pleadings, notices, certificates of service, discovery documents, etc. It does contain the documents in which the lawyer has recorded a legal analysis of the case, whether in advisory or advocacy mode.

The case file is, in some respects, artificial. Some of the file contents are labeled in the margins, to assist your reading and understanding of those items. In addition, two office memos are included to show two possible ana-

245

lytical approaches to the same facts and issues, even though an attorney would usually write only one office memo. (The first office memo explains the conclusions conveyed in the letter to the client.)

The case file is fixed in time, between the client interview in fall 1992 and the oral argument in spring 1994. Thus, the pertinent authorities are not necessarily current. If you encounter a research project on any of the topics in this case file, you should perform your own research to assure that you have current and correct authority and are using the current rules of court governing format.

Dick Weatherston's Assoc'd Mech'l Servs. v. Minnesota Mut. Life Ins. Co., 257 Minn. 184, 100 N.W.2d 819 (1960).

① case name

② docket number

DICK WEATHERSTON'S A. M. SERV. v. MINNESOTA M. L. I. CO.   Minn.   **819**
Cite as 100 N.W.2d 819

⑦

DICK WEATHERSTON'S ASSOCIATED MECHANICAL SERVICES, INC., Respondent,

v.

MINNESOTA MUTUAL LIFE INSURANCE COMPANY, Appellant.

No. 37730.

Supreme Court of Minnesota.

Jan. 22, 1960.

Action was brought for breach of contract between plaintiff's assignor and defendant for installation of air-conditioning equipment by assignor in defendant's building. The District Court, Ramsey County, Ronald E. Hachey, J., entered an order denying defendant's motion in the alternative for judgment notwithstanding the verdict for a new trial, and the defendant appealed. The Supreme Court, Murphy, J., held that contract between plaintiff's assignor and defendant for installation of air-conditioning equipment by assignor in defendant's building, was not illegal under statute providing that it is unlawful for a person to practice, among other occupations, architecture and professional engineering unless such person is qualified by registration under law, though contract involved elements of engineering work by preparation of plans and estimates, and though assignor was not licensed as an engineer under the statute, where plans, specifications, and estimates were furnished with understanding that they would be subject to approval by defendant's architect and engineer and were to be installed under supervision of that architect and engineer, and such professional work was incidental to and part of the contract for the entire job and was approved and accepted by defendant's architect and engineer.

Affirmed with directions.

1. Appeal and Error ⚖930(1)

Conflicts in evidence are to be resolved upon appeal by stating controlling facts as jury, in light of whole evidence, reasonably could and must have found them in arriving at its verdict, and reviewing court is controlled by such elementary rule, even though reviewing court might have, on basis of record, reached a different conclusion.

2. Contracts ⚖28(3)

In action to recover for breach of alleged contract between plaintiff's assignor and defendant for installation of air-conditioning equipment in defendant's building, evidence sustained jury's findings that a valid contract had been made by plaintiff's assignor and defendant.

3. Appeal and Error ⚖994(2, 3)

Question whether certain witnesses are worthy of belief is primarily for jury and trial court.

4. Licenses ⚖39.1

Generally, where a license or certificate is required by statute as a requisite for one practicing a particular profession, an agreement of professional character without such license or certificate is ordinarily held illegal and void.

5. Licenses ⚖39.40

Statute providing that it is unlawful for a person to practice, among other occupations, architecture and professional engineering unless such person is qualified by registration under law, is founded on sound public policy and has as its purpose the public health and welfare as well as the protection of the public against incompetence and fraud. M.S.A. § 326.02.

6. Licenses ⚖39.1

Justice and sound public policy do not always require literal and arbitrary enforcement of a licensing statute, and though general rule is that a contract executed in violation of a statute imposing a prohibition against carrying on of a business or occupation without first having secured a license is void, that rule is not to be

---

① case name
② docket number

③ court	⑥ West's headnotes
④ date of decision	⑦ citation
⑤ West's editorial matter	

applied in a particular case without first examining the statute as a whole to determine whether or not the Legislature intended such contract to be illegal.

7. Licenses ⬤=39.40

Contract between plaintiff's assignor and defendant for installation of air-conditioning equipment by assignor in defendant's building, was not illegal under statute providing that it is unlawful for a person to practice, among other occupations, architecture and professional engineering unless such person is qualified by registration under law, though contract involved elements of engineering work by preparation of plans and estimates, and though assignor was not licensed as an engineer under the statute, where plans, specifications, and estimates were furnished with understanding that they would be subject to approval by defendant's architect and engineer and were to be installed under supervision of that architect and engineer, and such professional work was incidental to and part of the contract for the entire job and was approved and accepted by defendant's architect and engineer. M.S.A. § 326.02.

8. Damages ⬤=40(2)

Generally, where breach of contract consists in the repudiation of the contract or prevention of performance of contract, party who is ready to perform may recover profits he would have realized had contract been performed.

9. Damages ⬤=45

In action for breach of contract between plaintiff's assignor and defendant for installation of air-conditioning equipment by assignor in defendant's building, it was proper for jury in determining amount of plaintiff's damages to consider $1,500 item representing time consumed by plaintiff's assignor, not only in preparation of plans and designs for approval by defendant's architect, but expense involved as well in time expended in conferences and in investigating prices and costs of components required for installation of the equipment.

10. Appeal and Error ⬤=221, 1178(6)
Costs ⬤=238(2)

Where appellant fails to call trial court's attention to error in jury's computation resulting in an excessive verdict, such error ordinarily will not be considered on appeal for the first time, but where apparent error in computation is substantial, question may be remanded for review by trial court in interests of justice without prejudice to respondent's rights to recover costs on appeal.

Syllabus by the Court.

1. Conflicts in the evidence are to be resolved upon appeal by stating the controlling facts as the jury in the light of the whole evidence reasonably could and must have found them in arriving at its verdict. An appellate court is controlled by this elementary rule even though it might have, on the basis of the record, reached a different conclusion.

2. It is the general rule that where a license or certificate is required by a statute as a requisite for one practicing a particular profession, an agreement of professional character without such license or certificate is ordinarily held illegal and void.

3. M.S.A. § 326.02, which requires persons engaged in the occupation of architecture and professional engineering to qualify by registration, is founded upon sound public policy, having as its purpose the public health and welfare as well as the protection of the public against incompetence and fraud.

4. Where an air-conditioning contractor enters into a contract for the installation of air-conditioning equipment, which contract involves elements of engineering work by preparation of plans and estimates, such contract is not rendered illegal within the meaning of § 326.02, even though the contractor is not licensed as an engineer under § 326.02, where the plans, specifications, and estimates are furnished with the understanding that they will be subject to approval by the architect and engineer re-

DICK WEATHERSTON'S A. M. SERV. v. MINNESOTA M. L. I. CO. Minn. **821**
Cite as 100 N.W.2d 819

tained by the other party and are to be installed under the supervision of the other party's architect and engineer. Such professional work was incidental to and part of the contract for the entire job and was approved and accepted by the architects and engineers responsible for the supervision of such construction.

5. The court correctly instructed the jury in accordance with the general rule that where a breach consists in repudiating the contract or preventing its performance the party who is ready to perform may recover the profits he would have realized had the contract been performed and that expenditures made in preparation to execute the contract may be recovered.

6. Where the appellant fails to call the trial court's attention to an error in computation by the jury resulting in an excessive verdict, such error ordinarily will not be considered on appeal for the first time. However, where the apparent error is substantial, the question may be remanded for review by the trial court in the interests of justice without prejudice to the respondent's rights to recover costs on appeal.

———•———

Richard J. Leonard and Eugene M. Warlich, St. Paul, Doherty, Rumble & Butler, St. Paul, of counsel, for appellant.

B. Jerome Loftsgaarden, Loftsgaarden & Loftsgaarden, St. Paul, for respondent.

MURPHY, Justice.

This case comes to us on appeal from an order denying the defendant's motion in the alternative for judgment notwithstanding the verdict or for a new trial. The plaintiff recovered a verdict in the sum of $5,691 in an action brought for breach of contract. The principal issue involved in this case requires a construction of M.S.A. § 326.02 as it applies to the particular facts before us. We are asked to determine if a contract which includes professional engineering services is in violation of that

statute and illegal so as to preclude recovery thereon under circumstances where the contractor is an unlicensed engineer whose services are rendered subject to the approval and supervision of an architect and engineer retained by the other party.

Viewing the record in the light most favorable to the verdict, the jury could have found these facts: The plaintiff's assignor, Dick Weatherston, at the time of the events involved in this action, was a contractor in the air-conditioning business. He had received a bachelor of science degree in mechanical engineering from the University of Michigan, after which he was employed by various companies, including General Mills and the Seeger Refrigerator Company, as a plant engineer. For some years before engaging in the contracting business in Minnesota he was employed as a project engineer, and in the course of that work he was registered in that profession under the laws of the States of Ohio and Texas. As a contractor he expected to receive work on projects designed and supervised by registered architects and engineers, and he stated in his testimony that in order to avoid a conflict of interest and to obviate the possibility of being considered a competitor with such architects and engineers he did not register as an engineer in Minnesota.

In the fall of 1956 the Minnesota Mutual Life Insurance Company was in the process of completing the construction of a large home office building in St. Paul. They had retained as their architects the firm of Ellerbe & Company. It appears that during the process of construction of this building the company determined to install certain electronic computing equipment on one of the upper floors of the building. Because of the great amount of heat this machine would give off in operation, there arose a serious problem in providing ventilation and air conditioning in the particular area where the equipment was to be installed.

In the fall of 1956 certain officers of the defendant company discussed the problem

⑨ attorneys ⑪ beginning of opinion ⑬ major issue
⑩ authoring justice ⑫ procedure ⑭ real-world facts

822   Minn.   100 NORTH WESTERN REPORTER, 2d SERIES

with plaintiff. He was advised that the plans submitted by Ellerbe & Company as to this particular phase of the construction and installation would involve costs in excess of the budget set up by the company. They asked him if he would be in a position to give them a proposal, including a design and cost price, to solve the air-conditioning problem in the particular area involved. After being told that Ellerbe & Company were the architects and engineers retained by the builder, Weatherston informed the defendant through its officers that a large part of his business was derived from architectural firms and that if these firms knew that he engaged in designing and engineering work they would discontinue dealing with him. He told them accordingly that he could not compete with Ellerbe in designing the system, but he could submit plans if he obtained the contract for the entire installation. He was told that an arrangement had been made whereby Ellerbe had withdrawn from the "air conditioning phase" of the installation but that they would remain as "consultant" to supervise and approve the system used. Weatherston agreed to this arrangement.

Preliminary plans and specifications were drawn up by Weatherston and submitted to the company with an offer about January 1, 1957. When these plans were submitted to the officers of the defendant company, Weatherston again explained that he was a contractor and did not want to conflict with Ellerbe in doing designing or engineering work. He was told that the company understood his position and that the plans submitted by him would have to be approved by Ellerbe. After some discussion and examination of his proposals, another plan was drawn up and submitted with a new offer for approval by Ellerbe & Company. Later, modifications were made which were suggested by Ellerbe and a final proposal appears to have been submitted some time in February 1957. During the course of these negotiations there were at least three conferences with Ellerbe & Company, the defendant's architects. The final plan, ex-

cept for some minor changes, proved satisfactory to Ellerbe & Company, and after a meeting at their office, it was agreed that the plaintiff would install the necessary equipment and furnish the materials for a price of $16,203. Weatherston testified that, after the final meeting with Ellerbe, the corporate officer who acted for the defendant company told him "to proceed with the work and get the equipment ordered, and then to, just to go ahead and get the job rolling." In the proposals Weatherston submitted, the sales price of all component parts of the air-conditioning system was included. So far as appears from the record no charge for design or plan was made. Weatherston considered the contract as one for the sale of an entire system and none of his actions in submitting the proposals are inconsistent with that conclusion.

On March 2, 1957, about 2 weeks after Weatherston claims his plans were submitted and his offer was accepted, he was informed that the defendant company had determined to give the work to another air-conditioning contractor. No loss was sustained by the plaintiff in the purchase of materials specified for the job. He was able to cancel the orders before delivery. The work was finally performed by Holmsten Refrigeration, Inc. It appears from the evidence that the latter company was not a registered architect or engineer.

[1–3] 1. There is a sharp conflict in the evidence in this case. The evidence of the defendant tended to show that no contract was ever entered into between the parties; that the plaintiff was one of a number of contractors invited to submit a bid or proposal setting forth the materials and labor he would furnish and the price he would charge for the proposed work; and that there was no acceptance of any proposal made by the plaintiff. On the other hand, there was evidence supporting the finding of the jury that an offer and acceptance constituting a valid contract had been made by the parties. Under the circumstances we are controlled by the well-

⑮

---

⑮   discussion of first issue: evidence supporting contract

DICK WEATHERSTON'S A. M. SERV. v. MINNESOTA M. L. I. CO. Minn. **823**

Cite as 100 N.W.2d 819

established rule that conflicts are to be resolved upon appeal by stating the controlling facts as the jury, in the light of the whole evidence, reasonably could and must have found them in arriving at its verdict. An appellate court is controlled by this elementary rule even though it might have, on the basis of the record, reached a different conclusion. Hardy v. Anderson, 241 Minn. 478, 63 N.W.2d 814; 1 Dunnell, Dig. (3 ed.) § 415b; 14 Id. §§ 7144, 7159. Whether certain witnesses are worthy of belief is primarily for the jury and the trial court. Becker v. Thomson, 208 Minn. 332, 294 N. W. 214.

⑯   [4] *2.* It is the contention of the defendant that the contract involved is one for professional engineering services and, since the plaintiff was unlicensed as an engineer, the contract is illegal so as to pre-

⑰   clude recovery. It may be generally stated that where a license or certificate is required by statute as a requisite for one practicing a particular profession, an agreement of professional character without such license or certificate is ordinarily held illegal and void.[1]

1. 53 C.J.S. Licenses, § 59; 33 Am.Jur., Licenses, §§ 68 to 74, 4 Dunnell, Dig. (3 ed.) § 1873.

2. Section 326.02, subd. 1, provides:
   "In order to safeguard life, health, and property, and to promote the public welfare, any person in either public or private capacity practicing, or offering to practice, architecture, professional engineering, or land surveying in this state, either as an individual, a co-partner, or as agent of another, shall be registered as hereinafter provided. It shall be unlawful for any person to practice, or to offer to practice, in this state, architecture, professional engineering, or land surveying, or to solicit or to contract to furnish work within the terms of sections 326.02 to 326.16, or to use in connection with his name or to otherwise assume, use or advertise any title or description tending to convey the impression that he is an architect, professional engineer (hereinafter called engineer) or land surveyor, unless such person is qualified by registration under sections 326.02 to 326.16."

[5] *3.* It is specifically provided by M.S.A. § 326.02 that it is unlawful for a person to practice, among other occupations, architecture and professional engineering unless such person is qualified by registration under law.[2] This statute is founded upon sound public policy, having as its purpose the public health and welfare as well as the protection of the public against incompetence and fraud.[3] It has been held in accordance with this principle that contracts made in violation of statutes requiring registration or licensing of engineers or architects are illegal and unenforceable because inimical to both the public policy and the actual, though implied, intent of the legislature.[4]

[6] *4.* While it is true that certain elements of the preliminary work performed by the plaintiff, such as calculations and design submitted by the plaintiff to the defendant and its architects, required an expertise in the area of engineering as defined by § 326.02, subd. 3,[5] the transaction as a whole must be considered in connection with its particular facts to determine if it comes within the prohibition of § 326.02.

3. In re Estate of Peterson, 230 Minn. 478. 42 N.W.2d 59, 18 A.L.R.2d 910; Leuthold v. Stickney, 116 Minn. 299, 133 N.W. 856, 39 L.R.A.,N.S., 231; cf. Vercellini v. U. S. I. Realty Co., 158 Minn. 72, 196 N.W. 672; Restatement, Contracts, § 580; 6 Corbin, Contracts, § 1512; 4 Dunnell, Dig. (3 ed.) § 1873; Annotations, 42 A.L.R. 1226 to 1228 and 118 A.L.R. 646.

4. Baer v. Tippett, 34 Cal.App.2d 33, 92 P.2d 1028; American Store Equipment & Const. Corp. v. Jack Dempsey's Punch Bowl, Inc., 174 Misc. 436, 21 N.Y.S.2d 117, affirmed 258 App.Div. 794, 16 N.Y.S. 2d 702, affirmed 283 N.Y. 601, 28 N.E.2d 23; 6 Williston, Contracts (Rev. ed.) § 1766.

5. Designing the plans and specifications called for knowledge of heating units (called British Thermal Units) which the equipment would give off when operating; calculating the amount of air conditioning needed to carry off the heat and control the room temperature; locating and installing the various component parts of the system; designing

---

⑯   discussion of second issue: ⑰   general rule
      legality of contract

Justice and sound public policy do not always require the literal and arbitrary enforcement of a licensing statute.[6] While recognizing the general rule that a contract executed in violation of a statute imposing a prohibition against the carrying on of a business or occupation without first having secured a license is void, that rule is not to be applied in a particular case without first examining the statute as a whole to determine whether or not the legislature intended such contract to be illegal.[7]

[7] If we apply the terms of the statute to the particular facts in this case we must readily come to the conclusion that the agreement between the parties was in no way inimical to life, health, property, or public welfare; nor should there by any difficulty in conceding that the transaction before us is free from any element of fraud, incompetence, or misrepresentation. Viewing the relationship of the parties, it must be recognized at the outset that the plaintiff was sought out by the defendant for his services as an air-conditioning contractor. It was clearly understood by the defendant that the plaintiff was engaged in the air-conditioning business and that in

addition to his qualifications as a contractor he had a background and education giving him a certain competence in the area of engineering. The plaintiff, however, made it clear to the defendant that he was not a registered engineer and architect. It is equally clear that the defendant had its own architects and engineers and did not wholly rely upon the qualifications of the plaintiff in that area. Because of the nature of the work to be performed, it was necessary for the plaintiff in order to give the defendant an estimate of the cost of the proposed work to specify the materials needed with plans and details of how the work was to be carried out. The defendant company was interested in having the work done at a price which would come within its budget. Since the plan for this work prepared by its own architects and engineers exceeded the budget, it was not surprising that it consulted a contractor who, because of his business, had specialized knowledge of methods of installing air-conditioning equipment. The design and plan he submitted to accomplish this purpose were approved by the defendant's architects and in effect were adopted by it and became its own plans.[8]

---

methods to comply with city ordinances on water regulation, all for the protection of the machinery and health and comfort of defendant's employees. Section 326.02, subd. 3, provides:

"Any person shall be deemed to be practicing professional engineering within the meaning of sections 326.02 to 326.-16 who shall furnish any technical professional service, such as planning, design or supervision of construction for the purpose of assuring compliance with specifications and design, in connection with any public or private structures, buildings, ultilities, machines, equipment, processes, works, or projects wherein the public welfare or the safeguarding of life, health, or property is concerned or involved, when such professional service requires the application of the principles of mathematics and the physical sciences, acquired by education or training."

6. 6 Corbin, Contracts, § 1512, p. 968.

7. 4 Dunnell, Dig. (3 ed.) § 1873; see, In re Estate of Peterson, 230 Minn. 478, 42 N.W.2d 59, 18 A.L.R.2d 910; Minter

Brothers Co. v. Hochman, 231 Minn. 156, 42 N.W.2d 562; Brimhall v. Van Campen, 8 Minn. 13, Gil. 1.

8. The necessity of examining the particular facts in each case so as to determine whether or not there is a violation of the statute becomes apparent from the testimony of Richard Holmsten, who was eventually awarded the contract for the work. He was not registered as an engineer or architect, yet he testified there were two methods by which air-conditioning contractors received work. He said, "One is to receive from a registered engineer a set of plans and specifications whereby he will outline the problem involved and we submit our quotation to accomplish this problem." The other, he said, is to call upon the customer and "ask him for the opportunity to design and work up a proposal to accomplish, for the problem which we quote a sum of money to accomplish this." He further testified that his company prepared plans where the job was of sufficient size "that it is to our benefit." It is

⑲

Since the professional work performed by the plaintiff in this case was incidental to and part of a contract for an entire job which was approved and accepted by architects and engineers responsible for the supervision of such construction, it is our view that it comes within those numerous exceptions which hold generally that the prohibitions of the statute involved are no broader than its purpose in protecting the public from misrepresentation and deceit.[9] The scope of the statute coincides with the reasons for its existence. Since those reasons have no bearing upon the transaction involved herein, the statute is without application. 6 Corbin, Contracts, § 1512; In re Estate of Peterson, 230 Minn. 478, 42 N.W.2d 59, 18 A.L.R.2d 910.

5. In support of its contention that the plaintiff violated the statute, the defendant points to the allegation of the plaintiff's amended complaint claiming damages in the sum of $1,500 for "work performed in designing and preparing drawings for said mechanical work" and to the testimony of the plaintiff to the effect that his contract price included the sum of $1,500 for that particular work. It argues that this evidence alone is determinative of the character of the work as being an architectural and engineering service requiring registration under the law.

[8, 9] In discussing this point it is necessary to keep in mind that this is not a suit to collect for an architectural or engineering fee. It is a suit to recover damages suffered by the plaintiff as a result of the defendant's alleged breach of contract. The only out-of-pocket expense involved in this transaction grew out of loss of the plaintiff's time in conferences with the defendant and its architects and in preparation of plans for the execution of the contract. We think the trial court correctly

perceived the issues as appears from his instructions. He told the jury that under the laws of Minnesota "an unregistered person is not permitted to practice professional engineering" and that "plaintiff would not be permitted to recover for the engineering services, that is, the consultation service, the drawing of plans, and the proposals standing alone because plaintiff is not a registered engineer in this state." He told the jury that the plaintiff could not recover for the services performed unless he could show that under the agreement "he was to prepare the plans and drawings or any other proposal and make the complete installation for a price certain and that the same was accepted by the defendant * * *." On the issue of damages he correctly instructed the jury in accordance with the general rule that where the breach consists in repudiating the contract or preventing its performance the party who is ready to perform may recover the profits he would have realized had the contract been performed. 15 Am.Jur., Damages, § 151; 5 Dunnell, Dig. (3 ed.) § 2568a. Further, with reference to expenditures made in preparation to execute the contract, the jury was instructed that recovery may be had for expense incurred in part performance or in preparation for performance, providing, of course, such items of damage are proven. Swanson v. Andrus, 83 Minn. 505, 86 N.W. 465; Periodical Press Co. v. Sherman-Elliott Co., 143 Minn. 489, 174 N.W. 516; Johnson v. Wright, 175 Minn. 236, 220 N.W. 946; 5 Dunnell, Dig. (3 ed.) § 2568a. In determining plaintiff's damage we think it was proper for the jury to take into consideration actual costs incurred by the plaintiff in connection with this work. We think it satisfactorily appears from the evidence that the $1,500 item represents time consumed by the plaintiff, not only in the preparation of the plans and designs

conceivable that under the latter method, depending upon the particular circumstances, the contractor might find that he is in fact engaging in professional engineering work without having registered as required by law.
100 N.W.2d—52½

9. Kennoy v. Graves, Ky., 300 S.W.2d 568; Edmonds v. Fehler & Feinauer Const. Co., 6 Cir., 252 F.2d 639; Dow v. United States, 10 Cir., 154 F.2d 707; Fischer v. Landisch, 203 Wis. 254, 234 N.W. 498.

---

⑲   holding; specific rule

826   Minn.   100 NORTH WESTERN REPORTER, 2d SERIES

for approval by the defendant's architect but expense involved as well in time expended in conferences and in investigating prices and costs of the components required for the installation of the work. We agree with the trial court that it was proper for the jury to consider the $1,500 item as an out-of-pocket expenditure in establishing the amount of plaintiff's damages.

6. In addition to the $1,500 representing the work performed in designing and preparing the drawings, the plaintiff claimed the further sum of $4,191.21 for loss of profit in the performance of the work. His total claim was $5,691.21. The jury awarded him $5,691, of which $4,191 appears to have been attributable to profit.

The record strongly supports the company's claim that the verdict is excessive. The plaintiff testified as to the cost of the various components, including two air conditioners, pneumatic controls, humidifiers, electrical wiring, and other items including labor and freight. He testified that his profit was $4,191.21, which was the difference between his cost price of $12,011.79 and his selling cost of $16,203. It appears from the record, however, that the plaintiff's estimated cost was $13,011.80, not $12,011.79. His profit, accordingly, would not be $4,191.21, but $3,191.20, or exactly $1,000.01 less than the error in addition showed it to be.

The defendant accordingly argues that a new trial should be granted on the ground that the verdict on the issue of damages is contrary to law and is not sustained by the evidence.

It must be noted, however, that the defendant made no motion in the trial court for a correction of this error. The trial court should have first been given the opportunity to examine the verdict and the record to determine how the error was made, if there was one, for the error could have been made in other ways than excessive computation by the jury. La Nasa v. Pierre, 225 Minn. 189, 30 N.W.2d 32; Fletcher v. German-American Ins. Co., 79 Minn. 337, 343, 82 N.W. 647, 649; Barnard-Curtiss Co. v. Minneapolis Dredging Co., 200 Minn. 327, 274 N.W. 229.

[10] In view of the substantial amount involved, we are of the view that in the interests of justice this particular issue should be remanded to the district court to give it an opportunity to pass upon the matter of the apparent error. The order of the trial court is affirmed and the case is remanded to the district court for the purpose only of reviewing the issue relating to the asserted error in computation. The case is remanded, however, only on condition that the appellant pay the full costs and disbursements on this appeal and such further costs as may be incurred on remand to the district court.

Affirmed with directions.

---

 discussion of third issue: excessive damages   procedural outcome

Weatherston's brief

Dick Weatherston's Associated Mechanical Services v. Minnesota Mutual Life Insurance Co., 100 N.W.2d 819 (Minn. 1960).

FACTS: P is contractor in air conditioning in MN. Although P's assignor Dick Weatherston (DW) had B.S. in mechanical engineering, he was not registered as engr in MN. D needed air conditioning for new building & asked P to submit design plans & pricing. DW told D he wasn't licensed & raised concern about conflict w/Ellerbe, D's architects & engrs. Ellerbe agreed to act as consultant. P submitted plans; they were modified after review by Ellerbe & approved. No charge for design or plan was included. P was told to start, but 2 weeks later, P was informed that D had given project to different contractor (also not reg'd engr).

PROCEDURE: P sued D for damages for breach of K. Jury found offer & acceptance & awarded damages. D moved for new trial or JNOV; denied. D appealed.

*ISSUE: Is K illegal, or can unregistered engr recover damages for breach of K, where statute requires regn as engr to practice engrg, work includes professional engr services, engr has training as engr, services are subject to approval of architect/engr retained by D, & D knows engr isn't regd?

HOLDING: Affirmed & remanded to trial ct w/directions re damages. Unregistered engr can recover damages for breach of K including engr services where engr has training, D's engr approves plans, & engr tells D of non-regn.

REASONING: General rule: Ks made in violation of licensing statutes typically are illegal & void. But statute must be viewed as whole to avoid arbitrary result & to determine whether legislature intended K to be illegal.
   Minn. Stat. § 326.02 requires that person who practices as profl engr be registered in MN. Statutory purpose is to protect public against fraud & incompetence & to promote public health & welfare.
   Here K should be enforced: K was incidental to & part of entire job. DW had training. Work was approved by registered engrs. D sought out P, & DW told D of unregd status. Case does not raise concerns about incompetence, harm to public welfare, fraud.
   Policy: Assure that parties who K for engr services are not harmed by fraud or work done by incompetent persons. Safeguard public welfare through properly engrd buildings (presumably).
   Nor does P's claim for "designing & preparing drawings" establish P's work was illegal engrg practice.

---

*Challenge to jury verdict & damages award are not covered.

Buckley v. Humason, 52 N.W. 385 (Minn. 1892).

BUCKLEY v. HUMASON *et al.*

(Supreme Court of Minnesota. June 15, 1892.)

VALIDITY OF CONTRACT—DOING BUSINESS WITHOUT LICENSE—REAL-ESTATE AGENTS.

1. Transactions in violation of law cannot be made the foundation of a valid contract.

2. Where a statute or an ordinance, duly authorized and enacted, makes a particular business unlawful for unlicensed persons, any contract made in such business by one not authorized is void.

3. Where, by a valid city ordinance, it was made unlawful for any person to exercise within the city the business of a real-estate broker without a license, *held*, that a person so engaged in negotiating the sale or exchange of real property, in violation of such ordinance, could recover no commissions for his services.

(Syllabus by the Court.)

Appeal from district court, Ramsey county; EGAN, Judge.

Action by Thomas A. Buckley against Emma A. Humason and others to recover commissions for services as real-estate agent. From an order dismissing the case on plaintiff's showing he appeals. Affirmed.

Stevens, O'Brien & Glenn and *Armand Albrecht,* for appellant. *Otis & Godfrey,* for respondents.

VANDERBURGH, J. This action is brought by plaintiff to recover commissions for services as a real-estate agent or broker in procuring a purchaser for certain real estate in Chicago. The cause of action is stated as follows in the complaint: "During the year 1890 the plaintiff, at the special instance and request of the defendants, performed services for said defendants in the city of Chicago, in the state of Illinois, in and about procuring a purchaser for certain property in the state of Illinois, which said services were then and there of the reasonable value of $4,375, and which said sum the defendants agreed and promised to pay plaintiff therefor." The plaintiff testified that at the time of the alleged services he resided in the city of Chicago. The transactions referred to occurred there, and the negotiations were there concluded, and the contract and purchase were consummated in that city, and the plaintiff claims to be entitled to the usual commissions charged and received in Chicago for such services. He also testified that he had been previously engaged in the real-estate business in Chicago, as an agent, and sold and exchanged property for others on commission; and the transaction in question appears clearly enough to have been in the line of his regular business as a real-estate agent or broker. In this connection we must observe that it is admitted in the pleadings that during the year 1890, and prior thereto, an ordinance of the city of Chicago, enacted in pursuance of a statute of that state, was in force, which provided that it should not be lawful for any person to exercise within that city the business of real-estate broker, without a license therefor, and defined a "real-estate broker" as a person who, for commissions or other compensation, is engaged in the selling of or in negotiating sales of real estate belonging to others. A license fee of $25 per annum is required to be paid by such broker, and any person violating the provisions of the ordinance is subject to a penalty of not less than $25, and to the same penalty for every subsequent violation thereof. The testimony shows that the plaintiff was using and exercising the business of a real-estate broker in the city of Chicago during the time in question, and in performing the services for which a recovery is sought in this action. It was made unlawful for him to do so by the terms of the ordinance referred to. It was not at all material that the parties for whom he negotiated a sale agreed to take property in St. Paul in payment or exchange for the Chicago property of which plaintiff negotiated a sale, and for which he found a purchaser. The ordinance, which is set out in full in the answer, was valid, and the case as presented by the evidence clearly falls within it. Braun v Chicago, 110 Ill. 187. It has the force of law within the city of Chicago. Bott v. Pratt, 33 Minn. 323, 23 N. W. Rep. 237. The particular transaction in question was therefore in violation of law, unless he was duly licensed, which was not shown. On the contrary, the answer alleges, and it stands admitted, for want of a reply, that the plaintiff was not duly licensed as a broker. The plaintiff cannot, therefore, recover his commissions. Hustis v. Pickands, 27 Ill. App. 270; Johnson v. Hulings, 103 Pa. St. 501; Holt v. Green, 73 Pa. St. 198. Business transactions, in violation of law, cannot be made the foundation of a valid contract; and the general rule is that where a statute makes a particular business unlawful generally, or for unlicensed persons, any contract made in such business by one not authorized is void, (Bish. Cont. §§ 471, 547; 1 Pom. Eq. Jur. § 402;) and the contract, being void where it was made and to be performed, will be so held here, (Bish. Cont. § 1383.) The case was properly dismissed upon the evidence.

Order affirmed.

Buckley brief

Buckley v. Humason, 52 N.W. 385 (Minn. 1892).

FACTS: P, real estate broker & resident of Chicago, was hired by D to find purchaser for D's property in Chicago in 1890. In 1890 Chicago ordinance stated that RE broker must obtain license to lawfully conduct RE business in Chicago. P was not licensed as RE broker during his K with D. P found purchaser, & D promised to pay P his commission. D did not pay P's commission.

PROCEDURE: P sued D to recover commission. Trial court dismissed P's suit, & P appeals.

ISSUE: Can person acting as RE agent without license in violation of city ordinance recover unpaid commission?

HOLDING: Affirmed. P cannot recover commission.

REASONING: Business transaction between P & D was unlawful because P was not licensed. Unlawful business transactions cannot be foundation of valid K, & K is void. P cannot enforce void K.

Solomon v. Dreschler, 4 Minn. 278 (1860).

SOLOMON *v.* DRESCHLER.   **197**

(4 Minn. R. p. 278.)

MEYER L. SOLOMON *vs.* WILLIAM DRESCHLER.

Contracts, Prohibited by Statute, Void.—Under the license law of 1855, a contract of sale of liquors, by one without a license, is void, and no action will lie thereon.

Ingersoll *vs.* Randall, vol. 14.

Onus of Proving License.—If a complaint for goods sold and delivered show that the articles sold were of such a character, that a sale of them without license would be invalid, the plaintiff must prove a license before he can recover.

Application of Payments. Legal and Illegal Demands.—Where a party claims two demands against another, one legal and the other illegal, and the debtor has made a payment which was not applied to either demand by the parties at the time, the law will apply it upon the legal demand.

Points and authorities for appellant not on file.

Points and authorities for respondent:—

1. The burden of proof is always upon the plaintiff to show that he has a legal claim against the defendant. Such claim is not shown by plaintiff showing that he has sold and delivered to the defendant spirituous liquors of certain value, where the sale of such liquors is prohibited by law, except under a license. In such a case, the court, taking judicial notice of the law, will require the plaintiff to show that he had authority or legal capacity to sell, and, until he does this, no indebtedness is shown.

2. A party can in no case recover upon a contract made in violation of the statute, and for making which he renders himself liable to fine and imprisonment. Chitty Cont. 420, and authorities there cited.

3. Where a plaintiff has brought his action to recover upon several contracts, and some of them appear to be legal and valid, and others to have been made in contravention of the statutes, and general payments have been made and no specific application made of the payments, the courts must apply the same upon the legal and valid

contracts, for they cannot countenance or reward violations of the public law.

Lawrence & Lochren, for appellant.

Sanborn & Lund, for respondent.

FLANDRAU, J.   The complaint was in the ordinary form for goods, wares, and merchandise, sold and delivered, with a bill of particulars attached, which showed the articles to be principally spirituous liquors.   The sale was alleged to have been at St. Anthony, in the County of Hennepin.   The answer sufficiently alleges that the plaintiff had no license to sell spirituous liquors at the time the sale was made, and the defendant proved it on the trial by calling the register of deeds of Hennepin County to the point.

The judge charged the jury that the allegation in the complaint, of the place where the liquor was sold, concluded the plaintiff on that point, nothing appearing to the contrary; and that place being within the operation of the license law of 1855, which was in force at the time of the sale, the burden of proof was upon the plaintiff to show that he was duly licensed to sell liquors, and that he could not recover if the liquors in question were sold without license.   He also charged that as part of the articles were not liquors, and not under the prohibition of the statute, that the payments which had been made, should be applied first to such lawful article, if there had been no specific application of them by the parties.   All these points of the charge were severally excepted to by the plaintiff.

There are two principal questions presented for decision: *First*, whether the statute of 1855 renders a contract made in contravention of its provisions irrecoverable? and, *second*, where the burden of proof lies to show the violation of the statute, or, in other words, whether the plaintiff must show that he had a license, or the defendant must show that he had not?   The law is now pretty well settled, that where a statute inflicts a penalty for doing an

SOLOMON *v.* DRESCHLER.   199

act, although the act is not prohibited in terms, yet it is thereby rendered unlawful, because the infliction of a penalty implies a prohibition. *De Begins* v. *Armistead*, 10 Bing. 107; *Forster* v. *Taylor*, 3 Nev. & Man. 224; *Forster* v. *Taylor*, 5 B. & Adolph, 887; *Cope* v. *Rowlands*, 2 Mee. & W. 149; 1 Binn. 110; 4 Serg. & R. 159; 14 Mass. 322

A distinction has been made between statutes, which, in requiring licenses, to engage in a particular business, have in view only the raising of revenue, and statutes which look to the protection of the public health or morals, or the prevention of fraud in the seller of goods. And it has been held that in the former cases, a contract would be valid, although it contravened the provisions of the statute, *Johnson* v. *Hudson*, 11 East. 180; *Brown* v. *Duncan*, 10 B. & C. 93; *Griffith* v. *Welles*, 3 Denio, 226; *Harris* v. *Runnels*, 12 How. U. S. 79; while in the latter it would be void; *Law* v. *Hodgson*, 2 Camp. 147; *Brown* v. *Duncan*, 10 B. & C. 93; *Forster* v. *Taylor*, 3 Nev. & Man. 224; *Little* v. *Poole*, 9 B. & C. 192; *Tyson* v. *Thomas*, McC. & Younge, 119; *Wheeler* v. *Russell*, 17 Mass. 258; *Bensley* v. *Bignold*, 5 B. & Ald. 335; *Drury* v. *Defontaine*, 1 Taunt. 136; *Cope* v. *Rowlands*, 2 Mee. & W. 149; *Houston* v. *Mills*, 1 Moody & R. 325. But in *Cope* v. *Rowlands*, 2 Mee. & W. 157, Baron Parke overrules this distinction, and says that if "the contract be rendered illegal, it can make no difference in point of law, whether the statute which has made it so has in view the protection of the revenue or any other object." And the supreme court of the United States in *Harris* v. *Runnels*, 12 How. U. S. 79, say that such is now (1851) the law in England, with many irreconcilable distinctions; leaving the question, in the opinion of the supreme court, in such a condition of uncertainty that they conclude the best rule is, to "examine the statute as a whole to find out whether or not the makers of it meant that a contract in contravention of it should be void, or that it was not to be so." Under this view we will examine the act of 1855. Section 1 of said act authorizes the granting of licenses by the county commissioners of the several counties outside of the Sioux purchases of 1851. Section 2 imposes the conditions upon which such licenses may be obtained; among which, besides the payment of a sum of money, is the giving of a bond of $5,000, conditioned that the licensed party will only sell in a designated building, and not on the Sabbath; that he will not permit any gambling for money in his house; that he will keep a quiet and orderly house, and will not sell to any minor or Indian. Section 3 authorizes suit to be brought on the bond in case of breach. Section 4 provides for the collection of the judgment recovered on the bond. Section 5 imposes a penalty for selling without license. Section 6 allows the county commissioners to revoke licenses granted by them, at will. The other sections of the act are not material to this examination.

It is quite clear that this act has in view more than the mere raising of revenue. If it had not, it would have been sufficient to have provided for a license at a stipulated sum, and imposed a penalty for selling without one. The bond and its conditions clearly indicate that the object of the act is, in the main, to protect the public against the evils which are generally supposed to result from the unrestrained traffic in spirituous liquors, and that the revenue is merely an incident. This view is much strengthened by the fact that a violation of the act may be punished by imprisonment as well as fine. We think that a violation of the statute is an act *contra bonos mores*, and that a court of justice should not lend its aid to help a party to enforce a contract thus tainted. On this point, the case of *Griffith* v. *Welles*, 3 Denio, 226, above cited, is exactly in point; and, in fact, it quadrates with the case at bar in every particular. The complaint was for whisky and beer. The defense, that it was sold without license. The justice of the peace gave judgment for the plaintiff for the value of the liquor. The common pleas reversed the judgment, on the ground that the plaintiff did not show a license to

MARTIN *v.* BROWN. 201

sell liquors, and the supreme court sustained the common pleas. Where the complaint shows that the articles sold are of such a character that the sale of them would be invalid without a license, the court knowing the law, then it is incumbent upon the plaintiff to show his authority to sell.

The general rule in regard to the application of payments where there are several accounts existing between the parties is this: The debtor, when he makes the payment, may apply it where he pleases; if he makes no specific application, then the creditor may appoint it. If neither do so, the law will apply it according to the justice of the case. But if a person have two demands upon another, one arising out of a lawful contract, and the other out of a contract forbidden by law, and the debtor make a payment which is not specifically appropriated at the time, the law will apply it to the legal demand. *Wright* v. *Laing*, 3 B. & C. 165.

We can find no error in the case which will authorize any interference with the judgment below. The judgment is therefore affirmed.

Solomon brief

Solomon v. Dreschler, 4 Minn. 278 (1860).

FACTS: Merchant P sold goods to D. Goods included "spirituous liquors" & other items. Territorial statute of 1855 required seller of liquors to obtain license, post bond of $5000, sell only in designated building, not sell on Sabbath or to minors or Indians, not permit gambling for money on premises, keep quiet & orderly house. Violations of statute are punishable by fine & imprisonment. P was not licensed.

PROCEDURE: P sued D to recover for price of goods sold to D. Lower court held for D. P appealed.

ISSUES: (1) Can seller recover under K for sale of liquor & other goods if K violates statute that imposes fine for selling liquor w/o license?
  (2) If sale of goods would be invalid without license, does burden of proof lie with P, to show there was no violation of licensing statute, or with D, to show violation of statute occurred?

HOLDING: (1) K for sale of liquor & other goods in violation of statute may not be enforced.
  (2) If sale of goods would be invalid w/o license, burden of proof lies with P to show P's authority & legal capacity to sell goods.

REASONING: Statute of 1855 is more than purely revenue statute. Policy behind statute is to protect public against problems that may result from unrestrained sale of "spirituous liquors." Violation of licensing statute may result in imprisonment & fine. Ct. should not enforce K that violates licensing statute. Therefore, K for sale of goods that violates licensing statute may not be enforced, & violator may be exposed to fine & imprisonment. Burden of proof lies with P to show P has legal claim against D.

Minn. Stat. § 481.02 (1992).

CHAPTER 481
ATTORNEYS-AT-LAW

481.01 BOARD OF LAW EXAMINERS; EXAMINATIONS.

The supreme court shall, by rule from time to time, prescribe the qualifications of all applicants for admission to practice law in this state, and shall appoint a board of law examiners, which shall be charged with the administration of such rules and with the examination of all applicants for admission to practice law. The board shall consist of not less than three, nor more than seven, attorneys at law, who shall be appointed each for the term of three years and until a successor qualifies. The supreme court may fill any vacancy in the board for the unexpired term and in its discretion may remove any member thereof. The board shall have a seal and shall keep a record of its proceedings, of all applications for admission to practice, and of persons admitted to practice upon its recommendation. At least two times a year the board shall hold examinations and report the result thereof, with its recommendations, to the supreme court. Upon consideration of such report, the supreme court shall enter an order in the case of each person examined, directing the board to reject or to issue to the person a certificate of admission to practice. The board shall have such officers as may, from time to time, be prescribed and designated by the supreme court. The fee for examination shall be fixed, from time to time, by the supreme court, but shall not exceed $50. Such fees, and any other fees which may be received pursuant to such rules as the supreme court may promulgate governing the practice of law shall be paid to the state treasurer and shall constitute a special fund in the state treasury. The moneys in such fund are appropriated annually to the supreme court for the payment of compensation and expenses of the members of the board of law examiners and for otherwise regulating the practice of law. The moneys in such fund shall never cancel. Payments therefrom shall be made by the state treasurer, upon warrants of the commissioner of finance issued upon vouchers signed by one of the justices of the supreme court. The members of the board shall have such compensation and such allowances for expenses as may, from time to time, be fixed by the supreme court.

History: *(5685) RL s 2278; 1921 c 161 s 1; 1953 c 167 s 1; 1959 c 384 s 1; 1963 c 718 s 1; 1973 c 492 s 14; 1976 c 149 s 57; 1985 c 248 s 70; 1986 c 444*

481.02 UNAUTHORIZED PRACTICE OF LAW.

Subdivision 1. **Prohibitions.** It shall be unlawful for any person or association of persons, except members of the bar of Minnesota admitted and licensed to practice as attorneys at law [1] to appear as attorney or counselor at law in any action or proceeding in any court in this state to maintain, conduct, or defend the same, except personally as a party thereto in other than a representative capacity, or, [2] by word, sign, letter, or advertisement, to hold out as competent or qualified to give legal advice or counsel, or to prepare legal documents, or as being engaged in advising or counseling in law or acting as attorney or counselor at law, or in furnishing to others the services of a lawyer or lawyers, or, [3] for a fee or any consideration, to give legal advice or counsel, perform for or furnish to another legal services, or, [4] for or without a fee or any consideration, to prepare, directly or through another, for another person, firm or corporation, any will or testamentary disposition or instrument of trust serving purposes similar to those of a will, or, [5] for a fee or any consideration, to prepare for another person, firm, or corporation, any other legal document, except as provided in subdivision 3.

title
scope
definition
general rule
   (elements 1–5)

25   ATTORNEYS-AT-LAW 481.02

not pertinent

Subd. 2. **Corporations.** No corporation, organized for pecuniary profit, except an attorney's professional corporation organized under chapter 319A, by or through its officers or employees or any one else, shall maintain, conduct, or defend, except in its own behalf when a party litigant, any action or proceeding in any court in this state, or shall, by or through its officers or employees or any one else, give or assume to give legal advice or counsel or perform for or furnish to another person or corporation legal services; or shall, by word, sign, letter, or advertisement, solicit the public or any person to permit it to prepare, or cause to be prepared, any will or testamentary disposition or instrument of trust serving purposes similar to those of a will, or hold itself out as desiring or willing to prepare any such document, or to give legal advice or legal services relating thereto or to give general legal advice or counsel, or to act as attorney at law or as supplying, or being in a position to supply, the services of a lawyer or lawyers; or shall to any extent engage in, or hold itself out as being engaged in, the business of supplying services of a lawyer or lawyers; or shall cause to be prepared any person's will or testamentary disposition or instrument of trust serving purposes similar to those of a will, or any other legal document, for another person, firm, or corporation, and receive, directly or indirectly, all or a part of the charges for such preparation or any benefits therefrom; or shall itself prepare, directly or through another, any such document for another person, firm, or corporation, except as provided in subdivision 3.

Subd. 3. **Permitted actions.** The provisions of this section shall not prohibit:

(1) any person from drawing, without charge, any document to which the person, an employer of the person, a firm of which the person is a member, or a corporation whose officer or employee the person is, is a party, except another's will or testamentary disposition or instrument of trust serving purposes similar to those of a will;

exception

(2) a person from drawing a will for another in an emergency if the imminence of death leaves insufficient time to have it drawn and its execution supervised by a licensed attorney-at-law;

not pertinent

(3) any insurance company from causing to be defended, or from offering to cause to be defended through lawyers of its selection, the insureds in policies issued or to be issued by it, in accordance with the terms of the policies;

(4) a licensed attorney-at-law from acting for several common-carrier corporations or any of its subsidiaries pursuant to arrangement between the corporations;

(5) any bona fide labor organization from giving legal advice to its members in matters arising out of their employment;

exception

(6) any person from conferring or cooperating with a licensed attorney-at-law of another in preparing any legal document, if the attorney is not, directly or indirectly, in the employ of the person or of any person, firm, or corporation represented by the person;

not pertinent

(7) any licensed attorney-at-law of Minnesota, who is an officer or employee of a corporation, from drawing, for or without compensation, any document to which the corporation is a party or in which it is interested personally or in a representative capacity, except wills or testamentary dispositions or instruments of trust serving purposes similar to those of a will, but any charge made for the legal work connected with preparing and drawing the document shall not exceed the amount paid to and received and retained by the attorney, and the attorney shall not, directly or indirectly, rebate the fee to or divide the fee with the corporation;

(8) any person or corporation from drawing, for or without a fee, farm or house leases, notes, mortgages, chattel mortgages, bills of sale, deeds, assignments, satisfactions, or any other conveyances except testamentary dispositions and instruments of trust;

not pertinent

(9) a licensed attorney-at-law of Minnesota from rendering to a corporation legal services to itself at the expense of one or more of its bona fide principal stockholders by whom the attorney is employed and by whom no compensation is, directly or indirectly, received for the services;

(10) any person or corporation engaged in the business of making collections from engaging or turning over to an attorney-at-law for the purpose of instituting and conducting suit or making proof of claim of a creditor in any case in which the attorney-at-law receives the entire compensation for the work;

(11) any regularly established farm journal or newspaper, devoted to general news, from publishing a department of legal questions and answers to them, made by a licensed attorney-at-law, if no answer is accompanied or at any time preceded or followed by any charge for it, any disclosure of any name of the maker of any answer, any recommendation of or reference to any one to furnish legal advice or services, or by any legal advice or service for the periodical or any one connected with it or suggested by it, directly or indirectly;

(12) any authorized management agent of an owner of rental property used for residential purposes, whether the management agent is a natural person, corporation, partnership, limited partnership, or any other business entity, from commencing, maintaining, conducting, or defending in its own behalf any action in any court in this state to recover or retain possession of the property, except that the provision of this clause does not authorize a person who is not a licensed attorney-at-law to conduct a jury trial or to appear before a district court or the court of appeals or supreme court pursuant to an appeal;

(13) any person from commencing, maintaining, conducting, or defending on behalf of the plaintiff or defendant any action in any court of this state pursuant to the provisions of section 566.175 or sections 566.18 to 566.35 or from commencing, maintaining, conducting, or defending on behalf of the plaintiff or defendant any action in any court of this state for the recovery of rental property used for residential purposes pursuant to the provisions of section 566.02 or 566.03, subdivision 1, except that the provision of this clause does not authorize a person who is not a licensed attorney-at-law to conduct a jury trial or to appear before a district court or the court of appeals or supreme court pursuant to an appeal, and provided that, except for a nonprofit corporation, a person who is not a licensed attorney-at-law shall not charge or collect a separate fee for services rendered pursuant to this clause;

(14) the delivery of legal services by a specialized legal assistant in accordance with a specialty license issued by the supreme court before July 1, 1995;

(15) the sole shareholder of a corporation from appearing on behalf of the corporation in court; or

(16) an officer, shareholder, director, partner, or employee from appearing on behalf of a corporation, partnership, sole proprietorship, or association in conciliation court in accordance with section 487.30, subdivision 4a, or in district court in an action that was removed from conciliation court.

Subd. 3a. **Real estate closing services.** Nothing in this section shall be construed to prevent a real estate broker, a real estate salesperson, or a real estate closing agent, as defined in section 82.17, from drawing or assisting in drawing papers incident to the sale, trade, lease, or loan of property, or from charging for drawing or assisting in drawing them, except as hereafter provided by the supreme court.

Subd. 4. **Mortgage foreclosure fees.** It shall be unlawful to exact, charge or receive any attorney's fee for the foreclosure of any mortgage, unless the foreclosure is conducted by a licensed attorney at law of Minnesota and unless the full amount charged as attorney's fee is actually paid to and received and retained by such attorney, without being, directly or indirectly, shared with or rebated to any one else; and it shall be unlawful for any such attorney to make any showing of receiving such a fee unless the attorney has received the same or to share with or rebate to any other person, firm, or corporation such fee, or any part thereof, received by the attorney; but such attorney

27   ATTORNEYS-AT-LAW 481.02

not pertinent

may divide such fee with another licensed attorney at law maintaining the other's place of business and not an officer or employee of the foreclosing party, if such attorney has assisted in performing the services for which the fee is paid, or resides in a place other than that where the foreclosure proceedings are conducted and has forwarded the case to the attorney conducting such foreclosure.

Subd. 5. **Corporate fiduciary agents.** It shall be unlawful for any corporation, appearing as executor, administrator, guardian, trustee, or other representative, to do the legal work in any action, probate proceeding or other proceeding in any court in this state, except through a licensed attorney at law of Minnesota maintaining the attorney's own place of business and not an officer or employee of such executor, administrator, guardian, trustee, or representative. No attorney's fee shall be charged or paid or received in any such case, unless actually paid to and received and retained by such an attorney at law maintaining the attorney's own place of business and not an officer or employee of such executor, administrator, guardian, trustee, or representative; and it shall be unlawful for such attorney to represent in any manner receiving any sum as a fee or compensation unless the same has been actually received or, directly or indirectly, to divide with or rebate to any person, firm, or corporation any part of any such fee or consideration received by the attorney in any such case; but such attorney may divide such fee with another licensed attorney at law maintaining the other's own place of business and not an officer or employee of such executor, administrator, guardian, trustee, or other representative, if such attorney has assisted in performing the services for which the fees are paid, or resides in a place other than that where the action or proceedings are conducted and has forwarded the case to the attorney conducting the action or proceedings.

Subd. 6. **Attorneys of other states.** Any attorney or counselor at law residing in any other state or territory in which the attorney has been admitted to practice law, who attends any term of the supreme court, court of appeals, or district court of this state for the purpose of trying or participating in the trial or proceedings of any action or proceedings there pending, may, in the discretion of the court before which the attorney appears in the action or proceeding, be permitted to try, or participate in the trial or proceedings in, the action or proceeding, without being subject to the provisions of this section, other than those set forth in subdivision 2, providing the state in which the attorney is licensed to practice law likewise grants permission to members of the state bar of Minnesota to act as an attorney for a client in that state under the same terms.

exception

Subd. 7. **Lay assistance to attorneys.** Nothing herein contained shall be construed to prevent a corporation from furnishing to any person lawfully engaged in the practice of law, such information or such clerical service in and about the attorney's professional work as, except for the provisions of this section, may be lawful, provided, that at all times the lawyer receiving such information or such services shall maintain full, professional and direct responsibility to the attorney's clients for the information and services so received.

consequences; enforcement

Subd. 8. **Penalty; injunction.** Any person or corporation, or officer or employee thereof, violating any of the foregoing provisions shall be guilty of a misdemeanor; and, upon conviction thereof, shall be punished as by statute provided for the punishment of misdemeanors. It shall be the duty of the respective county attorneys in this state to prosecute violations of this section, and the district courts of this state shall have sole original jurisdiction of any such offense under this section.

In lieu of criminal prosecution above provided for, such county attorney or the attorney general may, in the name of the state of Minnesota, or in the name of the state board of law examiners, proceed by injunction suit against any violator of any of the provisions above set forth to enjoin the doing of any act or acts violating any of said provisions.

not pertinent

Subd. 9. Nothing in subdivision 3a shall be construed to allow a person other than a licensed attorney to perform or provide the services of an attorney or be construed to otherwise conflict with this section.

History: *(5687-1) 1931 c 114 s 1; 1959 c 476 s 1; 1969 c 9 s 87; 1974 c 406 s 49; 1981 c 168 s 1; 1983 c 247 s 173,174; 1986 c 444; 1987 c 377 s 6; 1988 c 695 s 3-5; 1991 c 299 s 1; 1992 c 376 art 1 s 1; 1992 c 497 s 1; 1992 c 591 s 1*

§ 481.02 brief

IF any person/assn except members of MN bar admitted & licensed to practice

A. does 1 OR 2 OR 3 (all in subd. 1)

 1. gives legal advice or counsel
 or performs for or furnishes legal services
 to another
 for fee or considn

 2. prepares directly or thru another
 for another person/firm/corp.
 any will or testamentary disposition or instrument of trust serving purposes similar to will
 (for or w/o fee or considn)

 3. prepares for another person/firm/corp.
 any other legal document
 for fee or considn

  ■ common meaning of "legal" "document": official paper relied on as basis or proof, established by law or conforming to law
  ■ in pari materia: § 145B.04 equates living will with "legal document"

B. AND NOT person drafting will
 for another
 in emergency leaving insuff. time for atty supervn
 Subd. 3(2)

C. AND NOT person conferring or cooperating
 with licensed atty of another
 in preparing any legal document
 where atty is not empd by that person or by person/firm/corp. repd by that person
 Subd. 3(6)

D. AND NOT corp. furnishing
 lawful info or clerical services
 to atty
 who maintains responsibility to clients
 for info & services
 Subd. 7

THEN misdemeanor prosecuted by county atty in dist. ct; injunction brought by county atty or atty genl—Subd. 8.

  ■ *Peterson:* illegally drafted doc. is *not* voided
   — policy of statute is to penalize drafter, not testator
   — expressio unius

Minn. Stat. §§ 145B.01-.06 (1992).

CHAPTER 145B

ADULT HEALTH CARE DECISIONS

title

145B.01 CITATION.

This chapter may be cited as the "Minnesota living will act."

History: *1989 c 3 s 1; 1991 c 148 s 1*

definitions

145B.02 DEFINITIONS.

Subdivision 1. **Applicability.** The definitions in this section apply to this chapter.

Subd. 2. **Living will.** "Living will" means a writing made according to section 145B.03.

Subd. 3. **Health care.** "Health care" means care, treatment, services, or procedures to maintain, diagnose, or treat an individual's physical condition when the individual is in a terminal condition.

Subd. 4. **Health care decision.** "Health care decision" means a decision to begin, continue, increase, limit, discontinue, or not begin any health care.

Subd. 5. **Health care facility.** "Health care facility" means a hospital or other entity licensed under sections 144.50 to 144.58; a nursing home licensed to serve adults under section 144A.02; or a home care provider licensed under sections 144A.43 to 144A.49.

Subd. 6. **Health care provider.** "Health care provider" means a person, health care facility, organization, or corporation licensed, certified, or otherwise authorized or permitted by the laws of this state to administer health care directly or through an arrangement with other health care providers.

Subd. 7. **HMO.** "HMO" means an organization licensed under sections 62D.01 to 62D.30.

Subd. 8. **Terminal condition.** "Terminal condition" means an incurable or irreversible condition for which the administration of medical treatment will serve only to prolong the dying process.

History: *1989 c 3 s 2; 1991 c 148 s 6*

scope

145B.03 LIVING WILL.

Subdivision 1. **Scope.** A competent adult may make a living will of preferences or instructions regarding health care. These preferences or instructions may include, but are not limited to, consent to or refusal of any health care, treatment, service, procedure, or placement. A living will may include preferences or instructions regarding health care, the designation of a proxy to make health care decisions on behalf of the declarant, or both.

general rule

Subd. 2. **Requirements for executing a living will.** (a) A living will is effective only if it is signed by the declarant and two witnesses or a notary public.

(b) A living will must state:

(1) the declarant's preferences regarding whether the declarant wishes to receive or not receive artificial administration of nutrition and hydration; or

(2) that the declarant wishes the proxy, if any, to make decisions regarding the administering of artificially administered nutrition and hydration for the declarant if the declarant is unable to make health care decisions and the living will becomes operative. If the living will does not state the declarant's preferences regarding artificial administration of nutrition and hydration, the living will shall be enforceable as to all other preferences or instructions regarding health care, and a decision to administer, withhold, or withdraw nutrition and hydration artificially shall be made pursuant to section 145B.13. However, the mere existence of a living will or appointment of a proxy does not, by itself, create a presumption that the declarant wanted the withholding or withdrawing of artificially administered nutrition or hydration. *(exception)*

(c) The living will may be communicated to and then transcribed by one of the witnesses. If the declarant is physically unable to sign the document, one of the witnesses shall sign the document at the declarant's direction. *(exception)*

(d) Neither of the witnesses can be someone who is entitled to any part of the estate of the declarant under a will then existing or by operation of law. Neither of the witnesses nor the notary may be named as a proxy in the living will. Each witness shall substantially make the following declaration on the document:

"I certify that the declarant voluntarily signed this living will in my presence and that the declarant is personally known to me. I am not named as a proxy by the living will."

Subd. 3. **Guardian or conservator.** Except as otherwise provided in the living will, designation of a proxy is considered a nomination of a guardian or conservator of the person for purposes of section 525.544.

History: *1989 c 3 s 3; 1991 c 148 s 6*

145B.04 SUGGESTED FORM.

A living will executed after August 1, 1989, under this chapter must be substantially in the form in this section. Forms printed for public distribution must be substantially in the form in this section. *general rule*

"Health Care Living Will

Notice:

This is an important legal document. Before signing this document, you should know these important facts:

(a) This document gives your health care providers or your designated proxy the power and guidance to make health care decisions according to your wishes when you are in a terminal condition and cannot do so. This document may include what kind of treatment you want or do not want and under what circumstances you want these decisions to be made. You may state where you want or do not want to receive any treatment.

(b) If you name a proxy in this document and that person agrees to serve as your proxy, that person has a duty to act consistently with your wishes. If the proxy does not know your wishes, the proxy has the duty to act in your best interests. If you do not name a proxy, your health care providers have a duty to act consistently with your instructions or tell you that they are unwilling to do so.

(c) This document will remain valid and in effect until and unless you amend or revoke it. Review this document periodically to make sure it continues to reflect your preferences. You may amend or revoke the living will at any time by notifying your health care providers.

(d) Your named proxy has the same right as you have to examine your medical records and to consent to their disclosure for purposes related to your health care or insurance unless you limit this right in this document.

(e) If there is anything in this document that you do not understand, you should ask for professional help to have it explained to you.

145B.04 ADULT HEALTH CARE DECISIONS   1338

TO MY FAMILY, DOCTORS, AND ALL THOSE CONCERNED WITH MY CARE:

I, ..., born on .... (birthdate), being an adult of sound mind, will-fully and voluntarily make this statement as a directive to be followed if I am in a termi-nal condition and become unable to participate in decisions regarding my health care. I understand that my health care providers are legally bound to act consistently with my wishes, within the limits of reasonable medical practice and other applicable law. I also understand that I have the right to make medical and health care decisions for myself as long as I am able to do so and to revoke this living will at any time.

(1) The following are my feelings and wishes regarding my health care (you may state the circumstances under which this living will applies):

....
....
....
....

(2) I particularly want to have all appropriate health care that will help in the fol-lowing ways (you may give instructions for care you do want):

....
....
....
....

(3) I particularly do not want the following (you may list specific treatment you do not want in certain circumstances):

....
....

(4) I particularly want to have the following kinds of life-sustaining treatment if I am diagnosed to have a terminal condition (you may list the specific types of life-sustaining treatment that you do want if you have a terminal condition):

....
....
....
....

(5) I particularly do not want the following kinds of life-sustaining treatment if I am diagnosed to have a terminal condition (you may list the specific types of life-sustaining treatment that you do not want if you have a terminal condition):

....
....
....
....

(6) I recognize that if I reject artificially administered sustenance, then I may die of dehydration or malnutrition rather than from my illness or injury. The following are my feelings and wishes regarding artificially administered sustenance should I have a terminal condition (you may indicate whether you wish to receive food and fluids given to you in some other way than by mouth if you have a terminal condition):

....
....
....
....

(7) Thoughts I feel are relevant to my instructions. (You may, but need not, give your religious beliefs, philosophy, or other personal values that you feel are important. You may also state preferences concerning the location of your care.)

....
....
....
....

(8) Proxy Designation. (If you wish, you may name someone to see that your wishes are carried out, but you do not have to do this. You may also name a proxy without including specific instructions regarding your care. If you name a proxy, you should discuss your wishes with that person.)

If I become unable to communicate my instructions, I designate the following person(s) to act on my behalf consistently with my instructions, if any, as stated in this document. Unless I write instructions that limit my proxy's authority, my proxy has full power and authority to make health care decisions for me. If a guardian or conservator of the person is to be appointed for me, I nominate my proxy named in this document to act as guardian or conservator of my person.

Name: ....

Address: ....

Phone Number: ....

Relationship: (If any) ....

If the person I have named above refuses or is unable or unavailable to act on my behalf, or if I revoke that person's authority to act as my proxy, I authorize the following person to do so:

Name: ....

Address: ....

Phone Number: ....

Relationship: (If any) ....

I understand that I have the right to revoke the appointment of the persons named above to act on my behalf at any time by communicating that decision to the proxy or my health care provider.

I (have) (have not) agreed in another document or on another form to donate some or all of my organs when I die.

DATE: ....

SIGNED: ....

STATE OF ....

....

COUNTY OF ....

Subscribed, sworn to, and acknowledged before me by .... on this ..... day of ...., 19...

....

NOTARY PUBLIC

OR

(Sign and date here in the presence of two adult witnesses, neither of whom is entitled to any part of your estate under a will or by operation of law, and neither of whom is your proxy.)

I certify that the declarant voluntarily signed this living will in my presence and that the declarant is personally known to me. I am not named as a proxy by the living will, and to the best of my knowledge, I am not entitled to any part of the estate of the declarant under a will or by operation of law.

Witness .... Address ....

Witness .... Address ....

Reminder: Keep the signed original with your personal papers.

Give signed copies to your doctors, family, and proxy."

History: *1989 c 3 s 4; 1991 c 148 s 6; 1992 c 535 s 1*

145B.05 WHEN OPERATIVE.

A living will becomes operative when it is delivered to the declarant's physician or other health care provider. The physician or provider must comply with it to the fullest extent possible, consistent with reasonable medical practice and other applicable law, or comply with the notice and transfer provisions of sections 145B.06 and 145B.07. The physician or health care provider shall continue to obtain the declarant's informed consent to all health care decisions if the declarant is capable of informed consent.

History: *1989 c 3 s 5; 1991 c 148 s 6*

145B.06 COMPLIANCE WITH LIVING WILL.

Subdivision 1. **By health care provider.** (a) A physician or other health care provider shall make the living will a part of the declarant's medical record. If the physician or other health care provider is unwilling at any time to comply with the living will, the physician or health care provider must promptly notify the declarant and document the notification in the declarant's medical record. After notification, if a competent declarant fails to transfer to a different physician or provider, the physician or provider has no duty to transfer the patient.

(b) If a physician or other health care provider receives a living will from a competent declarant and does not advise the declarant of unwillingness to comply, and if the declarant then becomes incompetent or otherwise unable to seek transfer to a different physician or provider, the physician or other health care provider who is unwilling to comply with the living will shall promptly take all reasonable steps to transfer care of the declarant to a physician or other health care provider who is willing to comply with the living will.

Subd. 2. **By proxy.** A proxy designated to make health care decisions and who agrees to serve as proxy may make health care decisions on behalf of a declarant to the same extent that the declarant could make the decision, subject to limitations or conditions stated in the living will. In exercising this authority, the proxy shall act consistently with any desires the declarant expresses in the living will or otherwise makes known to the proxy. If the declarant's desires are unknown, the proxy shall act in the best interests of the declarant.

History: *1989 c 3 s 6; 1991 c 148 s 6*

Peterson v. Hovland (*In re Peterson's Estate*)
230 Minn. 478, 42 N.W.2d 59 (1950).

IN RE PETERSON'S ESTATE
Cite as 42 N.W.2d 59

Minn.   59

In re PETERSON'S ESTATE.

PETERSON et al. v. HOVLAND.

No. 35108.

Supreme Court of Minnesota.

March 31, 1950.

Proceeding in the matter of the estate of Peter H. Peterson, decedent, by Hans H. Peterson and others, heirs at law, against George M. Hovland, wherein validity of will was challenged. From a judgment of the District Court, Freeborn County, Martin A. Nelson, J., affirming an order of the probate court allowing the last will and testament of decedent, the heirs at law appealed. The Supreme Court, Matson, J., held that a will drawn for testator by bank cashier in violation of statute against the unlicensed practice of law is not invalid.

Judgment affirmed.

1. Contracts ⟐107

Generally, a contract in violation of statute which imposes prohibition and penalty is void, but before so ruling in a particular case, statute should be examined as a whole to determine whether legislature so intended.

2. Contracts ⟐105

Validity of instrument executed in violation of statute does not depend on whether the acts involved are malum in se or merely malum prohibitum.

3. Contracts ⟐108(1)

Generally, a contract is not void as against public policy unless it is injurious to interests of the public or contravenes some established interests of society, but contracts are contrary to public policy if they clearly tend to injure public health or morals, the fundamental rights of the individual, or if they undermine confidence in impartiality of the administration of justice.

4. Contracts ⟐107

If an act is expressly forbidden and a penalty is imposed for violation, intent of legislature is controlling factor in determining to what extent, in order to preserve requirements of public policy, contracts and other instruments made in connection with such violation are to be held illegal.

5. Contracts ⟐107

An inference of invalidity of contract executed in violation of statute does not necessarily follow from fact that statute prescribes a penalty.

6. Statutes ⟐181(2)

Where language of statute is not explicit and admits of construction, the courts in determining legislative intent will consider occasion and necessity for the law, mischief to be remedied, object to be obtained, and consequences of a particular interpretation. M.S.A. § 645.16.

7. Statutes ⟐241(1)

Where statute specifically prohibits and penalizes a certain act by members of one class, for protection of members of another class, a statutory construction which attributes to legislature an intent to bring about a consequence that is inconsistent with the protective purpose should not be adopted.

8. Statutes ⟐241(1)

Where legislature has carefully designated offense, offender, and the penalty and has made specific provisions to insure enforcement, inference is that legislature has dealt with subject completely and did not intend, in addition thereto, that by mere implication drastic consequences of invalidity should be visited upon victim of offender.

9. Courts ⟐107

No decision has authoritative value beyond the proportions established by its controlling facts.

10. Wills ⟐84

Will drawn by bank cashier for testator, at a time when no emergency existed which would leave insufficient time to have it drawn and its execution supervised by an attorney at law, was not invalid because it was prepared in direct violation of the statute which prohibits and penalizes as a misdemeanor the act of an unlicensed practitioner in preparing a will for another. M.S.A. § 481.02.

Syllabus by the Court.

1. Although the general rule is that a contract executed in violation of a statute which imposes a prohibition and a penalty for the doing of an act—such as the pursuit of an occupation, business, or profession without being possessed of a license as required by law for the protection of the public—is void, such rule is not to be applied in any particular case without first examining the statute as a whole to find out whether or not the legislature so intended.

2. The distinction between acts which are *malum in se* and those which are merely *malum prohibitum* is no longer controlling in this jurisdiction in determining the validity of an instrument executed in violation of statute.

IN RE PETERSON'S ESTATE
Cite as 42 N.W.2d 59

Minn. 61

3. If an act is expressly forbidden and a penalty is imposed for a violation, the intent of the legislature is the controlling factor in determining to what extent, in order to preserve the requirements of public policy, contracts and other instruments made in connection with such act of violation are to be held illegal, if at all.

4. An inference of invalidity does not necessarily follow from the fact that a statute prescribes a penalty.

5. Where a statute specifically prohibits and penalizes a certain act by the members of one class, for the protection of the members of another class, a statutory construction should not be adopted which attributes to the legislature an intent to bring about a consequence that is inconsistent with the protective purpose for which the law was enacted.

6. Where the legislature has carefully designated the *offense,* the *offender,* and the *penalty* and *has made specific provisions to insure enforcement,* the inference is that the legislature has dealt with the subject completely and did not intend, in addition thereto, that drastic consequences of invalidity should be visited upon the victim of the offender by mere implication.

7. No decision has authoritative value beyond the proportions established by **its** controlling facts.

8. A will does not become invalid and void by reason of the sole fact that it was drawn for the testator—when no emergency existed which left insufficient time to have it drawn and its execution supervised by a licensed attorney at law—by a layman in direct violation of M.S.A. § 481.02, which prohibits and penalizes as a misdemeanor the act of an unlicensed practitioner in preparing a will for another.

———◆·——

Moonan, Moonan & Friedel, Waseca, for appellants.

Peterson & Peterson, Albert Lea, for respondent.

MATSON, Justice.

Appeal from a district court judgment affirming an order of the probate court allowing decedent's last will and testament.

Peter H. Peterson, decedent, on September 7, 1948, which was several weeks prior to his death, executed his last will and testament, which, upon his request, had been drawn by the cashier of the Twin Lakes State Bank, a layman, who had never been admitted to the practice of law. The trial court specifically found that at the time the will was drawn "no emergency existed nor had the imminence of death left insufficient time to have this Will drawn and its execution supervised by a licensed attorney at law."

Appellants are heirs at law for whom no provision was made in the will. The only issue raised is whether a will which is otherwise valid is invalid and should be given no legal effect by reason of the *sole* fact that it was drawn by a layman—who at the time the will was drawn was not admitted and licensed to practice as an attorney at law—in direct violation of M.S.A. § 481.02, which provides:

Subd. 1. "It shall be unlawful for any person or association of persons, except members of the bar of Minnesota admitted and licensed to practice as attorneys at law, * * * *for or without a fee or any consideration,* to prepare, directly or through another, for another person, * * * any will or testamentary disposition or instrument of trust serving purposes similar to those of a will, * * *."[1] (Italics supplied.)

Subd. 8. "Any person or corporation, or officer or employee thereof, violating any of the foregoing provisions *shall be guilty of a misdemeanor;* and, upon conviction thereof, shall be punished as by statute provided for the punishment of misdemeanors. *It shall be the duty of the respective county attorneys in this state to prosecute violations of this section,* * * *

---

1. Subd. 3 of said statute permits a layman to draw a will for another in an emergency wherein the imminence of death leaves insufficient time to have the same drawn and its execution supervised by a licensed attorney at law.

62   Minn.   42 NORTH WESTERN REPORTER, 2d SERIES

"In lieu of criminal prosecution above provided for, such county attorney or the attorney general may, * * * proceed by injunction suit against any violator of any of the provisions above set forth to enjoin the doing of any act or acts violating any of said provisions." (Italics supplied.)

Does it follow that the will itself is tainted with such illegality as to be void by reason of having been drafted in a prohibited manner? Did the testator, in employing an unlicensed layman, so participate in the performance of a crime that his attempt to make a will resulted in a nullity? In considering the issue, it should be borne in mind that the direct violator of the statute, the unlicensed scrivener, is not a beneficiary under the will and is not a party to this litigation. He is in no manner seeking a fee for his services or any other benefit from his unlawful act. In other words, we are not asked to aid the wrongdoer himself. See, 5 Williston, Contracts (Rev.Ed.) § 1630; Bosshard v. County of Steele, 173 Minn. 283, 217 N.W. 354; Goodrich v. N. W. Tel. Exch. Co., 161 Minn. 106, 201 N.W. 290. A different situation arises where an unlicensed practitioner seeks to recover fees for his performance of legal services. See, Annotations, 4 A.L.R. 1087 and 42 A.L.R. 1228; Gionti v. Crown Motor Freight Co., 128 N.J.L. 407, 26 A.2d 282.

In most instances, decisions concerned with the validity of instruments executed in violation of a statute involve the issue of the enforceability or nonenforceability of contracts. Where an attempt is made to enforce a contract which was made in violation of a statute, many considerations enter which are not present where the validity of a will is assailed on the sole ground that it was drawn by an unlicensed scrivener. Nevertheless, the contract cases are illustrative of certain fundamental principles which are controlling.

See, 5 Williston, Contracts (Rev.Ed.) § 1630.

[1-6] 1-2-3-4. Although the general rule is that a contract executed in violation of a statute which imposes a prohibition and a penalty for the doing of an act—such as the pursuit of an occupation, business, or profession without being possessed of a license as required by law for the protection of the public—is void, such rule is not to be applied in any particular case without first examining the statute as a whole to find out whether or not the legislature so intended.[2] It is not an arbitrary rule which is applicable to all instruments executed in violation of statutory prohibitions. Its applicable scope coincides with the reason for its existence, and when that reason ceases the rule itself ceases to have a basis and becomes inoperative. See, Webster v. U. S. I. Realty Co., 170 Minn. 360, 363, 212 N.W. 806, 807; cf. Restatement, Contracts, §§ 598–604. In construing such a statute, the inference is that the legislature did not intend that an instrument executed in violation of its terms should be void unless that be necessary to accomplish its purpose. Barriere v. Depatie, 219 Mass. 33, 106 N.E. 572. Usually the rule that a contract so made is void finds application where the acts or things prohibited by statute are *malum in se,* in that they are by their nature iniquitous and void. Laun v. Pacific Mut. Life Ins. Co. of California, 131 Wis. 555, 111 N.W. 660, 9 L.R.A.,N.S., 1204; Walter A. Wood Mowing & Reaping Machine Co. v. Caldwell, 54 Ind. 270, 23 Am.Rep. 641. No longer, however, is the distinction between acts which are *malum in se* and those which are merely *malum prohibitum* controlling in this jurisdiction in determining the validity of an instrument executed in violation of a statute. Holland v. Sheehan, 108 Minn. 362, 122 N.W. 1, 23 L.R.A.,N.S., 510, 17 Ann. Cas. 687; 2 Dunnell, Dig. & Supp. § 1868.

---

2. Solomon v. Dreschler, 4 Minn. 278 (Gil. 197); Miller v. Ammon, 145 U.S. 421, 12 S.Ct. 884, 36 L.Ed. 759; Harris v. Runnels, 53 U.S. 79, 12 How. 79, 13 L.Ed. 901; Pangborn v. Westlake, 36 Iowa 546;

Barriere v. Depatie, 219 Mass. 33, 106 N.E. 572; see, 2 Dunnell, Dig. & Supp. § 1873; Annotations, 30 A.L.R. 834 and 42 A.L.R. 1226.

IN RE PETERSON'S ESTATE Minn. 63
Cite as 42 N.W.2d 59

Where contracts or other instruments which are merely *malum prohibitum* have been made in violation of statutory provisions— as in the instant case—they may or may not be void.[3] Generally speaking, a contract is not void as against public policy unless it is injurious to the interests of the public or contravenes some established interest of society. On the other hand, contracts are contrary to public policy if they clearly tend to injure public health or morals, the fundamental rights of the individual, or if they undermine confidence in the impartiality of the administration of justice. See, Solomon v. Dreschler, 4 Minn. 278 (Gil. 197); 2 Dunnell, Dig. & Supp. § 1870. These general principles are of little direct aid in a specific case and are but reflections of what the legislature has usually declared public policy to be. Primarily, it is the prerogative of the legislature to declare what acts constitute a violation of public policy and the consequences of such violation. Mathison v. Minneapolis St. Ry. Co., 126 Minn. 286, 148 N.W. 71, L.R.A.1916D, 412. If an act is expressly forbidden and a penalty is imposed for a violation, the intent of the legislature is the controlling factor in determining to what extent, in order to preserve the requirements of public policy, contracts and other instruments made in connection with such act of violation are to be held illegal, if at all. 3 Sutherland, Statutory Construction (3 ed.) § 5608. An inference of invalidity does not necessarily follow from the fact that a statute prescribes a penalty. De Mers v. Daniels, 39 Minn. 158, 39 N.W. 98. Each statute must be judged by itself as a whole. Solomon v. Dreschler, 4 Minn. 278 (Gil. 197); Bowditch v. New England Mut. Life Ins. Co. 141 Mass. 292, 4 N.E. 798, 55 Am.Rep. 474.

In construing a statute where the language is not explicit and admits of construction, in determining legislative intent the courts will consider the occasion and the necessity for the law, the mischief to be remedied, the object to be attained, and the consequences of a particular interpretation. M.S.A. § 645.16.

Section 481.02 had its origin with G.S. 1866, c. 88, § 8, which simply prohibited any person not a lawyer to appear, to maintain, or defend in any proceeding in court.[4] Although the wording was changed from time to time in certain inconsequential particulars, no major change was made until the enactment of L. 1901, c. 282, when it was made unlawful for an unlicensed practitioner not only to appear in court but also to hold himself out as competent to furnish legal services or to perform any legal services for a consideration. Undoubtedly this amendment by its application generally to the practice of law made it unlawful for a layman to prepare another's will for a fee. It was not, however, until the enactment of L. 1931, c. 114, § 1, that this statute was amended to apply in *express* terms to wills. Undoubtedly, the necessity for expressly prohibiting any person not licensed to practice as an attorney at law from preparing a will for another, *whether for or without a fee,* arose out of the deplorable situation frequently created for widows and children of testators whose wills had been drawn by laymen who meant well but had only a superficial knowledge of law. Through the bungling use of legal terms and an improper knowledge of estate planning, poorly drawn wills frequently were held invalid, specific bequests failed, estates were needlessly depleted by burdensome taxation, or the testator's intent was otherwise defeated.

3. De Mers v. Daniels, 39 Minn. 158, 39 N.W. 98; Pangborn v. Westlake, 36 Iowa 546; John E. Rosasco Creameries, Inc. v. Cohen, 276 N.Y. 274, 278, 11 N.E.2d 908, 909, 118 A.L.R. 641 (wherein a milk dealer was permitted to recover sale price of milk sold without having statutory license); Hartford Fire Ins. Co. v. Knight, 146 Miss. 862, 867, 111 So. 748; Irwin v. Curie, 171 N.Y. 409, 64 N.E. 161, 58 L.R.A. 830; Niemeyer v. Wright, 75 Va. 239, 40 Am.Rep. 720;

Warren People's Market Co. v. Corbett & Sons, 114 Ohio St. 126, 151 N.E. 51; 2 Dunnell, Dig. & Supp. § 1873.

4. Derivation of M.S.A. § 481.02: Mason St.1940 Supp. § 5687-1; L. 1931, c. 114, § 1; Mason St. 1927, § 5687; G.S. 1923, § 5687; G.S. 1913, § 4947; R.L. 1905, § 2280; L. 1901, c. 282; G.S. 1894, § 6179; L. 1891, c. 36, § 8; G.S. 1878, c. 88, § 8; G.S. 1866, c. 88, § 8.

64   Minn.   42 NORTH WESTERN REPORTER, 2d SERIES

Incompetency was accompanied by irresponsibility, in that these laymen, unlike members of the bar, by reason of their unlicensed status were not subject to the direct supervision and discipline of the courts. See, Matter of Co-operative Law Co., 198 N.Y. 479, 92 N.E. 15, 32 L.R.A.,N.S., 55, 139 Am.St.Rep. 839, 19 Ann.Cas. 879; cf. State v. Nowicki, 256 Wis. 279, 40 N.W.2d 377. The need for remedial legislation was acute. It was met by the enactment of an express statutory prohibition and penalty, *not against any act of the testator or against the drafting or making of wills generally,* but solely against the act of the *unlicensed* will draftsman, whose unskilled services and irresponsible status could no longer be tolerated. As a result, we have a typical example of legislation designed to protect one class of the public, those persons in need of a will, from imposition by another class, those individuals who, without adequate legal training, offer their services to the unwary. Similar protective legislation is not new to this jurisdiction.[5] In De Mers v. Daniels, 39. Minn. 158, 39 N.W. 98, we held a contract for the sale of certain lots to be valid and enforceable though the vendor was subject to a statutory penalty for having failed to execute and file the townsite plat as required by G.S. 1878, c. 29. In the De Mers case we said, 39 Minn. 159, 39 N.W. 99: "It must be conceded to be an established principle of law that when a statute prescribes a penalty for the doing of a specific act, that is *prima facie* equivalent to an express prohibition; and that, *when the object of such an enactment is deemed to have been the protection of persons dealing with those in respect to whose acts the penalty is declared,* or the accomplishment of purposes entertained upon grounds of public policy, not pertaining to mere administrative measures, such as the raising of a revenue, the act thus impliedly prohibited will, in general, be treated as *unlawful and void as to the party who is subjected to the penalty.* This rule is not, however, without qualification. The question is one of interpretation of the legislative intention. *The imposing of a penalty*

does not necessarily give rise to an implication of an intention that, where an act is done which subjects a party to the penalty, the act itself shall be void, and of no legal effect; and if it seems more probable, from the subject and the terms of the enactment, and from the consequences which were to be anticipated as likely to result from giving such an effect to the penal law, that it was not the intention of the legislature to make the transaction void, but only to punish the offending party in the manner specified, the law should be so construed. * * * *The fact that no penalty, forfeiture, or disability is declared with respect to purchasers, under any circumstances, is worthy of being considered* in this connection." (Italics supplied.)

In the De Mers case, as in the instant case, a specific penalty was imposed for the wrongful act of one party, but the statute was silent as to the consequences to the other party and as to the validity of a written instrument executed in connection with or in reliance upon such wrongful act. In ascertaining legislative intent under such circumstances, we may apply the maxim that "the expression of one thing is the exclusion of another." Sacketts Harbor Bank v. Codd, 18 N.Y. 240; Laun v. Pacific Mut. Life Ins. Co., 131 Wis. 555, 111 N.W. 660, 9 L.R.A.,N.S., 1204; 6 Dunnell, Dig. & Supp. § 8980. As indicative of legislative intent to rely upon the penalty alone for accomplishing the statutory purpose, without holding the will itself void, is the statutory emphasis placed upon the enforcement of the penalty. By express terms, the statute declares it to be the positive duty of county attorneys to institute criminal proceedings against any unlicensed practitioners who draw wills—in the absence of an actual emergency when no lawyer is available. The only alternative in lieu of criminal prosecution is the initiation of proceedings to enjoin future acts of violation.

[7, 8]   5-6. Where a statute specifically prohibits and penalizes a certain act by the members of one class, for the protection of the members of another class, a statutory

---

5. De Mers v. Daniels, 39 Minn. 158, 39 N.W. 98; Webster v. U. S. I. Realty Co., 170 Minn. 360, 212 N.W. 806.

IN RE PETERSON'S ESTATE   Minn.   **65**
Cite as 42 N.W.2d 59

construction should not be adopted which attributes to the legislature an intent to bring about a consequence that is inconsistent with the protective purpose for which the law was enacted. Where a penalty is imposed upon one party and not upon the other, they are not to be regarded as *in pari delicto.* Irwin v. Curie, 171 N.Y. 409, 414, 64 N.E. 161, 162, 58 L.R.A. 830. A testator is not *in pari delicto* with an unlicensed practitioner. He is a member of the class the statute was designed to protect. See, Webster v. U. S. I. Realty Co., 170 Minn. 360, 212 N.W. 806. Protective legislation is to be construed so that it does not become just another hazard for the unwary. If, by implication, we were to attribute to the legislature an intent that a will drawn by an unlicensed practitioner should in all cases be void, we would visit upon the unfortunate victims of unskilled draftsmen a penalty far greater than, and out of all proportion to, the penalty imposed upon the wrongdoer himself. Where the legislature has carefully designated the *offense,* the *offender,* and the *penalty* and *has made specific provisions to insure enforcement,* the inference is that the legislature has dealt with the subject completely and did not intend, in addition thereto, that drastic consequences of invalidity should be visited upon the victim of the offender by mere implication. See, Laun v. Pacific Mut. Life Ins. Co., 131 Wis. 555, 570–571, 111 N.W. 660, 665, 9 L.R.A.,N.S., 1204; Bowditch v. New England Mut. Life Ins. Co., 141 Mass. 292, 4 N.E. 798, 55 Am.Rep. 474.

Appellants cite Buckley v. Humason, 50 Minn. 195, 52 N.W. 385, 16 L.R.A. 423, 36 Am.St.Rep. 637, in support of their contentions. In that case the plaintiff, who conducted a Chicago real estate brokerage business without having the license required by an ordinance of that city, was denied the right to recover his brokerage commissions, on the ground that where a business is made unlawful for unlicensed persons any contract made in such business is void. In the Buckley case, the wrongdoer himself was seeking, *to his own advantage,* to enforce a contract made in violation of law. In the instant matter we do not have that situation. It is also significant that the earlier De Mers decision, 39 Minn. 158, 39 N.W. 98, was not called to the attention of or considered by the court. In a much later decision, Vercellini v. U. S. I. Realty Co., 158 Minn. 72, 196 N.W. 672, the court, after citing Buckley v. Humason, supra, expressly took notice of the error in the assumption that all contracts made in violation of law are necessarily void. In that case, the purchaser of certain lands under an investment contract made in violation of the blue sky law, L. 1917, c. 429, as amended by L. 1919, c. 105, was permitted to recover what he had paid. The court said therein that the purchaser was a member of the protected class and that he was not *in pari delicto* with the seller, who was the only party guilty of violating the statute. See, also, Marin v. Olson, 181 Minn. 327, 232 N.W. 523.

[9] 7. Our attention is directed to In re Estate of Calich, 214 Minn. 292, 8 N.W.2d 337, wherein this court discussed the serious losses resulting to innocent people from the unlicensed practice of law by laymen, and then, after vigorously condemning such unlawful practice, urged the prompt and aggressive prosecution of all violators. This court therein expressed a reluctance to give effect to a will drawn by a layman in violation of the statute, but it is significant to note that the alleged will was drawn by a layman who stood to profit by his own wrongful act, in that he was the sole beneficiary. What is of more significance is that the actual decision therein was not based upon any illegality resulting from an unauthorized practice of law, but on a determination that the finding of the trial court that no will had ever been executed was sustained by the evidence. It is elementary that no decision has any authoritative value beyond the proportions established by its controlling facts.[6]

---

6. Certain cases cited by appellants should be distinguished. In Waddell v. Traylor, 99 Colo. 576, 64 P.2d 1273, involving a

42 N.W.2d—5

suit upon a promissory note which, in violation of a penal statute, prescribed an unlawful rate of interest, the court

66   Minn.   42 NORTH WESTERN REPORTER, 2d SERIES

Appellants cite certain cases wherein unlicensed practitioners have appeared in court, and in consequence thereof the proceedings have been set aside and spoken of as void. These cases illustrate the confusion which results when the distinction between the words "void" and "voidable" is not observed. They also illustrate that the authoritative value of a decision is limited to the scope of its controlling or decisive facts. In practically all these decisions, the courts have either granted a new trial or taken other steps to protect the rights of the wrongdoer's clients and the interest of opposing parties. No purpose will be served by attempting to distinguish or discuss such decisions, in that the task has already been ably performed in Schifrin v. Chenille Mfg. Co. Inc., 2 Cir., 117 F.2d 92. In certain instances, court proceedings have failed for want of jurisdiction where the only effort made to invoke the court's jurisdiction has been by the issuance of a summons which was fatally defective in not having been subscribed by the plaintiff or by an officer of the court in his behalf, as required by statute. See, Jacobs v. Queen Ins. Co., 51 S.D. 249, 213 N.W. 14.

[10] 8. It follows that a will does not become invalid and void by reason of the sole fact that it was drawn for the testator —when no emergency existed which left insufficient time to have it drawn and its execution supervised by a licensed attorney at law—by a layman in direct violation of § 481.02, which prohibits and penalizes as a misdemeanor the act of an unlicensed practitioner in preparing a will for another.[7]

The judgment of the trial court is affirmed.

Affirmed.

FRANK T. GALLAGHER, J., took no part in the consideration or decision of this case.

---

held the note invalid *only* to the extent of the unlawful interest and allowed a recovery of the money actually loaned, together with lawful interest thereon. The court refused to increase the penalty beyond that expressly prescribed by the statute. In Hancock Co. Inc. v. Stephens, 177 Va. 349, 14 S.E.2d 332, the wrongdoer himself, an unlicensed real estate broker, was denied a right of recovery. Cf. Restatement, Contracts, §§ 598–604.

7. There is a question whether appellants are in a position to raise the issue of illegality. Usually the issue or defense of illegality may be raised only by the parties or those claiming under them and not by third parties. See, Marx v. Lining, 231 Ala. 445, 165 So. 207; Ferris v. Snively, 172 Wash. 167, 19 P.2d 942, 90 A.L.R. 278; White v. Little, 131 Okl. 132, 268 P. 221; Matta v. Katsoulas, 192 Wis. 212, 212 N.W. 261, 50 A.L.R. 291.

Peterson brief

Peterson v. Hovland (*In re Peterson's Estate*), 42 N.W.2d 59 (Minn. 1950).

FACTS: Decedent Peterson executed will several weeks before death. At his request, will was drawn by cashier of bank, layperson never admitted to practice of law. No emergency involving imminent death existed.

PROCEDURE: Heirs at law not provided for in will challenged it. Probate ct allowed will; dist ct affirmed. Heirs appealed.

ISSUE: Is otherwise valid will rendered invalid solely because it was drawn by layperson, where no emergency involving imminent death of testator existed?

HOLDING: Affirmed. Will is not invalid solely because it was drawn by layperson, even where no emergency existed.

REASONING: Unauthorized practice statute prohibits nonlawyer from drawing will for another with or without fee; stated penalties are misdemeanor & injunction.

This case is different from suit by layperson to secure fee; there wrongdoing layperson is seeking to benefit. Compare contract enforceability cases: general rule is that contract in violation of licensing statute is void—but one must examine legis intent behind statute to be sure voiding contract is in accord w/legis purpose. Contract is void where enforcement would injure public health or morals, harm fundamental rights of individual, undermine confidence in justice system. Cites to MN cases.

It is legis task to declare acts in violation of public policy & to set consequences. Where statute is not explicit as to conseqs, consider legis intent, derived from need for law, mischief to be remedied, object to be attained, etc. Cite to sec. 645.16. Sec. 481.02 is aimed at harm to widows & kids where well meaning but bungling layperson drafted defective will. Such laypeople are outside supervision of cts. So statute's purpose is to protect testators from drafters.

Where statute imposes penalty on wrongdoer & is silent as to effect of transaction, silence is significant. See expressio unius. Where penalty is imposed on one party & not on other, do not deem them in pari delicto. Here penalty goes against drafter. Do not penalize testator by invalidating will.

Buckley is distinguished as involving attempt by wrongdoer to benefit from transaction. Similarly case in which drafter was sole beneficiary of will & will was declared invalid is distinguishable. Cases involving litigation are distinguishable.

Gardner v. Conway, 234 Minn. 468, 48 N.W.2d 788 (1951).

788   Minn.   **48 NORTH WESTERN REPORTER, 2d SERIES**

GARDNER et al. v. CONWAY.
No. 35317.

Supreme Court of Minnesota.

July 6, 1951.

Action by Clifford W. Gardner and others, as constituting all the members of a committee on the unauthorized and illegal practice of the law, being a subcommittee of the Committee on Practice of the Law of the Ramsey County Bar Association, etc., against James L. Conway to perpetually enjoin defendant from further engaging in the unauthorized practice of law and to adjudge him in contempt of court therefor. The District Court, Ramsey County, Albin S. Pearson, J., entered an order denying defendant's motion for a new trial and defendant appealed. The Supreme Court, Matson, J., held that the resolution by tax expert of difficult legal questions incidental to the preparation of income tax return for another for a consideration constituted the practice of law and that a layman may not hold himself out to the public as a tax consultant or tax expert or describe himself by any similar phrase which implies that he has a knowledge of the law.

Order affirmed.

1. Attorney and client ⬅11

A proceeding to adjudge a person in contempt of court for unauthorized practice of law, regardless of whether such unauthorized practice occurred within or outside the presence of the court, is punitive and criminal in its nature and is primarily brought in the public interest to vindicate the authority of the court and to deter other like derelictions.

2. Contempt ⬅66(1)

A conviction for a criminal contempt, as distinguished from a civil contempt, must be reviewed by certiorari and is not appealable.

3. Injunction ⬅89

The district court has jurisdiction to enjoin the unauthorized practice of law, regardless of whether such practice takes place within or outside the presence of the court, and such jurisdiction is not destroyed by the criminality of defendant's misconduct which neither gives nor ousts jurisdiction in chancery. M.S.A. § 481.02.

4. Injunction ⬅89

Where purported acts of unauthorized practice of law were intentionally performed by defendant upon the mistaken assumption that he was advising a bona fide taxpayer and was preparing for him a tax return for use in reporting an actual taxpayer's income, action to enjoin unauthorized practice of law presented a justiciable issue, though the evidentiary basis of action consisted primarily of professional acts and service furnished for a consideration for a private investigator acting under a fictitious name upon a hypothetical state of facts in connection with preparation of an income tax return which was never intended to be filed. M.S.A. § 481.02.

5. Injunction ⬅22

In action to enjoin unauthorized practice of law, the controversy was not moot, since judgment would have a swift and definite impact upon defendant by forever enjoining him from giving regular advice and service in connection with the preparation of income tax returns. M.S.A. § 481.02.

6. Attorney and client ⬅11

The development of any practical criterion for determining what constitutes the practice of law, as well as the application of such criterion, must be closely related to the purpose for which attorneys are licensed as the exclusive occupants of their field. M.S.A. § 481.02.

7. Attorney and client ⬅11

The purpose for which attorneys are licensed as the exclusive occupants of their field is to protect the public from the intolerable evils which are brought upon people by those who assume to practice law without having the proper qualifications.

8. Attorney and client ⬅4

The law practice franchise or privilege is based upon the threefold requirements of ability, character, and responsible supervision. M.S.A. § 481.02.

9. Attorney and client ⬅36(1)

Attorneys as officers of the court are subject to its inherent supervisory jurisdic-

GARDNER v. CONWAY

tion, which embraces the power to remove from the profession those practitioners who are unfaithful or incompetent in the discharge of their trust.

10. Attorney and client ⊕4

While professional standards for safeguarding the public interest must be sufficiently flexible to allow for adaptation to changes in conditions, they must in any event be of such stability and permanence as to protect the individual practitioner in the enjoyment of his professional franchise, in order to induce men of ability and character to undergo the years of training necessary to qualify them as attorneys.

11. Attorney and client ⊕11

A layman's legal service activities constitute the "practice of law" unless they are incidental to his regular calling, but the mere fact that they are incidental is not decisive. M.S.A. § 481.02.

> See publication Words and Phrases, for other judicial constructions and definitions of "Practice of Law".

12. Attorney and client ⊕11

What constitutes the practice of law may be determined only from a consideration of the acts of service performed in each case.

13. Attorney and client ⊕11

Generally, whenever, as incidental to another transaction or calling, a layman, as part of his regular course of conduct resolves legal question for another at his request and for a consideration by giving him advice or by taking action for and in his behalf, the layman is "practicing law" if difficult or doubtful legal questions are involved which, to safeguard the public, reasonably demand the application of a trained legal mind. M.S.A. § 481.02.

> See publication Words and Phrases, for other judicial constructions and definitions of "Practicing Law".

14. Attorney and client ⊕11

What is a difficult or doubtful question of law demanding the application of a trained legal mind is not to be measured by the comprehension of a trained legal mind but by the understanding thereof which is possessed by a reasonably in-

telligent layman who is reasonably familiar with similar transactions. M.S.A. § 481.02.

15. Attorney and client ⊕11

In restricting laymen from unauthorized practice of law, the difficult question of law criterion is to be applied in a common sense way which will protect primarily the interests of the public and not hamper or burden such interest with impractical and technical restrictions which have no reasonable justification. M.S.A. § 481.02.

16. Broker ⊕4

As ancillary to the closing of a real estate transaction, a real estate broker may draw the ordinary instruments of conveyance.

17. Attorney and client ⊕11

A layman may not draw another's will, except where dire emergency prevents the calling of an attorney. M.S.A. § 481.02.

18. Attorney and client ⊕11

When an accountant or other layman who is employed to prepare an income tax return is faced with difficult or doubtful questions of the interpretation or application of statutes, administrative regulations and rulings, court decisions or general law, it is his duty to leave the determination of such questions to an attorney. M.S.A. § 481.02.

19. Attorney and client ⊕11

The work of an accountant disassociated from the resolving of difficult or doubtful questions of law is not the practice of law. M.S.A. § 481.02.

20. Attorney and client ⊕11

Where income tax expert incidental to the preparation of income tax return for a consideration resolved difficult legal questions as to whether taxpayer was in partnership with common-law wife in operation of a truck farm, whether he was entitled to claim as an exemption the woman with whom he had been living without ceremonial marriage, whether taxpayer and such woman should file a joint or separate returns, and whether cost of improvement of buildings on farm and produce losses sustained by frost and flood were deductible while preparation of return was not of itself the practice of law, the services rendered, taken as a whole, constituted the "practice of law". M.S.A. § 481.02.

21. Attorney and client ⚖11

A layman, regardless of whether he is an accountant, may not hold himself out to the public as a tax consultant or tax expert or describe himself by any similar phrase which implies that he has a knowledge of the law. M.S.A. § 481.02.

Syllabus by the Court.

1. A proceeding to adjudge a person in contempt of court for the unauthorized practice of law—whether such unauthorized practice occurred within or outside the presence of the court—is punitive and criminal in its nature and is primarily brought in the public interest to vindicate the authority of the court and to deter other like derelictions.

2. A conviction for a criminal contempt, as distinguished from a civil contempt, is not appealable, but must be reviewed by certiorari.

3. The district court has jurisdiction to enjoin the unauthorized practice of law, whether such practice takes place within or outside the presence of the court, and such jurisdiction is not destroyed by the criminality of the defendant's misconduct.

4. A justiciable issue may arise although the purported acts of unauthorized practice of law were intentionally performed by defendant upon the mistaken assumption that he was then advising a bona fide taxpayer and was preparing for him a tax return for use in reporting an actual taxpayer's income.

5. The purpose for which lawyers are licensed as the exclusive occupants of their field is to protect the public from the intolerable evils which are brought upon people by those who assume to practice law without having the proper qualifications.

6. The law practice franchise or privilege is based upon the threefold requirements of *ability, character,* and *responsible supervision.*

7. A layman's legal service activities are the practice of law unless they are in-cidental to his regular calling; but the mere fact that they are incidental is by no means decisive.

8. Generally speaking, whenever, as incidental to another transaction or calling, a layman, as part of his regular course of conduct, resolves legal questions for another—at the latter's request and for a consideration—by giving him advice or by taking action for and in his behalf, he is practicing law if difficult or doubtful legal questions are involved which, to safeguard the public, reasonably demand the application of a trained legal mind.

9. What is a difficult or doubtful question of law is not to be measured by the comprehension of a trained legal mind, but by the understanding thereof which is possessed by a reasonably intelligent layman who is reasonably familiar with similar transactions.

10. In restraining laymen from improper activity, *the difficult question of law criterion* is to be applied in a common-sense way which will protect primarily the interest of the public and not hamper or burden that interest with impractical and technical restrictions which have no reasonable justification.

11. When an accountant or other layman who is employed to prepare an income tax return is faced with difficult or doubtful questions of the interpretation or application of statutes, administrative regulations and rulings, court decisions, or general law, it is his duty to leave the determination of such questions to a lawyer.

12. The work of an accountant disassociated from the resolving of difficult or doubtful questions of law is not law practice.

13. Although the preparation of the income tax return was not of itself the practice of law, defendant herein, incidental to such preparation, resolved certain difficult legal questions which, taken as a whole, constituted the practice of law.

14. A layman, whether he is or is not an accountant, may not hold himself out to the public as a tax consultant or a tax expert, or describe himself by any sim-

GARDNER v. CONWAY

Minn. 791

Cite as 48 N.W.2d 788

ilar phrase which implies that he has a knowledge of tax law.

———◆———

Bundlie, Kelley, Finley & Maun, St. Paul, for appellant.

Clifford W. Gardner, C. Paul Smith, Calvin Hunt, Alric Anderson, Irving Gotlieb, Fred Kueppers, and Worth K. Rice, all of St. Paul, for respondents.

Fontaine C. Bradley, Washington, D. C. (American Institute of Accountants), Best, Flanagan, Rogers, Lewis & Simonet, Minneapolis (Minn. Assn. of Public Accountants and National Soc. of Public Accountants), Fowler, Youngquist, Furber, Taney & Johnson, G. Aaron Youngquist and John R. Goetz, all of Minneapolis (Minnesota Soc. of Certified Public Accountants), Robert J. Nowack, Minneapolis (Minnesota State Bar Assn., by its Standing Committee on Unauthorized Practice of Law), John D. Randall, Chairman, Cedar Rapids, Iowa, Cuthbert S. Baldwin, New Orleans, La., Thomas J. Boodell, Chicago, Ill., A. J. Casner, Cambridge, Mass., Edgar N. Eisenhower, Tacoma, Wash., Edwin M. Otterbourg, New York City and Warren H. Resh, Madison, Wis. (American Bar Assn., by its Standing Committee on Unauthorized Practice of Law), amici curiæ.

MATSON, Justice.

Defendant appeals from an order denying his motion for a new trial.

This action, to have the defendant perpetually *enjoined* from further engaging in the unauthorized practice of law and to have him *adjudged in contempt* of court therefor, was brought by the plaintiffs[1] in their own behalf as licensed lawyers and in a representative capacity in behalf of every other licensed lawyer in Minnesota, as well as in behalf of the courts and the public.[2]

Defendant, who is possessed of only a grade-school education, has never been admitted to the practice of law in Minnesota or elsewhere. During a two-year period immediately prior to the time of trial, he followed the occupation of a public accountant. Prior thereto, he served for three years as a United States deputy collector of internal revenue. Before that, he had worked for six years as the credit manager of a hardware company, about five years as the operator of a collection agency, and for four years as an insurance solicitor and risk inspector.

At and prior to the time with which we are concerned, defendant held himself out to the public by newspaper advertisements and by other advertising media as an "Income Tax Expert," duly qualified to give advice, aid, and assistance to the public generally in the discharge of a taxpayer's duty to make accurate returns of income to the federal government. Defendant alleges that he is thoroughly familiar with income tax rules and regulations. He has used a business card on which he describes himself as a "Tax Consultant" and prominently calls attention thereon to the fact that he was a former deputy collector of internal revenue.

On or about March 4, 1948, Cecil G. Germain, a private investigator employed by plaintiffs to obtain information as to whether defendant was engaged in the practice of law, went to the office of defendant under the assumed name and identity of an alleged taxpayer, George Heinl. Germain, as George Heinl, informed defendant that he operated a truck farm, that he had come to have his income tax return prepared, and that he needed help with certain questions. For a cash consideration, defendant prepared the income tax return and gave Germain professional advice for the determination of the following questions:

---

1. Plaintiffs are the members of a committee on the unauthorized and illegal practice of law, which is a subcommittee of the Committee on Practice of Law of the Ramsey County Bar Association.

2. As *amici curiae* the following organizations have filed briefs with the court:

Minnesota Association of Public Accountants, National Society of Public Accountants, Minnesota Society of Certified Public Accountants, American Institute of Accountants, Minnesota State Bar Association, and the American Bar Association.

(a) Whether the taxpayer, who himself had exclusive control of the operation of the truck farm, was in partnership with his wife, who had contributed one-half of the purchase price, who helped with the work, and who received one-half the profits.

(b) Whether the taxpayer was entitled to claim his wife as an exemption, since he had never been ceremonially married, though maintaining a common-law marriage status.

(c) Whether the taxpayer should file his separate return and advise his so-called common-law wife to file a separate return.

(d) Whether certain money expended on improvements of buildings on the truck farm was deductible from his earnings.

(e) Whether a certain produce loss sustained by frost and subsequent flood was a deductible item.

Aside from the fundamental issue of whether defendant's activities constituted the unauthorized practice of law, we are concerned with these procedural issues:

(1) Does the *district court* have the power to adjudge defendant in contempt of court and to punish him for the unauthorized practice of law?

(2) Does the district court have jurisdiction to enjoin the unauthorized practice of law where defendant's acts of purported law practice did not involve any act or appearance before said court?

(3) Is a justiciable issue presented when the evidentiary base of an action to enjoin the unauthorized practice of law consists primarily of professional acts of advice and service which were furnished for a consideration to a person who was not a bona fide taxpayer, upon a fabricated

and hypothetical state of facts, and in connection with the preparation of an income tax return which was never intended to be filed?

[1, 2] 1–2. We shall dispose of the procedural matters first. A proceeding to adjudge a person in contempt of court for the unauthorized practice of law—whether such unauthorized practice occurred within or outside the presence of the court—is punitive and criminal in its nature and is primarily brought in the public interest to vindicate the authority of the court and to deter other like derelictions. In re Frederick Bugasch, Inc., 175 A. 110, 12 N.J. Misc. 788, State ex rel. Indianapolis Bar Ass'n v. Fletcher Trust Co., 211 Ind. 27, 5 N.E.2d 538; Dangel, Contempt, National Lawyers' Manual (1939), §§ 353, 436; 7 C.J.S., Attorney and Client, § 16c. Although a prosecution for the unauthorized practice of law, as an offense against society, inures incidentally to the individual benefit of properly licensed lawyers, the criminal nature of the proceeding is unaffected. In re Frederick Bugasch, Inc., supra; see, Root v. MacDonald, 260 Mass. 344, 367, 157 N.E. 684, 692, 54 A.L.R. 1422.[3] Defendant, contending that the supreme court of Minnesota has the sole and exclusive jurisdiction to adjudge a person in contempt for the unauthorized practice of law, asks us upon this appeal to determine whether the district court had the power to adjudge him in contempt. This we cannot do. We have repeatedly held that a conviction for a criminal contempt, as distinguished from a civil contempt, is not appealable, but must be reviewed by certiorari. Swift & Co. v. United Packing House Workers, 228 Minn. 571, 37 N.W.2d 831, and cases cited therein.[4]

3. As to the distinction between a contempt proceeding, even though its object and result are wholly punitive, and an ordinary criminal proceeding, see Root v. MacDonald, 260 Mass. 344, 365, 157 N.E. 684, 691, 54 A.L.R. 1422; Dangel, Contempt, National Lawyers' Manual (1939) § 161.

4. As to contempt proceedings generally for the unauthorized practice of law, see Bump v. District Court, 232 Iowa 623, 5 N.W.2d 914; State ex rel. Wright v.

Barlow, 131 Neb. 294, 268 N.W. 95; State ex rel. Johnson v. Childe, 147 Neb. 527, 23 N.W.2d 720; People ex rel. Illinois State Bar Ass'n v. Peoples Stock Yards State Bank, 344 Ill. 462, 176 N.E. 901; People v. Securities Discount Corp. 361 Ill. 551, 198 N.E. 681; In re Frederick Bugasch, Inc., 175 A. 110, 12 N.J. Misc. 788; Matter of New York County Lawyers Ass'n (Bercu) 273 App.Div. 524, 78 N.Y.S.2d 209, 9 A.L.R.2d 787, affirmed, 299 N.Y. 728, 87 N.E.2d 451;

[3] 3. The district court has jurisdiction to enjoin the unauthorized practice of law, whether such practice takes place within or outside the presence of the court, and such jurisdiction is not destroyed by the criminality of the defendant's misconduct. The criminal nature of unauthorized practice neither gives nor ousts jurisdiction in chancery. Fitchette v. Taylor, 191 Minn. 582, 254 N.W. 910, 94 A.L.R. 356; Cowern v. Nelson, 207 Minn. 642, 290 N.W. 795; see, Miller v. Minneapolis Underwriters Ass'n, Inc. 226 Minn. 367, 371, 33 N.W.2d 48, 51; M.S.A. § 481.02.

[4] 4. Does a justiciable issue arise when the purported acts of unauthorized practice of law were intentionally performed by defendant upon the mistaken assumption that he was then advising a bona fide taxpayer and was preparing for him a tax return for use in reporting an actual taxpayer's income? Defendant's intentional acts were performed when plaintiffs' private investigator provided the occasion and the opportunity for such performance by calling at defendant's office under an assumed name with a purely fictitious and hypothetical state of facts. Although such investigator employed defendant's services for the sole purpose of obtaining evidentiary information as to the nature of defendant's regular activities, defendant did intentionally give his advice in the same manner as if a bona fide taxpayer had actually appeared. The fact that the income tax return was based upon fictitious facts and figures is not of itself a defense. Frequently decoy letters and other fictional devices have been employed in law enforcement cases, not to induce the commission of an unlawful act, but to secure information as to whether unlawful acts had been and were being committed. United States v. Lindenfeld, 2 Cir., 142 F. 2d 829. Defendant here assumes that because the tax return which he prepared

was not authentic he could not have committed any offense. He is mistaken. The leading case upon this point is Grimm v. United States, 156 U.S. 604, 609, 15 S.Ct. 470, 472, 39 L.Ed. 550, 552, where the court said:

"* * * it is insisted that the conviction cannot be sustained, because the letters of defendant were deposited in the mails at the instance of the government, and through the solicitation of one of its officers; that they were directed and mailed to fictitious persons; that no intent can be imputed to defendant to convey information to other than the persons named in the letters sent by him; and that, as they were fictitious persons, there could in law be no intent to give information to any one. * * *

"* * * The mere facts that the letters were written under an assumed name, and that he was a government official,—a detective, he may be called,—do not of themselves constitute a defense to the crime actually committed. The official, suspecting that the defendant was engaged in a business offensive to good morals, sought information directly from him, and the defendant, responding thereto, violated a law of the United States by using the mails to convey such information, and he cannot plead in defense that he would not have violated the law if inquiry had not been made of him by such government official."

This court followed the Grimm case in State v. Gibbs, 109 Minn. 247, 123 N.W. 810, 25 L.R.A., N.S., 449. When the investigator called at defendant's office he did not thereby induce or originate defendant's intent to perform the alleged acts of unauthorized practice, but merely provided the opportunity for defendant to exercise the intent which he already possessed.[5]

State ex rel. Indianapolis Bar Ass'n v. Fletcher Trust Co., 211 Ind. 27, 5 N.E. 2d 538; In re Morse, 98 Vt. 85, 126 A. 550, 36 A.L.R. 527, with Annotation at page 533; Rhode Island Bar Ass'n v. Automobile Service Ass'n, 55 R.I. 122, 179 A. 139, 100 A.L.R. 226, with Annotation at page 236; In re McCallum, 186 Wash. 312, 57 P.2d 1259; Appeal of Cichon, 227 Wis. 62, 278 N.W. 1.

48 N.W.2d—50½

5. United States v. Lindenfeld, 2 Cir., 142 F.2d 829; United States v. Becker, 2 Cir., 62 F.2d 1007; Fiunkin v. United States, 9 Cir., 265 F. 1; Rothman v.

[5] An actual intent by defendant to hold himself out to the public as willing to do and as customarily and regularly doing the acts which are here alleged to constitute the unauthorized practice of law is the very basis of these proceedings. In view of the evidentiary establishment of his intent and his regular doing of such acts, does it follow that no justiciable issue is presented simply because the evidence was obtained by the device of a fictitious tax return and a purely hypothetical set of facts? There is nothing fictitious or hypothetical about the basic issue between the parties. Instead of a fictitious, academic, or hypothetical issue, we have an actual, genuine, and live controversy as to whether defendant is guilty of the unauthorized practice of law. We are not concerned with some contingent or threatened event which may never occur. We are dealing with acts of alleged unlawful practice which have occurred. Furthermore, a controversy is not moot where, as here, the judgment of the court will have a swift and definite impact upon defendant by forever enjoining him from giving regular advice and service in connection with the preparation of income tax returns.

5. Was defendant, however, practicing law when, as a preliminary to and as part of his preparation of an income tax return, he advised the purported taxpayer as to whether he had acquired a partnership status, a valid marriage for exemption purposes, whether he should file a joint return with a woman to whom he had never been ceremonially married, and whether certain building and truck farm improvements, as well as certain losses sustained by frost and subsequent flood, were deductible items?

Much of what is law practice is conducted outside the courtroom, and as to that field of activity we have said: " * * * The line between what is and what is not

the practice of law cannot be drawn with precision. Lawyers should be the first to recognize that between the two there is a region wherein much of what lawyers do every day in their practice may also be done by others without wrongful invasion of the lawyers' field." Cowern v. Nelson, 207 Minn. 642, 646, 290 N.W. 795, 797.

[6,7] Although it is difficult to draw any precise dividing line, the task is ours to find some criterion for distinguishing that which is from that which is not law practice. The development of any practical criterion, as well as its subsequent application, must be closely related to the purpose for which lawyers are licensed as the exclusive occupants of their field. That purpose is to protect the public from the intolerable evils which are brought upon people by those who assume to practice law without having the proper qualifications. See, 29 Mich.L.Rev. 989. The need for public protection is not of new origin. As early as 1292,[6] the problem was recognized when Edward I, by royal ordinance, limited the number of attorneys and directed his justices "to provide for every county a sufficient number of attornies and apprentices from among the best, the most lawful and the most teachable, so *that king and people might be well served.*" (Italics supplied.) 1 Pollock and Maitland, History of English Law, p. 194. See, Herbert, Antiquities of the Inns of Court and Chancery, pp. 166, 167. The limitation and selection of lawyers, without strict regulation, proved inadequate.

"* * * The evil finally became so great that in the year 1402 Parliament this time took cognizance of it and enacted the now famous statute, 4 Henry IV, Ch. 18, which provided that all attorneys should be examined by the justices, and in their discretion, only those found to be good and virtuous, and of good fame, learned and sworn to do their duty, be allowed to be

---

United States, 2 Cir., 270 F. 31; Sorrells v. United States, 287 U.S. 435, 53 S.Ct. 210, 77 L.Ed. 413; see, People v. Alfani, 227 N.Y. 334, 125 N.E. 671.

6. What is probably the first Anglo-Saxon statute regulating the practice of the law was passed in 1275 as the Statute of

Westminster, the First, 3 Edward I, c. 29 (1 Stat. at Large, p. 94). The professional lawyer, however, began to appear in Anglo-Saxon England shortly after the Conquest. See, Cohen, The Law:— Business or Profession? (1924) pp. 84–86.

put upon the roll and all others put out."
Rhode Island Bar Ass'n v. Automobile
Service Ass'n, 55 R.I. 122, 133, 179 A. 139,
144, 100 A.L.R. 226. These early English
statutes illustrate that a licensed bar subject to the supervision of the courts origi-
nated with a public demand for the exclusion of those who assumed to practice
without being qualified therefor.

[8–10] 6. The protection of the public,
as the purpose of confining law practice to
a licensed bar, ancient as it is in its origin,
is of vital importance today. See, In re
Estate of Peterson, 230 Minn. 478, 42 N.
W.2d 59; Cowern v. Nelson, 207 Minn.
642, 290 N.W. 795; M.S.A. 481.02. Any
criterion for distinguishing law practice
from that which belongs to other fields
can be properly geared to the public welfare only if we keep in mind the manner in
which the licensing of lawyers serves its
purpose. The law practice franchise or
privilege is based upon the threefold requirements of *ability, character,* and *responsible supervision.* The public welfare
is safeguarded not merely by limiting law
practice to individuals who are possessed
of the requisite ability and character, but
also by the further requirement that such
practitioners shall thenceforth be officers
of the court and subject to its supervision.
See, 40 Dickinson L.Rev. 225, 229. In consequence, lawyers are not merely bound by
a high code of professional ethics, but as
officers of the court they are subject to its
inherent supervisory jurisdiction, which
embraces the power to remove from the
profession those practitioners who are unfaithful or incompetent in the discharge of
their trust. In re Tracy, 197 Minn. 35, 266
N.W. 88, 267 N.W. 142; see, In re Opinion
of the Justices, 289 Mass. 607, 194 N.E.
313. This is in itself an important reason
why law practice should be confined to
members of the bar. Protection of the
public is set at naught if laymen who are
not subject to court supervision are permitted to practice law. Although professional standards for safeguarding the public interest must be sufficiently flexible to
allow for adaptation to changes in conditions, they must in any event be of such
stability and permanence as to protect the

individual practitioner in the enjoyment
of his professional franchise; otherwise
men of ability and character will find no
inducement to undergo the years of training necessary to qualify them as lawyers.
This principle, as a part of the public weal,
is applicable to any profession which demands of its members high skill and pro-
ficiency based upon years of intensive preparatory training. State v. Bailey Dental
Co., 211 Iowa 781, 234 N.W. 260; 5 Ford-
ham L. Rev. 207.

[11] 7. If we bear in mind that any
choice of criterion must find its ultimate
justification in the interest of the public and
not in that of advantage for either lawyer
or nonlawyer, we soon cease to look for
an answer in any rule of thumb such as
that based upon a distinction between the
incidental and the primary. See, People
v. Title Guarantee & Trust Co., 227 N.
Y. 366, 379, 125 N.E. 666, 670; Merrick v.
American Security & Trust Co. 71 App.D.
C. 72, 107 F.2d 271. Any rule which holds
that a layman who prepares legal papers
or furnishes other services of a legal nature
is not practicing law when such services
are incidental to another business or profession completely ignores the public welfare. A service performed by one individual for another, even though it be incidental to some other occupation, may entail a difficult question of law which requires a determination by a trained legal
mind. See, 33 Minn.L.Rev. 445. Are we
to say that a real estate broker who examines an abstract of title and furnishes an
opinion thereon may not be held to practice
law merely because the examination of a
title is ancillary to a sale and purchase of
real estate? Can we say that a lawyer
employed to bring a suit for damages for
personal injuries is competent to diagnose
the nature of his client's injuries and that
he is not practicing medicine merely because such diagnosis is incidental to a proper presentation of his client's case? The
drawing of a simple instrument or the application of an elementary legal principle
is one thing in the incidental classification,
but it is wholly another when such incidental act or service requires professional
skill. The incidental test has no value ex-

cept in the negative sense that if the furnishing of the legal service is the primary business of the actor such activity is the practice of law, even though such service is of an elementary nature. In other words, a layman's legal service activities are the practice of law unless they are incidental to his regular calling; but the mere fact that they are incidental is by no means decisive. In a positive sense, the incidental test ignores the interest of the public as the controlling determinant.

[12–14] 8–9. In rejecting the incidental test, it follows that the distinction between law practice and that which is not may be determined only from a consideration of the nature of the acts of service performed in each case. No difficulty arises where such service is the primary business of the actor. We then have law practice. Difficulty comes, however, when the service furnished is incidental to the performance of other service of a nonlegal character in the pursuit of another calling such as that of accounting. In the field of income taxation, as in the instant case, we have an overlapping of both law and accounting. An accountant must adapt his accounting skill to the requirements of tax law, and therefore he must have a workable knowledge of law as applied to his field. By the same token, a lawyer must have some understanding of accounting. In the income tax area, they occupy much common ground where the skills of both professions may be required and where it is difficult to draw a precise line to separate their respective functions. The public interest does not permit an obliteration of all lines of demarcation. We cannot escape reality by hiding behind a facade of nomenclature and assume that "taxation," though composed of both law and accounting, is something *sui generis* and apart from the law. See, Matter of New York County Lawyers Ass'n (Bercu) 273 App.Div. 524, 78 N.Y.S.2d 209, affirmed, 299 N.Y. 728, 87 N.E.2d 451. If taxation is a hybrid of law and accounting, it does not follow that it is so wholly without the law that its legal activities may be pursued without proper qualifications and without court supervision. The interest of the public is not protected by the narrow specialization of an individual who lacks the perspective and the orientation which comes only from a thorough knowledge and understanding of basic legal concepts, of legal processes, and of the interrelation of the law in all its branches.[7] Generally speaking, whenever, as incidental to another transaction or calling, a layman, as part of his regular course of conduct, resolves legal questions for another—at the latter's request and for a consideration—by giving him advice or by taking action for and in his behalf, he is practicing law if difficult or doubtful legal questions are involved which, to safeguard the public, reasonably demand the application of a trained legal mind. What is a difficult or doubtful question of law is not to be measured by the comprehension of a trained legal mind, but by the understanding thereof which is possessed by a reasonably intelligent layman who is reasonably familiar with similar transactions. A criterion which designates the determination of a difficult or complex question of law as law practice, and the application of an elementary or simple legal principle as not, may indeed be criticized for uncertainty if a rule of thumb is sought which can be applied with mechanical precision to all cases. Any rule of law which purports to reflect the needs of the public welfare in a changing society, by reason of its essen-

7. The shortcomings of a narrow specialization is well illustrated by the service given by the respondent to his client in Matter of New York County Lawyers Assn. (Bercu) 273 App.Div. 524, 78 N.Y. S.2d 209, affirmed, 299 N.Y. 728, 87 N.E. 2d 451. On the other hand, the value of a well-rounded legal training in the income tax field was demonstrated by two Minnesota lawyers in Albright v. United States, 8 Cir., 173 F.2d 339, wherein the court held that sales of all dairy and breeding animals used in a farmer's business and owned more than six months were entitled, under § 117(j) of the Internal Revenue Code, 26 U.S.C.A. § 117(j), to be treated as sales of capital assets. It has been said that this decision has saved farmers millions of dollars in income taxes. See, 35 Iowa L.Rev. 49.

tial and inherent flexibility, will, however, be as variable in operation as the particular facts to which it is applied.

[15–17] 10–11–12. In restraining laymen from improper activity, *the difficult question of law criterion* is to be applied in a common-sense way which will protect primarily the interest of the public and not hamper or burden that interest with impractical and technical restrictions which have no reasonable justification. Cowern v. Nelson, 207 Minn. 642, 290 N.W. 795. We are therefore not concerned with a technical application which would ban the giving of any and all legal advice or the taking of any and all action for another.[8] Whether a difficult or doubtful question of law is resolved by the giving of advice to, or the doing of an act for, another must in each case depend upon the nature of the problem involved. As ancillary to the closing of a real estate transaction, a real estate broker may draw the ordinary instruments of conveyance. Cowern v. Nelson, supra. No layman, however, except when dire emergency prevents the calling of a lawyer, may draw another's will. In re Estate of Peterson, 230 Minn. 478, 42 N.W.2d 59; M.S.A. § 481.02. As applied to the preparation of income tax returns, it has been well said: " * * * Federal income taxation is founded on statute, elaborated and interpreted by administrative regulations and rulings, and construed by court decisions. Matters in this field, as in other statutory subjects, will at times involve difficult questions of interpretation of statute or court decision, and the validity of regulations or statute; they will also involve doubtful questions of nontax law on which the tax issues may depend, and questions of liability for criminal or civil penalties or of statutes of limitation or of liability as transferee for the taxes of another. Such questions, in general, are the kind for which lawyers are equipped by training and practice."[9]

[18, 19] When an accountant or other layman who is employed to prepare an income tax return is faced with difficult or doubtful questions of the interpretation or application of statutes, administrative regulations and rulings, court decisions, or general law, it is his duty to leave the determination of such questions to a lawyer. In so holding that the determination of difficult or doubtful questions is the practice of law, it does not follow that the entire income tax field has been preempted by lawyers to the exclusion of accountants. The work of an accountant disassociated from the resolving of difficult or doubtful questions of law is not law practice. See, Opinion of the Justices, 289 Mass. 607, 615, 194 N.E. 313, 318. In the determination of income—the subject of taxation—difficult accounting problems may arise by presenting "such aspects as inventory pricing methods (last-in-first-out, first-in-first-out, retail method, cost determination, actual costs, standard costs, cost of in-process merchandise, market price valuation, etc.), accrual and installment accounting, carryover and carryback of net operating losses, depreciation, depletion and corporate distributions. The taxation of such income may involve such concepts as consolidated returns, taxable years of less than twelve months, invested capital, etc. All of these are concepts of accounting, * * *." 36 Iowa L.Rev. 227, 229.

Where difficult accounting questions arise, the careful lawyer will naturally advise his client to enlist the aid of an accountant. In the income tax field, the lawyer and the accountant each has a function to perform in the interest of the public.[10]

[20] 13. In the instant case, the evidence sustains the trial court's findings and

---

8. " 'Giving any legal advice' would include telling a man whether it is lawful to write 'Please do not open until Christmas' on a parcels post package. 'Any action taken for others in any matter connected with the law' would include parking a man's automobile for him parallel to the curb not over six inches from it." 19 American Bar Assn. Journal 652.

9. Maurice Austin, Relations Between Lawyers and Certified Public Accountants in Income Tax Practice (1951), 36 Iowa L.Rev. 227, 228.

10. See, 1 Catholic University of America L.Rev. 21.

conclusions that defendant was engaged in the practice of law. For a consideration, and as part of his regular income tax work, defendant advised and determined for the taxpayer whether the latter had attained the status of a lawful marriage with a woman with whom he had been living but to whom he had never been ceremonially married. He further gave advice as to whether such taxpayer and his consort should file separate or joint returns. The purported taxpayer was likewise uncertain as to whether he occupied the status of a partner with his so-called common-law wife in the operation of a truck farm, over which he himself exercised exclusive control but in which the latter shared equally in the labor, investment, and profit. This question, the answer to which obviously required legal training, he also resolved. We do not here have the case of a taxpayer whose legal status was established or known beforehand. In addition, defendant gave advice as to the deductions which the taxpayer might claim for certain farm improvements and for certain produce loss by frost and subsequent flood. Although the preparation of the income tax return was not of itself the practice of law, defendant, incidental to such preparation, resolved certain difficult legal questions which, taken as a whole, constituted the practice of law.

[21] 14. In further confirmation of the conclusion that defendant was practicing law, the evidence establishes that he advertised and held himself out as a "Tax Consultant," which by reasonable implication advised the public that he was competent to give legal advice on the law of taxation. A layman, whether he is or is not an accountant, may not hold himself out to the public as a tax consultant or a tax expert, or describe himself by any similar phrase which implies that he has a knowledge of tax law. It should be noted that lawyers, by the canons of ethics of the American Bar Association and the opinions thereto pertaining, are likewise prohibited from advertising any special branch of law practice. Canons of Professional and Judicial Ethics, American Bar Association, Canons 27 and 45, and see Opinion 260.

The order of the trial court is affirmed.

Affirmed.

Gardner brief

Gardner v. Conway, 48 N.W.2d 788 (Minn. 1951).

FACTS: D held himself out to public through newspaper & other advertisements as "income tax expert" qualified to give assistance to public in filing of federal income tax returns. D attained formal education through grade school & was never admitted to practice law in any state. Ps are members of Ramsey County Bar Association. Ps hired private detective to investigate whether D was illegally engaged in practice of law.

Detective went to D under assumed name as alleged taxpayer. Detective told D he operated truck farm, needed to have income tax return prepared, requested D to resolve questions: 1. whether he had formed partnership with his wife regarding the truck business, 2. whether he could claim his wife as exemption even though they had never been formally married, 3. whether he & common law wife should file joint or separate returns, 4. whether certain business expenditures & certain business losses could be deducted from his income. D answered these questions for detective & prepared his tax return.

PROCEDURE: Ps sued D to have him perpetually enjoined from further engaging in unauthorized practice of law & to have him adjudged in contempt of ct. Dist ct found D illegally engaged in practice of law & denied D's motion for new trial. D appealed.

ISSUE: Did D engage in practice of law when he answered question of detective about tax implications of marital & business relations?

HOLDING: Affirmed. Evidence sustains district court's finding that D was engaged in practice of law when answering questions about tax implications of marital & business relations.

REASONING: Lawyers must be licensed to practice law to protect public from intolerable evils brought upon people by those who assume to practice law without having proper qualifications. Public welfare is safeguarded by limiting law practice to individuals who possess requisite ability & character & are officers of court & subject to its supervision. Focus of rule must be interest of public & not advantage for either lawyer or nonlawyer.

Rule permitting a layperson to prepare legal papers or perform other legal services when such services are incidental to another business completely ignores public welfare. Incidental act of performing legal services may require professional skill which actor does not possess. Thus, focus on nature of acts of service performed in each case.

Rule: If legal services are primary business of actor, then law practice. When layperson as part of regular course of conduct incidentally resolves legal questions for another upon request & for consideration, person practices law if difficult or doubtful legal questions are involved which reasonably demand application of trained legal mind. What is difficult or doubtful question of law is to be determined by reasonably intelligent layperson familiar with similar transactions. Criterion is not to be applied in impractical or technical manner. Application of rule demands common sense dependent on facts of each case.

Here preparation of income tax return was not in itself practice of law. However, incidental to completion of return, D resolved difficult legal questions regarding partnership law, marital status, & business deductions which, taken as whole, constituted practice of law. Further, D held himself out to public through advertisements that he was competent to give legal advice on tax law.

Annotation, *Activities of Law Clerks as Illegal Practice of Law*, 13 A.L.R.3d 1137 (1967).

ANNOTATION

ACTIVITIES OF LAW CLERKS AS ILLEGAL PRACTICE OF LAW

TABLE OF JURISDICTIONS REPRESENTED
Consult POCKET PART in this volume for later case service

§ 1. Introduction

[a] Scope

This annotation[1] collects the cases discussing the nature of activities by a law clerk which constitute the illegal practice of law. For purposes of this annotation, "law clerk" includes clerical personnel employed by an attorney but not admitted to the bar.

Attention is called to the fact that this annotation discusses statutes only insofar as they are reflected in reported cases within the scope of the annotation. The reader is advised to consult the most recent statutes of his jurisdiction.

1. Insofar as the earlier annotations in 111 ALR 19, 125 ALR 1173, and 151 ALR 781, contain cases within the scope of this annotation, such cases have been included herein.

TOTAL CLIENT SERVICE LIBRARY REFERENCES

7 Am Jur 2d, Attorneys at Law § 88
ALR Digests, Attorneys § 1.3
ALR Quick Index, Attorneys

Consult POCKET PART in this volume for later case service

[b] Related matters

Power of court to enjoin attorney from prosecuting actions secured through chasers or runners. 14 ALR2d 740.

Services in connection with tax matters as practice of law. 9 ALR2d 797.

Handling, preparing, presenting, or trying workmen's compensation claims or cases as practice of law. 2 ALR3d 724.

What amounts to practice of law. 111 ALR 19, 125 ALR 1173, 151 ALR 781.

Liability of attorney for services rendered to him by one not admitted to bar as affected by the fact that they amounted to practice of law by the latter. 90 ALR 288.

§ 2. Preparatory or ministerial work

In the following cases, it was held that the activities of an unlicensed law clerk did not constitute the practice of law where such acts were limited to work of a preparatory or ministerial nature.

Thus, it was held that an unlicensed law clerk was not engaged in the unlawful practice of law where the clerk was hired by an attorney to take charge of the management of the work to be done in his office to the extent of drawing pleadings and papers necessary to be drawn by such attorney in his practice, in Johnson v Davidson (1921) 54 Cal App 251, 202 P 159, ovrld on other grounds Crawford v State Bar of California, 54 Cal 2d 659, 7 Cal Rptr 746, 355 P2d 490, the court, in affirming a judgment which held that the law clerk owned an undivided interest in certain property purchased by the attorney-employer with firm funds, simply stating that it was lawful for the attorney to employ the clerk to perform such functions.

An unlicensed law clerk who prepared and presented an order to the court that a jury had disagreed on a case, appeared before a court at a later date, and in-

formed the court that the case had not been settled and that his employer, an attorney representing one of the parties to the suit, was engaged in a trial in another court, was held not to have engaged in the unauthorized practice of law in People v Alexander (1964) 53 Ill App 2d 299, 202 NE2d 841, 13 ALR3d 1132, the court reversing an order adjudging the law clerk guilty of contempt of court for the unauthorized practice of law. In holding that the clerk's preparation of the order showing the mistrial was not an unauthorized practice of law, the court noted that the order had been prepared with the collaboration of opposing counsel and at the request of the court, and then stated that the preparation of the order was a ministerial act for the benefit of the court and a mere recordation of what had transpired. As to the law clerk's appearance before the court regarding the availability of counsel and the status of the case as not constituting the unauthorized practice of law, the court said that they agreed with the trial court that clerks should not be permitted to make motions or participate in other proceedings which could be considered as "managing" the litigation, but if apprising the court of an employer's engagement or inability to be present constituted the making of a motion, then they must hold that clerks could make such motions for continuances without being guilty of the unauthorized practice of law.

And while Toth v Samuel Phillipson & Co. (1928) 250 Ill App 247, is not within the scope of this annotation in that the question whether activities of an unlicensed law clerk constituted an unauthorized practice of law was not considered, the court stated that it was well known that where numerous trial courts were sitting at the same time the exigencies of such a situation required that trial attorneys be represented by their clerical force to respond to some of the calls, that the court acted upon their response the same as if the attorneys of record themselves appeared in person, and that the litigant, or his attorney, in such instances was treated as having appeared, it being recognized that it was impracticable and impossible under such circumstances for the trial attorney to respond to each call in person or to employ a force sufficient to try every case as it was called.

And see Ferris v Snively (1933) 172 **Wash** 167, 19 P2d 942, 90 ALR 278, infra § 3, wherein the court in holding that a law clerk had been engaged in the unlawful practice of law stated that a law clerk would not be engaged in the practice of law if he limited his functions to work of a preparatory nature, such as research, investigation of details, assemblage of data, and like work that would enable the attorney-employer to carry a given matter to a conclusion through his own examination, approval, or additional effort.

§ 3. Performance of functions requiring legal knowledge

In the following cases, it was held that an unlicensed law clerk was involved in the unauthorized practice of law where he engaged in activities requiring legal knowledge or training, such as handling probate matters, examination of abstract titles, and preparation of wills, leases, mortgages, bills of sale, or contracts, without supervision from his employer.

A disbarred attorney working as an alleged law clerk in the office of his attorney son was found to be engaged in the unlawful practice of law in Crawford v State Bar of California (1960) 54 **Cal** 2d 659, 7 Cal Rptr 746, 355 P2d 490, where the court, in reproving the son for permitting his father to engage in such activities, noted that the father

had given advice concededly legal in nature directly to a client regarding certain mining claims, had handled an entire probate matter, including conferences with the client, handled an escrow that involved considerable controversy as to compliance with the underlying contract, and performed various routine services for tax clients. As to the son's contention that the acts complained of were not improper for they were within the functions of a law clerk, the court stressed the fact that the father had acted independently of the son, both in regard to matters involving legal advice and to matters that could be characterized as such because performed in a law office, and that the son merely had knowledge of the existence of them but not of their progress or disposition.

In Clements v State (1940) 141 **Tex** Crim 108, 147 SW2d 483, the court sustained a conviction for "practicing law" illegally where, without being admitted to the bar, an individual was associated with an attorney's office, and received and consulted with one who came there as a client, giving her advice which resulted in her filing a suit for divorce asking for alimony and a division of community property, and accompanied her to the courthouse or to the office of her husband's attorney, where she introduced him as her attorney, and upon the letterhead of the attorney with whom he was associated appeared his name, with that of the attorney, over the designation "law offices," followed by the address of the office, and a letter upon such a letterhead was addressed to the husband's attorney submitting terms of settlement, which was signed by a firm designation which included the defendant, and was followed by his name as agent, notwithstanding the defendant did not collect a fee but was paid a salary by the attorney in whose office he was working.

The activities of an unlicensed law clerk which included his handling uncontested probate matters, giving oral opinions on abstracts of title, and preparing wills, leases, mortgages, bills of sale, and contracts, upon his own initiative, with no supervision from his employer, a licensed attorney, were held to amount to the practice of law within the meaning of a statute providing that no person should be permitted to practice as an attorney or counselor at law or to do work of a legal nature for compensation unless he had been admitted to practice law in the state in Ferris v Snively (1933) 172 **Wash** 167, 19 P2d 942, 90 ALR 278, the court holding, however, that the clerk's violation of the statute as to the practice of law by an unlicensed person did not preclude him from enforcing a contract against the estate of his employer for services rendered. In thus holding, the court stated that it recognized that the nature of work performed by law clerks approached in a degree that of their employers, and that the line of demarcation as to where their work began and where it ended could not always be drawn with absolute distinction or accuracy. The court went on to say that the activities of a law clerk would not constitute the practice of law so long as they were limited to work of a preparatory nature, such as research, investigation of details, assemblage of data, and like work that would enable the attorney-employer to carry a given matter to a conclusion through his own examination, approval, or additional effort.

The preparation, drafting, or drawing of wills and the giving of advice with respect thereto by an unlicensed law clerk was held to constitute the unauthorized practice of law in violation of a statute which required that any person practicing law must be admitted to the state bar in State ex rel. Wyoming State Bar v Hardy (1945) 61 **Wyo** 172, 156 P2d 309, the court, however, dismissing the proceeding against the defendant for contempt for unlawful practice of law in view of the circumstances involved in the case. In dismissing the proceeding, the court noted that the defendant had been engaged in the preparation of wills, etc., for a number of years, that this fact was known to members of the bar residing in the vicinity and yet no suggestion of impropriety or warning was given the defendant and no steps were taken to stop such practices until the present proceeding was instituted, and that the defendant did not intend to engage in the unauthorized practice of law. The court went on to say that inasmuch as this was the first case of this character before them they preferred to refrain from being unduly severe with defendant notwithstanding he had mistakenly transgressed the boundaries that subsisted between lay and professional action in the matter of drawing wills.

✦

8 Dunnell's Minn. Digest *Contracts* § 3.20, at 163-64 (4th ed. 1990).

3.20 Contracts contrary to statutes

As a general rule, contracts in violation of a statute that imposes a penalty for the doing of an act are unlawful,[48] but they are not always so.[49] An inference of invalidity of an act or document does not necessarily follow from the fact that a statute prescribes a penalty.[50] Although the general rule is that a contract entered into in violation of a statute that imposes a prohibition and a penalty for the doing of an act, such as the pursuit of a business, profession, or occupation without procuring a license or permit required by law for the protection of the public, is void, the rule is not to be applied without first examining the nature and circumstances of the contract in light of the applicable statute or ordinance.[51] It is a question of legislative intention.[52]

48. *See* Lew Bonn Co v. Herman, 271 Minn. 105, 135 N.W.2d 222 (1965); *In re* Peterson's Estate, 230 Minn. 478, 42 N.W.2d 59 (1950); Suess v. Arrowhead Steel Prod Co, 180 Minn. 21, 230 N.W. 125 (1930) (statutes for protection of employees); Vercellini v. U S I Realty Co, 158 Minn. 72, 196 N.W. 672 (1924); Johnstown Land Co v. Brainerd Brewing Co, 142 Minn. 291, 172 N.W. 211 (1919) (contract for introduction of liquor into territory made dry by treaty with Indians); Thomas v. Knapp, 101 Minn. 432, 112 N.W. 989 (1907) (statute prescribing conditions of foreign corporations doing business in Minnesota); Berni v. Boyer, 90 Minn. 469, 97 N.W. 121 (1903) (lease of property to be used as brothel); Swedish-American Nat'l Bank v. First Nat'l Bank, 89 Minn. 98, 94 N.W. 218 (1903) (statute regulating pledges); G Heileman Brewing Co v. Peimeisl, 85 Minn. 121, 88 N.W. 441 (1901) (statute imposing restrictions on foreign corporations); National Inv Co v. National Sav Loan & Bldg Ass'n, 49 Minn. 517, 52 N.W. 138 (1892) (statute forbidding building associations from leasing money to certain persons); Bisbee v. McAllen, 39 Minn. 143, 39 N.W. 299 (1888) (statute regulating weights and measures); Ingersoll v. Randall, 14 Minn. 400 (Gil. 304) (1869) (statute for boxing knuckles and tumbling rods of threshing machine); Brimhall v. Van Campen, 8 Minn. 13 (Gil. 1) (1862)

(statute regulating observance of Sun.); Solomon v. Dreschler, 4 Minn. 278 (Gil. 197) (1860) (statute regulating sale of liquors).

49. *In re* Peterson's Estate, 230 Minn. 478, 42 N.W.2d 59 (1950); Tolerton v. Barck, 84 Minn. 497, 88 N.W. 19 (1901) (statute requiring foreign corporations to appoint local agent); De Mers v. Daniels, 39 Minn. 158, 39 N.W. 98 (1888) (statute relating to town plats).

50. *In re* Peterson's Estate, 230 Minn. 478, 42 N.W.2d 59 (1950).

51. Lew Bonn Co v. Herman, 271 Minn. 105, 135 N.W.2d 222 (1965) (failure of electrical contractor to file with city building inspector copy of plans and specifications as required by ordinance did not render contract illegal where failure was no more than slight breach relating to collateral duty and did not involve bad motives or design to deny protection of law to one of class for whose benefit ordinance was enacted). *See* Dick Weatherston's A M Serv v. Minnesota Mut Life Ins Co, 257 Minn. 184, 100 N.W.2d 819 (1960); Minter Bros Co v. Hochman, 231 Minn. 156, 42 N.W.2d 562 (1950); *In re* Peterson's Estate, 230 Minn. 478, 42 N.W.2d 59 (1950).

52. *In re* Peterson's Estate, 230 Minn. 478, 42 N.W.2d 59 (1950); Tolerton v. Barck, 84 Minn. 497, 88 N.W. 19 (1901) (statute requiring foreign corporations to appoint local

§ 3.20 CONTRACTS

The intent of the legislature is the controlling factor in determining to what extent, in order to preserve the requirements of public policy, contracts and other instruments made in connection with the act of violation are to be held illegal, if at all.[53] In construing a statute or ordinance, courts will infer that the legislature did not intend that an instrument executed in violation of its terms should be void unless that is necessary to accomplish its purpose.[54] A statute is not to be construed as abridging freedom of contract unless such an intention is clearly expressed.[55] For example, in the absence of fraud or mistake, the doctrine that invalidates contracts contemplating illegal performance does not prohibit a sale from a vendor to a vendee merely because the property has only limited value.[56]

Where a statute or an ordinance makes a particular business unlawful for unlicensed persons, a contract made in that business by an unlicensed person is unlawful.[57] Justice and sound public policy do not always require the literal and arbitrary enforcement of a licensing statute.[58] A party who enters into a contract, such as leasing out an airplane, by which he is required to perform an act or service for which a license, or permit is required by statute does not forfeit his right of recovery on the contract because of his failure to have the permit or license, unless it appears clearly that this result was intended by the legislative authority specifying such a requirement.[59]

If a party agrees to do a thing that it is lawful for him to do and it becomes unlawful by an act of the legislature, the act avoids the promise.[60] A contract entered into in contravention of express law is wholly void.[61] A _____ lease, authorizing the lessee to operate a theater under a _____ lessor has been held ill____

agent); De Mers v. Daniels, 39 Minn. 158, 39 N.W. 98 (1888) (statute relating to town plats).

53. *In re* Peterson's Estate, 230 Minn. 478, 42 N.W.2d 59 (1950).

54. Lew Bonn Co v. Herman, 271 Minn. 105, 135 N.W.2d 222 (1965). *See In re* Peterson's Estate, 230 Minn. 478, 42 N.W.2d 59 (1950).

55. Johnson v. Central Life Assur Soc'y, 187 Minn. 611, 246 N.W. 354 (1933).

56. Bernard v. Schneider, 264 Minn. 104, 117 N.W.2d 755 (1962) (purchasers were bound by terms of covenant in deed permitting no building except dwelling in spite of zoning ordinance excluding dwellings from areas zoned commercial).

57. Buckley v. Humason, 50 Minn. 195, 52 N.W. 385 (1892) (ordinance licensing real estate brokers); Solomon v. Dreschler, 4 Minn. 278 (Gil. 197) (1860) (sale of liquor without license). *See* Gunnaldson v. Nyhus, 27 Minn. 440, 8 N.W. 147 (1881).

58. Dick Weatherston's A M Serv v. Minnesota Mut Life Ins Co, 257 Minn. 184, 100 N.W.2d 819 (1960).

59. North Cent Co v. Phelps Aero, 272 Minn. 413, 139 N.W.2d 258 (1965).

60. Seaman v. Minneapolis & R R Ry, 127 Minn. 180, 149 N.W. 134 (1914).

61. Swedish-American Nat'l Bank v. First Nat'l Bank, 89 Minn. 98, 94 N.W. 218 (1903). *See* Schmidt v. Prudential Ins Co, 190 Minn. 239, 251 N.W. 683 (1933).

Howard Orenstein et al., *Minnesota's Living Will . . .*,
Bench & B. Minn., Aug. 1989, at 21.

Howard Orenstein, David Bishop and Leigh D. Mathison

Minnesota's Living Will...

One of the most controversial questions faced by medical providers and by families of the critically ill is whether and when to withdraw care from patients who are too sick to make that choice for themselves. Society continues to wrestle with questions of how to allocate scarce medical resources and whether care should be provided to a patient who has not requested it and does not want it. While there appears to be a consensus that competent adults have the right to refuse medical treatment, there is not a similar consensus regarding how that right should be extended to incompetent adults — especially on the question of withholding or withdrawing artificially provided nutrition and hydration.

After several unsuccessful attempts in previous years, in 1989 the Minnesota Legislature joined 39 other states and the District of Columbia in passing "living will" legislation. The so-called Adult Health Care Decisions Act, Laws 1989, chapter 3 (to be codified at Minn. Stat. §145B.01 et seq.), provides a statutory framework for competent adults to give advance direction as to the health care they wish to receive or not receive should they later become unable to make such decisions. This legislation, while certainly not dispositive of the controversial social issues surrounding the withdrawal of medical care, does give new direction to families, medical providers, and judges as they struggle with questions of medical ethics.

The Adult Health Care Decisions Act of 1989 provides a statutory framework for addressing several of the key issues regarding living wills in Minnesota but the law in this area will likely be unsettled for the forseeable future.

ILLUSTRATION BY REG SANDLAND

The Legal Bases

While the Adult Health Care Decisions Act was 12 pages long in its final legislative form, the legal principle underlying the act is simple and basic: each individual has the right to control his or her own body. As discussed below, that principle finds consistent support in the common law, the Constitution of the United States and the constitution of the state of Minnesota.

At common law, the right of each individual to control his or her body was recognized through the tort of battery. The simple law school definition of battery — an unconsented touching — goes directly to the question involved with living wills. The common law of battery requires a physician to obtain a patient's informed consent prior to rendering invasive medical treatment to the patient. However, if the patient has made a living will, the physician presumably knows the kind of treatment the patient is willing to accept and may render that treatment without committing a battery.

The United States Supreme Court has recognized the right to control one's body as a fundamental constitutional right. As early as 1891, the U.S. Supreme Court held that a plaintiff in a civil suit could not be required to submit to a surgical examination. The Court stated:

No right is held more sacred, or is more carefully guarded by the common law, than the right of every individual to the possession and control of his own person, free from all restraint or interference of others. . . . The right to one's person may be said to be a right of complete immunity: to be let alone. *Union Pacific Railroad Company v. Botsford*, 141 U.S. 250, 251 (1891), citations omitted.

The "right to be let alone" was described by Justice Brandeis as "the most comprehensive of rights and the right most valued by civilized men . . . ." *Olmstead v. United States*, 277 U.S. 438, 478 (1928) (dissenting opinion). *Also see, e.g., Rochin v. California*, 342 U.S. 165, 174 (1952) (forced stomach pumping is "brutal and offensive to human dignity"); *Schmerber v. California*, 384 U.S. 757, 772 (1966) ("the integrity of an individual's person is a cherished value

of our society"); and *Winston v. Lee*, 470 U.S. 753, 762 (1985) (compelling a criminal defendant to submit to surgery was unconstitutional since such an intrusion "damages the individual's sense of personal privacy and security").

This federally protected right to control one's health care has previously been given effect in Minnesota through statute and case law. The Patients' Bill of Rights, Minn. Stat. §144.651, guarantees the right of patients to participate in the planning of their health care (subd. 10) and to refuse treatment (subd. 12). The Minnesota Supreme Court relied on the Patients Bill of Rights and the federally recognized right of privacy in upholding a conservator's decision to order removal of life-sustaining treatment from a comatose man who had previously told friends and relatives he would not want such treatment. *In re Torres*, 357 N.W.2d 332 (Minn. 1984). *See also Price v. Sheppard*, 307 Minn. 250, 239 N.W.2d 905 (1976) (the right to privacy recognized in the federal Constitution requires that physicians obtain court approval in an adversary proceeding prior to administering intrusive medical treatment to a committed patient who either refuses to give consent or is incompetent to give consent).

Minnesota courts have recently recognized the right to privacy as a state constitutional right distinct from the federal Constitution. In *State v. Gray*, 413 N.W.2d 107 (Minn. 1987), the Minnesota Supreme Court, without elaborating on the breadth of such a right, held that Minnesotans do derive a right of privacy from the state constitution.

Just two months later, the Court held that the right to privacy under the Minnesota constitution includes the right not to receive invasive medical care without consent. *Jarvis v. Levine*, 418 N.W.2d 139 (Minn. 1988). In *Jarvis*, a man involuntarily committed to a security hospital challenged the right of his physicians to administer neuroleptic drugs to him without his consent. The Court held that absent extraordinary situations, a competent person has a constitutional right to refuse to accept invasive medical treatment. 418 N.W.2d at 149. More important for the living will debate, the Court held that where a person is incompetent to give consent to

invasive medical treatment, a court hearing must be held before such treatment can be given.

The effect of *Jarvis* was to recognize that a person's incompetence does not negate the person's right to bodily control; rather, the Court held, physicians must still obtain consent — albeit from some source other than the contemporaneous words of the patient — before administering invasive medical treatment. The Court stated: ". . . the final decision to accept or reject a proposed medical procedure and its attendant risks is ultimately *not* a medical decision, but a personal choice." 418 N.W.2d at 148, emphasis in original. The right to privacy, the Court held, "begins with protecting the integrity of one's own body and includes the right not to have it altered or invaded without consent." *Id.*

It seems clear from the reasoning and dicta in *Jarvis* that absent extraordinary circumstances, a physician would be prohibited from administering invasive medical treatment to an adult who, while competent, had made an advance directive refusing such treatment. Living will legislation provides a statutory framework for individuals to assert this constitutionally recognized right to control their own health care.

The Minnesota Adult Health Care Decisions Act was passed in the spirit of *Jarvis* and was intended by its authors to be construed liberally so as to give full effect to the constitutional right to privacy enunciated in *Jarvis*. While the act was, of course, the product of compromise within the legislative process, we believe nothing in the act should be read as the intent of the Legislature to restrict an individual's right to bodily integrity. Section 17 of the act (Minn. Stat. §145B.17) states explicitly:

Nothing in this chapter impairs or supersedes the existing rights of any patient or any other legal right or legal responsibility a person may have to begin, continue, withhold, or withdraw health care.

The Legislative Battle

Living will legislation has been introduced in the Minnesota Legislature since 1984. Only this year did a number of forces converge to enable passage of the Adult Health Care Decisions Act.

Various legal issues were battled out in the four previous legislative sessions. These disputes involved, on the one hand, a coalition of senior citizen groups, the bar association, and almost all medical provider associations in the state as proponents of the final 1989 bill, and, on the other hand, a vigorous opposition led by the Minnesota Citizens Concerned for Life (MCCL), widely regarded as the most politically potent special interest lobbying force in the Legislature.

The MCCL was successful in 1984 in defeating a prior bill in committee and in 1985 prevented the bill from even getting a hearing in the House. Another version in 1986 was stopped by the MCCL in a House committee. In 1987, extensive efforts were made to revise the bill and work out problems through mediation arranged and paid for by the House Judiciary Committee chairman, Rep. Randy Kelly. The MCCL decided in 1987 to offer its own bill, one that would mandate food and nutrition, unless shown to be medically counterproductive, for all incompetent patients. This aggressive proposal by the MCCL resulted in a virtual deadlock for living will legislation.

During the 1987-88 legislative interim, approximately 35 hours of hearings were held around the state by the House Judiciary Committee on the two opposing proposals. Again in the 1988 session, a deadlock between the two powerful forces resulted in no bill being approved, although the coalition proposal reached the floors of both the Senate and House. The House Judiciary Committee rejected the MCCL version as an amendment to the coalition bill by a margin of one vote. The MCCL then claimed it had the votes lined up on the floor to reverse that result. This became moot when the MCCL amendment effectively gutted the coalition bill on the floor of the Senate and its chief author, Sen. Clarence Purfeerst, pulled the bill.

During 1988, the battle over living will legislation raged on in many aspects of the political scene in Minnesota, from the June Independent Republican convention platform to the questionnaires

sent out by the MCCL and the Berean League to all the candidates for the Minnesota House of Representatives. The senior citizens were urged to respond with similar political pressure and did so with their own questionnaires and meetings. They put together a much broader and more active coalition of supporting organizations than previously existed. In the fall elections, the defeat of Rep. Allen Quist, the chief House leader for the MCCL, sent a signal to other legislators that the coalition in favor of the bill had mustered respectable political clout.

"The new Minnesota law is unusual in that it does not specifically provide immunity to health care providers who comply with the declaration."

After the elections, the living will coalition enlisted a new chief author in the Senate, Sen. Ember Reichgott, an attorney who studied the various issues involved and prepared for another vigorous battle in the 1989 session.

As the 1989 legislative session opened, the chief House author, Rep. David Bishop, devised a new strategy: to line obtain a substantial commitment of support from sufficient members long in advance of the final voting. Rep. Bishop and supporters of the legislation were successful in obtaining 66 separate members as coauthors.

The House Judiciary Committee chair announced that the bill would not get a hearing in the House until it had cleared

the Senate, since so much time had previously been devoted to the issue in House hearings in 1988. Sen. Reichgott then proceeded in the Senate, needing only a bit of collaboration on clarifying amendments which were acceptable to the House author and to the coalition.

At this point, several amendments or changes in the bill occurred, which were followed and expanded upon as it then proceeded through the House committee and on the House floor. These changes reflect legislative intent and may be of particular interest to lawyers.

First, the clause granting medical providers legal immunity from malpractice claims if they relied in good faith on a declaration was eliminated in a Senate committee and was never reinstated in the House. This bill thus became the only living will law, in the 40 states that now have adopted similar legislation, not to grant provider immunity. The representatives of the medical profession indicated to the Senate committee that they did not consider such a clause legally necessary as long as the threshold for choice and applicability of a living will remained as stated — "reasonable medical practice."

Another amendment responded to extensive opposition by the MCCL and other groups who claimed that the law would apply to every incompetent patient, regardless whether the patient had made a written declaration. Those groups also claimed that the bill would apply to every medical condition regardless whether the condition was terminal. Amendments were therefore offered in both the Senate and the House, making it clear that only those patients who had signed declarations would be affected, and only terminal conditions as defined in the bill and as diagnosed by an attending physician would qualify.

In addition, negotiations with representatives of the Minnesota Catholic Conference of Health Care Facilities resulted in some changes in the bill. The opposition of the Catholic Conference that had surfaced at the end of the 1988 session was thus removed.

These developments led, after ten hours of hearings in the House Judiciary Committee, to a 13-to-12 vote that defeated the same MCCL amendment that had stalled the bill in the Senate in 1988. The way was thus cleared and the bill was sent to the House floor.

Finally, an amendment on the House floor attempted to specify the form that should be used to make an advance health care declaration (the term "living will" is never used in the act). The document form, originally intended only to be "suggested," was made practically mandatory on the floor of the House by inclusion of a clause in Section 4 (Minn. Stat. §145B.04) that "a declaration executed after August 1, 1989 under this Chapter must be substantially in the form in this Section."

The authors believe that notwithstanding these statutory provisions relating to the form of the declaration, advance declarations using a different form from that in the statute will be given effect by courts reviewing them. As discussed above, abundant precedent exists to support construction of the new statute consistent with the underlying constitutional right to privacy which prevents administration of medical treatment contrary to the patient's expressed wishes.

A Practitioner's Guide

While a person need not obtain legal assistance before making an effective advance health care declaration under the new Adult Health Care Decisions Act, it seems likely that attorneys will be involved in advising both patients and health care providers in how best to comply with the act. The following practice pointers are offered to assist attorneys and the general public in understanding and effectively using the Adult Health Care Decisions Act.

When Is An Advance Declaration Effective? Section 2, subd. 3 of the act (Minn. Stat. §145B.02, subd. 3) restricts the definition of "health care" to mean "care, treatment, services or procedures to maintain, diagnose, or treat an individual's physical condition *when the individual is in a terminal condition*" (emphasis supplied), while subdivision 8 sets forth a definition of terminal condition in the law which was not included in the original bill. The definition of terminal condition is important because

The 20 organizations that compose the Living Will Coalition, of which the Minnesota State Bar Association is a member, have produced a booklet entitled "Questions & Answers about the Adult Health Care Decisions Act." This booklet includes the form and instructions to assist people in completing a health care declaration. Copies are being prepared for distribution at a nominal charge. For further information, contact the MSBA at (612) 333-1183 or (800) 292-4152.

the opening paragraph of the statutory form states that the declaration applies "when you are in a terminal condition." This narrows the scope of situations in which a person's advance directive is effective under the statute.

A terminal condition is defined as "an incurable or irreversible condition for which the administration of medical treatment will serve only to prolong the dying process." Section 2, subd. 8 (Minn. Stat. §145B.02, subd. 8). This definition is broader than that which is included in some other states' statutes in that it includes an irreversible coma and a permanently unconscious or persistent vegetative state. Therefore, if a person does not want to include these conditions within the scope of a declaration, the definition should be narrowed in paragraph (1) of the form wherein the declarant is to state the circumstances under which the declaration applies. Likewise, if a person specifically wants the declaration to cover an irreversible coma, although it is included under the present definition of terminal condition, it might be wise to so state, both for clarity and to be prepared in the event that the definition of "terminal condition" is narrowed in the future.

Executing an Effective Declaration. Section 3 of the act (Minn. Stat. §145B.03) sets forth the scope and requirements for a declaration. It is also important because pursuant to Section 15 (Minn. Stat. §145B.15), a declaration executed prior to August 1, 1989, is effective only if it "substantially

complies" with the requirements set forth in that section. The declaration may include preferences or instructions regarding health care, the designation of a proxy decision maker, or both. Because many health care providers feel that appointment of a proxy is a superior way to provide for decision making, completion of that part of the form should be encouraged. Subdivision 2 of that section provides that the declaration must be signed by the declarant and two witnesses or a notary public, none of whom may be named as a proxy. In addition, neither of the witnesses may be entitled to any part of the declarant's estate by will or by intestacy, and must make a certification to that effect. Subdivision 2(b) also requires the declarant to state either his or her preferences regarding the administration of artificial nutrition and hydration ("tube feeding") or that the declarant wishes a proxy to make that decision. However, it goes on to state that if the declaration does not include the declarant's preferences regarding artificial nutrition and hydration, the declaration is still enforceable and the decision as to the administration of artificial nutrition and hydration will be made consistent with reasonable medical practice as outlined in Section 13 (Minn. Stat. §145B.13). The proxy may not be able to participate in the decision in that event.

What Form To Use. Section 4 of the Act (Minn. Stat. §145B.04) is the statutory form. Although the section is entitled "suggested form," the prefatory language states that "a declaration executed after August 1, 1989 under this Chapter must be substantially in the form in this Section," possibly precluding the use of a different form (but see the discussion of constitutional issues, *supra*).

The form contains a notice and instructions to the person executing the form. It utilizes a fill-in-the-blank format, wherein the declarant may state not only the circumstances under which the declaration applies, but also instructions for care and treatment the person wants or does not want. A person may complete any or all of the blanks.

For example, paragraphs (2) and (4) of the form ask what care the person wants. The person may wish to state in paragraph (2) that he or she wants "medical procedures or medication to provide comfort care and to alleviate pain." If the person wishes to have a more aggressive course of treatment, this should be so stated. Paragraphs (3) and (5) of the form enable the person to specify what treatment he or she does not want. If a traditional "living will" format is desired, the person may wish to state that he or she does not want any treatment that would serve only to prolong the dying process.

Paragraph (6) of the form is particularly important in that it requires the person to state his or her feelings regarding the provision of artificial nutrition and hydration. It should be completed whenever possible, since failure to complete this paragraph may mean that the proxy cannot make this decision for the declarant. Paragraph (8) is the provision for appointment of a proxy, and may be completed whether or not the person has specified instructions earlier in the form. It should be kept in mind that the person named as proxy will have priority for appointment as a guardian or conservator of the person if such a proceeding is required. Section 3 of the act (Minn. Stat. §145B.03) gives the proxy priority for appointment as guardian or conservator of the person of the declarant as permitted by Minn. Stat. §525.544.

Health Care Provider's Obligations. A declaration becomes operative when it is delivered to the declarant's physician or other health care provider and the declarant can no longer give informed consent. Unless the declaration is revoked, a physician or other health care provider is required to follow the declaration, consistent with reasonable medical practice, or comply with the notice and transfer provisions of Section 6 (Minn. Stat. §145B.06).

The new Minnesota law is unusual in that it does not specifically provide immunity to health care providers who comply with the declaration. However, as discussed above, no liability should result so long as the health care provider complies with reasonable medical practice as set forth in Section 13 (Minn. Stat. §145B.13). That section provides, in part, that care to provide comfort and alleviate pain must always be given, and requires oral administration of food or water to a patient who accepts it, "except for clearly documented medical reasons."

Exclusions and Open Issues. The law states in several places that it has no effect upon a person who has not executed a declaration, and creates no presumption regarding the appropriate medical treatment to be provided to such a person. The law also states that it is not to be construed to condone, authorize, or approve mercy killing, euthanasia, suicide, or assisted suicide.

Practitioners should in all instances remember the underlying constitutional principle that each individual has the right to control his or her own health care. Where the new Minnesota statute results in some substantive or procedural roadblock to the effectuation of that constitutional right, practitioners may wish to assert their clients' rights to the full extent allowed by the Constitution and, where appropriate, litigate those issues for the clients' benefit.

Conclusion

The issues involved in the new Minnesota Adult Health Care Decisions Act are so deep and so pervasive that they will likely be with us in legislation and litigation in years to come. Already in 1989, the MCCL has indicated it intends to continue the fight in the legislative arena and attack the definition of "terminal." In addition, the whole subject of forced or natural supply of food and fluids is being litigated all over the country by organizations such as the MCCL.

The prospect of continued controversy surrounding these issues suggests taht the law in this area will not be settled soon. What is clear is that clients will require careful and informed counsel from attorneys from time to time, interpreting both the existing legislation and the underlying constitutional rights of medical patients. 🕮

Restatement (Second) of Contracts § 181 (1979)
(with comments and illustrations).

§ 181.   **Effect of Failure to Comply with Licensing or Similar Requirement**

If a party is prohibited from doing an act because of his failure to comply with a licensing, registration or similar requirement, a promise in consideration of his doing that act or of his promise to do it is unenforceable on grounds of public policy if

(a) the requirement has a regulatory purpose, and

(b) the interest in the enforcement of the promise is clearly outweighed by the public policy behind the requirement.

Comment:

a.   Scope.   One of the most frequent applications of the general rule stated in § 178 occurs where a party seeks to enforce an agreement although he has failed to obtain a license, to register or to comply with a similar requirement.   This Section states a specific version of

See Appendix for Court Citations and Cross References

21

§ 181 CONTRACTS, SECOND Ch. 8

that general rule as it applies to such cases. Whether there has been a violation of legislation that imposes the requirement is a matter of interpretation of the legislation itself and is beyond the scope of this Restatement.

b. Regulatory purpose. In deciding whether a party can enforce an agreement in spite of his failure to comply with such a requirement, courts distinguish between requirements that have a regulatory purpose and those that do not. The policy behind a requirement that has a regulatory purpose may be regarded as sufficiently substantial to preclude enforcement, while the policy behind one that is merely designed to raise revenue will not be. In determining whether a measure has a regulatory purpose, a court will consider the entire legislative scheme, including any relevant declaration of purpose. Common indications of regulation include provisions for examination or apprenticeship to ensure minimum standards on entrance and provisions for the posting of a bond or procedures for license revocation to ensure that standards are maintained.

Illustration:

1. A, an unlicensed broker, agrees to arrange a transaction for B, for which B promises to pay A $1,000. A city ordinance requires persons arranging such transactions to be licensed as a result of paying a fee, with no inquiry into competence or responsibility. A arranges the transaction. Since the licensing requirement is designed merely to raise revenue and does not have a regulatory purpose, enforcement of B's promise is not precluded on grounds of public policy.

c. Balancing where purpose is regulatory. If the court decides that the requirement has a regulatory purpose, it must then weigh the interests favoring enforcement of the promise against the public policy behind the requirement. The factors listed in § 178 are taken into account in this process. If the party who has failed to comply with the requirement has done nothing by way of preparation or performance, the interest in enforcement of the promise is easily outweighed. But if, as is usually the case, he has completely performed and is seeking the promised compensation for that performance, forfeiture to himself and enrichment to the other party may result from a refusal to enforce the other party's promise. In determining the extent to which forfeiture and enrichment will result, a court will consider the possibilities that part of the agreement may be enforceable (see § 183 and Illustration 1 to that section) and that restitution may be available (see § 197 and Illustration 4 to that section). In evaluating the gravity of the

Ch. 8   GROUNDS OF PUBLIC POLICY   § 181

public policy involved, the court will look to the interest that the regulation is designed to protect and will give greater weight, for example, to a measure intended to protect the public health or safety than one intended to have only an economic effect. Compare Illustrations 2 and 3. It will consider the magnitude of the penalty provided by the legislature as some indication of the weight that it attached to that interest. It will also take account of the extent to which the misconduct was deliberate or inadvertent. See Illustration 4.

Illustrations:

2. A, an unlicensed plumber, agrees to repair plumbing in B's home, for which B promises to pay A $1,000. A state statute, enacted to prevent the public from being victimized by incompetent plumbers and to protect the public health, requires persons doing plumbing to be licensed on the basis of an examination, the posting of a bond, and the payment of a fee, and makes violation a crime. A does the agreed work. A court may decide that the public policy against enforcement of B's promise outweighs the interest in its enforcement, and that B's promise is unenforceable on grounds of public policy. Compare Illustration 1 to § 183.

3. A, an unlicensed milk dealer, promises to deliver to B, a licensed milk dealer, milk for which B promises to pay $20,000. A state statute designed for the purpose of economic regulation of the milk industry provides that "no dealer shall buy or sell milk without a license," and makes violation a misdemeanor punishable by a fine of up to $500 and imprisonment for up to 6 months. A delivers the milk to B, but B refuses to pay the price. In view of all the circumstances, including the discrepancy between the forfeiture by A if B's promise were not enforced and the penalty provided by the statute, a court may decide that the public policy against enforcement of B's promise does not outweigh the interest in its enforcement and that enforcement of B's promise is not precluded on grounds of public policy.

4. The facts being otherwise as stated in Illustration 2, A had once been licensed but his license had expired the week before because, unknown to him, his clerk had inadvertently forgotten to send in the renewal fee, although the bond had been extended. The court may decide that in all the circumstances including A's ignorance of the fact that he was unlicensed, enforcement of B's promise is not precluded on grounds of public policy.

E. Allan Farnsworth, *Contracts* § 5.6, at 377-79
(2d ed. 1990).

• • • •
In cases of this second type, a party who seeks to recover the price of goods delivered or services performed under an agreement is met with the defense that the party failed to comply with a licensing requirement. Analogous problems arise under registration and similar requirements,[15] but most of the leading cases involve licensing.

Unlicensed claimant cases

In deciding the licensing cases, courts have traditionally distinguished between requirements that have a regulatory purpose and those that do not. A court may regard the policy underlying a licensing requirement that has a regulatory purpose as sufficiently strong to justify a refusal to enforce the agreement, even though forfeiture will result.[16] A court will not, however, regard the policy underlying a requirement designed merely to raise revenue as sufficiently strong to justify a refusal.[17]

Regulatory or other purpose

[15]For cases involving other types of requirements, *compare* Amoco Oil Co. v. Toppert, 56 Ill. App. 3d 595, 371 N.E.2d 1294 (1978) (since failure of seller of fertilizer to provide statement of chemical analysis as required by Fertilizer Act was "not seriously injurious," seller could recover price of fertilizer delivered) *with* Brooks v. R.A. Clark's Garage, 117 N.H. 770, 378 A.2d 1144 (1977) (failure of garage to give customer written estimate as required by consumer protection statute barred garage from recovering for repairs). *See also* Fields v. Hunter, 368 A.2d 1156 (D.C. App. 1977) (taking of postdated check by seller of liquor violated statute prohibiting sale of liquor on credit and barred him from recovering amount of check); Mascari v. Raines, 220 Tenn. 234, 415 S.W.2d 874 (1967) (taking of note by seller of liquor violated statute prohibiting sale of liquor on credit and barred him from recovering on note).

[16]Derico v. Duncan, 410 So. 2d 27 (Ala. 1982) (where "regulation and protection are the goal" of licensing statute, consumer loan in violation was "null, void, and unenforceable"); Truitt v. Miller, 407 A.2d 1073 (D.C. App. 1979) (unlicensed home improvement contractor could not recover for renovation of house); William Coltin & Co. v. Manchester Sav. Bank, 105 N.H. 254, 197 A.2d 208 (1964) (where statute requiring brokers to be licensed is "an exercise of the police powers and is designed to protect the public against fraud and incompetence, the lack of license will not only subject a violator to the express statutory penalties but he will be unable to enforce his bargain and collect his commission").

[17]M. Arthur Gensler, Jr., & Assocs. v. Larry Barrett, Inc., 7 Cal. 3d 695, 499 P.2d 503 (1972) (at most, failure to apply for amended building permit "affected only the revenue-raising provisions of the code and not those directed at public protection").

377

§5.6   Unenforceability on Grounds of Public Policy

In deciding whether the purpose is regulatory, a court will consider the
entire legislative scheme, including any legislative declaration of purpose and provisions for examination, apprenticeship, posting a bond,
and license revocation.[18]

Balancing of   Even if the court concludes that the purpose is regulatory, it will not
interests   refuse to enforce the agreement unless the policy underlying the licensing requirement clearly outweighs the interest in enforcing the agreement. Courts have been increasingly reluctant to refuse enforcement on
the ground of mere noncompliance with some regulatory law. A court
may disregard the noncompliance if the regulation is intended to serve
only an economic interest, and not an interest in health or safety,[19] if the
penalty provided by the legislature for violation is relatively modest,[20]
or if there has been substantial compliance with the licensing requirement.[21] And it may infer, from the legislation's silence on the question of
unenforceability when compared with explicit provisions in similar legislation, that this additional sanction is inappropriate.[22]

---

[18]Wilson v. Kealakekua Ranch, 551 P.2d 525 (Haw. 1976) ("while the provisions of
the statute requiring initial registration [of architects] are clearly designed to protect
the public from unfit and incompetent practitioners of architecture, we think that the
provision requiring renewal . . . is purely for the purpose of raising revenue" where no
reexamination or reinvestigation was required).

[19]John E. Rosasco Creameries v. Cohen, 276 N.Y. 274, 11 N.E.2d 908 (1937) (although
milk dealer was unlicensed, violation of statute did "not endanger health or morals").

[20]Town Planning & Engr. Assocs. v. Amesbury Specialty Co., 369 Mass. 737, 342
N.E.2d 706 (1976) (firm that performed engineering services without being registered
as professional engineers not barred from recovery under contract since any violation
"was punishable as a misdemeanor [and] we have to ask whether a consequence, beyond the one prescribed by statute, should attach"); John E. Rosasco Creameries v.
Cohen, *supra* note 19 (violations were punishable as misdemeanors, by fine of up to
$200 and imprisonment of up to six months, whereas denial of enforcement will "punish
the plaintiff to the extent of a loss of approximately $11,000 and permit the defendants
to evade the payment of a legitimate debt"). *But cf.* Gene Taylor & Sons Plumbing Co.
v. Corondolet Realty Trust, 611 S.W.2d 572 (Tenn. 1981) (distinguishing *Rosasco
Creameries* where statute providing penalty took effect subsequently).

[21]Asdourian v. Araj, 38 Cal. 3d 276, 696 P.2d 95 (1985) (contractor operated as sole
proprietorship using own name instead of name of business under which he obtained
license); Northwest Cascade Constr. v. Custom Component Structures, 83 Wash. 2d 453,
519 P.2d 1 (1974) (although employees of registered subcontractor completed job, subcontractor remained obligated and sufficiently involved).

[22]Mountain States Bolt, Nut & Screw Co. v. Best-Way Transp. Co., 116 Ariz. 123, 568
P.2d 430 (Ct. App. 1977) (where legislature expressly barred recovery by improperly
licensed contractors, but did not do so in the case of deficiently licensed carriers, such
a carrier was not barred from recovering for services); Murphy v. Mallos, 59 A.2d 514
(D.C. App. 1948) (where a related statutory provision barred suit by unlicensed broker,
but provision in question did not, court had "no right to read such additional punitive
provision into the section"). For a more extreme view, *see* Hiram Ricker & Sons v. Students Intl. Meditation Socy., 342 A.2d 262 (Me. 1975) ("In the absence of any *express*

C. Policies Derived from Legislation §5.6

That an agreement is unenforceable by an unlicensed party does not necessarily mean that it is unenforceable by the other party. If the regulatory legislation is designed to protect persons in a particular class, a court may conclude that the policy underlying the legislation will best be served by allowing a claimant who is a member of that class to hold the unlicensed party in damages for any defective performance.[23] It may also conclude that the claimant is entitled, in the alternative, to restitution of any payments made.[24]

May be enforceable by other party

---

legislative intention to declare contracts made and performed by unlicensed innkeepers void, we will not infer such intention."), appeal dismissed, 423 U.S. 1042 (1976). For a case holding a contract enforceable in spite of legislative history suggesting the contrary, *see* Davenport & Co. v. Spieker, 197 Cal. App. 3d 566, 242 Cal. Rptr. 911 (1988). *See* Restatement Second §181.

[23]Hedla v. McCool, 476 F.2d 1223 (9th Cir. 1973) (owners could recover damages for delay caused by inadequacy of plans furnished by architects who were unlicensed, though owners did not know this); Cohen v. Mayflower Corp., 196 Va. 1153, 86 S.E.2d 860 (1955) (owner could recover damages for defective waterproofing by contractor who had failed to get license since "to deny relief . . . would defeat the purpose of the statute and penalize the person intended to be protected"). *But cf.* In re Mahmoud & Ispahani, [1921] 2 K.B. 716 (C.A.) (unlicensed buyer who misrepresented that he was licensed not liable to seller for refusal to take delivery of goods).

[24]Truitt v. Miller, *supra* note 16 (owners of house entitled to restitution of payments made to unlicensed home improvement contractor before they knew he was not licensed).

Office Memo #1

TO: Partner
FROM: Associate
RE: HomeElderCare: drafting of living wills
DATE: October 20, 1992

ISSUES

law + facts

1. Do social workers illegally practice law when, at the request of their elderly clients, they draft living wills and advise clients about them for a set fee?

facts + law

2. Is a contract to provide such a service for a fee enforceable?

facts + law

3. Is the product of the contract, the living will, valid?

SHORT ANSWERS

law + facts + reasons

1. Social workers most likely practice law illegally when they prepare living wills and advise clients about them, because they thereby draft legal documents and answer difficult or doubtful legal questions.

facts + law + reason

2. A contract to provide such a service for a fee probably would be enforceable nonetheless, for public policy reasons.

facts + law + reason

3. The living will would be valid, based on the intent of the legislature in enacting the Minnesota Living Will Act and the unauthorized practice of law statute.

FACTS

introduction

HomeElderCare (our client) is a private, non-profit corporation in Minnesota that provides various services for elderly persons who still live in their own homes; it is interested in preparing living wills for its clients.

1st topic: HEC's services generally

Each HomeElderCare client contracts for the services he or she desires. Standard services include shopping, transportation, home maintenance, and personal finance advice. A staff of geriatric social workers coordinates these services for clients, and volunteers provide some services. The social workers also serve as liaisons between clients and attorneys working on legal transactions for the clients.

2nd topic: living will service

Over the past few months, several clients have asked whether the social workers would help the clients complete living wills. A living will is a document that specifies the signer's desires regarding medical treatment in the event the signer is incapacitated. One social worker has located a form living will. The form presents blanks to be filled in and indicates fairly clearly how the document is to be signed, witnessed, and notarized. According to the form's introduction, the form complies with the requirements of Minnesota law.

The social work staff and executive director believe that living wills are useful documents. They further believe that the staff could prepare the wills, especially after attending a seminar or two, and that preparation of living wills is a logical extension of the liaison work done with doctors and other health care providers.

3rd topic: staff competence and attitudes

HomeElderCare proposes to provide the following service: The client would be interviewed by a social worker, who also would talk through the significance of the living will, and the social worker would then prepare a draft based on the form. The client would be encouraged to review the document with his or her physician before signing it. The social worker would arrange for the signing, including notarization. Finally, the social worker would deliver the living will to the client's primary care physician. Each client would pay a fee based on the time the social worker spent on the living will.

4th topic: HEC's proposal in chronological form

The executive director of HomeElderCare is aware that only lawyers may legally draft wills disposing of property upon the death of the individual. She wonders whether the preparation of living wills by the social workers would violate the law. She also wonders whether HomeElderCare's contracts with their clients for the drafting of living wills would be enforceable and whether the living wills themselves would be valid.

client's concerns

DISCUSSION

Introduction

The Minnesota unauthorized practice of law statute essentially prohibits individuals from providing legal services unless they are members of the bar and licensed to practice law. The drafting of living wills by HomeElderCare (HEC) social workers would be an unauthorized practice of law, and the counseling service also would be unauthorized if answers to difficult or doubtful legal questions are given to clients. Despite the illegal practice of law, the contract between HEC and its clients may be enforceable, on public policy grounds. Finally, the living will would be valid, in light of public policy and the limited penalty provisions of the unauthorized practice of law statute.

thesis paragraph (general overview)

Unauthorized Practice of Law

Under the Minnesota unauthorized practice of law statute, it is unlawful

for any person, . . . except for members of the bar of Minnesota admitted and licensed to practice as attorneys at law, . . . for a fee or any consideration, to give legal advice or counsel, perform for or furnish or another legal services, or, for or without a fee or any consideration, to prepare, di-

1st part
statute as overview

rectly or through another, for another person, any will or testamentary disposition or instrument of trust serving purposes similar to those of a will, or, for a fee or any consideration, to prepare for another person, firm, or corporation any other legal document. . . .

Minn. Stat. § 481.02 subd. 1 (1992). The HEC social workers are not licensed or admitted attorneys in Minnesota. HEC's proposal would violate this statute in two respects.

beginning application

First, HEC social workers would prepare "legal documents" for a fee by preparing living wills for their clients. Although the unauthorized practice of law statute does not define "legal document," the Minnesota Living Will Act provides a suggested form for living wills that plainly states that the form is a legal document. Minn. Stat. § 145B.04 (1992). This interpretation accords with the dictionary definitions of "legal" and "document": "an original or official paper relied on as the basis, proof, or support" of matters that are "established by law; statutory; conforming to or permitted by law or established rules." Webster's New Collegiate Dictionary 333, 651 (1981). HEC would draft these legal documents for clients and charge a fee for this service, thereby violating the statute.

■ 1st subpart (IRAC in one paragraph)

Second, HEC social workers may give "legal advice or counsel" for a fee in the course of preparing living wills. See Minn. Stat. § 481.02 subd. 1. Although "the line between what is and what is not the practice of law cannot be drawn with precision," an individual who engages in lawyering activities incidental to his or her non-legal career practices law if "difficult or doubtful legal questions are involved which, to safeguard the public, reasonably demand the application of a trained legal mind." Gardner v. Conway, 48 N.W.2d 788, 794, 796 (Minn. 1951). For example, an accountant engaged in the unauthorized practice of law when he provided information on various tax issues in the course of preparing a tax return for a client. Id. at 797-98. He provided advice and analysis on business partnerships, the status of a common-law wife on joint tax returns, and the deductibility of various expenditures. Id. at 792.

■ 2nd subpart —introduction —rule: case brief

—application

The preparation of living wills would be an activity incidental to HEC's social work. HEC social workers likely would face difficult or doubtful legal questions. Such questions might arise when the social workers discuss the significance of a living will with the client or after the social workers prepare a draft of the document and present it to the client. The sample form provided in the Living Will Act contains numerous examples of terms which could easily give rise to questions of a legal nature, such as "limits of reasonable medical practice," "terminal condition," "legally bound," and "willfully and voluntarily." See Minn. Stat. § 145B.04. Furthermore, the suggested form in the Living

Will Act specifically states that a professional should be consulted if there are any questions pertaining to the document, an indication that the form may not be as simple as it appears at first blush. See also Howard Orenstein, et al., Minnesota's Living Will. . . ., Bench & B. Minn., Aug. 1989, at 21, 24-25 (legislators deemed lawyers' involvement in drafting of living wills likely).

The questions that HEC social workers may address are at least as complex as those in Gardner relating to tax issues. They involve legal interpretations of statutory terms, although the living will statute is shorter and simpler than the tax code. In some respects, the HEC questions may be even more difficult given the relatively brief history of living wills. The Living Will Act is three years old, see Act of Mar. 3, 1989, ch. 3, 1989 Minn. Laws 8, and no appellate courts have addressed or settled the legal issues it raises. Furthermore, it is only part of a broader body of law on patient autonomy. See generally Orenstein, supra, at 22.

—more application: comparison to case

Interpreting the unauthorized practice statute to bar this service accords with the primary purpose of the prohibition on unauthorized practice. That purpose is to "protect the public from the intolerable evils which are brought upon people by those who assume to practice law without having the proper qualifications." Gardner, 48 N.W.2d at 794.

—more application: policy

On the other hand, the Gardner rule must be applied in "a common sense way which will protect the public and not hamper or burden that public interest with impractical and technical restrictions which have no reasonable justification." Id. at 797; see also Cardinal v. Merrill Lynch Realty/Burnet, Inc., 433 N.W.2d 864 (Minn. 1988) (involving charging of a fee for simple real estate transactions). HEC could argue that completing a living will form does not necessarily require legal knowledge. Declarants may complete the form themselves, and many of the issues to be decided are medical or ethical, not primarily legal. Furthermore, the authors of the living will statute sought to facilitate the use of living wills as a means of effectuating the patient's right to choose his or her health care options, Orenstein, supra, at 21, and prohibiting social workers from assisting clients could deter some clients from using living wills.

—more application: counter-argument with policy

However, restrictions on social workers preparing living wills are neither impractical nor merely technical. While the restrictions may be somewhat burdensome, they are reasonably justified because very significant legal issues are involved, as in the context of regular wills. Cf. Minn. Stat. § 481.02 subd. 1 (explicit prohibition against testamentary will drafting). These issues literally involve "matters of life and death" and, therefore, warrant particularly careful attention from a legal perspective.

—more application: resolution

—*more application:*
   final subelement

Finally, the charging of a fee suggests that an activity involves the resolution of difficult legal questions. Cardinal, 433 N.W.2d at 869. HomeElderCare plans to charge a fee.

—conclusion

In conclusion, the social workers most likely would violate the unauthorized practice of law statute if they prepared living wills and answered difficult legal questions during counseling. The stated penalties are misdemeanor penalties or an injunction. Minn. Stat. § 481.02 subd. 8.

consequences
branchpoint

The remaining questions are the enforceability of the contract and the validity of the living will. If preparing the living will is not an unauthorized practice of law, then the contract is enforceable and the living will is valid. If the drafting and advising constitute unauthorized practice, further analysis is necessary.

2nd part

introduction
rule: general statement

Contract Enforceability

As a general rule, if a statute requires licensing to perform a professional service and an unlicensed practitioner enters into a contract, that contract would generally be considered void. E. Allan Farnsworth, Contracts § 5.6, at 377-79 (2d ed. 1990). For some years, Minnesota followed this rule. See, e.g., Buckley v. Humason, 52 N.W. 385 (Minn. 1892) (where a real estate broker was held unable to recover a fee for real estate services because he was not licensed as required by statute). The rule, however, has been modified, and courts in Minnesota now examine the legislative intent behind the licensing statute rather than automatically hold the contract to be illegal and void. See Dick Weatherston's Assoc'd Mech'l Servs. v. Minnesota Mut. Life Ins. Co., 100 N.W.2d 819, 824 (Minn. 1960).

more rule: case brief

In Dick Weatherston's, the court enforced a contract on behalf of an engineer who was not licensed as required by statute, although he was trained as an engineer. The court determined that the legislative intent behind the engineering licensing statute was to protect "the public against incompetence and fraud" and safeguard "public health and welfare." Id. at 823. It then examined the facts of the case and found that the air-conditioning installation contract at issue did not violate those statutory goals for several reasons. First, the unlicensed engineer nonetheless had a bachelor's degree in engineering, as well as job experience. Id. at 821, 824. Second, the building owner who was seeking to void the contract sought out the engineer's services and clearly knew of his unlicensed status. Id. at 824. Third, the building owner had its own architects and engineers who approved, supervised, and eventually accepted the engineer's work, so the owner did not rely completely on the unlicensed engineer's expertise. Id. at 824-25. Fourth, the engineering design work at issue was incidental to a much larger contract for air-conditioning installation. Thus, the transaction did not endanger public health and welfare, nor was it tainted with fraud or misrepresentation, so the purpose of the licensing statute was not violated by the contract at issue. Therefore, the contract was valid. Id. at 825.

Here too, the statute on unauthorized practice of law prohibits certain unlicensed professional services, and the contemplated living-will service may well constitute unauthorized practice.

application: first factor

The facts in favor of HomeElderCare are not as favorable as the facts in Dick Weatherston's, but the court nonetheless probably would uphold the contracts. The purpose of that statute is to protect the public from the potentially serious harm that can result from the practice of law by incompetent individuals not subject to the direct supervision and discipline of the courts. Peterson v. Hovland (In re Peterson's Estate), 42 N.W.2d 59, 63-64 (Minn. 1950). Enforcement of the HEC contract would not harm the public in this way. As in Dick Weatherston's, there would be several guarantees of competence, although they are not as substantial as those in Dick Weatherston's. The social workers have general experience in health care and legal matters. They could receive training in drafting living wills and be instructed to refer clients with legal questions to attorneys. However, they are not licensed as attorneys and would not be supervised by licensed attorneys.

more application: additional factor

In HomeElderCare's favor, the HEC clients would not be the target of fraud or misrepresentation. The social workers would be responding to client requests and would do so in a responsible manner. They presumably would inform clients that they are not lawyers and what the basis of their expertise is.

more application: additional factor

As in Dick Weatherston's, the legal services would be incidental to legitimate nonlegal services, namely the provision of emotional support and guidance as to medical and moral issues.

more application: additional factor

Furthermore, as noted above, the legislature, in enacting the Living Will Act subsequent to the unauthorized practice of law statute, intended to encourage the use of living wills. Permitting the social workers to assist their clients will promote this legislative purpose.

more application: policy

As noted in Dick Weatherston's, "[j]ustice and sound public policy do not always require the literal and arbitrary enforcement of a licensing statute." 110 N.W.2d at 824. The legislature would not intend the HEC contract to be unenforceable as a consequence of the violation of the unauthorized practice of law statute.

conclusion

Validity of Living Will

3rd part

The penalties provision of the unauthorized practice of law statute suggests that the living will would be valid notwithstanding any unauthorized practice by the social workers. The unauthorized practice of law statute pro-

*introduction
rule: statute and case law*

vides for the prosecution and enjoining of individuals who engage in the unauthorized practice of law. Minn. Stat. § 481.02 subd. 8. The statute makes no reference to voiding the product of such acts. Interpreting the statute accordingly, the Minnesota Supreme Court held that a testamentary will drawn by a layperson in violation of the statute was nevertheless valid. <u>Peterson</u>, 42 N.W.2d at 64.

application

Similarly, in the HEC situation the living will drafted in violation of the statute would be valid. HEC might be penalized for its breach of the law through unauthorized practice proceedings. The clients, who would not be at fault, should not be punished as well.

more application: policy

Furthermore, holding the HEC living wills to be valid comports with the purpose of the Living Will Act—namely, to encourage and support individuals who want to complete such documents. The living wills would express the desires of the patients. Holding the living wills invalid would be contrary to the underlying philosophy of the Living Will Act.

conclusion

Analysis of both statutes leads to the conclusion that the living wills would be valid, even if their drafting would constitute the unauthorized practice of law.

CONCLUSION AND RECOMMENDATIONS

conclusion

Although the current proposal could well yield enforceable contracts and very likely would yield valid living wills, it probably involves the unauthorized practice of law. The proposal by HEC to have social workers prepare living wills for its clients should not be pursued until the issue of the unauthorized practice of law is resolved. Alternative solutions are possible.

initial recommendation

1st alternative

The most cautious approach is to have attorneys perform this service instead of the social workers. This option presumably is the most expensive approach.

2nd alternative

It is my recommendation that an attorney educate the social workers on the unauthorized practice of law. This instruction should include specific examples of violations—particularly relating to the preparation of living wills. All difficult or doubtful legal questions then would be forwarded to the attorney for evaluation; the social workers would not answer such questions. The attorney also could monitor the drafting of the wills. This approach would entail permissible cooperation between the social workers and the attorney. <u>See</u> Minn. Stat § 481.02 subd. 3(6) (permitting a person to confer or cooperate with a licensed attorney); subd. 7 (permitting a corporation to provide information or clerical service to attorneys).

Office Memo #2

TO: Senior Attorney
FROM: Associate
DATE: October 20, 1992
RE: HomeElderCare's proposal to draft clients' living wills,
            File No. H-53

Your notes in margin

ISSUES

1.   Will the preparation of living wills constitute the unauthorized practice of law if HomeElderCare's geriatric social workers interview the signer, explain the will, prepare a draft, and arrange for the signing and notarization?

2.   Will these living wills be valid in Minnesota, when prepared by Home-ElderCare's social workers?

3.   Will HomeElderCare (a private, non-profit corporation) be able to enforce its contracts for the preparation of living wills with its clients, who are elderly persons living in their homes?

SHORT ANSWERS

1.   The preparation of living wills would be incidental to the services generally provided by the social workers and would not require them to resolve difficult or doubtful legal questions. Therefore, the preparation of living wills would not constitute the unauthorized practice of law.

2.   HomeElderCare's living will form meets the statutory requirements and is valid according to the Minnesota Living Will Act. Furthermore, the living wills would not be invalidated solely because the living wills are prepared by Home-ElderCare's social workers.

3.   HomeElderCare's contracts with its clients for the drafting of living wills would be enforceable, because the contracts would not include professional services in violation of the statute on unauthorized practice of law.

FACTS

Our client, HomeElderCare, serves an elderly population by providing the services that each client picks from a menu of services, including transportation, shopping, home maintenance, bill-paying and other individual financial services, and liaison work with the client's physician and attorney. HomeElderCare is a private, non-profit corporation that employs a staff of social workers trained and experienced in working with geriatric clients; volunteers provide some services.

Your notes in margin

Now several of HomeElderCare's clients have begun asking for an additional service—assistance in completing living wills. A living will gives its maker control over some medical treatment choices, especially extraordinary measures, in the event that the maker becomes incapacitated. HomeElderCare would like to honor its clients' wishes by adding this service. The service would begin with an interview by the social worker assigned to work with the client, which would include a discussion of the purpose and importance of a living will. Then the social worker would present the client with a living will form and ask the client the questions on the form in order to prepare a draft. The social worker would encourage the client to discuss the draft with the client's physician before signing it. Then the social worker would arrange to have the living will signed and notarized. Later, HomeElderCare would bill the client an hourly fee for its services.

The HomeElderCare social workers are enthusiastic about this proposed new service. They can see the value of living wills to their clients and are confident that they can easily be trained to competently provide this service by attending one or two seminars. However, HomeElderCare's executive director wonders whether there are legal barriers to this proposal. In particular, she wants to know whether social workers can legally prepare living wills, whether the living wills would be fully effective, and whether HomeElderCare could enforce its contracts for this service with its clients.

DISCUSSION

Unauthorized Practice of Law

According to Minnesota's unauthorized practice statute, "[i]t shall be unlawful for any person . . . except members of the bar of Minnesota admitted and licensed to practice as attorneys at law . . . for a fee . . . to prepare for another person . . . any . . . legal document . . . ." Minn. Stat. § 481.02 subd. 1 (1992). (Exceptions to this general rule exist, but the exceptions are not applicable to the HomeElderCare situations. Id. subd. 3.) Here, the living will probably is a "legal document" under the unauthorized practice statute, because the living will statute says that it is a "legal document," Minn. Stat. § 145B.04 (1992). Thus, HomeElderCare's social workers would be preparing legal documents for their clients, in return for fees.

In addition, the unauthorized practice statute prohibits anyone but a licensed Minnesota attorney from "giv[ing] legal advice or counsel" for a fee. Id. § 481.02 subd. 1. HomeElderCare's social workers might be in a position to give legal advice or counsel to some of its clients on some aspects of living wills, in return for the hourly fee to be charged for the living will service.

However, neither of these activities—document drafting or advice giving—would constitute the unauthorized practice of law unless (1) the person's primary business involves legal services or (2) the preparation is an incidental part of a person's business and the person answers "difficult and doubtful legal questions." Gardner v. Conway, 48 N.W.2d 788, 796 (Minn. 1951). The "difficult or doubtful legal question" test adds a common law gloss to the statute on unauthorized practice of law. Id. What is a difficult or doubtful legal question is measured by a reasonably intelligent person who has knowledge in similar transactions. Id. This test is "applied in a common-sense way which will protect primarily the interest of the public and not hamper or burden that interest with impractical and technical restrictions which have no reasonable justification." Id. at 797. The "difficult and doubtful legal question" test is flexible and demands a case-by-case analysis. Id. In Gardner, an accountant familiar with income tax rules and regulations gave advice on business partnerships, the status of a common-law wife on a joint tax return, and the deductibility of various expenses. These were deemed answers to difficult and doubtful legal questions and therefore violated the unauthorized practice of law statute. Id. at 798.

The HomeElderCare social workers would be using a living will form that meets the statutory requirements and gives instructions as to its completion. By following the instructions, the social workers could lead their clients through the preparation of the living will without interpreting the statute. They would discuss medical and ethical, but not legal, judgments with the clients. Because the social workers would not need to answer difficult or doubtful legal questions. they therefore would not engage in the unauthorized practice of law.

However, some elderly persons with living immediate family members may find that the living will form is not suited to their needs and is too legalistic. See Dallas M. High, Who Will Make Health Care Decisions for Me When I Can't, J. Aging & Health, Aug. 1990, at 291, 307. If a HomeElderCare client wishes to deviate from the form, the social workers may be asked to interpret the statute to determine whether deviations are permitted. Statutory interpretation by HomeElderCare social workers may involve difficult legal questions and require the skills of an attorney. Thus, the HomeElderCare social workers could avoid statutory interpretation problems by working only within the living will form.

In other cases, the charging of a fee has raised questions as to whether advice constitutes the practice of law. Cardinal v. Merrill Lynch Realty/Burnet, Inc., 433 N.W.2d 864, 869 (Minn. 1988). Yet HomeElderCare charges a fee for all of its services, and the preparation fee is charged for clearly non-legal services. Hence it should not pose problems here.

Your notes in margin

Your notes in margin

In summary, the statute on unauthorized practice of law covers the preparation of living wills by the HomeElderCare social workers. However, under the "difficult or doubtful legal question" test, the service would not violate the statute since it would not involve determining difficult or doubtful legal issues.

Validity of Living Wills

The HomeElderCare social workers would use a living will form that complies with the requirements of the Minnesota Living Will Act, Minn. Stat. § 145B.04 (1992). The form gives instructions that must be substantially followed. Id. Therefore, by following the given instructions on the form, the HomeElderCare social workers would produce valid wills for HomeElderCare's clients.

Even if the living will service violated the unauthorized practice statute, protecting the best interests of the client probably would be an important policy underlying a court's decision on whether a living will is valid. See Peterson v. Hovland (In re Peterson's Estate), 42 N.W.2d 59, 65 (Minn. 1950). In Peterson, a non-lawyer drafted a testamentary will for Peterson several weeks before Peterson's death without any known emergency, even though the unauthorized practice statute, Minn. Stat. § 481.02 subd. 1, prohibits a non-lawyer from drafting a will without an emergency. 42 N.W.2d at 61. The will protected the interests of Peterson and was held valid. Id. at 66. The court reasoned that the innocent testator would be punished if an otherwise valid will were held void. Id. at 65.

Likewise, the purpose of a living will is to communicate the signer's health care decisions if the signer becomes incapacitated. If the living will were deemed invalid when the signer was incapacitated, then the signer's health care decisions could be violated.

Accordingly, the living will prepared by the social workers and subject to review by the signer, physician, and proxy should be valid regardless of whether HomeElderCare's preparation of the wills is deemed the unauthorized practice of law.

Enforceability of Contracts

Generally, a contract for professional services provided by an unlicensed professional is not enforceable in Minnesota. Buckley v. Humason, 52 N.W. 385, 386 (Minn. 1892). In Buckley, an unlicensed real estate broker entered into a contract with a client who refused to pay the broker's commission. The broker sued for recovery of the commission and was unsuccessful because he had violated the licensing law. The court held that a contract is invalid if it is founded on an unlawful business transaction. Id.

However, in a later case, a contract for professional service by an unlicensed professional was valid since the activities to be undertaken under the contract were not the sort of activities the licensing statute was adopted to preclude. <u>Dick Weatherston's Assoc'd Mech'l Servs. v. Minnesota Mut. Life Ins. Co.</u>, 100 N.W.2d 819 (Minn. 1960). There, a contractor with a degree but no license in engineering was asked to design an air conditioning system; the job required some professional engineering. The defendant gave the contractor the job, including the engineering work, subject to review and approval by a defendant's licensed engineer. <u>Id.</u> at 821-22. This review and approval process, as well as the contractor's engineering training, helped to convince the court that this contract was not the type of contract that the licensing statute meant to prevent. <u>Id.</u> at 825. Also relevant to the court was the incidental nature of the engineering services to the contract as a whole, as well as the defendant's knowledge that the contractor was not licensed. <u>Id.</u> at 824-25.

Here, first and foremost, the HomeElderCare contracts would not be in violation of the unauthorized practice statute if the social workers do not attempt to answer difficult or doubtful legal questions. Thus there would be no grounds to invalidate the contracts.

However, if the social workers were deemed to be practicing law, the <u>Buckley/Weatherston's</u> rule might render the contract invalid. The unauthorized practice statute is designed to protect people from incompetent service by unlicensed professionals. <u>Peterson</u>, 42 N.W.2d at 63. It will be difficult to train the social workers sufficiently to understand the legal issues in living wills and the boundaries around activities that will constitute unauthorized practice of law. The legal issues in living wills are not just incidental to this form, which states that it is a "legal document," Minn. Stat. § 145B.04. Moreover, if an attorney does not supervise or review the resulting living wills, the "safety net" present in <u>Weatherston's</u> will not be present here. These likely deficiencies in HomeElderCare's proposed service might well result in one or more botched living wills, leading to the argument that these are the kind of contracts that the statute was designed to protect against, even if the social workers do not mislead the clients about their expertise. Then the contracts between HomeElderCare and its clients for such services could be unenforceable, because <u>Weatherston's</u> would be inapplicable.

CONCLUSION

HomeElderCare should offer the living will service to its clients, as long as the social workers are instructed to follow the living will form and not to answer any difficult or doubtful legal questions.

Your notes in margin

Your notes in margin

If some of HomeElderCare's clients are not satisfied with the living will form and want to modify it in some way, the service may be construed as involving the determination of difficult or doubtful legal issues and, therefore, the unauthorized practice of law. Because of this risk the social workers must refer clients who wish to modify the form to licensed attorneys.

So long as the HomeElderCare social workers follow this course of action, the proposed new service would not constitute the unauthorized practice of law, and HomeElderCare's contracts with its clients will be valid. Regardless of the social workers' actions, the clients' living wills likely would be valid.

Partner & Associates, P.A.
123 Main Street, Suite 400
Great Lake MN 50000
(210) 555-6543

Heading

November 6, 1992

Ms. Mary Mahoney, Executive Director
HomeElderCare, Inc.
678 Great Lake Boulevard
Great Lake MN 50000

CONFIDENTIAL
ATTORNEY-CLIENT
COMMUNICATION

Re: Drafting of living wills

Dear Ms. Mahoney:

I enjoyed talking with you about HomeElderCare last week, and I appreciate the opportunity to advise you on the preparing of living wills by HEC social workers for your elderly clients. From what you have told me, I certainly can see why your staff favors providing this service.

Introduction
■ *rapport, previous contact*

However, as this letter explains, there could be some legal risks. One concern is avoiding the illegal practice of law, which could lead to prosecution for a misdemeanor or a court order prohibiting the service. On the other hand, HEC probably would be able to enforce the contracts with its clients. Furthermore, the illegality would not invalidate the living wills.

■ *overview*

To help you understand these conclusions, I first have restated HEC's situation and the proposal, as I understand it from our conversation. Please be sure to contact me if my understanding is mistaken, because my advice rests on the stated facts. Then I have explained my conclusions under the law as it now stands. As you no doubt can appreciate, the law in this area is evolving fairly rapidly, and my conclusions could change if the law changes. I have concluded with a discussion of HEC's options. Please keep this letter confidential.

■ *ground rules of advice letter*

Summary of facts. As I understand it from our conversation, HEC is a private non-profit corporation that provides various services for hourly fees to

Summary of facts
■ *HEC*

elderly persons who still live in their own homes. The services are provided by geriatric social workers and volunteers, none of them lawyers.

■ *proposal*

In response to client requests, the social work staff would like to prepare living wills for clients who desire them. The social workers would attend a seminar or two first. The social worker would interview the client and talk through the significance of a living will. The social worker then would prepare a draft based on the form you have found, which indicates that it complies with Minnesota law. The social worker would encourage the client to confer with a doctor before signing the will. The social worker would arrange for the signing and notarizing of the will and then deliver it to the client's doctor. As with other HEC services, the client would pay a fee based on the time that the social worker spent on the service.

Explanation
■ *overview*

Explanation. As I recall, you expressed several legal concerns: that the service might be prohibited by law, that HEC's contracts with the clients might not be enforceable by HEC, and that the HEC-drafted living wills might not be valid. The first concern is well founded; the second and third are less troublesome.

■ *1st topic*

As for your first concern, with only a few exceptions not applicable here, Minnesota law prohibits persons who are not licensed lawyers from practicing law. The non-lawyer can be prosecuted for a misdemeanor, or the court may issue an order prohibiting the activity. Because your social workers lack licenses as lawyers, a very important question is whether the proposed service would amount to practicing law. Unfortunately, the answer is possibly yes, on two separate grounds.

The first ground is that preparing legal documents for someone else for a fee constitutes practicing law. The official form itself indicates that the living will is a "legal document."

The second ground is that providing legal advice or counsel for a fee can constitute practicing law. The Minnesota courts have recognized that some professions border quite closely on law; social work probably would be viewed as such a profession. In these professions, non-lawyers are permitted to handle easy and clear legal questions, but not difficult or doubtful ones. Some questions that might arise in your situation would be primarily medical, not legal. But others probably would be viewed as legal in nature and difficult or doubtful, given the law's significant and fast-changing regulation (for better or worse) of this area.

This conclusion—that the preparation of the living wills would entail practicing law—is not certain, because this precise question has not come before the courts before. If it did, HEC could make some good arguments. The

Minnesota statute setting out the living will form shows that living wills are desirable; permitting your staff to prepare living wills would encourage their use. The statute permits an individual to draft his or her own living will, unassisted. On the other hand, courts generally are very concerned about the harm to clients from mistakes made by non-lawyers as to legal questions of significance to clients.

Because it is not clear whether the preparation of the living wills would entail practicing law, we need to look at your second and third questions in both lights. If the preparation of the living wills would <u>not</u> entail practicing law, the courts would not deny enforcement to HEC's contracts with the clients or invalidate the living wills for that reason.

■ transition/branchpoint

Even if the service <u>would</u> entail practicing law and thus violate the prohibition against non-lawyers practicing law, HEC probably would not be precluded for this reason from enforcing its contracts with its clients. You might suspect that the courts would not assist HEC in such a situation. However, the courts look not only at whether the professional lacks a license to do the work, but also at several other factors that work in HEC's favor. The risk of incompetent service would be fairly minor, given the social workers' general expertise in geriatric health matters, the training you have proposed, and the social workers' reliance on the official form. The clients would not be the target of fraud, because (I presume) the social workers would identify their professional status and indicate the limits of their expertise. Any legal service that your staff provided would be incidental to legitimate nonlegal services of providing emotional support and guidance on medical and moral issues. Again, the service would promote living wills, so the court might favor it.

■ 2nd topic

Finally, even if the service <u>would</u> entail practicing law, an otherwise properly prepared living will would almost certainly be valid. The courts would not wish to invalidate the living will merely because the drafter acted illegally.

■ 3rd topic

<u>Advice</u>. Because your current proposal might draw the social workers into practicing law, even though the contracts between HEC and the clients probably would be enforced and the living wills would be valid, I suggest that you consider other options.

Advice
■ client proposal

HEC could provide this service by hiring attorneys instead of the social workers. Or HEC could hire an attorney to teach the social workers about living wills, monitor their work, and answer any difficult or doubtful questions that might come up. The social workers could confine their assistance to filling in the form. Or HEC could provide a more modest service, with the social workers serving as liaisons between the clients and their attorneys. The law does permit non-lawyers to cooperate with a licensed attorney who is provid-

■ other options

ing legal services. Each of these alternatives no doubt has practical and economic advantages and disadvantages for HEC as well as your clients.

Closing

I hope that this letter is helpful to you and your staff. I will call you in a week or so to answer any questions and explore any options you may wish to pursue. If you wish to talk with me before then, please feel free to call my direct dial number, 555-6543.

Sincerely,

Ann Irwin

Ann Irwin

STATE OF MINNESOTA   DISTRICT COURT

COUNTY OF LASALLE   SEVENTEENTH JUDICIAL COURT

)	
)	
State of Minnesota,)	Other Civil: Practice of Law
Plaintiff,)	
)	
vs.)	NOTICE OF MOTION
)	AND MOTION
HomeElderCare, Inc.,)	FOR TEMPORARY INJUNCTION
)	
Defendant.)	File No. CIV93-893
)	
)	

<u>Notice of Motion</u>

TO: Ms. Katherine Crawford, Attorney for Defendant HomeElderCare, Inc.:

Please take notice that the undersigned will move the Court for a temporary injunction at the Courthouse in the city of LaSalle on the 1st day of November, 1993, at 9:00 a.m. or as soon thereafter as counsel can be heard.

<u>Motion</u>

Pursuant to Minnesota Rule of Civil Procedure 65, Plaintiff State of Minnesota moves the court to temporarily enjoin Defendant from engaging in the drafting of living wills and all counseling services related to living wills. This motion is based on the pleadings, discovery record, and memorandum and argument in support of this motion.

Date: <u>Oct. 1, 1993</u> **Andrew McCampbell**

Andrew McCampbell
Counsel for Plaintiff State of Minnesota
LaSalle County Attorney
1234 Sherburne Avenue
LaSalle MN 55555
(507) 555-4567
Attorney Reg. No. 11111

STATE OF MINNESOTA   DISTRICT COURT

COUNTY OF LASALLE   SEVENTEENTH JUDICIAL COURT

	)	
	)	
State of Minnesota,	)	Other Civil: Practice of Law
Plaintiff,	)	
	)	
vs.	)	PROPOSED ORDER
	)	
HomeElderCare, Inc.,	)	File No. CIV93-893
	)	
Defendant.	)	
	)	
	)	

This matter came before the Court on November 1, 1993, upon Plaintiff's Motion for Temporary Injunction. This Court, having read the record and counsels' memoranda, having heard arguments of counsel and being fully apprised in the matter, hereby ORDERS:

Pursuant to Minnesota Rule of Civil Procedure 65, Defendant HomeElderCare, Inc., is hereby temporarily enjoined from engaging in the drafting of living wills and all counseling services related to living wills. This Order takes effect immediately and continues in effect until lifted by this Court or until judgment is entered following the trial in this case.

Date: _____   _____

                            Judge_____
                            Special Term Judge
                            District Court, Seventeenth Judicial District

STATE OF MINNESOTA

COUNTY OF LASALLE

DISTRICT COURT

SEVENTEENTH JUDICIAL COURT

State of Minnesota,
        Plaintiff,
 	
vs.
 	
HomeElderCare, Inc.,
 	
        Defendant.
	)
	)
	)
	)
	)
	)
	)
	)
	)
	)
	)
	)
	)

Other Civil: Practice of Law

PLAINTIFF'S MEMORANDUM
IN SUPPORT OF
PLAINTIFF'S MOTION
FOR TEMPORARY
INJUNCTION

File No. CIV93-893

SUMMARY

Kimberly Hall is not a lawyer. Rather, Ms. Hall is a geriatric social worker employed by HomeElderCare, Inc., a non-profit provider of social services for elderly individuals. Despite her lack of admission to the bar of any state and despite her lack of legal training, Ms. Hall has drafted living wills for Home-ElderCare clients, for a fee, without the assistance of a lawyer. Furthermore, she has counseled these clients about the legal effect of their living wills. So have other HomeElderCare social workers.

opening with factual emphasis

These activities violate Minnesota's unauthorized practice of law statute, which prohibits non-lawyers from drafting legal documents for others for a fee and from providing legal counsel to others for a fee. The statute explicitly provides for actions brought by a county attorney to enforce the statute and for injunctions against further unauthorized practice.

legal significance of facts

A temporary injunction is warranted here. First, the State likely will succeed in demonstrating that Defendant's preparation of and counseling about living wills for its elderly clients constitutes the illegal practice of law and affronts the public policies stated in the unauthorized practice and living will statutes. If Defendant prepares living wills that inaccurately reflect its elderly

summary of arguments (roadmap)

clients' choices concerning medical treatment or death, its clients will suffer ir-reparable harm, with no adequate remedy at law, and this harm will outweigh Defendant's loss of income if the injunction is granted. Finally, the temporary injunction sought by the State will be straightforward to enforce.

FACTS

opening: introduction of parties and why Plaintiff initiated suit

The State, through the LaSalle County Attorney, has brought this action against HomeElderCare, Inc., a non-profit social services agency serving el-derly individuals. The State has acted because the Defendant has overstepped its bounds as a social service agency and has illegally practiced law by drafting living wills for clients and providing related counseling. (Compl.)

1st topic: living wills

As the living will itself indicates, it is "an important legal document." (Ex. A to Hall Dep.) This label is apt. A living will states the declarant's wishes as to medical care in the event he or she is incapacitated and unable to make those wishes known. The living will states the declarant's views as to treatment in general, life-sustaining treatment, and sustenance. The living will identifies a proxy, who may act on behalf of the declarant and is thereby nominated to be the declarant's guardian. (Id.)

2nd topic: example of HEC incompetence (chronological ordering)

By way of example, Roger Nelson is seventy-eight years old, in declining health because of diabetes, and a widower. (R. Nelson Dep. at 2.) Several months before a recent hospitalization, Mr. Nelson had executed a living will. (Id. at 6.) The living will made the family's minister his proxy and thereby nominated the minister as his guardian. (Ex. A to R. Nelson Dep.) Yet Mr. Nel-son wished his minister to serve only as his proxy for medical decisionmaking; he wished his son, Albert Nelson, to serve as his guardian. (R. Nelson Dep. at 10.) When Albert Nelson discovered the error, he arranged for a substitute liv-ing will drafted by the family attorney. (A. Nelson Dep. at 6.)

3rd topic: HEC social worker's experience and training (emphasizing inadequacies as to legal matters)

The elder Mr. Nelson's original, erroneous living will was drafted by Kimberly Hall. (R. Nelson Dep. at 8.) Ms. Hall is a geriatric social worker em-ployed by HomeElderCare, Inc., a non-profit social service agency providing care for elderly individuals who live in their own homes. (Hall Dep. at 2.) HomeElderCare offers its clients assistance in maintaining their homes, man-aging personal finances, obtaining home maintenance and transportation, shopping, working with attorneys, and other aspects of their lives. These ser-vices are provided by social workers and volunteers. Ms. Hall is an experi-enced social worker. (Mahoney Dep. at 3-4.) However, Ms. Hall is not a lawyer, she has not attended law school, and she has never been admitted to practice in Minnesota or elsewhere. Neither have any of the other HomeElder-Care social workers. (Id. at 3-4.)

Nonetheless, Ms. Hall has prepared about ten living wills for HomeElder-Care clients, including Mr. Nelson. In all of these situations, Ms. Hall has actually prepared the living will by typing the entire document herself or typing multi-line insertions on a blank form. She has discussed the wishes of the client and sought to represent them in the living will. She has inquired whether her clients are adults of sound mind, acting willfully and voluntarily. She has explained how the living will should be used by doctors and other medical personnel, in conjunction with the requirements of reasonable medical practice, in the event of incapacitation. She has explained the form to the client's witnesses and proxy. She has answered their questions. She has supervised the execution of the living will. She also has charged a fee for these services, which varies according to the time spent on the project. (Id. at 8,15.) *4th topic: HEC will drafting process*

Ms. Hall has undertaken all of these tasks without the involvement of a lawyer. (Id. at 16.) She is aware of the legal issues surrounding living wills, because she heard a presentation (lasting forty-five minutes) by a lawyer on living wills at a workshop on social work for the terminally ill. (Id. at 19.) Furthermore, Ms. Hall is aware that the forms and the living wills she herself has written indicate that the will is "an important legal document." (Id.; Ex. A to R. Nelson Dep.)

Ms. Hall's ten living wills constitute only a quarter of the forty or so living wills prepared by HomeElderCare social workers. (Mahoney Dep. at 12.) Ms. Hall's services are typical of those provided in the other thirty situations. (Id. at 22.) Eight HomeElderCare clients have been hospitalized, and the living wills have been shown to their doctors. Fortunately, no client has yet been incapacitated so as to bring any of the living wills into effect. (Id. at 25-26.) *5th topic: HEC track record*

The State sued HomeElderCare on July 12, 1993, seeking an end to the practices just described, before HomeElderCare prepares more wills or the wills become effective. (Compl.) HomeElderCare answered, denying that its practices violate the law. (Answer.) Based on the pleadings, the documents produced during discovery, and the depositions of HomeElderCare staff and clients, the State now moves for a temporary injunction. *6th topic: procedural facts*

ARGUMENT

The party seeking an injunction must prove that it has no adequate remedy at law and that it would suffer irreparable injury if the injunction were not issued. See Sanborn Mfg. Co. v. Currie, 500 N.W.2d 161, 163 (Minn. Ct. App. 1993) (citing Cherne Indus., Inc. v. Grounds & Assoc., Inc., 278 N.W.2d 81, *procedural rules*

92 (Minn. 1979)). The court must take into account the following five factors when deciding whether to grant a temporary injunction:

> (1) [t]he likelihood that one party or the other will prevail on the merits when the fact situation is viewed in light of established precedents fixing the limits of equitable relief[;]
>
> (2) [t]he aspects of the fact situation, if any, which permit or require consideration of public policy expressed in the statutes, State and Federal[;]
>
> (3) [t]he harm to be suffered by plaintiff if the temporary restraint is denied as compared to that inflicted on defendant if the injunction issues pending trial[;]
>
> (4) [t]he administrative burdens involved in judicial supervision and enforcement of the temporary decree[; and]
>
> (5) [t]he nature and background of the relationship between the parties preexisting the dispute giving rise to the request for relief[.]

Dahlberg Bros., Inc. v. Ford Motor Co., 272 Minn. 264, 274-75, 137 N.W.2d 314, 321-22 (1965) (five factors reordered above). The Cherne standard is subsumed in the balance-of-harms factor (3). Yager v. Thompson, 352 N.W.2d 71, 75 (Minn. Ct. App. 1984).

roadmap

In this case, the law and public policy as expressed in state statutes (factors 1 and 2) favor the injunction. The harm suffered by the state's elderly citizens without the injunction is irreparable and easily outweighs any harm to HomeElderCare from grant of an injunction (factor 3). And the

(aside re omitted factor)

temporary injunction would be straightforward to enforce (factor 4). (The fifth Dahlberg factor is irrelevant because the parties do not have a preexisting relationship.) Thus, the court should grant the requested temporary injunction.

1st major heading (procedural and substantive law + facts)

I. The State likely will succeed in demonstrating that Defendant's preparation of and counseling about living wills for its elderly clients constitutes the illegal practice of law and affronts the public policies stated in the statutes on living wills and unauthorized practice of law.

1st minor point heading

A. Defendant's living will service constitutes the unauthorized practice of law, for a fee, by social workers.

overall rule from statute

Minnesota's statute on the unauthorized practice of law states in pertinent part:

> It shall be unlawful for any person or association of persons, except members of the bar of Minnesota admitted and licensed to practice as attorneys at law, . . . [1] for a fee or any consideration, to give legal advice or counsel, perform for or furnish to another legal services, or, [2] for or without a fee or any consideration, to prepare, directly or through another, for another person, firm, or corporation, any will or testamentary disposition or

instrument of trust serving purposes similar to those of a will, or, [3] for a fee or any consideration, to prepare for another person, firm, or corporation, any other legal document . . . .

Minn. Stat. § 481.02 subd. 1 (1992) (enumeration added). This prohibition is enforced through misdemeanor penalties or, as here, by an injunction action brought by the State, acting through county attorneys. See id. subd. 8.

Defendant falls squarely within the reach of the statute. Ms. Hall is not a member of the bar of Minnesota, nor are the other HomeElderCare social workers. No exception is applicable. See id. § 481.02 subd. 3. Furthermore, Defendant's actions violate two statutory prohibitions: against drafting legal documents (number 3 above) and against giving legal advice and counsel (number 1 above).

beginning application

roadmap

First, living wills are "legal documents" within the scope of the unauthorized practice statute. See id. subd. 1. While the unauthorized practice statute does not define the phrase "legal document," the Minnesota Living Will Act plainly states, in its suggested form, that the will is "an important legal document." Minn. Stat. § 145B.04 (1992). In addition, the plain meaning of "legal" is "conforms to rules or the law," Webster's New Collegiate Dictionary 656 (1976), and the plain meaning of "document" is "an original or official paper relied on as the basis, proof, or support of something," id. at 336. A living will is an official statement proving the declarant's wishes in the event of incapacitation, conforming to the requirements of the Minnesota Living Will Act, so it is a legal document in the plain meaning of the term. Furthermore, a living will is similar to a testamentary will, which is expressly covered by the preceding prohibition (number 2 above) and is the reference point for the phrase "any other legal document," see Minn. Stat. § 481.02 subd. 1. Like a testamentary will, a living will states the declarant's intentions about important personal matters to be carried out near the time of death and is enforceable through legal mechanisms. See id. §§ 145B.03-.05.

■ *1st subsubtopic*
—*rules*

In light of this definition, Defendant has illegally prepared legal documents for other people for a fee. Defendant's employees prepare the wills when they elicit information from the clients, type that information onto a form or draft or type the entire document, and arrange for the will's execution. Furthermore, clients pay Defendant a fee for these services—even when, as in Mr. Nelson's case, the living will is erroneous.

—*application*

Second, a non-lawyer engages in unauthorized legal practice when she "give[s] legal advice or counsel" for a fee. Minn. Stat. § 481.02 subd. 1.

■ *2nd subsubtopic*
—*rule*

This activity occurs when the non-lawyer engages in counseling activities incidental to another calling "if difficult or doubtful legal questions are involved which, to safeguard the public, reasonably demand the application of a trained legal mind." Gardner v. Conway, 234 Minn. 468, 481, 48 N.W.2d 788, 796 (1951). In Gardner, an accountant engaged in unauthorized law practice when he provided information on various tax issues in the course of preparing a tax return for a client. Included were advice about and analysis of business partnerships, the status of a common-law wife in joint tax returns, and the deductibility of various expenditures. See id. at 472, 48 N.W.2d at 792.

—application   Defendant's employees' counseling of clients about the living wills may be an incident of the general social services provided to clients—but it also is illegal law practice because it involves difficult and doubtful legal questions that require a trained legal mind. These questions may arise during the initial consultation, or during the drafting process, or at the time of the will's execution. These questions may pertain to phrases used in the will form or the will drafted by the social worker, or they may pertain to the will's effect. For example, the social workers counsel clients about

- the client's status as an adult of sound mind, acting willfully and voluntarily;
- the obligations of a physician to follow the directives of the living will;
- the concurrent obligation of the physician to comply with reasonable medical practice;
- the role of the proxy; and
- the declarant's power to revoke the will.

Ms. Hall has admitted to counseling her clients on many of these topics.

All of these matters are regulated in the Minnesota Living Will Act, Minn. Stat. §§ 145B.01-.17. Furthermore, living wills implicate legal concerns extending well beyond the Living Will Act. In Mr. Nelson's case, for example, the error arose because his identification of a proxy affected his choice of a legal guardian. Guardianship is, of course, extensively regulated by Minnesota law; this regulation covers both the powers and appointment of guardians. See Minn. Stat. §§ 525.532-.6198 (1992). More broadly, a living will is a manifestation of the declarant's constitutional right to privacy in the sense of bodily autonomy. See Howard Orenstein et al., Minnesota's Living Will . . . , Bench & B. Minn., Aug. 1989, at 22; Note, Pamela B. Goldsmith, Live and Let Die: The Constitutional Validity of a Living Will, 5 N.Y.L. Sch. J. Hum. Rts. 477, 486-90 (1988). A non-lawyer is unlikely to perceive or fully understand these legal dimensions of living wills. Indeed, the brief training that Defendant provided Ms. Hall on living wills was conducted by an attorney.

These issues and areas of law are certainly as difficult and doubtful as the tax issues addressed by the accountant in <u>Gardner</u>. They involve the drawing of fine lines with significant consequences. Indeed, the questions addressed by HomeElderCare's social workers may be even more difficult than the tax questions addressed by the accountant in <u>Gardner</u>. The Living Will Act is four years old, <u>see</u> Act of Mar. 3, 1989, ch. 3, 1989 Minn. Laws 8, and its subtleties have yet to be interpreted by the appellate courts. Legal regulation of medical decisionmaking is in a phase of rapid change. <u>See generally</u> Orenstein, <u>supra</u>.

In addition, HomeElderCare has charged a fee for its drafting and counseling services. The statute identifies charging a fee as an element of illegal practice. Furthermore, the Minnesota Supreme Court has noted that charging a fee suggests that the counseling involves a difficult and doubtful legal issue. <u>See</u> <u>Cardinal v. Merrill Lynch Realty/Burnet, Inc.</u>, 433 N.W.2d 864, 869 (Minn. 1988).

■ 3rd subsubtopic

Thus, Defendant has illegally drafted legal documents and provided legal counsel for a fee to elderly citizens—and erroneously so in at least Mr. Nelson's case. To secure a temporary injunction, the State need not demonstrate that it will win this case, but only that it is likely to. <u>Dahlberg Bros. v. Ford Motor Co.</u>, 272 Minn. 264, 275, 137 N.W.2d 314, 321 (1965). The State has successfully demonstrated that the Defendant has violated the unauthorized practice statute.

—conclusion to A. and reference to procedural rule

B. Defendant's living will service affronts the public policies stated in the unauthorized practice and living will statutes.

2nd minor heading

The purposes of the unauthorized practice statute would be furthered by a temporary injunction precluding HomeElderCare's preparation of living wills and related counseling services. The statute is designed to forestall poorly drawn legal documents caused by a non-lawyer's "bungling use of legal terms and improper knowledge" of the law that results in documents that either are invalid or operate contrary to the client's intent. <u>See</u> <u>Peterson v. Hovland</u> (<u>In re Peterson's Estate</u>), 230 Minn. 478, 484, 42 N.W.2d 59, 63 (1950) (involving drafting of a testamentary will). When Ms. Hall prepared Mr. Nelson's living will and counseled him, precisely these problems occurred—and they were corrected when an attorney drafted a revised living will.

■ 1st policy
—mandatory precedent and application

—persuasive precedent

Other jurisdictions that have faced the issue of non-lawyers completing and advising about legal forms have ruled in favor of protecting the public. The Florida Supreme Court has held that a non-lawyer may distribute legal forms and type in material as directed by the client, but may not provide specific assistance in the preparation of the form, answer questions, or correct errors or omissions. See Florida Bar v. Brumbaugh, 355 So. 2d 1186 (Fla. 1978). Other courts have similarly ruled that distributing legal forms is permissible, but personal contact between a non-lawyer and a client involving explanation, advice, or assistance is unauthorized law practice. See State Bar of Michigan v. Cramer, 249 N.W.2d 1 (Mich.1976); New York County Lawyers Ass'n v. Dacey, 234 N.E.2d 459 (N.Y. 1967); Oregon State Bar v. Gilchrist, 538 P.2d 913 (Or. 1975).

—rebuttal of counter-argument

Certainly, the unauthorized practice statute should not be used so as to impose "impractical and technical restrictions which have no reasonable justification." Gardner, 234 Minn. at 481-82, 48 N.W.2d at 797. See also Cardinal, 433 N.W.2d at 868-69. The restrictions imposed by the statute on HomeElderCare's social workers are not technical and impractical; they have a more than reasonable justification—implementation of the policy expressed in the living will statute.

■ 2nd policy and application

Minnesota's living will statute evinces a strong public policy in favor of giving a competent adult the means by which to

> make a living will of preferences or instructions regarding health care. These preferences or instructions may include, but are not limited to, consent to or refusal of any health care, treatment, service, procedure, or placement. A living will may include preferences or instructions regarding health care, the designation of a proxy to make health care decisions on behalf of the declarant, or both.

Minn. Stat. § 145B.03 subd. 1. This statute allows individuals "to assert [their] constitutionally recognized right to control their own health care." Orenstein, supra, at 22. If a person filling out a living will receives incompetent assistance, the intent of the statute and the underlying constitutional right will not be implemented. Thus, the public policies of both statutes support a temporary injunction.

conclusion to B.

2nd major heading (procedural law + facts)

II. If Defendant incompetently prepares living wills that inaccurately reflect its elderly clients' choices concerning medical treatment or death, its clients will suffer irreparable harm, with no adequate remedy at law, and this harm will outweigh Defendant's loss of income if the injunction is granted.

procedural rules

The party seeking an injunction must show irreparable harm, while the opposing party need show only substantial harm in order to bar the injunction. See Yager v. Thompson, 352 N.W.2d 71, 75 (Minn. Ct. App. 1984). Irreparable harm is defined as an injury that cannot be compensated by money alone. See Morse v. City of Waterville, 458 N.W.2d 728, 729-30 (Minn. Ct. App. 1990).

The State is acting in this case on behalf of Defendant's clients. They are elderly individuals, faced with their own mortality, contemplating difficult issues of how to bring a close to their lives in a way that is legally, medically, morally, and socially responsible. They must depend not only on the good faith and efforts of Defendant's social workers, but also on the professional competence of those social workers. Yet Defendant's social workers are not fully professionally competent for the task they have undertaken and for which they are charging fees. The clients' vulnerability justifies judicial intervention.

application (one side of balance)

As already noted, a living will sets out a person's instructions as to how medical treatment should be administered at his or her life's end in certain situations, as well as who has the authority to speak for the declarant. See generally Minn. Stat. §§ 145B.01-.17. If these instructions are recorded inaccurately, the person may receive unwanted medical treatment or may not receive the treatment he or she wanted. Worse yet, if the living will is drafted so poorly that it is unenforceable, see id. § 145B.03 subd. 2 (requirements for valid living will), the person's wishes will be totally disregarded, except insofar as the person's family members convey those wishes and the doctor honors those wishes, see In re Torres, 357 N.W.2d 332 (Minn. 1984). There is a grim and very real possibility that a client will die prematurely or be kept alive against his or her wishes as a consequence of a bungled living will.

In each of these scenarios, the person who is near life's end would suffer irreparable harm. Anxiety, confusion, worsened quality of life, pain and suffering, and possibly death are very difficult—if not impossible—to value and compensate. Death, by definition, is irreparable. For these losses, there is no adequate remedy at law.

By contrast, Defendant will suffer little harm from grant of the injunction. Although it will not be able to provide this single service pending the resolution of the litigation, it can, of course, maintain its client relationships by continuing to offer its other services, such as assistance with home maintenance, personal finances, and transportation. Therefore, the balance of harms favors the State.

application (other side of balance)

III. The temporary injunction sought by the State will be straightforward to enforce.

3rd major heading (procedural law)

The relief requested in this motion is nothing more than a short-term version of the remedy provided by the legislature—a permanent injunction against the unauthorized practice of law, requested by the State. <u>See</u> Minn. Stat. § 481.02 subd. 8. The State requests that this Court temporarily prohibit the living will services offered by Defendant. The injunction can be effected by Defendant notifying its own employees of the prohibition. Monitoring, if needed, could be accomplished by examining Defendant's billings to its clients. Thus, granting a temporary injunction in this case will not impose an excessive administrative burden on this Court.

CONCLUSION

summary

The State has established that the relevant factors weigh strongly in favor of a temporary injunction against Defendant, to preclude its further violation of the unauthorized practice of law statute and to protect the elderly citizens of this state, who otherwise might be irreparably harmed during the pen-

relief requested

dency of this case. Therefore, the State respectfully requests that the Court grant a temporary injunction against the living will services provided by Defendant.

Respectfully submitted,

Andrew McCampbell   Dated: **Oct. 1, 1993**

Andrew McCampbell
Counsel for Plaintiff State of Minnesota
LaSalle County Attorney
1234 Sherburne Avenue
LaSalle MN 55555
(507) 555-4567
Attorney Reg. No. 11111

Your notes in margin

STATE OF MINNESOTA   DISTRICT COURT

COUNTY OF LASALLE   SEVENTEENTH JUDICIAL COURT

_____

)
State of Minnesota,   )   Other Civil: Practice of Law
   Plaintiff,   )
)
 vs.   )   DEFENDANT'S MEMORANDUM
)   IN OPPOSITION TO
HomeElderCare, Inc.,   )   PLAINTIFF'S MOTION
)   FOR TEMPORARY
   Defendant.   )   INJUNCTION
)
_____   File No. CIV93-893

FACTS

Defendant HomeElderCare, Inc., is a private, non-profit corporation with a staff of geriatric social workers who provide services to help their elderly clients in their day-to-day activities. (Hall Dep. at 2.) HomeElderCare has been sued by the state of Minnesota, which seeks to terminate HomeElder-Care's valuable service of assisting its clients with filling in the statutory living will form. (Compl.) The State's pending motion for temporary injunction would prevent HomeElderCare's clients from obtaining the service during this litigation. (Temp. Injcn. Motion.)

HomeElderCare has many clients who are on fixed incomes. (Hall Dep. at 2.) When requested, HomeElderCare social workers assist clients in obtaining transportation, shopping, maintaining their homes and apartments, and managing personal finances. Volunteers sometimes provide services too. In addition, the social workers also serve as liaisons between clients and attorneys working on such matters as wills and real estate transactions. (Mahoney Dep. at 3-4.) Each client contracts with HomeElderCare for the services he or she desires and pays a fee based on the amount of time that the social worker spends on the services. (Mahoney Dep. at 5.)

Several clients recently asked HomeElderCare to fill a gap in the services provided to them by providing assistance in preparing living wills, because they needed the emotional support of a social worker while completing the form. (Id. at 10.) A living will is a document that specifies the signer's desires regarding medical treatment in the event the signer is incapacitated. (Id. at 12; Ex. A to Mahoney Dep.) In Minnesota, a state statute includes a living will form that is easily prepared by filling in blanks; the statute also indicates how the document is to be signed, witnessed, and notarized. (Ex. A to Mahoney Dep.) Thus far, the HomeElderCare social workers have prepared about forty living wills, relying on a living will form that complies with Minnesota law. The social workers decline to prepare wills deviating from the form, and they refrain from influencing clients' personal choices or pressuring clients to complete living wills. Furthermore, if a client demands a living will that does not adhere to the form, the social workers advise the client that this action is beyond their scope of employment duties, and they recommend that the client seek expert legal advice from a licensed attorney. (Mahoney Dep. at 10-12.) Eight of those HomeElderCare clients have been hospitalized since their living wills were drafted. The living wills were shown to their doctors, but none of the clients were incapacitated enough to bring any of the living wills into effect. (Id. at 25-26.)

Kimberly Hall is a social worker at HomeElderCare. She has a master's degree in social work and has worked in the field for twelve years. (Hall Dep. at 2-4.) She attended a one-day HomeElderCare workshop on care issues involving the terminally ill; this workshop included a forty-five-minute training session on preparing living wills. (Id. at 19.) Thus far, she has prepared ten living wills for HomeElderCare clients. (Id. at 9.)

When one of those clients, Roger Nelson, was hospitalized, Mr. Nelson's son, an attorney, realized that his father's living will made Mr. Nelson's proxy his guardian, but Mr. Nelson instead wanted his son to be his guardian. (A. Nelson Dep. at 5.) Mr. Nelson, who is a seventy-eight-year-old widower, is in declining health because of diabetes. (R. Nelson Dep. at 2.) Perhaps he did not understand Ms. Hall's standard explanation of the roles of proxies, guardians, and conservators, and he apparently did not consult an attorney with his questions, as she believes she suggested to him. (See Hall Dep. at 13-15.)

In any event, Mr. Nelson's son contacted the LaSalle County Attorney about HomeElderCare's living will service. (A. Nelson Dep. at 8.) The county attorney, representing the state of Minnesota, has sued HomeElderCare, seeking to end its living will services. (Compl.) HomeElderCare has answered the complaint by asserting the legality of its services (Answer) and now asks the Court not to prohibit HomeElderCare from offering this service to its clients.

ISSUES

Your notes in margin

I. Has the State proved, as it must to obtain a temporary injunction, that it will suffer great and irreparable injury if HomeElderCare continues to offer assistance with living wills to its clients?

II. Has the State met its burden as to the following factors needed for a temporary injunction to issue:

A. Would the State's alleged harm in the absence of a temporary injunction outweigh the harm to HomeElderCare's elderly clients and to the business relationships between HomeElderCare and its clients if an injunction is granted?

B. Is it likely that the State will ultimately succeed in convincing the Court that HomeElderCare's living will services to its clients constitute the unauthorized practice of law?

C. Will the public interest be served by prohibiting HomeElderCare's living will services during the pendency of the case?

ARGUMENT

A temporary injunction is an extraordinary equitable remedy that preserves the status quo pending a trial on the merits. Sunny Fresh Foods, Inc. v. Microfresh Foods Corp., 424 N.W.2d 309, 310 (Minn. Ct. App. 1988). "A party seeking the injunction must establish that [the] legal remedy is not adequate . . . and that the injunction is necessary to prevent great and irreparable injury." Id. (quoting Cherne Industrial, Inc. v. Grounds & Assocs., Inc., 278 N.W.2d 81, 92 (Minn. 1979)). Here, the State has failed to prove that a great and irreparable injury will result if a temporary injunction is not granted; this failure alone is grounds to deny the injunction.

Furthermore, this Court must consider and weigh the following factors:

(1) the relationship between the parties before the dispute;
(2) the harm the plaintiff will suffer if [the injunction] is denied compared with the harm inflicted on the defendant if the injunction is issued;
(3) the likelihood that one party or the other will prevail on the merits;
(4) the public policy involved, if any;
(5) the administrative burdens involved in enforcing the [injunction].

Overholt Crop Ins. Serv. v. Bredeson, 437 N.W.2d 698, 701 (Minn. Ct. App. 1989) (citing Dahlberg Bros., Inc. v. Ford Motor Co., 272 Minn. 264, 274-75, 137 N.W.2d 314, 321-22 (1965)).

The State has failed to carry its burden as to these factors, especially in light of the stringent standard of proof required of the movant. "Injunctive re-

Your notes in margin lief should be awarded only in clear cases, reasonably free from doubt . . . . The burden of proof rests upon the complainant to establish the material allegations entitling him to relief." Sunny Fresh Foods, Inc. v. Microfresh Foods Corp., 424 N.W.2d at 310 (citing AMF Pinspotters, Inc. v. Harkins Bowling, Inc., 260 Minn. 499, 504, 110 N.W.2d 348, 351 (1961)). This case focuses on the second, third, and fourth factors: The State has failed to establish that its alleged harm outweighs HomeElderCare's harm if an injunction is granted, that it likely will prevail on the merits at trial, or that the various public interests in this dispute favor a temporary injunction. The first factor is irrelevant because the State and HomeElderCare had no relationship before this dispute. The fifth factor is not at issue, because neither party foresees any administrative burden from a temporary injunction in this case.

I. The State has failed to prove that it will suffer great and irreparable injury if HomeElderCare continues to offer living will assistance to its clients.

The Cherne test requires the movant to show that an injunction would prevent a "great and irreparable injury" from occurring. 278 N.W.2d at 92. "[F]ailure to show irreparable harm [or injury] is, by itself, a sufficient ground upon which to deny an injunction." Carl Bolander & Sons Co. v. City of Minneapolis, 488 N.W.2d 804, 811 (Minn. Ct. App. 1992).

When a HomeElderCare social worker assists a client with a living will by helping the client to record his or her wishes in the blanks on the living will form, no injury occurs. In fact, a laudable service has been done—for the client, for his or her family, and for society. And in thirty-nine instances, that is exactly what happened.

Yet, the State wants to put a halt to this service for the duration of the trial process. The State's only factual ground for doing so is a disputed set of facts as to a single event. HomeElderCare's social worker believes that she helped an elderly gentleman in failing health accurately record his wishes, as he stated them, in response to the living will questions on the form. She also believes that she suggested that he discuss his legal questions with his attorney. The client, perhaps because of his precarious health, did not consult an attorney. His living will was amended when, as one would expect to occur quite often, the client reviewed his living will with his family. No action adverse to the client occurred pursuant to the living will. In any event, this one incident is not sufficient to establish that great and irreparable harm will occur to HomeElderCare's clients (and therefore to the state's citizens) if this Court denies the State's motion for a temporary injunction.

Furthermore, the State argues that its potential harm is the potential harm to HomeElderCare's clients, but the clients have articulated a need for assistance with the form. The State, in seeking an injunction, is acting contrary to the voiced needs of HomeElderCare's clients. Thus, the State has failed to clearly prove the crucial element of great and irreparable injury.

II. The State has not met its burden as to the factors needed for a temporary injunction to issue.

A. The State's alleged harm in the absence of a temporary injunction does not outweigh the harm to HomeElderCare's elderly clients and to the business relationships between HomeElderCare and its clients if an injunction is granted.

One of the five Dahlberg factors is that, absent the injunction, the State would suffer greater injury than would HomeElderCare and its clients upon the grant of the injunction. See Dahlberg Bros. v. Ford Motor Co., 272 Minn. at 274-75, 137 N.W.2d at 321-22. The party seeking to trigger the injunction must show irreparable harm, but the opposing party must only show substantial harm to bar it. Yager v. Thompson, 352 N.W.2d 71, 75 (Minn. Ct. App. 1984).

Here, the State has failed to show that HomeElderCare's living will service is causing irreparable harm; to the contrary, the service provides invaluable assistance on the crucial issues contained in a living will. Through its living will service—a service requested by its elderly clients—HomeElderCare seeks to help its elderly clients fill in the blanks of the living will form. The form raises difficult emotional, social, and even religious issues that may determine a person's quality of life in his or her final days. The resolution of these issues may also have a significant impact on the person's family members and friends. Many elderly persons find it helpful to discuss these issues with an informed person who does not have an emotional stake in their resolution yet understands the range of factors at issue. HomeElderCare is not influencing its clients in any way, nor is it pressuring its clients to complete living wills. In fact, the elderly clients originally requested HomeElderCare to provide this service to them.

If an injunction forced HomeElderCare to temporarily eliminate this service, its clients likely would not seek out attorneys to assist them in filling out the living will form because their needs as to the form are not legal needs; their needs are instead emotional and social. Moreover, clients on fixed incomes might not have the resources to engage an attorney for this service. Nor would the HomeElderCare clients who request this service be likely to complete the

Your notes in margin

living wills on their own without the emotional support of the HomeElderCare social workers.

In addition, HomeElderCare would suffer substantial harm because of an undeserved hindrance of its relationships with its clients. In <u>Dahlberg</u>, 272 Minn. at 277, 137 N.W.2d at 322, the court ruled that the potential harm resulting from a dealer's temporary interruption of business outweighed the manufacturer's potential harm from not being able to terminate the dealer's franchise right away, because the dealer's "[l]iaison with the buying public will be interrupted." Similarly, HomeElderCare would have to terminate this requested service and somehow explain that it cannot offer living will assistance until this trial is concluded.

The interests of HomeElderCare and its clients are far stronger than any interests that the State purports to represent. Accordingly, the State has not met its burden in proving that the State would suffer irreparable harm outweighing substantial harm to HomeElderCare.

B. The State is not likely to succeed in convincing the Court that HomeElderCare's provision of living will services to its clients constitutes the unauthorized practice of law.

Non-lawyers may not, of course, practice law in Minnesota. <u>See</u> Minn. Stat. § 481.02 (1992). But a non-lawyer may touch on legal matters incidental to her profession so long as she does not answer difficult or doubtful legal questions. <u>See</u> <u>Gardner v. Conway</u>, 234 Minn. 468, 481, 48 N.W.2d 788, 796 (1951). What is a difficult or doubtful legal question is measured by a reasonably intelligent person who has knowledge in similar transactions. <u>Id.</u> This test is "applied in a common-sense way which protects primarily the interests of the public and does not hamper or burden that interest with technical restrictions." <u>Id.</u> at 482, 48 N.W.2d at 797. The "difficult and doubtful legal question" test is flexible and entails a case-by-case analysis. <u>Id.</u> In <u>Gardner</u>, an accountant familiar with income tax rules and regulations answered difficult and doubtful legal questions in preparing a tax return and, therefore, violated the unauthorized practice of law statute. <u>See</u> <u>id.</u> at 472, 48 N.W.2d at 792.

HomeElderCare social workers use a straightforward living will form that meets the statutory requirements for living wills and gives instructions as to its completion. <u>See</u> Minn. Stat. § 145B.04 (1992). The form addresses various medical topics and designation of decisionmakers for the declarant should he become incompetent. <u>Id.</u> Indeed, the statute anticipates that many declarants will complete their own living wills. See id. § 145B.03. By leading their clients through the statutory living will form, the social workers meet their elderly clients' desire to complete the living will form. More important, for this case, by this process, the social workers avoid interpreting the living will statute and thereby avoid answering any difficult or doubtful legal questions. They thereby avoid engaging in the unauthorized practice of law.

Your notes in margin

The possibility of the social workers engaging in the unauthorized practice of law might exist if the social workers deviated from the living will form or interpreted the statute. However, the HomeElderCare social workers have done neither. The social workers refuse to alter the form. And if a client demands a living will that does not adhere to the living will form, the Home-ElderCare social workers advise the client that this action is beyond their scope of employment duties, and they recommend that the client seek expert legal advice from a licensed attorney—unlike the accountant in Gardner. That a single HomeElderCare client disregarded this advice does not convert the social worker's actions into the unauthorized practice of law.

Although charging a fee for services has in the past suggested that an issue may be "difficult and doubtful," Cardinal v. Merrill Lynch Realty/Burnet, Inc., 433 N.W.2d 864, 868 (Minn. 1989), HomeElderCare's fee is not for legal services. HomeElderCare charges a reasonable fee for all of its services. The preparation fee for living wills is an hourly rate charged all clients who select this service.

The State has argued that living wills are "legal documents" within the statutory prohibition against drafting "legal documents." See Minn. Stat. § 481.02. This argument fails for several reasons. There is no evidence that the reference in the living will form to "legal document" was meant to relate to the unauthorized practice statute. To the contrary, had the legislature intended this connection, it would have alerted declarants to the need for legal advice, whereas the form refers more broadly to seeking "professional advice." See Minn. Stat. § 145B.04.

Furthermore, the "difficult and doubtful" test was developed in response to a non-lawyer practicing in another form-driven setting—tax. See Gardner, 234 Minn. at 472, 48 N.W.2d at 792. Hence this test would apply to Home-ElderCare's filling out a living will form. As already argued, the living will service passes this test.

Thus, the service is permitted under the "difficult and doubtful legal question" test and is not prohibited by the unauthorized practice of law statute. Therefore, the State is not likely to succeed on the merits of the case.

Your notes in margin

C. The public interest will not be served by prohibiting HomeElder-Care's living will services during the pendency of the case.

The persons most affected by any temporary injunction granted in this case would be elderly persons and persons in failing health. These persons often are vulnerable, in need of emotional support, and on fixed incomes. Many attorneys are not as well prepared as social workers to provide the needed emotional support and the needed services; furthermore, the cost of obtaining these services from attorneys would not be an efficient use of these persons' meager or fixed incomes. Thus, the HomeElderCare service is an efficient and needed service. Elderly and ill clients ought to be able to use this service now; they should not have to await the outcome of trial.

Ultimately, the public is served well by HomeElderCare's assistance in preparing living wills. The service enhances the possibility that elderly persons will have living wills in place when and if they are needed. It is Minnesota's public policy to encourage living wills. See Minn. Stat. §§ 145B.03, 06.

Furthermore, living wills enable the health care system to better serve the needs of its patients and to better allocate scarce health care resources. "Patients without [living wills] have significantly higher terminal hospitalization charges than those with [living wills]." William Weeks, Advance Directives and the Cost of Terminal Hospitalization, 154 Archives Internal Med. *1 (1994), available in DIALOG, ARCHINTMED database, No. 2077. "[T]he preferences of patients with [living wills] are to limit care and these preferences influence the cost of terminal hospitalization." Id. Keeping this in mind, the possible total savings in the cost of health care if living wills were completed by all in the nation is somewhere between thirty-five and sixty percent. Id. at *6. Therefore, both the patient and the health care system benefit from the use of living wills.

Thus, the living will service of HomeElderCare serves the public interest. As a result, the public interest will not be served by prohibiting this service.

CONCLUSION

The State has not met its burden of proving its entitlement to the extraordinary equitable remedy of a temporary injunction. It has not demonstrated great and irreparable harm. It will not suffer a greater harm upon the denial of

the injunction than HomeElderCare would suffer upon the grant of such an in- *Your notes in margin*
junction. Nor is the State likely to succeed on the merits of this case, since the
living will service does not constitute the unauthorized practice of law. Finally,
the public interest would not be served by a temporary injunction. Thus, the
State's motion should be denied.

Respectfully submitted,

Katherine Crawford   Dated: Oct. 10, 1993

Katherine Crawford
Counsel for HomeElderCare, Inc.
5678 Sherburne Avenue
LaSalle MN 55555
(507) 555-4321
Attorney Reg. No. 12541

APPELLATE COURT CASE NO. 94-1234
STATE OF MINNESOTA
IN COURT OF APPEALS

Roger Nelson,
    Plaintiff-Respondent,

vs.

HomeElderCare, Inc.,
    Defendant-Appellant.

APPELLANT'S BRIEF

Katherine Crawford (No. 12541)   Albert Frank (No. 14711)
Attorney for Appellant   Attorney for Respondent
Crawford & Larson   Law Offices of Albert Frank
12 Main Avenue   672 Oak Street
Versailles, MN 50000   Versailles, MN 50001
Telephone: (222) 555-1234   (222) 777-7771

TABLE OF CONTENTS

TABLE OF AUTHORITIES

LAW REVIEW COMMENTARIES:

STATEMENT OF THE ISSUE

facts + law + more facts

Is a service contract between Appellant, a private geriatric services agency, and Respondent, an elderly client, invalid on the grounds that the agency practiced law when its trained social worker assisted the elderly client to fill in the blanks on a living will form?

trial court holding

procedural posture

The trial court ruled affirmatively by granting the Respondent client summary declaratory judgment and denying Appellant's cross-motion for summary judgment.

STATEMENT OF FACTS
The Case

commencement of suit

cause of action

On July 20, 1993, the Respondent, Roger Nelson, sued the Appellant, HomeElderCare, Inc., seeking to void his own contract with HomeElderCare for preparation of a living will—and, in effect, to prohibit HomeElderCare from offering its living will service to other HomeElderCare clients. (Compl.)

remedy

Mr. Nelson's suit sought a declaratory judgment (id.), HomeElderCare and Mr. Nelson stipulated to the facts, (Stip.), and both parties moved for summary

dispositive motion

judgment (Pl.'s Mot. for Summ. J.; Def.'s Cross-Mot. for Summ. J.). Judge Annelise Burton of the LaSalle County District Court granted Mr. Nelson's mo-

order

appeal

tion and issued a declaratory judgment in his favor. (Order for Decl. J.) HomeElderCare appeals.

The Facts

1st topic: HEC's services generally

Appellant HomeElderCare is a private, non-profit corporation with a staff of geriatric social workers who provide services to help their elderly clients with day-to-day activities. Volunteers assist with some services. Available services include shopping, transportation, home maintenance, and assistance with personal finances. The social workers also serve as liaisons between clients and attorneys working on such matters as testamentary wills and real estate transactions. (Stip. ¶ 2.) Each client contracts with HomeElderCare for the services he or she desires and pays a fee based on the services rendered. (Id. ¶ 3.)

2nd topic: living will service

Several clients recently asked HomeElderCare to fill a gap in the services provided to them by offering the service of preparing living wills. HomeElderCare decided to respond to its clients' requests and began preparing living wills for its clients. (Id. ¶ 4.) As with its other services, HomeElderCare charges a fee that varies with the time the social worker puts in on the project. (Id. ¶ 5.)

A living will is a document that specifies the signer's desires regarding medical treatment in the event the signer is incapacitated. In Minnesota, a state statute includes a living will form that is easily prepared by filling in the blanks; the statute also indicates how the document is to be signed, witnessed, and notarized. See Minn. Stat. § 145B.04 (1992). HomeElderCare's social workers use the living will form that complies with Minnesota law. The social workers do not deviate from the form, but rather advise clients to consult with attorneys in such situations. (Stip. ¶ 5.)

definition of living will and use of statutory form

To date, the HomeElderCare social workers have prepared forty living wills. Eight clients have since been hospitalized. The living wills were shown to their doctors, but none of the clients were incapacitated enough to bring any of the living wills into effect. Other than Mr. Nelson, HomeElderCare's clients have registered no objections to their living wills. (Id. ¶ 8.)

other clients served

Appellant Kimberly Hall is a social worker at HomeElderCare. She has a master's degree in social work and has worked in the field for twelve years. (Id. ¶ 4.) As is true of her colleagues, she attended a one-day HomeElderCare workshop on care issues involving the terminally ill; this workshop included a forty-five-minute presentation by a lawyer about preparing living wills. (Id. ¶ 6.) With this training, thus far, she has prepared ten living wills for Home-ElderCare clients. (Id. ¶ 8.)

3rd topic: social worker's training

Ms. Hall prepared a living will for Roger Nelson. (Id. ¶ 1.) When Mr. Nelson was hospitalized, his son, an attorney, realized that the living will made Roger Nelson's proxy for medical decisions also his guardian for financial decisions, although Roger Nelson now desires otherwise. (Id. ¶ 7.) Mr. Nelson, who is a seventy-eight-year-old widower, is in declining health because of diabetes. (Id. ¶ 1.) It is unknown how the terms of Mr. Nelson's living will came to diverge from his present desires. Ms. Hall usually provides a standard explanation of the roles of proxies, guardians, and conservators, and Mr. Nelson did not consult an attorney with his questions, as Ms. Hall believes she suggested to him. (See id. ¶ 5.)

4th topic: Roger Nelson's situation

SUMMARY OF ARGUMENT

HomeElderCare responsibly designed a program to provide assistance to its elderly clients who requested help in filling in the blanks on a living will form. The service in question did not constitute the unauthorized practice of law. Because the social worker confined her service to filling out the statutory form and would refer clients to attorneys as needed, there was no provision of legal advice. The living will form has many medical and ethical implications, but relatively few legal implications and no testamentary effect. Hence a living will is not a legal document that an attorney must draft.

However, even if the social worker's assistance was the practice of law, the social worker provided the living will services as an incident of its nonlegal consequences, competently and without fraud; the service did not contravene the purpose of the statute on the unauthorized practice of law. Thus, the service contract between the client and the agency was valid. Moreover, public policy favors living wills and therefore supports the agency's service of assisting its clients in filling in living will forms.

In the trial court, both parties, having stipulated to the facts, moved for summary judgment. The trial court erroneously granted summary judgment to Respondent, and this court should reverse that judgment and grant Appellant's cross-motion for summary judgment.

ARGUMENT

This Court should reverse the summary declaratory judgment in favor of Respondent and should instead grant Appellant's cross-motion for summary judgment, thereby upholding the contract under which a trained social worker for a private geriatric services agency assisted an elderly client to fill in the blanks on a living will form.

A declaratory judgment "may be reviewed as other orders, judgments and decrees." Minn. Stat. § 555.07 (1992). When reviewing an appeal from summary judgment, this Court determines whether there are any genuine issues of material fact and whether the trial court erred in its application of the law. See Offerdahl v. University of Minn. Hosp. & Clinics, 426 N.W.2d 425, 427 (Minn. 1988). See Minn. R. Civ. P. 56.03. Because the parties stipulated to the facts, this Court need decide only whether the trial court correctly applied the law.

A. The agency did not practice law when its trained social worker assisted the client in filling in the blanks on a living will form.

When HomeElderCare's social worker assisted its client, Mr. Nelson, in filling in the blanks on a state-approved living will form, it did not engage in the unauthorized practice of law because the social worker neither gave legal advice nor drafted a legal document.

According to Minnesota's unauthorized practice statute:

> It shall be unlawful for any person . . . , except . . . Minnesota . . . attorneys . . . [1] for a fee . . . , to give legal advice or counsel, perform for or furnish to another legal services, or, [2] for or without a fee . . . , to prepare . . . for another person . . . any will or testamentary disposition or instrument of trust serving purposes similar to those of a will, or, [3] for a fee . . . , to prepare for another person . . . any other legal document, except as provided in subdivision 3.[1]

overall rule: statute

Minn. Stat. § 481.02 subd. 1 (1992) (enumeration added).

Clause [1] forbids a layperson from giving legal advice or counsel, or performing for or furnishing to another legal services, for a fee. See Minn. Stat. § 481.02 subd. 1. The HomeElderCare social worker was assisting an elderly client with the medical and ethical issues in the living will form set out in the statute. The form asks the maker of the will questions about health care preferences, life-sustaining treatment, artificially administered sustenance, designation of a health care proxy, and organ donation, the answers to take effect when that person has an incurable or irreversible condition and is no longer able to participate in decisions regarding his or her health care. To avoid the rendering of legal advice, HomeElderCare practice calls for the social worker to suggest that the client consult an attorney if the client wishes to deviate from the form or has legal questions. Thus, the social worker did not provide legal advice.[2]

■ *1st subtopic: legal advice or counsel —first point*

However, even if the social worker touched on legal matters, the service would not constitute unauthorized practice of law under Minnesota case law. The Minnesota Supreme Court held that a layperson can dispense legal advice and services in the course of his or her business so long as it is incidental (not primary) to the business and the layperson does not answer difficult or doubtful legal questions. See Gardner v. Conway, 234 Minn. 468, 480-81, 48 N.W.2d 788, 796 (1951). A difficult or doubtful legal question exists when it must be answered by someone with a trained legal mind, in

—argument in the alternative

—rule: case

---

1. Subdivision 3 lists 16 exceptions, none of which apply to these facts. Minn. Stat. § 481.02 subd. 3 (1992).
2. As it does for all of its services, HomeElderCare charged a fee for its living will service. The charging of a fee should not render this service the practice of law, any more than the charging of a fee for home maintenance services would render that service the practice of law. Cf. Cardinal v. Merrill Lynch Realty/Burnet, Inc., 433 N.W.2d 864 (Minn. 1988) (charging a fee suggests, but does not establish, practice of law).

(tangential points in footnotes)
(rebuttal)

(inapplicable case)

order to safeguard the public. See id. In Gardner, an accountant gave a client opinions on tax questions concerning lawful marital status, joint versus separate returns, and partnership status, all of which required analysis by someone with legal training. Thus, the accountant was engaging in the unauthorized practice of law. See id. at 483-84, 48 N.W.2d at 798. The court emphasized that the test of what is a difficult or doubtful legal question should be

> applied in a common-sense way which will protect primarily the interest of the public and not hamper or burden that interest with impractical and technical restrictions which have no reasonable justification. We are therefore not concerned with a technical application which would ban the giving of any and all legal advice or the taking of any and all action for another.

Id. at 481-82, 48 N.W.2d at 797 (citations omitted).

—policy argument

It is not common sense to bar a HomeElderCare social worker from helping a client fill in the blanks on a statutory form dominated by medical and ethical questions, just because the form includes some incidental legal topics. So long as the social worker declines to answer any difficult or doubtful questions of law, there is no unauthorized practice of law. Here there is no evidence that

—application of case rule

Ms. Hall addressed such questions. She provided an explanation of proxies, guardians, and conservators—concepts that must not be that difficult, since these roles are routinely filled by laypeople. See generally Minn. Stat. §§ 145B.06 subd. 2; 145B.08; 525.539 subds. 2, 3; 525.56 (1992). There is no evidence that she counseled Mr. Nelson about how to apply these concepts to his individual situation. HomeElderCare's practice calls for referral to attor-

conclusion to 1st subtopic

neys when clients raise questions or wish to deviate from the form. Thus, unlike the tax accountant in Gardner, Ms. Hall did not exceed her bounds, and HomeElderCare did not violate the statutory prohibition against giving legal advice or counsel.

■ *2nd subtopic: legal document*

The living will form that HomeElderCare fills in for its clients is not a "legal document" under clause [3] of the unauthorized practice statute. Although the form states that it "is an important legal document," the form is designed to provide medical and ethical instructions to medical caregivers. It focuses mostly on medical concepts like "specific treatments," "life-sustaining treatments," "artificially administered sustenance," and death from "dehydration or malnutrition." See Minn. Stat. § 145B.04. The Act suggests that a declarant seek "professional help" to understand unclear provisions, id.; the legislature could have specified a lawyer's assistance, but did not. Thus, the living will form in question is not a "legal document" within the meaning of the unauthorized practice statute.

Nor does the living will come within the scope of clause [2], which pertains to "any will or testamentary disposition or instrument of trust serving purposes similar to those of a will." Minn. Stat. § 481.02 subd. 1. A living "will" does not convey any rights posthumously, nor is it designed to be filed in a court of law. It deals only with the patient's wishes in the event of a terminal illness that renders the patient unable to communicate his or her rational wishes for medical treatment or lack thereof.[3]

■ 3rd subtopic: will or trust

In summary, HomeElderCare did not violate clauses [1], [2], or [3] of the statute on the unauthorized practice of law.

conclusion to A.

B. Even if the social worker practiced law, the contract is valid because the social worker provided the living will services without fraud or incompetence and incidentally to nonlegal counseling.

2nd minor point heading (law + facts)

A contract for professional services by an unlicensed professional is enforceable if the activities under the contract are not the kind of activities that the licensing statute was adopted to preclude. See Dick Weatherston's Assoc'd Mech'l Servs. v. Minnesota Mut. Life Ins. Co., 257 Minn. 184, 191, 100 N.W.2d 819, 824 (1960). In Dick Weatherston's, the court upheld the validity of an engineering contract with an unlicensed professional because the engineering licensing statute was intended to protect the public from fraud and incompetence, neither of which were present in that case. The client knew the engineer's status, the client had its own engineers and architects who approved and accepted the services, and the engineering services were incidental to an air conditioning contract. See id. at 191-92, 100 N.W.2d at 824-25.

rule: case

Similarly, the law defining unauthorized practice of law is intended to safeguard the public from fraud and incompetence. See generally Gardner, 234 Minn. at 478, 48 N.W.2d at 795. There is no evidence that Ms. Hall fraudulently held herself out as having legal expertise. Indeed, HomeElderCare practices call for referral to an attorney should the client have questions or wish to deviate from the form, and Ms. Hall believes she so referred Mr. Nelson. He could not have been mistaken as to her professional status.

application (analogy to case)

Nor is there any clear evidence of incompetence. Although the client's living will contained a misstatement of his intentions, the evidence does not show that he accurately stated his intentions to Ms. Hall. Nor does the evidence

---

3. Peterson v. Hovland (In re Peterson's Estate), 230 Minn. 478, 42 N.W.2d 59 (1950), is inapplicable to this case because it deals with a bank cashier who drafted a customer's testamentary will, rather than a living will. The Peterson court allowed the will to stand, even though the act of drafting it violated clause [2] of the unauthorized practice statute; however, this appeal does not address the question of the living will's validity. Thus, this appeal is distinguishable from Peterson on both its facts and its issues.

(distinguish case)

show that the social worker, rather than the client himself, was responsible. Moreover, there is no evidence of incompetence or even misunderstandings in the other thirty-nine living wills prepared with HomeElderCare assistance. HomeElderCare trained its social workers for this specific service, and Home-ElderCare instructed its social workers to urge clients with legal questions to consult an attorney, as Ms. Hall believes that she so instructed Mr. Nelson.

conclusion to B.

Furthermore, as in Dick Weatherston's, HomeElderCare's allegedly legal services were incidental to its provision of primarily nonlegal services, namely assistance with medical care and ethical decisionmaking. Thus, this case is analogous to Dick Weatherston's. Accordingly, the living-will service contract between HomeElderCare and its client is valid.

3rd minor point heading (policy + facts)

C. Public policy favors living wills and therefore also favors a service provider who assists a client in filling in the blanks on the statutory living will form.

rules setting policy

Minnesota's state constitution recognizes the right to privacy and a derivative "right not to have [one's body] altered or invaded without consent." Jarvis v. Levine, 418 N.W.2d 138, 149 (Minn. 1988). If the patient is incompetent and cannot give consent, the physician cannot administer invasive medical treatment without first obtaining consent "from some source other than the contemporaneous words of the patient." Id. at 147. This rule is based on the "right of every individual to the possession and to control of his own person, free from all restraint or interference of others, unless by clear and unquestionable authority of law." Union Pac. R.R. Co. v. Botsford, 141 U.S. 250, 251 (1891), cited in Howard Orenstein et al., Minnesota's Living Will . . ., Bench & B. Minn. Aug. 1989, at 21, 22. The Living Will Act, passed after Jarvis, furnishes a legal mechanism by which a patient can give advance instructions and preferences to the physician while the patient is still competent. It allows "a competent adult [to] make a living will of preferences or instructions regarding . . . health care, treatment, service, procedure, or placement." Minn. Stat. § 145B.03 subd. 1.

Furthermore, living wills enable the health care system to better serve the needs of its patients and to better allocate scarce health care resources. "Patients without [living wills] have significantly higher terminal hospitalization charges than those with [living wills]." William Weeks, Advance Directives and the Cost of Terminal Hospitalization, 154 Archives Internal Med. *1 (1994), available in DIALOG ARCHINTMED database, No. 2077. "[T]he preferences of patients with [living wills] are to limit care and these preferences influence the cost of terminal hospitalization." Id. Keeping this in mind, the possible total savings in the cost of health care if living wills were completed by all in the nation is somewhere between thirty-five and sixty percent. Id. at *6.

Therefore, both the patient and the health care system benefit from the use of living wills.

To maximize the use of living wills in light of these public policies, the Act includes a suggested form for a living will and mandates that "[f]orms printed for public distribution . . . be substantially in the form in this section." Id. § 145B.04. The Act does not restrict these forms to the offices of attorneys, but instead promotes public distribution so that they can be made widely available—most probably by hospitals, physicians, and geriatric care organizations. Of course, many of the persons filling out these forms will be elderly.

general application

HomeElderCare has sought to effectuate public policy and the Living Will Act through its living will service. Responding to the requests of elderly clients, it has sought to make living wills more available to the elderly, who have an undeniable interest in self-determination as to medical issues and an equally clear potential for unduly protracted medical care. Mr. Nelson himself sought out the help of a HomeElderCare social worker when he made out his living will. That social worker had been trained in how to fill in the blanks on the form and knew to refer legal questions to the client's attorney. Thus, the trial court's declaratory judgment invalidating the contract in this case is contrary to public policy and should be reversed.

specific application

conclusion to C.

CONCLUSION

HomeElderCare respectfully requests this Court to vacate the trial court's summary declaratory judgment in favor of Mr. Nelson and grant summary judgment to HomeElderCare.

overall conclusion with procedural recommendation

Dated: _____J a n. 8, 1994_____   Respectfully submitted,

signature block

By: *Katherine Crawford*
Katherine Crawford (No. 12541)
Crawford & Larson
12 Main Avenue
Versailles, MN 50000
Telephone: (222) 555-1234
ATTORNEY FOR APPELLANT
HomeElderCare, Inc.

APPELLATE COURT CASE NO. 94-1234
STATE OF MINNESOTA
IN COURT OF APPEALS

Roger Nelson,
      Plaintiff-Respondent,

    vs.

HomeElderCare, Inc.,
      Defendant-Appellant.

RESPONDENT'S BRIEF

Albert Frank (No. 14711)
Attorney for Respondent
Law Offices of Albert Frank
672 Oak Street
Versailles, MN 50001
(222) 777-7771

Katherine Crawford (No. 12541)
Attorney for Appellant
Crawford & Larson
12 Main Avenue
Versailles, MN 50000
Telephone: (222) 555-1234

TABLE OF CONTENTS

TABLE OF AUTHORITIES

OTHER AUTHORITIES:

Your notes in margin

ISSUES

I. Did a social worker—who is not licensed to practice law—engage in the unauthorized practice of law when she prepared a defective living will for an elderly client for a fee?

The trial court held that the social worker violated the Minnesota Unauthorized Practice of Law Statute.

II. If there was unauthorized practice of law, is the contract between the social work agency and the client unenforceable, so as to excuse the client from paying for the defective document?

The trial court held that, because of the violation of the Unauthorized Practice of Law Statute, the contract is not enforceable.

STATEMENT OF CASE AND FACTS

Statement of Case

Plaintiff Roger Nelson commenced this action against Defendant Home-ElderCare, Inc. in LaSalle County District Court on July 20, 1993. Mr. Nelson sought a declaratory judgment that he is not legally obligated to pay Home-ElderCare for preparing his living will on the grounds that HomeElderCare engaged in the unauthorized practice of law, rendering the contract unenforceable. (Compl.) The parties stipulated to the facts, (Stip.), and filed cross-motions for summary judgment, (Pl's Mot. for Summ. J.; Def's Mot. for Summ. J.).

On November 3, 1993, Judge Annelise Burton granted summary judgment in favor of Mr. Nelson. The Order for Declaratory Judgment states:

(1) HomeElderCare's social workers engaged in the unauthorized practice of law, in violation of Minn. Stat. § 481.02 (1992);

(2) the contract between Mr. Nelson and HomeElderCare is not enforceable, and, therefore, Mr. Nelson is not legally obligated to pay Home-ElderCare for preparing his living will.

(Order for Decl. J.) HomeElderCare appeals.

Statement of Facts

Roger Nelson is seventy-eight years old and a widower. He is in declining health because of diabetes. (Stip. ¶ 1.) Contemplating the time when his condition might worsen and he would become incapacitated, Mr. Nelson set out to arrange his personal affairs as he wished. Among other steps, Mr. Nelson wrote a living will, a statement of his desires regarding health care when he is in a terminal state. Unfortunately, Mr. Nelson initially turned to Defendant HomeElderCare, Inc., to prepare his living will. (Id. ¶ 7.)

HomeElderCare is a private, non-profit corporation that provides various social services for elderly persons. Among the useful services provided by HomeElderCare are shopping, transportation, and home maintenance. The social workers also serve as liaisons between clients and other professionals, such as attorneys working on the clients' testamentary wills and real estate transactions. (Id. ¶ 2.) The elderly clients contract for the particular services desired, HomeElderCare's staff makes the necessary arrangements, and the clients pay a fee for the services. (Id. ¶ 3.) Volunteers also provide some free services.

As befits a social work agency, HomeElderCare is staffed by social workers. These social workers are not attorneys. These social workers do not have law degrees. These social workers have not been admitted to practice law in Minnesota or anywhere else. (Id. ¶ 4.)

Nonetheless, HomeElderCare social workers have prepared at least forty living wills for their clients. (Id. ¶ 8.) For some reason, HomeElderCare chose not to follow its established practice and serve as liaison between the clients and their attorneys, as it does with other legal transactions, (id. ¶ 2), but rather elected to prepare the living wills itself, (id. ¶ 5). The sole training received by the social workers was a forty-five minute seminar taught by an attorney. (Id. ¶ 6.)

In particular, social worker Kimberly Hall, a non-lawyer, prepared a living will for Mr. Nelson on October 10, 1992. In this living will, Mr. Nelson's minister was designated as the proxy authorized to make medical decisions on behalf of Mr. Nelson should he become mentally incapacitated. (Id. ¶ 7.) The proxy is also, by operation of statute, nominated to be the declarant's guardian. See Minn. Stat. § 145B.04 (1992). Mr. Nelson actually wanted his minister to serve only as his proxy for medical decisionmaking; he wanted his son, Albert Nelson, to serve as his guardian. (Stip. ¶ 7.) Thus the living will fundamentally misstated Mr. Nelson's wishes about the handling of his affairs in the last days of his life.

While neither Ms. Hall nor Mr. Nelson can remember the details of their interaction leading up to the defective document, (id. ¶ 7), HomeElderCare social workers, including Ms. Hall, have followed certain procedures. First, the social worker talks with the client, and then a draft of the living will is prepared by the social worker. The social worker explains various legal implications of the living will, such as the doctor's obligation to follow its provisions and the role of the proxy. The social worker also explains the living will to the proxy and then arranges for it to be signed and notarized. The social worker then delivers the living will to the client's primary care physician. (Id. ¶ 5.)

The client is charged a fee that is based on the amount of time the social worker spends on the project. (Id.) Mr. Nelson paid $80 for his defective living will. (Id. ¶ 7.)

Fortunately, Mr. Nelson's son, who is an attorney, became concerned when he realized his father did not agree with the terms of the living will that had been prepared for him. Subsequently, the younger Mr. Nelson arranged for a substitute living will to be drafted by the family's attorney. The revised will accurately states Mr. Nelson's wishes. (Id. ¶ 9.)

ARGUMENT

Summary

The trial court properly concluded that HomeElderCare's social worker engaged in the unauthorized practice of law and that the contract between Mr. Nelson and HomeElderCare thus is unenforceable. To protect the public, the Minnesota statute on unauthorized practice of law prohibits non-attorneys from practicing law. Yet HomeElderCare's social worker did precisely that when she drafted Mr. Nelson's defective living will, counseled him about it, and charged him for it. Because enforcement of the contract between Home-ElderCare and Mr. Nelson for the preparation of his living will would be plainly contrary to the intent of the legislature, the contract is unenforceable. A social worker should not be paid for defective legal work.

Standard of Review

When reviewing an appeal from summary judgment, this Court determines whether there are any genuine issues of material fact and whether the trial court erred in its application of the law. See Offerdahl v. University of Minn. Hosp. & Clinics, 426 N.W.2d 425, 427 (Minn. 1988). In the present case, there are no genuine issues of material fact because the parties stipulated to the facts. Therefore, the sole issue is whether the trial court correctly applied the law.

I. The trial court properly ruled that HomeElderCare's social worker engaged in the unauthorized practice of law when she prepared Mr. Nelson's living will for a fee.

Your notes in margin

Minnesota's Unauthorized Practice of Law Statute is designed to forestall poorly drawn legal documents due to "bungling use of legal terms and improper knowledge" of the law by non-lawyers. Peterson v. Hovland (In re Peterson's Estate), 230 Minn. 478, 484, 42 N.W.2d 59, 63 (1950) (involving drafting of a testamentary will). Such poorly drawn documents may be invalid or operate contrary to the client's intent, yet their non-lawyer authors would not be subject to the supervision of the courts. Id.

The situation involving Mr. Nelson is a perfect example of the sort of situation that gave rise to the prohibition on the unauthorized practice of law. As a consequence of the actions of Ms. Hall, Mr. Nelson designated his minister as both his proxy and guardian—even though this arrangement was not what he desired. It took a lawyer to correct the defective document to properly implement his desires.

More precisely, the Minnesota Unauthorized Practice of Law Statute renders it unlawful for non-lawyers to engage in the following activities:

> [1] for a fee or any consideration, to give legal advice or counsel, perform for or furnish to another legal services, . . .
> [2] to prepare . . . any will or [similar] testamentary disposition. . . , or,
> [3] "for a fee or any consideration, to prepare for another person, firm, or corporation, any other legal document . . . .

Minn. Stat. § 481.02 subd. 1 (1992) (numbers added).

HomeElderCare social worker Kimberly Hall is not an attorney. She has not been trained as a lawyer, has not passed the bar, and is not subject to the supervision of the Minnesota courts. Nonetheless, Ms. Hall practiced law in two respects.

First, contrary to the third prohibition (quoted above), social worker Hall prepared a legal document when she prepared Mr. Nelson's living will. While the unauthorized practice statute does not define "legal document," the Minnesota Living Will Act provides a suggested form for living wills which plainly states that the form is an "important legal document." Minn. Stat. § 145B.04 (1992). Furthermore, Mr. Nelson's living will is a "legal document" according to the plain meaning of the term. Webster's New Collegiate Dictionary defines "document" as "an original or official paper relied on as basis, proof, or support of something" and "legal" as something that "conforms to rules or the law." Webster's New Collegiate Dictionary 336, 656 (1976). A living will is an official statement proving the declarant's wishes in the event of incapacitation, conforming to the requirements of the Minnesota Living

Your notes in margin

Will Act and imposing upon physicians the responsibilities set out in that statute. See Minn. Stat. § 145B.03 subd. 1. In addition, HomeElderCare charged Mr. Nelson a fee for this service, thereby completing the violation of the statute.

Second, contrary to the first prohibition (quoted above), social worker Hall gave legal advice and counsel to Mr. Nelson in the course of preparing his living will. The line between what is and what is not "legal advice and counsel" cannot be drawn with precision, because law practice overlaps with many other professions. For instance, in Gardner v. Conway, 234 Minn. 468, 480, 48 N.W.2d 788, 796 (1951) (citations omitted), the court observed that

> [i]n the field of income taxation, . . . we have an overlapping of both law and accounting. An accountant must adapt his [or her] accounting skills to the requirements of tax law, and therefore he [or she] must have a workable knowledge of law as applied to his [or her] field. By the same token, a lawyer must have some understanding of accounting. In the income tax area, . . . it is difficult to draw a precise line to separate their respective functions. The public interest does not permit an obliteration of all lines of demarcations. We cannot escape reality by hiding behind a facade of nomenclature and assume that "taxation," though composed of both law and accounting, is something sui generis and apart from the law. If taxation is a hybrid of law and accounting, it does not follow that it is so wholly without the law that its legal activities may be pursued without proper qualifications and without court supervision.

The Gardner court ruled that "whenever, as incidental to another . . . calling, a lay[person] . . . resolves legal questions for another . . . by giving . . . advice or by taking action . . . , he [or she] is practicing law if difficult or doubtful legal questions are involved which, to safeguard the public, reasonably demand the application of a trained legal mind." Id. at 481, 48 N.W.2d at 796. The tax accountant in Gardner illegally practiced law when he provided information on various tax issues in the course of preparing a tax return for a client. He gave advice on tax treatment of business partnerships, the status of a common law wife on joint tax returns, and the deductibility of various expenditures. See id. at 483-84, 48 N.W.2d at 792.

Ms. Hall, a social worker, similarly ventured into the realm of legal advice. Neither she nor Mr. Nelson can recall exactly what advice she gave Mr. Nelson when she prepared his living will. The parties have, however, stipulated that Ms. Hall would normally discuss the roles of proxies, guardians, and conservators to clients. It also has been her practice to explain the legal obligations of doctors and other medical personnel in the event of a client's incapacitation. Furthermore, she has explained the document to the client's witness

Your notes in margin

and proxy, explained their roles to them, and supervised the execution of the living will.

These legal topics are as difficult and doubtful as the tax issues covered by the accountant in <u>Gardner</u>. They are legal matters covered in detail in the living will statute. <u>See</u> Minn. Stat. §§ 145B.01-.17 (1992). Because the living will statute was enacted in 1989, <u>see</u> Act of Mar. 3, 1989, ch. 3, 1989 Minn. Laws 8, and has yet to be interpreted by the appellate courts, its application to specific situations is uncertain. In addition, the specific issue on which Ms. Hall failed Mr. Nelson—the appointment of a guardian—is regulated not only by the living will statute, but also by a separate extensive and complex statute on guardianship. <u>See</u> Minn. Stat. §§ 525.532-.6198 (1992). In general, legal regulation of medical decisionmaking is in a phase of rapid change, with both statutory and constitutional dimensions. <u>See generally</u> Howard Orenstein et al., <u>Minnesota's Living Will . . .</u>, Bench & B. Minn., Aug. 1989, at 21-25 (citing <u>Jarvis v. Levine</u>, 418 N.W.2d 139 (Minn. 1988)).

The <u>Gardner</u> rule must be applied in a "common sense way which will protect the public and not hamper or burden that public interest with impractical and technical restrictions which have no reasonable justification." <u>Gardner</u>, 234 Minn. at 481-82, 48 N.W.2d at 797. The restriction on social workers preparing living wills may burden the social worker who wishes to practice law. But the restriction is not impractical or merely technical; it is more than reasonably justified when viewed from the proper perspective—the client's. The client's need for legal assistance is recognized in the statutory living will form itself, which states that a professional should be consulted if there are any questions. <u>See</u> Minn. Stat. § 145B.04. That professional should be a lawyer because very significant legal issues are covered in the document. These issues touch on important aspects of client autonomy, as in Mr. Nelson's case, and also—literally—matters of life and death. The living will thus resembles a testamentary will. Only lawyers may prepare testamentary wills for other people, Minn. Stat. § 481.02 subd. 1 (second prohibition stated above); so too should a lawyer be consulted for assistance in preparation of a living will. The proper role for a social worker is to serve as a liaison for a client needing assistance in obtaining legal services, a role permitted by the unauthorized practice statute, <u>see</u> Minn. Stat. § 481.02 subd. 3(6), subd. 7.[1]

Furthermore, the charging of a fee suggests that the services offered in-

---

[1] Of course, in both testamentary and living will situations, the client can also choose to draft the document himself, for reasons of cost or personal choice.

Your notes in margin

volve a difficult and doubtful legal issue. See generally Cardinal v. Merrill Lynch Realty/Burnet, Inc., 433 N.W.2d 864, 869 (Minn. 1988). HomeElderCare charged Mr. Nelson a fee for the preparation of his living will.

The trial court's ruling in favor of Mr. Nelson is consistent with the law in other jurisdictions. For example, the Florida Supreme Court held that a non-lawyer could distribute and type standardized legal forms, but prohibited the non-lawyer from providing any specific assistance in the preparation of the forms, answering questions on how to complete the form, or correcting any errors and omissions made by her customers. See Florida Bar v. Brumbaugh, 355 So. 2d 1186 (Fla. 1978). New York, Michigan, and Oregon courts also have held that distributing standardized legal forms with general instructions may be permitted, but personal contact between a non-lawyer and a client is an unauthorized practice of law when there is explanation, advice, or assistance in filling out the form. See State Bar v. Cramer, 249 N.W.2d 1 (Mich. 1976); New York County Lawyers' Ass'n v. Dacey, 234 N.E.2d 459 (N.Y. 1967); Oregon State Bar v. Gilchrist, 538 P.2d 913 (Or. 1975).

In summary, social worker Hall violated the unauthorized practice statute when she prepared Mr. Nelson's defective living will and again when she counseled him about it, both for a fee. The declaratory judgment should be affirmed so as to protect Mr. Nelson and others like him from the potentially very serious consequences of incompetent legal practice.

II. Because of this unauthorized practice of law, the contract between Home-ElderCare and Mr. Nelson for preparation of the living will is unenforceable, as the trial court properly held.

If a statute requires a license to perform a professional service and an unlicensed practitioner enters into a contract to perform that service, that contract is generally void. See E. Allan Farnsworth, Contracts § 5.6, at 377-79 (2d ed. 1990). Minnesota has followed this rule. See, e.g., Buckley v. Humason, 50 Minn. 195, 52 N.W. 385 (1892) (real estate broker held unable to recover fee for real estate services because he was not licensed as required by statute). However, the courts also examine the legislative intent behind the licensing statute to determine whether the contract should be illegal and void. See Dick Weatherston's Assoc'd Mech'l Servs. v. Minnesota Mut. Life Ins. Co., 257 Minn. 184, 191, 100 N.W.2d 819, 823-24 (1960).

In Weatherston's, on an unusual set of facts, the court enforced a contract involving an engineer who was not licensed as required by statute. Id. at 191-92, 100 N.W.2d at 824-25. The contract involved installation of an air-conditioning system and associated incidental design work. The court there found that the agreement between the customer and the engineer was "free from any element of fraud, incompetence, or misrepresentation" and was "in no way inimical to life, health, property or public welfare." Id. at 191, 100 N.W.2d at 824. The same, unfortunately, cannot be said about the contract between HomeElderCare and Mr. Nelson.

There are significant factual differences between the situation in Weatherston's and the present case as to the critical issue of competence. Mr. Weatherston, though unlicensed, was nonetheless competent and supervised. He had a bachelor of science degree in mechanical engineering, several years of experience in project engineering, and licensure in other states. He was clearly a competent professional. In addition, he was supervised by another engineer and an architect on behalf of the client; his proposals were actually subject to their approval. See id. at 186-88, 100 N.W.2d at 821-22.

By contrast, social worker Hall is not well trained in the law. She is not licensed as an attorney in Minnesota or any other state. She has not attended law school. She simply heard a brief presentation on the general subject of living wills. Having completed only ten living wills, Ms. Hall can boast of only minimal experience in this area. Thus, Ms. Hall cannot meet the standards of a fully competent professional, unlike the engineer in Weatherston's. Furthermore, Hall works independently and is not under the supervision of a lawyer.

The issue of competence is critical, given Weatherston's focus on legislative purpose, id. at 191, 100 N.W.2d at 823-24, and the intent of the legislature in enacting the unauthorized practice statute. The purpose of that statute is to protect the public from the very serious harm that can result from the practice of law by incompetent individuals not subject to direct supervision of the courts. See Peterson, 230 Minn. at 484-85, 42 N.W.2d at 63-64. The error in Mr. Nelson's living will, drafted by social worker Hall, is a perfect example of the type of harm the legislation is designed to prevent. Enforcement of the contract would effectively endorse activity that harmed Mr. Nelson and runs contrary to the public interest as determined by the legislature.

Finally, HomeElderCare clearly stands to gain from enforcement of the contract as a result of the fee charged Mr. Nelson. Although the living will itself might be enforceable, the Minnesota Supreme Court indicated in Peterson that "a different situation arises where an unlicensed practitioner seeks to recover fees for his performance of legal services." Id. at 481, 42 N.W.2d at 62. And unlike Weatherston's, HomeElderCare is seeking payment precisely for the unauthorized legal services, not for a broader contract that incidentally includes legal services. A social worker should not be paid for defective legal work.

Your notes in margin

In summary, the contract between HomeElderCare and Mr. Nelson is tainted by incompetence, thus violates the statutory purpose of protecting the public from defective legal work performed by non-lawyers, and yet provides compensation to HomeElderCare for that work. The trial court properly deemed the contract unenforceable, and the declaratory judgment should be affirmed.

CONCLUSION

The trial court's grant of summary declaratory judgment for Mr. Nelson should be affirmed because the trial court properly ruled that

(1) HomeElderCare engaged in the unauthorized practice of law, in violation of Minn. Stat. § 481.02;

(2) the contract between HomeElderCare and Mr. Nelson is thus unenforceable.

Dated: Feb. 10, 1994   Respectfully submitted,

                                              By: Albert Frank
                                              Albert Frank (No. 14711)
                                              Attorney for Respondent Roger Nelson
                                              Law Offices of Albert Frank
                                              672 Oak Street
                                              Versailles, MN 50001
                                              (222) 777-7771

Nelson v. HomeElderCare Argument
Before Intermediate Appellate Court

Note to Readers:

This is a transcript of a mock appellate oral argument for *Nelson v. HomeElderCare* at the Minnesota Court of Appeals, which is the intermediate appellate court in Minnesota. The judges were portrayed by Professors Ken Kirwin, Denise Roy, and Curt Stine; they are on the faculty at William Mitchell College of Law. Arguing the case are law students Katie Crosby Lehmann and Tony Massaros. The time limits being observed in this case were 12 minutes for the appellant's main argument, 12 minutes for the respondent's argument, and 3 minutes for the rebuttal.

As you read each question from the judge, ask yourself how you would have answered the question; then read the advocate's answer and evaluate it against your own.

Judge 2: You may begin, counsel.

Chief judge recognizes Appellant's counsel

Appellant's Counsel: May it please the court. My name is Katie Crosby Lehmann, and I represent appellant HomeElderCare. I wish to reserve three minutes for rebuttal.

Introduction of counsel and client; reserve rebuttal time

There are two issues that we will discuss today. The first deals with whether HomeElderCare social workers engage in the unauthorized practice of law while preparing living wills for their clients. The second issue is whether Respondent Nelson's contract for the living will preparation is valid due to unauthorized practice of law concerns, fraud, and incompetency concerns.

Roadmap of 2 main issues (Introduction)

The facts have been stipulated to by the parties. HomeElderCare is a private, non-profit corporation that employs a staff of geriatric social workers. The social workers provide various services to their clients upon their clients' request. HomeElderCare clients asked HomeElderCare to offer them an additional service: the service of preparing living wills for them. HomeElderCare agreed with their clients' request and now offers the service. The fee for this service is based on the time of completion. The fee is no different for this service than any other service.

Fact statement
■ *HomeElderCare*

Kimberly Hall is a social worker for HomeElderCare. She is highly educated and trained in living will preparation. She has been a social worker for over twelve years. She prepared Mr. Nelson's living will. A living will states the signer's medical treatment desires if and when the signer becomes incapacitated. Mr. Nelson is 78 years old and in declining health due to diabetes. Mr. Nelson's living will did not exactly reflect his wishes. However, there is no evidence that it was Ms. Hall versus Mr. Nelson himself who caused this misstatement. Ms. Hall believes she suggested Mr. Nelson to see an attorney if he had any further questions regarding his living will. Mr. Nelson's own son is an attorney, and he did not speak to his son or any other attorney.

■ *preparation of living will*

■ *procedural posture*

Respondent sued HomeElderCare seeking to void his contract for the living will preparation service and requested a declaratory judgment to determine the validity of the contract. Both parties moved for summary judgment. The district court granted Respondent's declaratory judgment and summary judgment. The district court held that the living will preparation service constituted the unauthorized practice of law and that the contract for such services was invalid. HomeElderCare appeals. The standard of review of appeal is de novo.

■ *standard of review*

Argument
■ *1st argument: unau-
   thorized practice of
   law*

The first issue addresses the unauthorized practice of law concern, joined with the difficult and doubtful legal question test. The Minnesota Supreme Court held that when a person's primary business is not to provide legal services, a person may dabble in the law so long as he or she is not answering difficult or doubtful legal questions. The unauthorized practice of law statute states that "it shall be unlawful for any person except members of the Bar of Minnesota for a fee to give legal advice or counsel or to prepare for another person any other legal document." The unauthorized practice of law statute must be analyzed with the supreme court's difficult and doubtful legal question test. This test is measured by a reasonably intelligent person, not a lawyer, with knowledge of similar transactions. The test is to be applied in a common sense way with the goal of protecting primarily the interests of the public without burdening the public with technical restrictions. It is a flexible test and demands a case-by-case analysis.

*difficult and doubtful
legal question test*

*3 examples that were
not difficult and doubtful
legal questions*

What is and what is not a difficult and doubtful question is not crystal clear. The following examples, all involving the charging of a fee, have been held to not be difficult and doubtful legal questions. The first is preparing a tax return, including calculating income in taxable years. The second is preparing documents for a real estate closing, answering questions on the real estate closing documents, and lastly, completing an affidavit and assignment for contract for deed.

*question about whether
real estate example is
distinguishable*

Judge 3: Counsel, my understanding is that real estate documents are pretty fixed in their content, whereas the living will statute talks about the form being substantially in the form as in the statute. Doesn't that suggest that deviation from the form is permitted so that's somewhat different from the real estate documents?

answer clarifying facts

Appellant's Counsel: That's a question that really is beyond what the HomeElderCare service does. HomeElderCare social workers do not deviate from the forms. They think that if they deviate or interpret the form at all, then you could be reaching the line of what is a difficult and doubtful question.

*further question about
HEC's practices*

Judge 3: But if they don't deviate from the form, is it possible that they are channeling people into a particular format, whether it fits that particular person's needs or not?

*further clarification of
facts*

Appellant's Counsel: The form they use is the statutorily approved living will form. This is the only service that they offer their clients. The clients come to them, and they ask them to help them guide them through the completion of this form. If their clients wish to alter or deviate or if they have any concerns about following the form, then the social worker stops what they are doing and directs the person to see an attorney.

final clarifying question

Judge 3: So that any deviation from the form would constitute the practice of law, you think?

Appellant's Counsel: It could be. It's reaching that fuzzy line of what may be the difficult and doubtful question, but it's really not an issue here because our social workers do not deviate from the form whatsoever.

 An example of what is a difficult and doubtful legal question is when a person holding himself out as a tax expert gives advice on partnerships, valid marriages, common-law marriages, and approvements. Considering these examples, it is clear that a person can complete legal documents or guide another through a legal document as long as it is only an incidental part of the person's business and it does not involve answering difficult and doubtful legal questions.

Judge 1: Well, counsel, doesn't the last page of the living will form refer to such concepts as proxy and guardian and conservator? Aren't those just as difficult or complicated concepts as the ones that you just referred to?

Appellant's Counsel: Those are legal terms, but the social workers have been trained by an attorney on the definitions of those terms. The social workers in return offer those definitions to their clients. If that does not satisfy their clients' needs, the social worker recommends that the client seek an attorney's advice for further explanation. Because they are limiting themselves on what they do explain to the clients, they are not reaching the line of a difficult and doubtful legal question. The social workers simply lead their clients through the living will form. They answer simple questions on definitions and, therefore, because they are not deviating from the form or altering the form in any way, they do not reach the line of answering difficult and doubtful legal questions and are not practicing law.

Judge 2: Can you help us by telling us what kind of problems the clients have in filling out the forms? Why do they need assistance at all in going through the form?

Appellant's Counsel: The clients came to HomeElderCare and asked them to offer this service to them. They want HomeElderCare to provide the statutorily approved form to them, read through the form with them, and answer simple questions as they go along. What the social workers do is take the clients' answers to the forms and fill in the form. After it is filled in, the client and the social worker go over the form to make sure it fits the clients' needs. At the end, the social worker recommends that if the client has any further questions, they seek an attorney for more detailed explanation.

 HomeElderCare does charge a fee for this service. The fee in the past has triggered the difficult and doubtful legal question test. However, it is only a factor in the unauthorized practice of law analysis. Charging a fee cannot convert an otherwise lawful transaction into the unauthorized practice of law. Because the service is lawful and the fee is reasonable, the service is valid.

Judge 1: Excuse me, Counsel. Isn't this quite different from the previous cases where the work was really incident to some other transaction, like preparing a tax return or closing a real estate transaction? Here the work is actually just doing the document.

Appellant's Counsel: It is different from the previous examples; however, it is different in a better way. The HomeElderCare clients are only being charged for exactly the time it takes a social worker to lead them through the forms. In the real estate example, the client was being charged whether or not

---

answer

4 examples that were difficult and doubtful legal questions

question about whether examples are analogous to HEC

answer distinguishing HEC's practices

factual question

answer

relevance of fee

question about whether HEC's practices are distinguishable from cases that were not difficult or doubtful legal questions

answer that the factual differences are not distinguishing differences

the work was performed or not. So we think this is an even fairer way to establish the fee calculation system.

The beginning of the statutory living will form states that the living will is a legal document. A driver's license, employee handbook, and purchase agreements are also legal documents. The unauthorized practice of law statute refers to legal documents but surely it does not require all legal documents to be completed by attorneys. The purpose of the unauthorized practice of law statute is to protect the public from fraudulent legal service. This purpose is not served by limiting the living will preparation to attorneys only. Requiring attorneys to complete the living will form runs counter to the purpose of the living will statute; the living will is to be distributed and used by members of the public. Therefore, completing the living will does not constitute the unauthorized practice of law.

The second issue deals with the validity of Mr. Nelson's contract with HomeElderCare for the living will preparation service. Respondent must prove two issues to establish the invalidity of the contract. First, Respondent must prove that the contract constitutes unauthorized practice of law and second, that the contract involved fraudulent or incompetent service. The unauthorized practice of law has already been discussed, and it's clear that social workers are not answering difficult and doubtful legal questions and are not engaging in the unauthorized practice of law. Even if it is found that the unauthorized practice of law exists, the contract is valid if there is no harm to the public due to fraudulent or incompetent service. The social workers have completed over forty forms for satisfied clients. There is no evidence that it was Ms. Hall versus Respondent himself who caused misstatement of Respondent's living will.

Judge 3: Counsel, have any of the living wills executed under the supervision of your client's employees actually been used? Have any of the persons who executed them become terminal and, therefore, someone had to take a careful look at the document?

Appellant's Counsel: None of the clients have become terminal; however, we are confident in our social workers' ability to complete the living will forms competently.

Judge 2: Counsel, does anyone such as an attorney periodically review the forms that have been completed to see how the social workers are performing?

Appellant's Counsel: No. The social workers follow all the instructions on the living will form, and that is not one of the instructions included on the form.

There is no evidence of fraudulent or incompetent service by the social workers. If we deem the living contracts invalid, we are only harming the people who ask for the service—the elderly clients in need of the emotional support of HomeElderCare social workers. The social workers can ably perform this service and provide their clients with the emotional support.

In conclusion, HomeElderCare and Ms. Hall request the court to vacate the district courts' declaratory judgment, reverse the summary judgment in favor of Respondent, and rule that HomeElderCare's preparation of Mr. Nelson's living will does not involve unauthorized practice of law or incompetent service, and rule that the contract is valid.

Judge 2: All right, counsel. Go ahead.

Respondent's Counsel: May it please the Court, my name is Tony Massaros, and I am counsel for Mr. Roger Nelson.

*Introduction of counsel and client
Theme (Introduction)*

The issue in this case is whether a social worker should be paid for incompetent legal work.

Fact statement (clarification of Appellant's facts)

While opposing counsel has generally stated the facts accurately, I would like to make a few clarifications so as to make perfectly clear what it is we are dealing with in this case. In light of Mr. Nelson's age and condition he desired to put his affairs in order now so that if he became incapacitated his wishes would be respected. A HomeElderCare social worker, a non-lawyer, prepared a living will in a way that did not reflect Mr. Nelson's wishes as to the person to be designated as his guardian. Fortunately, a lawyer corrected the document before any serious harm occurred to Mr. Nelson.

My argument today has two points. First, HomeElderCare engaged in the unauthorized practice of law. Second, the contract between HomeElder-Care and Mr. Nelson is, therefore, unenforceable. In short, the decision by the district court was correct and should be affirmed by this court. The main point that I would like you to remember is that a social worker should not receive payment for poorly performed legal work.

*Argument
—roadmap of 2 main issues; summary*

—theme reiterated

Beginning first with the unauthorized practice of law: the Minnesota unauthorized practice of law statute was violated by HomeElderCare in two ways. First, non-lawyer Kimberly Hall prepared a legal document. Second, she provided legal advice and counsel. Either one of these actions is sufficient to find a violation of the statute.

■ *1st argument: unauthorized practice of law
two violations*

The Minnesota unauthorized practice of law statute makes it unlawful for non-attorneys to prepare legal documents for a fee. A living will is a legal document. Indeed, the legislature specifically characterized the sample form as "an important legal document." The plain meaning of the term also supports such an interpretation. Kimberly Hall is not an attorney. She is a social worker who prepared a living will for a fee and thereby engaged in the unauthorized practice of law.

1st violation: "legal document" preparation

Secondly, while opposing counsel characterizes the social worker's actions as merely guiding the elderly patients through the process of creating a living will, a more accurate characterization is that the social worker in this case actually gave legal advice and counsel to Mr. Nelson. An individual practices law if difficult or doubtful legal questions are involved which, to safeguard the public, require legal expertise.

2nd violation: legal advice and counsel

Judge 3: Counsel, my understanding is that the legislature enacting the living will statute intended for the document to be very easily executed. It did adopt two different ways to execute the document. Wouldn't it be appropriate for this court to authorize persons other than lawyers, such as social workers, to help with the execution of these documents? The legislature has indicated that it is the policy of the state to encourage this document for persons.

question about legislative intent and policy

Respondent's Counsel: It is true that the legislature has made clear that it believes it is good public policy to encourage the use of living wills. We don't see that there is really any conflict between that policy and the policy underlying the unauthorized practice of law statute. We think the two can coexist very comfortably. What we have here, though, is a situation where the policies that guide the unauthorized practice of law statute—namely, to protect the public from the very serious harm that can result from activities or actions by individuals who are not lawyers—that should be given the primary consideration.

answer reconciling policies of the 2 statutes

question about medical
issues in living will

Judge 3: But don't the issues that arise under the content of the living will—they are medical issues, are they not, not legal issues—decisions as to what kind of medical care someone might take? Isn't it true that geriatric social workers might indeed have more knowledge of medical issues than would a lawyer?

answer highlighting
legal issues in living will

Respondent's Counsel: It is true that there are certainly a lot of medical issues involved in the living will form, but there are also a good number of legal issues as well that we believe require expertise in order to provide a proper service to these clients. We see a social worker discussing the role of proxies, guardians, and conservators; explaining the legal obligations of doctors; explaining the document to the client's witness and proxy.

question about whether
they are difficult and
doubtful questions
answer highlighting
HEC facts

Judge 1: Are those really such difficult and doubtful issues? Isn't it fairly simple to explain in everyday language what a proxy or a conservator is?

Respondent's Counsel: Well, we think that it is difficult and doubtful, and we think the proof of that is actually the fact of this case. And we had a situation here where the person that Mr. Nelson wanted to be his guardian was in fact not made his guardian as a result of the actions of HomeElderCare. So we believe that indeed there are difficult and doubtful legal questions being addressed here, and therefore the actions of the HomeElderCare social workers did indeed constitute the unauthorized practice of law.

question about purpose
of living will statute

Judge 1: Isn't it likely that if we don't allow this to be done by the social workers that it won't be done at all? Wouldn't that run contrary to the legislature's purpose to encourage living wills?

answer countering with
purpose of unauthorized
practice of law statute

Respondent's Counsel: We believe that there are certainly a lot of other options, a lot of other ways, that the living will can be completed for these individuals. What we're saying here is that in this case the HomeElderCare social workers should not be providing legal advice and counsel in the process of creating those living wills. We believe that the individuals themselves could easily do it—could complete the form. They could have friends and family do it. But the key that we have here is, we have legal advice and counsel being provided by somebody who is not authorized and licensed to practice law. And that's really the issue that we have here, not so much the question of whether or not living wills are appropriate or whether or not the legislature is encouraging the use of living wills. What we have here is a need to protect the public from people practicing law who are not competent to practice law. We believe that the difficult and doubtful questions are clearly evidenced by the facts of this case and that it took somebody trained in the law to fix the document that was drafted by the HomeElderCare social workers.

question challenging as-
sumptions in previous
answer

Judge 1: Well, don't the facts of this case indicate that the friends and relatives or other people that you mentioned are apparently not filling this need, because HomeElderCare apparently did do some forty wills and charged, at least in this case, $80, and that shows that there is a need for the service, doesn't it?

clarifying answer

Respondent's Counsel: It shows that they did that. I don't know that it shows that that is the only alternative that was available. They do provide other services that require legal expertise in those areas—for example, testamentary wills, with real estate transactions—there they have also provided service to the HomeElderCare clients and there they have acted primarily as a liaison with attorneys, recognizing that they really don't have the skill and ability to engage in this sort of activity.

Judge 3: Counsel, I'm a bit concerned as to where you would have us draw the line. Are you saying that if a person were brought to a hospital losing consciousness—about to lose the capacity to execute a document of this sort—that the people at the medical facility could not assist in the execution of the document? We'd have to wait until an attorney was called to come?

Respondent's Counsel: No, I don't think that we would say that that was the case. I think if a person in that situation—a hospital worker, for example—just wrote down exactly what the patient wanted, there was no discussion of what the terms mean but basically did it in a sort of clerical way, I don't think that we would have the unauthorized practice of law in such a situation.

Judge 3: But isn't that what happened here?

Respondent's Counsel: Well, we don't believe that it is. In fact, we have the record which indicates that they explain the document to the doctors, they explain it to the proxies, they explain it to the witnesses, and they actually oversee the execution of the document. So we have something very much more involved here than simply completing a form.

The second point that I would like to cover is the question of the enforceability of the contract between HomeElderCare and Mr. Nelson. It's clearly established that if a statute requires licensing a person to perform a professional service and a person who is unlicensed enters into a contract to do that, then that contract is generally considered void. And we believe that that's what we have here and that the contract between HomeElderCare and Mr. Nelson should therefore be unenforceable.

Judge 2: Counsel, don't you also have to show fraud or incompetence in order to prevail on the contract claim?

Respondent's Counsel: That is true, Your Honor, and we believe that we have clear evidence of incompetence here. The proof of this is that the living will had to be redone; it had to be revised so that the interests of Mr. Nelson were met, so that his desires were satisfied. So we believe that indeed we do have evidence of incompetence in this case.

Judge 1: Well, opposing counsel indicates that the record is unclear as to whether it was maybe Mr. Nelson's own misunderstanding that caused this. We don't really have it clear on the record that it was the HomeElderCare worker's incompetence that produced this. Isn't that true?

Respondent's Counsel: I think that we can make the assumption that indeed it was the incompetence of the HomeElderCare social worker. I think that this further demonstrates why you need somebody with a trained legal background to make these kinds of decisions so that these kinds of questions are not at issue after we have the living will being formed.

Judge 3: Counsel, real estate agents often execute legal documents related to real estate; they have expertise in the area. Here we're dealing with social workers who have expertise in this particular area. Why shouldn't we treat them like real estate agents, who are authorized to conduct these affairs?

*answer on separate leg-
islative treatment*

*Conclusion and request
for relief*

*Chief Judge recognizes
Appellant's counsel for
rebuttal*
■ *2 main points*

*response to counter-
argument on unautho-
rized practice of law*

no changes in form

*suitability of social
workers for answering
living will questions*

clients' needs

*response to counter-
argument on contract
validity; no incompe-
tence*

*question about trust and
vulnerability of clients*

answer clarifying facts

Respondent's Counsel: Well, I think the difference, Your Honor, is that with the real estate transactions the legislature has chosen to carve out an exception for real estate agents who engage in certain activities such as closing and other real estate related matters. So I think that we have a very different situation there than we do in the situation involving HomeElderCare.

In conclusion, the district court's decision should be affirmed. There was an unauthorized practice of law, and the contract between HomeElderCare and Mr. Nelson is therefore unenforceable. A social worker should not be paid for incompetent, unlicensed, irresponsible legal work.

Thank you.

Judge 2: You may begin.

Appellant's Counsel: HomeElderCare social workers do not hold themselves out as attorneys. The social workers simply want to offer their clients a complete range of services to meet their clients' medical and emotional needs.

Opposing counsel stated that Ms. Hall gave legal advice and counsel to Mr. Nelson. In order to practice law, Ms. Hall and any HomeElderCare social worker would need to answer difficult and doubtful legal questions and violate the unauthorized practice of law statute. Ms. Hall and all HomeElderCare social workers do not make deviations or alterations to the living will form. They simply provide the form to their clients, read the form through with their clients, and fill in the blanks with the answers the clients provide them. They are not answering difficult or doubtful legal questions, and they are not engaging in the unauthorized practice of law.

The social workers are exactly the people who should provide this service to their elderly clients. They can build on their existing relationship with their clients. They are trained in medical and ethical issues affecting the elderly and the terminally ill. The social workers are better qualified than an attorney to answer these medical and ethical questions. There is no need for an attorney to complete this living will form because the social workers are competent and they are not engaging in the unauthorized practice of law or answering difficult and doubtful legal questions.

The living will service by HomeElderCare is a service created at their HomeElderCare clients' request. The social workers do not answer difficult and doubtful legal questions; therefore, there is no concern about the unauthorized practice of law.

Mr. Nelson is 78 years old and in declining health. There is no evidence that the misstatement in his living will was due to Ms. Hall's incompetence versus an answer Mr. Nelson provided to Ms. Hall when Ms. Hall completed Mr. Nelson's living will.

Judge 2: Counsel, I'm concerned about the trust level that the HomeElderCare clients have in the social workers. It seems to me that the very trust that they place in those workers could lead them to give undue weight to any kind of—it wouldn't be legal advice, but—legal definitions provided by the social workers, and that they could be lulled into a sense of security in filling out these forms where they ought to be more questioning about what the meaning of the form is.

Appellant's Counsel: At t\he end of the preparation of each living will, the social worker does recommend that the client seek an attorney's advice if they have any further questions or concerns. HomeElderCare does provide their social workers with training and education in the preparation of these forms. The training was done by an attorney, so there really is no concern that the definitions would be inaccurate.

The social workers are protecting their clients' interest and serving the public interest by offering this living will preparation service. Without this service it is likely that the clients will not have a living will if and when they become incapacitated.

Judge 2: Counsel, your time's up. Thank you.

Appellant's Counsel: Thank you.

Chief Judge ends oral argument time period

APPENDIX A

SENTENCE STRUCTURE

AND WORD USAGE

Easy-Reference List
A. Reader Expectations and Energy Expenditures
B. The Relationship Between Subject and Verb
C. Verbs
D. Relationships Among Clauses and Phrases
E. Nouns and Pronouns
F. Word Choice
G. Punctuation

EASY-REFERENCE LIST FOR APPENDIX A

This appendix examines sentence structure and word usage from the perspective of reader expectation theory—that is, how to tailor sentences to meet the reader's underlying linguistic assumptions and preferences, to produce text that the reader can easily read and understand. This appendix highlights issues of sentence structure and word usage that frequently are a concern in legal writing or are commonly troublesome to legal writers. If you have questions about topics not covered here, consult a grammar book.

A. READER EXPECTATIONS AND ENERGY EXPENDITURES

Readers come to the activity of reading with expectations about grammar, word usage, punctuation, and other aspects of sentence structure. The more formal the prose, the more likely that its readers expect their expectations to be honored. Legal writing is fairly formal prose, so reader expectations are high. To increase your awareness of reader expectations, imagine a crowd of prospective readers hovering over your shoulder, asking you questions like the following: "How does this part fit with that part?" "Must I really read this long sentence?" "What does this passage mean?"

Furthermore, legal readers are well educated, so they have acquired extensive and precise expectations about the prose they read. And legal readers value (and often bill) their professional time, so they want writing that they can read quickly. If the writer's prose is grammatically correct and easy to read, the reader will think more highly of the written analysis. The greater the number of grammatical errors and difficult-to-read passages, the more convinced the reader becomes that the writer does not have a mastery of the English language. The reader may then question the validity of the writer's analysis. This is due to the "halo effect": If we judge a person positively or negatively on one aspect, we have a tendency to judge that person similarly on other aspects.

Reader expectations can be requirements or preferences. *Requirements* outrank all other writing considerations. Writing that does not meet these requirements jars the reader, prompts the reader to re-read some material, and causes a major break in the reader's progress. For instance, readers expect that a singular verb will follow a singular noun. Note your reaction to the following sentence:

A reader expect that a singular verb will follow a singular noun.

Was your attention jarred at some point? Did you reread a portion of the sentence?

Other reader expectations are merely *preferences*. Writing that does not conform to these preferences may slow down and distract the reader, who then devotes mental energy to figuring out the sentence's structure and therefore pays less attention to the sentence's meaning. For instance, consider the following sentence:

> Although the validity of the patient's living will is debatable because its form deviates from the form in the statute, it is doubtful that there will be any challenge to its validity because everyone knows that the wishes in the living will are clearly those of the patient.

Did your attempts to decipher the structure distract your attention from the meaning?

Thus, some reader expectations are based on requirements, and others are based on preferences. Requirements are unavoidable, while preferences are norms that occasionally can be disregarded in favor of countervailing considerations. This appendix will cover both.[1]

B. THE RELATIONSHIP BETWEEN SUBJECT AND VERB

This part discusses the core of the sentence—the subject and its verb. A reader starts to read a sentence by looking for these: a subject, because it usually tells who the actor of the sentence is, and its verb, because the verb usually tells what the actor is doing. Everything else in the sentence is secondary.

1. Subject-Verb Agreement

The reader expects that a plural verb will describe the action of a plural subject and that a singular verb will describe the action of a singular subject. This *requirement* is violated when the subject is singular and its verb is plural, or vice versa. Subject-verb disagreement often occurs when many words intrude between subject and verb (in italics). For example:

> The living will *form* that appears in the statute and that was used by the clients *are* valid.

The easiest way to catch this error is to find the core of the sentence and then match subject to verb. In the example above, the word "clients" lured the writer into using a plural verb instead of the required singular verb. The true subject is "form," and its verb should be "is."

---

1. For additional help with grammar, consult the following books written for legal writers: Lynn B. Squires et al., *Legal Writing in a Nutshell* (2d ed. 1996); Richard Wydick, *Plain English for Lawyers* (4th ed. 1998). *See also* any college-level grammar book, such as H. Ramsey Fowler, Jane E. Aaron, & Jo Koster Tarvers, *The Little, Brown Handbook* (6th ed. 1995).

2. Subject-Verb Proximity

Readers *prefer* the subject and verb of a sentence to be close together, so their connection is clear. If too many words appear between the subject and verb, the reader probably will skim over the intervening words. For example:

> The *contract* for payment, **the illegality of which may not be raised by a non-party to the contract,** *may be enforced* by the unpaid party if the contract does not violate public policy.

The subject and its verb (in italics) are separated by a lengthy intervening clause (in boldface) that seems like a parenthetical remark.

Sentences with many words between subject and verb can be revised in various ways:

(1) Reduce the number of words between subject and verb.
(2) Move the intervening words elsewhere in the sentence.
(3) Break the sentence into two sentences, and add an appropriate connector.

In the sample sentence above, the intervening clause cannot be shortened without losing meaning. However, the intervening clause (in boldface) can be moved elsewhere in the sentence, so that the main subject and verb (in italics) are now close together:

> The *contract* for payment *may be enforced* by the unpaid party if the contract does not violate public policy, <u>and</u> **the illegality of** ~~which~~ <u>the contract</u> **may not be raised by a non-party to the contract.**

(The text deleted from the original is printed in strike-out typeface. The added text is underlined.) Or you could break the sentence in two:

> The *contract* for payment *may be enforced* by the unpaid party if the contract does not violate public policy. **The illegality of** ~~which~~ <u>the contract</u> **may not be raised by a non-party to the contract.**

Because subject-verb proximity is a preference, not a requirement, you might decide that some material between the subject and its verb is workable. For instance, the following sentence reads well:

> The *living will,* **which the patient drew up more than fifteen years ago,** *may not reflect* the patient's current views.

The clause between the subject and its verb is brief enough that the reader can process it easily. In addition, the intervening clause gets added reader attention in its location between the subject and its verb.

3. Active and Passive Voice

Each sentence core follows one of five patterns:

subject	verb (intransitive)		
subject	verb (linking)	subject complement	
subject	verb (transitive)	direct object	
subject	verb (transitive)	indirect object	direct object
subject	verb (transitive)	direct object	object complement

Below are examples of these patterns:

client agreed
client was male; client is satisfied
attorney wrote a will
attorney wrote the client a letter
client declares the will accurate

All of these patterns are in "active voice" because (1) the subject noun is the actor of the verb and (2) the verb is in active voice. Active-voice sentences are readily readable because the verb describes the actions of its subject. Hence readers *prefer* active voice.

The latter three patterns (those with transitive verbs) can be transformed into "passive voice" when (1) an object (direct object, indirect object, or object complement) rather than the actor occupies the position of the subject and (2) the verb is in passive voice. Below are the passive-voice versions of the latter three patterns:

will was written by attorney
letter was written to client by attorney
will is declared accurate by client

Passive voice is more difficult for the reader for five reasons. First, contrary to the reader's expectation, the verb does not describe the actions of the subject of the sentence. Second, the passive-voice form of the verb ("was paid," "is declared") is more complex; it consists of a "to be" helping verb ("is," "are," "was," "were", "has been," "had been") and the past participle of the verb. Third, the resulting sentence is wordier. Fourth, the true actor sometimes appears in a prepositional phrase ("by attorney") and sometimes does not appear at all in a passive-voice sentence. For example:

The will is declared accurate. (by whom? the court? the client's relatives?)

Unless the actor is apparent from context, the reader wonders who did the action in the sentence. Fifth, passive voice increases the chance of a misplaced modifier, which is a word or phrase that seems to modify an adjacent word but really modifies a more distant word. For example:

Active: Satisfied with the will, the *client* paid the attorney.
Passive: Satisfied with the will, the attorney was paid by the *client.*

The reader expects the subject of the sentence also to be the actor of this introductory verb clause. The active-voice sentence above meets that expectation ("satisfied with will" modifies "client"). The passive-voice sentence does not.

You can test for passive voice in two ways: (1) Discern whether the verb is in passive voice ("to be" helping verb + past participle of verb). (2) Or locate the verb in question ("to pay," "to declare"), and ask who is the actor of that verb (who's paying? who's declaring?). If that actor is in the subject position, the sentence is in active voice, but if that actor is missing or is elsewhere in the sentence (usually in a prepositional phrase), the sentence is in passive voice.

Active voice is a *preference,* not a requirement, but you should not use passive voice when you do not know why you are using it. Here are eight settings in which passive voice is useful:

First, use passive voice when the actor (in italics) of the action is unknown. For example:

Active: *Someone* delivered the living will to the physician.
Passive: The living will was delivered to the physician.

Second, use passive voice when you want to de-emphasize the true actor (in italics) of the verb.

Third, use passive voice when you want to dilute the power of the verb (in boldface). Both are illustrated below:

Active: *My client* **drafted** a defective living will.
Passive: A defective living will **was drafted.**

Fourth, use passive voice when you want to emphasize the direct object (in italics). For example:

Active: Only the parties to the contract can raise the *defense* of the contract's illegality.
Passive: The *defense* of the contract's illegality can be raised only by the parties to the contract.

Fifth, use passive voice to avoid some misplaced modifiers. As already noted, the reader expects an introductory verb clause to modify the word in the subject position (in italics). If the introductory clause really modifies the direct object (in boldface), then active voice creates a misplaced modifier, while passive voice does not. For example:

Active: Being of sound mind but weak body, the *attorney* urged the **testator** to update her will. (misplaced modifier)
Passive: Being of sound mind but weak body, the *testator* was urged to update her will. (no misplaced modifier)

Sixth, use passive voice to facilitate the use of pronouns or to avoid pronoun confusion (in italics). For example:

> Active: The testator's brother urged the testator to cancel *his* bequest. (Does "his" mean the bequest going to the brother, or does it mean some other bequest by the testator?)
> Passive: The testator was urged to cancel *his* bequest. (Now "his" can mean only the testator's.)

Seventh, use passive voice to avoid gender-based pronouns. For example:

> Active: The social worker drafts the living will. *He or she* then notifies the proxy when the signing will be.
> Passive: The social worker drafts the living will. The proxy then is notified when the signing will be.

Eighth, use passive voice so that you can use a single subject for two verbs. For example:

> Both active: The legal community *had anticipated* the ruling for years. Therefore, the ruling *raised* nary an eyebrow.
> Passive, then active: This ruling *had been anticipated* for years and therefore *raised* nary an eyebrow.

Thus, although active voice is the norm, passive voice has a place in carefully crafted prose when you know why you are using it.

4. Postponed Subjects

Some sentences mimic the effect of passive voice because the true actor is not in the subject position. Instead, the main clause of the sentence begins with "there is," "there exists," or "it is [adjective] that . . . ." The remainder of the sentence contains the true actor and its action. For that reason, this type of construction is called a "postponed subject." For example:

> *There is* a living will form in the statute.
> *There existed* some concern that the living will was not accurate.
> *It is possible that* the client will not understand the language of the form.

The reader must expend mental energy looking for the real actor and the real action, buried later in the sentence. The sentence sounds diluted in its power because the opening clause has little or no meaning, while the true actor and its action lie embedded in the remainder of the sentence.

The solution is to delete the weak opening and rewrite the remainder. For example:

The statute contains a living will form.
_____ was concerned that the living will was not accurate.
The client may not understand the language of the form.

C. VERBS

Verbs are the most powerful words in the English language and hence have considerable impact on readers. Legal readers expect legal writing to follow general conventions for verb tense, as well as the conventions of the legal profession.

1. Verb Tenses

Readers expect consistency in the writer's verb tense decisions, so that a particular event is always discussed in the same tense, such as past or present, throughout the paper. Experienced legal readers expect even more consistency; in legal writing, the following aspects are nearly always discussed in the following tenses:

> *Rules of law, reasoning*
>   former (repealed, overturned)   past tense
>   current (in force, in use, valid)   present tense
>   future (not yet in effect, proposed)   future tense
> *Facts, actions of courts and legislatures*
>   past facts and actions   past tense
>   pending facts and actions   present tense
>   future facts and actions   future tense

Pending facts and actions may include current negotiations of a dispute or an undecided motion before the court. The following passage demonstrates these tenses:

> In 1960, the <u>Weatherston's</u> court *held* that the contract between an unlicensed professional and a client *was* enforceable. The court *based* its holding on the policy that the public should be protected against certain kinds of hazards but that other contracts should remain valid. Since this case, the rule in Minnesota *is* that an unlicensed professional *can* enter into a valid contract if the following conditions *are* met: . . .

Sometimes a writer needs more time-frames than just the *simple tenses* of past, present, and future. The writer also can use the *perfect tenses,* which show completion of an action before a particular time ("had held," "has held," "will have held"), and the *progressive tenses,* which show that an action continues over a particular time period ("was holding," "is holding," "will be holding"). Below is a list of these verb tenses, ordered from distant past to future:

Tense	Examples	Timing
past perfect	had held	action completed in past before another past action

past perfect progressive	had been holding	action continuing and completed in past before another past action
past progressive	was holding	continuing action in past
simple past	held	past
present perfect	has held	action that began in past and is linked to present
present perfect progressive	has been holding	action that began in past and is continuing in present
present progressive	is holding	continuing action in present
simple present	holds	present
future perfect	will have held	action that will be completed before another future action
future perfect progressive	will have been holding	action that will be continuing and completed before another future action
future progressive	will be holding	continuing action in future
future	will hold	future

For example, a fact statement might include the following tenses:

past perfect	HomeElderCare *had instituted* a will drafting service three years before Mr. Nelson's contract with HEC.
past perfect progressive	Its social workers *had been assisting* clients with various projects.
past	When Mr. Nelson and the HEC social worker *met*,
past	she *explained* to him his responsibilities.
past	Subsequently, the client's son *discovered*
past perfect	that the social worker *had drafted* the living will against his father's wishes.
past	and the client then *sued* HEC

present progressive	and the state *is contemplating* whether to seek an injunction.
present	The client *claims* that
past	HEC *engaged* in the unauthorized practice of law
past	when it *drafted* . . . .

Note that the transition words "subsequently" and "then" tell the reader that the past tense covers earlier and later time frames. Transition words like this help make your gradations of time even clearer to the reader.

Verb tense consistency is a *requirement*. Using the verb tense conventions of the legal profession is a *preference*.

2. Verb Moods

Verb mood gives additional information about the verb beyond its tense. The three verb moods are indicative, imperative, and subjunctive:

Mood	*Attitude*	*Example*
indicative	fact, opinion, or question	The contract *is* valid. *Is* the contract valid?
imperative	command or direction	*Ignore* irrelevancies. *Be* unbiased.
subjunctive	suggestion, desire, requirement, or condition contrary to fact	She suggested that he *consult* . . . . The statute requires that signatures *be* notarized. . . . Had she *advised* him otherwise, . . . If she *were* to draft the living will, . . .

The above uses of verb mood are *requirements,* except that a condition contrary to fact may or may not be stated in subjunctive mood. The subjunctive mood can be skillfully used in legal advocacy to state a condition contrary to fact (a hypothetical) when that condition is contrary to a client's interest, so you want to make it sound as unlikely as possible. A hypothetical sounds more likely when stated in indicative mood and less likely when stated in subjunctive mood, as shown below:

> Indicative: If a social worker *drafts* a living will erroneously, the client and the client's family *will suffer.*
> Subjunctive: If a social worker *were to draft* a living will erroneously, the client and the client's family *would suffer.*

Either statement is correct, so your choice of mood for hypotheticals depends on how likely or unlikely you want the hypothetical to sound. The attorney representing HomeElderCare would choose the subjunctive mood, while the opposing attorney would choose the indicative mood.

2. Split Infinitives and Other Verb Phrases

Generally, a verb phrase (in italics) can be interrupted with a single-word adverb (in boldface) without disrupting the sentence. For example:

The client *had* **recently** *asked* the social workers about a living will.

However, lengthier interruptions (in boldface) typically dilute the power of the verb and read awkwardly. For example:

HomeElderCare *had,* **based on client input,** *instituted* a living will service.

The solution is to move the interruption elsewhere in the sentence:

Based on client input, HomeElderCare *had instituted* a living will service.

The same problem occurs with "infinitives," which are verbs preceded by the word "to" (for example, "to draft," "to argue"). When one or more words occur between "to" and the verb, this construction is called a "split infinitive." Split infinitives regularly occur in spoken English and are acceptable under modern grammar rules when the interruption is small and the result is not awkward.[2] For example:

To **boldly** *go* where no man has gone before . . .

Larger interruptions should always be avoided. For example:

Split: Are the social workers trained well enough *to,* **in every instance,** *draft* an accurate living will?
Unsplit: Are the social workers trained well enough *to draft* an accurate living will **in every instance?**

After this point, though, grammatical consensus disappears. Some readers still adhere to the "old school" and think poorly of a writer who splits any infinitive. Thus, the absolutely safest course is never to split an infinitive. However, some sentences become more awkward when the infinitive is not split. For example:

Split: The issue is whether the social workers are trained well enough *to* **competently** *draft* living wills.
Unsplit: The issue is whether the social workers are trained well enough *to draft* **competently** living wills.

---

2. *See* H. W. Fowler, *A Dictionary of Modern English Usage* 429, 579-82 (2d ed. Ernest Gowers, ed. 1965) (out of the frying pan, split infinitives); Maxine Hairston & John J. Ruskiewicz, *The Scott, Foresman Handbook for Writers* 316-17 (4th ed. 1996); H. Ramsey Fowler, Jane E. Aaron, & Jo Koster Tarvers, *The Little, Brown Handbook* 288 (6th ed. 1995).

Of course, the ideal solution is to know your reader's preference and cater to it. However, in the legal profession, that solution usually is not possible. You will have to decide for yourself whether (1) to refrain from splitting all infinitives, even when the result is awkwardness, in order to avoid alienating readers who adhere to the outdated rule or (2) to risk occasional reader alienation by occasionally splitting an infinitive with a small interruption in order to avoid awkwardness.

D. RELATIONSHIPS AMONG CLAUSES AND PHRASES

This part looks at how clauses are joined with each other and how their structure affects the meaning of the sentence.

1. One Point per Sentence

A short sentence is more readable than a long sentence because the reader does not have to work so hard to locate the subject and verb of the sentence. A reader who is confronted with a long, bulky sentence may slow down to parse through its structure, or the reader may just move on to the next sentence. Consider the following sentence, which is grammatically correct but very bulky:

> Although the validity of the patient's living will is debatable because its form deviates from the form in the statute, no one likely will challenge its validity because everyone knows that the wishes in the living will are clearly those of the patient.

This sentence is trying to get the following two points across to the reader: "form deviates from statute so living will may not be valid" and "no one will challenge it because it embodies the patient's wishes." To make this sentence more readable, break the sentence into two sentences, as follows:

> The form of the patient's living will deviates from the form in the statute, so it may not be valid. However, no one likely will challenge its validity because it clearly embodies the patient's wishes.

Sometimes this reader *preference* must be disobeyed to meet a format requirement or reader expectations in a particular setting. For instance, a point heading in a brief to the court may be a long sentence, rather than two shorter sentences, because the format demands (and the reader expects) a single sentence.

2. Short Introductory Clauses

Long introductory clauses keep the reader from easily locating the core of the sentence. If the introductory clause is too long, the reader probably will skim over it. Readers *prefer* short introductory clauses. Sentences with long introductory clauses can be revised as follows:

(1) Delete unnecessary words from the introductory clause.
(2) Move the introductory clause to the end of the sentence.
(3) Make the introductory clause into the main clause, and make the former main clause into a dependent clause.
(4) Break the sentence into two sentences, and add an appropriate connector.

In the following sentence, the introductory clause (in italics) cannot be shortened without losing meaning, so the first solution is not possible:

If the company carefully trains its social workers not to give legal or medical advice, the company safely can allow its social workers to assist clients in filling out living wills.

The second solution moves the dependent clause to the end of the sentence and places the main subject and verb at the outset of the sentence, a position that enhances the sentence's readability:

The company safely can allow its social workers to assist clients in filling out living wills, *if it carefully trains its social workers not to give legal or medical advice.*

The third solution turns the introductory clause into the main clause and the main clause into a dependent clause, as follows:

~~If~~ The company <u>*may be able to*</u> carefully ~~trains~~ its social workers not to give legal or medical advice, <u>so that</u> the company safely can allow its social workers to assist clients in filling out living wills.

Be careful that the needed word changes do not subtly change the sentence's meaning. The fourth solution breaks the sentence in two, yielding the following result:

~~If~~ The company <u>*may be able to*</u> carefully ~~trains~~ its social workers not to give legal or medical advice. <u>With this training,</u> the company safely can allow its social workers to assist clients in filling out living wills.

You should choose the solution that best fits with the surrounding text and the emphasis you want to convey. Or you might decide to retain the long introductory clause.

3. "That," "Which," and "Who"

"That" and "which" are relative pronouns; they introduce dependent clauses modifying nouns. Using them properly is a *requirement* of sound writing. In the following correct examples, the relative pronouns are in underlined italics, the dependent clauses are in italics, and the modified nouns are in boldface:

The client's **intent** _that she not remain in an extended coma_ was noted in the living will.

The client's **living will,** _which was drafted in her home,_ accurately reflected her intent.

The choice between the two depends on whether the clause narrows (and thereby "restricts") the modified noun. Clauses that narrow the modified noun begin with "that," are known as "restrictive clauses," and are not set off from the rest of the sentence with commas. Clauses that do not narrow the modified noun, but merely describe some aspect of that noun, begin with "which," are known as "nonrestrictive clauses," and are set off from the rest of the sentence with commas.

In the first example above, the that-clause narrows and restricts which portion of the client's intent is being described; it describes the client's particular intent as to an extended coma. The that-clause is not set off from the rest of the sentence by commas.

In the second example above, the which-clause does not narrow or restrict which living will is being described; it merely describes one aspect of the living will—where it was drafted. The which-clause is set off from the rest of the sentence with commas.

"Who" is used to introduce a dependent clause that modifies a noun describing a person. Who-clauses can be either restrictive or non-restrictive. For example:

The **client** _who wanted a living will_ was pleased with the social worker's assistance.

In this example, the who-clause is not set off from the rest of the sentence with commas because it is restrictive; it specifies which client was pleased.

4. Misplaced and Dangling Modifiers

The reader usually links a modifying word or phrase to the nearest word that could be modified. When the word seemingly modified is the wrong one, the modifier is "misplaced." Avoiding misplaced modifiers is a _requirement_ of good writing. In the following examples, the phrase in italics modifies the noun in boldface, for better or for worse:

Misplaced: The social worker drafted the form for the **client** _using a computer._ (Is the client using the computer?)
Correct: _Using a computer,_ the **social worker** drafted the form for the client.

"Limiting modifiers" (only, hardly, merely, nearly, etc.) frequently are misplaced. They should appear immediately before the word or phrase being modified. In the three correct sentences below, the placement of "only" changes the meaning:

The social workers *only* drafted the living wills in the first month. (They did not do anything besides draft.)

The social workers drafted *only* the living wills in the first month. (They did not draft anything else.)

The social workers drafted the living wills *only* in the first month. (After the first month, they did not draft living wills.)

A common instance of a misplaced modifier involves a "verb phrase," a phrase with a verb but not a subject. The implied subject of an introductory verb phrase (in italics) is supposed to be the subject of the sentence (in boldface). If it is not, the phrase is misplaced. For example:

Misplaced: *Trying not to give legal advice,* the **client** was referred to an attorney by the social worker.
Correct: *Trying not to give legal advice,* the **social worker** referred the client to the attorney.

The misplaced phrase above is caused by passive voice; the corrected sentence is in active voice. Similarly, the misplaced phrase below is caused by a postponed subject; the corrected sentence eliminates that construction.

Misplaced: *Assuming the living will form to be adequate,* **there** was no motivation for the client to raise any other topics.
Correct: *Assuming the living will form to be adequate,* the **client** was not motivated to raise any other topics.

When a modifier does not seem to modify anything in the sentence, the modifier is "dangling," rather than misplaced. In the example below, passive voice is the culprit:

Dangling: *Wondering whether the contracts would be valid,* **counsel** was hired to research the question.
Correct: *Wondering whether the contracts would be valid,* **HomeElder-Care** hired counsel to research the question.

5. Parallel Structure

Readers expect compound sentence elements to use a similar grammatical form. This *requirement* of "parallel structure" applies to lists and to series. A series is a collection of two or more items joined by a coordinating conjunction (and, or, nor, but, yet). In the following correct examples, the series are in italics, and the coordinating conjunctions are in boldface:

The form was *accurate, available,* **and** *helpful.* (series of three adjectives)

The attorney *drafted* the will **and** *met* with the client to make sure the will was accurate. (series of two verbs, both in same tense)

The social worker approached the counseling session *efficiently*, **yet** *compassionately*. (series of two adverbs)

When parallel structure is missing, the result is awkward, jarring, or confusing. As is often the case with parallel structure errors, the sentence below can be read with either of two series in mind (one in italics, and one in boldface), but neither series is in parallel structure:

The living will form in the statute **asks** the signer to state preferences about appropriate health *care*, life-sustaining **treatment**, **giving** artificially administered sustenance, and **explains** the proper use of the form.

Most lists are series and therefore should be in parallel structure. For example:

The statute has four parts: (1) *purpose*, (2) *definitions*, (3) *duties of the officers*, **and** (4) *damages and penalties*. (all nouns)

However, the following "exploded sentence" does not contain compound sentence elements joined by a conjunction, so it is not required to be in parallel structure:

The maker of the living will must (1) sign it (2) in the presence of a witness (3) who is not the proxy.

The numbers above merely segment the sentence into non-coordinate parts.

Parallel structure is required for items joined by correlative conjunctions (either/or, neither/nor, both/and, not only/but also). Note the following correct use of parallel structure (in italics) with correlative conjunctions (in boldface):

The living will was **both** *valid* under the statute **and** *accurate* about the maker's wishes. (two adjectives)

The contract **not only** *set* the flat rate for the living will service, **but also** *specified* that a living will form would be used. (two verbs)

Parallel structure also is required between items being compared or contrasted. Note the following correct sentences:

The living will was **better** *judged* invalid **than** *acted* upon in error. (comparison of two verbs in same tense)

The clients wanted help from *social workers*, **rather than** *attorneys*. (comparison of two nouns)

The clients wanted help *from* social workers, **rather than** *from* attorneys. (comparison of two prepositional phrases)

In the third sentence, the repeated (optional) use of "from" emphasizes the parallel structure.

E. NOUNS AND PRONOUNS

Nouns are words that name people, places, and things. A pronoun can take the place of a nearby noun.

1. Collective Nouns

Legal writing contains many collective nouns that are singular because the group represented by the collective noun functions as a single legal entity. Proper treatment of collective nouns is a *requirement*. For example:

Collective noun (singular)	*Noun representing group members (plural)*
jury	jurors
court	judges or justices
legislature	legislators
board	board members
commission	commissioner
corporation	shareholders
partnership	partners

Once you know whether you are discussing the group (the collective noun) or the persons in the group, you can write the sentence correctly. For example:

> **HomeElderCare** (a corporation) *offers its* clients the services of *its* social workers.

> The supreme **court** *has ruled* against the appellants. But several **justices** *have written* concurring opinions to express *their* concern about the policy implications of the court's holding.

Note the agreement between noun and pronoun, as well as the agreement between subject and verb.

2. Indefinite Pronouns

Indefinite pronouns do not refer to a specific person or thing. Although grammar books differ as to which are singular and which are plural, the chart below reflects formal and college usage:[3]

---

3. Maxine Hairston & John J. Ruskiewicz, *The Scott, Foresman Handbook for Writers* 343 (4th ed. 1996)

Singular	*Variable (singular or plural)*	*Plural*
any-body, -one, -thing	all	few
each	any	many
every-body, -one, -thing	either	several
no-body, -one, -thing	more	
some-body, -one, -thing	most	
	neither	
	none	
	some	

The following examples are correct:

> *Either* of the employees *is* willing to serve this client.
> *None* of the employees *is* willing to serve this client.
> *Each* of the clients *was* satisfied with *his or her* living will.

To view these sentences properly, focus on the pronoun as the subject of the verb. For example, "either . . . is . . . ."

3. Pronoun-Antecedent Agreement

A pronoun takes the place of a nearby noun, its "antecedent." The pronoun must agree with its antecedent in number, person, and gender. "Number" is whether the pronoun is singular or plural (for instance, it or they). "Person" is whether the pronoun is in first-, second-, or third-person (for instance, we, you, or they). "Gender" is whether a singular third-person pronoun is feminine, masculine, or neuter (for instance, she, he, or it).

Except in rare circumstances, two or more antecedents (in italics) joined by "and" take a plural pronoun (in boldface), regardless of the number of either antecedent. For instance:

> When *HomeElderCare and its clients* initiated the living-will service, **they** believed that it was a valuable addition.

However, when two or more antecedents are joined by "or" or "nor," the pronoun must agree with the antecedent nearer to the pronoun. For instance:

> Neither *HomeElderCare nor its clients* believed that **their** contract was void.

When collective nouns and indefinite pronouns are involved, follow the rules in the preceding sections regarding number.

4. Implied Antecedents

When "this" and "that" are used as free-standing pronouns, they often result in unclear implied antecedents. Because the reader has to surmise the unnamed antecedent of the pronoun, readers *prefer* greater clarity. In the example below, "this" could be "this defective drafting," "this defect," or "this kind of living will":

> If defectively drafted, the living will may not represent the wishes of the patient as to his or her treatment for the final illness or injury preceding death. **This** can trigger difficult questions about mortality and medical practices.

The solution is to place the appropriate noun after the word "this." You also may need to reword the preceding sentence to make the connection clearer.

5. Gender-Neutral Wording

Formerly, legal writing used masculine pronouns when the gender was not specified. However, during the past one or two decades, the convention has shifted. Society has begun to take more notice of issues that affect women, women occupy more positions of power, and the legal profession has gone from a nearly exclusively male profession to a profession with increasing numbers of women (forty to fifty percent of current law school classes). These changes have affected reader expectations within the profession. Gender-biased wording now carries an implied message that the writer does not care about (or is not aware of) offending women readers, as well as many men who are sensitive to these issues.

Gender-neutral wording is a *preference*, not a requirement. It involves using pronouns carefully so as to avoid implying a particular gender when the gender is unknown. Gender-neutral wording presents your client's message in the most effective light for a wide audience.

The first step in gender-neutral wording is to replace gender-biased words, such as the following:

Former usage	*Replacement*
chairman	chairperson, chair
fireman	firefighter
policeman	police officer
manpower	resources
reasonable man	reasonable person

For more examples, consult one of the new dictionaries on gender-neutral terms.

The second step is to figure out the gender of any known person being discussed and then use the appropriate gender-specific pronoun for that person. In discussing a hypothetical situation, you could generate names for the hypothetical characters and then use the appropriate gender-specific pronouns for those characters. Balance the genders of your hypothetical characters by having nearly equal numbers of male and female characters, if appropriate to the situation.

The third step is to omit as many gender-specific pronouns as possible in the following ways:

EXHIBIT A.1

REPLACEMENT PRONOUNS FOR GENDER-NEUTRAL WORDING

Replacement		Disadvantages
Subjective	*Possessive*	
he/she	his/her	too colloquial for formal writing; still has masculine pronoun first
he or she	his or her	bulky but often workable; favors masculine pronoun by placing it in initial position
she or he	her or his	bulky and somewhat unexpected by the reader, but often workable; favors feminine pronoun by placing it in initial position
alternating between he or she	alternating between his and her	sometimes confusing to reader; may disrupt readability

(a) Repeat the noun instead of using the pronoun.

(b) Change the person being discussed from singular to plural, so that "he or she" becomes "they."

(c) Change the discussion from third person to second person, so that "he or she" becomes "you."

(d) Change the person being discussed to an indefinite pronoun (anyone, everybody, no one, nobody, someone, somebody, one).

(e) Change the noun being discussed so that the pronoun can be neuter (it).

(f) Omit the possessive pronoun; for instance, "his or her drafting" becomes "drafting."

(g) Replace the pronoun with a noun, so that "he or she" becomes "the drafter," while "his or her contract" becomes "the contract."

(h) Change the sentence to passive voice and eliminate the actor entirely, so that "he or she" disappears.

The fourth step is to reword the remaining pronouns to avoid any implication of gender where the gender is unknown. Exhibit A.1 presents the alternatives with their disadvantages. Weigh the disadvantages in light of the audience and purpose of your document. "He or she" is probably the most common alternative.

F. WORD CHOICE

The following material addresses wording choices that yield text that is precise and concise—both important attributes of good legal writing.

1. Consistent and Distinct Wording Choices

In some fields, elegant variation in writing is prized. However, in legal writing, if you use different words to mean the same thing, the result is usually ambiguity. In the following example, "arrangement," "contract," and "agreement" may or may not all refer to the same set of terms between HomeElderCare and its clients:

> HomeElderCare's *arrangement* with its clients allows the social workers to furnish services under the *contract* and to bill the clients at the rate in the *agreement*.

Thus, in legal writing, you always should use the same word for a concept, for consistency. And you should use different words for different concepts, so that distinct concepts are perceived as distinct.

2. Nominalization

Readers *prefer* the action of the sentence to be expressed in verbs, not nouns. The reader can more easily find the action of the sentence if it has not been turned into a noun, i.e., "nominalized." For example:

Verb	*Nominalization*
refer	referral
admit	admission
agree	agreement
injure	injury

In addition, verbs have more "punch" than nominalizations do.

An occasional nominalization is a normal occurrence, but a heavily nominalized sentence is a reader's nightmare. When nominalization pervades a sentence, the resulting nouns often appear in consecutive prepositional phrases. The following sentence begins with five consecutive prepositional phrases (prepositions in boldface), two of them containing nominalizations (in italics). The remaining portion of the sentence is a nominalized version of passive voice ("will be referred" became "will be subject to a referral").

> **In** the event **of** a *refusal* **by** a client **to** the *use* **of** the living will form, the client will be subject **to** a *referral* **to** an attorney immediately.

To revise a nominalized sentence:

(1) Find the core message of the sentence, and state it as briefly as possible.
(2) Build the rest of the sentence around that core message.

In the example above, the core message is, "If client refuses to use living will form, _____ will refer client to attorney immediately." Note that the revised version is now in active voice. Although the true actor does not appear in the original sentence, the context suggests that the true actor is a social worker. Thus, the revised sentence would read as follows:

If a client refuses to use the living will form, the social worker immediately will refer the client to an attorney.

3. Unneeded Adverbs

Be alert for adverbs that weaken your text. They violate a *preference* that each word carry some useful meaning. For instance, words like "very," "somewhat," and "rather" sometimes can be deleted with no loss in meaning but a gain in power of the remaining words. For example:

The living will ~~very~~ accurately represented the wishes of the client.

4. Multiple Negatives

When two or more negative expressions occur in the same sentence, they often slow down the reader and obscure meaning. For those reasons, readers *prefer* to avoid multiple negatives (in italics). For example:

It is *unlawful* for a social worker to *fail* to use the living will form when assisting clients.

To revise, cancel out each pair of negatives, and then assess whether the resulting meaning is accurate. For example:

A social worker must use the living will form when assisting clients.

5. Other Surplus Words

Readers *prefer* lean text because it makes meaning easier to ascertain and thereby makes reading faster. Eliminate redundant legal phrases—strings of synonyms where one would do. Examples include "cease and desist," "null and void," and "last will and testament."[4] Also eliminate bulky constructions that waste words and space, such as the following:[5]

Bulky	*Simplified*
at that point in time	then
by means of	by
by reason of	because of
by virtue of	by, under
for the purpose of	to
for the reason that	because
in accordance with	by, under

---

4. For the historical roots of these redundant phrases, see Richard C. Wydick, *Plain English for Lawyers* 19-20 (4th ed. 1998).
5. *See id.* at 9-16, 57-58, 60-61.

inasmuch as	since
in connection with	with, about, concerning
in favor of	for
in order to	to
in relation to	about, concerning
in the event that	if
in the nature of	like
prior to	before
subsequent to	after
with a view to	to
with reference to	about, concerning
the fact that she had ____	her ____
was aware of the fact that	knew
despite the fact that	although, even though
because of the fact that	because
in some instances	sometimes
in many cases	often
in the majority of instances	usually
that was a situation in which	there
during the time that	during, while
for the period of	for
there is no doubt but that	doubtless, no doubt
this is a ____ that	this ____
until such time as	until
said	the, this, those
insofar as ____ is concerned	(delete)
aforementioned	(delete)
hereinaftermentioned	(delete)
whereas	(delete)

6. Precise Word Choices

Some words have several meanings, while other words carry but one meaning. Legal usage *prefers* that, when you have a choice among synonyms, you choose the word with the single meaning, so that the reader will not have to decide which meaning was intended out of two or more.

"Because," "since," and "as" sometimes are used interchangeably as conjunctions, but they are not always synonyms:

"Because" shows causation—that something happened by reason of or on account of something else.

"Since" can show causation, or it can show a temporal relationship after a particular event in the past.

"As" can show a causative relationship (because), or it can show a contrary relationship (though), or it can show a concurrent temporal relationship (while, when), or it can show sameness (as if, in the same manner or degree, in accordance with).

Thus, when you want to show a causative relationship between clauses, you should use "because" rather than "since" or "as" so that the reader will know right away which meaning was intended.

Likewise, "although," "while" and "as" sometimes are used interchangeably as conjunctions, but they are not always synonyms:

"Although" shows a contrary relationship in the same manner as "even though" or "in spite of the fact that."

"While" can show a contrary relationship in the same manner as "although" and "whereas," or it can show a concurrent temporal relationship.

"As" can show a contrary relationship (though), or it can show a concurrent temporal relationship (while, when), or it can show a causative relationship (because), or it can show sameness (as if, in the same manner or degree, in accordance with).

When you want to show a contrary relationship between clauses, you should use "although" rather than "while" or "as," because "although" always shows a contrary relationship. When you want to show a concurrent temporal relationship, you should use "while" rather than "as," preferring the two meanings of "while" to the four meanings of "as."

Another overlapping pair of conjunctions is "whether" and "if":

"Whether" shows an alternative relationship between two upcoming items.

"If" can show a condition ("in the event that"), or it can show an alternative relationship in the same manner as "whether."

Thus, when you want to show an alternative relationship between clauses, you should use "whether" rather than "if."

"Among" and "between" are not synonyms. "Between" is used to connect two items; "among" is used to connect three or more items.

G. PUNCTUATION

Punctuation marks are compact signals, each conveying a specific message to the reader about the connections among words. If you use a punctuation mark incorrectly, you will send the wrong signal.

1. Choosing among "Stops": Commas, Semicolons, Periods, Dashes, Parentheses, and Colons

"Stops" are the punctuation marks that signal a pause; they are periods, semicolons, commas, dashes, parentheses, and colons. A key punctuation dilemma for most legal writers is which "stop" to choose in the three situations shown in Exhibit A.2.

a. Joining Main Clauses

One choice among stops occurs when you want to join two or more main clauses. You can use a period, a semicolon, or a comma for this task. Your choice should reflect how closely you want to link the two clauses. If you want to link the two clauses very closely, you should use a comma and a co-ordinating conjunction (and, but, or, nor). For example:

> The living wills likely will be valid, *but* the social workers cannot advise clients how to revise the form.

If you want to link the two clauses less closely but still show their connection to each other, you should use a semicolon but no coordinating conjunction.

EXHIBIT A.2	
CHOICES AMONG STOPS	
Purpose	**Stop** (listed in each box from smallest to largest amount of pause)
Joining two or more main clauses	• comma (and coordinating conjunction) • semicolon • period
Setting apart an interrupting word or phrase	• parentheses • commas • dashes
Introducing quote, list, or other material set off from sentence	• no stop • comma • colon

You might also choose to add some other connecting word or phrase (in italics):

> The living wills likely will be valid; *however,* the social workers cannot advise clients how to revise the form.

If you want a distinct break between the clauses, you should use a period, creating two separate sentences. Again, no conjunction should be used, but you might choose to add a connecting word or phrase (in italics):

> The living wills likely will be valid. *However,* the social workers cannot advise clients how to revise the form.

The last example is the most readable, because two short sentences are more readable than a single longer sentence. However, the first and second examples are desirable choices when the writer wants more linkage between the clauses than separate sentences can show.

When two independent clauses are joined incorrectly, the result is known as a "run-on sentence" or "fused sentence." For example:

> Incorrect: The living wills likely will be valid the social workers cannot advise clients how to revise the form.

> Incorrect: The living wills likely will be valid, the social workers cannot advise clients how to revise the form.

> Correct: The living wills likely will be valid, but the social workers cannot advise clients how to revise the form.

> Correct: The living wills likely will be valid; the social workers cannot advise clients how to revise the form.

Avoiding fused sentences is a *requirement.*

b. Interrupting the Text

Another choice among stops occurs when an interrupting word or phrase needs to be set apart from the rest of the sentence by a pause on either side. For this task, you can use parentheses, a pair of commas, or a pair of dashes. Your choice should reflect how much of a pause you want. If you want the interruption de-emphasized, use parentheses. If you want a medium pause, set off the interruption with a comma on either side (known as parenthetical commas). If you want a longer pause, use a dash on either side. For example:

> The living will *(also known as an "advance directives declaration")* was delivered to the maker's primary physician.

> The living will, *once shown to be authentic,* was delivered to the maker's primary physician.

The living will—*although disputed by the patient's relatives*—was delivered to the patient's primary physician.

A dash can be made with two hyphens if your word processing program or printer will not generate a dash. Dashes are flush against adjacent text with no open spaces on either side.

c. Introducing Quotes, Lists, and Other Set-apart Material

Yet another choice among stops occurs at the outset of a quotation, a list, or other material that is set apart from text. You may precede this material with no stop at all, a comma, or a colon. Your choice should reflect how much of a connection you want between the preceding text and the set-apart material. Sometimes you want the quoted or listed material to flow smoothly into the sentence, without any introduction, as it would if the numbers and the quotation marks were absent. For this effect, do not use any stops, and do not capitalize the initial letter of the quoted or listed material. For example:

The five factors **are (1) the** maker's intent, (2) . . .

HomeElderCare's president told us that she wanted to **know "whether** the living wills will be valid."

The court ruled **that "[t]hese** contracts are enforceable if they do not run contrary to public policy."

In the third sentence, "[t]" shows that "these" had an initial capital letter in the original source but the writer changed that capitalization to make the quotation fit the rules of this punctuation format.

If you want a medium amount of pause to set apart a quotation from the accompanying text and if the quotation is an independent clause, precede the quote with a comma and an identifying verb (in boldface). For example:

HomeElderCare's president **said, "We** want to know whether the living wills will be valid."

The court **ruled, "These** contracts are enforceable if they do not run contrary to public policy."

Note that each quotation begins with a capital letter (also in boldface).

If you prefer an emphatic break before the set-apart material, use a more formal introduction, followed by a colon (in boldface). For example:

The five factors are **as follows: (1) the** maker's intent, (2) . . . .

HomeElderCare's president clearly **expressed her concern: "We** want to make sure that the living wills will be valid."

In the second example, the set-apart quotation begins with a capital letter.

When a colon is not followed by a quoted sentence, whether to capitalize the first word after the colon depends on what follows the colon. If what follows is a complete sentence, it may or may not be capitalized. Otherwise, it should not be.

d. Other Uses and Misuses of Commas

In addition to the comma usages discussed above, use a comma (1) on either side of the year when it follows the month and the day (in that order), (2) after an introductory phrase or word at the beginning of a sentence, and (3) after all but the last item in a series of three or more items. The first is a *requirement;* the latter two are *preferences* derived from majority rules. For example:

> Interestingly, the client made a second living will on May 15, 1999, when he changed his mind about his do-not-resuscitate preference, his hydration preference, and the person he had named as a proxy in his December 1998 will.

However, if one item in a series contains an internal comma, semicolons (rather than commas) should appear after all of the items in a series of three or more. For example:

> The client changed his mind regarding (1) his do-not-resuscitate preference; (2) his hydration preference; and (3) the person he had named as a proxy, who subsequently lost the client's trust.

Recall that a clause beginning with "which" must be bounded by commas, but a clause beginning with "that" should not be.

Although a comma, semicolon, or period is required between independent clauses, it is erroneous to place a comma between the subject and verb of the same clause, or between a verb and its object, unless some other usage requires the comma. For example:

> Incorrect: The client and his estate-planning attorney, made a second living will.

> Incorrect: The client had decided to amend, the provision on hydration.

2. Hyphens

Hyphens are used in two settings: (1) in words that are hyphenated in the dictionary and (2) between two or more words that serve as a single adjective and precede the noun. The first usage is *required.* The second usage is a reader *preference,* because it removes ambiguity. The discussion below will address the second usage.

Usually each word preceding and modifying a noun stands on its own, so that if the other words modifying the noun were taken away, that single modifying word would still carry its intended meaning. For example:

valid testamentary will   valid will,
                                       testamentary will

intended statutory section   intended section,
                                       statutory section

However, sometimes two or more words preceding a noun need to be tied together to convey the correct meaning. These words (not usually hyphenated on their own) are hyphenated when they occur together before the noun. For example:

seeing-eye dog   *not* seeing dog,
                                       not eye dog

do-not-resuscitate preference   *not* do preference,
                                       not not preference,
                                       not resuscitate preference

Grammarians disagree about whether to hyphenate when one of the words preceding the noun is an adverb, but the majority rule is not to hyphenate. For example:

very serious error
commonly used form

The adverb (very, commonly) could never modify the noun (error, form), so the adverb need not be attached its adjacent verb or adjective (serious, used) with a hyphen.

Some legal terms almost never are hyphenated, even when they precede a noun. These terms are words like "common law," the names of legal rules and doctrines, the names of statutes, and foreign terms. For instance:

common law rule
lost volume damages
good faith effort
living will statute
unauthorized practice act
bona fide purchaser

A final word of differentiation: A pair of hyphens in text to set off a word or phrase from the rest of the sentence is known as a "dash," not a hyphen.

3. Apostrophes

Apostrophes are *required* in contractions (can't, won't, don't) and in the possessive form of nouns. Add an apostrophe and "s" to form the possessive of most singular nouns, plural nouns not ending in "s" or "z," and indefinite pronouns. For example:

HomeElderCare's service
women's concerns
everyone's health

If a singular noun ends in "s" or "z," the majority rule says to form the possessive by adding an apostrophe and "s" unless the resulting pronunciation is difficult, in which case, add only an apostrophe. For example:

Dr. Ferris's opinion
Professor Berenz's office
the business' lobbyist
for goodness' sake

The possessive form of a plural noun ending with "s" or "z" is formed by adding an apostrophe to the noun. For example:

social workers' counseling

The possessive pronoun "its" does not contain an apostrophe, but the contraction "it's" does, because it is the contraction of "it is." Likewise, the possessive pronoun "whose" does not contain an apostrophe, but the contraction "who's" does, because it is the contraction of "who is." In the following passage, the italicized usages are correct, but the boldface usages are not:

It's disheartening that an *apostrophe's* commercial use is often *its* misuse. Store and advertising signs are the most common abusers of *apostrophes'* usage. For instance, this morning I passed a restaurant called "Tom & **Marys**" with a sign that read, "**TACO'S**." But *who's* to object if the tacos are good? And *whose* sensitivities will be offended?

4. Quotation Marks

Quotation marks appear on either side of quoted text or a new term that is yet undefined. A quote within a quote is bounded by single quotation marks. For example:

The social worker reported, "The client told me to 'deliver this living will right away.'"

Legal style rules governing quotations appear in Rule 5 of *The Bluebook: A Uniform System of Citation*. These rules are *requirements, not preferences,* and they differ somewhat from style rules outside the legal profession.

A comma or period at the end of quoted matter always goes inside of the final quotation mark, regardless of whether it was part of the quote. All other punctuation at the end of quoted matter goes outside of the final quotation mark unless it appeared in the original text from which the quote was taken.

If the quote is blocked and indented (50 words or more, under *Bluebook* standards), quotation marks are not used to open and close the quotation.

APPENDIX B

EDITING

A. **Distancing Yourself from Your Draft**
B. **Immersing Yourself in Your Draft**
C. **Your Final Responsibility**

To edit your own work effectively, you must both distance yourself from your draft and immerse yourself thoroughly in it. This is an apparent, but not actual, paradox. You must distance yourself emotionally from your draft, so that you are able to review it dispassionately. And you must immerse yourself in it intellectually, reviewing every aspect of the draft and reforming what needs improvement.

This appendix discusses the processes of distancing and immersion. While each writer has his or her own way of editing, we hope that this appendix presents some useful ideas for you.[1]

A. DISTANCING YOURSELF FROM YOUR DRAFT

Editing your own work generally is much more difficult than editing someone else's work. It is difficult to see your work as someone else sees it. It is difficult to delete or revise a passage on which you expended significant time and effort.

An excellent means of gaining the necessary perspective on your work is, of course, to ask an intelligent and careful reader to review your draft and give you suggestions. If your situation does not permit this assistance, or even if it does, you may wish to try the following strategies:

---

1. For further editing suggestions, see Mary Barnard Ray & Jill J. Ramsfield, *Legal Writing: Getting It Right and Getting It Written* 228, 357-59 (2d ed. 1993); Lynn B. Squires et al., *Legal Writing in a Nutshell* 78-84 (2d ed. 1996).

As you write the draft, think of it not as a final product, but rather as a work-in-progress. Do not aim for perfection. Write yourself notes about problems to come back to at the editing stage.

Leave your draft for a few days. It will seem less familiar, less a part of you when you return to it—and some good ideas may come to you during your respite.

Try editing the draft somewhere other than where you wrote it. The change of location may help you shift from the writing phase to the editing phase. Similarly, try shifting from one mode of writing to another. For example, if you wrote the draft at the computer, start your editing on a print-out of the paper.

Re-read the assignment, and think again about your various audiences and their needs in reading the paper. As you turn to the draft, imagine you are a member of each audience.

Imagine a reader over your shoulder, who is intelligent and interested, but not informed about your client's case. What questions would he or she ask?

When you begin your editing, read your draft aloud.

B. IMMERSING YOURSELF IN YOUR DRAFT

It almost always helps to work through a draft several times, with a specific task for each run-through. Different people begin and end with different tasks. Whatever order you choose, you should be sure to accomplish all of the following tasks:

Verify the accuracy of the factual and legal assertions you have made. Re-read the factual material on which the paper is based, and review your legal research. Then you should compare your draft to the content of these materials. If at any point you have any doubt about the accuracy of a factual or legal point, you should look it up.

Discern and affirm or re-work the major and minor points of the paper. Read the draft fairly quickly, put it aside, and then jot down the major and minor points you can remember. Then think about whether the points make sense:

- Do they fit the facts, conform to the law, and lead to a just and sensible result?
- Do they relate to each other in a logical and consistent way? (If your points are in the alternative, they should be discernible as alternatives.)
- Can you proceed through the analysis without wondering "why" or "how" at any point?

If any answer is "no," the next step is to re-think and re-work your analysis so that all answers are "yes."

Review the organization of the paper, and revise it as needed. To edit carefully, you should consider each level of an organization in a separate step of the editing process. Here are some mechanisms for doing so:

Check the draft against format requirements for the paper, making sure you have written all necessary components and that each component conforms to the requirements of the format.

Make a retrospective outline (or flowchart or other depiction) of the longer sections, typically the discussion or argument as well as the facts. You first may wish to work through the paper with several colors of highlighters, highlighting major topics in yellow, minor ones in pink, and so on. Another preparatory step is to label portions of the draft in the margin. You then can write a traditional outline, or you can extract the topic or thesis sentences from each paragraph. Then review the retrospective outline:

- Is there a sensible overall organizing scheme? (For example, does the fact statement flow chronologically or topically? In the discussion, are any threshold or pivotal issues handled first?)
- Is each subtopic aligned properly under the corresponding topic?
- Are there excessive cross-references or redundancies?

You may well find that your organization needs adjustment. In general, it is more efficient to re-organize the outline first and then proceed to make changes in the draft itself.

Examine the headings and transitions between topics and subtopics. Make sure that they clearly convey what is coming and how this topic relates to what has come before.

Also examine whether the facts and discussion have adequate introductory or roadmap paragraphs at the beginning and wrap-ups at the end. If the discussion is complex, check for a roadmap at the start of each major topic.

Refine your paragraphs. Review each paragraph as a distinct unit and in relation to adjacent paragraphs:

- Does the paragraph have a distinct point or topic? Does all material pertain to this point or topic?
- Is that point or topic clearly stated—typically at the beginning of the paragraph?
- Do the sentences providing development or support proceed logically?
- Are there clear transitions linking this paragraph to the preceding and following paragraphs?

To sharpen your focus on individual paragraphs, you may find it helpful to work on them out of order. Consider highlighting the topic or thesis sentence, to see where it is in the paragraph and whether the paragraph amplifies this sentence.

Refine your sentences. Check each sentence against the guidelines of Appendix A. Look especially carefully at long sentences, where the risk of grammar errors and poor readability rises. As you gain practice in editing your own work, make note of the grammatical rules and guidelines you are prone to violate; focus on them. At this stage, you also should review your spelling and typing. If you edit initially on paper, the following standard editing symbols may be useful:

re͜d	insert word, letter, punctuation mark
readȇ	delete word, letter, punctuation mark
ra͡ed	invert order of letters or words
c̲ourt	capitalize
⊘ourt	lower case
co͜urt	close space
it͜and	insert space

As with paragraphs, you may find that working on sentences out of order helps you to focus on the details of each sentence.

Refine your citations. You should include rough citations in your first draft and adjust them as you edit. Once your text is in close-to-final form, you should verify that you have provided citations for your factual and legal points and have done so properly. You should wait until your paper is nearly finished because some citation aspects (such as long versus short forms and signals) may change as the text evolves. Appendix C, which covers citation, suggests various steps in crafting citations: formulating the proper citation form for the source, placing the citation in your text, inserting a signal, appending information, and assembling string cites (where appropriate). Review each citation to be sure you have accomplished these steps correctly.

Computer-assisted editing. You most likely will have available to you various computer-assisted programs, to "check" your spelling, composition, or citation. Although it may make sense to run your text through these programs (especially a spell-check program), remember they are neither infallible nor as intelligent as you are. For example, a spell-check program will not correct the following misspelling, because it does not understand context: "The court red the case narrowly."

C. YOUR FINAL RESPONSIBILITY

Once you have refined your paper, you most likely will rely on some form of technology to produce your paper. Of course, technology can fail: word processors and printers can delete text or adjust margins, photocopiers can skip pages. Your paper is not done until you have checked over the final product, as it clears these machines, to be sure it is printed and copied correctly. Ultimately, you are responsible for the quality of your written work. Be sure to keep a copy, as any responsible attorney would do.

APPENDIX C

CITATION

A. Citation to Legal Materials
B. Citation to Materials About Your Case
C. *The Bluebook* as a Style Manual

Citation is the practice of providing references to legal and factual materials supporting the assertions made in a legal memorandum or brief. This appendix draws on *The Bluebook: A Uniform System of Citation* (16th ed. 1996), the most established and exhaustive text on legal citation.

You may wonder why a "uniform system" is necessary or desirable. A uniform system of citation functions much like a uniform system of punctuation and grammar: it facilitates and therefore speeds the processing of information by the reader. Just as we all know, almost without thinking, that a period signifies the end of a sentence and a complete thought, legal readers know what N.W.2d or U.S.C. means. Furthermore, to experienced readers of legal papers, proper citation is a hallmark of the professionalism of the writer, and readers may infer that the research and analysis in a paper are only as good as the citation.

For many newcomers to *The Bluebook*, it is a difficult source to use. Exhibit C.1 presents both a schematic of *The Bluebook*'s structure and a sequence of steps for using it. It does not encompass all features of *The Bluebook*, but rather focuses on those you are most likely to use early in your career as a legal writer.

EXHIBIT C.1

STRUCTURE OF *THE BLUEBOOK*

First, locate the pertinent rule, using:	*Second, read the main rule covering your source:*	*Third, consult tables augmenting that rule:*	*Fourth, consult the rules that govern many sources:*

broad table of contents on back cover
detailed table of contents at pp. vii-xv
index at pp. 327-65
quick reference citations inside *back* cover
Note: *The quick reference citations inside the front cover are for scholarly writing—not for law-practice writing.*
typical citations analyzed at pp. 5-9
	10 on cases (also P.3 on state court cases)
	11 on constitutions
	12 on statutes
	13 on legislative materials
	14 on administrative agency materials
	15 on treatises and similar sources
	16 on periodical articles
	17 on non-print sources
		1 United States jurisdictions
		6 case names
		7 court names
		9 explanatory phrases
		10 geographical terms
		11 judges and officials
		12 months
		13 periodicals
		16 subdivisions
		Note that the tables are in the blue pages near the end.
			P.1 typeface conventions
			P.2 citation sentences and clauses
			1 structure and use of citations, including
			   1.2 and 1.3 signals
			   1.4 order of authorities
			   1.5 parenthetical information
			   1.6 related authority (two sources linked together)
			3 subdivisions (pages, footnotes, sections, paragraphs, appendices, volumes)
			4 and P.4 short citation forms (used when a source has been cited in full already in the same discussion)
			6.1 abbreviations and spacing

Note the following rules on citation to the record generated for your case:
P.7 abbreviations for court documents
Table 8 court documents

Remember that The Bluebook is also a style manual:
5 quotations, including alterations and omissions
6 abbreviations, numerals, and symbols
7 and P.1 italicization
8 and P.6 capitalization
9 titles of judges and officials

Note that the P rules are the Practitioners' Notes in the blue pages near the front.

A. CITATION TO LEGAL MATERIALS

1. Functions of Legal Citations

A citation to a legal source, such as a case or periodical article, permits the reader to locate the authority, should he or she desire to verify its content, assess the authoritativeness of the source, and discern the strength of the source's support for the legal proposition stated in the paper. The first two functions are fulfilled by the citation itself, while the third is fulfilled by the "signal," or link between the text and the citation, and also by parenthetical information.

2. Long Citation Forms for Commonly Cited Sources

The following is a list of illustrative citations, drawn from the HomeElder-Care sample office memos. Note that each citation provides information permitting you to ascertain the name of the source; its location, including the page or section number where the specific information appears within the source; the author of the source; and its date. Key *Bluebook* rule and table numbers as well as a brief explanation follow.

Dick Weatherston's Assoc'd Mech'l Servs. v. Minnesota Mut. Life Ins. Co., 100 N.W.2d 819, 820-21 (Minn. 1960).

> See rules 10 and P.3, tables 1 and 6, rules P.1 and 6.1.
> "100 N.W.2d 819" permits the reader to locate the source.
> "Minn. 1960" tells the reader that the case is a fairly recent mandatory precedent from the Minnesota Supreme Court. The lack of information indicating that the case has been adversely treated shows that it remains good law.
> (Note that this citation refers you to a commercial case reporter and that rule P.3 would require citation to the court's official reporter if you were writing to a Minnesota state court.)

Minn. Stat. § 481.02 subd. 1 (1992).

> See rule 12, tables 1 and 16, rules 3.4 and P.1.
> The entire citation permits the reader to locate the source. Minn. Stat. tells the reader it is a binding statute from Minnesota, and 1992 suggests that it is current law (the memo was written in 1993, Minnesota Statutes is published in even years, and presumably there is no updating information in a supplement).

E. Allan Farnsworth, *Contracts* § 5.6 (2d ed. 1990).

> See rules 15, 3.4, and P.1.
> The entire citation permits the reader to locate the source.
> The reader can judge the treatise's credibility by its author, fairly recent publication date, and republication in second edition (weak treatises tend not to be republished).

Howard Orenstein et al., *Minnesota's Living Will . . .* , Bench & B. Minn., Aug. 1989, at 21, 28-29.

> See rule 16; tables 10, 12, and 13; rules 3.3 and P.1.
> The entire citation permits the reader to locate the source.

The reader can judge the article's credibility by its author, journal, and date.

3. Short Citation Forms

The four citations presented above are complete citations that would appear the first time a source is cited. Fortunately, you need not repeat this long form when you refer to the source again within the same general discussion. Rules P.4 and 4 provide various "short form" citations; each of the rules governing a specific source (such as rule 10 on cases) also contains a section on short forms. Here are short forms for the four sources cited above:

> *Weatherston's,* 100 N.W.2d at 820.
> Minn. Stat. § 481.02 subd. 3 (or § 481.02 subd. 3).
> Farnsworth, *supra,* § 5.8.
> Orenstein, *supra,* at 29.

Note that *supra* cannot be used for cases and statutes, according to rule 4.2, except in the rarest of circumstances.

When a source is cited twice (or more) in a row, with no intervening citation, an even shorter form may be used. For example, the *id.* short forms for the case and treatise would be the following:

> Case: *Id.* at 820.
> Treatise: *Id.* § 5.8.

Id. may be used by itself when the subsequent citation is identical to the preceding, i.e., there is no change in page or section number.

4. Placement of Citations Within Text

Under rule P.2, citations may be placed within your text in various ways. In the least intrusive, the citation appears in its own "citation sentence" immediately following the text it supports; the citation sentence is punctuated as a separate sentence. For example:

> If the unlicensed individual answers difficult or doubtful legal questions, she has committed the unlawful practice of law. *See Gardner v. Conway,* 48 N.W.2d 788, 796 (Minn. 1951).

If a citation supports only a portion of the textual sentence, it should be inserted immediately after that portion and punctuated as a clause, set off by commas or by a comma and a period. For example:

> The courts have suggested that the drafting of a testamentary will by a non-lawyer is the unauthorized practice of law, *see Peterson v. Hovland (In re Peterson's Estate),* 42 N.W.2d 59, 63 (Minn. 1950), as is the preparation of complicated tax returns, *see Gardner v. Conway,* 48 N.W.2d 788, 796 (Minn. 1951).

In some situations, you may wish to refer to a source in your text, so that the reader is more aware of the source itself. For example:

The Minnesota Supreme Court established the "difficult or doubtful question" test in *Gardner v. Conway,* 48 N.W.2d 788, 796 (Minn. 1951).

This case involves two facets of the prohibition on legal practice by non-lawyers found in § 481.02 subd. 1.

Note that rule 10.2 calls for fewer abbreviations within the case name when it is used in a text sentence in this way than when the case name is found in a citation sentence or clause. And rule 6.2 covers whether to spell out "section."

5. Linking Your Citations and Your Text

You are obligated to provide a citation for every legal proposition you assert—not just for direct quotations. Some propositions will be supported very directly by a legal source, as is true of the examples given above. Other propositions will be supported only indirectly by a source or even contradicted by a source.

Rather than take up space in a textual sentence explaining the links between your proposition and your source, you should take advantage of the "signals" listed in rule 1.2.[1] The continuum below shows these signals arrayed from the strongest support for your proposition to the strongest contradiction of your proposition:

[none]   *accord*   *see also*   *see generally*   *compare*   *cf.*   *but cf.*   *but see*
         see

strongest   strongest
support   ⟵─────────────────────────────⟶   contradiction

Here are classic situations in which you might use some of the more commonly used signals:

[none] for a direct quote

see when the supporting statement is not a direct quote or when the statement refers to your client's case along with a legal concept drawn from the cited source;

compare when you have derived a rule from a set of cases with varying outcomes;

---

1. The sixteenth edition of *The Bluebook* reconfigured some signals and their meaning. Some law schools and practitioners probably will continue to use the signal rules from the fifteenth edition. The older version used no signal in some situations now covered by *see;* it used *contra* for some situations covered currently by *but see.* This book uses the sixteenth-edition rules.

but see when you are urging the court to adopt one rule found in persuasive precedent and you need to alert the court that there is contrary authority elsewhere.

You can add *e.g.* to show that other uncited authorities bear the same relationship to your source as the one you have cited.

You also can use signals, along with textual discussion of sources, for persuasive effect. For example, you can raise an adverse case quickly and in little space by using a *but see* citation. On the other hand, you might want to provide a full textual discussion of a leading favorable case. The *accord* and *see, e.g.,* signals permit you to convey to the reader that there is substantial additional authority in support of your proposition.

6. Parentheticals and Other Appended Information

In some situations, a citation with a signal may raise questions for the reader. For example, the reader may wish to know how two cases in a *compare* cite relate to each other. *The Bluebook* provides an economical way of providing this information and allows you to avoid a textual discussion. Under rules 1.2 on signals and 1.5 on parentheticals, you would insert a parenthetical explanation, containing a phrase or two explaining the facts and holding of each case, immediately after each case in the *compare* citation. For example:

> The court has been inconsistent in its application of the unauthorized practice statute. *Compare Peterson v. Hovland (In re Peterson's Estate)*, 42 N.W.2d 59 (Minn. 1950) (holding that drafting of a testamentary will is unauthorized) *with Cardinal v. Merrill Lynch Realty/Burnet, Inc.*, 433 N.W.2d 864 (Minn. 1988) (suggesting that drafting real estate documents is not unauthorized).

This mechanism is standard with several other signals, such as *cf.* and *see generally.*

More broadly, parentheticals are used when a phrase or two of explanation would further your reader's understanding. For example, if you are referring to a non-majority opinion, you must append a parenthetical indicating this, according to rule 10.6.

Other important information is appended to the citation. In particular, some cases and statutes develop over time. For example, a case from an intermediate appellate court may be affirmed on appeal, or a case from a supreme court may be overruled some years later. A statute may be amended or repealed. Your reader should have this information about the case's or statute's "subsequent history." Under rules 10.7 on cases and 12.6 on statutes, this information is appended to the end of the citation; it consists of a phrase signifying what happened and then the location of the pertinent development. If, for example, the *Weatherston's* case had overruled the *Buckley* case, the citation to *Buckley* would read as follows:

Buckley v. Humason, 52 N.W. 385 (Minn. 1892), *overruled by Dick Weatherston's Assoc'd Mech'l Servs. v. Minnesota Mut. Life Ins. Co.,* 100 N.W.2d 819 (Minn. 1960).

Finally, you may wish to note how one source relies on another. For example, you may wish to note that a recent case draws key language from an earlier case. Or you may wish to note that a law review's language has been cited with approval in a case in your jurisdiction. Under rule 1.6 on related authority, you would follow the form in these two examples:

newer case (quoting older case).
law review article, *cited with approval in* case.

7. Multiple Sources Supporting a Single Point

On occasion, more than one source will support your proposition, and you will provide a "string cite." String cites should be used when the reader needs to consult a range of sources to find your legal proposition credible; typical examples are a statute bearing judicial gloss and a statement about a trend in the law. String cites typically support the most critical propositions in a paper. You should not overuse string cites because excessive string citing clutters up text.

The sources in the string cite may all be linked to the proposition in the same way; that is, they all may be introduced by the same signal. Rule 1.4's order of authorities within a signal relies on the hierarchy of the legal system, reverse chronology, and the alphabet. The sources in the string cite may be linked in different ways to the proposition, requiring the use of various signals. Rule 1.3 outlines the order of signals. For example, if you were to provide a very full citation to a statement about prohibitions on the unauthorized practice of law, it might read as follows:

Minnesota prohibits the unauthorized practice of law by a wide variety of non-lawyer professionals. *See* Minn. Stat. § 481.02 (1992); *Gardner v. Conway,* 48 N.W.2d 788, 796 (Minn. 1951) (tax accountant); *Peterson v. Hovland (In re Peterson's Estate),* 42 N.W.2d 59 (Minn. 1950) (bank cashier).

B. CITATION TO MATERIALS ABOUT YOUR CASE

When writing to a court about your client's case, you also are responsible for directing the court to the record—the pleadings, the documents created during the discovery conducted by the parties before trial, the trial transcript, motions made by the parties and the judge's rulings on them, and so on. References to the record appear in parentheses, in citation sentences or clauses as appropriate, under rule P.7. Table 8 provides a list of abbreviations for commonly cited documents.

C.   THE BLUEBOOK AS A STYLE MANUAL

While *The Bluebook* does not purport to be a composition text, it does address certain issues of style and usage. It provides answers to such issues as when to spell out numbers, when to capitalize plaintiff and defendant and court names, and when to indent long quotes. See Exhibit C.1 for a list of the style matters covered in *Bluebook* rules.

EXERCISES

This series of exercises involves the liability of a seller of liquor to persons who are injured by the acts of an intoxicated buyer of liquor. Most pertain to the following client situation, which you may wish to review from time to time:

> One evening in Stamford, Connecticut, Gary Masters visited two bars over the course of four to six hours. He drank three shots of tequila and six bottles of beer at the first. When he arrived at the second bar, the smell of liquor was on his breath. He kept to himself and appeared sullen and withdrawn. He paid for and drank three more shots and six more bottles of beer at the second bar. Shortly after leaving the second bar, he drove his car across the highway into oncoming traffic. He struck a car carrying a child, who was killed. (At this point, you do not know Gary Masters' age.)
>
> The child's father has brought suit against your client, the second bar, for negligence and for damages under the state dram shop act, which applies to commercial vendors of liquor.

The materials referred to here are real legal materials from Connecticut on this topic, but they are not necessarily exhaustive or current.

(*Note:* Do not discard any pages in this section; you will need to refer to them frequently in working through the exercises that follow.)

EXERCISES FOR CHAPTER 2

THE STRUCTURE OF LEGAL RULES

1.   Restate each of the following rules in if/then form; use letters or numbers to set off the various elements and legal consequences. Identify the relationships among the elements, e.g., conjunctive, aggregate, a combination. Finally, note whether the consequence is an ultimate practical consequence or intermediate legal consequence.

"Two conditions [ ] must coexist before statutory negligence can be actionable. First, the plaintiff must be within the class of persons protected by the statute. Second, the injury must be of the type which the statute was intended to protect." *Wright v. Brown*, 356 A.2d 176, 179 (Conn. 1975).

If _____

_____

_____

_____

then _____

_____

Elements are: ❑ conjunctive
                ❑ disjunctive
                ❑ aggregate
                ❑ balancing
                ❑ mix of _____

Legal consequence is:
                ❑ ultimate practical consequence
                ❑ intermediate legal consequence

"Failure to exercise due care is negligence, and whether there is such a failure must depend on the circumstances of a particular case. Generally, in the absence of some rule of conduct specifically prescribed by legislation, the standard of due care is that of the ordinary prudent person under the circumstances." *Burritt v. Plate*, 481 A.2d 425, 427 (Conn. Super. 1984).

If _____

_____

_____

_____

then _____

_____

Elements are: ❑ conjunctive
               ❑ disjunctive
               ❑ aggregate
               ❑ balancing
               ❑ mix of _____

Legal consequence is:
               ❑ ultimate practical consequence
               ❑ intermediate legal consequence

"The inquiry whether, in a particular case, a party conducted himself with ordinary care, always involves the consideration of the difficulties and obstacles to be encountered, his knowledge of their existence, and his means and power to overcome them. And if men of ordinary prudence would regard the ability of the party insufficient for the purpose, without hazard, there is want of ordinary care in making the attempt." *See Fox v. Town of Glastonbury,* 29 Conn. 204, 208-09 (1860).

If _____

_____

_____

_____

then _____

_____

Elements are: ❑ conjunctive
               ❑ disjunctive
               ❑ aggregate
               ❑ balancing
               ❑ mix of _____

Legal consequence is:
               ❑ ultimate practical consequence
               ❑ intermediate legal consequence

2.   Select one of these rules, and depict it in a flowchart.

(Workspace for #2. continued)

3. Write your own rule about the liability of a bar for injuries caused by a customer who consumed liquor at the bar and afterward injured someone (the customer or a third party). Try to state an ultimate practical consequence in the then-clause. Present your rule in if/then form, and identify how the elements are related to each other.

If _____

_____

_____

_____

then _____

_____

Elements are: ❑ conjunctive
               ❑ disjunctive
               ❑ aggregate
               ❑ balancing
               ❑ mix of _____

EXERCISES FOR CHAPTER 3

READING CASES

1. Read the following case and the introductory material. Label the case according to the components of the case brief presented in Chapter 3, e.g., facts, issues, reasoning.

By way of background: The case set out below involves a claim that the defendants acted negligently. "Negligence" is a common law claim involving "a departure from the conduct expectable of a reasonably prudent person under like circumstances." *Black's Law Dictionary* 1032 (6th ed. 1990). "Negligence per se" arises when the breached duty involves violation of a statute or municipal ordinance. Because *Moore* involves negligence per se, there are several references to Connecticut statutes. (You will learn more about statutes in Chapters 5 and 6.) To establish negligence, the plaintiff must show that the defendant's acts "proximately caused" the plaintiff's injury, that is, that the defendant's conduct "created the risk of a particular harm and was a substantial factor in causing that harm." *Quinnett v. Newman*, 568 A.2d 786, 790 (Conn. 1990).

Milton MOORE, Administrator (ESTATE of
John H. MOORE)

v.

Bradford E. BUNK et al.

Supreme Court of Connecticut.

March 23, 1967.

Action for death of plaintiff's decedent
allegedly caused by defendants' furnishing
alcoholic liquor to him. The Superior
Court, New Haven County at Waterbury,
Benjamin M. Leipner, J., sustained demurrers by defendants and plaintiff having
failed to plead over rendered judgment for
defendants, and plaintiff appealed. The Supreme Court, King, C. J., held that 16-year-
old minor who consumes liquor is presumed
to have done so voluntarily and minor's
consumption of liquor and not the furnishing of the liquor was proximate cause of
intoxication and resulting injuries and
death.

No error.

1. Intoxicating Liquors ⬅291

The general common-law rule is that
proximate cause of intoxication is voluntary consumption, rather than furnishing,
of intoxicating liquor.

2. Negligence ⬅56(3)

Common-law rule as to proximate cause
applies in any common-law action of negligence, even though that action includes,
as specifications of negligence, one or more
alleged violations of applicable statutes.

3. Evidence ⬅62

Minor aged 16 or over is presumed to
have capacity to decide whether to violate
law, and if he consumes intoxicating liquor,
he is presumed to have done so voluntarily.
C.G.S.A. §§ 30–77, 30–86.

4. Intoxicating Liquors ⬅291

Where 16-year-old voluntarily consumed intoxicating liquor, his consumption
rather than any violation of statutes by
person furnishing intoxicating liquor to
minor was proximate cause of his intoxication and of injuries and death claimed
to have resulted therefrom. C.G.S.A. §
30–86.

5. Negligence ⬅121(5)

Negligence, whether common-law or
statutory, must be proved to have been
proximate cause of injuries complained of if
it is to constitute actionable negligence.

6. Pleading ⬅214(5)

Allegations of legal conclusions are
not admitted by demurrer.

7. Intoxicating Liquors ⬅306

  Pleading ⬅8(3)

Allegations of complaint that defendants' furnishing of liquor to minor decedent
was proximate cause of his intoxication, injuries and death were legal conclusions
and were ineffective to negate common-law
rule that voluntary consumption, rather than
furnishing, of liquor was proximate cause

of intoxication and resulting injuries and death. C.G.S.A. §§ 30–77, 30–86.

8. Pleading ⬅8(17), 214(5)

Allegation of complaint that defendants, having allowed minor decedent to become intoxicated, neglected and failed to exercise any degree of care or control to prevent his injury and death at time when they were under duty so to do was mere legal conclusion and in absence of allegation of any specific duty or facts giving rise to any duty defendants' demurrers did not admit existence of any such duty. C.G.S.A. §§ 30–77, 30–86.

9. Intoxicating Liquors ⬅291

Any violation by holder of club liquor permit of duty to prevent persons on permit premises from giving or delivering intoxicating liquor to minor decedent was not proximate cause of minor's intoxication or of any injuries resulting from such intoxication. C.G.S.A. §§ 30–77, 30–86.

--◆--

Joseph H. Sylvester, Shelton, with whom was David B. Cohen, Derby, for appellant (plaintiff).

Alan H. W. Shiff, New Haven, with whom, on the brief, was Philip R. Shiff, New Haven, for appellees (defendants Bunk et al.).

John H. Cassidy, Jr., Watertown, for appellee (defendant Zalenski).

Thomas J. Hagarty, Hartford, with whom, on the brief, was Joseph T. Sweeney, Hartford, for appellee (defendant Smith).

Before KING, C. J., and ALCORN, HOUSE, THIM and RYAN, JJ.

KING, Chief Justice.

This action was brought by the administrator of the estate of John H. Moore to recover damages for his death. The first count runs against the defendants Bradford

E. Bunk and St. Stanislawa Benefits and Mutual Society, Inc., hereinafter referred to as Society, as permittee and backer, respectively, of Society's club liquor permit. The second count runs against the defendants Joseph Zalenski, George Smith, and George Morey.

The complaint alleges that on July 18, 1964, the decedent, a minor sixteen years of age, while he was on Society's club premises, was given, and consumed, intoxicating liquors in such quantity that he became intoxicated and, as a consequence of that intoxication, so operated a motor vehicle as to cause it to collide with some trees, which resulted in the injuries from which he died.

The second count alleges that Zalenski, Smith, and Morey gave the liquor to the decedent, or permitted him to consume it, and that these acts were violations of General Statutes §§ 30–77 and 30–86 and constituted a proximate cause of his intoxication.

The first count alleges that Society and Bunk rented to the defendant Zalenski, who was not a member of Society, a portion of the club premises, knowing, or chargeable with knowledge, that intoxicating liquors would therein be dispensed to minors. It is further alleged that the decedent's intoxication, injuries, and death were proximately caused by Society and Bunk in that they rented the club premises to a nonmember, failed to obtain the signatures of the guests in a guest book, and failed to seal off the club barroom from the rented portion of the premises, all in violation of regulations of the liquor control commission; in that they allowed minors to loiter on the premises in violation of General Statutes § 30–90; in that they gave intoxicating liquor or allowed it to be given to a minor on the club premises; and in that they knew or should have known that minors were on the premises and were being given intoxicating liquor, but they failed or neglected to prevent such action from taking place.

All defendants demurred to the complaint, and, upon the sustaining of the demurrers, the plaintiff declined to plead over. From the judgment rendered for the defendants, the plaintiff appealed.

The plaintiff's primary claims are based on alleged violations of various general statutes and of regulations of the liquor control commission claimed to have been enacted for the benefit and protection of persons in the general circumstances of this plaintiff's decedent. Although it is not stated with the precision desirable in pleadings, it appears that the plaintiff is claiming that the violations of these statutes and regulations constituted negligence per se.

[1, 2] The crucial allegations of the complaint are that these violations were the proximate cause of the decedent's intoxication. It is, however, the general common-law rule that the proximate cause of intoxication is the voluntary consumption, rather than the furnishing, of intoxicating liquor. Nolan v. Morelli, 154 Conn. 432, 436, 226 A.2d 383. Thus, the furnishing of intoxicating liquor was not the proximate cause of intoxication or of any damage proximately resulting from such intoxication, whether sustained by the intoxicated person himself or by another. The common-law rule as to proximate cause, of course, applies in any common-law action of negligence, even though that action includes, as specifications of negligence, one or more alleged violations of applicable statutes. This would include, of course, General Statutes § 30–86, which prohibits the furnishing of intoxicating liquor to minors, whether gratuitously or by sale.

The complaint alleges that the decedent consumed the liquor furnished, or permitted to be furnished, by the defendants. The voluntariness of that consumption, while not expressly alleged, is in nowise negated, as it must be to avoid the common-law rule.

There remains for consideration the question whether the portion of § 30–86 which prohibits, with certain exceptions not applicable to the present case, the furnishing of intoxicating liquor to minors, whether gratuitously or by sale, amounts to a legislative declaration that minors are legally incapable of consenting to the consumption of liquor and thus preclude their action in drinking the liquor from being voluntarily within the meaning of the common-law rule.

[3] Although a minor is subject to a legal disability in the management of his property and in his contractual obligations, he nevertheless is permitted to make a will at the age of eighteen (General Statutes § 45–160), and he may be licensed to operate a motor vehicle after he becomes sixteen. General Statutes § 14–36. A minor may be held criminally responsible for his violations of law at age sixteen. General Statutes §§ 17–53, 17–65, 17–72. Under General Statutes § 52–217, in actions for recovery of damages for injury to person or property, a minor under sixteen is entitled to have the trier of fact determine whether his violation of a statutory duty was negligence, while one sixteen years of age or older is subject to the general rule that the violation of an applicable statute is negligence per se. Santor v. Balnis, 151 Conn. 434, 436, 199 A.2d 2; Bevins v. Brewer, 146 Conn. 10, 15, 147 A.2d 189. Thus, a minor aged sixteen or over is presumed to have the capacity to decide whether or not to violate the law. As a sixteen-year-old minor may be held accountable for violating § 14–227a by operating a motor vehicle while he is intoxicated, he may certainly be held accountable for deciding to consume intoxicating liquor in the first place. Furthermore, § 30–89 provides a criminal penalty for any minor who purchases or attempts to purchase intoxicating liquor. Thus, at least in the case of a minor aged sixteen or over, he may be presumed, if he consumes liquor, to have done so voluntarily.

[4, 5] Since here the decedent's consumption of intoxicating liquor was voluntary, his consumption, rather than any

violation, by any of the defendants, of § 30–86 or of other statutes or liquor control commission regulations, was, under the common-law rule, the proximate cause of his intoxication and of the injuries and death claimed to have resulted therefrom. Of course, negligence, whether common-law or statutory, must be proved to have been a proximate cause of the injuries complained of if it is to constitute actionable negligence. Nolan v. Morelli, 154 Conn. 432, 443, 226 A.2d 383.

[6, 7] It is true that the complaint specifically alleges that the giving of liquor to the decedent was a proximate cause of his intoxication, injuries and death. But allegations of legal conclusions are not admitted by demurrer. Rossignol v. Danbury School of Aeronautics, Inc., 154 Conn. —, 227 A.2d 418; McAdam v. Sheldon, 153 Conn. 278, 282, 216 A.2d 193; Barnes v. Viering, 152 Conn. 243, 244, 206 A.2d 112. Consequently, the allegations of proximate cause are ineffective to negate the common-law rule that the voluntary consumption, rather than the furnishing, of the liquor was the proximate cause of the intoxication and the resulting injuries and death.

[8] Finally, we consider briefly certain other allegations of duty appearing in the complaint. As to Zalenski, Smith, and Morey, the complaint alleges that, having allowed the decedent to become intoxicated, they neglected and failed to exercise any degree of care or control to prevent his injury and death at a time when they were under a duty so to do. But the allegation of the existence of such a duty is merely a legal conclusion. Neither any specific duty nor any facts giving rise to any duty are alleged. The demurrers, therefore, did not admit the existence of any such duty. Rossignol v. Danbury School of Aeronautics, Inc., supra; McAdam v. Sheldon, supra; see Nolan v. Morelli, supra.

[9] As to Bunk and Society, the complaint, construed favorably to the plaintiff, alleges a duty to prevent others on the permit premises from giving or delivering intoxicating liquor to the decedent as a minor. But if such a duty exists, as to the minor decedent in the present case, under the common-law rule any violation of that duty was not a proximate cause of intoxication resulting from the decedent's voluntary consumption of that liquor or of any injuries resulting from such intoxication.

There is no error.

In this opinion the other judges concurred.

2.   Read the following three sample briefs of *Moore*, and critique them according to the criteria in Chapter 3. For example: Are all relevant facts presented? Does the issue link facts and law in question form?

Sample #1

Moore v. Bunk, Connecticut Supreme Court 1967

FACTS: 16 year old P drank too much liquor provided by Ds. P drove car, collided with trees, died as result of injuries.

PROCEDURE: P sued; Ds demurred; trial ct sustained demurrers. P appeals demurrer.

ISSUE: Does absence of proximate cause bar lawsuit against liquor seller for death of minor?

HOLDING: Yes, proximate cause bars suit, bcz minor caused own injuries.

REASONING: "It is the general common-law rule that the proximate cause of intoxication is the voluntary consumption, rather than the furnishing, of intoxicating liquor." This rule applies to minors. Minors voluntarily consume liquor, as they make other legal decisions voluntarily.

Strengths	Weaknesses

Sample #2

Moore v. Bunk, Connecticut Supreme Court 1967

FACTS: Administrator of John H. Moore estate brought action to recover damages for his death. First count against Bradford Bunk & St. Stanislaws Benefits & Mutual Society (Society). Second count against Joseph Zalenski, George Smith, George Morey.

July 18, 1964, Moore became intox'd on Society's premises & then operated motor vehicle so as to cause it to collide with trees, which resulted in injuries, from which he died.

Violations of statutes 30-77, 30-86, 30-90 alleged (renting to nonmember, failing to obtain signatures in book, failing to seal off barroom, allowing minors to loiter, etc.).

PROCEDURE: Admin. of estate sued Bunk, Society, Zalenski, Smith, Morey. All Ds demurred. Trial ct sustained demurrers. P did not re-plead. P appeals jmt rendered for Ds.

ISSUE: Is Society neg where minor Moore becomes intox'd after defendants Zalenski etc. give him liquor on Society premises, drives & wrecks car, & therefore dies?

HOLDING: No, defendants aren't neg where minor Moore becomes intox'd after defendants Zalenski etc. give him liquor on Society premises, drives & wrecks car, & therefore dies. Affirmed.

REASONING: Claims are not well pleaded, but basically allege neg per se. There must be proximate cause. There is no proximate cause where furnishing liquor doesn't cause injury, whether sustained by intox'd person or another, whether minor buys or is given liquor. Minors can make many legally binding decisions: will at 18, drive at 16, criminal acts at 16, neg per se at 16, driving while intox'd at 16, buying liquor at ?? So their decision to drink & drive should preclude suits agst liquor sellers. This goes for suit agst Zalenski, Smith, Morey for letting Moore drink.

Strengths	Weaknesses

Sample #3

Moore v. Bunk, Connecticut Supreme Court 1967

FACTS: Minor person drank liquor on premises of one D, where another had liquor permit, & 3 other Ds were there giving liquor to minor. Minor then became drunk, drove, killed himself by running into tree. Two counts were agst permittee, backer, 3 other Ds. Ds won at trial court (they are respondents).

ISSUE: Was it error to sustain demurrers agst P's cause of action?

HOLDING: There is no error. This is neg per se lawsuit, based on violations of liquor laws re minors drinking. There must be proximate cause. Ds did not cause minor to drink.

REASONING: Minors can choose to drink, just as they can choose to make wills, drive, commit crimes. Therefore Ds did not violate statutes. Nor did Ds fail to control minor when they had duty to do so.

Strengths	Weaknesses

3.   *Moore* does not include concurrences or dissents. Imagine that you are a concurring justice; what outcome would you urge, and what might your reasoning be? What if you dissented? Do you personally agree with the actual decision, or your concurrence, or your dissent?

Concurrence _____

_____

_____

_____

Dissent _____

_____

_____

_____

Your personal view _____

_____

_____

_____

4.   Which state and federal courts would be bound by the decision in *Moore*, and under what circumstances? Which state and federal courts might use the decision as persuasive precedent, and under what conditions?

	Bound by *Moore*	***Moore* is persuasive**
State Courts		
Federal Courts		

5.   Write your own brief of *Moore*.

EXERCISES FOR CHAPTER 4

FUSING CASES

1.   Read the following five case briefs:*

Ely v. Murphy, Connecticut Supreme Court 1988

FACTS: Ds hosted high school graduation party involving youth drinking all night. Legal drinking age is 19. No bartenders or security staff; no one monitored drinking. Ds said they took car keys of drunk partygoers. 18 year old guest became very drunk, said keys were in car (& Ds never got keys), left early in morning, drove into another guest, killing him.

PROCEDURE: Among other claims, father of killed guest sued Ds for common law neg in serving liquor. Court granted motion to strike neg count re serving liquor. P appeals.

ISSUE: Is there neg cause of action where social host provides liquor to minor, minor becomes drunk, drives, & fatally injures third party?

HOLDING: Reversed & remanded. Social host may be liable in neg for serving liquor to minor who thereafter becomes drunk & injures third party; proximate cause is not lacking.

REASONING: General rule at common law is: no neg cause of action agst person who by sale or gift serves liquor to person who becomes intox'd & then injures self or another, bcz proximate cause of intox'n is consumption, not furnishing of liquor. Rule assumes knowing & intelligent exercise of choice to drink. But statutes on drinking by minors & public attitudes indicate that minors are incompetent by reason of youth & inexperience to deal with liquor. Thus consumption of liquor by youth is not intervening act necessary to break proximate cause chain. *Moore* & *Nelson* are overruled. Court also cites persuasive precedent in support of new rule. Proximate cause in minor case is now question of fact.

*   *   *   *   *

Kowal v. Hofher, Connecticut Supreme Court 1980

FACTS: According to complaint: D restaurant owner served liquor to already intox'd person, who then negligently drove into car in which decedent was riding.

PROCEDURE: Admin of estate sued D for neg & reckless conduct. D moved to strike those counts; ct granted motion. P appeals.

ISSUES: Are there (1) neg or (2) reckless conduct causes of action where commercial seller of liquor serves intox'd person who drives into third party's car, killing him?

---

*The cases may be found as follows: *Ely* at 540 A.2d 54; *Kowal* at 436 A.2d 1; *Moore* at 228 A.2d 510; *Nelson* at 365 A.2d 1174; and *Nolan* at 226 A.2d 383.

HOLDING: Affirmed in part, reversed & remanded in part. Where seller of liquor serves intox'd person who then injures third party, (1) there is no neg cause of action, but (2) there may be reckless conduct cause of action.

REASONING: General rule at common law is: no neg cause of action agst person who by sale or gift serves liquor to person who becomes intox'd & then injures self or another, bcz proximate cause of intox'n is consumption, not furnishing of liquor. This rule covers neg claim.

Where, however, conduct is not neg but wanton & reckless, i.e., in reckless disregard of another's safety, one must bear greater responsibility for injuries due to conduct. Causation is expanded in reckless conduct cases. Therefore there may be proximate cause in this case as to recklessness claim. Cites persuasive precedent & Restatement of Torts.

CONCURRENCE WITHOUT OPINION: One justice.

CONCURRENCE/DISSENT: Majority is correct as to reckless conduct; should hold similarly as to neg as well. (One justice.)

DISSENT: Decision affronts court's precedent that there is no tort cause of action on these facts. Difference bet neg & reckless conduct is only theoretical & unwise; in any event, distinction pertains not to causation but to degree of care. Distinguishes majority's persuasive precedent. (One justice.)

*　　*　　*　　*　　*

Moore v. Bunk, Connecticut Supreme Court 1967

FACTS: According to complaint, Moore (decedent), 16 yrs old, was given & drank liquor on premises of defendant Society. Other defendants are Bunk, liquor permittee of Society, & persons who rented premises & gave liquor to decedent. Society & Bunk engaged in acts violating liquor laws in renting premises knowing liquor would be served to minors, failing to close off bar, allowing minors to loiter, etc. Decedent became intox'd, drove car, collided with trees, died as result of injuries.

PROCEDURE: Admin. of estate sued. All Ds demurred. Trial ct sustained demurrers. P did not replead. P appeals jmt rendered for Ds.

ISSUE: Is there neg cause of action agst commercial seller of liquor which permits serving of liquor to minor in violation of liquor laws, where minor becomes intox'd, drives & wrecks car, & dies as result of wreck?

HOLDING: Affirmed; demurrer upheld. There is no cause of action agst seller of liquor based on injuries sustained by minor who became intox'd on liquor provided by seller, in violation of liquor laws, & thereafter died as result of car accident due to minor/driver's intox'n.

REASONING: General common law rule: Proximate cause of intox'n—as well as injury— is voluntary consumption of liquor, not furnishing of liquor. This applies to bar common law neg & neg per se, based on statute re furnishing liquor to minors. Rule does not differ where drinker is minor. Tho statute prohibits furnishing liquor to minor, minor still is legally capable of consenting to consumption. See statutes recognizing minor's legal capacity, especially statutes holding minor accountable for driving while intox'd & for purchasing liquor. Here intox'n was cause of injury, not furnishing of liquor, as to all duties alleged. Complaint fails for lack of proximate cause.

* * * * *

Nelson v. Steffens, Connecticut Supreme Court 1976

FACTS: D sold liquor to already intox'd minor who then drove with two other boys in car. Car went out of control. One passenger was killed; other injured.

PROCEDURE: Mother of dead/injured boys sued D. D demurred. Ct sustained demurrer. P appeals.

ISSUE: Is there neg cause of action where commercial seller of liquor furnishes liquor to intox'd minor who then drives car so as to injure/kill passengers?

HOLDING: Affirmed. There is no neg cause of action agst commercial seller who furnishes liquor to minor who thereafter injures passengers in car wreck.

REASONING: General rule at common law is no neg cause of action agst person who by sale or gift serves liquor to person who becomes intox'd & then injures self or another, bcz proximate cause of intox'n is consumption, not furnishing of liquor. This is rule suggested in earlier decisions in Connecticut & majority rule elsewhere. P does not cite any reason not to follow this rule.

CONCURRENCE WITHOUT OPINION: Three justices.

DISSENT: Conduct alleged is neg conduct: failure to conform to duty set by statute (here statute prohibiting service of liquor to minor) or duty to exercise reasonable care. Rule adopted by majority is antiquated. Seller should foresee situation that occurred here, so that minor driver's conduct does not break chain of causation. Proximate cause should be jury judgment.

* * * * *

Nolan v. Morelli, Connecticut Supreme Court 1967

FACTS: D restaurants served adult liquor. He became intox'd, drove car into tree, was injured & died.

PROCEDURE: Driver's wife sued D for neg (among other claims). Ds demurred, ct sustained demurrer. P appeals.

ISSUE: Is there neg cause of action (common law or neg per se) agst commercial seller of liquor for furnishing liquor to adult who then becomes intox'd & kills self in car wreck?

HOLDING: Affirmed. There is no cause of action agst commercial seller of liquor for furnishing liquor to adult who then killed himself when driving while intox'd.

REASONING: General rule at common law is: no neg cause of action agst person who by sale or gift serves liquor to person who becomes intox'd & then injures self or another, bcz proximate cause of intox'n is consumption, not furnishing of liquor. This rule has been followed by lower court in Connecticut. To provide compensation to intox'd person for overindulgence might encourage, rather than discourage, intox'n. Intox'n is voluntary act that is superseding act bet sale & injury. This reasoning covers both common law neg & neg per se.

Construct a hierarchical array of these five cases.

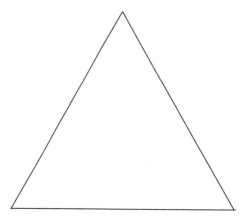

2. Construct a chronological array of the cases.

first
case

most recent
case

3. Fuse the cases, to derive one or more rules as appropriate, by use of textual fusion, rule flowchart, or features chart.

Why did you choose the method you used?

_____

_____

4.   State your fused rule (or one of them if you derived more than one) in if/then form, and identify the relationship among the elements and type of consequence.

If _____

_____

_____

_____

then _____

_____

Rule is ❑ conjunctive
        ❑ disjunctive
        ❑ aggregate
        ❑ balancing
        ❑ mix of _____

Legal consequence is:
        ❑ ultimate practical consequence
        ❑ intermediate legal consequence

5.   Are you certain about the rule you have developed from these cases, or are there uncertain aspects? If so, what is uncertain?

_____

_____

_____

_____

_____

_____

6.   Does the fused rule express your sense of what the law should be? Why, or why not? (You may wish to compare the fused rule to the rule you created in response to question 3 for Chapter 2.)

_____

_____

_____

_____

_____

_____

Exercises for Chapter 5

Reading Statutes

1. Read the following Connecticut statute, reprinted from West's Connecticut General Statutes Annotated (1990). Determine whether any of it is *not* pertinent to your client's situation (stated at p. 431), and cross out those portions.

§ 30-102.   Dram shop act; liquor seller liable for damage by intoxicated person

If any person, by himself or his agent, sells any alcoholic liquor to an intoxicated person, and such purchaser, in consequence of such intoxication, thereafter injures the person or property of another, such seller shall pay just damages to the person injured, up to the amount of twenty thousand dollars, or to persons injured in consequence of such intoxication up to an aggregate amount of fifty thousand dollars, to be recovered in an action under this section, provided the aggrieved person or persons shall give written notice to such seller within sixty days of the occurrence of such injury to person or property of his or their intention to bring an action under this section. In computing such sixty-day period, the time between the death or incapacity of any aggrieved person and the appointment of an executor, administrator, conservator or guardian of his estate shall be excluded, except that the time so excluded shall not exceed one hundred twenty days. Such notice shall specify the time, the date and the person to whom such sale was made, the name and address of the person injured or whose property was damaged, and the time, date and place where the injury to person or property occurred. No action under the provisions of this section shall be brought but within one year from the date of the act or omission complained of.

(1949 Rev., § 4307; 1955, Supp. § 2172d; 1957, P.A. 306; 1959, P.A. 631, § 1, eff. July 1, 1959; 1961, P.A. 432; 1974, P.A. 74-144, § 1, eff. May 8, 1974; 1986, P.A. 86-338, § 7, eff. Oct. 1, 1986; 1987, P.A. 87-227, § 11.)

2. Label the portions of the statute that are pertinent to your situation according to the statutory components presented in Chapter 5, e.g., definitions, general rule, exceptions, consequences.

3. Read the following three sample briefs. Then critique each brief according to the criteria in Chapter 5. For example: Is the statutory language presented accurately? Is all pertinent information presented? Are related ideas presented together?

Sample #1

TITLE: Dram Shop Act

DEFINITIONS: None

SCOPE: None

GENERAL RULES: Illegal for any person:

   to sell alcohol to intoxicated person
   where purchaser injures another person.

EXCEPTIONS: Injured person does not:

   give notice within 60 days of intent to sue
   and sue within one year.

CONSEQUENCES/ENFORCEMENT: Just damages paid in action brought by injured person.

Strengths	Weaknesses

Sample #2

IF   any person sells alcoholic liquor to intoxicated person who as consequence injures
       another person or property

THEN   seller pays $20,000–$50,000 to injured persons.

IF   aggrieved person(s) does not give written notice to seller within 60 days (or up to
       120 days in case of death) of injury of intent to bring action
            which includes information re sale, injured person, injury

THEN   seller is not liable.

IF   suit is not brought within one year of injury

THEN   seller is not liable.

Strengths	Weaknesses

Sample #3

GENERAL RULE: If any person by himself or agent sells any alcoholic liquor to an intoxicated person, and the purchaser in consequence of intoxication thereafter injures person or property of another, seller pays just damages.

EXCEPTIONS: None.

CONSEQUENCES/ENFORCEMENT: Damages are $20,000 to person injured, up to aggregate of $50,000 to persons injured.

Aggrieved person(s) shall give written notice to seller within 60 days of occurrence of injury to person or property of intention to sue within this statute; time between death or incapacity of injured person and appointment of executor, administrator, conservator, guardian is excluded up to 120 days; notice must include time/date/person to whom sale occurred; name/address of injured person/property; time/date/place of injury to person/property.

No action unless within one year of date of act or omission complained of.

Strengths	Weaknesses

4.   Write your own if/then brief of section 30-102 in quasi-outline or flowchart form.

5.   Does the statutory rule express your sense of what the law should be? Why or why not? (You may want to compare the statutory rule to the rule you created in response to question 3 for Chapter 2.)

_____

_____

_____

_____

_____

_____

EXERCISES FOR CHAPTER 6

INTERPRETING STATUTES

1. Return to your own brief of the statute presented in the exercise for Chapter 5, or read the sample brief set out below. Recall the client situation at page 431.

> IF   any person or his/her agent (seller)
> sells
> alcoholic liquor
> to intoxicated person (purchaser)
>
> and purchaser
> in consequence of intoxication
> injures person/property of third party
>
> and third party
> gives written notice of intent to sue
> stating time and date of sale, purchaser;
>   name and address of third party;
>   time, date, place of injury
> to seller
> within 60 days of injury
>   (excluding time between death or incapacity of third party and
>   appointment of executor, up to 120 days)
> and suit is brought within one year of act/omission
>
> THEN   seller pays to third party just damages
> up to $20,000 per person, $50,000 aggregate.

Do you see any ambiguities in this rule as it relates to your client's situation? If so, what is ambiguous? If you were a court deciding the case, how would you resolve the ambiguity?

_____

_____

_____

_____

_____

2. Read the following points about your statute, beginning on the next page. Rank the points by how authoritative they are. Review Exhibit 6.1; remember that the authoritativeness of a case is fixed by factors such as jurisdiction and currency. Explain your rankings.

A. A 1985 case decided by the Connecticut Supreme Court holds that a person may be found to be intoxicated when the following symptoms are manifest to an observer: the person's walk or conversation is abnormal, judgment is disturbed, or will power is temporarily suspended.

B. The prior version of the statute required that the plaintiff establish a causal connection between the provision of the liquor by the defendant and the injury suffered by the plaintiff.

C. According to a 1957 decision by the Connecticut Supreme Court, the legislature was concerned about the danger to public health, safety, and morals from liquor sales and, more specifically, about drunk driving.

D. Under the state's penal code, "intoxication" is "a substantial disturbance of mental or physical capacities resulting from the introduction of substances into the body."

E. Several decisions by the Connecticut Supreme Court indicate that the Dram Shop Act does not alter one's ability to sue under the common law or the common law cause of action, but rather provides a statutory claim for limited damages in specified circumstances.

F. In 1957, the Connecticut Supreme Court upheld the statute against the argument that it was unconstitutional in providing a penalty against the seller even though there was no causal connection between the sale and the injury. The court noted that the statute was a proper exercise of the legislature's broad power to regulate liquor.

G. At the time the statute was passed, a state commerce law deemed the dispensing of food or drink in a restaurant or tavern a "service" rather than a "sale."

H. The Connecticut Supreme Court held in 1957 that a jury could properly infer that two individuals who drank two beers in a bar were sold the beers at the bar; there need not be direct proof of the sale (such as the bartender's testimony).

I. In various cases, the Connecticut Supreme Court has identified three elements of a dram shop case: (1) a sale of intoxicating liquor; (2) to an intoxicated person; (3) who, in consequence of such intoxication, causes injury to the person or property of another.

J. In a 1967 decision by the Connecticut Supreme Court, the court ruled that the Dram Shop Act does not provide recovery where the intoxicated buyer is the injured party.

K. In a 1990 case decided by the Appellate Court of Connecticut, the court accepted the seller's evidence that the buyer was "shut off" when he became obnoxious, found that evidence that the buyer was seen with a beer can thereafter would not establish a sale, and yet ruled that the jury could find an illegal sale based on sales before the buyer was "shut off."

Note: The points listed above are drawn directly or indirectly from the following cases: *Sanders v. Officers Club of Connecticut Inc.*, 493 A.2d 184 (Conn. 1985); *Kowal v. Hofher*, 436 A.2d 1 (Conn. 1980); *Nelson v. Steffens*, 365 A.2d 1174 (Conn. 1976); *Nolan v. Morelli*, 226 A.2d 383 (Conn. 1967); *Pierce v. Albanese*, 129 A.2d 606 (Conn. 1957); *Kelehear v. Larcon, Inc.*, 577 A.2d 746 (Conn. Ct. App. 1990).

Rank	Reason for ranking
Most authoritative	
Least authoritative	

3. To which portion of the statute does each point pertain? Has your understanding of any portion of the statute changed as a result of any of these points?

Point	Statutory language it addresses	Impact on your understanding of statute
A		
B		
C		
D		
E		
F		
G		
H		
I		
J		
K		

4.   How might you use canons of construction to enable you better to interpret the statute?

_____

_____

_____

_____

_____

5.   As you consider the client situation (stated at p. 431), is there any ambiguity remaining in the statute once these points are used to interpret the statute? If so, what remains ambiguous?

_____

_____

_____

_____

_____

6.   Does the statute as interpreted express your sense of what the law should be? Why or why not? (You may wish to compare the statutory rule as you interpret it to the rule you created in response to question 3 for Chapter 2.)

_____

_____

_____

_____

_____

Exercises for Chapter 7

Reading Commentary

Read the following pages from 4 Fowler V. Harper et al., *The Law of Torts* § 20.5 (2d ed. 1986 & Supp. 1999).

1.   If you read this material as you were researching the liability of a liquor seller in Connecticut, which specific references to primary authority would be of particular interest to you? Why? Draw an asterisk beside them.

_____

_____

_____

_____

2.   If you read this material for the primary purpose of better understanding the law of proximate cause as it now stands, what can you learn from this material? Draw a bracket beside the key passage(s).

_____

_____

_____

_____

3.   If you looked to this material for critique of the law of proximate cause, what can you learn from this material? Draw a bracket beside the key passage(s).

_____

_____

_____

_____

4.   What would you take into account as you assess how authoritative this material is?

_____

_____

_____

_____

§20.5   LEGAL CAUSE

Much of what has been said about the scope of common law
duties is applicable also to duties imposed by statutes. Here,
however, the emphasis is on the statutory purpose in determining the interests protected by the duty and the evils sought to
be prevented by legislative proscription of conduct, rather than
on what a reasonable person in defendant's place would foresee.[19] Because the statutory purpose doctrine was probably
clearly and expressly articulated at an earlier time than its coun-
terpart, the limitation on the scope of common law duties, there
has been perhaps slightly less urge to obfuscate the former
inquiry by pursuing it in terms of proximate cause, but this is
done all too often even today. Thus where plaintiff's playmate
pushed him under a middle car of defendant's train which was
passing at a speed in violation of a local ordinance, the court
admitted that the defendant was guilty of negligence per se but
found that the "intervening, independent, sole, proximate
cause" of the injury was the other boy's push.[20] And where
defendant has parked his unlocked car on the street, with the key
in the ignition switch in violation of an ordinance, and the car
is stolen by a person who, while driving it, causes some damage,
the owner has been held not liable on the ground that the

---

[19]See Morris, Duty, Negligence and Causation, 101 U. Pa. L. Rev. 189, 203
(1952) (complaining that "the judicially invented statutory purpose doctrine
can produce highly restrictive and somewhat irrational limitations on civil
liability"); C. Morris and C. R. Morris, Morris on Torts 167-172 (2d ed. 1980).
[20]Lineberry v. North Carolina Ry. Co., 187 N.C. 786, 123 S.E. 1 (1924). Cf.
Daggett v. Keshner, 284 A.D. 733, 134 N.Y.S.2d 524 (1954), criticized in Note,
40 Cornell L.Q. 810 (1955). Green suggested that courts often use the "proximate cause" doctrine "to get rid of the compulsion of the statute." See Green,
Proximate Cause in Texas Negligence Law, 28 Tex. L. Rev. 621, 634-635, 764,
771 (1950), and Green, Proximate Cause in Connecticut Negligence Law, 24
Conn. B.J. 24, 28-30 (1950). Cf. James, Statutory Standards and Negligence
in Accident Cases, 11 La. L. Rev. 95, 121 (1950).

proximate cause of the injury was the action of the thief and not the negligence of the owner.[21]

[21]See, e.g., Wannebo v. Gates, 227 Minn. 194, 34 N.W.2d 695 (1948), and Note, 14 Mo. L. Rev. 128 (1949), which make the error pointed out in the text. See annot., 45 A.L.R.3d 787 (1970). Perhaps the leading case *contra* is Ross v. Hartman, 139 F.2d 14 (D.C. Cir. 1943), *cert. denied,* 321 U.S. 790 (1944). See also Note, 34 Iowa L. Rev. 376 (1949), which treats this problem and properly distinguishes the issues of cause and of duty. Variant results in these cases persist but most cases deny recovery. Some do so on the ground that the act of the thief or intermeddler breaks the chain of causation. Cf. State of West Virginia v. Fidelity & Casualty Co. of N.Y., 263 F. Supp. 88 (S.D. W.Va. 1967); Hersh v. Miller, 169 Neb. 517, 99 N.W.2d 878 (1959); Ross v. Nutt, 177 Ohio St. 113, 203 N.E.2d 118 (1964) (because unforeseeable); Nolan v. Bacon, 216 A.2d 126 (R.I. 1966) (same). Others, more accurately it is believed, seek the answer by examining the statutory purpose. Ney v. Yellow Cab Co., 2 Ill. 2d 74, 117 N.E.2d 74, 51 A.L.R.2d 624 (1954) (safety found to be a purpose); Kacena v. Geo. W. Bowers Co., 63 Ill. App. 2d 27, 211 N.E. 563 (1965) (same); Zegarelli v. Colp, 91 Misc. 2d 430, 398 N.Y.S.2d 103 (1977) (same). See also Vining v. Avis Rent-a-Car Systems, Inc., 354 So. 2d 54 (Fla. 1977); Davis v. Thornton, 384 Mich. 138, 180 N.W.2d 11 (1970); Zinck v. Whalen, 120 N.J. Super. 432, 294 A.2d 727 (App. Div. 1972); see §17.6 note 40 *supra;* Restatement (Second) of Torts §281, Comment *i,* §286, and Comments and Illuss. (1965); id., Appendix 346-363 (Reporter's Notes and court citation) (1966). (Note that the motorist's liability insurance may not include coverage of liability for harm caused by unauthorized use of the car in which the key is left. Cf., e.g., Owen v. Wagner, 426 So. 2d 1262 (Fla. App. 1983).)

The key-in-ignition problem too is treated in Petition of Kinsman Transit Co., 338 F.2d 708, 717-718 (2nd Cir. 1964).

The same error as is discussed in the text has appeared in cases absolving a defendant who illegally served alcohol to a visibly intoxicated adult, or to a minor, from liability to the foreseeable victim of the drunk driving of the person so illegally served, on the specious ground that it was the drinking of the alcohol and not its illegal service that caused the accident, e.g., Nelson v. Steffens, 170 Conn. 356, 365 A.2d 1174 (1976). See able analysis *contra* in Vesely v. Sager, 5 Cal. 3d 153, 95 Cal. Rptr. 623, 486 P.2d 151 (1971). (Unfortunately the *Vesely* opinion has apparently been nullified in California, at least in some applications, by a remarkable 1978 statute which stated "the intent of the Legislature to abrogate the holdings in cases such as Vesely v. Sager . . . and to reinstate the prior judicial interpretation of this section as it relates to proximate cause for injuries incurred as a result of furnishing alcoholic beverages to an intoxicated person, namely that the furnishing of alcoholic beverages is not the proximate cause of injuries resulting from intoxication, but rather the consumption of alcoholic beverages is the proximate cause of injuries inflicted upon another by an intoxicated person." Cal. Civ. Code §1714(b) (West 1985). See also Cal. Bus. & Prof. Code §25602(b), (c)

(West Supp. 1985).). Cf., also rejecting the older no-cause doctrine, Corrigan v. United States, 595 F. Supp. 1047 (E.D. Va. 1984); Buchanan v. Merger Enterprises, Inc., 463 So. 2d 121, 126 (Ala. 1984); Nazareno v. Urie, 638 P.2d 671 (Alaska 1981); Ontiveros v. Borak, 136 Ariz. 500, 667 P.2d 200 (1983); Lewis v. Wolf, 122 Ariz. 567, 596 P.2d 705 (App. 1979) (including useful compendium of citations to more enlightened opinions, at 596 P.2d 707-708); Elder v. Fisher, 247 Ind. 598, 217 N.E.2d 847 (1966); Ono v. Applegate, 62 Haw. 131, 612 P.2d 533 (1980); Clark v. Mincks, 364 N.W.2d 226 (Iowa 1985); Rappaport v. Nichols, 31 N.J. 188, 156 A.2d 1 (1959); Brookins v. The Round Table, Inc., 624 S.W.2d 547, 549 (Tenn. 1981); Sorensen v. Jarvis, 119 Wis. 2d 627, 350 N.W.2d 108 (1984); McClellan v. Tottenhoff, 666 P.2d 408 (Wyo. 1983); §§17.5 note 21 and 17.6 note 12 *supra*.

Cf. K-Mart Enterprises of Florida, Inc. v. Keller, 439 So. 2d 283 (Fla. App. 1983) (retailer who unlawfully sold firearm to purchaser who was subject of felony information and also unlawful user of marijuana, who entrusted gun to his brother, subject to liability to police officer who was shot in head by the purchaser's brother).

144

§20.5 n.21, p.144.   After carryover paragraph of notes, add the following:

Cf., also rejecting older notion that the supplying of alcohol is not a cause of the harm caused by the person intoxicated by it, Largo Corp. v. Crespin, 727 P.2d 1098 (Colo. 1986); Ely v. Murphy, 207 Conn. 88, 540 A.2d 54 (1988) (in case of alcohol furnished to and consumed by minors); Grayson Fraternal Order of Eagles v. Claywell, 736 S.W.2d 328, 333-334 (Ky. 1987); McGuiggan v. New England Tel. & Tel. Co., 398 Mass. 152, 496 N.E.2d 141 (1986); Brigance v. Velvet Dove Rest., Inc., 725 P.2d 300 (Okla. 1986). Compare Samson v. Smith, 560 A.2d 1024 (Del. 1989) (adhering to older view); Charles v. Seigfried, 165 Ill. 2d 482, 209 Ill. Dec. 226, 651 N.E.2d 154 (1995) (similar).

South Dakota has enacted legislation similar to California's to the effect that the furnishing of alcohol is not a proximate cause of injury resulting from a drunk's intoxication. S.D. Codified Laws Ann. §35-11-1 (1986); cf. id. §35-11-2 (further immunizing social hosts from liability).

In 1986 the Iowa legislature also passed a law similar to the California post-*Vesely* legislation, explicitly providing that "the holding of Clark v. Mincks . . . is abrogated in favor of prior judicial interpretation finding the consumption of alcoholic beverages . . . rather than the serving . . . as the proximate cause of injury inflicted upon another by an intoxicated person." Iowa Code §123.49 para. 1b (1987).

In 1986 an attempt was made in the Tennessee legislature to repudiate *Brookins* and reinstate the older rule on causation. It was partly successful; a provision like the California post-*Vesely* legislation was enacted. A partial exception to this provision was

53

also enacted. The exception permits liability in two cases, if a 12-member jury finds "beyond a reasonable doubt" that harm was caused by the serving of "alcoholic beverage or beer" to a known minor (under the age of 21), or to someone already obviously intoxicated. Tenn. Code Ann. §§57-10-101, 57-10-102 (1989).

A curiosity may be noted in connection with the view of some courts and legislatures that the illegal provider of alcoholic beverages should not be subject to liability in negligence for harm caused by the drunk, on the theory that it was not the serving of the drink, but only its consumption, that was the proximate cause of the harmful conduct. Under certain dram shop statutes that provide a civil remedy against the supplier for harm caused by those who were furnished alcohol illegally, cf. §17.5 note 15 *supra*, it is not necessary to show that the harm was caused by the intoxication; it is instead sufficient to show that the harm was caused by the intoxicated person, who had been served illegally by the defendant. Cf., e.g., Sanders v. Officers Club of Connecticut, 196 Conn. 341, 493 A.2d 184 (1985) (under Connecticut dram shop statute, which prohibits sale to an intoxicated person, seller's liability to the injured party depends on proof that injury was caused by the first person's intoxication, not by the prohibited sale); Thorp v. Casey's Gen. Stores, Inc., 446 N.W.2d 457 (Iowa 1989); Meshefski v. Shirnan, 385 N.W.2d 474 (N.D. 1986) (citing, inter alia, annot., 64 A.L.R.2d 705, 722 (1959)). Cf. Attala Golf and Country Club, Inc. v. Harris, 601 So. 2d 965, 970 (Ala. 1992); Slager v. HWA Corp., 435 N.W.2d 349, 352 (Iowa 1989) (in Iowa "an injured party . . . does not have to show a causal relationship between the intoxication and the injuries" but "the legislature [has] made proximate cause an affirmative defense.").

Cf. O'Toole v. Carlsbad Shell Serv. Station, 202 Cal. App. 3d 151, 247 Cal. Rptr. 663 (1988) (potential liability for negligent entrustment of automobile to drunk driver through sale of gasoline) and Blake v. Moore, 162 Cal. App. 3d 700, 208 Cal. Rptr. 703 (1984) (negligent entrustment of automobile to drunk driver, by the supplier of the drinks) for examples of the partial

LEGAL CAUSE   §20.5

survival of the reasoning of *Vesely* in California jurisprudence notwithstanding the post-*Vesely* legislation; compare Knighten v. Sam's Parking Valet, 202 Cal. App. 3d 69, 253 Cal. Rptr. 365 (1988).

See also, on "key in ignition" issue, note 39 *infra*.

EXERCISES FOR CHAPTER 8

APPLYING A RULE TO FACTS: DEDUCTIVE REASONING

1.   Read the following case law rules, drawn from the case law presented in the exercises for Chapter 4. (Other rules could be drawn from the same cases.) Apply both rules to your client's facts (stated at p. 431); assume Masters is 36 years old. If you need additional facts, make appropriate assumption(s), and proceed.

Major premise: IF   A.   commercial seller of liquor
                      B.   negligently furnishes liquor to
                      C.   adult
                      D.   who then injures
                           1.   self or
                           2.   other
                 THEN   no proximate cause; therefore no cause of action for negligence against seller.

Minor premise: _____

                 _____

                 _____

                 _____

                 _____

                 _____

Conclusion: _____

Elements	Client Facts	Element Met/Not Met
IF A. commercial seller of liquor		
B. recklessly furnishes liquor to		
C. intoxicated person		
D. who then injures		
1. self or		
2. other		

Consequences	Effect on Client Facts
THEN potential cause of action for recklessness against seller.	

2. Consider either rule stated in question 1. Identify which of the six classic journalist questions—who, what, when, where, why, and how—is involved in each element.

A. _____   C. _____

B. _____   D. _____

3. Read the following if/then statute brief, used in the exercises to Chapters 5 and 6.

> IF   A. any person or his/her agent (seller)
>   sells
>   alcoholic liquor
>   to intoxicated person (purchaser)
>
> B. and purchaser
>   in consequence of intoxication
>   injures person/property of third party
>
> C. and third party
>   gives written notice of intent to sue
>   stating time and date of sale, purchaser;
>   name and address of third party;
>   time, date, place of injury
>   to seller within 60 days of injury
>   (excluding time between death or incapacity of third party and
>   appointment of executor, up to 120 days)
>
> D. and suit is brought within one year of act/omission
>
> THEN seller pays to third party just damages up to $20,000 per person,
> $50,000 aggregate.

Apply that rule to your client's facts (stated at p. 431). If you need additional facts, make appropriate assumption(s) and proceed. Use one of the methods presented in Chapter 8 for depicting deductive reasoning, or develop your own. Show your work, as well as your conclusion.

(Workspace for #3 continued)

Why did you use the method you used for question 3?

_____

_____

_____

_____

4.   Compare the results of your answers to questions 1 and 3. Are they similar or different? How so?

_____

_____

_____

_____

_____

5.   If you were the court deciding the case, what result would you prefer? Why?

_____

_____

_____

_____

_____

6.   Now assume that in your client's situation, the intoxicated driver injured only himself. Assume further that the applicable rule is that stated in question 3, without if-clauses C and D (deleted for simplicity's sake). Recast the rule in negative form, and state it below. Then state the outcome of your client's case under the rule.

Outcome _____

_____

_____

EXERCISES FOR CHAPTER 9

APPLYING A RULE TO FACTS: REASONING BY EXAMPLE AND POLICY ANALYSIS

1.   Look at the case briefs presented in the exercises to Chapter 4, in light of your client's situation (stated at p. 431). Select a case you would emphasize in analyzing your client's situation if Mr. Masters is 36 years old, and explain why you chose that case.

_____

_____

_____

_____

Use the Venn diagram below to compare that case to your client's case. If you need additional facts, make appropriate assumption(s), and proceed. Indicate whether the case you chose and your client's situation are analogous or distinguishable.

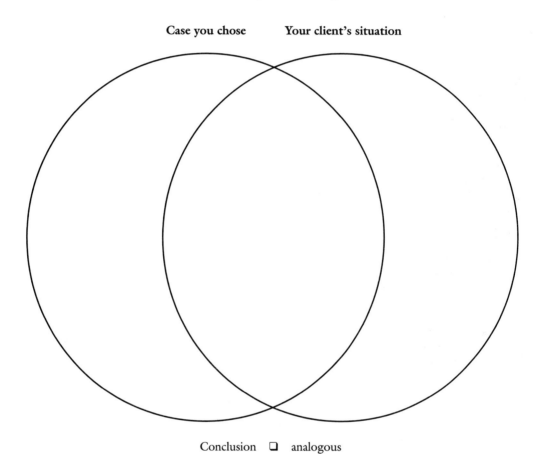

Case you chose   **Your client's situation**

Conclusion   ❑   analogous
             ❑   distinguishable

2.   Now select a case (briefed in the exercises to Chapter 4) that you would emphasize in analyzing your client's situation if Gary Masters is 16, and explain why you chose that case.

_____

_____

_____

_____

Use the checkerboard chart to compare that case to your client's case. If you need additional facts, make appropriate assumption(s), and proceed. Show your work, as well as your conclusion whether the case is analogous or distinguishable.

Client's case		Decided case
Issue		Issue
	same? ⟶	
Facts		Facts
	similar enough? ⟶	
Predicted result		Holding
	analogy or distinction justified? ⟵	

3.   Present one of the two case comparisons from your answers to questions 1 and 2 in textual form.

_____

_____

_____

_____

_____

4.   Perform a stakeholder analysis to determine the underlying policy or policies of the statute presented in Chapter 5's exercises. First, sketch the stakeholders on the spider-web diagram; then, state the policy or policies served by the statute; then identify the interest and desired outcome of each stakeholder.

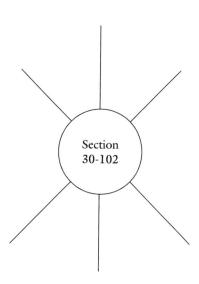

Statutory policy or policies:

_____

_____

_____

5.   How would a rule read if it favored only the bar's interest? How would a rule read if it favored only the injured third party's interest?

Bar _____

_____

_____

Injured party _____

_____

_____

6.   Apply the statutory policy (or policies) you developed in your answer to question 5 to the Masters situation.

Facts

↓

Rule

↓

Policy/Policies

↓

Conclusion

Exercises for Chapter 11

The Office Memo: The Discussion

Review your work on the exercises to this point. If you have not done all of them, review the following material:

- ❑ the client situation, at page 431;
- ❑ the case briefs, at pages 447 to 450;
- ❑ the statutory brief and abstracts regarding the statute, at pages 459 to 460.

Assume that you do not know the age of Gary Masters.

1.   Prepare a classic outline, a typeface outline, a box chart, or other sketch of the discussion of a memo on your topics, displaying your large-scale and middle-scale organization.

Explain how you chose your sequence of topics. Did you use any of the standard legal conventions set out in part D of Chapter 11?

_____

_____

_____

_____

_____

Do any topics appear twice? How would you handle any such topic?

_____

_____

_____

_____

_____

2.   Read the following paragraph, and label the sentences I, R, A, and C. (Citations are omitted.)

> The second statutory element is that the individual was intoxicated when he was served by the defendant commercial seller. Witnesses will testify that he had trouble walking and was using foul language when he entered Joe's and for a while thereafter. This was no doubt because Mr. Masters had consumed three shots of tequila and six beers at the first bar, before being served at Joe's. This case is thus reminiscent of a 1990 Connecticut Court of Appeals case where the bar was held liable under the statute for serving beer to an obnoxious individual. Therefore, this element is met. Furthermore, the facts meet the definition of a 1985 Connecticut Supreme Court decision indicating that someone is intoxicated when an observer perceives that the drinker's walk or conversation is abnormal, judgment is disturbed, and will power is temporarily suspended. Mr. Masters' ability to play pool well while at Joe's is not significant in light of the other aspects of his behavior.

Does the paragraph follow IRAC well? How so, or how not? How might you improve the paragraph?

_____

_____

_____

_____

_____

3.   Select an element of one of the rules that applies to the facts in a straightforward way. Write an IRAC paragraph on that element. You need not include proper citations, but should provide simple references to the law. Label your sentences I, R, A, or C.

_____

_____

_____

_____

_____

_____

_____

_____

_____

_____

_____

_____

4.   Select an element of one of the rules as to which the law is clear but both sides have sound arguments on the facts. Write an IRAC paragraph on that element. You need not include proper citations but should provide simple references to the law. Label your sentences I, R, A, or C.

_____

_____

_____

_____

_____

_____

_____

_____

_____

_____

_____

_____

5.   Select an element of one of the rules to which several authorities pertain. Write the I
and R components of an IRAC discussion of that element. You need not include proper citations, but should provide simple references to the law.

_____

_____

_____

_____

_____

_____

_____

_____

_____

6.   Does the analysis of this problem involve any branchpoints? If so, state the type of
branchpoint(s)—ambiguous or unsettled rules, unknown or disputed facts, unclear application of law to facts, interlocking rules, multiple options under consideration by the client.
Diagram the two branches.

_____

_____

Exercises for Chapter 12

The Office Memo: Issues, Short Answers, and Conclusions

1.   Read the following sample issues and short answers, which draw on the statutory material at pages 459–460. Critique each pair according to the criteria developed in Chapter 12.

Sample #1

ISSUE: Is our client liable under the Connecticut Dram Shop Act to the child killed by Gary Masters?

SHORT ANSWER: Our client clearly is liable under the Dram Shop Act.

Strengths	Weaknesses

Sample #2

ISSUE: Under the Connecticut Dram Shop Act, is a restaurant liable to a child killed when a drunk driver drives across oncoming traffic and into the car carrying the child after the driver consumed three shots of tequila and six beers at the restaurant and, prior to that, also consumed three shots of tequila and six beers at a different restaurant?

SHORT ANSWER: The restaurant is most likely liable under these facts because the driver was intoxicated.

Strengths	Weaknesses

Sample #3

ISSUE: When is a restaurant liable under the Connecticut Dram Shop Act to a third party injured by a drunk driver?

SHORT ANSWER: A restaurant is liable under the Dram Shop Act when the restaurant serves liquor to an intoxicated person who, as a consequence of intoxication, injures another.

Strengths	Weaknesses

2.   Write your own issue and short answer for a memo discussing the client situation at page 431. Assume Mr. Masters is 36 years old. Base your drafts on the following case law rule:

IF   A. commercial seller of liquor
         B. negligently furnishes liquor to
         C. adult
         D. who then injures
              1. self or
              2. other
THEN   no proximate cause; therefore no cause of action for negligence against
         seller.

Issue _____

_____

_____

Answer _____

_____

_____

3.   Frame a draft conclusion for an office memo regarding the client situation at p. 431, analyzed under the rule stated in question 2 above and the following rule:

IF   any person or his/her agent (seller)
     sells
     alcoholic liquor
     to intoxicated person (purchaser)

     and purchaser
     in consequence of intoxication
     injures person/property of third party

     and third party
     gives written notice of intent to sue
     stating time and date of sale, purchaser;
         name and address of third party;
         time, date, place of injury
     to seller
     within 60 days of injury
         (excluding time between death or incapacity of third party
         and appointment of executor, up to 120 days)

     and suit is brought within one year of act/omission

THEN   seller pays to third party just damages
            up to $20,000 per person, $50,000 aggregate.

First, write a sentence or two summarizing your answers to the legal issues.

_____

_____

_____

_____

Then depict your recommendations to your client in full sentences, a decision tree, or another form of your own making.

4.   In advising your client, the bar, would you factor in nonlegal considerations? Why or why not?

_____

_____

_____

_____

—

Exercises for Chapter 13

The Office Memo: The Facts

Note: These exercises involve a different situation from that used in the other exercises in this series, although it is governed by the same legal authorities.

Read the following facts. Assume your client is Jody Harrison, who is considering a suit against Hillside Country Club.

Taken from police report:
1. A car driven by Marsha Lewis (age 26) crashed going around a bend on Highway 56 near the Simpson farm at about 3:30 p.m.
2. The car was going approximately 80 m.p.h.
3. Weather and road conditions were fine.
4. There was no oncoming traffic.
5. Both Lewis and passenger Jody Harrison (age 24) were severely injured and taken to the county hospital by ambulance.
6. Both Lewis and Harrison smelled of alcohol.
7. A search of the car revealed no valid driver's license for Lewis.

Statement of Marsha Lewis:
8. My car spun out near the Simpson farm when it hit a wet spot in the road.
9. The car's speed was approximately 40 m.p.h.
10. Harrison was hurt so badly because she wasn't wearing her seat belt.
11. Harrison and I each drank about four beers during the early afternoon, over two hours, stopping at 3:00 p.m.
12. We drank them at Hillside Country Club after finishing a round of golf; we also ate lunch.
13. One bartender, Mark Johnson, served us the first two beers; a second, Gary Martinez, served us the second two.
14. We were never drunk, either of us (maybe tipsy).

Statement of Gary Martinez:
15. I served both Harrison and Lewis two beers between 2:30 and 3:15 p.m. along with an order of nachos.
16. They were eating, but not drinking, when I arrived on shift.
17. Harrison was becoming loud and boisterous, so I told her I had decided not to serve her more if she was driving, which she said she was not.
18. Shortly after, Lewis and Harrison left angrily.
19. Lewis showed no signs of being inebriated.

Statement of Andrew Harrison (Jody's husband):
20. Doctors say Jody has suffered long-term memory loss and diminished concentration, although her abdominal injuries have healed.
21. Our marriage is showing signs of strain due to Jody's disability and reduced earning capacity.

22. Jody and Marsha often drank, Marsha heavily, after golf on Saturdays, so Jody generally drove.

23. Marsha drove that Saturday because our car was being fixed.

Laboratory report:

24. Lewis's blood alcohol level was .10.

25. Harrison's blood alcohol level was .12

1. Use the factual matrix chart below to weave the facts together.

Topic	Police report	Marsha Lewis	Gary Martinez	Andrew Harrison	Lab report

2. Use a timeline to weave the facts together.

$$\longleftarrow \hspace{9cm} \longrightarrow$$

3. Did you discern discrepancies in these facts? Identify two, and explain how you would deal with each.

(1)_____

_____

_____

(2)_____

_____

4. Assume the following three rules of law apply:

    IF   A. commercial seller of liquor
         B. negligently furnishes liquor to
         C. adult
         D. who then injures
             1. self or
             2. other
    THEN no proximate cause; therefore no cause of action for negligence against seller.

    IF   A. commercial seller of liquor
         B. recklessly furnishes liquor to
         C. intoxicated person
         D. who then injures third party
    THEN there may be proximate cause and cause of action for recklessness.

IF   any person or his/her agent (seller)
      sells
      alcoholic liquor
      to intoxicated person (purchaser)

      and purchaser
      in consequence of intoxication
      injures person/property of third party

      and third party
      gives written notice of intent to sue
      stating time and date of sale, purchaser,
          name and address of third party;
          time, date, place of injury
      to seller
      within 60 days of injury
          (excluding time between death or incapacity of third party and
          appointment of executor, up to 120 days)

      and suit is brought within one year of act/omission
THEN   seller pays to third party just damages
          up to $20,000 per person, $50,000 aggregate.

In light of these rules, list the relevant, background, and residual facts.

	Relevant	Background	Residual
Police report			
Marsha Lewis			
Gary Martinez			
Andrew Harrison			
Lab report			

Which facts would you exclude from your fact statement? Why?

_____

_____

_____

5. Write an introductory paragraph to set the stage for the rest of the fact statement.

_____

_____

_____

_____

_____

_____

_____

6. By what principle(s) would you organize the remaining facts? List your main topics.

_____

_____

_____

_____

_____

_____

_____

7. Critique the following sentence according to the criteria in Chapter 13; then revise it.

    After drinking heavily and annoying the bartender, Lewis and Harrison left Hillside.

Critique _____

_____

Revision _____

_____

_____

_____

8.   Are there additional facts you would like to know? If so, what are they?

_____

_____

_____

_____

_____

_____

Exercises for Chapter 14

Advocacy Writing: The Function and Format of the Advice Letter

For the following exercises, refer to the client situation stated at page 431, the statute presented at page 453, and the material regarding the statute at pages 459–460.

1.   Read the following sample introduction; then critique it according to the principles set forth in Chapter 14.

> Dear Client:
>
>   This letter presents our analysis of the facts you recounted last Friday in light of the pertinent statute. That statute provides for liability on the part of any person ("seller") who sells alcoholic liquor to an intoxicated person ("purchaser") where that purchaser then injures a third party ("victim"), the victim's injury/death being a consequence of the purchaser's intoxication. On the assumption that the procedural requirements of the statute are met (see below), such liability most probably follows in your situation (see below for further explanation). The victim's recovery would be capped at $20,000.
>
>   This letter is current as of the date of this writing and is based on the following facts as you have recounted them to this office.

Strengths	Weaknesses

2.   Assume that your client is *the bar*, a regular client. Rewrite the introduction presented above.

_____

_____

_____

_____

_____

_____

3.   Now assume that your client, a first-time client, is *the father of the killed child*. Rewrite the introduction presented above.

_____

_____

_____

_____

_____

_____

4.   Write a paragraph for the explanation component on the issue of whether Mr. Masters was "intoxicated" within the meaning of that term in the Connecticut Dram Shop Act. Assume that *the bar* is your client.

_____

_____

_____

_____

_____

_____

Would this paragraph differ at all if *the father* were your client? If so, how so?

_____

_____

_____

5.   Assume that you have concluded that *the bar*, your client, probably would be ordered to pay $20,000 under the Dram Shop Act if the procedural requirements were met by the claimant. Assume further that the claimant sent a notice to the bar, but it was three days late. Write your summary and advice section.

_____

_____

_____

_____

_____

_____

_____

6.   If *the bar* were your client, which model of lawyering—hired gun, godfather, guru, or friend—would you employ? Why?

_____

_____

_____

_____

_____

_____

EXERCISES FOR CHAPTER 15

ADVOCACY WRITING IN THE PRE-TRIAL AND TRIAL SETTING: THE FUNCTION AND FORMAT OF THE MOTION PRACTICE MEMO

The following is the factual record for the case of *Harrison v. Hillside Country Club:*

Taken from police report:

1. A car driven by Marsha Lewis (age 26) crashed going around a bend on Highway 56 near the Simpson farm at about 3:30 p.m.
2. The car was going approximately 80 m.p.h.
3. Weather and road conditions were fine.
4. There was no oncoming traffic.
5. Both Lewis and passenger Jody Harrison (age 24) were severely injured and taken to the county hospital by ambulance.
6. Both Lewis and Harrison smelled of alcohol.
7. A search of the car revealed no valid driver's license for Lewis.

Deposition of Marsha Lewis:

8. My car spun out near the Simpson farm when it hit a wet spot in the road.
9. The car's speed was approximately 40 m.p.h.
10. Harrison was hurt so badly because she wasn't wearing her seat belt.
11. Harrison and I each drank about four beers during the early afternoon, over two hours, stopping at 3:00 p.m.
12. We drank them at Hillside Country Club after finishing a round of golf; we also ate lunch.
13. One bartender, Mark Johnson, served us the first two beers; a second, Gary Martinez, served us the second two.
14. We were never drunk, either of us (maybe tipsy).

Deposition of Gary Martinez:

15. I served both Harrison and Lewis two beers between 2:30 and 3:15 p.m. along with an order of nachos.
16. They were eating, but not drinking, when I arrived on shift.
17. Harrison was becoming loud and boisterous, so I told her I had decided not to serve her more if she was driving, which she said she was not.
18. Shortly after, Lewis and Harrison left angrily.
19. Lewis showed no signs of being inebriated.

Deposition of Andrew Harrison (Jody's husband):

20. Doctors say Jody has suffered long-term memory loss and diminished concentration, although her abdominal injuries have healed.
21. Our marriage is showing signs of strain due to Jody's disability and reduced earning capacity.
22. Jody and Marsha often drank, Marsha heavily, after golf on Saturdays, so Jody generally drove.
23. Marsha drove that Saturday because our car was being fixed.

Laboratory report:
24. Lewis's blood alcohol level was .10.
25. Harrison's blood alcohol level was .12

Ms. Harrison has sued the club on three counts, one under Connecticut common law for negligence and a second for recklessness (presented at pages 447 to 450) and a third under the Connecticut Dram Shop Act (presented at page 453 with supporting materials at 459 to 460). The club is moving for summary judgment on the common law counts (not the Dram Shop count). Assume that Connecticut law requires the movant to establish (1) that there is no genuine issue of material fact and (2) that the movant is entitled to judgment as a matter of law.

1. Assume that the Connecticut trial courts operate on a block system. As counsel for Defendant *Hillside,* would you bring this motion? Why or why not?

_____

_____

_____

2. Assume that the Connecticut trial courts operate on a block system. As counsel for Plaintiff *Ms. Harrison,* would you defend against the motion? State your rationale.

_____

_____

_____

3. If you did not have to follow a particular format, and you represented *Hillside,* which of the following components would you present first: introduction or summary, procedure, facts? Explain your choice.

_____

_____

_____

4. If you did not have to follow a particular format, and you represented *Ms. Harrison,* which of the following components would you present first: introduction or summary, procedure, facts? Explain your choice.

_____

_____

_____

5. Read the following sample issues. First, analyze their content by marking each as follows: straight underline for substantive law and squiggly underline for procedural law. Do not mark the facts. Second, indicate for each sample whether you were inclined to answer "yes" or "no" or neither. Third, critique each sample according to the criteria presented in Chapter 15.

Sample #1

I. Are there genuine issues of material fact precluding summary judgment on the common law claim?
II. Is Defendant entitled to judgment as a matter of law on the common law claim?

Issues suggest:
- ❑ yes
- ❑ no
- ❑ neither

Strengths	Weaknesses

Sample #2

Is a commercial seller of alcoholic beverages liable under the common law where an adult purchased and consumed beverages at the seller's establishment and then injured the Plaintiff by driving recklessly?

Issue suggests:
- ❑ yes
- ❑ no
- ❑ neither

Strengths	Weaknesses

Sample #3

Is a country club entitled to summary judgment under the common law where the Plaintiff was injured by the reckless driving of a patron, that patron drank several beers at the club over the course of several hours and ate food as well, the Plaintiff also ate and drank at the club, the Plaintiff but not the patron appeared drunk to the club's bartenders, and the patron's blood alcohol level was .10?

Issue suggests:
- ❑ yes
- ❑ no
- ❑ neither

Strengths	Weaknesses

Sample #4

Where a club served an adult golfer and friend four drinks over two hours and also served the golfer food, the golfer did not become loud or obnoxious (although her friend did), the golfer and her friend left, the golfer then drove recklessly and crashed, and the friend was injured:
A. are there genuine issues of material fact, and
B. is the club entitled to judgment as a matter of law where the law permits recovery in cases where a commercial seller of liquor acts recklessly, but not negligently?

Issue suggests:
- ❑ yes
- ❑ no
- ❑ neither

Strengths	Weaknesses

6. Write an introduction or summary on behalf of *Hillside.*

_____

_____

_____

_____

_____

_____

7. Write an introduction or summary on behalf of *Ms. Harrison.*

_____

_____

_____

_____

_____

_____

8.   a. Review the list of facts stated above. If you represented *Hillside,* which facts would you include in your fact statement? List them by number.

_____

_____

   b. Are any of them residual facts you would not have included in an office memorandum? Explain.

_____

_____

   c. Draft the opening paragraph of your fact statement.

_____

_____

_____

_____

_____

d. Which organization would you use for the body of your fact statement: topical, chronological, perceptual, or a combination? Why?

_____

_____

e. Draft the closing paragraph of your fact statement; assume that you have not included a procedure component.

_____

_____

_____

_____

9. a. Review the list of facts stated above. If you represented *Ms. Harrison,* which facts would you include in your fact statement? List them by number.

_____

_____

b. Are any of them residual facts you would not have included in an office memorandum? Explain.

_____

_____

c. Draft the opening paragraph of your fact statement.

_____

_____

_____

_____

_____

d. Which organization would you use for your fact statement: topical, chronological, perceptual, or a combination? Why?

_____

_____

e. Draft the closing paragraph of your fact statement; assume that you have not included a procedure component.

_____

_____

_____

_____

10. Assume that you represent *Hillside*. Use a traditional outline, flowchart, or other device to show how you would combine the substantive and procedural law with the facts in your argument section. (For an example of one format, see Exhibit 15.3.)

11. Assume that you represent *Ms. Harrison*. Use a traditional outline, flowchart, or other device to show how you would combine the substantive and procedural law with the facts in your argument section. (For an example of one format, see Exhibit 15.3.)

12. Read the following sample point headings. First, analyze their content by marking each as follows: straight underline for substantive law; squiggly underline for procedural law; no marking for the facts. Then critique each according to the criteria presented in Chapter 15.

Sample #1

The club is not liable because it did not act recklessly when it served a patron several drinks over a period of two hours and the patron showed no signs of intoxication.

Strengths	Weaknesses

Sample #2

A. There is no genuine issue of material fact because the testimony of all witnesses on the relevant facts is in accord.

B. The club is entitled to judgment as a matter of law, where the law affords recovery only when a liquor seller acts recklessly, because the club acted at most negligently in serving several drinks during an afternoon to a patron who was not intoxicated in the eyes of anyone present.

Strengths	Weaknesses

Sample #3

Summary judgment is not appropriate where there is a genuine issue of material fact and the moving party is not entitled to judgment as a matter of law.
    A.   There are fact issues because the testimony of some parties conflict.
    B.   Defendant is not entitled to judgment as a matter of law because the law does afford a cause of action for recklessness.

Strengths	Weaknesses

Sample #4

The club is liable because it did act recklessly when it served an apparently drunk patron several drinks over two hours.
    A.   Entitlement to judgment as a matter of law
    B.   Genuine issues of material fact

Strengths	Weaknesses

13. Write an improved point heading (or headings) on behalf of *Hillside*.

_____

_____

_____

_____

_____

_____

_____

_____

_____

14. Write an improved point heading (or headings) on behalf of *Ms. Harrison*.

_____

_____

_____

_____

_____

_____

_____

_____

_____

EXERCISES FOR CHAPTER 16

THE SCIENCE OF ADVOCACY

Read the factual record in the introductory material for the Chapter 15 exercises, as well as the legal materials referred to there. Continue with the same facts and assumptions.

1.   a. Identify a conflict in the record as to an important fact, and note the conflict here.

_____

_____

    b. How would you handle that fact if you represented *Hillside?*

_____

_____

    c. How would you handle that fact if you represented *Ms. Harrison?*

_____

_____

2.   a. Review the procedural rule on summary judgment. What type of rule is it: conjunctive, disjunctive, aggregate, or balancing?

_____

    b. Review the substantive rule on liability of liquor sellers, as developed in the common law. What type of rule is it: conjunctive, disjunctive, aggregate, or balancing?

_____

    c. As *Hillside's* counsel, what must or may you do to succeed in your motion?

_____

_____

_____

_____

    d. As *Ms. Harrison's* counsel, what must or may you do to successfully defend against the motion?

_____

_____

_____

_____

3.   a. If you represented *Hillside*, would any of your potential arguments be alternatives to each other? If so, explain.

_____

_____

_____

_____

   b. If you represented *Ms. Harrison*, would any of your potential arguments be alternatives to each other? If so, explain.

_____

_____

_____

_____

4.   List the main assertions Hillside is likely to make and the probable responses of Ms. Harrison. Identify the points of clash by drawing an X between the clashing assertions.

Hillside assertions	Harrison assertions

5.   a. If you represented *Hillside,* would you deem your case overall to be strong on facts, law, or policy (or some combination)? What is its overall weakness? Explain.

_____

_____

_____

_____

_____

   b. Which case(s) would you emphasize? Why? How would you emphasize that case?

_____

_____

_____

_____

   c. Is there any unfavorable case you deem yourself ethically bound to raise even if opposing counsel does not? Explain. How would you handle that case?

_____

_____

_____

_____

_____

   d. Would you seek to emphasize or de-emphasize the procedural rule? Explain.

_____

_____

_____

_____

   e. Which facts would you emphasize? Why? How would you emphasize those facts?

_____

_____

_____

_____

f. Which facts would you de-emphasize? Why? How would you de-emphasize those facts?

_____

_____

_____

_____

g. Is there any policy you would seek to emphasize? Explain.

_____

_____

_____

_____

h. Is there any policy you would seek to de-emphasize? Explain.

_____

_____

_____

_____

i. Based on your analysis above, state your theory of the case. Write it into the pie chart, or state it in a brief sentence, or both.

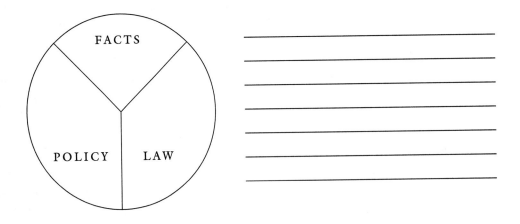

6. a. If you represented *Ms. Harrison,* would you deem your case overall to be strong on facts, law, or policy (or some combination)? What is its overall weakness? Explain.

_____

_____

_____

_____

_____

b. Which case(s) would you emphasize? Why? How would you emphasize that case?

_____

_____

_____

_____

c. Is there any unfavorable case you deem yourself ethically bound to raise even if opposing counsel does not? Explain. How would you handle that case?

_____

_____

_____

_____

d. Would you seek to emphasize or de-emphasize the procedural rule? Explain.

_____

_____

_____

e. Which facts would you emphasize? Why? How would you emphasize those facts?

_____

_____

_____

_____

f. Which facts would you de-emphasize? Why? How would you de-emphasize those facts?

_____

_____

_____

_____

g. Is there any policy you would seek to emphasize? Explain.

_____

_____

_____

_____

h. Is there any policy you would seek to de-emphasize? Explain.

_____

_____

_____

_____

i. Based on your analysis above, state your theory of the case. Write it into the pie chart, or state it in a brief sentence, or both.

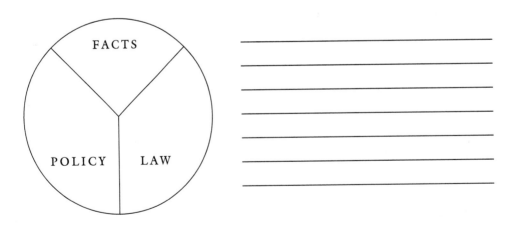

_____

_____

_____

_____

_____

_____

Exercises for Chapter 17

Advocacy Writing in the Appellate Setting: The Function and Format of the Appellate Brief

Read the material at pages 447 to 450, 459 to 460, and 466 to 471; this material forms the law pertinent to the following case.

> The plaintiff, Phillip E. Quinnett, as administrator of the estate of his five year old son, Benjamin L. Quinnett, brought this action seeking damages for the wrongful death of his son.
>
> The jury might reasonably have found that on December 1, 1983, at approximately 5:15 p.m., Gary Mastrobattisto stopped at Gindee's bar in New Haven, an establishment operated by the defendants Virginia Newman and Gindee's Corporation, where he remained for two to three hours. During that time, Mastrobattisto consumed three shots of tequila and six twelve-ounce bottles of beer. He thereafter drove to Pickles bar in Branford, an establishment operated by the defendants Brett Kerr and Pacarrie, Inc. (defendants), where he remained for an additional two to three hours. While there, Mastrobattisto drank three more shots of tequila and six more twelve-ounce bottles of beer. Shortly after leaving Pickles bar, Mastrobattisto drove his vehicle across the highway into the lane for oncoming traffic and struck the car carrying the plaintiff's decedent, causing the injuries that thereafter led to his death.
>
> The suit involving Gindee's bar was resolved by stipulated judgment. The case involving Pickles bar was thereafter submitted to the jury solely on the issue[ ] of wanton and reckless misconduct. The trial court, J. Flanagan, J., directed the jury to render a verdict for the defendants on the remaining count of the complaint, concluding that, as a matter of law, there is no cause of action based upon negligence . . . in selling alcohol to an adult who thereafter injures another by reason of his intoxication. The jury returned a verdict in favor of the defendants on the recklessness count and as directed by the court on the remaining count[ ]. The trial court denied the plaintiff's motion to set aside the verdicts . . . and thereafter rendered judgment for the defendants.*

Assume that the Connecticut Appellate Court affirmed, Mr. Quinnett has appealed to the Connecticut Supreme Court, and that court has granted review.

Assume that the following procedural law and standards of review apply:

jury verdict and denial of motion to set aside the verdict (for Defendant on recklessness claim):

> A jury verdict is entitled to acceptance unless the reviewing court can say as a matter of law that the jury's conclusions were such that reasoning minds could not reasonably have reached them.

> The trial court has broad discretion in deciding a motion to set aside the verdict on the grounds it is contrary to law and the evidence; that decision will not be disturbed in the absence of clear abuse.

---

*The citation to this material appears *infra*.

directed verdict (for Defendant on negligence claim):

> In reviewing a trial court decision to direct a verdict for the defendant, the appeals court considers the evidence in the light most favorable to the plaintiff and then determines whether the jury reasonably and legally could have reached a conclusion other than in the defendant's favor.

1.   If the Plaintiff were to appeal its losses on both counts, would the appeal fall within the scope of appellate review? Explain your answer by applying the following rules:

final judgment rule _____

_____

_____

rule prohibiting new facts on appeal _____

_____

_____

rule prohibiting new theories on appeal _____

_____

_____

reversible error rule _____

_____

_____

2.   Assume that the Connecticut Supreme Court uses the factors stated in Chapter 17 in deciding whether to grant discretionary review. Why should it grant review in this case?

_____

_____

_____

3.   What legal points must the Plaintiff show to win on appeal? As to each claim, your statement should reflect the standard of review, the procedural law, and the substantive law.

negligence claim _____

_____

_____

_____

recklessness claim _____

_____

_____

_____

Which issue (if either) is the Plaintiff more likely to win? Why?

_____

_____

_____

_____

Notes. The following questions appear twice—in questions 4–8 you represent Mr. Quinnett; in questions 9–13 you represent Pickles bar. If you have not yet read Chapter 18, you should think of your answers here as works-in-progress. You may wish to return to these exercises to refine your answers once you have read that lesson.

Assume that you represent Mr. Quinnett, the Appellant.

4.   Here are two neutral, broad ways of phrasing the issues that could be raised on appeal:

Does a cause of action in negligence exist against a commercial vendor who sells intoxicating liquor to an adult who thereafter, by reason of his intoxication, injures another?

On the facts of this case, could the jury find that the commercial vendor did not act recklessly?

Rephrase the two issues so as to subtly suggest an answer favoring your client. (Ideally the answers to both would be "yes" or "no.") You may introduce subissues.

Underline the procedural law or standard of review, draw a dotted underline under the substantive law, draw a squiggly line under policy, and leave the facts without an underline.

State the trial court's holding on each issue, as you would phrase it from your client's perspective.

_____

_____

_____

_____

_____

5.   Write a paragraph setting forth the nature of the case and its relevant procedural history. Be sure to include appropriate citations to the pleadings and record.

_____

_____

_____

_____

_____

_____

_____

6.   a. The facts stated above are presented as a court would phrase them, dispassionately, in a straight chronological order. Would you exclude any of the stated facts? Explain.

_____

_____

_____

    b. On the assumption that the record contained the information you needed, would you include any of the following facts? Why or why not?

physical or emotional effects of the loss suffered by Mr. Quinnett _____

_____

_____

the events prompting Mr. Mastrobattisto to drink that day _____

_____

_____

the condition of his car or of the road _____

_____

_____

the economic state of the Pickles bar _____

_____

_____

c. List three ways you would alter the presentation of the facts stated above, other than adding or deleting facts.

_____

_____

_____

_____

d. Write the first sentence of the body of your fact statement.

_____

_____

_____

_____

7. Sketch out the main topics to be covered in your argument. (See Exhibit 17.4 for one example.) Be sure to include the substantive and procedural law, policy, and facts, and to convey the relationships among them.

(Workspace for #7. continued)

8.   Write a set of point headings for your argument. You may write more than one major heading; you may use minor headings as well.   OR   Write a summary for your argument. Aim for one paragraph, three to five sentences long.

Underline the procedural law or standard of review, draw a dotted underline under the substantive law, draw a squiggly line under policy, and leave the facts without an underline. OR   Circle up to ten words you hope your reader will remember best from your summary, and from the argument.

Assume that you represent the owners of Pickles bar, the Appellee.

9. Here are two neutral, broad ways of phrasing the issues that could be raised on appeal:

    Does a cause of action in negligence exist against a commercial vendor who sells intoxicating liquor to an adult who thereafter, by reason of his intoxication, injures another?

    On the facts of this case, could the jury find that the commercial vendor did not act recklessly?

Rephrase the two issues so as to subtly suggest an answer favoring your client. (Ideally the answers to both would be "yes" or "no.") You may introduce subissues if you wish.

Underline the procedural law or standard of review, draw a dotted underline under the substantive law, draw a squiggly line under policy, and leave the facts without an underline.

State the trial court's holding on each issue, as you would phrase it from your client's perspective.

_____

_____

_____

_____

_____

10. Write a paragraph setting forth the nature of the case and its relevant procedural history. Be sure to include appropriate citations to the pleadings and record.

_____

_____

_____

_____

_____

_____

_____

11. a. The facts stated above are presented as a court would phrase them, dispassionately, in a straight chronological order. Would you exclude any of the stated facts? Explain.

_____

_____

_____

b. On the assumption that the record contained the information you needed, would you include any of the following facts? Why, or why not?

physical or emotional effects of the loss suffered by Mr. Quinnett _____

_____

_____

the events prompting Mr. Mastrobattisto to drink that day _____

_____

_____

the condition of his car or of the road _____

_____

_____

the economic state of the Pickles bar _____

_____

_____

c. List three ways you would alter the presentation of the facts stated above, other than adding or deleting facts.

_____

_____

_____

_____

d. Write the first sentence of the body of your fact statement.

_____

_____

_____

12.   Sketch out the main topics to be covered in your argument. (See Exhibit 17.4 for one example.) Be sure to include the substantive and procedural law, policy, and facts, and to convey the relationships among them.

(Workspace for #12. continued)

13.   Write a set of point headings for your argument. You may write more than one major heading; you may use minor headings as well.   <u>OR</u>   Write a summary for your argument. Aim for one paragraph, three to five sentences long.

Underline the procedural law or standard of review, draw a dotted underline under the substantive law, draw a squiggly line under policy, and leave the facts without an underline. <u>OR</u>   Circle up to ten words you hope your reader will remember best from your summary, and from the argument.

EXERCISES FOR CHAPTER 18

THE ART AND PHILOSOPHY OF ADVOCACY

Read the material at pages 447 to 450, 459 to 460, and 466 to 471, as well as the fact situation at 517.

Consider the following two grounds for appeal in this case: first, that the jury erred in its verdict on the recklessness count; second, that the trial court erred in directing a verdict on the negligence count.

1.   Assess the two grounds for appeal from the perspectives of both Mr. Quinnett and Pickles bar by filling in the following grids. In each space, write "strength," "weakness," or "mixed,"and a phrase explaining your choice.

Jury verdict on recklessness		
	Quinnett perspective	**Pickles perspective**
Substantive law		
Procedural law/ standard of review		
Policy		
Facts		

Directed verdict on negligence		
	Quinnett perspective	**Pickles perspective**
Substantive law		
Procedural law/ standard of review		
Policy		
Facts		

Note: the following questions appear twice—in questions 2–10, you represent Mr. Quinnett; in questions 11–19, you represent Pickles bar.

Assume that you represent Mr. Quinnett, the Appellant.

2.   Develop a theory of your case linking its legal, policy, and factual dimensions. Remember that the legal dimension is both substantive and procedural. Draw it into the pie chart, write it out, or both.

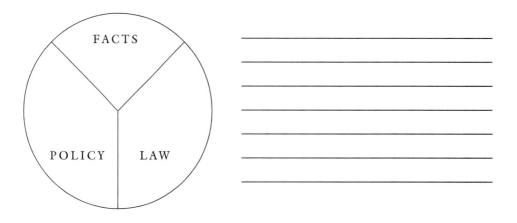

3. In light of the strengths and weaknesses of your client's case, allocate percentages of the argument to the two main topics and to the law, policy, and facts by filling in the following chart. Note that the three numbers for substantive law, procedural law, and facts under each count should be added to derive the total for that count. Those two count totals plus the policy number should add up to 100%.

Recklessness count	Negligence count	Policy	T O T A L
substantive law _____ procedural law _____ facts _____	substantive law _____ procedural law _____ facts _____	(may appear in either of two main topics or by itself)	
Total _____	Total _____	Policy _____	100%

4. In which order would you present your main arguments? Explain why you would choose that sequence.

_____

_____

_____

5. Write the topic sentences for your argument on the negligence cause of action. Draw a star by the assertions you deem the strongest for your client, and write a question mark by the least convincing assertions.

_____

_____

_____

_____

_____

_____

_____

_____

Did you use the sandwich, running-start, or momentum sequences? Explain.

_____

_____

6. Below are sentences that could appear in a discussion of the recklessness cause of action. Number them as you would present them in order to state your client's position most effectively. As appropriate, after each sentence, write a transition to the next sentence. Then write in your introductory and concluding sentences.

Introductory sentence _____

_____

_____

_____ A jury verdict is to be accepted unless, as a matter of law, reasoning minds could not reasonably have reached the jury's conclusion. _____

_____ When a liquor seller recklessly serves an intoxicated person who then injures a third party, the seller may be liable to the third party. _____

_____ One who acts recklessly must bear great responsibility for his actions, great enough to overshadow the responsibility of the drunk driver. _____

_____ Gary Mastrobattisto drank three shots of tequila and six twelve-ounce bottles of beer over two to three hours at Gindee's bar. _____

_____ Afterward, he drove to Pickles bar, where he stayed for two to three hours. _____

_____ While at Pickles bar, Mastrobattisto drank three more shots of tequila and six more twelve-ounce bottles of beer. _____

_____ Shortly after leaving Pickles bar, Mastrobattisto drove into oncoming traffic and struck the car carrying Benjamin Quinnett. _____

Concluding sentence _____

_____

_____

_____

Does your sequence follow IRAC? Explain.

_____

_____

_____

7. Reread the second paragraph of the case description at page 517. Rewrite it so as to favor your client, without changing its content, by use of the syntax and semantic strategies discussed in Chapter 18. (You may re-order the material if you wish.) In the margin, identify your strategies, such as passive voice and vivid language.

rewrite **strategies**

_____   _____

_____   _____

_____   _____

_____   _____

_____   _____

_____   _____

_____   _____

_____   _____

_____   _____

_____   _____

8. Write a sentence or two using one or more of the following rhetorical devices. Check the device(s) you selected.

_____ juxtaposition   _____ alliteration   _____ anaphora

_____ aphorism   _____ allusion   _____ question

_____

_____

_____

_____

9. Identify a point on which both sides concur and that favors your opponent. Write out your statement of the point and the surrounding material.

_____

_____

_____

How did you minimize the concession?

_____

_____

What type of concession did you present, e.g., confession and avoidance, assuming arguendo?

_____

10.   Identify an assertion of your opponent that you might choose to state explicitly and rebut. Write out that passage.

_____

_____

_____

_____

How did you minimize the statement of the opponent's assertion and maximize your rebuttal?

_____

_____

Assume that you represent Pickles bar.

11.   Develop a theory of your case linking its legal, policy, and factual dimensions. Remember that the legal dimension is both substantive and procedural. Draw it into the pie chart, write it out, or both.

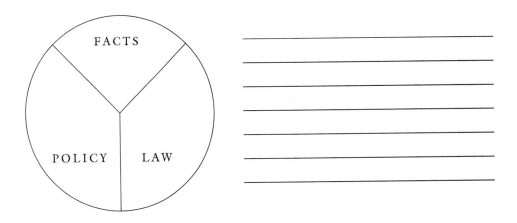

_____

_____

_____

_____

_____

_____

_____

12.   In light of the strengths and weaknesses of your client's case, allocate percentages of
the argument to the two main topics and to the law, policy, and facts by filling in the following chart. Note that the three numbers for substantive law, procedural law, and facts
under each count should be added to derive the total for that count. Those two count totals plus the policy number should add up to 100%.

Reckless count	Negligence count	Policy	T
substantive law _____ procedural law _____ facts _____	substantive law _____ procedural law _____ facts _____	(may appear in either of two main topics or by itself)	O T A L
Total _____	Total _____	Policy _____	100%

13.   In which order would you present your main arguments? Explain why you would
choose that sequence.

_____

_____

_____

14.   Write the topic sentences for your argument on the negligence cause of action. Draw
a star by the assertions you deem the strongest for your client, and write a question mark by
the least convincing assertions.

_____

_____

_____

_____

_____

_____

Did you use the sandwich, running-start, or momentum sequences? Explain.

_____

_____

15.   Below are sentences that could appear in a discussion of the recklessness cause of action. Number them as you would present them in order to state your client's position most effectively. As appropriate, after each sentence, write a transition to the next sentence. Then write in your introductory and concluding sentences.

Introductory sentence _____

_____

_____   A jury verdict is to be accepted unless, as a matter of law, reasoning minds could not reasonably have reached the jury's conclusion._____

_____   When a liquor seller recklessly serves an intoxicated person who then injures a third party, the seller may be liable to the third party. _____

_____   One who acts recklessly must bear great responsibility for his actions, great enough to overshadow the responsibility of the drunk driver._____

_____   Gary Mastrobattisto drank three shots of tequila and six twelve-ounce bottles of beer over two to three hours at Gindee's bar. _____

_____   Afterward, he drove to Pickles bar, where he stayed for two to three hours. _____

_____   While at Pickles bar, Mastrobattisto drank three more shots of tequila and six more twelve-ounce bottles of beer._____

_____   Shortly after leaving Pickles bar, Mastrobattisto drove into oncoming traffic and struck the car carrying Benjamin Quinnett._____

Concluding sentence _____

_____

_____

_____

Does your sequence follow IRAC? Explain.

_____

_____

_____

16.   Reread the second paragraph of the case description at page 517. Rewrite it so as to favor your client, without changing its content, by use of the syntax and semantic strategies discussed in Chapter 18. (You may re-order the material if you wish.) In the margin, identify your strategies, such as passive voice and vivid language.

rewrite   **strategies**

_____   _____
_____   _____
_____   _____
_____   _____
_____   _____
_____   _____
_____   _____
_____   _____
_____   _____
_____   _____

17.   Write a sentence or two using one or more of the following rhetorical devices. Check the device(s) you selected.

_____   juxtaposition   _____   alliteration   _____   anaphora

_____   aphorism   _____   allusion   _____   question

_____
_____
_____
_____

18.   Identify a point on which both sides concur and that favors your opponent. Write out your statement of the point and the surrounding material.

_____
_____
_____

How did you minimize the concession?

_____
_____

What type of concession did you present, e.g., confession and avoidance, assuming arguendo?

_____

19.   Identify an assertion of your opponent that you might choose to state explicitly and rebut. Write out that passage.

_____

_____

_____

_____

How did you minimize the statement of the opponent's assertion and maximize your rebuttal?

_____

_____

Assume for the remaining questions that you are a member of the Connecticut Supreme Court.

20.   How would you respond to the following sentences if they appeared in the parties' briefs? If you believe any sentence needs editing, write in your changes.

a. Moments after leaving Pickles, Mastrobattisto slaughtered an innocent and unsuspecting child.

_____

_____

b. This Court's opinion in *Kowal* disregards the legitimate interests of the driving public in favor of the interests of commercial establishments that place drunk drivers on our state's roads.

_____

_____

c. Counsel for Appellant has shown little regard for the principle of stare decisis in her argument on the negligence cause of action.

_____

_____

d. How many more children must die before the rule of *Nolan v. Morelli* is overruled?

_____

_____

e. Appellant's counsel would have us believe that it is law-abiding establishments, such as the restaurant sued in this case, that cause the regrettable injuries in cases of this sort. But, as this Court knows, it is clear that the culprits are the Gary Mastrobattistos of this world, who are unable to control their deadly impulses.

_____

_____

21.   If you were to rule in favor of Mr. Quinnett on the negligence cause of action and thereby change the law, how would you construct your opinion? More specifically, what would you say as to the following:

a. current case law _____

_____

_____

_____

b. persuasive precedent _____

_____

_____

_____

c. the equities of the new rule _____

_____

_____

_____

d. the fairness of applying the new rule to the present case _____

_____

_____

_____

e. the limits of the new rule (situations falling within and outside its scope) _____

_____

_____

_____

f. the public policies favoring the new rule _____

_____

_____

_____

22.   If you were to rule in favor of Pickles bar and thereby adhere to current law, how would you construct your opinion? More specifically what would you say as to the following:

a. current case law _____

_____

_____

_____

b. persuasive precedent _____

_____

_____

_____

c. the equities of the current rule _____

_____

_____

_____

d. the fairness of applying the proposed rule to the present case _____

_____

_____

_____

e. the limits of the proposed rule (situations falling within and outside its scope) ____

_____

_____

_____

f. the public policies favoring the current rule _____

_____

_____

_____

Exercises for Chapter 19

Oral Advocacy

Read the material at pages 447 to 450, 459 to 460, and 466 to 471, as well as the fact situation at 517.

Note: The following questions appear twice: in questions 1–7, you represent Mr. Quinnett; in questions 8–14, you represent Pickles bar.

Assume first that you represent Mr. Quinnett, the Appellant.

1.   Write out the introduction to your oral argument before the Connecticut Supreme Court. Include the introduction and roadmap, summarizing the issues or arguments to be discussed.

_____

_____

_____

_____

_____

_____

_____

2.   List the key facts in the order in which you would state them.

_____

_____

_____

_____

_____

_____

_____

_____

Time yourself. How long does it take you to state these facts? _____

3.   Write out the procedural posture of the case.

_____

_____

_____

Time yourself. How long does it take you to state the procedural posture? _____

4.   In the space below, prepare an outline of your planned argument. Try to note your assertions concisely, rather than write out lengthy sentences, and be sure to include transitions. Assume you have thirty minutes to argue; allocate fifteen minutes to the assertions you have identified. Mark stars next to the most important material to convey.

5. Write out the conclusion to your oral argument.

_____

_____

_____

_____

_____

6. Select the three sources you deem the most likely to be discussed extensively in an oral argument. Write out "index cards" for these three sources:

```
┌──────────────────────────────────────────────────────┐
│                                                      │
│   source name _____       │
│                                                      │
│   important points                                   │
│                                                      │
│                                                      │
│                                                      │
│                                                      │
│                                                      │
└──────────────────────────────────────────────────────┘
```

```
┌──────────────────────────────────────────────────────┐
│                                                      │
│   source name _____       │
│                                                      │
│   important points                                   │
│                                                      │
│                                                      │
│                                                      │
│                                                      │
│                                                      │
└──────────────────────────────────────────────────────┘
```

```
┌──────────────────────────────────────────────────────┐
│                                                      │
│   source name _____       │
│                                                      │
│   important points                                   │
│                                                      │
│                                                      │
│                                                      │
│                                                      │
│                                                      │
└──────────────────────────────────────────────────────┘
```

7.   Write out questions you might be asked, and sketch out your answers.

Question about the facts

_____

_____

Answer to the question

_____

_____

_____

Question about the law

_____

_____

Answer to the question

_____

_____

_____

Question about public policy

_____

_____

Answer to the question

_____

_____

_____

Question about a hypothetical situation

_____

_____

Answer to the question

_____

_____

_____

Question seeking concession

_____

_____

Answer to the question

_____

_____

_____

Question about your opponent's argument

_____

_____

Answer to the question

_____

_____

_____

Assume now that you represent Pickles bar, the Appellee.

8. Write out the introduction to your oral argument before the Connecticut Supreme Court. Include the introduction and roadmap, summarizing the issues or arguments to be discussed.

_____

_____

_____

_____

_____

_____

9. List the key facts you would highlight in the order in which you would state them.

_____

_____

_____

_____

_____

Time yourself. How long does it take you to state these facts? _____

10.   Would you plan to remark at all on the cases's procedural posture? If so, state the point(s) you would make.

_____

_____

_____

Time yourself. How long does it take you to state the procedural points? _____

11.   In the space below, prepare an outline of your planned argument. Note the major and minor assertions you would make. Try to note your assertions concisely, rather than write out lengthy sentences, and be sure to include transitions. Assume you have twenty-five minutes to argue; allocate fifteen minutes to the assertions you have identified. Mark with stars the most important material to convey.

12. Write out the conclusion to your oral argument.

_____

_____

_____

_____

_____

13. Select the three sources you deem the most likely to be discussed extensively in an oral argument. Write out "index cards" for these three sources:

source name _____

important points

source name _____

important points

source name _____

important points

14.   Write out questions you might be asked, and sketch out your answers.

Question about the facts

_____

_____

Answer to the question

_____

_____

_____

Question about the law

_____

_____

Answer to the question

_____

_____

_____

Question about public policy

_____

_____

Answer to the question

_____

_____

_____

Question about a hypothetical situation

_____

_____

Answer to the question

_____

_____

_____

Question seeking concession

_____

_____

Answer to the question

_____

_____

_____

Question about your opponent's argument

_____

_____

Answer to the question

_____

_____

_____

POSTSCRIPT

In *Quinnett v. Newman*, 568 A.2d 786 (Conn. 1990), the Connecticut Supreme Court noted its longstanding rule that there is no proximate cause in such a case, as well as the "limited exception" of *Ely v. Murphy*, 540 A.2d 54 (1988), that there is proximate cause when the drinker is a minor and the provider is a social host. *Quinnett*, 568 A.2d at 787. In *Quinnett*, the court declined to expand the *Ely* exception. Instead the court noted that the legislature had provided a remedy for cases such as this (unlike the situation in *Ely*) in the Dram Shop Act, Conn. Gen. Stat. § 30-102 (1990), albeit with a limitation on the amount of recovery. *Quinnett*, 568 A.2d at 788. The majority also found no error in the trial court's denial of Mr. Quinnett's motion to set aside the jury verdicts, *id.* at 787, and declined to recognize a claim for public nuisance. *id.* at 788-89.

Chief Justice Peters and Justice Hull dissented. *Id.* at 789-91. "The continued existence of the present law is a blot on the social conscience and will, sooner or later, be corrected by this court. Why not now?" *Id.* at 791 (Hull, J., dissenting).

TABLE OF AUTHORITIES

INDEX

M

O